VOLUME

6

CARING VOICES AND WOMEN'S MORAL FRAMES

GILLIGAN'S VIEW

Edited with introductions by
BILL PUKA

GARLAND PUBLISHING, INc.
New York & London
1994

Library of Congress Cataloging-in-Publication Data

Moral development : a compendium / edited with introductions by Bill
Puka.
     p.   cm.
     Includes bibliographical references.
     Contents: v. 1. Defining perspectives in moral development — v.
2. Fundamental research in moral development — v. 3. Kohlberg's
original study of moral development — v. 4. The great justice
debate — v. 5. New research in moral development — v. 6. Caring
voices and women's moral frames — v. 7. Reaching out.
     ISBN 0–8153–1553–8 (v. 6 : alk. paper).
     1. Moral development.   I. Puka, Bill.
BF723.M54M66   1994
155.2'5—dc20   94–462
                               CIP

Printed on acid-free, 250-year-life paper
Manufactured in the United States of America

CONTENTS

Contents

Series Introduction

Moral development is an interdisciplinary field that researches moral common sense and interpersonal know-how. It investigates how children evolve a sense of right and wrong, good and bad, and how adults hone their abilities to handle ethical issues in daily life. This includes resolving value conflicts, fermenting trusting, cooperative, and tolerant relationships, and setting ethical goals. It focuses most on how we think about these ethical issues (using our cognitive competences) and how we act as a result.

These seven volumes are designed to function as a standard, comprehensive sourcebook. They focus on central concerns and controversies in moral development, such as the relation between moral socialization and development, moral judgment and action, and the effects of culture, class, or gender on moral orientation. They also focus on central research programs in the field, such as the enduring Kohlberg research on moral stages, Gilligan research on ethical caring and women's development, and related prosocial research on altruism.

The studies contained here were compiled from the "wish lists" of researchers and educators in the field. These are the publications cited as most important (and, often, least available) for effective teaching and research training and for conveying the field to others. Unfortunately, the most crucial studies and essays in moral development are widely scattered across hard-to-find (sometimes out-of-print) volumes. Compiling them for a course is difficult and costly. This compendium eases these problems by gathering needed sources in one place, for a single charge. Regrettably, rising reprint fees frustrated plans to include *all* needed resources here, halving the original contents of these volumes and requiring torturous excising decisions. Even so, compared to other collections, this series approaches a true "handbook" of moral development, providing key sources on central issues rather than "further essays" on specialized topics.

A major aim of this series is to represent moral development accurately to related fields. Controversies in moral development have sparked lively interest in the disciplines of philosophy, education, sociology and anthropology, literary criticism, political science, gender and cultural studies, critical legal studies, criminology and corrections, and peace studies. Unfortunately, members of these fields were often introduced to moral development through the highly theoretical musings of Lawrence Kohlberg, Carol Gilligan, or Jean Piaget—or by highly theoretical commentaries on them. Jumping into the fray over gender or culture bias in stage theory, theorists in the humanities show virtually no familiarity with the empirical research that gave rise to it. Indeed, many commentators seem unaware that these controversies arise in a distinct research field and are context-dependent.

This compendium displays moral development as a social science, generating research findings in cognitive developmental, and social psychology. (Students are invited to recognize and approach the field as such.) Theory is heavily involved in this research—helping define the fundamental notions of "moral" and "development," for example. But even when philosophically or ethically cast, it remains psychological or social scientific theory. It utilizes but does not engage in moral philosophy per se. Otherwise, it is not moral development theory, but meta-theory. (Several extensively criticized Kohlberg articles on justice are meta-theory.) The confusion of these types and levels of theory has been a source of pervasive confusion in the field. The mistaken assessment of psychological theory by moral-philosophical standards has generated extremely damaging and misguided controversy in moral development. Other types of theory (moral, social, interpretive, anthropological) should be directed at moral development science, focusing on empirical research methods and their empirical interpretation. It should be theory of data, that is, not meta-theoretical reflection on the "amateur" philosophizing and hermeneutics interpolations of psychological researchers. (Likewise, social scientific research should not focus on the empirical generalizations of philosophers when trying to probe social reality or seek guidance in doing so from this theoretical discipline.) The bulk of entries in this compendium present the proper, empirically raw material for such "outside" theoretical enterprise.

To researchers, theorists, and students in related fields, this series extends an invitation to share our interest in the fascinating phenomena of moral development, and to share our findings thus far. Your help is welcomed also in refining our treacherously qualitative research methods and theories. In my dual disciplines of psychology and philosophy, I have found no more inspiring area of study. Alongside its somewhat dispassionate research orientation, this field carries on the ancient "cause" of its pre-scientific past. This is to show that human nature is naturally good—that the human psyche spontaneously unfolds in good will, cleaving toward fair-mindedness, compassion, and cooperative concern.

The first volume, *Defining Perspectives*, presents the major approaches to moral development and socialization in the words of chief proponents: Kohlberg, Bandura, Aronfreed, Mischel, Eysenck, and Perry. (Piaget is discussed in detail.) This first volume is required reading for those needing to orient to this field or regain orientation. It is crucial for clarifying the relations and differences between moral development and socialization that define research.

The second volume, *Fundamental Research*, compiles the classic research studies on moral levels and stages of development. These studies expose the crucial relation of role-taking and social perspective to moral judgment and of moral judgment to action. They also divine the important role of moral self-identity (viewing oneself as morally interested) in moral motivation.

The third volume contains *Kohlberg's Original Study*, his massive doctoral research project. The study, which has never before been published, sets the parameters for moral development research, theory, and controversy. (Major critical alternatives to Kohlberg's approach share far more in common with it than they diverge.) Here the reader sees "how it all started," glimpsing the sweep of Kohlberg's aspiration: to uncover the chief adaptation of humankind, the evolving systems of reasoning and meaning-making that, even in children, guide effective choice and action. Most major Kohlberg critiques fault features of this original study, especially in the all-male, all-white, all-American cast of his research sample. (Why look here for traits that characterize all humans in all cultures through all time?) It is worth checking these criticisms against the text, in context, as depictions of unpublished work often blur into hearsay. It is also worth viewing this study through the massive reanalysis of its data (Colby, Kohlberg, et al.) and the full mass of Kohlberg research that shaped stage theory. Both are liberally sampled in Volume Five.

The Great Justice Debate, the fourth volume, gathers the broad range of criticisms leveled at moral stage theory. It takes up the range of "bias charges" in developmental research—bias by gender, social class, culture, political ideology, and partisan intellectual persuasion. Chief among these reputed biases is the equation of moral competence and development with justice and rights. Here key features of compassion and benevolence seem overlooked or underrated. Here a seemingly male standard of ethical preference downplays women's sensibilities and skills. Responses to these charges appear here as well.

Volume Five, *New Research*, focuses on cross-cultural research in moral development. Studies in India, Turkey, Israel, Korea, Poland, and China are included. While interesting in itself, such research also supports the generalizability of moral stages, challenged above. Indeed, Volume Five attempts to reconceive or re-start the central research program of moral development from the inception of its matured research methods and statistically well-validated findings. From this point research is more data-based than theory-driven. It can address criticism with hard evidence. Regarding controversy in moral development, Volumes Four and Five go together as challenge and retort.

Volume Six, *Caring Voices*, is devoted to the popular "different voice" hypothesis. This hypothesis posits a distinct ethical orientation of caring relationship, naturally preferred by women, that complements justice. Compiled here is the main record of Gilligan's (and colleagues') research, including recent experiments with "narrative" research method. The significant critical literature on care is well-represented as well, with responses. While Gilligan's empirical research program is more formative than Kohlberg's, her interpretive observations have influenced several fields, especially in feminist studies. Few research sources have more common-sense significance and "consciousness-raising" potential. The student reader may find Gilligan's approach the most personally relevant and useful in moral development.

Reaching Out, the final volume, extends moral development concerns to "prosocial" research on altruism. Altruistic helping behavior bears close relation to caring and to certain ideals of liberal justice. This volume emphasizes the role of emotions in helping (and not helping), focusing on empathic distress, forgiveness, and guilt. It also looks at early friendship and family influences. Moral emotions are related to ethical virtues here, which are considered alongside the "vices" of apathy and learned helplessness. Leading researchers are included such as Hoffman, Eisenberg, Batson, and Staub.

INTRODUCTION

This volume provides a comprehensive account of Gilligan's research on ethical caring and women's development. It also includes major empirical and theoretical criticisms of care research with replies. Gilligan's essay "In a Different Voice" has had an enormous impact on a variety of fields, especially on education, feminist and women's studies, and the humanities. Its main thesis is that there are primarily two broad and complementary themes of commonsense ethics, caring, and justice. They operate first, and most importantly, in perceiving, defining, and orienting to ethical matters. Justice is a minimalist orientation, marked by general rules for not treading on each other. Caring is a far more proactive and procedural orientation born of personal experience and interpersonal know-how. It ethically binds us to each other by reinforcing natural bonds and helping us better negotiate and deepen our relations.

According to Gilligan, women spontaneously prefer caring. While they can think and act through the ethics of justice and individual rights preferred by males, they find them somewhat alien, flawed, and limited—except when balanced with caring. This "feminine preference" apparently has been missed by researchers in moral development because they judge moral competence and development by male standards. This causes them to underrate caring, female competencies.

Most readers will find ethical caring more appealing and ideal than justice or rights. Compared to care, justice seems judgmental and negative (anti-injustice), stingy (confined to obligations), and constraining (through its burdens of obligations). Likewise, individual rights wax aggressive and demanding, if not punitive, as we wield them against one another. Together these ethics strike a callous, impersonal pose—rendering each, impartially, his due—that is quite out of spirit with the spirit of ethics. By contrast, care shows a more generous, trusting, and compassionate spirit. Yet unlike "unconditional love" or utilitarianism, it is neither over-idealistic nor threatening to individual liberty or equality.

As noted, care was a long-awaited voice in moral development, a missing link in the Piaget-Kohlberg paradigm. Other kindly candidates had been posed to fill the yawning gap at the upper end of Kohlberg's stages. Even Kohlberg proposed one ("Stage 7" agape). But none before had arisen from empirical sources comparable to initial justice research. None were so neatly tailored to make up Kohlbergian shortfalls or compensate for perceived biases.

This sixth volume gathers the main studies that gave voice to ethical caring (by Gilligan, Belenky, Lyons, Attanucci, and Johnston). Focus is also placed on Brown's attempts to develop narrative research methods that preserve the rich detail of care (responsiveness, dialogue, non-harm, consensus-seeking, compassion, empathy, etc. The previous Lyons measure captured only a few care features).

Most major criticisms of Gilligan's research methodology and theoretical claims are gathered in this volume as well. They focus on the "dual themes/separate tracks" hypothesis (regarding care and justice) and on sex differences. Commentaries by Maccoby, Luria, Greeno, and Walker (in his review of sex differences) are best known. But more extensive research by Bebeau and Brabeck and Nunner-Winkler deserves attention. Replies to criticism by Gilligan, Attanucci, Brown, and Tappan are also provided.

Of special note is the inclusion of Broverman's study on gender stereotypes. This oft-cited research grounds the feminist implications of Gilligan's care as a struggle against stereotyped female roles. But it also grounds feminist criticisms of care as a backhanded endorsement of feminine stereotypes. My "liberation" essay explores that criticism. Tronto's essay may point to the best direction for rising above these disputes and moving forward. In two additional essays I suggest that we view Kohlberg's and Gilligan's research developmentally—as highly limited, in-process inquiries that cannot be compared, much less rated, until they are helped farther along together.

In a Different Voice: Women's Conceptions of Self and of Morality

CAROL GILLIGAN
Harvard University

As theories of developmental psychology continue to define educational goals and practice, it has become imperative for educators and researchers to scrutinize not only the underlying assumptions of such theories but also the model of adulthood toward which they point. Carol Gilligan examines the limitations of several theories, most notably Kohlberg's stage theory of moral development, and concludes that developmental theory has not given adequate expression to the concerns and experience of women. Through a review of psychological and literary sources, she illustrates the feminine construction of reality. From her own research data, interviews with women contemplating abortion, she then derives an alternative sequence for the development of women's moral judgments. Finally, she argues for an expanded conception of adulthood that would result from the integration of the "feminine voice" into developmental theory.

The arc of developmental theory leads from infantile dependence to adult autonomy, tracing a path characterized by an increasing differentiation of self from other and a progressive freeing of thought from contextual constraints. The vision of Luther, journeying from the rejection of a self defined by others to the assertive boldness of "Here I stand" and the image of Plato's allegorical man in the cave, separating at last the shadows from the sun, have taken powerful hold on the psychological understanding of what constitutes development. Thus, the individual, meeting fully the developmental challenges of adolescence as set for him by Piaget, Erikson, and Kohlberg, thinks formally, proceeding from theory to fact, and defines both the self and the moral autonomously, that is, apart from the identification and conventions that had comprised the particulars of his childhood world. So

The research reported here was partially supported by a grant from the Spencer Foundation. I wish to thank Mary Belenky for her collaboration and colleagueship in the abortion decision study and Michael Murphy for his comments and help in preparing this manuscript.

Harvard Educational Review Vol. 47 No. 4 November 1977

equipped, he is presumed ready to live as an adult, to love and work in a way that is both intimate and generative, to develop an ethical sense of caring and a genital mode of relating in which giving and taking fuse in the ultimate reconciliation of the tension between self and other.

Yet the men whose theories have largely informed this understanding of development have all been plagued by the same problem, the problem of women, whose sexuality remains more diffuse, whose perception of self is so much more tenaciously embedded in relationships with others and whose moral dilemmas hold them in a mode of judgment that is insistently contextual. The solution has been to consider women as either deviant or deficient in their development.

That there is a discrepancy between concepts of womanhood and adulthood is nowhere more clearly evident than in the series of studies on sex-role stereotypes reported by Broverman, Vogel, Broverman, Clarkson, and Rosenkrantz (1972). The repeated finding of these studies is that the qualities deemed necessary for adulthood—the capacity for autonomous thinking, clear decision making, and responsible action—are those associated with masculinity but considered undesirable as attributes of the feminine self. The stereotypes suggest a splitting of love and work that relegates the expressive capacities requisite for the former to women while the instrumental abilities necessary for the latter reside in the masculine domain. Yet, looked at from a different perspective, these stereotypes reflect a conception of adulthood that is itself out of balance, favoring the separateness of the individual self over its connection to others and leaning more toward an autonomous life of work than toward the interdependence of love and care.

This difference in point of view is the subject of this essay, which seeks to identify in the feminine experience and construction of social reality a distinctive voice, recognizable in the different perspective it brings to bear on the construction and resolution of moral problems. The first section begins with the repeated observation of difference in women's concepts of self and of morality. This difference is identified in previous psychological descriptions of women's moral judgments and described as it again appears in current research data. Examples drawn from interviews with women in and around a university community are used to illustrate the characteristics of the feminine voice. The relational bias in women's thinking that has, in the past, been seen to compromise their moral judgment and impede their development now begins to emerge in a new developmental light. Instead of being seen as a developmental deficiency, this bias appears to reflect a different social and moral understanding.

This alternative conception is enlarged in the second section through consideration of research interviews with women facing the moral dilemma of whether to continue or abort a pregnancy. Since the research design allowed women to define as well as resolve the moral problem, developmental distinctions could be derived directly from the categories of women's thought. The responses of women to structured interview questions regarding the pregnancy decision formed the basis for describing a developmental sequence that traces progressive differentiations in their understanding and judgment of conflicts between self and other. While the sequence of women's moral development follows the three-level progression of all social developmental theory, from an egocentric through a societal to a universal perspective, this progression takes place within a distinct moral conception. This conception differs from that derived by Kohlberg from his all-male longitudinal research data.

This difference then becomes the basis in the third section for challenging the current assessment of women's moral judgment at the same time that it brings to bear a new perspective on developmental assessment in general. The inclusion in the overall conception of development of those categories derived from the study of women's moral judgment enlarges developmental understanding, enabling it to encompass better the thinking of both sexes. This is particularly true with respect to the construction and resolution of the dilemmas of adult life. Since the conception of adulthood retrospectively shapes the theoretical understanding of the development that precedes it, the changes in that conception that follow from the more central inclusion of women's judgments recast developmental understanding and lead to a reconsideration of the substance of social and moral development.

Characteristics of the Feminine Voice

The revolutionary contribution of Piaget's work is the experimental confirmation and refinement of Kant's assertion that knowledge is actively constructed rather than passively received. Time, space, self, and other, as well as the categories of developmental theory, all arise out of the active interchange between the individual and the physical and social world in which he lives and of which he strives to make sense. The development of cognition is the process of reappropriating reality at progressively more complex levels of apprehension, as the structures of thinking expand to encompass the increasing richness and intricacy of experience.

Moral development, in the work of Piaget and Kohlberg, refers specifically to the expanding conception of the social world as it is reflected in the understanding and resolution of the inevitable conflicts that arise in the relations between self and others. The moral judgment is a statement of priority, an attempt at rational resolution in a situation where, from a different point of view, the choice itself seems to do violence to justice.

Kohlberg (1969), in his extension of the early work of Piaget, discovered six stages of moral judgment, which he claimed formed an invariant sequence, each successive stage representing a more adequate construction of the moral problem, which in turn provides the basis for its more just resolution. The stages divide into three levels, each of which denotes a significant expansion of the moral point of view from an egocentric through a societal to a universal ethical conception. With this expansion in perspective comes the capacity to free moral judgment from the individual needs and social conventions with which it had earlier been confused and anchor it instead in principles of justice that are universal in application. These principles provide criteria upon which both individual and societal claims can be impartially assessed. In Kohlberg's view, at the highest stages of development morality is freed from both psychological and historical constraints, and the individual can judge independently of his own particular needs and of the values of those around him.

That the moral sensibility of women differs from that of men was noted by Freud (1925/1961) in the following by now well-quoted statement:

> I cannot evade the notion (though I hesitate to give it expression) that for women the level of what is ethically normal is different from what it is in man. Their superego is never so inexorable, so impersonal, so independent of its emotional origins as we require it to be in men. Character-traits which critics of every epoch have brought up against women—that they show less sense of justice than men, that they are less ready to submit to the great exigencies of life, that they are more often influenced in their judgments by feelings of affection or hostility—all these would be amply accounted for by the modification in the formation of their super-ego which we have inferred above. (pp. 257–258)

While Freud's explanation lies in the deviation of female from male development around the construction and resolution of the Oedipal problem, the same observations about the nature of morality in women emerge from the work of Piaget and Kohlberg. Piaget (1932/1965), in his study of the rules of children's games, observed that, in the games they played, girls were "less explicit about agreement [than boys] and less concerned with legal elaboration" (p. 93). In contrast to the boys' interest in the codification of rules, the girls adopted a more pragmatic attitude, regarding "a rule as good so long as the game repays it" (p. 83). As a result, in comparison to boys, girls were found to be "more tolerant and more easily reconciled to innovations" (p. 52).

Kohlberg (1971) also identifies a strong interpersonal bias in the moral judgments of women, which leads them to be considered as typically at the third of his six-stage developmental sequence. At that stage, the good is identified with "what pleases or helps others and is approved of by them" (p. 164). This mode of judgment is conventional in its conformity to generally held notions of the good but also psychological in its concern with intention and consequence as the basis for judging the morality of action.

That women fall largely into this level of moral judgment is hardly surprising when we read from the Broverman et al. (1972) list that prominent among the twelve attributes considered to be desirable for women are tact, gentleness, awareness of the feelings of others, strong need for security, and easy expression of tender feelings. And yet, herein lies the paradox, for the very traits that have traditionally defined the "goodness" of women, their care for and sensitivity to the needs of others, are those that mark them as deficient in moral development. The infusion of feeling into their judgments keeps them from developing a more independent and abstract ethical conception in which concern for others derives from principles of justice rather than from compassion and care. Kohlberg, however, is less pessimistic than Freud in his assessment, for he sees the development of women as extending beyond the interpersonal level, following the same path toward independent, principled judgment that he discovered in the research on men from which his stages were derived. In Kohlberg's view, women's development will proceed beyond Stage Three when they are challenged to solve moral problems that require them to see beyond the relationships that have in the past generally bound their moral experience.

What then do women say when asked to construct the moral domain; how do we identify the characteristically "feminine" voice? A Radcliffe undergraduate, responding to the question, "If you had to say what morality meant to you, how would you sum it up?," replies:

> When I think of the word morality, I think of obligations. I usually think of it as conflicts between personal desires and social things, social considerations, or personal desires of yourself versus personal desires of another person or people or whatever. Morality is that whole realm of how you decide these conflicts. A moral person is one who would decide, like by placing themselves more often than not as equals, a truly moral person would always consider another person as their equal . . . in a situation of social interaction, something is morally wrong where the individual ends up screwing a lot of people. And it is morally right when everyone comes out better of.[1]

Yet when asked if she can think of someone whom she would consider a genuinely moral person, she replies, "Well, immediately I think of Albert Schweitzer because he has obviously given his life to help others." Obligation and sacrifice override the ideal of equality, setting up a basic contradiction in her thinking.

Another undergraduate responds to the question, "What does it mean to say something is morally right or wrong?," by also speaking first of responsibilities and obligations:

> Just that it has to do with responsibilties and obligations and values, mainly values. . . . In my life situation I relate morality with interpersonal relationships that have to do with respect for the other person and myself. [Why respect other people?] Because they have a consciousness or feelings that can be hurt, an awareness that can be hurt.

The concern about hurting others persists as a major theme in the responses of two other Radcliffe students:

> [Why be moral?] Millions of people have to live together peacefully. I personally don't want to hurt other people. That's a real criterion, a main criterion for me. It underlies my sense of justice. It isn't nice to inflict pain. I empathize with anyone in pain. Not hurting others is important in my own private morals. Years ago, I would have jumped out of a window not to hurt my boyfriend. That was pathological. Even today though, I want approval and love and I don't want enemies. Maybe that's why there is morality—so people can win approval, love and friendship.

> My main moral principle is not hurting other people as long as you aren't going against your own conscience and as long as you remain true to yourself. . . . There are many moral issues such as abortion, the draft, killing, stealing, monogamy, etc. If something is a controversial issue like these, then I always say it is up to the individual. The individual has to decide and then follow his own con-

[1] The Radcliffe women whose responses are cited were interviewed as part of a pilot study on undergraduate moral development conducted by the author in 1970.

science. There are no moral absolutes. . . . Laws are pragmatic instruments, but they are not absolutes. A viable society can't make exceptions all the time, but I would personally. . . . I'm afraid I'm heading for some big crisis with my boyfriend someday, and someone will get hurt, and he'll get more hurt than I will. I feel an obligation to not hurt him, but also an obligation to not lie. I don't know if it is possible to not lie and not hurt.

The common thread that runs through these statements, the wish not to hurt others and the hope that in morality lies a way of solving conflicts so that no one will get hurt, is striking in that it is independently introduced by each of the four women as the most specific item in their response to a most general question. The moral person is one who helps others; goodness is service, meeting one's obligations and responsibilities to others, if possible, without sacrificing oneself. While the first of the four women ends by denying the conflict she initially introduced, the last woman anticipates a conflict between remaining true to herself and adhering to her principle of not hurting others. The dilemma that would test the limits of this judgment would be one where helping others is seen to be at the price of hurting the self.

The reticence about taking stands on "controversial issues," the willingness to "make exceptions all the time" expressed in the final example above, is echoed repeatedly by other Radcliffe students, as in the following two examples:

I never feel that I can condemn anyone else. I have a very relativistic position. The basic idea that I cling to is the sanctity of human life. I am inhibited about impressing my beliefs on others.

I could never argue that my belief on a moral question is anything that another person should accept. I don't believe in absolutes. . . . If there is an absolute for moral decisions, it is human life.

Or as a thirty-one-year-old Wellesley graduate says, in explaining why she would find it difficult to steal a drug to save her own life despite her belief that it would be right to steal for another: "It's just very hard to defend yourself against the rules. I mean, we live by consensus, and you take an action simply for yourself, by yourself, there's no consensus there, and that is relatively indefensible in this society now."

What begins to emerge is a sense of vulnerability that impedes these women from taking a stand, what George Eliot (1860/1965) regards as the girl's "susceptibility" to adverse judgments of others, which stems from her lack of power and consequent inability to do something in the world. While relativism in men, the unwillingness to make moral judgments that Kohlberg and Kramer (1969) and Kohlberg and Gilligan (1971) have associated with the adolescent crisis of identity and belief, takes the form of calling into question the concept of morality itself, the women's reluctance to judge stems rather from their uncertainty about their right to make moral statements or, perhaps, the price for them that such judgment seems to entail. This contrast echoes that made by Matina Horner (1972), who differentiated the ideological fear of success expressed by men from the personal conflicts about succeeding that riddled the women's responses to stories of competitive achievement.

486

> Most of the men who responded with the expectation of negative consequences because of success were not concerned about their masculinity but were instead likely to have expressed existential concerns about finding a "non-materialistic happiness and satisfaction in life." These concerns, which reflect changing attitudes toward traditional kinds of success or achievement in our society, played little, if any, part in the female stories. Most of the women who were high in fear of success imagery continued to be concerned about the discrepancy between success in the situation described and feminine identity. (pp. 163–164)

When women feel excluded from direct participation in society, they see themselves as subject to a consensus or judgment made and enforced by the men on whose protection and support they depend and by whose names they are known. A divorced middle-aged woman, mother of adolescent daughters, resident of a sophisticated university community, tells the story as follows:

> As a woman, I feel I never understood that I was a person, that I can make decisions and I have a right to make decisions. I always felt that that belonged to my father or my husband in some way or church which was always represented by a male clergyman. They were the three men in my life: father, husband, and clergyman, and they had much more to say about what I should or shouldn't do. They were really authority figures which I accepted. I didn't rebel against that. It only has lately occurred to me that I never even rebelled against it, and my girls are much more conscious of this, not in the militant sense, but just in the recognizing sense. . . . I still let things happen to me rather than make them happen, than to make choices, although I know all about choices. I know the procedures and the steps and all. [Do you have any clues about why this might be true?] Well, I think in one sense, there is less responsibility involved. Because if you make a dumb decision, you have to take the rap. If it happens to you, well, you can complain about it. I think that if you don't grow up feeling that you ever had any choices, you don't either have the sense that you have emotional responsibility. With this sense of choice comes this sense of responsibility.

The essence of the moral decision is the exercise of choice and the willingness to accept responsibility for that choice. To the extent that women perceive themselves as having no choice, they correspondingly excuse themselves from the responsibility that decision entails. Childlike in the vulnerability of their dependence and consequent fear of abandonment, they claim to wish only to please but in return for their goodness they expect to be loved and cared for. This, then, is an "altruism" always at risk, for it presupposes an innocence constantly in danger of being compromised by an awareness of the trade-off that has been made. Asked to describe herself, a Radcliffe senior responds:

> I have heard of the onion skin theory. I see myself as an onion, as a block of different layers, the external layers for people that I don't know that well, the agreeable, the social, and as you go inward there are more sides for people I know that I show. I am not sure about the innermost, whether there is a core, or whether I have just picked up everything as I was growing up, these different influences. I think I have a neutral attitude towards myself, but I do think in terms of good and bad. . . . Good—I try to be considerate and thoughtful of other people and I try to be fair in situations and be tolerant. I use the words but I try and work

them out practically. . . . Bad things—I am not sure if they are bad, if they are altruistic or I am doing them basically for approval of other people. [Which things are these?] The values I have when I try to act them out. They deal mostly with interpersonal type relations. . . . If I were doing it for approval, it would be a very tenuous thing. If I didn't get the right feedback, there might go all my values.

Ibsen's play, *A Doll House* (1879/1965), depicts the explosion of just such a world through the eruption of a moral dilemma that calls into question the notion of goodness that lies at its center. Nora, the "squirrel wife," living with her husband as she had lived with her father, puts into action this conception of goodness as sacrifice and, with the best of intentions, takes the law into her own hands. The crisis that ensues, most painfully for her in the repudiation of that goodness by the very person who was its recipient and beneficiary, causes her to reject the suicide that she had initially seen as its ultimate expression and chose instead to seek new and firmer answers to the adolescent questions of identity and belief.

The availability of choice and with it the onus of responsibility has now invaded the most private sector of the woman's domain and threatens a similar explosion. For centuries, women's sexuality anchored them in passivity, in a receptive rather than active stance, where the events of conception and childbirth could be controlled only by a withholding in which their own sexual needs were either denied or sacrificed. That such a sacrifice entailed a cost to their intelligence as well was seen by Freud (1908/1959) when he tied the "undoubted intellectual inferiority of so many women" to "the inhibition of thought necessitated by sexual suppression" (p. 199). The strategies of withholding and denial that women have employed in the politics of sexual relations appear similar to their evasion or withholding of judgment in the moral realm. The hesitance expressed in the previous examples to impose even a belief in the value of human life on others, like the reluctance to claim one's sexuality, bespeaks a self uncertain of its strength, unwilling to deal with consequence, and thus avoiding confrontation.

Thus women have traditionally deferred to the judgment of men, although often while intimating a sensibility of their own which is at variance with that judgment. Maggie Tulliver, in *The Mill on the Floss* (Eliot, 1860/1965) responds to the accusations that ensue from the discovery of her secretly continued relationship with Phillip Wakeham by acceding to her brother's moral judgment while at the same time asserting a different set of standards by which she attests her own superiority:

I don't want to defend myself. . . . I know I've been wrong—often continually. But yet, sometimes when I have done wrong, it has been because I have feelings that you would be the better for if you had them. If *you* were in fault ever, if you had done anything very wrong, I should be sorry for the pain it brought you; I should not want punishment to be heaped on you. (p. 188)

An eloquent defense, Kohlberg would argue, of a Stage Three moral position, an assertion of the age-old split between thinking and feeling, justice and mercy, that underlies many of the clichés and stereotypes concerning the difference between the sexes. But considered from another point of view, it is a moment of co⌐

488

8

frontation, replacing a former evasion, between two modes of judging, two differing constructions of the moral domain—one traditionally associated with masculinity and the public world of social power, the other with femininity and the privacy of domestic interchange. While the developmental ordering of these two points of view has been to consider the masculine as the more adequate and thus as replacing the feminine as the individual moves toward higher stages, their reconciliation remains unclear.

The Development of Women's Moral Judgment

Recent evidence for a divergence in moral development between men and women comes from the research of Haan (Note 1) and Holstein (1976) whose findings lead them to question the possibility of a "sex-related bias" in Kolhberg's scoring system. This system is based on Kohlberg's six-stage description of moral development. Kohlberg's stages divide into three levels, which he designates as preconventional, conventional, and postconventional, thus denoting the major shifts in moral perspective around a center of moral understanding that equates justice with the maintenance of existing social systems. While the preconventional conception of justice is based on the needs of the self, the conventional judgment derives from an understanding of society. This understanding is in turn superseded by a postconventional or principled conception of justice where the good is formulated in universal terms. The quarrel with Kohlberg's stage scoring does not pertain to the structural differentiation of his levels but rather to questions of stage and sequence. Kohlberg's stages begin with an obedience and punishment orientation (Stage One), and go from there in invariant order to instrumental hedonism (Stage Two), interpersonal concordance (Stage Three), law and order (Stage Four), social contract (Stage Five), and universal ethical principles (Stage Six).

The bias that Haan and Holstein question in this scoring system has to do with the subordination of the interpersonal to the societal definition of the good in the transition from Stage Three to Stage Four. This is the transition that has repeatedly been found to be problematic for women. In 1969, Kohlberg and Kramer identified Stage Three as the characteristic mode of women's moral judgments, claiming that, since women's lives were interpersonally based, this stage was not only "functional" for them but also adequate for resolving the moral conflicts that they faced. Turiel (1973) reported that while girls reached Stage Three sooner than did boys, their judgments tended to remain at that stage while the boys' development continued further along Kohlberg's scale. Gilligan, Kohlberg, Lerner, and Belenky (1971) found a similar association between sex and moral-judgment stage in a study of high-school students, with the girls' responses being scored predominantly at Stage Three while the boys' responses were more often scored at Stage Four.

This repeated finding of developmental inferiority in women may, however, have more to do with the standard by which development has been measured than with the quality of women's thinking per se. Haan's data (Note 1) on the Berkeley Free Speech Movement and Holstein's (1976) three-year longitudinal study of

489

9

adolescents and their parents indicate that the moral judgments of women differ from those of men in the greater extent to which women's judgments are tied to feelings of empathy and compassion and are concerned more with the resolution of "real-life" as opposed to hypothetical dilemmas (Note 1, p. 34). However, as long as the categories by which development is assessed are derived within a male perspective from male research data, divergence from the masculine standard can be seen only as a failure of development. As a result, the thinking of women is often classified with that of children. The systematic exclusion from consideration of alternative criteria that might better encompass the development of women indicates not only the limitations of a theory framed by men and validated by research samples disproportionately male and adolescent but also the effects of the diffidence prevalent among women, their reluctance to speak publicly in their own voice, given the constraints imposed on them by the politics of differential power between the sexes.

In order to go beyond the question, "How much like men do women think, how capable are they of engaging in the abstract and hypothetical construction of reality?" it is necessary to identify and define in formal terms developmental criteria that encompass the categories of women's thinking. Such criteria would include the progressive differentiations, comprehensiveness, and adequacy that characterize higher-stage resolution of the "more frequently occurring, real-life moral dilemmas of interpersonal, empathic, fellow-feeling concerns" (Haan, Note 1, p. 34), which have long been the center of women's moral judgments and experience. To ascertain whether the feminine construction of the moral domain relies on a language different from that of men, but one which deserves equal credence in the definition of what constitutes development, it is necessary first to find the places where women have the power to choose and thus are willing to speak in their own voice.

When birth control and abortion provide women with effective means for controlling their fertility, the dilemma of choice enters the center of women's lives. Then the relationships that have traditionally defined women's identities and framed their moral judgments no longer flow inevitably from their reproductive capacity but become matters of decision over which they have control. Released from the passivity and reticence of a sexuality that binds them in dependence, it becomes possible for women to question with Freud what it is that they want and to assert their own answers to that question. However, while society may affirm publicly the woman's right to choose for herself, the exercise of such choice brings her privately into conflict with the conventions of femininity, particularly the moral equation of goodness with self-sacrifice. While independent assertion in judgment and action is considered the hallmark of adulthood and constitutes as well the standard of masculine development, it is rather in their care and concern for others that women have both judged themselves and been judged.

The conflict between self and other thus constitutes the central moral problem for women, posing a dilemma whose resolution requires a reconciliation between femininity and adulthood. In the absence of such a reconciliation, the moral prob-

490

lem cannot be resolved. The "good woman" masks assertion in evasion, denying responsibility by claiming only to meet the needs of others, while the "bad woman" forgoes or renounces the commitments that bind her in self-deception and betrayal. It is precisely this dilemma—the conflict between compassion and autonomy, between virtue and power—which the feminine voice struggles to resolve in its effort to reclaim the self and to solve the moral problem in such a way that no one is hurt.

When a woman considers whether to continue or abort a pregnancy, she contemplates a decision that affects both self and others and engages directly the critical moral issue of hurting. Since the choice is ultimately hers and therefore one for which she is responsible, it raises precisely those questions of judgment that have been most problematic for women. Now she is asked whether she wishes to interrupt that stream of life which has for centuries immersed her in the passivity of dependence while at the same time imposing on her the responsibility for care. Thus the abortion decision brings to the core of feminine apprehension, to what Joan Didion (1972) calls "the irreconcilable difference of it—that sense of living one's deepest life underwater, that dark involvement with blood and birth and death" (p. 14), the adult questions of responsibility and choice.

How women deal with such choices has been the subject of my research, designed to clarify, through considering the ways in which women construct and resolve the abortion decision, the nature and development of women's moral judgment. Twenty-nine women, diverse in age, race, and social class, were referred by abortion and pregnancy counseling services and participated in the study for a variety of reasons. Some came to gain further clarification with respect to a decision about which they were in conflict, some in response to a counselor's concern about repeated abortions, and others out of an interest in and/or willingness to contribute to ongoing research. Although the pregnancies occurred under a variety of circumstances in the lives of these women, certain commonalities could be discerned. The adolescents often failed to use birth control because they denied or discredited their capacity to bear children. Some of the older women attributed the pregnancy to the omission of contraceptive measures in circumstances where intercourse had not been anticipated. Since the pregnancies often coincided with efforts on the part of the women to end a relationship, they may be seen as a manifestation of ambivalence or as a way of putting the relationship to the ultimate test of commitment. For these women, the pregnancy appeared to be a way of testing truth, making the baby an ally in the search for male support and protection or, that failing, a companion victim of his rejection. There were, finally, some women who became pregnant either as a result of a failure of birth control or intentionally as part of a joint decision that later was reconsidered. Of the twenty-nine women, four decided to have the baby, one miscarried, twenty-one chose abortion, and three remained in doubt about the decision.

In the initial part of the interview, the women were asked to discuss the decision that confronted them, how they were dealing with it, the alternatives they were considering, their reasons for and against each option, the people involved, the conflicts entailed, and the ways in which making this decision affected their self-concepts and their relationships with others. Then, in the second part of the interview, moral judgment was assessed in the hypothetical mode by presenting for resolution three of Kohlberg's standard research dilemmas.

While the structural progression from a preconventional through a conventional to a postconventional moral perspective can readily be discerned in the women's responses to both actual and hypothetical dilemmas, the conventions that shape women's moral judgments differ from those that apply to men. The construction of the abortion dilemma, in particular, reveals the existence of a distinct moral language whose evolution informs the sequence of women's development. This is the language of selfishness and responsibility, which defines the moral problem as one of obligation to exercise care and avoid hurt. The infliction of hurt is considered selfish and immoral in its reflection of unconcern, while the expression of care is seen as the fulfillment of moral responsibility. The reiterative use of the language of selfishness and responsibility and the underlying moral orientation it reflects sets the women apart from the men whom Kohlberg studied and may be seen as the critical reason for their failure to develop within the constraints of his system.

In the developmental sequence that follows, women's moral judgments proceed from an initial focus on the self at the *first level* to the discovery, in the transition to the *second level*, of the concept of responsibility as the basis for a new equilibrium between self and others. The elaboration of this concept of responsibility and its fusion with a maternal concept of morality, which seeks to ensure protection for the dependent and unequal, characterizes the *second level* of judgment. At this level the good is equated with caring for others. However, when the conventions of feminine goodness legitimize only others as the recipients of moral care, the logical inequality between self and other and the psychological violence that it engenders create the disequilibrium that initiates the *second* transition. The relationship between self and others is then reconsidered in an effort to sort out the confusion between conformity and care inherent in the conventional definition of feminine goodness and to establish a new equilibrium, which dissipates the tension between selfishness and responsibility. At the *third level,* the self becomes the arbiter of an independent judgment that now subsumes both conventions and individual needs under the moral principle of nonviolence. Judgment remains psychological in its concern with the intention and consequences of action, but it now becomes universal in its condemnation of exploitation and hurt.

Level I: Orientation to Individual Survival

In its initial and simplest construction, the abortion decision centers on the self. The concern is pragmatic, and the issue is individual survival. At this level, "should" is undifferentiated from "would," and others influence the decision only through their power to affect its consequences. An eighteen-year-old, asked what she thought when she found herself pregnant, replies: "I really didn't think anything except that I didn't want it. [Why was that?] I didn't want it, I wasn't ready for it, and next year will be my last year and I want to go to school."

Asked if there was a right decision, she says, "There is no right decision. [Why?]

492

12

I didn't want it." For her the question of right decision would emerge only if her own needs were in conflict; then she would have to decide which needs should take precedence. This was the dilemma of another eighteen-year-old, who saw having a baby as a way of increasing her freedom by providing "the perfect chance to get married and move away from home," but also as restricting her freedom "to do a lot of things."

At this first level, the self, which is the sole object of concern, is constrained by lack of power; the wish "to do a lot of things" is constantly belied by the limitations of what, in fact, is being done. Relationships are, for the most part, disappointing: "The only thing you are ever going to get out of going with a guy is to get hurt." As a result, women may in some instances deliberately choose isolation to protect themselves against hurt. When asked how she would describe herself to herself, a nineteen-year-old, who held herself responsible for the accidental death of a younger brother, answers as follows:

> I really don't know. I never thought about it. I don't know. I know basically the outline of a character. I am very independent. I don't really want to have to ask anybody for anything and I am a loner in life. I prefer to be by myself than around anybody else. I manage to keep my friends at a limited number with the point that I have very few friends. I don't know what else there is. I am a loner and I enjoy it. Here today and gone tomorrow.

The primacy of the concern with survival is explicitly acknowledged by a sixteen-year-old delinquent in response to Kohlberg's Heinz dilemma, which asks if it is right for a desperate husband to steal an outrageously overpriced drug to save the life of his dying wife:

> I think survival is one of the first things in life and that people fight for. I think it is the most important thing, more important than stealing. Stealing might be wrong, but if you have to steal to survive yourself or even kill, that is what you should do. . . . Preservation of oneself, I think, is the most important thing; it comes before anything in life.

The First Transition: From Selfishness to Responsibility

In the transition which follows and criticizes this level of judgment, the words selfishness and responsibility first appear. Their reference initially is to the self in a redefinition of the self-interest which has thus far served as the basis for judgment. The transitional issue is one of attachment or connection to others. The pregnancy catches up the issue not only by representing an immediate, literal connection, but also by affirming, in the most concrete and physical way, the capacity to assume adult feminine roles. However, while having a baby seems at first to offer respite from the loneliness of adolescence and to solve conflicts over dependence and independence, in reality the continuation of an adolescent pregnancy generally compounds these problems, increasing social isolation and precluding further steps toward independence.

To be a mother in the societal as well as the physical sense requires the assumption of parental responsibility for the care and protection of a child. However, in

493

13

order to be able to care for another, one must first be able to care responsibly for oneself. The growth from childhood to adulthood, conceived as a move from selfishness to responsibility, is articulated explicitly in these terms by a seventeen-year-old who describes her response to her pregnancy as follows:

> I started feeling really good about being pregnant instead of feeling really bad, because I wasn't looking at the situation realistically. I was looking at it from my own sort of selfish needs because I was lonely and felt lonely and stuff. . . . Things weren't really going good for me, so I was looking at it that I could have a baby that I could take care of or something that was part of me, and that made me feel good . . . but I wasn't looking at the realistic side . . . about the responsibility I would have to take on . . . I came to this decision that I was going to have an abortion [because] I realized how much responsibility goes with having a child. Like you have to be there, you can't be out of the house all the time which is one thing I like to do . . . and I decided that I have to take on responsibility for myself and I have to work out a lot of things.

Stating her former mode of judgment, the wish to have a baby as a way of combating loneliness and feeling connected, she now criticizes that judgment as both "selfish" and "unrealistic." The contradiction between wishes for a baby and for the freedom to be "out of the house all the time"—that is, for connection and also for independence—is resolved in terms of a new priority, as the criterion for judgment changes. The dilemma now assumes moral definition as the emergent conflict between wish and necessity is seen as a disparity between "would" and "should." In this construction the "selfishness" of willful decision is counterposed to the "responsibility" of moral choice:

> What I want to do is to have the baby, but what I feel I should do which is what I need to do, is have an abortion right now, because sometimes what you want isn't right. Sometimes what is necessary comes before what you want, because it might not always lead to the right thing.

While the pregnancy itself confirms femininity—"I started feeling really good; it sort of made me feel, like being pregnant, I started feeling like a woman"—the abortion decision becomes an opportunity for the adult exercise of responsible choice.

> [How would you describe yourself to yourself?] I am looking at myself differently in the way that I have had a really heavy decision put upon me, and I have never really had too many hard decisions in my life, and I have made it. It has taken some responsibility to do this. I have changed in that way, that I have made a hard decision. And that has been good. Because before, I would not have looked at it realistically, in my opinion. I would have gone by what I wanted to do, and I wanted it, and even if it wasn't right. So I see myself as I'm becoming more mature in ways of making decisions and taking care of myself, doing something for myself. I think it is going to help me in other ways, if I have other decisions to make put upon me, which would take some responsibility. And I would know that I could make them.

In the epiphany of this cognitive reconstruction, the old becomes transformed in terms of the new. The wish to "do something for myself" remains, but the terms of its fulfillment change as the decision affirms both femininity and adulthood in its integration of responsibility and care. Morality, says another adolescent, "is the way you think about yourself . . . sooner or later you have to make up your mind to start taking care of yourself. Abortion, if you do it for the right reasons, is helping yourself to start over and do different things."

Since this transition signals an enhancement in self-worth, it requires a conception of self which includes the possibility for doing "the right thing," the ability to see in oneself the potential for social acceptance. When such confidence is seriously in doubt, the transitional questions may be raised but development is impeded. The failure to make this first transition, despite an understanding of the issues involved, is illustrated by a woman in her late twenties Her struggle with the conflict between selfishness and responsibility pervades but fails to resolve her dilemma of whether or not to have a third abortion.

> I think you have to think about the people who are involved, including yourself. You have responsibilities to yourself . . . and to make a right, whatever that is, decision in this depends on your knowledge and awareness of the responsibilities that you have and whether you can survive with a child and what it will do to your relationship with the father or how it will affect him emotionally.

Rejecting the idea of selling the baby and making "a lot of money in a black market kind of thing . . . because mostly I operate on principles and it would just rub me the wrong way to think I would be selling my own child," she struggles with a concept of responsibility which repeatedly turns back on the question of her own survival. Transition seems blocked by a self-image which is insistently contradictory:

> [How would you describe yourself to yourself?] I see myself as impulsive, practical—that is a contradiction—and moral and amoral, a contradiction. Actually the only thing that is consistent and not contradictory is the fact that I am very lazy which everyone has always told me is really a symptom of something else which I have never been able to put my finger on exactly. It has taken me a long time to like myself. In fact there are times when I don't, which I think is healthy to a point and sometimes I think I like myself too much and I probably evade myself too much, which avoids responsibility to myself and to other people who like me. I am pretty unfaithful to myself. . . I have a hard time even thinking that I am a human being, simply because so much rotten stuff goes on and people are so crummy and insensitive.

Seeing herself as avoiding responsibility, she can find no basis upon which to resolve the pregnancy dilemma. Instead, her inability to arrive at any clear sense of decision only contributes further to her overall sense of failure. Criticizing her parents for having betrayed her during adolescence by coercing her to have an abortion she did not want, she now betrays herself and criticizes that as well. In this light, it is less surprising that she considered selling her child, since she felt herself to have, in effect, been sold by her parents for the sake of maintaining their social status.

495

15

The Second Level: Goodness as Self-Sacrifice

The transition from selfishness to responsibility is a move toward social participation. Whereas at the first level, morality is seen as a matter of sanctions imposed by a society of which one is more subject than citizen, at the second level, moral judgment comes to rely on shared norms and expectations. The woman at this level validates her claim to social membership through the adoption of societal values. Consensual judgment becomes paramount and goodness the overriding concern as survival is now seen to depend on acceptance by others.

Here the conventional feminine voice emerges with great clarity, defining the self and proclaiming its worth on the basis of the ability to care for and protect others. The woman now constructs the world perfused with the assumptions about feminine goodness reflected in the stereotypes of the Broverman et al. (1972) studies. There the attributes considered desirable for women all presume an other, a recipient of the "tact, gentleness and easy expression of feeling" which allow the woman to respond sensitively while evoking in return the care which meets her own "very strong need for security" (p. 63). The strength of this position lies in its capacity for caring; its limitation is the restriction it imposes on direct expression. Both qualities are elucidated by a nineteen-year-old who contrasts her reluctance to criticize with her boyfriend's straightforwardness:

> I never want to hurt anyone, and I tell them in a very nice way, and I have respect for their own opinions, and they can do the things the way that they want, and he usually tells people right off the bat. . . . He does a lot of things out in public which I do in private. . . . it is better, the other [his way], but I just could never do it.

While her judgment clearly exists, it is not expressed, at least not in public. Concern for the feelings of others imposes a deference which she nevertheless criticizes in an awareness that, under the name of consideration, a vulnerability and a duplicity are concealed.

At the second level of judgment, it is specifically over the issue of hurting that conflict arises with respect to the abortion decision. When no option exists that can be construed as being in the best interest of everyone, when responsibilities conflict and decision entails the sacrifice of somebody's needs, then the woman confronts the seemingly impossible task of choosing the victim. A nineteen-year-old, fearing the consequences for herself of a second abortion but facing the opposition of both her family and her lover to the continuation of the pregnancy, describes the dilemma as follows:

> I don't know what choices are open to me; it is either to have it or the abortion; these are the choices open to me. It is just that either way I don't . . . I think what confuses me is it is a choice of either hurting myself or hurting other people around me. What is more important? If there could be a happy medium, it would be fine, but there isn't. It is either hurting someone on this side or hurting myself.

While the feminine identification of goodness with self-sacrifice seems clearly to dictate the "right" resolution of this dilemma, the stakes may be high for the woman herself, and the sacrifice of the fetus, in any event, compromises the altruism of an abortion motivated by a concern for others. Since femininity itself is in conflict in an abortion intended as an expression of love and care, this is a resolution which readily explodes in its own contradiction.

"I don't think anyone should have to choose between two things that they love," says a twenty-five-year-old woman who assumed responsibility not only for her lover but also for his wife and children in having an abortion she did not want:

> I just wanted the child and I really don't believe in abortions. Who can say when life begins. I think that life begins at conception and . . . I felt like there were changes happening in my body and I felt very protective . . . [but] I felt a responsibility, my responsibility if anything ever happened to her [his wife]. He made me feel that I had to make a choice and there was only one choice to make and that was to have an abortion and I could always have children another time and he made me feel if I didn't have it that it would drive us apart.

The abortion decision was, in her mind, a choice not to choose with respect to the pregnancy—"That was my choice, I had to do it." Instead, it was a decision to subordinate the pregnancy to the continuation of a relationship that she saw as encompassing her life—"Since I met him, he has been my life. I do everything for him; my life sort of revolves around him." Since she wanted to have the baby and also to continue the relationship, either choice could be construed as selfish. Furthermore, since both alternatives entailed hurting someone, neither could be considered moral. Faced with a decision which, in her own terms, was untenable, she sought to avoid responsibility for the choice she made, construing the decision as a sacrifice of her own needs to those of her lover. However, this public sacrifice in the name of responsibility engendered a private resentment that erupted in anger, compromising the very relationship that it had been intended to sustain.

> Afterwards we went through a bad time because I hate to say it and I was wrong, but I blamed him. I gave in to him. But when it came down to it, I made the decision. I could have said, 'I am going to have this child whether you want me to or not,' and I just didn't do it.

Pregnant again by the same man, she recognizes in retrospect that the choice in fact had been hers, as she returns once again to what now appears to have been missed opportunity for growth. Seeking, this time, to make rather than abdicate the decision, she sees the issue as one of "strength" as she struggles to free herself from the powerlessness of her own dependence:

> I think that right now I think of myself as someone who can become a lot stronger. Because of the circumstances, I just go along like with the tide. I never really had anything of my own before . . . [this time] I hope to come on strong and make a big decision, whether it is right or wrong.

Because the morality of self-sacrifice had justified the previous abortion, she now must suspend that judgment if she is to claim her own voice and accept responsibility for choice.

She thereby calls into question the underlying assumption of Level Two, which leads the woman to consider herself responsible for the actions of others, while holding others responsible for the choices she makes. This notion of reciprocity, backwards in its assumptions about control, disguises assertion as response. By reversing responsibility, it generates a series of indirect actions, which leave everyone feeling manipulated and betrayed. The logic of this position is confused in that the morality of mutual care is embedded in the psychology of dependence. Assertion becomes personally dangerous in its risk of criticism and abandonment, as well as potentially immoral in its power to hurt. This confusion is captured by Kohlberg's (1969) definition of Stage Three moral judgment, which joins the need for approval with the wish to care for and help others.

When thus caught between the passivity of dependence and the activity of care, the woman becomes suspended in an immobility of both judgment and action. "If I were drowning, I couldn't reach out a hand to save myself, so unwilling am I to set myself up against fate" (p. 7), begins the central character of Margaret Drabble's novel, *The Waterfall* (1971), in an effort to absolve herself of responsibility as she at the same time relinquishes control. Facing the same moral conflict which George Eliot depicted in *The Mill on the Floss,* Drabble's heroine proceeds to relive Maggie Tulliver's dilemma but turns inward in her search for the way in which to retell that story. What is initially suspended and then called into question is the judgment which "had in the past made it seem better to renounce myself than them" (Drabble, p. 50).

The Second Transition: From Goodness to Truth

The second transition begins with the reconsideration of the relationship between self and other, as the woman starts to scrutinize the logic of self-sacrifice in the service of a morality of care. In the interview data, this transition is announced by the reappearance of the word selfish. Retrieving the judgmental initiative, the woman begins to ask whether it is selfish or responsible, moral or immoral, to include her own needs within the compass of her care and concern. This question leads her to reexamine the concept of responsibility, juxtaposing the outward concern with what other people think with a new inner judgment.

In separating the voice of the self from those of others, the woman asks if it is possible to be responsible to herself as well as to others and thus to reconcile the disparity between hurt and care. The exercise of such responsibility, however, requires a new kind of judgment whose first demand is for honesty. To be responsible, it is necessary first to acknowledge what it is that one is doing. The criterion for judgment thus shifts from "goodness" to "truth" as the morality of action comes to be assessed not on the basis of its appearance in the eyes of others, but in terms of the realities of its intention and consequence.

A twenty-four-year-old married Catholic woman, pregnant again two months following the birth of her first child, identifies her dilemma as one of choice: "You have to now decide; because it is now available, you have to make a decision. And if it wasn't available, there was no choice open; you just do what you have to do." In the absence of legal abortion, a morality of self-sacrifice was necessary in order to

18

insure protection and care for the dependent child. However, when such sacrifice becomes optional, the entire problem is recast.

The abortion decision is framed by this woman first in terms of her responsibilities to others: having a second child at this time would be contrary to medical advice and would strain both the emotional and financial resources of the family. However, there is, she says, a third reason for having an abortion, "sort of an emotional reason. I don't know if it is selfish or not, but it would really be tying myself down and right now I am not ready to be tied down with two."

Against this combination of selfish and responsible reasons for abortion is her Catholic belief that

> . . . it is taking a life, and it is. Even though it is not formed, it is the potential, and to me it is still taking a life. But I have to think of mine, my son's and my husband's, to think about, and at first I think that I thought it was for selfish reasons, but it is not. I believe that too, some of it is selfish. I don't want another one right now; I am not ready for it.

The dilemma arises over the issue of justification for taking a life: "I can't cover it over, because I believe this and if I do try to cover it over, I know that I am going to be in a mess. It will be denying what I am really doing." Asking "Am I doing the right thing; is it moral?," she counterposes to her belief against abortion her concern with the consequences of continuing the pregnancy. While concluding that "I can't be so morally strict as to hurt three other people with a decision just because of my moral beliefs," the issue of goodness still remains critical to her resolution of the dilemma:

> The moral factor is there. To me it is taking a life, and I am going to take that upon myself, that decision upon myself and I have feelings about it, and talked to a priest . . . but he said it is there and it will be from now on, and it is up to the person if they can live with the idea and still believe they are good.

The criteria for goodness, however, move inward as the ability to have an abortion and still consider herself good comes to hinge on the issue of selfishness with which she struggles to come to terms. Asked if acting morally is acting according to what is best for the self or whether it is a matter of self-sacrifice, she replies:

> I don't know if I really understand the question. . . . Like in my situation where I want to have the abortion and if I didn't it would be self-sacrificing, I am really in the middle of both those ways . . . but I think that my morality is strong and if these reasons—financial, physical reality and also for the whole family involved— were not here, that I wouldn't have to do it, and then it would be a self-sacrifice.

The importance of clarifying her own participation in the decision is evident in her attempt to ascertain her feelings in order to determine whether or not she was "putting them under" in deciding to end the pregnancy. Whereas in the first transition, from selfishness to responsibility, women made lists in order to bring to their consideration needs other than their own, now, in the second transition, it is the needs of the self which have to be deliberately uncovered. Confronting the

499

19

reality of her own wish for an abortion, she now must deal with the problem of selfishness and the qualification that she feels it imposes on the "goodness" of her decision. The primacy of this concern is apparent in her description of herself:

> I think in a way I am selfish for one thing, and very emotional, very . . . and I think that I am a very real person and an understanding person and I can handle life situations fairly well, so I am basing a lot of it on my ability to do the things that I feel are right and best for me and whoever I am involved with. I think I was very fair to myself about the decision, and I really think that I have been truthful, not hiding anything, bringing out all the feelings involved. I feel it is a good decision and an honest one, a real decision.

Thus she strives to encompass the needs of both self and others, to be responsible to others and thus to be "good" but also to be responsible to herself and thus to be "honest" and "real."

While from one point of view, attention to one's own needs is considered selfish, when looked at from a different perspective, it is a matter of honesty and fairness. This is the essence of the transitional shift toward a new conception of goodness which turns inward in an acknowledgement of the self and an acceptance of responsibility for decision. While outward justification, the concern with "good reasons," remains critical for this particular woman: "I still think abortion is wrong, and it will be unless the situation can justify what you are doing." But the search for justification has produced a change in her thinking, "not drastically, but a little bit." She realizes that in continuing the pregnancy she would punish not only herself but also her husband, toward whom she had begun to feel "turned off and irritated." This leads her to consider the consequences self-sacrifice can have both for the self and for others. "God," she says, "can punish, but He can also forgive." What remains in question is whether her claim to forgiveness is compromised by a decision that not only meets the needs of others but that also is "right and best for me."

The concern with selfishness and its equation with immorality recur in an interview with another Catholic woman whose arrival for an abortion was punctuated by the statement, "I have always thought abortion was a fancy word for murder." Initially explaining this murder as one of lesser degree—"I am doing it because I have to do it. I am not doing it the least bit because I want to," she judges it "not quite as bad. You can rationalize that it is not quite the same." Since "keeping the child for lots and lots of reasons was just sort of impractical and out," she considers her options to be either abortion or adoption. However, having previously given up one child for adoption, she says: "I knew that psychologically there was no way that I could hack another adoption. It took me about four-and-a-half years to get my head on straight; there was just no way I was going to go through it again." The decision thus reduces in her eyes to a choice between murdering the fetus or damaging herself. The choice is further complicated by the fact that by continuing the pregnancy she would hurt not only herself but also her parents, with whom she lived. In the face of these manifold moral contradictions, the psychological demand for honesty that arises in counseling finally allows decision:

500

20

> On my own, I was doing it not so much for myself; I was doing it for my parents. I was doing it because the doctor told me to do it, but I had never resolved in my mind that I was doing it for me. Because it goes right back to the fact that I never believed in abortions. . . . Actually, I had to sit down and admit, no, I really don't want to go the mother route now. I honestly don't feel that I want to be a mother, and that is not really such a bad thing to say after all. But that is not how I felt up until talking to Maureen [her counselor]. It was just a horrible way to feel, so I just wasn't going to feel it, and I just blocked it right out.

As long as her consideration remains "moral," abortion can be justified only as an act of sacrifice, a submission to necessity where the absence of choice precludes responsibility. In this way, she can avoid self-condemnation, since, "When you get into moral stuff then you are getting into self-respect and that stuff, and at least if I do something that I feel is morally wrong, then I tend to lose some of my self-respect as a person." Her evasion of responsibility, critical to maintaining the innocence necessary for self-respect, contradicts the reality of her own participation in the abortion decision. The dishonesty in her plea of victimization creates the conflict that generates the need for a more inclusive understanding. She must now resolve the emerging contradiction in her thinking between two uses of the term right: "I am saying that abortion is morally wrong, but the situation is right, and I am going to do it. But the thing is that eventually they are going to have to go together, and I am going to have to put them together somehow." Asked how this could be done, she replies:

> I would have to change morally wrong to morally right. [How?] I have no idea. I don't think you can take something that you feel is morally wrong because the situation makes it right and put the two together. They are not together, they are opposite. They don't go together. Something is wrong, but all of a sudden because you are doing it, it is right.

This discrepancy recalls a similar conflict she faced over the question of euthanasia, also considered by her to be morally wrong until she "took care of a couple of patients who had flat EEGs and saw the job that it was doing on their families." Recalling that experience, she says:

> You really don't know your black and whites until you really get into them and are being confronted with it. If you stop and think about my feelings on euthanasia until I got into it, and then my feelings about abortion until I got into it, I thought both of them were murder. Right and wrong and no middle but there is a gray.

In discovering the gray and questioning the moral judgments which formerly she considered to be absolute, she confronts the moral crisis of the second transition. Now the conventions which in the past had guided her moral judgment become subject to a new criticism, as she questions not only the justification for hurting others in the name of morality but also the "rightness" of hurting herself. However, to sustain such criticism in the face of conventions that equate goodness

501

21

with self-sacrifice, the woman must verify her capacity for independent judgment and the legitimacy of her own point of view.

Once again transition hinges on self-concept. When uncertainty about her own worth prevents a woman from claiming equality, self-assertion falls prey to the old criticism of selfishness. Then the morality that condones self-destruction in the name of responsible care is not repudiated as inadequate but rather is abandoned in the face of its threat to survival. Moral obligation, rather than expanding to include the self, is rejected completely as the failure of conventional reciprocity leaves the woman unwilling any longer to protect others at what is now seen to be her own expense. In the absence of morality, survival, however "selfish" or "immoral," returns as the paramount concern.

A musician in her late twenties illustrates this transitional impasse. Having led an independent life which centered on her work, she considered herself "fairly strong-willed, fairly in control, fairly rational and objective" until she became involved in an intense love affair and discovered in her capacity to love "an entirely new dimension" in herself. Admitting in retrospect to "tremendous naiveté and idealism," she had entertained "some vague ideas that some day I would like a child to concretize our relationship . . . having always associated having a child with all the creative aspects of my life." Abjuring, with her lover, the use of contraceptives because, "as the relationship was sort of an ideal relationship in our minds, we liked the idea of not using foreign objects or anything artificial," she saw herself as having relinquished control, becoming instead "just simply vague and allowing events to just carry me along." Just as she began in her own thinking to confront "the realities of that situation"—the possibility of pregnancy and the fact that her lover was married—she found herself pregnant. "Caught" between her wish to end a relationship that "seemed more and more defeating" and her wish for a baby, which "would be a connection that would last a long time," she is paralyzed by her inability to resolve the dilemma which her ambivalence creates.

The pregnancy poses a conflict between her "moral" belief that "once a certain life has begun, it shouldn't be stopped artificially" and her "amazing" discovery that to have the baby she would "need much more [support] than I thought." Despite her moral conviction that she "should" have the child, she doubts that she could psychologically deal with "having the child alone and taking the responsibility for it." Thus a conflict erupts between what she considers to be her moral obligation to protect life and her inability to do so under the circumstances of this pregnancy. Seeing it as "my decision and my responsibility for making the decision whether to have or have not the child," she struggles to find a viable basis on which to resolve the dilemma.

Capable of arguing either for or against abortion "with a philosophical logic," she says, on the one hand, that in an overpopulated world one should have children only under ideal conditions for care but, on the other, that one should end a life only when it is impossible to sustain it. She describes her impasse in response to the question of whether there is a difference between what she wants to do and what she thinks she should do:

> Yes, and there always has. I have always been confronted with that precise situation in a lot of my choices, and I have been trying to figure out what are the things that make me believe that these are things I should do as opposed to what I feel I want to do. [In this situation?] It is not that clear cut. I both want the child and feel I should have it, and I also think I should have the abortion and want it, but I would say it is my stronger feeling, and that I don't have enough confidence in my work yet and that is really where it is all hinged, I think . . . [the abortion] would solve the problem and I know I can't handle the pregnancy.

Characterizing this solution as "emotional and pragmatic" and attributing it to her lack of confidence in her work, she contrasts it with the "better thought out and more logical and more correct" resolution of her lover who thinks that she should have the child and raise it without either his presence or financial support. Confronted with this reflected image of herself as ultimately giving and good, as self-sustaining in her own creativity and thus able to meet the needs of others while imposing no demands of her own in return, she questions not the image itself but her own adequacy in filling it. Concluding that she is not yet capable of doing so, she is reduced in her own eyes to what she sees as a selfish and highly compromised fight

> for my survival. But in one way or another, I am going to suffer. Maybe I am going to suffer mentally and emotionally having the abortion, or I would suffer what I think is possibly something worse. So I suppose it is the lesser of two evils. I think it is a matter of choosing which one I know that I can survive through. It is really. I think it is selfish, I suppose, because it does have to do with that. I just realized that. I guess it does have to do with whether I would survive or not. [Why is this selfish?] Well, you know, it is. Because I am concerned with my survival first, as opposed to the survival of the relationship or the survival of the child, another human being . . . I guess I am setting priorities, and I guess I am setting my needs to survive first. . . . I guess I see it in negative terms a lot . . . but I do think of other positive things; that I am still going to have some life left, maybe. I don't know.

In the face of this failure of reciprocity of care, in the disappointment of abandonment where connection was sought, survival is seen to hinge on her work which is "where I derive the meaning of what I am. That's the known factor." While uncertainty about her work makes this survival precarious, the choice for abortion is also distressing in that she considers it to be "highly introverted—that in this one respect, having an abortion would be going a step backward; going outside to love someone else and having a child would be a step forward." The sense of retrenchment that the severing of connection signifies is apparent in her anticipation of the cost which abortion would entail:

> Probably what I will do is I will cut off my feelings, and when they will return or what would happen to them after that, I don't know. So that I don't feel anything at all, and I would probably just be very cold and go through it very coldly. . . . The more you do that to yourself, the more difficult it becomes to love again or to trust again or to feel again. . . . Each time I move away from that, it

503

becomes easier, not more difficult, but easier to avoid committing myself to a relationship. And I am really concerned about cutting off that whole feeling aspect.

Caught between selfishness and responsibility, unable to find in the circumstances of this choice a way of caring which does not at the same time destroy, she confronts a dilemma which reduces to a conflict between morality and survival. Adulthood and femininity fly apart in the failure of this attempt at integration as the choice to work becomes a decision not only to renounce this particular relationship and child but also to obliterate the vulnerability that love and care engender.

The Third Level: The Morality of Nonviolence

In contrast, a twenty-five-year-old woman, facing a similar disappointment, finds a way to reconcile the initially disparate concepts of selfishness and responsibility through a transformed understanding of self and a corresponding redefinition of morality. Examining the assumptions underlying the conventions of feminine self-abnegation and moral self-sacrifice, she comes to reject these conventions as immoral in their power to hurt. By elevating nonviolence—the injunction against hurting—to a principle governing all moral judgment and action, she is able to assert a moral equality between self and other. Care then becomes a universal obligation, the self-chosen ethic of a postconventional judgment that reconstructs the dilemma in a way that allows the assumption of responsibility for choice.

In this woman's life, the current pregnancy brings to the surface the unfinished business of an earlier pregnancy and of the relationship in which both pregnancies occurred. The first pregnancy was discovered after her lover had left and was terminated by an abortion experienced as a purging expression of her anger at having been rejected. Remembering the abortion only as a relief, she nevertheless describes that time in her life as one in which she "hit rock bottom." Having hoped then to "take control of my life," she instead resumed the relationship when the man reappeared. Now, two years later, having once again "left my diaphragm in the drawer," she again becomes pregnant. Although initially "ecstatic" at the news, her elation dissipates when her lover tells her that he will leave if she chooses to have the child. Under these circumstances, she considers a second abortion but is unable to keep the repeated appointments she makes because of her reluctance to accept the responsibility for that choice. While the first abortion seemed an "honest mistake," she says that a second would make her feel "like a walking slaughter-house." Since she would need financial support to raise the child, her initial strategy was to take the matter to "the welfare people" in the hope that they would refuse to provide the necessary funds and thus resolve her dilemma:

> In that way, you know, the responsibility would be off my shoulders, and I could say, it's not my fault, you know, the state denied me the money that I would need to do it. But it turned out that it was possible to do it, and so I was, you know, right back where I started. And I had an appointment for an abortion, and I kept calling and cancelling it and then remaking the appointment and cancelling it, and I just couldn't make up my mind.

Confronting the need to choose between the two evils of hurting herself or ending the incipient life of the child, she finds, in a reconstruction of the dilemma itself, a basis for a new priority that allows decision. In doing so, she comes to see the conflict as arising from a faulty construction of reality. Her thinking recapitulates the developmental sequence, as she considers but rejects as inadequate the components of earlier-stage resolutions. An expanded conception of responsibility now reshapes moral judgment and guides resolution of the dilemma, whose pros and cons she considers as follows:

> Well, the pros for having the baby are all the admiration that you would get from, you know, being a single woman, alone, martyr, struggling, having the adoring love of this beautiful Gerber baby . . . just more of a home life than I have had in a long time, and that basically was it, which is pretty fantasyland; it is not very realistic. . . . Cons against having the baby: it was going to hasten what is looking to be the inevitable end of the relationship with the man I am presently with. . . . I was going to have to go on welfare, my parents were going to hate me for the rest of my life, I was going to lose a really good job that I have, I would lose a lot of independence . . . solitude . . . and I would have to be put in a position of asking help from a lot of people a lot of the time. Cons against having the abortion is having to face up to the guilt . . . and pros for having the abortion are I would be able to handle my deteriorating relation with S. with a lot more capability and a lot more responsibility for him and for myself . . . and I would not have to go through the realization that for the next twenty-five years of my life I would be punishing myself for being foolish enough to get pregnant again and forcing myself to bring up a kid just because I did this. Having to face the guilt of a second abortion seemed like, not exactly, well, exactly the lesser of the two evils but also the one that would pay off for me personally in the long run because by looking at why I am pregnant again and subsequently have decided to have a second abortion, I have to face up to some things about myself.

Although she doesn't "feel good about having a second abortion," she nevertheless concludes,

> I would not be doing myself or the child or the world any kind of favor having this child. . . . I don't need to pay off my imaginary debts to the world through this child, and I don't think that it is right to bring a child into the world and use it for that purpose.

Asked to describe herself, she indicates how closely her transformed moral understanding is tied to a changing self-concept:

> I have been thinking about that a lot lately, and it comes up different than what my usual subconscious perception of myself is. Usually paying off some sort of debt, going around serving people who are not really worthy of my attentions because somewhere in my life I think I got the impression that my needs are really secondary to other people's, and that if I feel, if I make any demands on other people to fulfill my needs, I'd feel guilty for it and submerge my own in favor of other people's, which later backfires on me, and I feel a great deal of resentment for other people that I am doing things for, which causes friction and the eventual

25

deterioration of the relationship. And then I start all over again. How would I describe myself to myself? Pretty frustrated and a lot angrier than I admit, a lot more aggressive than I admit.

Reflecting on the virtues which comprise the conventional definition of the feminine self, a definition which she hears articulated in her mother's voice, she says, "I am beginning to think that all these virtues are really not getting me anywhere. I have begun to notice." Tied to this recognition is an acknowledgement of her power and worth, both previously excluded from the image she projected:

> I am suddenly beginning to realize that the things that I like to do, the things I am interested in, and the things that I believe and the kind of person I am is not so bad that I have to constantly be sitting on the shelf and letting it gather dust. I am a lot more worthwhile than what my past actions have led other people to believe.

Her notion of a "good person," which previously was limited to her mother's example of hard work, patience and self-sacrifice, now changes to include the value that she herself places on directness and honesty. Although she believes that this new self-assertion will lead her "to feel a lot better about myself" she recognizes that it will also expose her to criticism:

> Other people may say, 'Boy, she's aggressive, and I don't like that,' but at least, you know, they will know that they don't like that. They are not going to say, 'I like the way she manipulates herself to fit right around me.' . . . What I want to do is just be a more self-determined person and a more singular person.

While within her old framework abortion had seemed a way of "copping out" instead of being a "responsible person [who] pays for his mistakes and pays and pays and is always there when she says she will be there and even when she doesn't say she will be there is there," now, her "conception of what I think is right for myself and my conception of self-worth is changing." She can consider this emergent self "also a good person," as her concept of goodness expands to encompass "the feeling of self-worth; you are not going to sell yourself short and you are not going to make yourself do things that, you know, are really stupid and that you don't want to do." This reorientation centers on the awareness that:

> I have a responsibility to myself, and you know, for once I am beginning to realize that that really matters to me . . . instead of doing what I want for myself and feeling guilty over how selfish I am, you realize that that is a very usual way for people to live . . . doing what you want to do because you feel that your wants and your needs are important, if to no one else, then to you, and that's reason enough to do something that you want to do.

Once obligation extends to include the self as well as others, the disparity between selfishness and responsibility is reconciled. Although the conflict between self and other remains, the moral problem is restructured in an awareness that the occurrence of the dilemma itself precludes non-violent resolution. The abortion decision is now seen to be a "serious" choice affecting both self and others: "This is a life that I have taken, a conscious decision to terminate, and that is just very heavy, a very heavy thing." While accepting the necessity of abortion as a highly compromised resolution, she turns her attention to the pregnancy itself, which she now considers to denote a failure of responsibility, a failure to care for and protect both self and other.

As in the first transition, although now in different terms, the conflict precipitated by the pregnancy catches up the issues critical to development. These issues now concern the worth of the self in relation to others, the claiming of the power to choose, and the acceptance of responsibility for choice. By provoking a confrontation with these issues, the crisis can become "a very auspicious time; you can use the pregnancy as sort of a learning, teeing-off point, which makes it useful in a way." This possibility for growth inherent in a crisis which allows confrontation with a construction of reality whose acceptance previously had impeded development was first identified by Coles (1964) in his study of the children of Little Rock. This same sense of possibility is expressed by the women who see, in their resolution of the abortion dilemma, a reconstructed understanding which creates the opportunity for "a new beginning," a chance "to take control of my life."

For this woman, the first step in taking control was to end the relationship in which she had considered herself "reduced to a nonentity," but to do so in a responsible way. Recognizing hurt as the inevitable concomitant of rejection, she strives to minimize that hurt "by dealing with [his] needs as best I can without compromising my own . . . that's a big point for me, because the thing in my life to this point has been always compromising, and I am not willing to do that any more." Instead, she seeks to act in a "decent, human kind of way . . . one that leaves maybe a slightly shook but not totally destroyed person." Thus the "nonentity" confronts her power to destroy which formerly had impeded any assertion, as she consider the possibility for a new kind of action that leaves both self and other intact.

The moral concern remains a concern with hurting as she considers Kohlberg's Heinz dilemma in terms of the question, "who is going to be hurt more, the druggist who loses some money or the person who loses their life?" The right to property and right to life are weighed not in the abstract, in terms of their logical priority, but rather in the particular, in terms of the actual consequences that the violation of these rights would have in the lives of the people involved. Thinking remains contextual and admixed with feelings of care, as the moral imperative to avoid hurt begins to be informed by a psychological understanding of the meaning of nonviolence.

Thus, release from the intimidation of inequality finally allows the expression of a judgment that previously had been withheld. What women then enunciate is not a new morality, but a moral conception disentangled from the constraints that formerly had confused its perception and impeded its articulation. The willingness to express and take responsibility for judgment stems from the recognition of the psychological and moral necessity for an equation of worth between self and other. Responsibility for care then includes both self and other, and the obligation not to hurt, freed from conventional constraints, is reconstructed as a universal guide to moral choice.

The reality of hurt centers the judgment of a twenty-nine-year-old woman, married and the mother of a preschool child, as she struggles with the dilemma posed by a second pregnancy whose timing conflicts with her completion of an advanced degree. Saying that "I cannot deliberately do something that is bad or would hurt another person because I can't live with having done that," she nevertheless confronts a situation in which hurt has become inevitable. Seeking that solution which would best protect both herself and others, she indicates, in her definition of morality, the ineluctable sense of connection which infuses and colors all of her thinking:

> [Morality is] doing what is appropriate and what is just within your circumstances, but ideally it is not going to affect—I was going to say, ideally it wouldn't negatively affect another person, but that is ridiculous, because decisions are always going to affect another person. But you see, what I am trying to say is that it is the person that is the center of the decision making, of that decision making about what's right and what's wrong.

The person who is the center of this decision making begins by denying, but then goes on to acknowledge, the conflicting nature both of her own needs and of her various responsibilities. Seeing the pregnancy as a manifestation of the inner conflict between her wish, on the one hand, "to be a college president" and, on the other, "to be making pottery and flowers and having kids and staying at home," she struggles with contradiction between femininity and adulthood. Considering abortion as the "better" choice—because "in the end, meaning this time next year or this time two weeks from now, it will be less of a personal strain on us individually and on us as a family for me not to be pregnant at this time," she concludes that the decision has

> got to be, first of all, something that the woman can live with—a decision that the woman can live with, one way or another, or at least try to live with, and that it be based on where she is at and other people, significant people in her life, are at.

At the beginning of the interview she had presented the dilemma in its conventional feminine construction, as a conflict between her own wish to have a baby and the wish of others for her to complete her education. On the basis of this construction she deemed it "selfish" to continue the pregnancy because it was something "I want to do." However, as she begins to examine her thinking, she comes to abandon as false this conceptualization of the problem, acknowledging the truth of her own internal conflict and elaborating the tension which she feels between her femininity and the adulthood of her work life. She describes herself as "going in two directions" and values that part of herself which is "incredibly passionate and sensitive"—her capacity to recognize and meet, often with anticipation, the needs of others. Seeing her "compassion" as "something I don't want to lose" she regards it as endangered by her pursuit of professional advancement. Thus the self-deception of her initial presentation, its attempt to sustain the fiction of her own innocence, stems from her fear that to say that *she* does not want to have another baby at this time would be

> an acknowledgement to me that I am an ambitious person and that I want to

have power and responsibility for others and that I want to live a life that extends from 9 to 5 every day and into the evenings and on weekends, because that is what the power and responsibility means. It means that my family would necessarily come second . . . there would be such an incredible conflict about which is tops, and I don't want that for myself.

Asked about her concept of "an ambitious person" she says that to be ambitious means to be

power hungry [and] insensitive. [Why insensitive?] Because people are stomped on in the process. A person on the way up stomps on people, whether it is family or other colleagues or clientele, on the way up. [Inevitably?] Not always, but I have seen it so often in my limited years of working that it is scary to me. It is scary because I don't want to change like that.

Because the acquisition of adult power is seen to entail the loss of feminine sensitivity and compassion, the conflict between femininity and adulthood becomes construed as a moral problem. The discovery of the principle of nonviolence begins to direct attention to the moral dilemma itself and initiates the search for a resolution that can encompass both femininity and adulthood.

Developmental Theory Reconsidered

The developmental conception delineated at the outset, which has so consistently found the development of women to be either aberrant or incomplete, has been limited insofar as it has been predominantly a male conception, giving lip-service, a place on the chart, to the interdependence of intimacy and care but constantly stressing, at their expense, the importance and value of autonomous judgment and action. To admit to this conception the truth of the feminine perspective is to recognize for both sexes the central importance in adult life of the connection between self and other, the universality of the need for compassion and care. The concept of the separate self and of the moral principle uncompromised by the constraints of reality is an adolescent ideal, the elaborately wrought philosophy of a Stephen Daedalus, whose flight we know to be in jeopardy. Erikson (1964), in contrasting the ideological morality of the adolescent with the ethics of adult care, attempts to grapple with this problem of integration, but is impeded by the limitations of his own previous developmental conception. When his developmental stages chart a path where the sole precursor to the intimacy of adult relationships is the trust established in infancy and all intervening experience is marked only as steps toward greater independence, then separation itself becomes the model and the measure of growth. The observation that for women, identity has as much to do with connection as with separation led Erikson into trouble largely because of his failure to integrate this insight into the mainstream of his developmental theory (Erikson, 1968).

The morality of responsibility which women describe stands apart from the morality of rights which underlies Kohlberg's conception of the highest stages of moral judgment. Kohlberg (Note 3) sees the progression toward these stages as

509

resulting from the generalization of the self-centered adolescent rejection of societal morality into a principled conception of individual natural rights. To illustrate this progression, he cites as an example of integrated Stage Five judgment, "possibly moving to Stage Six," the following response of a twenty-five-year-old subject from his male longitudinal sample:

> [What does the word morality mean to you?] Nobody in the world knows the answer. I think it is recognizing the right of the individual, the rights of other individuals, not interfering with those rights. Act as fairly as you would have them treat you. I think it is basically to preserve the human being's right to existence. I think that is the most important. Secondly, the human being's right to do as he pleases, again without interfering with somebody else's rights. (p. 29)

Another version of the same conception is evident in the following interview response of a male college senior whose moral judgment also was scored by Kohlberg (Note 4) as at Stage Five or Six:

> [Morality] is a prescription, it is a thing to follow, and the idea of having a concept of morality is to try to figure out what it is that people can do in order to make life with each other livable, make for a kind of balance, a kind of equilibrium, a harmony in which everybody feels he has a place and an equal share in things, and it's doing that—doing that is kind of contributing to a state of affairs that go beyond the individual in the absence of which, the individual has no chance for self-fulfillment of any kind. Fairness; morality is kind of essential, it seems to me, for creating the kind of environment, interaction between people, that is prerequisite to this fulfillment of most individual goals and so on. If you want other people to not interfere with your pursuit of whatever you are into, you have to play the game.

In contrast, a woman in her late twenties responds to a similar question by defining a morality not of rights but of responsibility:

> [What makes something a moral issue?] Some sense of trying to uncover a right path in which to live, and always in my mind is that the world is full of real and recognizable trouble, and is it heading for some sort of doom and is it right to bring children into this world when we currently have an overpopulation problem, and is it right to spend money on a pair of shoes when I have a pair of shoes and other people are shoeless. . . . It is part of a self-critical view, part of saying, how am I spending my time and in what sense am I working? I think I have a real drive to, I have a real maternal drive to take care of someone. To take care of my mother, to take care of children, to take care of other people's children, to take care of my own children, to take care of the world. I think that goes back to your other question, and when I am dealing with moral issues, I am sort of saying to myself constantly, are you taking care of all the things that you think are important and in what ways are you wasting yourself and wasting those issues?

While the postconventional nature of this woman's perspective seems clear, her judgments of Kohlberg's hypothetical moral dilemmas do not meet his criteria for scoring at the principled level. Kohlberg regards this as a disparity between normative and metaethical judgments which he sees as indicative of the transition

510

30

between conventional and principled thinking. From another perspective, however, this judgment represents a different moral conception, disentangled from societal conventions and raised to the principled level. In this conception, moral judgment is oriented toward issues of responsibility. The way in which the responsibility orientation guides moral decision at the postconventional level is described by the following woman in her thirties:

> [Is there a right way to make moral decisions?] The only way I know is to try to be as awake as possible, to try to know the range of what you feel, to try to consider all that's involved, to be as aware as you can be to what's going on, as conscious as you can of where you're walking. [Are there principles that guide you?] The principle would have something to do with responsibility, responsibility and caring about yourself and others. . . . But it's not that on the one hand you choose to be responsible and on the other hand you choose to be irresponsible—both ways you can be responsible. That's why there's not just a principle that once you take hold of you settle—the principle put into practice here is still going to leave you with conflict.

The moral imperative that emerges repeatedly in the women's interviews is an injunction to care, a responsibility to discern and alleviate the "real and recognizable trouble" of this world. For the men Kohlberg studied, the moral imperative appeared rather as an injunction to respect the rights of others and thus to protect from interference the right to life and self-fulfillment. Women's insistence on care is at first self-critical rather than self-protective, while men initially conceive obligation to others negatively in terms of noninterference. Development for both sexes then would seem to entail an integration of rights and responsibilities through the discovery of the complementarity of these disparate views. For the women I have studied, this integration between rights and responsibilities appears to take place through a principled understanding of equity and reciprocity. This understanding tempers the self-destructive potential of a self-critical morality by asserting the equal right of all persons to care. For the men in Kohlberg's sample as well as for those in a longitudinal study of Harvard undergraduates (Gilligan & Murphy, Note 5) it appears to be the recognition through experience of the need for a more active responsibility in taking care that corrects the potential indifference of a morality of noninterference and turns attention from the logic to the consequences of choice. In the development of a postconventional ethic understanding, women come to see the violence generated by inequitable relationships, while men come to realize the limitations of a conception of justice blinded to the real inequities of human life.

Kohlberg's dilemmas, in the hypothetical abstraction of their presentation, divest the moral actors from the history and psychology of their individual lives and separate the moral problem from the social contingencies of its possible occurrence. In doing so, the dilemmas are useful for the distillation and refinement of the "objective principles of justice" toward which Kohlberg's stages strive. However, the reconstruction of the dilemma in its contextual particularity allows the understanding of cause and consequence which engages the compassion and tolerance considered by previous theorists to qualify the feminine sense of justice. Only

511

31

when substance is given to the skeletal lives of hypothetical people is it possible to consider the social injustices which their moral problems may reflect and to imagine the individual suffering their occurrence may signify or their resolution engender.

The proclivity of women to reconstruct hypothetical dilemmas in terms of the real, to request or supply the information missing about the nature of the people and the places where they live, shifts their judgment away from the hierarchical ordering of principles and the formal procedures of decision making that are critical for scoring at Kohlberg's highest stages. This insistence on the particular signifies an orientation to the dilemma and to moral problems in general that differs from any of Kohlberg's stage descriptions. Given the constraints of Kohlberg's system and the biases in his research sample, this different orientation can only be construed as a failure in development. While several of the women in the research sample clearly articulated what Kohlberg regarded as a postconventional metaethical position, none of them were considered by Kohlberg to be principled in their normative moral judgments of his hypothetical moral dilemmas (Note 4). Instead, the women's judgments pointed toward an identification of the violence inherent in the dilemma itself which was seen to compromise the justice of any of its possible resolutions. This construction of the dilemma led the women to recast the moral judgment from a consideration of the good to a choice between evils.

The woman whose judgment of the abortion dilemma concluded the developmental sequence presented in the preceding section saw Kohlberg's Heinz dilemma in these terms and judged Heinz's action in terms of a choice between selfishness and sacrifice. For Heinz to steal the drug, given the circumstances of his life (which she inferred from his inability to pay two thousand dollars), he would have "to do something which is not in his best interest, in that he is going to get sent away, and that is a supreme sacrifice, a sacrifice which I would say a person truly in love might be willing to make." However, not to steal the drug "would be selfish on his part . . . he would just have to feel guilty about not allowing her a chance to live longer." Heinz's decision to steal is considered not in terms of the logical priority of life over property which justifies its rightness, but rather in terms of the actual consequences that stealing would have for a man of limited means and little social power.

Considered in the light of its probable outcomes—his wife dead, or Heinz in jail, brutalized by the violence of that experience and his life compromised by a record of felony—the dilemma itself changes. Its resolution has less to do with the relative weights of life and property in an abstract moral conception than with the collision it has produced between two lives, formerly conjoined but now in opposition, where the continuation of one life can now occur only at the expense of the other. Given this construction, it becomes clear why consideration revolves around the issue of sacrifice and why guilt becomes the inevitable concomitant of either resolution.

Demonstrating the reticence noted in the first section about making moral judgments, this woman explains her reluctance to judge in terms of her belief

512

that everybody's existence is so different that I kind of say to myself, that might be something that I wouldn't do, but I can't say that it is right or wrong for that person. I can only deal with what is appropriate for me to do when I am faced with specific problems.

Asked if she would apply to others her own injunction against hurting, she says:

See, I can't say that it is wrong. I can't say that it is right or that it's wrong because I don't know what the person did that the other person did something to hurt him . . . so it is not right that the person got hurt, but it is right that the person who just lost the job has got to get that anger up and out. It doesn't put any bread on his table, but it is released. I don't mean to be copping out. I really am trying to see how to answer these questions for you.

Her difficulty in answering Kohlberg's questions, her sense of strain with the construction which they impose on the dilemma, stems from their divergence from her own frame of reference:

I don't even think I use the words right and wrong anymore, and I know I don't use the word moral, because I am not sure I know what it means. . . . We are talking about an unjust society, we are talking about a whole lot of things that are not right, that are truly wrong, to use the word that I don't use very often, and I have no control to change that. If I could change it, I certainly would, but I can only make my small contribution from day to day, and if I don't intentionally hurt somebody, that is my contribution to a better society. And so a chunk of that contribution is also not to pass judgment on other people, particularly when I don't know the circumstances of why they are doing certain things.

The reluctance to judge remains a reluctance to hurt, but one that stems now not from a sense of personal vulnerability but rather from a recognition of the limitations of judgment itself. The deference of the conventional feminine perspective can thus be seen to continue at the postconventional level, not as moral relativism but rather as part of a reconstructed moral understanding. Moral judgment is renounced in an awareness of the psychological and social determinism of all human behavior at the same time as moral concern is reaffirmed in recognition of the reality of human pain and suffering.

I have a real thing about hurting people and always have, and that gets a little complicated at times, because, for example, you don't want to hurt your child. I don't want to hurt my child but if I don't hurt her sometimes, then that's hurting her more, you see, and so that was a terrible dilemma for me.

Moral dilemmas are terrible in that they entail hurt; she sees Heinz's decision as "the result of anguish, who am I hurting, why do I have to hurt them." While the morality of Heinz's theft is not in question, given the circumstances which necessitated it, what is at issue is his willingness to substitute himself for his wife and become, in her stead, the victim of exploitation by a society which breeds and legitimizes the druggist's irresponsibility and whose injustice is thus manifest in the very occurrence of the dilemma.

513

33

The same sense that the wrong questions are being asked is evident in the response of another woman who justified Heinz's action on a similar basis, saying "I don't think that exploitation should really be a right." When women begin to make direct moral statements, the issues they repeatedly address are those of exploitation and hurt. In doing so, they raise the issue of nonviolence in precisely the same psychological context that brought Erikson (1969) to pause in his consideration of the truth of Gandhi's life.

In the pivotal letter, around which the judgment of his book turns, Erikson confronts the contradiction between the philosophy of nonviolence that informed Gandhi's dealing with the British and the psychology of violence that marred his relationships with his family and with the children of the ashram. It was this contradiction, Erikson confesses,

> which almost brought *me* to the point where I felt unable to continue writing *this* book because I seemed to sense the presence of a kind of untruth in the very protestation of truth; of something unclean when all the words spelled out an unreal purity; and, above all, of displaced violence where nonviolence was the professed issue. (p. 231)

In an effort to untangle the relationship between the spiritual truth of Satyagraha and the truth of his own psychoanalytic understanding, Erikson reminds Gandhi that "Truth, you once said, 'excludes the use of violence because man is not capable of knowing the absolute truth and therefore is not competent to punish'" (p. 241). The affinity between Satyagraha and psychoanalysis lies in their shared commitment to seeing life as an "experiment in truth," in their being

> somehow joined in a universal "therapeutics," committed to the Hippocratic principle that one can test truth (or the healing power inherent in a sick situation) only by action which avoids harm—or better, by action which maximizes mutuality and minimizes the violence caused by unilateral coercion or threat. (p. 247)

Erikson takes Gandhi to task for his failure to acknowledge the relativity of truth. This failure is manifest in the coercion of Gandhi's claim to exclusive possession of the truth, his "unwillingness to learn from *anybody anything* except what was approved by the 'inner voice'" (p. 236). This claim led Gandhi, in the guise of love, to impose his truth on others without awareness or regard for the extent to which he thereby did violence to their integrity.

The moral dilemma, arising inevitably out of a conflict of truths, is by definition a "sick situation" in that its either/or formulation leaves no room for an outcome that does not do violence. The resolution of such dilemmas, however, lies not in the self-deception of rationalized violence—"I was" said Gandhi, "a cruelly kind husband. I regarded myself as her teacher and so harassed her out of my blind love for her" (p. 233)—but rather in the replacement of the underlying antagonism with a mutuality of respect and care.

Gandhi, whom Kohlberg has mentioned as exemplifying Stage Six moral judgment and whom Erikson sought as a model of an adult ethical sensibility, instead is criticized by a judgment that refuses to look away from or condone the infliction of harm. In denying the validity of his wife's reluctance to open her home to strangers and in his blindness to the different reality of adolescent sexuality and temptation, Gandhi compromised in his everyday life the ethic of nonviolence to which in principle and in public he was so steadfastly committed.

The blind willingness to sacrifice people to truth, however, has always been the danger of an ethics abstracted from life. This willingness links Gandhi to the biblical Abraham, who prepared to sacrifice the life of his son in order to demonstrate the integrity and supremacy of his faith. Both men, in the limitations of their fatherhood, stand in implicit contrast to the woman who comes before Solomon and verifies her motherhood by relinquishing truth in order to save the life of her child. It is the ethics of an adulthood that has become principled at the expense of care that Erikson comes to criticize in his assessment of Gandhi's life.

This same criticism is dramatized explicitly as a contrast between the sexes in *The Merchant of Venice* (1598/1912), where Shakespeare goes through an extraordinary complication of sexual identity (dressing a male actor as a female character who in turn poses as a male judge) in order to bring into the masculine citadel of justice the feminine plea for mercy. The limitation of the contractual conception of justice is illustrated through the absurdity of its literal execution, while the "need to make exceptions all the time" is demonstrated contrapuntally in the matter of the rings. Portia, in calling for mercy, argues for that resolution in which no one is hurt, and as the men are forgiven for their failure to keep both their rings and their word, Antonio in turn foregoes his "right" to ruin Shylock.

The research findings that have been reported in this essay suggest that women impose a distinctive construction on moral problems, seeing moral dilemmas in terms of conflicting responsibilities. This construction was found to develop through a sequence of three levels and two transitions, each level representing a more complex understanding of the relationship between self and other and each transition involving a critical reinterpretation of the moral conflict between selfishness and responsibility. The development of women's moral judgment appears to proceed from an initial concern with survival, to a focus on goodness, and finally to a principled understanding of nonviolence as the most adequate guide to the just resolution of moral conflicts.

In counterposing to Kohlberg's longitudinal research on the development of hypothetical moral judgment in men a cross-sectional study of women's responses to actual dilemmas of moral conflict and choice, this essay precludes the possibility of generalization in either direction and leaves to further research the task of sorting out the different variables of occasion and sex. Longitudinal studies of women's moral judgments are necessary in order to validate the claims of stage and sequence presented here. Similarly, the contrast drawn between the moral judgments of men and women awaits for its confirmation a more systematic comparison of the responses of both sexes. Kohlberg's research on moral development has confounded the variables of age, sex, type of decision, and type of dilemma by presenting a single configuration (the responses of adolescent males to hypothetical dilemmas of conflicting rights) as the basis for a universal stage sequence. This paper underscores the need for systematic treatment of these variables and points toward their study as a critical task for future moral development research.

515

For the present, my aim has been to demonstrate the centrality of the concepts of responsibility and care in women's constructions of the moral domain, to indicate the close tie in women's thinking between conceptions of the self and conceptions of morality, and, finally, to argue the need for an expanded developmental theory that would include, rather than rule out from developmental consideration, the difference in the feminine voice. Such an inclusion seems essential, not only for explaining the development of women but also for understanding in both sexes the characteristics and precursors of an adult moral conception.

Reference Notes

1. Haan, N. *Activism as moral protest: Moral judgments of hypothetical dilemmas and an actual situation of civil disobedience.* Unpublished manuscript, University of California at Berkeley, 1971.
2. Turiel, E. *A comparative analysis of moral knowledge and moral judgment in males and females.* Unpublished manuscript, Harvard University, 1973.
3. Kohlberg, L. *Continuities and discontinuities in childhood and adult moral development revisited.* Unpublished paper, Harvard University, 1973.
4. Kohlberg, L. Personal communication, August, 1976.
5. Gilligan, C., & Murphy, M. *The philosopher and the "dilemma of the fact": Moral development in late adolescence and adulthood.* Unpublished manuscript, Harvard University, 1977.

References

Broverman, I., Vogel, S., Broverman, D., Clarkson, F., & Rosenkrantz, P. Sex-role stereotypes: A current appraisal. *Journal of Social Issues,* 1972, **28**, 59–78.

Coles, R. *Children of crisis.* Boston: Little, Brown, 1964.

Didion, J. The women's movement. *New York Times Book Review,* July 30, 1972, pp. 1–2; 14.

Drabble, M. *The waterfall.* Hammondsworth, Eng.: Penguin Books, 1969.

Eliot, G. *The mill on the floss.* New York: New American Library, 1965. (Originally published, 1860.)

Erikson, E. H. *Insight and responsibility.* New York: W. W. Norton, 1964.

Erikson, E. H. *Identity: Youth and crisis.* New York: W. W. Norton, 1968.

Erikson, E. H. *Gandhi's truth.* New York: W. W. Norton, 1969.

Freud, S. "Civilized" sexual morality and modern nervous illness. In J. Strachey (Ed.), *The standard edition of the complete psychological works of Sigmund Freud* (Vol. 9). London: Hogarth Press, 1959. (Originally published, 1908.)

Freud, S. Some psychical consequences of the anatomical distinction between the sexes. In J. Strachey (Ed.), *The standard edition of the complete psychological works of Sigmund Freud* (Vol. 19). London: Hogarth Press, 1961. (Originally published, 1925.)

Gilligan, C., Kohlberg, L., Lerner, J., & Belenky, M. Moral reasoning about sexual dilemmas: The development of an interview and scoring system. *Technical Report of the President's Commission on Obscenity and Pornography* (Vol. 1) [415 060–137]. Washington, D.C.: U.S. Government Printing Office, 1971.

Haan, N. Hypothetical and actual moral reasoning in a situation of civil disobedience. *Journal of Personality and Social Psychology,* 1975, **32**, 255–270.

Holstein, C. Development of moral judgment: A longitudinal study of males and females. *Child Development,* 1976, **47**, 51–61.

516

Horner, M. Toward an understanding of achievement-related conflicts in women. *Journal of Social Issues*, 1972, 29, 157–174.

Ibsen, H. *A doll's house*. In *Ibsen plays*. Hammondsworth, Eng.: Penguin Books, 1965. (Originally published, 1879.)

Kohlberg, L. From is to ought: How to commit the naturalistic fallacy and get away with it in the study of moral development. In T. Mischel (Ed.), *Cognitive development and epistemology*. New York: Academic Press, 1971.

Kohlberg, L., & Gilligan, C. The adolescent as a philosopher: The discovery of the self in a postconventional world. *Daedalus*, 1971, **100**, 1051–1056.

Kohlberg, L., & Kramer, R. Continuities and discontinuities in childhood and adult moral development. *Human Development*, 1969, **12**, 93–120.

Piaget, J. *The moral judgment of the child*. New York: The Free Press, 1965. (Originally published, 1932.)

Shakespeare, W. *The merchant of Venice*. In *The comedies of Shakespeare*. London: Oxford University Press, 1912. (Originally published, 1598.)

Discrepancies between hypothetical judgments and reasoning about an actual choice can predict the clinical outcome of crisis and the occurrence of developmental change.

A Naturalistic Study of Abortion Decisions

Carol Gilligan
Mary Field Belenky

In this chapter, we bring together two literatures, seemingly disparate but actually convergent — the clinical study of human irrationality and the developmental study of the logic of thought. This clinical-developmental integration takes place around an empirical center, a naturalistic study of women deciding whether to continue or abort a pregnancy. The study was designed to investigate the relationship of judgment and action in a real situation of conflict and choice. From a developmental perspective, our interest lay in determining how the structures of thought shape the experience of ongoing events and how experience in turn gives rise to new modes of understanding. From a clinical perspective, we were interested in whether an understanding of developmental transition and of the adaptive potential inherent in the developmental process could elucidate the experience of crisis and predict the occurrence and direction of change. Thus, on the one hand, we sought to observe the process of developmental transition in the context of an actual choice and, on the other hand, to see if this analysis could provide a basis for clinical assessment and prediction.

New Directions for Child Development, 7, 1980 **69**

While the constructive developmental psychology elucidated by Piaget indicates how the present transforms the past through the changing relation of knower and known, clinical psychology has focused instead on the continuing hold of the past on the present. In setting out this distinction between a clinical and a developmental understanding, we point not to an absolute contrast but rather to a difference in emphasis. This difference is especially apparent in the literature on pregnancy and abortion, where clinicians have tended to delineate past conflicts manifest in present behavior while developmental psycholog-ists have focused instead on the potential in the present for growth. In practice, however, both clinicians and developmentalists share a common underlying concern with understanding the narrative of human development in order to foster its ongoing course. In understanding the experience of a pregnancy whose continuation is problematic, both approaches can illuminate the crisis at hand.

Pregnancy invariably involves the past through associations with experience of the parent-child relationship and through its relation to previous development around issues of sexuality and impulse control. Thus a considerable clinical literature exists, particularly on the subject of teenage pregnancy, illustrating how childhood wishes and conflicts can be acted out through sexual behavior and lead to pregnancies which arouse unconscious and ambivalent feelings. In this literature, a problematic pregnancy is seen as a crisis that magnifies and reveals existing psychological vulnerabilities and developmental faults in character structure. Freud indicates how crisis can illuminate the past by comparing the psyche under stress to a crystal that is thrown to the floor and breaks "not into haphazard pieces [but] comes apart along its lines of cleavage into fragments whose boundaries, though they were invisible, were predetermined by the crystal's structure" (1964, p. 59). Certainly the statistics about teenage pregnancy, the occurrence of unwanted pregnancies despite knowledge of reproductive functioning and despite access to birth control, as well as the high frequency of repeated abortions among the teenage population, signify the power of human sexuality to generate manifestly irrational behavior that seems elusive of conscious control and impervious to sex education.

However, the common implication in the work of Freud and Piaget is that, even in the most apparently irrational behavior, there is a logic to be found. While for Freud this is the illogical logic of feelings, for Piaget it is the developing logic of thought. By showing understanding to be a continuing acitivity of an evolving intelligence, Piaget indicates how the function of adaptation is served by an ongoing transformation in the structures of thought. Each stage in this structural developmental progression signifies a more equilibrated understanding that articulates with greater differentiation and integration the relationship between subject and object, between self and other or knower and known. Thus Piaget has taught a generation of psychologists to decipher the logic of apparently illogical thought by abstracting the structures of thinking within which a given understanding or behavior can be seen to make sense. In doing so, he indicates how conflict or crisis can be the harbinger of growth by initiating the process of reorganization through which an adaptive equilibrium is reached.

It was this constructive-developmental approach that guided our study of the pregnancy dilemma (Belenky, 1978; Gilligan, 1977). By holding the dilemma constant, we could demonstrate how the structures of thinking engage an actual experience of choice so that at different stages of cognitive development the same events appear in a radically different light. However, by focusing on the role of conflict in the process of developmental transition, we sought to determine how experience leads to the discovery of contradiction and gives rise to discrepancies in understanding. The developmental and clinical significance of such discrepancies is the subject of this chapter.

Predicting the Developmental and Clinical Outcomes of Crisis

In speculating about the relationship between the verbal or theoretical thought used in judging hypothetical dilemmas and the concrete or effective thought used in actual life situations, Piaget notes that "verbal thinking consists of a progressive coming into consciousness, or conscious realization, of schemas that have been built up by action. In such cases, verbal thought simply lags behind concrete thought, since the former has to reconstruct symbolically and on a new plane operations that have already taken place on a preceding level" (1965, p. 117).

With specific reference to the development of moral judgment, Piaget observes that "we shall meet with children who, for example, take no account of intentions in appraising actions on the verbal plane, but who, when asked for personal experiences, show that they take full account of intentions that come into play" (p. 117). On the basis of such observed discrepancies between theoretical and practical reasoning, Piaget advances the hypothesis that new structures of thinking arise first in action and are only later manifest on a purely reflective plane.

In order to assess the developmental significance of personal experiences of conflict and choice, we compared thinking about actual dilemmas with the judgment of hypothetical problems. If the judgments that guided the resolution of the crisis of a problematic pregnancy only later appeared in theoretical reasoning about hypothetical situations, there would be evidence to support Piaget's hypothesis regarding the onset of developmental change. Furthermore, the existence of such discrepancies between theoretical and practical reasoning could, if the time-lag hypothesis is correct, alert clinicians to a potential for development in the crisis situation.

In the study of the pregnancy dilemma, the analysis of the structures of thought was based on stages that describe the development of social and moral understanding. These stages were initially elaborated by Piaget (1965) and subsequently expanded by Kohlberg (1969), who extended Piaget's study of moral judgment into adolescence and adulthood. On the basis of changes in the understanding and resolution of moral dilemmas, Kohlberg delineates a six-stage progression that describes the evolution of the concept of justice. This progression charts the course of moral development from an egocentric through a conventional to a principled understanding of dilemmas of moral conflict and choice. While the theoretical constructs of Kohlberg's progression were derived from responses to hypothetical dilemmas, such theoretical judgments may correspond, as Piaget suggests, with the judgments people apply in actual life situations. This correspondence was apparent in our analysis of women's thinking about the actual dilemma of whether to continue or abort a pregnancy. For example, the preconventional or egocentric understanding evident in the response to Kohlberg's dilemma that a husband should save his wife because he probably would need someone to help take care of the kids is also apparent in a woman's decision to continue a pregnancy because she believes having a baby would be the perfect chance to get married and move away from home. In both instances the decision is considered only from an egocentric perspective and judgment is guided by the wish to satisfy a single individual's need. More generally, the judgments that women apply in thinking about continuing or aborting a pregnancy reflect the structural distinction between preconventional, conventional, and postconventional thought. By comparing the women's understanding of the actual dilemma they faced with their thinking about Kohlberg's hypothetical moral problems, we were able to analyze the relationship between their effective and their theoretical reasoning and, on that basis, to ascertain the existence of structural discrepancies in their thought.

In applying this discrepancy analysis to predicting the outcome of choice, we adopted an Eriksonian view of crisis as "a turning-point for better or worse" (Erikson, 1964, p. 139). Thus we combined the clinical understanding of how the present is tied to the past with a developmental analysis of the present's potential for transforming both past and future. In doing so, we brought together the developmental view of conflict as initiating the process of reorganization and growth and the clinical view of crisis as precipitating disorganization and regression. For those women whose understanding of the pregnancy decision was discrepant with their thinking about hypothetical dilemmas, both outcomes seemed clinically possible. But in analyzing the direction of the discrepancy between thinking about real and hypothetical choices, we sought to predict the direction of change. We therefore assumed that, just as new structures of thought can first arise in action, so too can existing structures of thought be eroded when action is guided by less adequate modes of understanding. In other words, cognitive disequilibrium and clinical crisis do not always eventuate in developmental advance but may also result in regression or a continuing state of disorganization. This regressive potential inherent in crisis, while commonly observed in clinical settings, is less likely to become manifest in laboratory situations, where the relationship between theoretical and practical reasoning can never be as fully explored and where incidents of personal conflict and stress are less likely to occur.

The significance of naturalistic research for understanding the relationship of judgment and action and illuminating the process of developmental change, while originally demonstrated by Piaget (1965) in his study of the rules of the game, has been underscored more recently in the work of Damon (1977), Haan (1975), and Selman and Jaquette (1978). In all of these studies, reasoning about hypothetical social and moral dilemmas has been compared with reasoning about real life events and the existence of discrepancies between these two types of thinking has been shown to have developmental or clinical significance.

Selman and Jaquette (1978), in a study of preadolescent boys in a school for children with emotional disturbances, report that discrepancies in thinking about real and hypothetical interpersonal conflicts are predictive of subsequent clinical course. Children who showed consistency between their reasoning about actual relationships in school and their highest demonstrated levels of capacity in resolving hypothetical friendship dilemmas also showed the greatest clinical improvement and were soon returned to regular schools. In contrast, children who oscillated in their interpersonal reasoning, often using lower levels of reasoning in real situations than they applied to the resolution of hypothetical problems, showed greater evidence of anxiety and stress. Thus Selman and Jaquette observe that children's inability to bring their cognitive capacities to bear in thinking about real life situations is associated with the greatest incidence of disturbance.

In studies of normal children in regular classroom settings, Damon (1977) also investigates the relationship between hypothetical and real life thought. In one of his studies, Damon compared the conceptions of distributive justice manifest in children's reasoning about hypothetical distribution dilemmas with the conceptions that were apparent in their resolution of the actual problems of how to distribute candy bar prizes. While approximately half of the children used the same stage of reasoning in both situations, over a third used more mature reasoning in the hypothetical dilemma, while the rest (about 20 percent) were more mature in their thinking about the actual distribution.

While Damon claims that these findings contradict "predictions made by Piaget concerning the developmental priority of active to reflective knowledge" (1977, p. 109), his cross-sectional study does not provide an adequate test of Piaget's time-lag hypothesis. Although Piaget claims that new structures of thought will arise first in action, he does not claim that these structures will consistently be applied in action situations. Thus Damon's interpretation that in actuality the children's self-interest often overrode the structures of their moral understanding does not refute Piaget's hypothesis. However, if the 20 percent of the children who used higher stages of reasoning in the actual distribution problem than in the hypothetical dilemma were subsequently found to have matured in their theoretical conceptions of distributive justice, then Piaget's hypothesis would be supported. Only a longitudinal study could assess the accuracy of Piaget's predictions with respect to the patterns of discrepancy that Damon found in children's thinking.

Similarly, the absence of a longitudinal design limits the findings of Haan, Smith, and Block (1968) as well as the subsequent analysis by Haan (1975) of discrepancies between hypothetical and real life reasoning. Haan, Smith, and Block studied the relationship of judgment and action by comparing the structure of student's reasoning about Kohlberg's hypothetical dilemmas with the actions that they had taken in the Berkeley Free Speech Movement (FSM) demonstration. On the basis of this comparison, they report a correlation between stage of moral reasoning and participation in acts of civil disobedience. However, the developmental significance of these findings is qualified by the fact that judgments were assessed following action rather than prior to its occurrence.

Haan goes on to compare the stage of moral reasoning retrospectively used to justify action decisions with the reasoning brought to bear on the resolution of hypothetical dilemmas. From this comparison, she reports three patterns of reasoning — two patterns of discrepancy between hypothetical and real life reasoning and a group that shows no differences. While her designation of the three groups (Gain, Loss, and Stable) implies a longitudinal design, her cross-sectional data did not allow her to test the developmental implications of her interpretation. Observing that the students who were more likely to have participated in the demonstration were those who reasoned about the actual FSM decision at a higher stage than they used in resolving Kohlberg's hypothetical dilemmas, Haan suggests that the commitment to moral action may have energized moral development. Speculating that these students may have been in the process of developmental transition, she reiterates Piaget's hypothesis regarding the relation of hypothetical and real life thought: "When the action is nontrivial, it may well be the first, rather than the last manifestation of an evolving comprehension of more sufficient moral structuring than can yet be articulated in a cognitive-hypothetical way" (Haan, 1975, p. 268).

Conversely, Haan speculates that the students whose thinking about the actual FSM demonstration was at a lower stage than their judgment of hypothetical dilemmas may have experienced malaise and "the diminution of the self" (p. 269).

Building on Piaget's hypothesis and these previous naturalistic studies, our own research places the discrepancy analysis within the framework of a longitudinal design. By assessing judgment prior to action and then again at one year following choice, we were able to test the significance of developmental discrepancies for subsequent developmental transition. Furthermore, by combining developmental measures of stage discrepancies and stage transition with clinical assessments of conflict and stress and changes in life circumstance, we were able to assess the relationship between clinical crisis and developmental transition or, more generally, between developmental and clinical change. In combining clinical and developmental measures and adopting a longitudinal design, we sought to replicate and extend previous findings and test the power of a discrepancy analysis for predicting the developmental and clinical outcomes of choice.

On the basis of the existence and direction of discrepancies between thinking about real and hypothetical choices, we divided the women we studied into three prediction groups—*transitional, stable,* and *at risk.* The transitional group consisted of women whose understanding of the actual decision they made showed more mature structures of thought than were apparent in their judgment of Kohlberg's dilemmas. The stable group was composed of women who showed no structural differences in their thinking about real and hypothetical dilemmas. The women whom we considered at risk were those whose thinking about their actual decision was less mature than their thinking about hypothetical problems.

On the basis of this analysis, we predicted that in a one year follow-up interview these three groups would differ with respect to structural changes in thought and that these changes would in turn be associated with changes in life circumstance. Specifically, the different out-comes predicted for each group as measured by evidence and direction of change in level of moral judgment and evidence and direction of change in actual life situation were as follows: The transitional group was expected to show increased maturity in moral judgment of hypo-thetical dilemmas and improvement in life situation; the stable group was expected to show no change on either measure; and the at risk group was expected to show regression in moral judgment and deteri-oration in life situation. Before turning to the discussion of findings, we will briefly describe the study itself.

The Abortion Decision Study

Most of the women who participated in the abortion decision study were referred through pregnancy counseling services or abortion clinics in a large metropolitan area. A few came through a university health service or through private physicians or associations. The only criteria for inclusion in the sample were (1) that the woman be in the first trimester of a confirmed pregnancy; and (2) that for one reason or another the woman was considering abortion. The interviews were conducted between the eighth and the twelfth weeks of pregnancy, prior to any definitive resolution, and all of the women who met our criteria were included in the sample. Our aim was to gather a sample that represented different stages of cognitive and moral development, with each woman's thinking assessed before and after her choice over the longitudinal interval studied.

The twenty-four women who took part in the study ranged in age from fifteen to thirty-three and came from different social classes and different racial and cultural groups. The women were both married and unmarried; several had had previous abortions, and three were mothers of a preschool child. Because the women were selected through pregnancy and abortion counseling services, they all were at least considering abortion, and twenty out of twenty-four subsequently made that decision. One year follow-up interviews were conducted with twenty-one of these women, although one of these interviews did not include the hypothetical Kohlberg dilemmas. Of the three women for whom follow-up data were not obtained, one had moved out of the state and two could not be contacted. This attrition rate is the lowest reported in the literature on longitudinal studies of abortion (see Adler, 1976).

We had no expectation that our sample would be characteristic of the larger population of women considering, seeking, or having abortions. In fact, we have reason to believe that we saw women who were in greater than usual conflict over this decision since referral to our study was seen by some counselors as an effective means of crisis intervention.

The women were interviewed at two times, first while they were pregnant and making the decision (Time 1) and second, a year later (Time 2). The Time 1 interview was conducted after the pregnancy was confirmed and prior to any definitive solution. The interview was designed to elicit the woman's understanding of the problem posed by the pregnancy, the decision that she was facing, the alternatives she was considering, and the way in which she thought about each. Following the initial question — How did you get pregnant and how have you been thinking about it so far? — the interviewer asked questions that were designed to clarify the underlying structure of the woman's thought process. Then the interview turned to questions about self-concept (How would you describe yourself to yourself?) and finally to moral judgments (Is there a difference between what you want to do and what you think you should do? Is there a right thing to do in this situation? Right just for you or for anyone?). While moral terms like *should* or *ought* or judgments about the "right" or "best" thing to do were questioned whenever they spontaneously appeared, moral terminology was introduced by the interviewer only in the last section of the interview. This was done first with respect to the actual pregnancy dilemma, as indicated by the previous questions, and then with regard to hypothetical dilemmas, one about abortion and the three that compose the standard Kohlberg Form A interview.

The Time 2 interview followed the same format as the first, though now the discussion of the pregnancy decision was reconstructive (Thinking back now about the decision you made a year ago, what was your thinking about what to do?), and the interviewer inquired about the woman's experience during the intervening year. The second interview also included the same questions about self-concept and the same hypothetical moral dilemmas.

In our data analyses, responses to the hypothetical Kohlberg dilemmas were scored by Kohlberg and his colleagues' (1978) revised scoring manual, which distinguishes five stages of moral judgment. A separate but similar manual was constructed by Belenky (1978) for assigning a structural stage score to the types of reasoning that guided the actual resolutions of the pregnancy dilemma. Belenky's manual was based on an earlier manual for scoring responses to sexual dilemmas (Gilligan and others, 1971) and expanded to include Kohlberg and his colleagues' recent revisions in the descriptions of his stages as well as to incorporate Gilligan's (1977) description of the stages and sequence of women's moral development, based on her analysis of the Time 1 data. While this manual was thus something of a composite, satisfactory interrater reliability was obtained on the scores.

The different moral judgment scores allowed comparison of thinking about real and hypothetical dilemmas, and this comparison served as the basis for designating the transitional, stable, and at risk groups in our study. We were also able to compare Moral Maturity Scores (MMS) on hypothetical moral reasoning between Time 1 and Time 2 and thus to obtain an index of moral judgment development during the intervening year.

In addition to these cognitive developmental measures, we devised a scale to rate changes in reported life circumstance between the Time 1 and Time 2 interviews. This scale measured the occurrence and direction of change in the areas of love and work as well as the woman's report of her feelings about her life in the intervening year. One point was entered in the relevant outcome category (Better/Worse/ Same) each time there was evidence of expansion, constriction, or stability in the woman's educational or occupational roles, in her interpersonal relationships, or in her descriptions of her overall psychological state. For example, a student who was out of school at Time 1 and at Time 2 had returned to school, reported a change for the better in her life, had better friends, and had a more satisfying relationship with her parents, was called Better. Another woman, who had abandoned her occupation at Time 2 and was bedridden, alone, and full of self-doubt, was called Worse. These scores were weighted and averaged to yield a mean Life Outcome Score (LOS).

The prediction that different patterns of discrepancy between stages of reasoning about real and hypothetical dilemmas would be associated with different outcomes in the one year follow-up interview was tested by both developmental and clinical measures—changes in moral judgment scores and changes in life circumstance. The relationship between discrepancy scores at Time 1 and changes in moral judgment and life circumstance at Time 2 is shown in Table 1. As the table indicates, most of the women in the predicted transition group (whose reasoning about their actual choice had been higher than their reason-

Table 1. Time 2 Outcomes of Women Predicted to be Transitional, Stable, or At Risk at Time 1

Subject Classification at Time 1	Outcome in Moral Maturity Score at Time 2			Outcome in Life Outcome Score at Time 2		
	Higher	Same	Lower	Better	Same	Worse
Transitional	7	1	1	4	4	1
Stable	1	5	2	2	5	1
At Risk	2*	0	1	2*	0	2
	(Subject N = 20)			(Subject N = 21)		

*Women who reported an unplanned pregnancy within the follow-up year.

ing about hypothetical dilemmas) advanced in their moral judgment over the intervening year and reported improvements in life circumstance. The women in the stable group (who showed no discrepancies in thinking at Time 1) most often showed no evidence of change at Time 2 in either moral judgment or life situation.

The findings with respect to the group of women who were predicted to be at risk on the basis of the decrements in their reasoning about the actual pregnancy decision were complicated by the fact that two of the four women in this group became pregnant again during the intervening year. These were the only women in the sample who reported unplanned pregnancies during the one year follow-up interval. While both of the women described the second pregnancy as posing the same dilemma as the first, the second time they resolved the dilemma differently, following a mode of resolution that they had considered but rejected in the first pregnancy. While one woman chose to continue the second pregnancy and the other to have an abortion, their reasoning about these decisions was, at least in retrospective report, at the highest level of capacity they had demonstrated in the Time 1 interview. (Had they adopted this mode of resolution in the first pregnancy, they would have been placed in the predicted transition group.) Thus while the occurrence of the second pregnancy fits the clinical description of repetition compulsion (the unconscious drive to repeat past conflicts), it also can be seen from a developmental perspective as a return to a missed opportunity for growth. The evidence of discrepancy in the women's thinking about the pregnancy decision at Time 1 had indicated a potential for growth in this crisis that had not been realized in its resolution. The fact that the recurrence of a problematic pregnancy was limited in this sample to those women who had resolved their initial crisis by reasoning below their demonstrated level of capacity illustrates the power of the developmental process and the strength of the motivation to remake decisions which leave the woman developmentally at risk and which she herself has the capacity to criticize.

The findings reported in Table 1 were tested statistically by chi square analyses of the relationship between our predictions and each of the outcome measures. For both sections of the table, prediction-outcome relationships were significant at $p < .01$. However, since several cells in each table had expected frequencies of less than 5, we also calculated an asymmetric Lambda test of association, finding positive values of .45 for the relation between predicted and actual moral judgment change and .17 for life outcome scores. This analysis indicates a positive association between predicted and actual change on both outcome measures with a strong association with moral judgment scores.

With respect to relations between the outcomes, we find that changes in life situation are strongly connected with parallel changes in moral judgment. A correlation r = .61 was found between moral development and improvement in life circumstance. This relation was significant even when the effects of moral reasoning at Time 1 were controlled (R^2 change in MMS growth = .35, p<.01, controlling for MMS Time 1).

Thus the discrepancy patterns in thinking predict the developmental outcome of choice as measured by changes in moral reasoning and changes in life situation. These changes are in turn related; changes in moral judgment are associated with parallel changes in life situation. This association between developmental and clinical ratings of change substantiates the underlying developmental assumption of this study that the structures of social and moral understanding are related to the level of social adaptation. In this study the move toward more equilibrated structures of thought was accompanied by a change toward more adaptive relationships in life as well as the report of greater satisfaction in the activities of love and work.

While the findings of this study are provocative, they must be viewed with caution pending replication. The sample size was small, the same data served as the basis for constructing the manual for coding the pregnancy dilemmas and for testing predictions, and the satisfactory interrater reliability does not preclude experimenter bias since the original coder was familiar with the data and could not conduct the analyses blindly. Finally, our discrepancy findings are subject to an alternative explanation in the absence of baseline data obtained prior to the conflict experience. The Time 1 judgments of the hypothetical dilemma may have been depressed by anxiety and stress or by the distraction of the actual dilemma and may not have been an accurate measure of the woman's developmental capacity. This interpretation would suggest that the changes observed at Time 2 were due to the absence of stress at that time rather than to structural developmental change. Evidence against this interpretation comes from the changes in life circumstance that accompanied developmental transitions, since the initial life situations predated the crisis experience. The case study that follows illustrates this point and supports a developmental interpretation of our results by indicating how a growth in moral understanding is accompanied by a substantial improvement in the life of an adolescent girl.

Clinical Crisis and Developmental Transition

To illustrate the relationship of crisis and transition and demonstrate the complementarity of a clinical and developmental approach, we turn to the experience of a sixteen-year-old girl for whom the pregnancy brought to the surface conflicts that were rooted in her past as well as issues in her present development to which she had not been attending. In charting the process and the experience of her growth, we indicate how a clinical crisis can initiate a developmental transition that eventuates in a reorganization of thought and a dramatic change in behavior but only after a continuing struggle that occupied most of a year. This adolescent's experience, though in some ways extreme, was typical of the transitional process observed in the sample in general and characteristic of the kinds of developmental changes that occurred in the lives of other adolescents in the study.

Betty was referred to the study by a counselor at the abortion clinic where she had come for a second abortion within a period of six months. Concerned about the repetition of pregnancy and abortion in a sixteen-year-old girl who appeared highly intelligent but also angry and disturbed, the counselor believed that Betty would benefit from the opportunity the study provided to reflect on her decision and consider more generally what she was doing.

Betty's adolescence was a record of trouble with drugs, with authorities, with school, and with family—a history of ongoing conflict and fighting at home, in school, and in the community. She had been arrested by the police for drinking and disorderly conduct and, following a violation of probation, was hospitalized briefly for observation and then sent to a reform school. Betty said that her previous pregnancy had occurred when she was raped while hitchhiking. That pregnancy was terminated by an abortion, which she remembered as very unpleasant because of the physical pain.

While Betty's impulsive and out of control behavior can be seen, in clinical terms, to reflect problems in ego functioning or a deficiency in character structure, in developmental terms it is consonant with the stage structures of preconventional thought. Together, these two languages describe the feelings of helplessness and powerlessness that pervade Betty's account of her own behavior and of her dealings with the outside world. Betty describes these feelings in the face of sexual demands by indicating that, as far as she is concerned, the second pregnancy, like the first one, was not her fault.

> I started going with this guy, and he wanted me to go to bed with him, and I didn't want to . . . Then he kept asking me to go on the pill so I could go to bed with him, and that is why I didn't want to, because I really did like him. So I asked my mother if I could go on the pill, and she said she didn't think it was good because she read all these articles about cancer and everything. So then I just didn't go on it because of that, and I

went to bed with him anyway, because I got sick of him asking me, and then I got pregnant.

Wishing now that she had used birth control but seeing others as responsible for the fact that she did not ("He kept telling me to go on the pill, but he would never take me down to see about getting it or anything"), she says that when she found out she was pregnant, she did not know what she wanted to do: "When I first found out, I wanted to kill myself because I just couldn't face the fact. I knew that I wanted to get an abortion. I knew that I couldn't have the kid, but I just couldn't face the fact of going through that again."

Having felt both helpless and powerless to obtain contraception for herself ("I figured that you have to have parents' permission . . . I didn't have any money"), Betty had also been unable to deal with her boyfriend's continuing harassment. In the end, she gave in to his assurance that he knew what he was doing and would not get her pregnant. Her feelings of powerlessness stemmed in part from her belief that if she refused to have intercourse he would probably break up with her.

> [Why?] Because guys, if they are going out with you and buying you things, they expect to make out, most of them. [Was he taking you out and buying you things?] Yeah, he did everything for me. [What kind of things?] Just called me, picked me up, take me anywhere I wanted to go, buy me cigarettes, buy me beer if I wanted. Most of the guys I went out with before that would not be like that. They wouldn't call me, pick me up, and treat me good, instead of just treat me like shit . . . He treated me different than anybody I ever went out with.

Given her expectation that if she went to bed with him, he would continue to meet her needs for attention, cigarettes, and beer, her disappointment afterwards was great: "After I went to bed with him, he just treated me like shit. He was too possessive with me, he just wanted me to do everything that he wanted to do . . . I was more like a wife than a girlfriend, and I didn't like it." Describing the relationship in terms of instrumental exchange, she concludes that he "was really one way," seeking only to meet his own needs and disregarding "the fact that [she] wanted more freedom."

Upon reflection, however, Betty considers that perhaps the pregnancy is her own fault: "I should have tried to get [the pill] myself and I didn't." Concluding from this experience that she should listen to herself and not to other people, she says, "I know more than I ever did that I am right." Her reasons for having listened to others before ("because I figure if I do, I will get something out of it, or it will make things better, and they will stop bothering me, or leave me alone, if I do what they want me to do"), have been belied by her experience.

Thus she begins to question the assumptions that had pervaded her thinking at the beginning of the interview. Her consideration of abortion only in terms of the physical pain, her wish to keep the pregnancy secret in order to avoid getting a "wicked reputation," her concern with maintaining her freedom rather than having to do things for others, all indicate her preoccupation with her own needs and her struggle to ensure her survival in a world she perceives as exploitative and threatening. This construction of social reality is vividly apparent in her response to Kohlberg's dilemma as to whether a husband should steal an overpriced drug to save the life of his dying wife:

> [Should Heinz steal the drug?] Yeah, the guy is ripping him off, and his wife is dying. So, he [the druggist] deserves to be ripped off. [Is it the right thing to do?] Probably. I think survival is one of the first things in life that people fight for. I think it is the most important thing, more important than stealing. Stealing might be wrong, but if you have to steal to survive yourself, or even kill, that is what you should do. [Why is that so?] Preservation of oneself, I think, is the most important thing. It comes before anything in life. A lot of people say sex is the most important thing to a lot of people, but I think that preservation of oneself is the most important thing to people.

Thus the same concern with self-preservation that motivated Betty's sexual behavior also informs her judgment of this hypothetical moral dilemma.

While the overriding concern with survival and the satisfaction of need describes the preconventional structures of thought that are manifest in Betty's judgments, the salience of these issues for Betty stems directly from her experience of having been an adopted child and thus one whose survival seemed particularly endangered. Betty's feelings about her own precarious survival come to light in her discussion of the abortion decision as her focus begins to shift from her own needs to those of the baby. This shift to the consideration of the needs of others, which is the harbinger of conventional thought, is announced by the appearance of conventional moral language in her statement, "Abortion is *the right thing to do* in a situation like mine, if someone was in the middle of school, or if they have to [go back to school] like I do." Thus beginning by considering her own needs, albeit from the somewhat different perspective of a perceived obligation to go back to school, she indicates a shift in moral concern, saying, "It would be unfair for me to have a baby, unfair to the baby more than to me."

While at the time of the previous pregnancy (which followed her experience of rape) she "just couldn't stand the thought of the baby," this time she says, "I have thought a lot about it," and her use of the concept of fairness indicates the moral nature of her concern. Thinking about the baby, she says, makes her "feel kind of strange," because "I am adopted, and I was thinking like my mother didn't want me, otherwise she wouldn't have put me up for adoption. But I was thinking if I could have been an abortion or maybe was intended to be, or something, and that kind of gives me strange feelings about it."

From a clinical standpoint, the feelings of this adopted adolescent about getting pregnant and having an abortion are obviously complicated in a variety of ways. Her behavior in the present reaches back to the past, bringing to the surface residual conflicts, her uncertainties about herself, doubts about her biological mother's feelings for her as, in some sense, an unwanted child, as well as her own hope that she was wanted in the sense that maybe her mother "really loved the guy but . . . couldn't take care of" her. These feelings and identifications, however, tie in as well with Betty's present developmental concerns about her own adolescent identity and with the theme of responsibility, which becomes critical in the transition from childhood to adulthood. Thus for Betty, the abortion decision evokes the past but points toward the future, leading her to examine the contradictions in her present behavior and to consider the possibility of change:

> In a lot of ways [this pregnancy] has helped me, because I have stopped getting high and stopped drinking, and this is the first time in three years I stopped getting high and stopped drinking, because it was wrong. And now that I have, I know that I can do it, and I am just going to completely stop. [How did the pregnancy help you to do that?] Because when I first got pregnant, I wasn't sure what I was going to do. And when I first found out, I thought to myself, this time it was my fault, and I have to keep this baby. This is what I thought to myself. I thought that since it was my fault, that I shouldn't have an abortion. But then I stopped drinking and stopped getting high because I didn't want to hurt the baby. And then after a couple of weeks, I thought about it again, and I said, "No, I can't have it because I have to go to school."

Thus Betty indicates that she began to take care of herself because she did not want to hurt the baby, and even her sense of having to go back to school stems from "the thought about having a kid and not having any education and not having any skills." Recognizing her inability to raise a child in her present life situation and believing that the baby might have been damaged because, during the first month of the pregnancy, she was taking a lot of drugs, Betty sees the need to grow up herself before she will be able to take care of a child.

As Betty identifies herself with the endangered and damaged baby, she begins to consider the issue of care that had been a theme from the beginning of the interview. At first, however, this theme appeared only in terms of who was caring for her. Thus, while she was "mad" at the counselor in the clinic who interfered with her wish to have an abortion that day ("I just wanted to get it over with"), when asked what she thought the counselor's concern was, she said, "I think that they just wanted to make sure that my mind would be stable when I left there," adding, "I think it is good, because at least they care."

When asked then to describe herself, Betty says, "I guess that I am kind of hard to get along with sometimes because I like to do what I want to do. I don't like people to tell me what to do. But then, on the other hand, I am easily led." The same contradiction in her self-description between being willful and easily led, emerges again in her descriptions of others as either interfering with her freedom or not caring enough to interfere. Thus she says that her mother, "was never really strict enough with me. She just kind of let me get away with a lot of stuff," and adds that in school "I think I probably need somebody to be over me telling me to do it."

While the issue of care reaches back to her feelings about the mother who gave her up for adoption, in this pregnancy it also reaches forward to the child whose mother she could now be. In this shift, Betty begins to consider herself as a person capable of caring, eventually for a child but first for herself, in the realization that to be a responsible mother she would first have to become responsible for herself. Thus she says, "I guess I am going to start having to take care of myself better." In Betty's thinking about the termination of this pregnancy, there is evidence of a change in orientation and structure from a preconventional egocentrism to a conventional moral preoccupation with responsibility, fairness, and care. Saying, "I don't think it would be fair to give life to a child if it couldn't have its own mother," she indicates her incipient identification with the good, responsible, and caring mother, and concludes that "sooner or later you have to make up your mind to start taking care of yourself; being your own person instead of having everybody else tell you what to do." Given her new sense of internal responsibility and control, Betty begins to envision the future in a new and more positive light.

In the follow-up interview one year later, Betty's thinking indicates a consolidation of the shift evident in the text of the first interview from the language of egocentric concern (of avoiding pain and not getting a bad reputation) to the language of relationship and care evident in her talk about love and responsibility. The shift in concern from survival to goodness that describes the transition in women's thinking from a preconventional to a conventional moral understanding (Gilligan, 1977) is evident in the move from selfishness to responsibility that describes Betty's progress in the intervening year.

Following the abortion, she describes a period of depression and recounts her feelings of sadness and loss as she tells of giving up a puppy, staying at home all day watching television, fighting with her mother, and gaining weight: "I was the heaviest I have ever been, and I was so depressed. I just stayed home all winter . . . I would never go out of the house. I would be so ashamed." Then in June, "I said I have to lose, and it was such a change for me because I had been fat for so many years. And being thin, I never knew what it was like to be able to wear clothes . . . that looked good. I just felt dynamite, because so many people and so many guys were trying to go out with me . . . It was the first summer I was able to wear a bathing suit."

The dramatic change that Betty reports began at the time that the baby would have been born had the pregnancy been continued. In the rest of the sample, this date was often marked by significant life changes, either for better or for worse. For the women in the predicted transitional group, this tended to be the time when depression ended, as though the extension of the pregnancy had marked a natural period of mourning whose completion led to activities that resulted in substantial improvements in the woman's life situation. For the women in the predicted at risk group, this was the time when things fell apart.

For Betty, the improvement was marked. At the time of the second interview, she was enrolled in an alternative school where she had become interested in learning and very active in the school's community life. She had a steady relationship with a boyfriend, and from her description, this relationship seemed substantially different from those she had previously described in that activities of mutual care had replaced coercive and exploitative deals. Betty was also preparing with the encouragement of her school to attend a community college.

The fundamental change in Betty's moral understanding is evident in her response to the Kohlberg dilemma at Time 2 when she says that the husband should steal the drug "because his wife is dying, near death, and he loves his wife." While she said, referring to the content of her responses, that she was going to "answer this the same way I answered it before," on a structural level her answer has changed. Whereas previously she indicated the primacy of survival, now she discusses the importance of relationships. Where she spoke of entitlement, now instead, she speaks about guilt. "Because he loves his wife, and if she dies, he is going to feel like he could have done something but he didn't. So if she does die, he might feel really guilty and wish that he had stolen it, taken any means he could have to get it." Thus security, which she formerly saw as self-preservation in a dog-eat-dog world, now instead, is seen to depend on relationships of love and care.

The transformation in Betty's moral judgments is paralleled by a change in her perception of herself. Whereas at Time 1 she had described herself as "kind of hard to get along with," willful, impulsive, and easily led, now she says, "I think I am a person who likes challenge. I like to learn. I like things that are interesting, I like to talk to people. I am very sensitive." Asked whether she thinks there is a change in the way she sees herself now, compared to the past, she says, "Definitely. Like now, I really care about myself and then I didn't really care. I was so disgusted with everything . . . now I am starting to get a better attitude, and I feel like I can change a lot of things that I thought before I would never be able to change." No longer feeling so powerless, exploited, and endangered, Betty now feels more in control. "Things have changed drastically over a year" in a way that convinced her that she can "make it in life."

In Betty's retrospective account, the abortion decision itself is reconstructed in line with her new understanding, reflecting conventional structures of thought that were absent from her initial discussion. Thus she elaborates at Time 2 what might have been the alternative of having the baby and putting it up for adoption but indicates her concern that, because of the drugs she had taken, "if it came out deformed or something, then nobody would want it." Articulating her feeling that she should have had the baby as punishment "because it was really [her] fault," she indicates the conventional moral judgments that could be applied to the action she took. "Thinking about abortion, I don't know what to think, what it is, if I am killing something, or I am really not doing anything that bad. I am not a Jesus freak or anything like that, but I wonder about it, if it is something that is morally wrong, or what. It kind of bothered me for awhile."

Just as the world of morality has replaced a world in which everyone was getting ripped off, so too the world of mutuality succeeded relationships that were exploitative or disappointingly "one way." While Betty remembers the time of the pregnancy as having been a hard time, she thinks maybe "it is better to learn the hard way because then it stays. You really learn; it sticks with you. It just stays with you."

Thus in Betty's life the second pregnancy provoked a crisis that brought to the fore the residual conflicts from her past and the contradictions in her current behavior and thought. The intervention of the

abortion counselor, who cared enough to interfere with the emerging
pattern of repeated abortions and referred Betty to the study in order to
provide an opportunity for thought and reflection, initiated a clinical
crisis and a developmental transition. The process of growth consumed
most of the year that separated the first and second interviews and was
marked by a period of mourning, disorganization, and despair. At the
end of the year, in the second interview, Betty showed evidence of a
major reworking in her understanding of the events of her past and her
thinking about the future. Past conflicts had been revisited in a way
that allowed her to address in the present the pending issues of her adolescent development. In the second interview, she articulated clearly
her emerging sense of her own identity and gave evidence of a new
level of psychosocial adaptation in her interactions with the world.
While the second pregnancy recapitulated the past and illustrated the
repetitive phenomenon of acting out, it also looked forward to the
future, providing a chance to confront the issues of responsibility and
care that were critical to Betty's ongoing development.

In the first volume of his series on *Children of Crisis,* Robert
Coles observes that crisis can lead to growth when it presents an opportunity to confront impediments to further development. To illustrate
this point, he describes John Washington, a black adolescent living in
poverty whose parents showed symptoms of "serious mental disorder."
Yet, in volunteering to participate in the desegregation of the Little
Rock schools, John Washington begins a progress toward growth
under conditions of extraordinary stress. When Coles asked "what had
enabled him to do it," John Washington said, "That school glued me
together; it made me stronger than I ever thought I could be, and so
now I don't think I'll ever be able to forget what happened. I'll probably
be different for the rest of my life" (Coles, 1964, p. 122).

The occurrence of development through the encounter with
stress, the notion of conflict as providing a dangerous opportunity
for growth, is at the center of Coles' analysis which, in turn, derives
from Erikson's work. Under different circumstances of stress, the
women we studied make a similar point. Betty says, comparing present
with past,

> I am really happy with where my life is going now. Compared
> with last year, it has changed so much and is so much better.
> [How would you describe the change?] Myself? I feel better
> about what I am doing. I get up in the morning and I go to
> school. I was just sitting around for a year and a half doing
> nothing. Like, I wasn't going anywhere in life. I didn't know
> what I was doing, and now I feel like I have a direction, in a
> way. I know what I am interested in.

Anchored firmly in the everyday, getting up in the morning and going to school, Betty indicates a new sense of herself as a responsible person who has a direction that connects her to a coherent social world and to the line of her ongoing adolescent development.

Conclusion

In this clinical-developmental analysis of women's experience of an actual choice, the developmental understanding of transition complements and extends the clinical understanding of crisis. Together, these approaches combine to explain how conflicts in adaptation can lead in some instances to growth, while in others to disorganization and despair. While our analysis confirmed the clinical importance of past conflicts in present events, it also indicated how development can change the understanding of past, present, and future. By applying a constructivist developmental framework to the analysis of women's thinking about an actual choice, we were able to identify the growing edge of development and to assess the potential for development in the crisis situation. On this basis we were able to predict the developmental and clinical outcomes of choice, showing how crisis can precipitate developmental transition and indicating its likely course.

By bringing a clinical analysis of life-history data to the developmental understanding of the process of growth, we have demonstrated the need to account for the phenomena of both regression and advance and indicated the fluidity of change. By bringing developmental knowledge of stage transition to the clinical understanding of crisis, we have shown how depression and disorganization can signify not only psychopathology but also the mourning that precedes the consolidation of growth. In indicating the power of a clinical-developmental approach, both for predicting the outcomes of crisis and for understanding the experience of change, our naturalistic study shows the artificiality of the division between the cognitive and affective processes that have been separately studied by developmental and clinical psychologists. Instead, a developmental analysis of the structures of thought informs the clinical understanding of the crisis experience just as the clinical understanding of life-history data shows thought and feelings to be intricately entwined.

For the developmental researcher, this study argues strongly for the importance of naturalistic, longitudinal research. For the clinician, it points to the length of time between the onset and consolidation of developmental change, to the difficulty of the intervening period, and toward the kinds of therapeutic and environmental supports that could sustain the person in crisis by sharing the costs of growth and fostering the emergence of developing strengths.

References

Adler, N. "Sample Attrition in Studies of Psychological Sequelae of Abortion: How Great a Problem?" *Journal of Applied Social Psychology,* 1976. *6,* 240–259.

Belenky, M. F. "Conflict and Development: A Longitudinal Study of the Impact of Abortion Decisions on Moral Judgments of Adolescent and Adult Women." Unpublished doctoral dissertation, Harvard University, 1978.

Coles, R. *Children of Crisis.* Boston: Little, Brown, 1967.

Damon, W. *The Social World of the Child.* San Francisco: Jossey-Bass, 1977.

Erikson, E. H. *Insight and Responsibility.* New York: Norton, 1964.

Freud, S. "New Introductory Lectures on Psychoanalysis." Vol. 22. In J. Strachey (Ed.), *The Standard Edition of the Complete Psychological Works of Sigmund Freud.* London: Hogarth Press, 1964. (Originally published 1933.)

Gilligan, C. "In a Different Voice: Women's Conceptions of Self and Morality." *Harvard Educational Review,* 1977, *47* (4), 481–517.

Gilligan, C., and others. "Moral Reasoning About Sexual Dilemmas: The Development of an Interview and Scoring System." *Technical Report of the U.S. Commission on Obscenity and Pornography,* Vol. 1. Washington, D.C.: U.S. Government Printing Office, 1971.

Haan, N. "Hypothetical and Actual Moral Reasoning in a Situation of Civil Disobedience." *Journal of Personality and Social Psychology,* 1975, *32* (2), 255–270.

Haan, N., Smith, M., and Block, J. "Moral Reasoning of Young Adults: Political-Social Behavior, Family Background, and Personality Correlates." *Journal of Personality and Social Psychology,* 1968, *10* (3), 183–201.

Kohlberg, L. "Stage and Sequence: The Cognitive-Developmental Approach to Socialization." In D. Goslin (Ed.), *Handbook of Socialization Theory and Research.* Chicago: Rand McNally, 1969.

Kohlberg, L., and others. *Assessing Moral Stages: A Manual.* Cambridge, Mass.: Center for Moral Education, Harvard University, 1978.

Piaget, J. *The Moral Judgment of the Child.* New York: Free Press, 1965. (Originally published 1932.)

Selman, R., and Jaquette, D. "Stability and Oscillation in Interpersonal Awareness: A Clinical-Developmental Analysis." In C. B. Keasy (Ed.), *Twenty-Fifth Nebraska Symposium on Motivation.* Lincoln: University of Nebraska Press, 1978.

Carol Gilligan is associate professor of Education at the Harvard Graduate School of Education.

Mary Field Belenky is research associate at the Harvard Graduate School of Education.

JOURNAL OF APPLIED DEVELOPMENTAL PSYCHOLOGY 2, 211–226 (1981)

Reasoning in the Personal and Moral Domains: Adolescent and Young Adult Women's Decision-Making Regarding Abortion

JUDITH G. SMETANA

University of Rochester

The present investigation of adolescent and young adult women's reasoning, and decision-making about abortion was conducted to determine whether reasoning about abortion could be described by moral, social-conventional, and personal concepts and to examine relationships between domain of reasoning and action choices. Seventy single women, ranging in age from 13 to 31 and divided between 25 women having abortions, 23 women continuing their pregnancies, and 22 never-pregnant women, were administered a semi-structured clinical interview about abortion and two hypothetical moral judgment dilemmas. A classification task was developed to provide an additional measure of reasoning in different domains. Another 29 single, first-pregnant women provided a comparison of the effects of these procedures on decision-making. Content analysis of the protocols revealed that responses to the abortion interview could be reliably distinguished between concepts of morality and personal issues and their coordination or lack of coordination. Subjects treating abortion as a moral issue were more likely to continue their pregnancies while subjects treating abortion as a personal issue were more likely to obtain an abortion. Differences in reasoning between pregnant and nonpregnant subjects were not observed. Moral responses to the abortion interview were found to be highly related to hypothetical moral judgments.

Although abortion continues to be one of the most volatile issues of this era, psychological research on women's decision-making regarding abortion has been limited. Psychological variables, most frequently defined as attitudes toward abortion, have contributed little either to our understanding of judgments about this decision, or to the empirical relationships observed. Evidence from a variety of sources suggests that judgments about abortion are multidimensional, and that

the complexity and richness of this thought has been inadequately conceptualized.

The results of several studies suggest that different types of social cognition
may be particularly relevant to judgments about abortion. Studies of beliefs and
attitudes towards abortion reveal that acceptance or rejection of abortion is related to different types of beliefs which can be empirically distinguished (Knutson, 1973; Rossi, 1967; Schur, 1965; Smetana & Alder, 1979; Werner, Note 5).
Beliefs about abortion can be clustered into components which are either related
to beliefs about the fetus as a life and abortion as an act of murder, or concepts
concerning women's choices and self-determination (Knutson, 1973; Smetana &
Adler, 1979; Werner, Note 5). Similar distinctions also appear in the philosophical literature on abortion (Callahan, 1973; Potter, 1969). Further, several studies
also suggest that social conventions about sex roles or appropriate sexual behavior
for women might also be an important component in judgments about abortion
(Rossi, 1967; Schur, 1965). Finally, several investigators (Gilligan, 1977; Gilligan & Belenky, 1980) have described all judgments about abortion as within the
moral domain. However, the results obtained suggest that this conceptualization
does not sufficiently account for all the observed judgments about this decision.

Thus, previous research on abortion suggests that some but not all women
reason about abortion as a moral issue of life, and that the moral issues of
abortion should be conceptually and empirically distinguished from the social-
conventional issues of appropriate sex-role behavior and sexual mores, and from
the personal issues of autonomous choice and control over one's body. Moral
(Kohlberg, 1969), social-conventional (Turiel, 1975,1978,1979) and personal
(Nucci, Note 2, 1981) issues have all been described within a conceptual
model of structural development (Turiel, 1979, in press). According to this
model, moral, social-conventional, and personal concepts are developmentally
distinct and irreducible to one another. Research on these domains has to date
focused upon events and actions that are clear examples of content for each
domain (Nucci, 1981; Smetana, Note 4, in press, a; Turiel, 1978). The research
cited above suggests, however, that concepts in all three domains may be coordinated in women's judgments and decision-making about abortion.

The research reported in the present article employs a domain analysis of
structural development to examine adolescent and young adult women's reasoning about abortion. The first purpose of the present study was to describe the
coordination of moral, social-conventional, and personal concepts in women's
judgments about abortion, and also to develop reliable criteria for distinguishing
between responses in each domain. It was expected that while individuals share
similar ways of defining these three domains and have similar ways of classifying stimuli within each domain, they would vary in their judgments of how these
criteria should be applied to abortion.

The second question of the present study concerns the relationship of
judgments about abortion to decision-making regarding unplanned pregnancy.
The present research examined judgments about abortion in the decision-making

context. It was hypothesized that the domain of reasoning would be highly associated with women's decisions to terminate or continue a pregnancy. That is, it was hypothesized that women's actions would be consistent with their different interpretations of abortion. While developmental analyses of a moral judgment level were also conducted, no specific predictions about the relationship between a moral development stage and behavior were made.

The final purpose of the present research was to examine the relationship between hypothetical and actual moral judgments once moral judgments about abortion were differentiated from social-conventional and personal reasoning about abortion. It was expected that their distinction would result in higher correlations between hypothetical and actual judgments than if all reasoning about abortion were considered within the moral domain.

In summary, the present study sought (1) to describe reasoning about abortion in terms of the moral, social-conventional, and personal domains of social-cognitive development, (2) to determine the relationships between domain of reasoning about abortion and women's decisions to continue or terminate an unplanned pregnancy, and (3) to clarify relationships between hypothetical and actual moral judgments.

METHODS

Subjects and Design

Subjects consisted of 99 never-pregnant and first-pregnant women. Subjects ranged in age from 13 to 32. Thirty-seven percent were between the ages of 13–18; 35% were between 19–22, and 38% were between 23–32. Subjects were recruited from five family planning agencies and one high school continuation program for teenage mothers in a small university town in California. Subjects were selected on the basis of their decisions to continue or terminate their pregnancies, and were divided into four groups. The first group consisted of 25 women who were deciding to obtain an abortion. The second group consisted of 23 women, 16 from agencies and seven from the high school program, who were deciding to continue their unplanned pregnancies. Subjects were obtained from the high school program because of the difficulty in locating single women who were continuing unplanned pregnancies. These participants were within the first five months of their pregnancies. The third group consisted of 22 never-pregnant women who were matched in age to the previous two groups and recruited from the agencies' other family planning services. The fourth group consisted of 29 first-pregnant women, who were divided between 20 women terminating and nine women continuing their pregnancies. These subjects provided a comparison to the other pregnant subjects of the effects of the research intervention on decisions and actions. Only their intentions and subsequent actions were assessed, and they were not interviewed.

Subjects having an abortion did not differ significantly in age, education or religion from either subjects continuing their pregnancies, or from the never-pregnant subjects. The mean age was 20.8; they had, on the average, some college education although they ranged from high school students to those with professional degrees, and they came, on the average, from lower-middle class families. They were 36% Catholic, 40% Protestant, 15% Jewish and other religions, and 9% atheist in background. Subjects deciding to have an abortion reported attending church less frequently, having mothers with more education, and being earlier in their pregnancies than subjects choosing to continue their pregnancies. The difference in gestation time was still significant when subjects from the high school program were excluded from the analyses.

The frequency of agency clientele participating in the study and the distribution of subjects' ages compared to the general clinic populations were assessed to obtain an estimate of the volunteer effects in subject selection. These analyses revealed that participation rates were quite low (with one exception, approximately 10% of the confirmed pregnancies at each agency), and that participants were significantly younger than the general clinic populations. However, the exclusion of married women and women with repeat pregnancies from the study may provide a partial account for these factors. Unfortunately, data on the marital status or parity were not available from any of the agencies.

Procedure

Currently, single women in first, unplanned pregnancies were invited to participate by agency counselors when they were informed of their pregnancies. Consenting women were contacted by phone by the investigator, randomly assigned to either the interviewed or non-interviewed groups, and scheduled for an interview. Never-pregnant women attending family planning clinics at the same agencies were also invited to participate by counselors at those agencies, and were then contacted by the investigator. The cooperation of women in the high school program was obtained through their teacher.

Subjects were interviewed within a week after the initial contact at the agency; for subjects having abortions, the interview occurred prior to their procedures. Subjects were interviewed once, for approximately two hours, by the investigator. They were administered a semistructured clinical interview (Piaget, 1928) about abortion, two standardized moral judgment dilemmas (Kohlberg et al., Note 1) and a classification task. These interviews were audio tape-recorded and then transcribed. Self reports of subsequent actions were obtained by phone from interviewed pregnant subjects two to three weeks after the interview, and from non-interviewed pregnant subjects about a month following the initial contact.

Measures

Semistructured Abortion Interviews. The abortion interview contained a set of standardized questions designed to elicit the moral, social-conventional, and personal issues about abortion and the bases for the subjects' decisions about their own pregnancies. The subjects responded to questions concerning the salient issues in each domain. Moral issues included justice considerations and relationships between abortion and other decisions involving human life; personal issues included control over one's body, and choices; and social-conventional issues included beliefs about sexuality and motherhood. The interview also included questions concerning the woman's definition of human life, the importance of these beliefs to the abortion decision, and the role of significant others and social institutions such as the law in decision-making. Prescriptive data (e.g., what role should the partner have in the decision?) as well as descriptive data (e.g., what role did he actually have?) were obtained. The interviews were structured so that each subject responded to the same set of issues, but flexible probe questions were used to pursue and clarify issues of importance to a particular subject. [The abortion interview is described in greater detail elsewhere (Smetana, Note 3, in press, b)].

Moral Judgment Interviews. Two standardized moral judgment dilemmas concerning life vs. law and punishment (IIIA) and property vs. law (VIIIA) (Kohlberg et al., Note 1) were administered. They were scored blind for the moral maturity level and developmental stage by an independent, trained scorer.

Classification Task. This task was designed to obtain an independent assessment, using a different measure, of the subjects' reasoning about abortion, and was based on a procedure which has been used successfully in other research investigating the individuals' ability to discriminate between domains of social-cognitive development (Nucci, Note 2, 1981; Smetana, Note 4). Subjects were given cards representing 14 social actions, and were asked to sort them into categories representing the moral, social-conventional, and personal domains. They were told to sort the cards according to the following categories: "This action is (right) (wrong) whether or not there is a rule or law," "This action is (right) (wrong) only if there is a rule or law," and "Not an issue of right or wrong—there should be no rules or laws against this action," which correspond to the moral, social-conventional, and personal domains, respectively.

During a pilot test, it was found that subjects agreed in their placement of the items, with the exception of three items related to abortion, "having an abortion in the first trimester," "having an abortion in the second trimester," and "having an abortion in the third trimester." The items designated as content for the moral domain were "killing," "stealing," "helping someone," "rape," and "slavery." The items designated as content for the social-conventional domain were "calling a judge 'Your Honor' in court," "driving on the right side of the road," and "eating with hands." The items designated as content for the personal domain were "length of hair," "masturbation," and "premarital sex."

Post-Interview Follow-Up. Pregnant subjects were recontacted by phone two to three weeks after their interview or initial phone contact. The follow-up was scheduled so that subjects intending to have abortions were contacted one week to 10 days following their procedures. At that time, the follow-up of the subjects' initial declaration of their intentions regarding their pregnancies were obtained.

Scoring of the Abortion Interview

Development of a Scoring Manual. Responses to the abortion interview were found to differ conceptually in two major ways. Some responses were organized around the issue of personal decision-making and the autonomy of the individual. These responses were considered within the personal domain (Nucci, Note 2, 1981). Other responses involved reasoning about the issue of life, and were considered within the moral domain (Kohlberg et al., Note 1). A third type of response entailed coordinations between the two domains; these were considered coordinated responses. Finally, for some, concepts in the two domains were uncoordinated and were categorized as such. The criterion distinguishing these four types of responses, described in greater detail in the Results section, was identified as the point at which subjects ascribed value to the unborn as a life to be considered in the decision, and their characteristic definition of an equal human life.

These findings were organized within a scoring manual. This manual was developed from a content analysis of half the protocols. A global scoring method was employed, and protocols were assigned to a single category using scoring criteria and exemplars from transcripts. The protocols used in developing the scoring scheme and the remaining 50% of the protocols were scored by the investigator ; 97% of the protocols (n = 68) were scorable by this scheme. An independently trained rater scored a subset (50%) of the protocols; 89% agreement between the two raters was obtained.

Level of Reasoning. Following the differentiation of domains, moral reasoning about abortion was further analyzed for the developmental stage and moral maturity score by an independent, trained scorer blind to the subjects' ages. Moral maturity scores (MMS) represent the subject's use of each stage, multiplied by that stage's numerical designation, summed across the stages and multiplied by 100. This produces a score ranging from 100 to 600 for each subject.

Personal reasoning about abortion was not scored for developmental level, as the responses to the abortion questions were too homogenous to score with high reliability.

RESULTS

The findings from the semistructured interviews and the classification task indicate that reasoning about abortion can be described by moral and personal concepts and their coordination or lack of coordination. Social-conventional concepts were found to be unrelated to subjects' reasoning about abortion. That is, questions about social-conventional issues, as defined here, were considered unimportant by all subjects and were not spontaneously raised in the course of the interview. Reasoning about abortion was found to be highly associated with decisions to continue or terminate a pregnancy. Finally, moral reasoning about abortion was found to be highly related to moral reasoning about other (hypothetical) issues. These findings are elaborated below.

Domains of Reasoning about Abortion

The modes of reasoning that emerged from the content analysis and their observed frequency in the present sample are described below.

Moral Reasoners. Subjects treating abortion as a moral issue, referred to as *moral* reasoners, were those for whom moral issues, or issues of justice concerning two human lives were salient for the entire course of the pregnancy. They considered the genetic or spiritual potential of the embryo at conception sufficient to define it as a human life and were thus concerned with the possible justifications, or lack of justifications, for taking life. However, they varied in the value they ascribed to this life, as well as in their judgments about the acceptability of abortion.

Personal Reasoners. Subjects for whom personal issues were salient for the entire pregnancy, and who considered the criterion of physical and/or emotional independence from the mother (occurring at birth) as the relevant feature in considering the child a human life were referred to as personal reasoners. These subjects considered the unborn an equal human life only after birth, and thus made clear distinctions between the act of abortion and killing a (born) human life. Because the unborn was viewed as a physical/ emotional extension of the woman during the pregnancy, their judgments concerned the woman's control over her reproductive life and the necessity of autonomous decision-making. Abortion was considered an action outside the realm of societal regulation and moral concern. Either decision (to have an abortion or to have a child) was viewed as a personal issue.

Coordinations Between Domains. In addition to responses that could be classified in only one domain, there was one mode of response involving coordination between the two domains. Subjects who considered abortion first a personal and then a moral issue were referred to as *coordinated personal/moral* reasoners. For these subjects, concepts in (successively) the personal and moral domains were coordinated by their definition of life, full fetal development and/or resemblance to human form, which was seen to occur with varying biological accuracy between three and six months in a pregnancy. After the point at which these subjects believed human life begins, abortion was considered a justice issue similar to other issues of life.

Uncoordinated Responses. Finally, there were three types of thought that lacked coordination between the domains. Subjects who treated abortion as a personal issue until viability, and then experienced conflict between issues in the personal and moral domains, were referred to as personal/conflict reasoners. Subjects for whom issues in both the personal and moral domains were in conflict when considering the entire course of a pregnancy were referred to as the *conflict* group. Subjects whose responses were characterized by equivocation and confusion, and who lacked a clear definition of life were referred to as the *confusion* group.

The most prevalent mode of response was to consider abortion a personal issue (35% of the subjects), but substantial portions of the sample engaged in moral reasoning about abortion (25%), or coordinated the two domains (24%). The three types of response where the domains were partially or totally uncoordinated constituted only a small proportion of the sample (personal/conflict, 9%; conflict, 3%, and confusion, 4%). There were no age differences in mode of response about abortion.

Level of Reasoning. The modal stage of moral reasoning about abortion, scored from the responses of the moral reasoners (n = 17), and from the moral responses of the coordinated reasoners (n = 16) was Stage 3, and the mean MMS was 284. The percentage of subjects scored at each moral judgment stage was as follows: Stage 1: 15%; Stage 2: 21%; Stage 3: 42%; Stage 4: 12%; Stage 5: 9%.

Classification Task

While the criteria for classification of the interview data were developed from the protocols themselves, the classification task provides an independent assessment of subjects' ability to discriminate between personal and moral actions in general and abortion in particular. The results indicate that, overall, subjects agree in their placement of most stimulus items within a domain. However, subjects' placement of the abortion items was highly related to their reasoning about abortion. As Table 1 indicates, with four exceptions, subjects placed the items in the hypothesized domains. Both "abortion in the third trimester" and "helping someone who is hurt" were placed with nearly equal frequencies in both the moral and personal categories, while "calling a judge 'Your Honor' in court" was placed in both the social-conventional and personal categories. "Eating with your hands," originally defined as a social-conventional issue, was most frequently categorized as a personal issue.

Subjects' placement of the items in different domains was further analyzed according to responses to the abortion interview. Subjects whose responses to the abortion dilemma were classified in different domains did not differ in the fre-

TABLE 1

Frequency Distributions and χ^2 for Moral, Social-Conventional and Personal Stimulus Items

Hypothesized moral items	Moral		Social-Conventional		Personal		χ^2	P
	%	n	%	n	%	n		
Killing	92.9	(65)	5.7	(4)	1.4	(1)	111.80	.001
Rape	95.7	(67)	2.9	(2)	1.4	(1)	122.60	.001
Stealing	81.4	(57)	12.9	(9)	5.7	(4)	73.40	.001
Slavery	95.7	(67)	2.9	(2)	1.4	(1)	122.60	.001
Helping someone who is hurt	51.4	(36)	5.7	(4)	41.5	(29)	24.61	.001
Hypothesized Social-Conventional Items								
Driving on right side	20.0	(14)	77.1	(54)	2.9	(2)	63.54	.001
Calling a judge "Your Honor"	2.9	(2)	45.7	(32)	51.4	(36)	29.60	.001
Eating with hands	1.4	(1)	2.9	(2)	94.0	(66)	120.61	.001
Personal Items								
Length of Hair	0		0		100.0	(70)	0	
Premarital Sex	0		1.4	(1)	98.6	(69)	0	
Masturbation	0		0		100.0	(70)	0	
Abortion Items								
Abortion in 1st Trimester	7.1	(5)	2.9	(2)	90.0	(63)	101.34	.001
Abortion in 2nd Trimester	21.4	(15)	5.7	(4)	72.9	(51)	51.80	.001
Abortion in 3rd Trimester	34.3	(24)	10.0	(7)	55.8	(39)	21.97	.001

quency with which they categorized each item in a domain, with the exception of two abortion stimulus items, ''abortion in the second trimester'' ($\chi^2 = 22.67$, df = 6, p < .001), and ''abortion in the third trimester'' ($\chi^2 = 30.89$, df = 6, p < .001). Subjects considering abortion a personal or uncoordinated issue consistently placed the abortion items in the personal category. One hundred percent of subjects in these groups placed the items pertaining to abortion in the first and second trimester in the personal category. Eighty-three percent of subjects treating abortion as an uncoordinated issue, and 92% of the personal reasoners placed ''abortion in the third trimester'' in the personal category. Subjects considering abortion a moral or coordinated issue were more likely to place these items in the moral rather than personal category. Forty-seven percent of the moral reasoners, and 38% of the coordinated reasoners placed ''abortion in the second trimester'' in the moral category; 60% and 70% of these two groups, respectively, placed ''abortion in the third trimester'' in the moral category. Subjects' reasoning regarding their placement of items was also probed. This revealed that some moral reasoners perceived the task as requiring an absolute judgment about the rightness or wrongness of abortion that they were reluctant to make. This resulted in their placement of the abortion items in the personal category (interpreted as moral relativism) at a slightly higher frequency than would be predicted from the results of the abortion interview.

Actual Reasoning and Behavior

The measure of behavioral intention, the original basis for subject selection, was found to be an equivalent measure of subsequent behavior. A comparison of intentions and behavior for interviewed and non-interviewed subjects revealed that there were no changes in decisions for interviewed subjects choosing either alternative, and that the number of changes that occurred among non-interviewed pregnant subjects was not significant. These results suggest that the interview had no adverse effects in changing the subjects' decisions or actions regarding their unplanned pregnancies.

Support for the second hypothesis was obtained; reasoning and behavior were found to be highly related. Subjects varying in reasoning about abortion were found to choose different resolutions to their unplanned pregnancies ($\chi^2 = 26.66$, df = 4, $p < .001$; see Table 2). Women who considered abortion a moral issue were more likely to continue their pregnancies; 93% of pregnant respondents treating abortion as a moral issue made this choice. Personal reasoners were more likely to obtain abortions; 93% of pregnant respondents considering abortion a personal issue sought abortions. Subjects considering abortion a coordinated issue were also more likely to continue their pregnancies (64%), although these subjects considered first trimester abortions personal actions. Moreover, never-pregnant and pregnant subjects did not differ significantly in their reasoning about abortion ($\chi^2 = 6.77$, ns, see Table 3). This indicates that although

TABLE 2

Distribution and χ² Analyses for Behavioral Comparison Groups on Reasoning Categories

	Reasoning Groups													
	Moral		Personal/Moral		Personal/Conflict		Personal		Conflict & Confusion[1]		Total[2]		χ^2	P
	%	n	%	n	%	n	%	n	%	n	%	n		
Abortion group	(4)	1	(15)	4	(8)	2	(63)	15	(8)	2	(100)	24		
Continuing group	(61)	14	(30)	7		0	(4)	1	(4)	1	(99)	23	26.66	.001
	(32)	15	(24)	11	(4)	2	(34)	16	(6)	3	(100)	47		

[1]The conflict and confusion groups were combined in these analyses due to the small numbers in each category.

[2]Percentages may not equal 100 due to rounding.

TABLE 3

Distribution and χ² Analyses for Pregnant and Non-Pregnant Subjects on Reasoning Categories

	Reasoning Groups													
	Moral		Personal/Moral		Personal/Conflict		Personal		Conflict & Confusion[1]		Total[2]		χ^2	P
	%	n	%	n	%	n	%	n	%	n	%	n		
Pregnant Subjects	(32)	15	(23)	11	(4)	2	(34)	16	(6)	3	(99)	47		
Non-Pregnant Subjects	(10)	2	(24)	5	(19)	4	(38)	8	(10)	2	(100)	21	6.77	.15
Total	(25)	17	(24)	16	(9)	6	(36)	24	(7)	5	(102)[2]	68		

[1]The conflict and confusion groups were combined in these analyses due to the small numbers in each category.

[2]Percentages may not equal 100 due to rounding.

reasoning and specific behavioral choice are highly related, reasoning in the context of making actual decisions about abortion is consistent with the more abstract and hypothetical reasoning about abortion obtained from never-pregnant subjects. Moreover, moral maturity scores, as assessed on the hypothetical moral judgment dilemmas, did not differentiate decisions.

Hypothetical and Actual Dilemmas

The third aim of the present study was to examine relationships between hypothetical and actual moral judgments. This was investigated in two ways. To test the hypothesis that personal reasoning about abortion is not less adequate moral reasoning, the responses of subjects treating abortion as a nonmoral issue (e.g., personal and uncoordinated reasoners) were scored for moral reasoning by a trained scorer blind to subjects' ages and previous scoring of the abortion interview. Then, correlations between moral reasoning, as assessed on hypothetical moral dilemmas and moral reasoning in the abortion interview, were compared for those subjects considering abortion solely or partially a moral issue (n = 33), and those subjects considering abortion a nonmoral issue (n = 35). According to the distinct conceptual domain approach, a strong relationship between moral responses to the hypothetical dilemmas and the abortion interview would be predicted. As expected, a highly significant relationship between hypothetical and actual moral judgments was observed ($r = .70$; $p < .001$). This differed significantly ($p < .001$) from the correlation obtained ($r = .27$, ns) when the nonmoral group's judgments about abortion were (incorrectly) considered moral judgments and compared with their reasoning on hypothetical moral judgment dilemmas. These analyses indicate that moral reasoning about abortion is highly related to reasoning about hypothetical moral judgment dilemmas. However, personal reasoning about abortion, considered as moral judgment, bears no systematic relationship to the same subjects' reasoning about hypothetical moral dilemmas.

Next, differences between the reasoning groups, in response to hypothetical moral dilemmas, were assessed. This analysis demonstrated that subjects who considered abortion a personal issue did not differ significantly in moral maturity scores from subjects who treated abortion as a(n) moral, coordinated, or uncoordinated, issue ($\overline{X}$ = 323, 293, 304, 331, respectively). Significant differences were found to be entirely due to the effects of the higher moral maturity level of subjects classified as personal/conflict ($\overline{X}$ = 417; F = 8.03; $p < .001$). Thus, subjects who considered abortion a nonmoral issue were not found to be less adequate moral reasoners, as assessed on hypothetical moral dilemmas.

DISCUSSION

The present research began with the hypothesis that reasoning about abortion is multifaceted and that this thinking can be described by different conceptual domains of social-cognitive development. This hypothesis was supported, even though all the proposed domains were not used by subjects in this sample. Reasoning about abortion was described in terms of moral and personal concepts, and it was demonstrated that adolescents and young adults who use moral precepts in thinking about abortion can be reliably distinguished from those who consider abortion a personal issue. The classification task and content analysis of the interviews indicate that individuals agree in their criteria for defining moral or personal events, but that they vary in their interpretation of how abortion fits these criteria. While all subjects clearly engaged in moral thought when reasoning about human life after birth, the present subjects differed in their beliefs about when human life begins. Therefore, they differed as to whether they treated abortion as a moral issue.

The present findings support the notion that conceptual differences in thinking about abortion have their source in different developmental domains, and that personal thought cannot be considered less adequate moral reasoning. First, this was indicated by the discontinuity which occurred at the point of transition from personal to moral thought in all but the moral reasoners' thinking about abortion. This was perhaps most strikingly demonstrated in the responses of the subjects who coordinated the personal and moral domains when thinking about different times in a pregnancy. Second, subjects who treated abortion as a personal issue did not differ from subjects who treated abortion as a moral issue in their reasoning about hypothetical moral dilemmas. On the contrary, significantly higher levels of moral reasoning about hypothetical dilemmas were observed among subjects treating abortion as a personal/conflict issue.

That social-conventional issues were unimportant in the present sample's reasoning about abortion was surprising, since social norms have been considered a salient variable in relation to abortion (Smetana & Alder, 1979). While this may represent a methodological artifact of inadequate or inappropriate measures of the social-conventional issues about abortion, it appears more likely that these findings are the product of societal trends toward greater permissiveness in beliefs about abortion (Jones & Westoff, 1978). It is possible that in social contexts which are more restrictive about abortion, the social-conventional issues of pregnancy, abortion and childbearing would become more predominant.

Although developmental differences in moral judgments about abortion were observed and were found to be highly related to reasoning about more hypothetical moral issues, the present findings indicate that developmental differences in moral judgment were less salient in understanding reasoning about abortion and relationships between judgments and actions than domain distinctions. To the extent that individuals' constructions about the nature of the situation vary, the domain of reasoning may be a more salient variable than the developmental stage in any one domain in understanding or predicting behavior.

In the present design, the pregnant subjects' reasoning was only assessed in the context of actual decision-making. Thus, whether the pregnant subjects' responses reflect "reason" rather than truly causal attributions (Buss, 1978) could not be determined. However, the finding that pregnant and never-pregnant women's reasoning about abortion can be similarly described, and that both groups of women were found to construct different concepts about abortion provides strong evidence for the validity of the domain distinctions described in the present study. These findings suggest that reasoning in the present context reflects more than different styles of coping and defending (Haan, 1978) with an unplanned pregnancy. It represents relatively stable ways of organizing thinking about this issue.

Finally, these findings raise issues of applied concern. First, the findings suggest that in counseling women with unwanted pregnancies, counselors should be aware of the issues that are of concern to women constructing different conceptual solutions to the abortion dilemma. In addition, various authors have suggested the predictiveness of pre-abortion ambivalence to post-abortion psychological sequelae (Osofsky & Osofsky, 1972). The characteristics of conflict described in the present research might serve as a diagnostic tool in identifying women at risk. Finally, others (Rest, Turiel, & Kohlberg, 1968) have described the structure of messages that individuals at given developmental levels find most preferable and comprehensible. Using age norms rather than individual data, such knowledge could be incorporated into programs on unwanted pregnancy and birth control to help provide more effective communications.

In summary, the present findings indicate that adolescent and young adult women's reasoning about abortion can be described as the product of different conceptual domains of social-cognitive development. Besides abortion, there are many other issues that are multifaceted and involve coordinations between moral, social-conventional, and personal concepts. The presently employed domain analysis of structural development provides a method of examining judgments about such complex, real-life issues and of elucidating relationships between naturally occurring judgments and choice.

ACKNOWLEDGMENTS

The research reported in this article was taken from the author's doctoral dissertation in partial fulfillment of the requirements for the Ph.D. at the University of California, Santa Cruz. The author gratefully acknowledges the support and guidance of Elliot Turiel, Nancy Adler, and M. Brewster Smith on the dissertation. Nancy Adler, Judith Barkwick, Sherri Oden, Jacqueline Parsons, and Elliot Turiel provided helpful comments on earlier versions of this manuscript. The author also wishes to thank Martha Morehouse, Doreen Schack, Clark Power, and Richard Weiss for their assistance with scoring. This research was supported by grant no. BNS76-83384 from the National Science Foundation. Portions of this research were presented at the 1977 and 1978 meetings of the American Psychological Association Convention in San Francisco and Toronto, respectively.

Requests for reprints may be sent to the author, Graduate School of Education and Human Development, University of Rochester, Rochester, New York, 14627.

REFERENCE NOTES

1. Kohlberg, L., Colby, A., Gibbs, J. C., Speicher-Dubin, D., & Power, C. Identifying moral stages: A manual. Unpublished manuscript, Harvard University, 1976.
2. Nucci, L. Social development: Personal, conventional and moral concepts. Unpublished doctoral dissertation, University of California, Santa Cruz, 1977.
3. Smetana, J. Personal and moral concepts: A study of women's reasoning and decision-making regarding abortion. Unpublished doctoral dissertation, University of California, Santa Cruz, 1978.
4. Smetana, J. Prosocial events and transgressions in the moral and societal domains. Unpublished manuscript, University of Rochester, 1980.
5. Werner, P. A canonial correlation analysis of beliefs and attitudes regarding abortion. Paper presented at the 56th Annual Convention of the Western Psychological Association, Los Angeles, April, 1976.

REFERENCES

Buss, A. R. Causes and reasons in attribution theory: A conceptual critique. *Journal of Personality & Social Psychology*, 1978, *36* (11), 1311–,1321.

Callahan, D. *Abortion: Law, Choice and Morality*. New York: The Macmillan Company, 1970.

Gilligan, C. In a different voice: Women's conceptions of self and of morality. *Harvard Educational Review*, 1977, *47* (4), 481–518.

Gilligan, C., & Belenky, M. A naturalistic study of abortion decisions. In R. L. Selman, and R. Yando, (Eds.) *New Directions in Child Development: Clinical Developmental Psychology*. San Francisco, Ca.: Jossey-Bass, Inc., 1980.

Jones, E. F., & Westoff, C. F. How attitudes toward abortion are changing. *Journal of Population*, 1978, *1* (1), 5–21.

Kohlberg, L. Stage and sequence: The cognitive-developmental approach to socialization. In D. Goslin (Ed.) *Handbook of Socialization Theory and Research*. New York: Rand McNally & Co., 1969.

Knutson, A. L. A new human life and abortion: Beliefs, ideal values, and value judgments. In J. T. Fawcett (Ed.) *Psychological Perspectives on Population*. New York: Basic Books, 1972.

Nucci, L. The development of personal concepts: A domain distinct from moral or societal concepts. *Child Development*, 1981, *52*, 114–121.

Osofsky, J., & Osofsky, H. The psychological reaction of patients to legalized abortion. *American Journal of Orthopsychiatry*, 1972, *42*, 48–60.

Piaget, J. (1928). *The Child's Conception of the World*. Paterson, N.J.: Littlefield, Adams & Company, 1960.

Piaget, J. (1932). *The Moral Judgment of the Child*. Glencoe, Il.: Free Press, 1948.

Potter, R. B., Jr. The Abortion Debate. In D. R. Cutler (Ed.) *Updating Life and Death: Essays in Ethics and Medicine*. Boston, Ma.: Beacon Press, 1969.

Rest, J., Turiel, E., & Kohlberg, L. Level of moral judgment as a determinant of preference and comprehension of moral judgments made by others. *Journal of Personality and Social Psychology*, 1969, *37*, 225–252.

Rossi, A. A. Public views on abortion. In A. P. Guttmacher (Ed.) *The Case for Legalized Abortion Now*. Berkeley, Ca.: Diablo Press, 1967, 26–53.

Schur, E. M. *Crimes Without Victims: Deviant Behavior and Public Policy—Abortion, Homosexuality, Drug Addiction*. Englewood Cliffs, N.J.: Prentice-Hall, 1965.

Smetana, J., & Adler, N. Understanding the abortion decision: A test of Fishbein's expectancy X value model. *Journal of Population*, 1979, *2*, 338–357.

Smetana, J. Preschool children's conceptions of moral and social rules. *Child Development,* in press, a.

Smetana, J. *Concepts of Self and Morality: Women's Reasoning about Abortion.* New York: Praeger Publishing Co., in press, b.

Turiel, E. The development of social concepts: Mores, customs and conventions. In D. J. DePalma, & J. M. Foley (Eds.) *Moral Development: Current Theory and Research.* Hillsdale, N.J.: Lawrence Erlbaum Associates, 1975.

Turiel, E. The development of concepts of social structure. In J. Glick, & A. Clarke-Stewart (Eds.) *Personality and Social Development.* (Vol. 1) New York: Gardner Press, 1978.

Turiel, E. Distinct conceptual and developmental domains: Social-convention and morality. *Nebraska Symposium on Motivation.* Lincoln, Neb.: University of Nebraska Press, 1979.

Turiel, E. Domains and categories in social cognition. In W. Overton (Ed.) *The Relationship between Social and Cognitive Development,* in press.

Two Perspectives:
On Self, Relationships, and Morality

NONA PLESSNER LYONS
Harvard University

Nona Plessner Lyons offers interview data from female and male children, adolescents, and adults in support of the assertions of Carol Gilligan (HER, 1977) that there are two distinct modes of describing the self in relation to others—separate/objective and connected—as well as two kinds of considerations used by individuals in making moral decisions—justice and care. She then describes a methodology, developed from the data, for systematically and reliably identifying these modes of self-definition and moral judgment through the use of two coding schemes. Finally, an empirical study testing Gilligan's hypotheses of the relationship of gender to self-definition and moral judgment is presented with implications of this work for psychological theory and practice.

Asked in the course of an open-ended interview to respond to the question, "What does morality mean to you?" two adults give different definitions.[1] A man replies:

> Morality is basically having a reason for or a way of knowing what's right, what one ought to do; and, when you are put into a situation where you have to choose from among alternatives, being able to recognize when there is an issue of "ought" at stake and when there is not; and then . . . having some reason for choosing among alternatives.

A woman responds:

> Morality is a type of consciousness, I guess, a sensitivity to humanity, that you can affect someone else's life. You can affect your own life, and you have the responsibility not to endanger other people's lives or to hurt other people. So morality is complex. Morality is realizing that there is a play between self and others and that you are going to have to take responsibility for both of them. It's sort of a consciousness of your influence over what's going on.

---

[1] Responses are taken from interview data of the sample and study described in full beginning on page 137.

Harvard Educational Review   Vol. 53   No. 2   May 1983
Copyright © by President and Fellows of Harvard College. Permission to copy
Appendices B and C must be granted by Nona Plessner Lyons or the *Harvard Educational Review*.
0017-8055/83/$01.25

77

In contrast to the man's notion of morality — as "having a reason," "a way of knowing what's right, what one ought to do" — is the woman's sense of morality as a type of "consciousness," "a sensitivity" incorporating an injunction not to endanger or hurt other people. In the first image of an individual alone deciding what ought to be done, morality becomes a discrete moment of rational "choosing." In the second image, of an individual aware, connected, and attending to others, morality becomes a "type of consciousness" which, although rooted in time, is not bound by the single moment. Thus, two distinct ways of making moral choices are revealed.

The representation in psychological theory of these two different images and ideas of making moral choices is the concern of this paper. One view has come to dominate modern moral psychology — the image of the person in a discrete moment of individual choice. The identification of a second image — the individual connected and attending to others — and the systematic description of both views from empirical data are presented in this work. In her critique of moral philosophy, Murdoch (1970), the British novelist and philosopher, indicates the importance of this investigation. She elaborates two issues raised by this second image of the self which apply as well to moral psychology: the need for a conception of self not limited to that of a rational, choosing agent, and a concern for acknowledging a conception of love as central to people and to moral theory.

Describing present-day moral philosophy as "confused," "discredited," and "regarded as unnecessary," Murdoch focuses on philosophy's idea and image of the self. Believing that modern moral philosophy has been "dismantling the old substantial picture of the self," Murdoch sees the moral agent reduced to an "isolated principle of will or burrowing point of consciousness." The self as moral agent, "thin as a needle, appears only in the quick flash of the choosing will" (pp. 47, 53). Murdoch rejects this classic Kantian image of the self as pure, rational agent. For her, moral choice is "as often a mysterious matter, because, what we really are seems much more like an obscure system of energy out of which choices and visible acts of will emerge at intervals in ways that are often unclear and often dependent on the condition of the system in between the moments of choice" (p. 54).

The picture of the self as ever capable of detached objectivity in situations of human choice is thus rejected by Murdoch. Yet this is the image assumed in Kohlberg's (1969, 1981) model of moral development. That model, which is a hierarchically ordered sequence of stages of moral judgment-making based in part on the pioneering work of Piaget (1932/1966), is the dominant model of modern moral psychology. In addition, Murdoch's challenge to philosophy "that we need a moral philosophy in which the concept of love, so rarely mentioned now . . . can once again be made central," can also be directed to moral psychology (1970, p. 46). Murdoch's assumption is that love is a central fact of people's everyday lives and morality. But modern moral psychology, grounded in the concepts of justice and rights, subsumes any notion of care or concern for another we might call love. It was Gilligan (1977) who first revealed this distortion of moral psychological theory.

Gilligan (1977, 1982), listening to women's discussions of their own real-life moral conflicts, recognized a conception of morality not represented in Kohlberg's work. To her, women's concerns centered on care and response to others. Noting too that women often felt caught between caring for themselves and caring for others, and characterized their failures to care as failures to be "good" women, Gilligan suggested that conceptions of self and morality might be intricately linked. In sum, Gilligan hypothesized (1) that there are two distinct modes of moral judgment—justice and care—in the thinking of men and women; (2) that these are gender-related; and (3) that modes of moral judgment might be related to modes of self-definition.

The research described here includes the first systematic, empirical test of these hypotheses. This paper reports on the identification, exploration, and description from data of two views of the self and two ways of making moral choices. The translation of these ideas into a methodology made possible the testing of Gilligan's hypotheses.

The empirical data consist of responses of thirty-six individuals to questions asked in open-ended interviews designed to draw out an individual's conception of self and orientation to morality. The data were analyzed first for descriptions of self, then for considerations individuals presented from their own real-life moral conflicts, and finally for correlations between the two.

The first part of this article presents interview data on ways that individual males and females—children, adolescents, and adults—describe themselves. These data reveal two characteristic modes of describing the self-in-relation-to-others: a self separate or objective in its relations to others and a self connected or interdependent in its relations to others. Then, from individuals' discussions of their own real-life moral conflicts, two ways of considering moral issues are distinguished: a morality of rights and justice and a morality of response and care. These data are then used to develop two coding schemes, methodologies for systematically and reliably identifying peoples' modes of self-definition and bases of moral choice. Finally, results of the study designed to test Gilligan's hypotheses and a discussion of the implications of this work for psychological theory and practice are presented. Thus, this article moves between the discursive essay and the research report, to show the evolution of a conceptual framework based on peoples' real-life experiences, and the translation of that framework into a systematic methodology for analyzing data and testing hypotheses.

A social dimension emerges as central in this work: in each of the two images of people making moral choices, there is a distinct way of seeing and being in relation to others. Although Kohlberg has identified a developmental pattern of a morality of justice, he has not elaborated the connection between his conceptualization of moral development and an understanding of relationships. Because this present work assumes that an understanding of relationships is central to a conception of morality, it is not directly parallel to Kohlberg's, yet it does maintain an indebtedness to it.[2] Gilligan and her associates (Gilligan, 1977, 1982; Langdale & Gilligan, Note 1; Lyons, Notes 2, 3) have outlined, but only broadly, the developmental patterns of an orientation to care. What remains then is the task of examining the developmental patterns of a morality of justice and of care within a framework of relationships. This present work supports, modifies, and elaborates Gilligan's ideas and confirms Piaget's central insight that "apart from our relations to other people, there can be no moral necessity" (Piaget, 1932/1966, p. 196).

---

[2] Kohlberg's coding scheme focuses on analyzing moral judgments. It does not analyze the construction, resolution, and evaluation of moral choices, or considerations other than judgments in the resolution of conflict. In addition, it does not deal with real-life data, focusing instead on hypothetical moral dilemma data.

127

Data

When asked to talk about themselves, individuals differ in how they describe themselves in relation to others. Because these differences became central to the construction of the coding schemes for identifying modes of self-definition and moral choice, it is useful to look closely at the differences in the responses of adolescents, children, and adults. These data reveal two distinct conceptions of relationships, each characterized by a unique perspective toward others.

For two fourteen-year-olds taking part in an open-ended interview, the question was the same: "How would you describe yourself to yourself?" Jack begins:

> What I am? (pause) That's a hard one . . . Well, I ski — I think I'm a pretty good skier. And basketball, I think I'm a pretty good basketball player. I'm a good runner . . . and I think I'm pretty smart. My grades are good . . . I get along with a lot of people, and teachers. And . . . I'm not too fussy, I don't think — easy to satisfy, usually — depending on what it is.

Presenting ways by which he evaluates himself, Jack comments on how he measures up in terms of some ranking of abilities: good skier, basketball player, runner, pretty smart. Talking about his relations with others, Jack continues to focus on his abilities: "I get along with a lot of people and teachers."

Fourteen-year-old Beth's response begins as Jack's did with the activities that engage her; however, she then tells of the network of relations that connect her to others:

> I like to do a lot of things. I like to do activities and ski and stuff. I like people. I like little kids and babies. And I like older people, too, like grandparents and everything; they're real special and stuff. I don't know, I guess I'd say I like myself. I have a lot of stuff going on. I have a lot of friends in the neighborhood. And I laugh a lot.

The interviewer asks, "Why do you like yourself?" and Beth replies:

> I don't know. I think it's the surroundings around me that make my life pretty good. And I have a nice neighborhood and a lot of nice friends and older people. . . . We visit new people everywhere we go. And there's my grandmother, and every time I go to my grandmother's, she makes me see all her friends and stuff. And I think that helps me along the line, 'cause you get to know them, and it makes you more friendly.

The contrast between these two responses may not at first glance seem striking, but there is a difference between the images and ideas of each person's relationships to others. Jack connects himself to others through his abilities. Like his ranking of himself as a "pretty good skier" and a "good runner," Jack's way of relating to others is another measure of his abilities: "I get along with a lot of people and teachers." Jack's perspective toward others is in his own terms, through the self's "I." Beth's connection to others is through the people who make up her "surroundings" — nice friends, older people, little kids, and babies. Her connections *through* others are in turn *to* others: "My grandmother . . . she makes me see all her friends and stuff." Thus, Beth's perspective towards others is to see them in their own terms. She sees, for example, her grandmother with her own friends, in her own context. Further, Beth seems to see a circle of interdependence in these relationships: "And I think that helps me along the line, 'cause you get to know them, and it makes you more friendly." Although both young people discuss relational topics that sound similar, they reflect different perspectives towards others: seeing others in their own terms, or through the self's perspective.

These different ways of seeing others also emerge in individuals' considerations when talking about moral conflict. When asked, "Have you ever been in a situation where you had to make a decision about what was right but you weren't sure what to do?" Jack relates an experience of being with a group of his peers who wanted to wax windows on Halloween. To an earlier question, "What makes something a moral problem?" Jack had replied, "Somewhere I have to decide . . . whether I should do this or not . . . whether it's right that I should do something or whether it's wrong." Now, talking about his conflicts about that Halloween, he echoes the earlier response: "I knew it wasn't right, but they, the kids, they would think, 'Oh, he's no fun, he doesn't want to do it, he's afraid he's going to get in trouble,' stuff like that." Urged by the interviewer to describe the consequences he considered when making his decision, Jack mentions "getting in trouble,'""my mother and father would have been upset by something like that—they wouldn't like it," and "if I didn't go, some of my friends would think . . . 'Well, he's no fun'." Jack also describes his major consideration in making a decision: "Well, you have to think about what would be right . . . and then . . . are you gonna stand up for what's right and wrong to your friends, or are you gonna let them—get you into going." Revealing that in the end he didn't go with his friends, he elaborates why: "I didn't think it was right . . . and if somebody wanted to wax my windows, I wouldn't like it, so I wasn't going to do that to someone else."

Through reciprocity Jack resolves this moral conflict. Asked if he had made the right decision, Jack replies, "Well . . . my parents would have been pleased that I had not gone. . . . If the kids had gotten into trouble, I would have known that I made the right decision, 'cause I wouldn't have wanted to have been in that group." When challenged, "What if no one knew about it?" Jack resorts again to his "principle" for choice: "I don't think you could think that was the right decision if you were to do that—to wax somebody's windows and go away thinking that was the right thing to do."

For Jack, the moral problem hinges on knowing what is right and acting on that in spite of pressures or taunts from his friends. Solving the problem, then, becomes a matter of thinking about what would be right and standing up to that. His reciprocity-based justification is derived from the self's perspective: "If somebody wanted to wax my windows, I wouldn't like it, so I wasn't going to do that to someone else." Like the measure of self-in-relation-to-others found in his self-description, Jack sees and resolves moral conflict through the self's perspective.

Beth's moral problem arises from a different set of concerns as well as a different perspective towards others. First she narrates the events surrounding her conflict: "I had a decision to give up my paper route. And I had a decision over two people, like two people wanted it. And I didn't know what was the right decision." Asked to describe the conflicts for her in that situation, she says: "Well, some friends of the person that I said could not have the route were going against me and saying that, you know, 'You did it' and 'What a stupid thing to do, to give it to the other person.' The person got kinda upset, and kinda turned against me."

Reconstructing how she thought through the problem, Beth illuminates her way of thinking in choice:

129

[at first] I was trying to think mostly who I thought was going to do better at it. I don't know, it kinda got me all upset because I didn't want to hurt somebody, one person's feelings by telling them they couldn't have it. And going to the other person and saying you can. I think that's mostly what bothered me. . . . And then it bothered me more when I thought of what person was mostly gonna get it, I was thinking, well, are they really gonna do a good job? . . . I didn't want anybody doing it that was gonna be nasty to anybody. Because I have some older people that I do on the route, and they like to talk to you and everything. And I didn't want to give it to anybody that was gonna walk away. I wanted them to get along. . . . I didn't want anybody getting in fights or anything.

As she envisions the elderly people on her paper route, Beth's decision turns on her considerations of their needs. The moral problem at first hinges on seeing the possible fractures between people and trying to avert them. Caught between wanting someone good for the paper route job and not wanting to hurt the person she had to turn down, Beth's concerns for relationships and for the welfare of others conflict.

Asked, "How did you know that it was the right decision?" Beth tells us how things worked out: "The person that was bad for the job finally realized that the person [chosen] was going to be a good person to do it." She also describes how she evaluates the decision: "I told my friends about it and my parents, and they said, 'Yeah.' And I told my paper route people that there was gonna be a new person, and they said 'Yeah,' they liked that person. And so I thought, 'Well, I think I did a pretty good job, if everybody's happy'." Beth measures the rightness of her choice by how things worked out. Having told her friends, parents, and "my paper route people," and having their concurrence, she finds in the restoration of relationships the validation of her choice.

Although Jack and Beth both wrestle with issues raised by friendships, two different kinds of moral problems concern them. Through two different perspectives — the perspective of self or the perspective of others — different problems arise and different resolutions are sought. These distinctions are found in data from younger children and adults as well.

Two eight-year-olds are asked, "How would you describe yourself to yourself?" Jeffrey answers in the third person, saying that "he's got blond hair" and "has a hard time going to sleep." He also focuses on abilities: "He learns how to do things; when he thinks they're going to be hard, he learns how to do them." Describing his way of relating to others, Jeffrey says, "He bugs everybody and he fights everybody," concluding with, "That's it. I'm lazy."

To the interviewer's question, eight-year-old Karen replies in the first person, "I don't know. I do a lot of things. I like a lot of things." Adding, "I get mad not too easy," she comments that she has "made a lot of new friends" and concludes, "And, um, I don't know if everyone thinks this, but I think I tell the truth most of the time."

Echoing themes of Jack, the adolescent, Jeffrey presents a measure of himself by abilities: "He learns how to do things; when he thinks they're going to be hard, he learns how to do things." Karen's observation that she has "made a lot of new friends" echoes adolescent Beth's self-description of her connection to the people surrounding her. It is in contrast to Jeffrey's "he bugs everybody and he fights everybody."

Themes in the real-life conflicts which the children report repeat those of the adolescents. Jeffrey talks with the interviewer about a real-life conflict. "Like when I really

want to go to my friends and my mother's cleaning the cellar. I don't know what to do."
Urged by the interviewer to say why this is a conflict, Jeffrey elaborates:

> 'Cause it's kinda hard to figure it out. Unless I can go get my friends and they can help me
> and my mother clean the cellar.
>
> *Why is it hard to figure it out?*
> 'Cause you haven't thought about it that much.
>
> *So what do you do in a situation like that?*
> Just figure it out, and do the right thing that I should do.
>
> *And how do you know what you should do?*
> 'Cause when you think about it a lot, then you know the right thing to do first.
>
> *How do you know it's the right thing?*
> 'Cause you've been thinking about it a lot.
>
> *Can you tell me how you think about it?*
> It's really simple if you think about it real quick. I think about my friends and then I think
> about my mother. And then I think about the right thing to do.

To the interviewer's question, "But how do you know it's the right thing to do?" Jeffrey concludes, "Because usually different things go before other things. Because your mother — even though she might ask you second — it's in your house."

For Jeffrey, having a rule — "different things go before other things" — allows him to resolve the dilemma of choice. Like Jack's use of the Golden Rule, Jeffrey finds a resolution to his conflict in the rule of "some things go first." For both Jack and Jeffrey it is through the self's perspective — the self's rule or standard — that moral conflict is cast and resolved.

Different issues concern eight-year-old Karen. She describes conflicts with friends: "I have a lot of friends and I can't always play with all of them, so I have to take turns. Like, they get mad sometimes when I can't play with them. And then that's how it all starts." Asked what kinds of things she considers when trying to decide with whom to play, Karen replies, "Um, someone all alone, loneliness. Um, even if they are not my friends, not my real friends, I play with them anyways because not too many people do that. . . . They never think of the right person."

Describing the "right person" as someone who is "quiet who . . . doesn't talk too much, who doesn't have any brothers or sisters," Karen, like Beth, tries to connect people to one another, "to make them feel more like at home." Asked to elaborate, Karen responds: "If a person's all alone . . . if that person never has anyone to talk to or anything . . . they are never going to have any friends. Like when they get older they are gonna have to talk. And if they never talk or anything, then nobody's going to know them. . . . If that person always stays alone, she's not going to have any fun."

For Karen, as for Beth, moral conflicts arise from having to maintain connections between people, not wanting people to be isolated, alone, or hurt. For both, resolutions are found by considering the needs of those involved. Like their adolescent counterparts, these two eight-year-olds reflect different perspectives towards others. They see and attend to different things.

These distinguishing characteristics and different ways of seeing others are manifest in adulthood. John, the thirty-six-year-old professional educator quoted at the begin-

131

ning of this paper, reveals a "logic" consistent with that of Jack and Jeffrey. He describes the decision to fire a colleague as a personal moral conflict. Although believing that the firing breached a prior agreement, he describes his conflict as "lack of confidence in my own judgment . . . feeling like maybe the others were right." His co-workers had decided, after the deadline, to fire the staff member. Describing how he felt in trying to think about what to do, he says: "I felt I had a commitment to live with . . . [we] all had a commitment to honor. . . . But for me it was a serious matter of principles."

Later, reflecting on his decision to offer his resignation in protest, he comments on how he thought about the decision:

> Well, I guess I will never know for sure . . . but I am comfortable with it, in the sense that given the pressures, and given the fact I had to decide and I don't feel I perverted any principle I hold now in making that decision. For me it was a test, in a way it became a symbol, because all this had been weighing on me. In a way the principle was commitment to principle, and I had to decide whether I had it or not, and if I let it go by, then maybe I didn't have the right to ever challenge anybody else.

In childhood and adulthood, a line of thinking in moral choice is revealed in the conflicts expressed by Jack, Jeffrey, and John in which issues of morality hinge on "moments of choice" and "knowing how to decide," thus conjuring up Murdoch's image of the self in the "quick flash of the choosing will."

Answering the question, "How would you describe yourself to yourself?" John goes on to talk explicitly about his own perspective towards others. He acknowledges: "I happen to be a person who likes the world of ideas," who can "delight myself for hours on end reading and thinking, puzzling over things. . . . I am not the sort of person who has a natural outreaching towards other people. That for me is always sort of an effort . . . an effort that I need to be nudged to do." Suggesting the importance of relationships to him, he continues talking about their difficulties and rewards for him personally:

> I am nudged [towards others] in several ways — by other people . . . but also by my convictions that tell me that I have responsibilities to other people; and, once nudged though, the interesting thing is that it is always rewarding. And I am grateful because most of the personal growth I have gone through has been through these other people and not through thinking about the world of ideas and that sort of stuff. But somehow I always retreat into the corner and want to be off by myself. It is a paradox about me, one that I still haven't fully understood. . . . Gregarious people I think can't fully understand sometimes how hard it is for certain people to become involved with people because what they regard as either minor personal risks or non-risks altogether, can strike a person like me sometimes as insurmountable obstacles. So that is one aspect of myself that just happens to come to mind. This is interesting because I had never thought about this much.

John picks up the themes of relating to others from the self's perspective heard earlier in the responses of Jack and Jeffrey. So, too, an adult woman repeats themes found in the concerns of Karen and Beth.

Forty-six-year-old Sarah, a lawyer, who describes herself as "perceptive" and "responsive" to others, tells about a moral dilemma she faced. She discovered in the course of a contested custody case that her client's boyfriend was an illegal alien. Although withholding this information was not technically illegal, she sensed that the information could affect the judge's ruling. She asked herself if telling would really make a difference in the long run and decided that it would not, "that it would resolve itself one way or the other." She concludes, "nobody is getting particularly hurt by this." Talking about her dilemma in a larger context, she describes the conflict her role creates:

> I think that I run into a dilemma in doing domestic relations work in the sense that I am dealing with a legal system that is dealing with something that it doesn't know how to deal with very well and I get very distressed because it is hard for me to put together exactly what my role is supposed to be . . . you are presiding over some pretty emotional moments in people's lives, and I never know whether I should be sort of, here is the lawbook, and not do anything to try to do whatever kind of counseling, whatever kind of support one might provide for people without costing them a fortune. . . . On the other hand, I think people need something like this. I end up in a dilemma in dealing with custody decisions, which are very messy. And God knows, there is no right and no wrong. It is a question of how can you work out something that is going to be the least painful alternative for all the people involved. . . .

The ultimate principle for resolving moral conflict, for Sarah, seems to be to work out "the least painful alternative for all the people involved."

From these examples, we see that individuals describe different kinds of considerations in moral choice tied to different ways of being with, and seeing, others: to treat others as you would like to be treated or to work out something that is "the least painful alternative for all involved." To treat others as you would be treated demands distance and objectivity. It requires disengaging oneself from a situation to ensure that each person is treated equally. In contrast, to work out the least painful alternative for all those involved means to see the situation in its context, to work within an existential reality and ensure that all persons are understood in their own terms. These two ways of perceiving others and being in relation to them are thus central both to a way of describing the self and to thinking in moral choice.

Development of the Coding Schemes

When moving from data to the conceptual constructs on which a coding scheme is based, a circular interaction occurs: the data account for the constructs and are in turn explained by them. Indeed, as Loevinger (1979) argues, such circularity is necessary to validate the coding schemes and to build the theory of which they are a part. This interactive process is described below to illuminate how ideas about human relationships, identified first in the statements of individuals, were translated into systematic categories of a coding scheme, a methodology for analyzing data.

Many researchers (Broverman, Vogel, Broverman, Clarkson, & Rosenkrantz, 1972; Erikson, 1968; Freud, 1925/1961; Piaget, 1932/1966) have commented on the relational bias of women's conceptions of self and morality. But it was Gilligan (1977) who first suggested that this relational bias might represent a unique construction of social reality. The study discussed below, designed by Gilligan, hypothesized that men and women do think differently about themselves in relation to others. That there is such a difference was supported in an examination of data—such as the comments of those quoted above—and then elaborated conceptually on the basis of that data. In that process two different ideas and ways of experiencing human relationships were revealed that seemed tied to two characteristic ways of seeing others. This distinction was then

133

conceptualized as two perspectives towards others. Table 1 presents schematically the two modes of being-in-relation-to-others, separate/objective and connected, and their respective perspective towards others, reciprocity or response.

Each of these two ideas of relationships with their characteristic perspective towards others implies a set of related ideas. The perspective of the separate/objective self — labeled "reciprocity" — is based on impartiality, objectivity, and the distancing of the self from others. It assumes an ideal relationship of equality. When this is impossible, given the various kinds of obligatory role relationships and the sometimes conflicting claims of individuals in relationships, the best recourse is to fairness as an approximation of equality. This requires the maintenance of distance between oneself and others to allow for the impartial mediation of relationships. To consider others in reciprocity implies considering their situations as if one were in them oneself. Thus, an assumption of this perspective is that others are the same as the self.

The perspective of the connected self — labeled "response" — is based on interdependence and concern for another's well-being. It assumes an ideal relationship of care and responsiveness to others. Relationships can best be maintained and sustained by consid-

TABLE 1
Relationships[a] of Reciprocity and Relationships of Response

The Separate/Objective Self

Relationships are experienced in terms of	mediated through	and grounded in
RECIPROCITY between separate individuals, that is, as a concern for others considering them as one would like to be considered, with objectivity and in fairness;	RULES that maintain fairness and reciprocity in relationships;	ROLES which come from duties of obligation and commitment.

The Connected Self

Relationships are experienced as	mediated through	and grounded in
RESPONSE to OTHERS in THEIR TERMS that is, as a concern for the good of others or for the alleviation of their burdens, hurt, or suffering (physical or psychological);	THE ACTIVITY OF CARE which maintains and sustains caring and connection in relationships;	INTERDEPENDENCE which comes from recognition of the interconnectedness of people.

[a]Relationships—the ways of being with or towards others that all individuals experience but that may be understood in either of two ways.

134

ering others in their specific contexts and not always invoking strict equality.[3] To be responsive requires seeing others in their own terms, entering into the situations of others in order to know them as the others do, that is, to try to understand how they see their situations. Thus, an assumption of this perspective is that others are different from oneself.

In Table 2 the relationship between these conceptions of self and orientations to morality, as they emerged from the empirical data, are presented schematically. The data revealed that separate/objective individuals tend to use a morality of "justice," while connected individuals use a morality of "care."

The conceptions of morality and the perspectives towards others are constructs, and as such represent ideals containing strengths and weaknesses. Equality is an ideal and a strength of a morality of justice; the consideration of individuals' particular needs — in their own terms — is both an ideal and a strength of a morality of care. On the other hand, an impartial concern for others' rights may not be sufficient to provide for care, and caring for others may leave individuals uncaring of their own needs and rights to care for themselves. In addition, the response perspective may suggest an unqualified and overly emotional concern for meeting the needs of others.[4] However, the present research suggests a greater complexity of meaning. Response to another is an interactive process in which a developing and changing individual views others as also changing across the life cycle.

Within most psychological models the ability to see another's perspective is considered a cognitive capacity which gradually becomes more objective and abstract (Kohlberg, 1969, 1981; Mead, 1934; Selman, 1980). In contrast, the perspective of response described here emphasizes the particular and the concrete. While it is assumed that this perspective changes over the course of development, the nature of these changes is not yet known. It may be that in "maturity" one generalizes the particular, that is, one always looks at the particular, and this *is* the general principle. This research suggests that our current unitary models of perspective-taking may need revision. Perspective-taking and a "perspective-towards-others" conceptualized here are separate phenomena.

It is important also that the use of the word "response" or "reciprocity" in subjects' re-

---

[3] A fourteen-year-old girl suggested the subtlety of the process of considering others in their terms. Asked by the interviewer, in response to a comment she had made, "How do you think about what someone else's reaction is going to be?" she says: "Well, first I look at the person and I think about what they are like and how they have reacted in similar situations and how they react in general and, then, I put myself away from that person and say, 'This is how they would react probably in this situation.' " Asked, "What do you mean when you put yourself away from another person?" she replies, "Um — (pause) I guess maybe I don't put myself away from them, more the opposite. I put myself in that person and try to put together a way that they would feel about this and this and this with the ideas that I have." She continues her explanation, "I guess I put myself away from me for a minute, put myself in their — but I am not relating myself to the subject at all, I am not relating the way that I feel about it, what's important to me — to what I let them think, to what I think that they'll feel." This interview is from a study of adolescent girls currently being conducted with Carol Gilligan at the Emma Willard School (Troy, New York) through the support of the Geraldine R. Dodge Foundation and with the collaboration of Robert Parker, Principal, Trudy Hammer, Associate Principal, and the students and staff.
[4] In considering the "emotional aspect of concern for another," it is useful to note Blum's work, *Friendship, Altruism and Morality* (1980). Blum argues for a second mode of morality concerned with the good of the other and challenges the dominant Kantian view to argue that altruistic concerns and emotions can be morally good. The work presented here assumes Blum's philosophical argument and demonstrates empirically the psychological phenomenon that individuals do act out of concern for the good of another.

135

TABLE 2
The Relationship of Conceptions of Self and of Morality to Considerations Made in Real-Life Moral Choice: An Overview

A Morality of Justice

Individuals defined as SEPARATE/ OBJECTIVE in RELATION to OTHERS: see others as one would like to be seen by them, in objectivity; and	tend to use a morality of *Justice as Fairness* that rests on an understanding of RELATIONSHIPS as RECIPROCITY between separate individuals, grounded in the duty and obligation of their roles;	moral problems are generally construed as issues, especially decisions, of conflicting claims between self and others (including society); resolved by invoking impartial rules, principles, or standards,	considering: (1) one's role-related obligations, duty, or commitments; or (2) standards, rules, or principles for self, others, or society; including reciprocity, that is, fairness—how one should treat another considering how one would like to be treated if in their place;	and evaluated considering: (1) how decisions are thought about and justified; or (2) whether values, principles, or standards are (were) maintained, especially fairness.

A Morality of Response and Care

Individuals defined as CONNECTED in RELATION to OTHERS: see others in their own situations and contexts; and	tend to use a morality of *Care* that rests on an understanding of RELATIONSHIPS as RESPONSE to ANOTHER in their terms;	moral problems are generally construed as issues of relationships or of response, that is, how to respond to others in their particular terms; resolved through the activity of care;	considering: (1) maintaining relationships and response, that is, the connections of interdependent individuals to one another; or (2) promoting the the welfare of others or preventing their harm; or relieving the burdens, hurt, or suffering (physical or psychological) of others;	and evaluated considering: (1) what happened/ will happen, or how things worked out; or (2) whether relationships were/are maintained or restored.

sponses not be assumed to indicate automatically the possession of that particular perspective on morality or relationships. For example, an individual using a morality of justice and having a perspective of reciprocity might state, as did fourteen-year-old Jack, "I would not do that because I would not like someone to do that to me." However, an individual using a morality of care and having a perspective of response might use the *word* "reciprocity" but with a different meaning. "I want to reciprocate because they will need that kind of help and I will be able to do that for them." In a perspective of response, the focus is always on the needs of others; it is the welfare or well-being of others in their terms that is important, not strictly what others might do in return or what the principle of fairness might demand or allow.[5]

What follows from these distinctions is that the language of morality must always be scrutinized for differences in underlying meaning. For example, words like "obligation" or "responsibility" cannot be taken at face value. (The moral imperatives of what one is "obliged" to do, "should" do, or what "responsibilities" one has are, in fact, shaped by one's perspective towards others.)

Research is needed to elaborate the conceptualizations presented here — of two perspectives on self, relationship, and morality — across the life cycle, especially attending to the issues of change and development. Research should also address potential interactions, that is, ways in which one orientation to morality may affect or be affected by the other.[6] In addition, individuals' understanding and awareness of their own perspectives of themselves-in-relation-to-others needs to be elaborated. The work presented here shows how the logic of each mode of morality and self-description has been elicited from interview data. The next section will describe how that logic was captured in a methodology, that is, in two coding schemes and used to test a set of hypotheses.

An Empirical Study Testing Gilligan's Hypotheses

In this empirical study,[7] male and female subjects were interviewed in order to ascertain their modes of self-definition and of moral choice, and to explore the connection between self-definition and modes of moral choice. A wider age-range was sampled to help elaborate modes of moral choice and of self-definition previously observed by Gilligan (1977) in a narrower age span of women. Both men and women were included to

[5] "Response" is an ancient word in English meaning "an answer, a reply; an action or feeling which answers to some stimulus or influence." "Responsibility" — usually associated with moral accountability and obligation and most frequently with contractual agreements related to a morality of justice — itself carried in its earliest meaning "answering to something." It was only in the nineteenth century that "responsibility" became attached to moral accountability and rational conduct. *(Shorter Oxford English Dictionary*, 3rd ed., s.v. "response," "responsibility.")

For a useful discussion of "responsibility" as a new symbol and image in ethics, see Niebuhr's *The Responsible Self* (1963). Niebuhr makes the interesting argument that "responsibility" as a new image of man — "man the answerer, man engaged in dialogue . . . acting in response to action upon him" — when used of the self as agent, as doer "is usually translated with the aid of older images [of man] as meaning directed toward goals or as ability to be moved by respect for the law." Further, Niebuhr says, "the understanding of ourselves as responsive beings who in all our actions answer to action upon us in accordance with our interpretation of such actions is a fruitful conception, which brings into view aspects of our self-defining conduct that are *obscured* when the older images are exclusively employed" (p. 57). Niebuhr's point is relevant to the argument here. The meaning of "responsibility" in its sense of "responsiveness" is, or may be, obscured by teleological or deontological conceptions of morality.

[6] This interaction is not to be confused with the fact that an individual with a major, or predominant, orientation may call upon considerations within either orientation when dealing with moral choice. But how a major orientation is influenced by the other, or minor, mode in its own sequence of development has not yet been elaborated and requires future work.

[7] The data for this study were originally collected by Carol Gilligan and Michael Murphy in 1978 to test Gilligan's hypotheses of the relations between sex and conceptions of self and between conceptions of self and of morality.

137

avoid the bias of a single-sex sample and to allow for the exploration of both justice and care orientations across the life-cycle. If — as Gilligan suggested — the absence of women subjects in past research obscured an understanding of the morality of care, the inclusion of men and women within this study may reveal its complexity for both sexes.

A secondary purpose of the study was to explore a suggestion of Kohlberg and Kramer (1969) that when women are engaged professionally outside the home and occupy equivalent educational and social positions as do men, they will reach higher stages of moral development than the typical adult women's stage (stage three — interpersonal mode) of his six stage system of moral judgment-making. Therefore, a sample of professional women was essential. It was also expected that such a sample would provide evidence concerning Gilligan's hypothesis that women consistently demonstrate a morality of care regardless of their profession.

Sample. The sample of thirty-six people consisted of two males and two females at each of the following ages: 8, 11, 14-15, 19, 22, 27, 36, 45, and 60-plus years. The sample was identified through personal contact and recommendation, and all subjects referred met the sampling criteria of high levels of intelligence, education, and social class.

Procedure. The data were collected in a five-part, open-ended interview which was conducted in a clinical manner, a method derived from Piaget (1929/1976). The interview proceeds from structured questions to a more unstructured exploration and clarification of each person's response. (See Appendix A for interview schedule.) Interview questions were developed to illuminate how the individual constructs his or her own reality and meaning, in this case, the experience of self and the domain of morality.

Data Analysis. The data were analyzed first for modes of self-definition, then for the subjects' orientations within considerations[8] of real-life moral conflicts. Finally, they were analyzed for correlations between the two (Lyons, 1982, Note 3).

Considerations of Justice or Care in Moral Conflicts

By examining the considerations individuals present in the construction, resolution, and evaluation of real-life moral dilemmas, the relative predominance of justice or care orientations to morality was determined. Considerations were categorized as either response (care) or rights (justice) (see Coding Scheme, Appendix B), and scored by counting the number of considerations each individual presented within either mode. In addition to identifying the presence of justice or care considerations, predominance of mode within this scoring system was determined by the higher frequency of one or the other mode in a subject's responses. Results were also expressed as percentages indicating the relationship of the dominant mode to all considerations the individual gave.

Intercoder reliability was established by two additional coders for both identification of considerations within real-life dilemmas (Step 1) and categorization of considerations as belonging to response or rights modes within the subjects' construction, resolution, and evaluation of their moral conflict (Step 2). Agreements for Step 1 were 75 and 76 percent, for Step 2, 84 and 78 percent.

Table 3 summarizes the predominance of response and rights considerations in real-life moral dilemmas for both males and females. The table shows that in real-life con-

---

[8] A consideration — the unit of analysis of the coding scheme — is an idea presented by the individual in the framing, resolution, or evaluation of choice.

138

TABLE 3

Predominance of Considerations of Response or Rights in Real-Life Dilemmas by Females and Males

Sex	Response Predominating	Rights Predominating	Equal Response/ Rights Considerations
	%(N)	%(N)	%(N)
Females (N = 16)	75 (12)	25 (4)	0 (0)
Males (N = 14)	14 (2)	79 (11)	7 (1)

Note: $x^2(2) = 11.63$ p < .001

flicts, while women use considerations of response more frequently than rights and men use considerations of rights more frequently than response, in some instances the reverse is true.

Table 4 illustrates this pattern in another way, indicating that all the females in this sample presented considerations of response, but 37 percent (6) failed to mention any considerations of rights. Similarly, all the males presented considerations of rights, but 36 percent (6) failed to mention any considerations of response. These findings show that, in real-life moral conflict, individuals in this sample call upon and think about both care and justice considerations but use predominantly one mode which is related to but not defined or confined to an individual by virtue of gender.

TABLE 4

Absence of Considerations of Response or Rights: by Females and Males

Sex	No Considerations of Response	No Considerations of Rights
	%(N)	%(N)
Females (N = 16)	0 (0)	37 (6)
Males (N = 14)	36 (6)	0 (0)

Although this study did not specifically consider developmental changes in moral thinking and self-definition, some results suggest possible developmental issues. It is clear that considerations of both response and rights are found across the life cycle. However, after age 27, women show increased consideration of rights in their conceptualization of moral problems or conflict, although they still use considerations of response more frequently than rights in the resolution of conflict. This may be related to a second finding: the disappearance of the response consideration of "care of the self" at the same age. These findings suggest the possibility of an interaction between the rights and response orientations for women in their late twenties. Another finding with implications for developmental change is the greater persistence of considerations of response among male adolescents. In general, however, across the life cycle men's considerations of rights maintain greater consistency than do women's considerations of response. Taken

139

together, these findings suggest separate developmental shifts for men and women which deserve further study.

Keeping in mind that the sample is small (N = 36), the results reported here support the hypothesis that there are two different orientations to morality — an orientation towards rights and justice, and an orientation towards care and response to others in their own terms. Morality is not unitarily justice and rights, nor are these orientations mutually exclusive: individuals use both kinds of considerations in the construction, resolution, and evaluation of real-life moral conflicts, but usually one mode predominantly. This finding of gender-related differences, however, is not absolute since individual men and women use both types of considerations.

Modes of Self-Definition: Separate/Objective or Connected

This study also tested the hypothesis that individuals use two distinct modes of self-definition. Respondents were asked "How would you describe yourself to yourself?" and responses were analyzed to determine the predominance of one of two modes of self-definition — separate/objective or connected. In a manner similar to that used for the analysis of the moral conflicts data, these self-descriptive responses were categorized according to four components: general and factual; abilities and agency; psychological; and relational (see Coding Scheme, Appendix C). Each individual was scored by counting the number of separate/objective or connected relational characterizations, and then the predominant mode was determined.

Intercoder reliability for the self-description data was established using two independent coders in a two-step coding process which was more rigorous than most correlational reliability procedures. Every statement about self-definition was coded. In Step 1, in which each idea about the self was identified, intercoder reliability was 70 and 71 percent. In Step 2, in which each idea was categorized according to specific aspects within components, intercoder reliability was 74 and 82 percent.

A summary of male and female modes of self-definition is given in Table 5. As the table indicates, women more frequently use characterizations of a connected self, while men more frequently use characterizations of a separate/objective self. Although these different gender-related modalities occur systematically across the life-cycle, they are not absolute; some women and some men define themselves with elements of either mode. In addition, and perhaps most striking, is the finding that both men and women define themselves in relation to others with equal frequency, although their characterizations of these relationships are different.

TABLE 5
Modes of Self-definition: Females and Males

Sex	Predominately Connected	Predominately Separate/ Objective	Equally Connected and Separate	No Relational Component Used
	%(N)	%(N)	%(N)	%(N)
Females (N = 16)	63 (10)	12 (2)	6 (1)	19 (3)
Males (N = 14)	0 (0)	79 (11)	7 (1)	14 (2)

Note: $x^2(3)$ = 16.3 p < .001

140

Relationship of Definitions of Self to Considerations in Real-Life Moral Choice
Some of the most important results of this study concern the testing of the hypothesis of
the relationship between modes of moral choice and modes of self-definition. Table 6
presents these findings. In this sample, regardless of sex, individuals who characterized
themselves predominantly in connected terms more frequently used considerations of
response in constructing and resolving real-life moral conflicts; and individuals who
characterized themselves predominantly in separate/objective terms more frequently
used considerations of rights.

TABLE 6
Modes of Self-definition Related to Modes of Moral Choice

Predominant Modes of Moral Choice	Modes of Self-definition: Connected	Separate/ Objective	Other (S/C or none)[a]
Response N = 13 (1M, 12F)	10 (10F)	0	3 (1M, 2F)
Rights N = 16 (12M, 4F)	0	13 (11M, 2F)	3 (1M, 2F)

Note: $x^2(2) = 15.77$ p < .005. In order to calculate the x^2 statistic, 1 was added to each cell in order to
eliminate 0 cells.
[a]S/C indicates individuals having an equal number of separate/objective and connected characterizations;
none indicates an individual having no relational characterizations.

Although these results do not allow us to claim a causal relationship between modes of
self-definition and modes of moral choice, we can say an important relationship exists.
Further research is needed to see if these results hold over larger samples of a broader
socio-economic status. Furthermore, research is needed to test the possibility that patterns of decision-making in areas other than moral choice may also be related to these
modes of self-definition.

Implications

The development of the methodologies presented here — the coding schemes for identifying modes of self-definition and moral judgment — made possible the testing of a set of
hypotheses important for theories of ego and moral development and for educational
and clinical practice as well. Although all of the implications cannot be addressed fully,
some of the most important ones are identified as an invitation to others to join in further clarification.

1. Psychological theories of moral development should recognize a morality of care as a
systematic, lifelong concern of individuals. It should not be identified solely as a temporary, stage- or level-specific concern, or as subsumed within a morality of justice, as
Kohlberg's work posits.
2. Psychological theories of ego and identity development need to consider a relational
conception — the self-in-relation-to-others — as central to self-definition. This concern for connection to others should not be considered as present only at particular
stages or as issues pertaining only to women. Although men and women tend to un-

141

derstand and define relationships in different ways, definition of self in relation to others is found *in both sexes* at all ages.

3. Theories of cognitive and social development should recognize that individuals construct, resolve, and evaluate problems in distinctively different ways. These differences are not simply in content, but seem to be related to two different perspectives towards others. Theories of cognitive and social development built on unitary models of social perspective-taking should be reconsidered.

4. Counselors, teachers, and managers, when dealing with conflicts within relationships, need to take into account that the language of morality in everyday speech has different meanings for people and that these may carry behavioral implications. For example, what people feel obliged to do or what their responsibilities to others are may be defined and understood differently.

5. Designs for psychological research need to reflect in their subjects of study the centrality of interpersonal interactions. This means research should focus not just on the individual but on both members of an interacting unit — husband and wife, friends, mother and child, teacher and student, manager and staff, and so forth.

6. Sex as a variable for study ought to be included in research designs and methodologies as a matter of course. This paper suggests both the difficulty in understanding sex differences and their importance to an improved understanding of theory and practice.

To accommodate the problems of modern moral philosophy, Murdoch (1970) has called for psychology and philosophy to join in creating a "new working philosophical psychology" (p. 46). This paper offers to psychologists and philosophers alike some new premises and methodologies by which to explore further the meaning of morality in our lives.

I wish to thank Carol Gilligan for her continuing support and encouragement, and Jane Attanucci, Miriam Clasby, Maxine Greene, Kay Johnston, Lawrence Kohlberg, Sharry Langdale, Jane Martin, Michael Murphy, Erin Phelps, Sharon Rich, Linda Stuart, Sheldon White, Bea Whiting, and Robert Lyons for their help and insights in the development of this work. I want to acknowledge, too, the support and personal encouragement of Marilyn Hoffman. The National Institute of Education funded the research reported here. The Geraldine R. Dodge Foundation is supporting a study of adolescent girls, part of which is also reported.

Reference Notes

1. Langdale, C., & Gilligan, C. *The contribution of women's thought to developmental theory (Interim Report to the National Institute of Education)*. Cambridge, Mass.: Harvard University, 1980.
2. Lyons, N. *Seeing the consequences*. Unpublished qualifying paper, Harvard University, 1980.
3. Lyons, N. *Manual for coding responses to the question: How would you describe yourself to yourself?* Unpublished manuscript, Harvard University, 1981.
4. Gilligan, C., Langdale, S., Lyons, N., & Murphy, J. M. *The contribution of women's thought to developmental theory (Final Report to the National Institute of Education)*. Cambridge, Mass.: Harvard University, 1982.

References

Blum, L. *Friendship, altruism and morality*. Boston: Routledge & Kegan Paul, 1980.
Broverman, I., Vogel, S., Broverman, D., Clarkson, F., & Rosenkrantz, P. Sex-role stereotypes: A current appraisal. *Journal of Social Issues*, 1972, 28, 58-78.
Erikson, E. *Identity: Youth and crisis*. New York: Norton, 1968.

142

Freud, S. [Some psychical consequences of the anatomical distinction between the sexes.] In J. Strachey (Ed. and trans.), *Standard Edition 19*. London: Hogarth Press, 1961. (Originally published, 1925.)

Gilligan, C. In a different voice: Women's conceptions of the self and of morality. *Harvard Educational Review*, 1977, **47**, 481-517.

Gilligan, C. *In a different voice*. Cambridge, Mass.: Harvard University Press, 1982.

Kohlberg, L. Stage and sequence: The cognitive developmental approach to socialization. In D. Goslin (Ed.), *The handbook of socialization theory and research*. Chicago: Rand McNally, 1969.

Kohlberg, L. *The philosophy of moral development: Moral stages and the idea of justice*. San Francisco: Harper & Row, 1981.

Kohlberg, L., & Kramer, R. Continuities and discontinuities in childhood and adult moral development. *Human Development*, 1969, **12**, 93-120.

Loevinger, J. *Scientific ways in the study of ego development*. Worcester, Mass.: Clark University Press, 1979.

Lyons, N. *Conceptions of self and morality and modes of moral choice*. Unpublished doctoral dissertation, Harvard University, 1982.

Mead, G. H. *Mind, self, and society*. Chicago: University of Chicago Press, 1934.

Murdoch, I. *The sovereignty of good*. Boston and London: Routledge & Kegan Paul, 1970.

Niebuhr, H. R. *The responsible self*. New York: Harper & Row, 1963.

Perry, W. *Forms of intellectual and ethical development in the college years*. New York: Holt, Rinehart & Winston, 1968.

Piaget, J. *The moral judgment of the child*. New York: Free Press, 1966. (Originally published, 1932.)

Piaget, J. *The child's conception of the world*. Totowa, N.J.: Littlefield, Adams, 1976. (Originally published, 1929.)

Selman, R. L. *The growth of interpersonal understanding: Developmental and clinical analyses*. New York: Academic Press, 1980.

Appendix A

Interview Schedule

1. A general introductory question: "Looking back over the past year/five years, what stands out for you?" (from Perry, 1968).

2. Hypothetical, moral dilemma questions: the classic Kohlberg justice dilemma, the "Heinz dilemma," and a "responsibility," or caring, dilemma developed from Gilligan's research.

3. Discussion of a real-life dilemma generated by questions about personal moral conflict and choice asked in several ways: "Have you ever been in a situation where you weren't sure what was the right thing to do?" or, "Have you ever had a moral conflict?" or, "Could you describe a moral conflict?" These were followed by a more consistent set of questions: "Could you describe the situation?" "What were the conflicts for you in that situation?" "What did you do?" "Did you think it was the right thing to do?" "How did you know it was the right thing to do?"

4. A set of self-description questions: "How would you describe yourself to yourself?" "Is the way you see yourself now different from the way you saw yourself in the past?" "What led to the change?"

143

5. General questions: "What does morality mean to you?" "What makes something a moral problem to you?" "What does responsibility mean to you?" "When responsibility to self and responsibility to others conflict, how should one choose?" (Gilligan, Langdale, Lyons, & Murphy, Note 4).

Appendix B

Morality as Care and Morality as Justice: A Scheme for Coding Considerations of Response and Considerations of Rights

I . *The Construction of the Problem*
   A. Considerations of Response (Care)
      1. General effects to others (unelaborated)
      2. Maintenance or restoration of relationships; or response to another considering interdependence
      3. Welfare/well-being of another or the avoidance of conflict; or, the alleviation of another's burden/hurt/suffering (physical or psychological)
      4. Considers the "situation vs./over the principle"
      5. Considers care of self; care of self vs. care of others

   B. Considerations of Rights (Justice)
      1. General effects to the self (unelaborated including "trouble" "how decide")
      2. Obligations, duty or commitments
      3. Standards, rules or principles for self or society; or, considers fairness, that is, how one would like to be treated if in other's place
      4. Considers the "principle vs./over the situation"
      5. Considers that others have their own contexts

II. *The Resolution of the Problem/Conflict*
   [same as part I]

III. *The Evaluation of the Resolution*
   A. Considerations of Response (Care)
      1. What happened/how worked out
      2. Whether relationships maintained/restored

   B. Considerations of Rights (Justice)
      1. How decided/thought about/justified
      2. Whether values/standards/principles maintained

144

Appendix C

A Scheme for Coding Responses to the "Describe Yourself" Question

I. *General and Factual*
   A. General factual
   B. Physical characteristics
   C. Identifying activities
   D. Identifying possessions
   E. Social status

II. *Abilities and Agency*
   A. General ability
   B. Agency
   C. Physical abilities
   D. Intellectual abilities

III. *Psychological*
   A. Interests (likes/dislikes)
   B. Traits/dispositions
   C. Beliefs, values
   D. Preoccupations

IV. *Relational Component*
   A. Connected in relation to others:
      1. Have relationships: (relationships are there)
      2. Abilities in relationships: (make, sustain; to care, to do things for others)
      3. Traits/dispositions in relationships: (help others)
      4. Concern: for the good of another in *their* terms
      5. Preoccupations: with doing good for another; with *how* to do good

   B. Separate/objective in relation to others
      1. Have relationships: (relationships part of obligations/commitments; instrumental)
      2. Abilities in relationships: (skill in interacting with others)
      3. Traits/dispositions in relationships: (act in reciprocity; live up to duty/obligations; commitment; fairness)
      4. Concern: for others in light of principles, values, beliefs or general good of society)
      5. Preoccupations: with doing good for society; with *whether* to do good for others)

V. *Summary Statements*

VI. *Self-evaluating Commentary*
   A. In self's terms
   B. In self in relation to others
      1. Connected self
      2. Separate self

3

ADOLESCENTS' SOLUTIONS TO DILEMMAS IN FABLES:
TWO MORAL ORIENTATIONS--TWO PROBLEM SOLVING
STRATEGIES

D. Kay Johnston

Recent discussions of moral development have dealt with controversies relating to sex differences in moral development (Kohlberg, 1984;
Baumrind, 1986; Walker, 1986), cultural differences (Snarey, Reimer, &
Kohlberg, 1985; Snarey, 1985), and socialization versus developmental
theories of morality (Gibbs & Schnell, 1985). In these discussions one
definition of morality is offered, that of Kohlberg who followed Piaget
(1932/1965); thereby a theory of morality as the development of justice
reasoning is, in essence, taken for granted.

Other work has identified two moral orientations (Gilligan, 1977,
1982; Lyons, 1982, 1983) and explored how these two orientations are
used in people's thinking about real-life moral conflict and in hypothetical
dilemmas (Langdale, 1983). This work offers a theory about the morality
of care.

These two moral orientations--one of justice and rights and one
of care and response--have been shown to be represented in people's
descriptions of moral conflicts, but people tend to focus their attention
either on considerations of justice or on considerations of care so that
one orientation is predominant and the other minimally represented. In
addition, it has been demonstrated that in descriptions of real-life moral
conflict "care focus" dilemmas are more likely to be presented by females

99

and "justice focus" dilemmas by males (Lyons, 1982, 1983; Gilligan & Attanucci, in press and see Chapter 4). The discovery and exploration of moral orientations has largely been confined to data in which subjects were interviewed and asked to discuss an actual moral conflict which they faced. This question and its elaboration generate data called "real-life moral dilemmas." The moral orientations of justice and care appeared spontaneously in these discussions, but there was no attempt to systematically explore the person's understanding of the moral orientation that was not focused upon or used spontaneously.

The present study begins with the hypothesis that there is no reason to assume that because a person uses an orientation spontaneously, she or he would not use the other orientation if asked whether there is another way to see the problem. Thus, the study considers the question: Can both males and females understand both moral orientations? This question is addressed by using a standard method (Johnston, 1983) to investigate the ability of one person to use both orientations in solving moral dilemmas. The dilemmas used are embedded in fables.

The study varied age and gender to test the premise that eleven and fifteen-year-old boys and girls can use both the justice and the care orientations. Consistent questions were asked of each participant and elicited not only alternative ways to solve the problem presented but also the participant's evaluation of different ways of solving the problem.

METHOD

The author used two of Aesop's fables ("The Porcupine and the Moles" and "The Dog in the Manger") in two previous studies (see Appendix for fables). One study focused on different definitions of the moral problems posed in the fables;[1] another showed that boys and girls tended to solve the problems differently.[2] These two studies also found that the two moral orientations identified by Kohlberg and Gilligan emerged in the solutions of the subjects interviewed. These two orientations are characterized here as "rights orientation" and "response orientation," reflecting that the solution focused on issues of justice or issues of care. Subjects interviewed had solved the fable dilemmas either in the rights orientations by applying a universal rule which was seen as the fair way of solving a problem of conflicting rights or claims as, "it is the mole's house; therefore, the porcupine must leave," or in the response orientation by trying to attend to and respond with care to the needs of all the animals in the fable, for example, "the moles and the porcupine must talk and share the house."

Thus, the fables present a standard method for interviewing a subject about his/her understanding of the justice and care orientation. The method is similar to that used in eliciting real-life dilemmas in that it engages a person in discussing a moral problem; however, it is different in three ways. First, the fable offers a constant context which is specific and consistent for all interviewees so that comparisons can be made among and between peoples' discussion of the same dilemma. In this way it is similar to standard measures of moral development that use hypothetical dilemmas. Second, the fables were not a reconstruction of a difficult moral problem faced by the interviewee. Because these dilemmas were not as personal as the real-life dilemmas, this interviewer felt less constrained in challenging the interviewee's construction of the problem and in making counter-suggestions which indicated reasons why solutions offered by the interviewee might not work. Finally, in this method the interviewee constructed both the moral problem and the solution, since he or she first was asked to identify the problem posed in the fable story and then to solve that problem.[3]

Subjects

The subjects for this study were sixty adolescents who live and attend public school in a middle class suburban community north of Boston. The subjects were equally divided between boys and girls who were eleven and fifteen years of age.

The students were volunteers from four sixth-grade classes in two different elementary schools and from mixed levels of sophomore English classes. These students were recruited by the author who spoke to several classes and asked for student volunteers. Parental permission was obtained for each participant.

Task and Procedure

The interviews were conducted in the schools. Following a brief explanation of the purpose of the interview, the interviewer read either "The Dog in the Manger" or "The Porcupine and the Moles." Following the first fable and discussion, the second fable was read; the fables were alternated in their order of presentation.

After the first fable was read the interviewer began a technique of interviewing which utilized standard questions combined with the method Piaget called the "clinical examination" (1979, p. 10). The first standard question was, "What is the problem?" followed by questions (or probes) which clarified what the subject had in mind, and how the problem had been defined. Then the subject was asked, "How would you solve it?" During this phase of the interview, counter-suggestions were made in order to examine the student's commitment to her/his initial solution. Questions were also asked to clarify the solution the subject had in mind and strategies being used to reach the solution.

Two solutions to each fable were coded: the "spontaneous" solution and the "best" solution. The student's first solution was considered the spontaneous, and the preferred solution was the best. The codes were assigned to the answers to the question, "Why is that a good solution?" These codes made a distinction between answers in the rights orientation or in the response orientation by following the logic of the Lyons coding scheme (1983).

In the overview of Lyons' coding scheme, the two moral orientations of rights and response are presented. The logic of a morality of rights is defined as construing moral problems as "issues/decisions of conflicting claims between self and others (including society). These issues are resolved by invoking impartial rules, principles, or standards which consider one's obligations, duty, or commitment; or standards, rules, or principles for self, others, and society." The response logic is defined as construing problems as issues of how to respond to others in their situations. In order to do so one considers how to "maintain relationships" or "promote the welfare of others or prevent them harm or relieve their burdens, hurt, or suffering, physical or psychological" (Lyons, 1983, p. 134). The coding of the fables relied on this logic.

When the solution for the fable relied on a principle such as "the right to own property" or "the right to life" expressed as a universal or impartial understanding, the solution was coded in the "rights" mode. Some examples of answers coded in the rights mode are:

The porcupine has to go definitely. It's the mole's house.

It's their ownership and nobody else has the right to it.

Send the porcupine out since he was the last one there.

Answers which responded to the needs of both animals in the dilemmas were coded "response" mode. Examples of these solutions are:

Wrap the porcupine in a towel.

If there's enough hay, well, this is one way, split it. Like, if they could cooperate. Like, take some of the hay so the dog can rest on it and take some of the hay so the ox can eat it. That's the only way to work it out.

There'd be times that the moles would leave or the porcupines would stand still or they'd take turns doing stuff--eating and stuff and not moving.

The both of them should try to get together and make the hole bigger.

Answers to the dilemmas which incorporated elements of both orientations were coded "both." Answers including both typically tried to incorporate or integrate the ideas that relied on a principle with the idea that the needs of both the participants in the dilemmas must somehow be met. Examples of these solutions are:

If the porcupine used the mole's house for the winter, then went back to where he used to live.

They (moles) should help the porcupine find a new house.

I think the moles should just ask him again to leave and if he says no, they should ask him, why not. If he says, "I can't find another place to live," then they should maybe enlarge their home. If he says, "I just don't feel like it," then they should send him out.

While relying on Lyons' exposition of the logic of the rights and response orientation, the fable coding departs from the actual coding procedure outlined by Lyons. Unlike Lyons' method which identified distinct ideas (i.e., "considerations"), the unit of analysis in the fable coding is the entire solution offered by the subject. Similarly, in Lyons' procedure there is a delineation of separate ideas into "chunks" which fall under either the response or the rights orientation. In other words, the coder's task is to mark separate ideas presented by the interviewee and code each idea as either justice or care. This also is not done in the fable coding, since the concern is not to quantify the considerations which appear in one or the other orientation, but rather to ascertain whether each orientation is represented by each subject.

The final difference in this coding is a category called "both." "Both" indicates that the logics of both orientations were represented and/or integrated in the solution. Once the orientation of the solution was identified, it was coded either Response, Rights, or Both. It could also be labeled Uncodable, which meant the answer did not clearly represent any identified logic.

This four-category coding is desirable for two reasons: (1) the range of answers is represented and (2) the possibility of reducing these moral orientations to an either/or dichotomy is eliminated.

Intercoder Reliability

Intercoder reliability was determined for two coding categories in the fable data. These two categories were: (1) orientation used spontaneously and (2) orientation used for best solution.

The criterion of agreement was that the two judges identically coded each participant's spontaneous solution and best solution. The reliability of this coding method is reported in Table 1. It is worth noting that the second coder had not been previously reliable on the Lyons real-life coding

TABLE 1

Intercoder Reliability

Solution Coded	Agreement	Cohen's Kappa[*]
Spontaneous solution to The Dog in the Manger	100	1.00
Spontaneous solution to The Porcupine and the Moles	90	0.81
Best solution to The Dog in the Manger	100	1.00
Best solution to The Porcupine and the Moles	100	1.00

[*]*Cohen's Kappa is the measurement of agreement that takes chance into account (1960).*

104

scheme. This suggests that this standardized fable method may be easily replicated.[4]

As the interview continued, the student was asked, "Is there another way to solve the problem?" This standard question began the process of discovering the interviewee's ability to switch orientations. When the subject offered an alternative solution, the questioning process was repeated. If the subject was unable to spontaneously switch orientations, the interviewer used the following procedure. If the spontaneous solution given had been in the rights orientation, the interviewer said:

> *Is there a way to solve the dilemma so that all of the animals will be satisfied?*

If this did not help the subject adopt the response orientation, the interviewer said:

> *Some people would say that you can solve this problem by having the animals talk together and decide on a way in which they could all be happy. What do you think of that?*

This question was followed by another standard question:

> *How do you think someone who solved the problem in that way would think about the problem?*

If the spontaneous solution had been in the response orientation, the interviewer said:

> *Is there a rule you could use to solve the problem?*

If this did not elicit a rights solution, the interviewer said:

> *Some people would say that you could solve this problem by using a rule such as "This is the mole's house (or the ox's stable), so the porcupine (or dog) must leave." What do you think of that?*

This question was followed by:

> *How do you think someone who solved the problem in that way would think about the problem?*

Each of the interviewer's questions more clearly defined the thinking inherent in the second orientation for the subject. The idea of asking for the second orientation assumed the interviewer recognized the spontaneous orientation while interviewing. The author has had extensive experience coding the orientations in real-life dilemmas and did recognize the rights or response orientation while interviewing for the 1983 pilot study. If there was any question about which orientation was used spontaneously, the interviewer went through both sets of standard questions to elicit the subject's thinking in both orientations.

Finally, the interviewer asked:

Of all the solutions we discussed, which one is best?

RESULTS

The central question in this research is: How do adolescents use and explain both moral orientations while discussing the problem in the two fables. To address this question, this article will focus on results pertaining to: (1) the use of moral orientation for the spontaneous solution and (2) the use of moral orientation for the best solution.

In addressing each question, age and gender differences will be discussed. The results for each fable are presented separately because they were sometimes different. These differences are important and in some cases lead to different interpretations and implications. In the *Fable Effects* section there is an examination of the effects of discussing both orientations in one fable on the consideration of moral orientation in the second fable. For the sake of brevity, "The Porcupine and the Moles" will be referred to as the Porcupine Fable, and "The Dog in the Manger" as the Dog Fable.

Moral Orientation Used for Spontaneous Solution

Tables 2 and 3 show use of spontaneous orientation by gender for each fable. These results are collapsed across ages, since there was no significant difference in the use of spontaneous orientation by eleven and fifteen-year-olds.

As can be seen in Table 2, the orientation used spontaneously in the Dog Fable was significantly related to gender. The expected pattern is demonstrated with 73.3 percent of males using the rights orientation for their initial solution. In contrast, 50 percent of the girls used the response

TABLE 2

Moral Orientation of Spontaneous Solution for The Dog in the Manger Fable, by Gender

	Female	Male
Rights	12	22
Response	15	5
Both	3	1
Uncodable	0	2

$\chi^2 = 10.94$, *d.f.* $= 3$, *p* $= 0.01$.

Note: The expected values in the tables presented here are frequently lower than 5, the recommended minimum (Siegel, 1956). To check the significance of these tables, the categories Both *and* Uncodable *were eliminated because they often had low frequencies. Statistics were then calculated on the resulting two–by–two tables. The results were virtually the same. The tables presented here were selected because they represent the complexity of the responses more adequately than the two–by–two tables.*

TABLE 3

Moral Orientation of Spontaneous Solution for The Porcupine and the Moles Fable, by Gender

	Female	Male
Rights	15	21
Response	10	7
Both	5	1
Uncodable	0	1

$\chi^2 = 5.20$, *d.f.* $= 3$, *p* $= 0.16$.

orientation, 40 percent used rights, and 10 percent used both orientations in their initial solution.

In Table 3, it can be seen that the use of spontaneous orientation had no significant relationship to gender in the Porcupine Fable. It is interesting that 60 percent of all subjects interviewed spontaneously solved this Porcupine Fable in the rights mode. This presents a difference in the spontaneous solutions to the two fables.

Moral Orientations Used for Best Solutions

The following tables show the choice of moral orientation for the best solution by gender for both fables. Again, there was no significant relationship with age and the use of moral orientations for the best solutions; therefore, the results are not presented by age.

TABLE 4

Moral Orientation of Best Solution for The Dog in the Manger Fable, by Gender

	Female	Male
Rights	3	13
Response	24	13
Both	3	3
Uncodable	0	1

$\chi^2 = 10.52$, $d.f. = 3$, $p = 0.01$.

Table 4 shows that 80 percent of the females chose the response orientation as the best way to solve the problem, and 10 percent decided that a solution which included both orientations provided the best solution. This finding confirmed initial predictions. For the males it can be seen that 43.3 percent used the rights orientation and 43.3 percent used the response orientation for the best solution. This is different from the predicted outcome which was that males would use the rights orientation predominantly.

TABLE 5

Moral Orientation of Best Solution for The Porcupine and the Moles Fable, by Gender

	Female	*Male*
Rights	6	17
Response	18	5
Both	5	6
Uncodable	1	2

$\chi^2 = 13.03$, d.f. = 3, p = 0.0046.

The results for the use of moral orientation for the best solution to the Porcupine Fable (Table 5) show a highly significant relationship between orientation and gender. Sixty percent of the females chose response and 56.7 percent of the males chose rights as the orientation providing the best solution. This is the pattern predicted by previous research (Gilligan, Johnston, Langdale, Lyons). Also of interest here is that five females (16.7 percent) and six males (20 percent) used both moral orientations in their best solution, thus integrating the two orientations.

Fable Effects

Analysis was also done to determine if the discussion of both orientations in the first fable influenced the use of orientations in the discussion of the second fable. For each order of presentation, contingency tables were used to explore the associations between: the spontaneous orientation used in the first fable and the spontaneous orientation used in the second fable; the best orientation used in the first fable and the best orientation used in the second fable; the best orientation used in the first fable and the spontaneous orientation used in the second fable. None of these associations were significant, regardless of which fable was discussed first.

DISCUSSION

This study demonstrates that within the specific discussion of the two fables, the two moral orientations described by Gilligan and Kohlberg are used by adolescents of both ages to solve the fables' moral problems and can be reliably identified. Then the question becomes: What leads to the use of these orientations? These fable data suggest that both gender and fable speak to that question. These findings:

1. present gender differences in moral orientation
2. show the influence of context on use of orientation as shown by the fable differences
3. question the assumption that there is one problem-solving strategy for moral problems
4. point to avenues for further research

Gender Differences

Age was not related to use of moral orientation but gender was. The pattern of girls using the care orientation and boys using the rights orientation was present in one of the spontaneous solutions and in both of the best solutions. The spontaneous solution to the Porcupine Fable did not replicate this pattern and will be discussed in the section *Fable Differences.*

Two aspects of the findings are of particular interest. All of the boys and girls represented the two orientations in some way. They either used both orientations in their varying solutions or they switched orientations spontaneously when asked, "Is there another way to solve the problem?" Thus, by at least eleven years of age, most children indicate knowledge of both orientations. This shows that the gender difference does not reflect knowing or understanding only one orientation, but rather choosing and/or preferring one over the other as a solution to a moral dilemma. Thus, the gender difference represents a relationship between gender and choice of moral orientation. This relationship arises from the fact that the girls as a group choose both orientations more frequently than the boys who tend as a group to use the rights orientation more exclusively. In other words, boys use the moral orientation of care much less often than girls use the moral orientation of justice. This is interesting because even though the boys know both moral orientations, they most often choose and prefer only the rights orientation, while girls choose and prefer both. This finding corroborates Gilligan's original hypothesis that if only males are studied there *is* a predominant voice of morality, but studying girls complicates a unitary view of morality. It also suggests that girls may learn the dominant voice of morality, that of justice, and be able to represent this culturally valued dominant voice (see Kohlberg and also Miller, 1976, for a view of dominance in culture), but in addition, may represent a less well articulated voice of morality and shift voices with greater flexibility than boys. This flexibility may be a strength which is more evident in girls' development than in boys, and it raises the question of whether this is a characteristic of girls in particular or of subordinate groups in general.

Fable Differences

The context of the fables influences the choice of moral orientation in two ways. As previously noted, the spontaneous solution to the Porcupine Fable did not yield significant gender differences. Although males predominantly used the rights orientation, females did not use the care orientation predominantly but used the care and justice orientations equally. When the females are divided by age, it is the fifteen-year-olds who choose the moral orientation of rights, while the eleven-year-olds use the moral orientation of response. The data suggest two explanations for this finding. The greater frequency of the spontaneous use of rights solutions by fifteen-year-old girls in the Porcupine Fable may reflect the nature of the conflict presented in this fable: The moles' claim to property and the porcupine's claim to shelter can readily be construed in the rights mode, especially in a rights-oriented culture such as the United States. The older fifteen-year-old girls may be more aware of our cultural norms and values. Another explanation for this finding is that older girls may be afraid of looking naive when they propose an inclusive solution like "They could build a bigger house" to solve this conflict. This would explain their use of the rights orientation spontaneously in this dilemma.

The second fable difference is that the Dog Fable elicits more best solutions using the response orientation from the boys. In both fables if there is a change from the moral orientation used spontaneously to that used for the best solution, it tends to be from the rights to the response orientation or to a solution using both orientations. This suggests that a more circumspect appraisal of the dilemma produces a more inclusive solution.

TABLE 6

Moral Orientation of the Spontaneous and Best Solutions to Both Fables

	Rights	*Response*	*Both*	*Uncodable*
Spontaneous Solution				
Dog	56% (34)	33.3% (20)	6.7% (4)	3.3% (2)
Porcupine	60% (36)	28.3% (17)	10.0% (6)	1.7% (1)
Best Solution				
Dog	26.0% (16)	61.7% (37)	10.0% (6)	1.7% (1)
Porcupine	38.3% (23)	38.3% (23)	18.3% (11)	5.0% (3)

One can see in Table 6 that there are not major differences in the use of response in the best solution. In both fables there is a trend toward using response after both orientations have been discussed, but in the Dog Fable the trend is larger.

In the Porcupine Fable almost half of the changes (seven of fifteen) are accounted for by the fifteen-year-old females. This is not the case in the Dog Fable, where males account for thirteen of the twenty-two switches. It is important in this context to keep in mind that a significant relationship exists between gender and use of orientation for both spontaneous and best solutions in the Dog Fable. Thus, females began in the response orientation and ended there as well. But many males moved from rights to response. The question regarding the Dog Fable, therefore, becomes: What is it about *this* fable makes the boys want to try to meet the needs of the animals in this problem more than in the porcupine problem?

Initially the author believed that although the dog in the fable is cast in the villain role by taking over the ox's stable, adolescents might feel benevolent toward the dog since they probably knew many dogs and possibly have had one for a pet. However, when asked at the end of the interview if their solution would have been different if the dog were a raccoon, almost all of the respondents answered, "No." In the words of a fifteen-year-old male, "Well, probably not, the same alternatives are there." So the simplistic notion that the fable difference comes from the knowledge and liking of a more familiar animal was dismissed.

A question was added to this study after the pilot was conducted to get at the issue of switching moral orientations. When an individual solved one fable by using the rights orientation and the other by using the response orientation, he/she was asked why. Over half of the eleven and fifteen-year-old male adolescents were asked this question because 59 percent solved the two fables differently. The boys that changed were like the fifteen-year-old girls who changed in the Porcupine Fable in that their discussion also began to include the needs of both parties involved. One of the fifteen-year-old males who exemplified this pattern explains:

> S: Realize one another's needs, I guess. It's hard to do with animals though.

> I: *How would they get to do that if they had all kinds of human power? How would they get to that point?*

> S: Well, like the ox has to realize that the dog wants a place to sleep, he's tired, and the dog has to realize that the ox wants something to eat. So if they compromise they can each have half the stall and some hay.

> I: *How do you compromise? What does that mean?*

> S: Each give in on what you think to, ah, don't take your own side, compromise and like something that both would be [think would be] pretty fair.

This quote represents the central idea expressed by all the male adolescents who change orientations. The idea is that this dilemma does not have to be seen in a way that only deals with the needs of one of the participants. Both male and female adolescents recognize that if one can respond to the needs of all involved one removes the dilemma.

The differences found appear to arise from the question of when or under what circumstances do males abandon a rights orientation to problem solving and choose to use a response orientation. The data suggest the answer to this question. The boys' responses imply that the fundamental difference between these two fables lies in the possibility of the animals getting along after the problem is solved. For example, the eleven-year-old boys specifically address the ability of the moles and the porcupine to have a continuing relationship as indicated in the following excerpts:

> They (moles) get scratched all the time.

> The moles might still be annoyed even after all of the [pause], even if they tried lots of solutions and most of them might not work.

One boy, in explaining why there was a difference in the way he solved the two fables, said that the porcupine was "bothering the moles" and the dog was "just kicking the ox out." It is not immediately apparent why these are different, but one can distinguish between the suggestion of an ongoing difficulty (bothering the moles) and one incident (kicking the ox out). The implication is that, once the problem is solved between the ox and the dog, the conflict will be over. In contrast, one boy says, even "if they tried lots of solution," the porcupine, because of his fundamental difference from the moles (i.e., his quills) will continue to bother them. This theme is elaborated by a fifteen-year-old male.

> I: *Why do you see a difference in those two problems--the first one to have sharing the best, and this one to have the porcupine leave?*

> S: I think it depends mainly on the people involved. The dog and the ox, you can see where they might be able to live together, but a porcupine and a mole, the porcupine could be dangerous, so I guess it depends on the parties involved.

> I: *How can you sort out the situation? Thinking about what the people are like and how they are in the situation? How do you learn to do that?*

> S: See beyond what they look like and see inside. Some people are harsh or kind. Some people are prejudiced and some aren't. You can't put, for example, a person who wants to save the whales with someone who wants to kill them. You can't put them together and expect them to get along all the time. They won't even get along, maybe, so one will have to go. There's no good reason why they should be roommates in the first place.

> I: *What would happen?*

> S: If they become roommates?

I: Yes.

S: It would probably be the worst thing that ever happened. They'd be fighting, because like in the back of their mind, like that subject of killing whales, for example, and other topics, they'd probably pick at it.

To those boys, the response orientation provides the best solution only if there is the possibility of relationship beyond the conflict. They share an implicit criterion which they use to judge whether the relationship will continue over time. In the fables the impediment they see to a long lasting relationship is one of differences. This is a fundamental divergence in the problem solving of these boys and girls. By using the response orientation significantly more than the boys, girls *assume* that the relationship exists and can continue. The boys assume that the relationship does not exist if the differences in those involved in the problem appear too great. Gilligan's analogy to the figure/ground problem is helpful here in calling attention to the fact that, looking at the same image, one can focus on different aspects of it. Girls looking at the dilemma tend to see the relationships as prominent whereas boys tend to see the individual differences in the participants rather than their potential relationship as salient. These boys only focus on the relationship if the differences recede to the background.

Thus, the fable data have interesting implications for understanding differences in moral judgments. If morality signifies the understanding of relationships with other people and serves as a guide to solving problems in relationships, then the fables pose a cognitive exercise in resolving conflicts in relationship. The ways that differences are conceived lead to different strategies for negotiating conflicts in these relationships. In contrast to a simplistic representation of the theory which holds that the importance of relationships is more salient to females than to males, is the idea that males and females tend to negotiate conflict in relationship in different ways. The clearest difference is that 70 percent of the boys initially negotiated conflict by applying rules; when rules don't work or when counter-suggestions indicate rules will not work, they must make a choice. This choice tends to center on whether to invoke power--"The porcupine just has to go"--or whether to begin to talk and find a way to meet specific needs. The data in this study suggest that talking may only make sense to the boys if the possibility of a continuing relationship exists beyond the conflict. In the fables they tend to evaluate this possibility by judging how fundamental the differences in the participants are. Girls, in contrast, use both strategies in negotiating conflict but frequently begin by trying to attend to specific needs. When this seems to be unworkable, they then may resort to rules. The idea of different assumptions regarding relationships is the most compelling explanation for the finding that more boys use response in the best solution to the Dog Fable than in any other solution. However, future research should attempt to test alternative explanations of these data and examine whether assumptions about relationships are different for male and female adolescents when discussing other dilemmas.

IMPLICATIONS

Strategies for Moral Problem Solving

Past research on moral development assumes one theory of morality-- that of Kohlberg. Implicit in this theory is that only one problem-solving strategy, "justice reasoning," is employed in moral problem solving. This system is a hierarchical system like Piaget's description of cognitive operations. It orders priorities in a moral problem with the goal of being fair and objective. Like Piaget's exclusion of variables problems (Inhelder & Piaget, 1958/1983, p. 302), this problem-solving strategy excludes variables until the most important variable remains. In other words, Kohlberg documents a formal system of thinking which systematically chooses the best solution to a problem by isolating the "most moral claim" (Colby *et al.*, 1986).

The fable data indicate a second problem-solving strategy for moral problems. This system *includes* variables or needs of participants in the dilemmas until a solution which integrates these needs is reached. Polanyi writes of two conflicting aspects of formalized intelligence: (1) acquisition of formal instruments and (2) the pervasive participation of the knowing person in the act of knowing by virtue of an art which is essentially inarticulate (Polanyi, 1958, p. 70).

This study begins to render Polanyi's second aspect of intelligence articulate. One girl says that to reason one needs to "care," and "caring" means "understanding." When the boys and girls in this study begin to understand the needs of all participants in the dilemmas, they begin to employ a logic which includes the moral claims of all involved in the dilemma. The subjects in this study described this logic as "seeing everybody's side" of the problem. This is not done intuitively; rather, it is done by attending to all the variables in a particular situation. This logic does not systematically discard variables, but integrates as many variables as possible. These data demonstrate that both male and female adolescents do this kind of reasoning within the context of the fables, but girls are more likely to rely on this logic to provide solutions for the fable problems.

Therefore, gender may be related to the use of the problem-solving strategies in the following way. Vygotsky presents a theory of thinking in which the learner interacts with the society in which she/he participates, and he emphasizes the influence of that society on the individual. He believes children first learn in an interaction with adults and as this learning gradually becomes internalized, "an interpersonal process is transformed into an intrapersonal one. All the higher functions (voluntary attention, logical memory, formation of concepts) originate as actual relations between human individuals" (Vygotsky, 1978, p. 57). This theory allows for individual and group differences.

Keeping this idea that different interpersonal interactions may lead to different intrapersonal functions leads to the work of Chodorow. She suggests that men and women learn to relate differently. "Most generally I would suggest that a quality of embeddedness in social interaction and personal relationship characterize women's life relative to men's" (Chodorow, 1974, p. 66). She states that men, in order to develop, must separate or deny their attachment to their mothers; women do not need to do either of these things in their development.

Chodorow's idea of developing in a separate way or in a connected way would clearly imply two different experiences of interpersonal functions. Then, following Vygotsky's idea of thinking being transformed from inter- to intrapersonal, it would follow that the intrapersonal thinking would be different for people who identify themselves through connection with others as opposed to those who identify themselves through separation from others.

This idea of different interpersonal interactions leading to different cognitive strategies would suggest patterns of gender differences in cognitive functioning. But this discussion differs from Chodorow in that, rather than defining these different cognitive strategies as absolutely associated with gender, it posits that these two strategies are used by both males and females. Gilligan suggests that both males and females have the experiences of connection and separation, so these two types of interpersonal interaction shared by both males and females lead to two types of interpersonal functions employed by both genders. The interesting question, then, becomes not how do females think and how do males think, but *when* do males and females use these strategies? This study suggests that the use of these strategies may be dependent on the problem solver's view of the relationship in the problem.

Further Research Questions

Of interest in these data are the two unpredicted findings that older girls use the moral orientation of rights in the Porcupine Fable, and boys use response as frequently as rights for the best solution in the Dog Fable. Further research would investigate the development of the moral orientation of rights in girls between the ages of eleven and fifteen. Does this development of the rights voice silence the spontaneous voice of care? Is it a developmental gain or loss for these girls? Also of interest are the different assumptions about relationship made by boys and girls. Is it true that boys make different assumptions than girls? It is interesting that in these data boys speak of similarities between those involved when describing relationships and girls do not.

Finally, the problem-solving strategy that the data suggest needs to be carefully described. Is it a strategy that is more frequently associated with girls, and is it a strategy viable outside the domain of moral problem solving? Cunnion (1984) began this investigation in the field of abstract reasoning, but it is not described adequately in the psychological literature.

In summary, this study:

1. Supports Gilligan's original hypothesis that there is a gender difference in moral problem solving; therefore, recent questions (Walker, 1984, 1986; Pratt *et al.*, 1984) regarding whether gender differences in moral reasoning exist are answered in the affirmative.

2. Demonstrates that both genders employ both systems of reasoning, although they employ these systems differently. This differential use seems to be related to the context of the fables and the view of relationships held by the problem solver.

3. Begins to articulate a system of problem solving that is related to the logic of the moral orientation of response.

The results of the present study indicate that any description of moral development which omits either moral orientation is not a sufficient description of moral reasoning. Further, any description of moral development which either omits or oversimplifies the gender difference found in this study would not provide an accurate description of moral development in either sex. The fact that this study found gender differences using a standard research design is important. Of equal importance is the complicated way these differences appeared. The most general conclusion is that individuals use and understand both moral orientations; however, the use of these orientations is influenced by gender and by the context of the problem.

An interview which does not probe for a subject's understanding of both moral orientations will not provide adequate data for exploring the ways in which both moral orientations inform an individual's solution to a given moral problem. Furthermore, the assumption that the initial way a subject solved a moral dilemma is the only way or the best way to solve a problem cannot be held.

NOTES

1. Johnston, D.K. "Adolescents' Responses to Moral Dilemmas in Fables." Unpublished manuscript, Harvard Graduate School of Education (1979).

2. Johnston, D.K. "Responding to Moral Dilemmas in Fables, Ages Six to Eleven: A Brief Study of Gender Differences." Unpublished manuscript, Harvard Graduate School of Education (1982).

3. In Langdale's research (1983), the problem of "closed" research, or research directed by the interviewer's question, is addressed. This problem is avoided in the fables.

4. Six people were trained to code the fables over a six-week period. Reliability tests were run on the spontaneous and best solutions to both fables. The average reliability score was 80 percent.

APPENDIX

Fables

The Porcupine and the Moles

It was growing cold, and a porcupine was looking for a home. He found a most desirable cave but saw it was occupied by a family of moles.

"Would you mind if I shared your home for the winter?" the porcupine asked the moles.

The generous moles consented and the porcupine moved in. But the cave was small and every time the moles moved around they were scratched by the porcupine's sharp quills. The moles endured this discomfort as long as they could. Then at last they gathered courage to approach their visitor. "Pray leave," they said, "and let us have our cave to ourselves once again."

"Oh no!" said the porcupine. "This place suits me very well."

The Dog in the Manger

A dog, looking for a comfortable place to nap, came upon the empty stall of an ox. There it was quiet and cool and the hay was soft. The dog, who was very tired, curled up on the hay and was soon fast asleep.

A few hours later the ox lumbered in from the fields. He had worked hard and was looking forward to his dinner of hay. His heavy steps woke the dog who jumped up in a great temper. As the ox came near the stall the dog snapped angrily, as if to bite him. Again and again the ox tried to reach his food but each time he tried the dog stopped him.

Both fables are adapted from *Aesop's Fables*, retold by A. McGovern, which is published by Scholastic Book Company, 1963.

ACKNOWLEDGMENTS

I acknowledge the teachers and the administrators who allowed me to talk with their students. I thank Jane Attanucci for her help with reliability coding and data analysis. Many friends and my family encouraged my work, and I owe them more than thanks. Finally, and most important, I thank the adolescents with whom I spoke.

Two Moral Orientations:
Gender Differences and Similarities

Carol Gilligan and Jane Attanucci
Harvard University

Recent discussions of sex differences in moral development equate moral stage in Kohlberg's justice framework with moral orientation—the distinction between justice and care perspectives. The present study of real-life dilemmas from 46 men and 34 women, primarily adolescents and young adults, shows that: (a) Concerns about both justice and care are represented in people's thinking about real-life moral dilemmas, but people tend to focus on one set of concerns and minimally represent the other. And (b) There is an association between moral orientation and gender such that men and women use both orientations, but Care Focus dilemmas are most likely to be presented by women and Justice Focus dilemmas by men. Consideration of moral orientation transforms the debate over sex differences in moral reasoning into serious questions about moral perspectives that are open to empirical study.

Recent discussions of sex differences in moral development have equated moral stage in Kohlberg's justice framework with moral orientation—the distinction between justice and care perspectives. Kohlberg (1984), Walker (1984, 1986), Baumrind (1986), and Haan (1985) address the question of whether women and men score differently on the Kohlberg scale of justice reasoning, and report contradictory findings. In the present study, evidence of two moral perspectives in people's discussions of actual moral conflicts is examined. Also considered is whether there is an association between moral orientation and gender.

The research was supported by grants from the NIE, the Picker Foundation, and the Blake School, Minneapolis, MN. The authors acknowledge the generous support of the Mailman Foundation and Mrs. Marilyn Brachman Hoffman, thank the participants in these studies for their time and thoughtful responses, and also thank the interviewers and the coders. Diana Baumrind's detailed commentary on earlier drafts was immensely helpful. The authors are also indebted to Terry Tivnan, for his statistical assistance, and to their colleagues at the Center for the Study of Gender, Education, and Human Development. Correspondence should be sent to Jane Attanucci, Graduate School of Education, Harvard University, Roy E. Larsen Hall, Appian Way, Cambridge, MA 02138.

Merrill-Palmer Quarterly, July 1988, Vol. 34, No. 3, pp. 223–237.

The distinction between justice and care perspectives was made in the course of studying the relationship between judgment and action. These studies (Gilligan, 1977; Gilligan & Belenky, 1980; Gilligan & Murphy, 1979) of college students describing experiences of moral conflict and choice and pregnant women considering abortion, shifted the focus from people's thinking about hypothetical dilemmas to their construction of real-life choices. With this change in approach, it became possible to see how people describe moral problems in their lives and to explore the relationship between the understanding of moral problems and the strategies used in resolving them.

For example, some men who scored at the highest level of the Kohlberg scale and defined moral conflicts in their lives as problems of justice, described themselves as not acting on principles of justice because they considered just solutions to be morally problematic (Gilligan & Murphy, 1979). It was also observed that some women, especially when describing their own experiences of moral conflict and choice, often defined and resolved moral problems in a way that differed from those described in established theories of moral development and in the measures for its assessment.

Previous interpretations of individual, cultural, and sex differences in moral reasoning have been constrained by the assumption that there is a single moral perspective, that of justice. The analysis of women's moral judgments clarified an alternative approach to moral decision making which was designated the *care perspective* (Gilligan, 1982).

The language of the public abortion debate, for example, reveals a justice perspective. Whether the abortion dilemma is cast as a conflict of rights or in terms of respect for human life, the claims of the fetus and the pregnant woman are balanced or placed in opposition. The morality of abortion decisions thus considered hinges on the question of whether the fetus is a person, and, if so, whether its claims take precedence over those of the pregnant woman. Framed as a problem of care, the dilemma posed by abortion shifts. The connection between the fetus and the pregnant woman becomes the focus and the question becomes whether it is responsible or irresponsible, caring or careless, to extend or to end this connection. To ask what actions constitute care or are more caring directs attention to the parameters of connection and the costs of detachment, which become subjects of moral concern.

The distinction made here between a justice orientation and a care orientation pertains to the ways in which moral problems are conceived and reflects different dimensions of human relationships that give rise to moral concern. A justice perspective draws attention to problems of inequality and oppression and holds up an ideal of reciprocal rights and equal respect for individuals. A care perspective draws attention to problems of detachment or abandonment and holds up an ideal of attention and response to need.

Two moral injunctions, not to treat others unfairly and not to turn away from someone in need, capture these different concerns. From a developmental standpoint, both inequality and attachment are universal human experiences: All children are born into a situation of inequality and no child survives in the absence of some kind of adult attachment. These two intersecting dimensions of equality and attachment characterize all forms of human relationship. All relationships can be described in both sets of terms: as unequal or equal and as attached or detached. Because everyone has been vulnerable both to oppression and to abandonment, two moral visions—one of justice and one of care—recur in human experience.

Psychologists studying moral development have equated morality with justice, characterized the parent-child relationships as a relationship of inequality, and contrasted it with the equality of peer relations. Previous discussions of "two moralities" (Haan, 1978; Youniss, 1980) have been cast in terms of inequality and equality, following the Piaget (1932/1965) equation of moral development with the development of the idea of justice and his distinction between relationships of constraint and relationships of cooperation.

Although the dimensions of constraint and cooperation represent the opposite poles of inequality and equality in relationships, neither addresses the dimension of attachment and detachment, responsiveness and failures to respond, in those relationships. The present discussion of two moral orientations refers instead to the dimensions of attachment and equality in all relationships and considers moral development in terms of both changes in the understanding of what fairness means and in terms of changes in the understanding of what constitutes care. Because problems of inequality and problems of detachment arise throughout human life and in both public and private realms, it would be expected that equality and attachment would persist as moral concerns.

The present paper is a report of the results of three studies undertaken to investigate the two moral orientations and to determine to what extent men and women differentially raise concerns about justice and care in discussing moral conflicts in their lives. The examples presented in Table 1, drawn from discussions of real-life dilemmas, illustrate the concept of moral orientation. Each pair of dilemmas reveals how a problem is seen from a justice perspective and from a care perspective. In each pair of examples, the justice construction is

Table 1. Examples of Justice Care Perspectives in
Real-Life Moral Domain Data

Justice	Care
1J [If people were taking drugs and I was the only one who wasn't I would feel it was stupid, I know for me what is right is right and what's wrong is wrong . . . it's like a set of standards I have.] (*High School Student*)	1C [If there was one person it would be a lot easier to say no, I could talk to her, because there wouldn't be seven others to think about. I do think about them, you know, and wonder what they say about me and what it will mean . . . I made the right decision not to because my real friends accepted my decision.] (*High School Student*)
2J [The conflict was that by all rights she should have been turned into the honor board for violation of the alcohol policy.] [I liked her very much.] [She is extremely embarrassed and upset. She was contrite, she wished she had never done it. She had all the proper levels of contriteness and guilt and] [I was supposed to turn her in and didn't.] (*Medical Student*)	2C [It might just be his business if he wants to get drunk every week or it might be something that is really a problem and that should be dealt with professionally; and to be concerned about someone without antagonizing them or making their life more difficult than it had to be; maybe there was just no problem there.] [I guess in something like a personal relationship with a proctor you don't want to just go right out there and antagonize people, because that person will go away and if you destroy any relationship you have, I think you have lost any chance of doing anything for a person.] (*Medical Student*)
3J [I have moral dilemmas all the time, but I have no problem solving them usually. I usually resolve them according to my internal morality . . . the more important publicly your office is, to me the more important it is that you *play by the rules* because society hangs together by these rules and in my view, if you cheat on them, even for a laudatory purpose, eventually you break the rules down, because it is impossible to draw any fine lines.] (*Lawyer*)	3C [I have to preside over these decisions and try to make them as nondisastrous as possible for the people who are most vulnerable. The fewer games you play the better, because you are really dealing with issues that are the very basis to people's day-to-day well-being, and it is people's feelings, people's potential for growth, and you should do everything in your power to smooth it.] (*Lawyer*)

the more familiar one, capturing the way such problems are usually defined from a moral standpoint.

In 1J, a peer pressure dilemma is presented in terms of how to uphold one's moral standards and how to withstand the pressure from one's friends to deviate from what one knows for oneself to be right. In 1C, a similar decision (not to smoke) is cast in terms of how to respond both to one's friends and to oneself. The rightness of the decision not to smoke is established in terms of the fact that it did not break relationships: "My real friends accepted my decision." Attention to one's friends, to what they say and how choices affect the friendship, is presented as a moral concern.

In the second pair of examples, the dilemma of whether to report someone who has violated the medical school's alcohol policy is posed differently from the justice and care perspectives. The decision not to tell is reasoned in different ways. A clear example of justice tempered by mercy is presented in 2J. The student believes that the violator should be turned in ("I was supposed to turn her in") and justifies not doing so on the grounds that she deserved mercy because "She had all the proper level of contriteness" that was appropriate for the situation.

In 2C, a student decides not to turn a proctor in for drinking because it would "destroy any relationship you have" and therefore would "hurt any chance of doing anything for that person." In this construction, turning in the person is seen as impeding efforts to help. The concern about maintaining the relationship in order to be able to help is not mentioned in 2J. Similarly, the concern about maintaining the honor board policy is not mentioned in 2C.

A further illustration of how justice and care perspectives restructure moral understanding can be seen by observing that in 2J the student justifies not turning in the violator because of questions about the rightness of the alcohol policy itself. But in 2C the student considers whether what was deemed a problem was really a problem for the other person. The case of 2C illustrates what is meant by striving to see the other person in his or her own particular terms. It also exemplifies the contrast between this endeavor and the effort to establish, independently of persons, the legitimacy of existing rules and standards.

The third pair of examples further illustrates the distinction between establishing and maintaining existing rules and universal impartial standards (3J) and attending to people in their particular circumstances and minimizing the damaging effects of legal decisions (3C). In 3J, the lawyer affirms the value of the American legal system, dismissing the "impossible . . . fine lines." In 3C, the lawyer struggles with those same fine lines in order to protect those personally vulnerable to society's "game." These interpretations of the same legal system differ; neither is entirely wrong or naive. In 3J, the lawyer asserts the necessity of our legal system to hold society together. But in 3C, the lawyer appeals to the injunction not to abandon those in need.

It is important to emphasize that these examples were selected to highlight the contrast between a justice perspective and a care perspective. It must be stressed, however, that most people who participated in this research used considerations of both justice and care in discussing a moral conflict they faced.

In the present study two questions were posed: (a) In the evidence of justice and care orientations in people's discussion of real-life moral conflict, do people represent both orientations equally or do they tend to focus on one and minimally represent the other? And (b) Is there a relationship between moral orientation and gender?

METHOD

Subjects

Subjects were drawn from three research studies. In each study, the subjects were asked to describe a real-life moral dilemma. All three samples consisted of men and women who were matched for levels of education; the adults were matched for professional occupations. See Table 2 for the distribution of subjects, by sample, in age and gender categories.

Study 1. The design matched participants for high levels of education and professional occupations to examine the variables of age, gender, and type of dilemma. The adolescents and adults included were 11 women and 10 men. The racial composition (19 white and 2 minority) was not statistically random, as race was not a focal variable of the study.

Study 2. First-year students were randomly selected from two prestigious northeastern medical schools to be interviewed as part of a longitudinal study of stress and adaptation in physicians.[1] The 26 men and 13 women students represented the proportions of each gender in the class at large. The 19 white and 20 minority students (Black, Hispanic and Asian Americans) were selected to balance the

---

[1]Nineteen other medical students who could not (two would not) describe a situation of moral conflict are not in the present study. We acknowledge the bias created by such attrition. Their response may reflect the pressures on first-year medical students in a context which discourages the uncertainty about knowing what is the right thing to do. Generalizations about physicians from this specific study would be unwarranted, however, as several physicians who participated in Study 1 provided both care and justice perspectives on their experiences of conflict and choice.

Table 2. Gender and Age of Subjects By Study

	15–22 Years	23–34 Years	35–77 Years	n
Study 1				
Women	4	2	5	11
Men	4	1	5	10
Study 2				
Women	9	4	0	13
Men	12	14	0	26
Study 3				
Women	10	0	0	10
Men	10	0	0	10

sample's racial composition (the only sample in the present study with such a design). The students ranged in age from 21 to 27 years.

Study 3. The 10 female and 10 male participants were randomly selected from a coeducational private school in a midwestern city. The 19 white and 1 minority student ranged in age from 14 to 18 years.

Research Interview

All participants were asked the following series of questions about their personal experience of moral conflict and choice:

1. Have you ever been in a situation of moral conflict where you had to make a decision but weren't sure what was the right thing to do?
2. Could you describe the situation?
3. What were the conflicts for you in that situation?
4. What did you do?
5. Do you think it was the right thing to do?
6. How do you know?

The interviewer asked questions to encourage the participants to clarify and elaborate their responses. For example, participants were asked what they meant by words like *responsibility, obligation, moral, fair, selfish,* and *caring.* The interviewers followed the participants' logic in presenting the moral problem, most commonly querying, "Anything else?"

The interviews were conducted individually, tape recorded, and later transcribed. The moral conflict questions were one segment of an interview which included questions about morality and identity (Gilligan et al., 1982). The interviews lasted about 2 hours.

Data Analysis

The real-life moral dilemmas were analyzed by using methods described in Lyons's *Manual for Coding Real-Life Dilemmas* (1982). The Lyons procedure[2] is a content analysis which identifies moral considerations. The unit of analysis is the *consideration*, defined as each idea the participant presents in discussing a moral problem. The units are designated in Table 1 with brackets.

To reach an acceptable level of reliability in identifying considerations required extensive training. The three coders trained by Lyons were blind to the gender, age, and race of the participants and achieved high levels of intercoder reliability (a range of 67% to 95%, and a mean of 80% agreement, across samples of randomly selected cases). Typically, a real-life moral dilemma consisted of 7 considerations, with a range of 4 to 17. A minimum of four considerations was required for the present analysis. When only four considerations were present, in all but one case, the four considerations were in one orientation. The coder classified these considerations as either justice or care.

The Lyons score was simply the predominant, most frequent, mode of moral reasoning (justice or care). For the present study, *predominance* was redefined so that a real-life moral dilemma consisting of only care or justice considerations was labeled *Care Only* or *Justice Only*. A dilemma consisting of 75% or more care or justice considerations was labeled *Care Focus* or *Justice Focus*, respectively. A dilemma in which less than 75% of the total number of considerations were care or justice was placed in the *Care Justice* category.

---

[2]Lyons's coding sheet (Lyons, 1983) specifies five categories that establish whether the consideration is assigned to justice or care. Intercoder reliability is computed across categories. In the present study, most of the considerations coded fit Categories 2 and 3 under justice and care. When we ran our analysis using only these categories, some subjects were lost due to an insufficient number of considerations, but the direction of the findings as reported in the results section (with all categories included) remained. This fact is significant because Categories 2 and 3 under justice and care best capture our distinction between justice and care: concern with fulfilling obligations, duty or commitments, or maintaining standards or principles of fairness (justice), and concern with maintaining or restoring relationships, or with responding to the weal and woe of others (care). Lyons's Categories 1, 4, and 5 under justice and care are consistent with her focus on the perspective taken toward others. Yet Categories 1, 4, and 5 can readily be confused with a conception of justice and care as bi-polar opposites of a single dimension of moral reasoning or as mirror image conceptions where justice is egoistic and uncaring and caring is altruistic and unjust. Because these categories were rarely evident in the current data, these questions, although important for other researchers to consider, are only marginally relevant to the present discussion.

Table 3. Number of Participants by Moral Orientation Category

	Care Only	Care Focus	Care Justice	Justice Focus	Justice Only
Observed	5	8	27	20	20
Expected	.64	4	70	4	.64

RESULTS

The real-life dilemma data are summarized from three studies with comparable designs. That is, samples with male and female subjects are matched for high socioeconomic status. Frequencies and statistical tests are presented across samples. The statistical comparison of samples on moral orientation is not significant ($\chi^2(4, N = 80) = 9.21$ n.s.). Parallel tests have been performed for each sample and discrepancies from the overall pattern are reported and discussed.

Two observations can be made from the data in Table 3. First, the majority of people represent both moral orientations; 69% compared to the 31% who use Care or Justice Only. Second, two thirds of the dilemmas are in the Focus categories (Care Only, Care Focus, Justice Only, Justice Focus), and only one third are in the Care Justice category. The question addressed by Table 3 is, Do people tend to focus their discussion of a moral problem in one or the other orientation?

For the typical case, the ratio of care to justice considerations is Care Only 7:0; Care Focus 6:1; Care Justice 5:2, 4:3, 3:4, 2:5; Justice Focus 1:6; and Justice Only 0:7. Using a binomial model, if an equal probability of care and justice considerations in an account of a real-life moral dilemma ($p = .5$) is assumed, then a random sampling of moral considerations (typically $N = 7$) over 80 trials (80 participants' single dilemmas) would result in an expected binomial distribution. To test whether the distribution of scores fit the expected distribution, the χ^2 goodness of fit test is applied. The observed distribution differs significantly from the expected, $\chi^2(4, N = 80) = 133.8$, $p < .001$, and provides supporting evidence for the contention that an individual's moral considerations are not random but tend to be focused in either the care or justice orientation.

In Table 4 the distribution of moral orientations for each gender is presented. The statistical test of gender differences is based on a combination of Care Only and Care Focus, as well as a combination of Justice Only and Justice Focus in order to have expected values greater than 5: $\chi^2(2, N = 80) = 18.33$, $p < .001$. This test demonstrates the relationship between moral orientation and gender in which both men and women present dilemmas in the Care Justice category, but Care Focus is much more likely in the moral dilemma of a woman and Justice Focus more likely in the dilemma of a man. In

Table 4. Frequency of Moral Orientation Categories by Gender of Participants

	Care Only	Care Focus	Care Justice	Justice Focus	Justice Only
Women	5	7	12	6	4
Men	0	1	15	14	16

fact, if women were excluded from a study of moral reasoning, Care Focus could easily be overlooked.

The relationship between moral orientation and age was not tested because the majority of participants were adolescents and young adults, providing little age range. Furthermore, in the present study, age was confounded with sample (i.e., the young adults were the medical students), making interpretation difficult.

The medical student data (Study 2) raised further questions of interpretation which bear on the issues addressed in this analysis. First, the dilemmas from the medical students, when tested separately, do not show the same relationship between gender and moral orientation, $\chi^2(2, n = 39) = 4.36$, n.s. However, consistent with the overall findings, the two Care Focus dilemmas were presented by women.

As for the pattern of difference in this racially diverse sample, the Care Focus dilemmas were presented by one white woman and one minority woman. The relationship between moral orientation and race for both men and women was that the dilemmas presented by white students were more likely to fall in the Care Justice category and dilemmas of minority students in the Justice Focus category (Fisher's Exact $p = .045$ for women, and $p = .0082$ for men).

DISCUSSION

The present exploration of moral orientation has demonstrated that: (a) Concerns about justice and care are both represented in people's thinking about real-life moral dilemmas, but people tend to focus on one set of concerns and minimally represent the other. And (b) there is an association between moral orientation and gender such that both men and women use both orientations, but Care Focus dilemmas are more likely to be presented by women and Justice Focus dilemmas by men.

Analysis of care and justice as distinct moral orientations that address different moral concerns leads to a consideration of both perspectives as constituitive of mature moral thinking. The tension between these perspectives is suggested by the fact that detachment, which is the mark of mature moral judgment in the justice perspective, becomes the moral problem in the care perspective, that is, the failure to attend to need. Conversely, attention to the particular needs and circumstances of individuals, the mark of mature moral judgment in the care perspective, becomes the moral problem in the justice perspective, that is, failure to treat others fairly, as equals. Care Focus and Justice Focus reasoning suggest a tendency to lose sight of one perspective in arriving at moral decision. That the focus phenomenon was demonstrated by two thirds of both men and women in the present study suggests that this liability is shared by both sexes.

This finding provides an empirical explanation for the equation of morality with justice in the theories of moral development that are derived from all-male research samples (Kohlberg, 1969, 1984; Piaget, 1932/1965). If women were eliminated from the present study, the focus on care would virtually disappear. Given the presence of justice concerns, most of the dilemmas described by women could be analyzed for justice considerations without reference to care considerations.

In addition, the Care Focus dilemmas presented by women offer an explanation for the fact that within a justice conception of morality, moral judgments of girls and women have appeared anomalous and difficult to interpret; Piaget (1932/1965) cites this explanation as the reason for studying boys. Furthermore, finding Care Focus mainly among women indicates why the analysis of women's moral thinking elucidated the care perspective as a distinct moral orientation and why the considerations of care that has been noted in dilemmas presented by men did not seem fully elaborated (Gilligan & Murphy, 1979).

The evidence of orientation focus as an observable characteristic of moral judgment does not justify the conclusion that focus is a desirable attribute of moral decision. However, careful attention to women's articulation of the care perspective has led to a different conception of the moral domain and to a different way of analyzing the moral judgment of both men and women.

The category Care Justice in our findings raises important questions that merit investigation in future research. Dilemmas in this "bifocal" category were equally likely among men and women in our study. It is possible that interviews involving more dilemmas and further questioning might reveal the focus phenomenon to be more common. But it is also possible that such studies might find and elucidate further an ability to sustain two moral perspectives, an ability, which according to the present data, seems equally characteristic of men and women.

The findings presented here suggest that people know and use both moral orientations. Although Care Focus dilemmas are raised by women, it is important to emphasize that the focus phenomenon in two moral orientations is replicated in an all-female sample of students in a private girls' high school. The moral dilemmas of these 48 adolescent girls are distributed as follows: Care Focus, 22; Care Justice, 17; and Justice Focus, 9. This distribution differs significantly from the expected binomial distribution, as well. The statistical test is based on a combination of Care Only and Care Focus, as well as a combination of Justice Only and Justice Focus in order to have expected values greater than 5: $\chi^2(2, N = 48) = 154.4, p < .001$).

Further evidence is provided in a study by Johnston (1985) who created a standard method for studying spontaneous orientation and orientation preference. She found in a sample of 60 11- and 15-year-olds from a middle-class suburban community that most children could understand and use the logic of both orientations. She also found sex differences in spontaneous and preferred orientation. Her findings underscore our contention that moral orientation must be considered a variable in moral judgment research.

If people know both moral orientations, as our theory and data suggest, researchers can cue perception in one or the other direction in a real-life dilemma by the questions they raise or by their failure to ask questions. The context of the research study as well as the interview itself must be considered for its influence on the likelihood of eliciting care or justice reasoning. In the case of the medical student data (Study 2) presented in this paper, the findings raise just such contextual questions.

In this large-scale study of stress and adaptation which included extensive standard, evaluative inventories, as well as the clinical interview, is it possible that the first-year medical students might have been reluctant to admit uncertainty? Some could not or would not describe a situation in which they were not sure what the right thing to do was. Also, is it possible that the focus on justice represents efforts by the students to align themselves with the perceived values of the prestigious institution they are entering rather than with the values inherent in a caring profession. The focus on justice by minority students is of particular interest because it counters the suggestion that a care orientation is the perspective of social subordinates or people of lower social power and status.

Evidence that moral orientation organizes moral judgment as well as the discovery of the focus phenomenon has led us to make the following changes in our research interview, which we offer as suggestions for other researchers:

1. That interviewers proceed on the assumption that people can adopt both a justice and a care perspective and that they encourage participants to generate different perspectives on a moral problem

("Is there another way to think about this problem?") and to examine the relationship between them.

2. That interviewers seek to determine the conception of justice and care that organizes the moral thinking in the discussion of a particular dilemma. The Kohlberg stages describe the development of justice reasoning. The description by Gilligan (1977, 1982) of the different ways that women think about care and of changes in care reasoning over time offers a guide to thinking about developmental transitions in the care perspective. These empirical efforts are necessary prior to any further discussion of the relationship between stage and orientation.

3. That interviewers should attend to where the self stands with respect to the two moral orientations. In our present research we included the question, "What is at stake for you in the conflict?" to encourage subjects to reveal where they see themselves in the dilemmas they describe and how they align themselves with different perspectives on the problem.

The evidence of two moral perspectives suggests that the choice of moral standpoint, whether implicit or explicit, may indicate a preferred way of seeing. If so, the implications of the preference need to be explored. Orientation preference may be a dimension of identity or self-definition, especially when moral decision becomes more reflective or "postconventional" and the choice of moral standpoint becomes correspondingly more self-conscious.

The evidence accumulated, using the Lyons procedure, has lead to the interview changes just outlined and to insights that necessitate new coding procedures (Brown et al., 1987). Although some moral considerations can be assigned to mutually exclusive categories of justice and care, other considerations can be seen as both justice and care concerns. Awareness of both perspectives highlights the issue of interpretation. The entire research endeavor is thereby rendered more self-conscious. Researchers must ask not only the moral standpoint of participants but simultaneously address the question of their own perspectives on the interview. As Mishler (1986) has argued, the interview becomes a jointly constructed understanding rather than a participant's response to standard research questions.

The promise of approaching moral development in terms of moral orientation lies in its potential to transform debates over sex differences in moral reasoning into serious questions about moral perspectives that are open to empirical study. If moral maturity consists in the ability to sustain concerns about justice and care and if the focus phenomenon indicates a tendency to lose sight of one set of concerns, then the encounter with orientation difference can tend to offset errors in moral perception. Like the moment when the ambiguous figure shifts from a vase to two faces, the recognition that there is another way to look at a problem may expand moral understanding.

REFERENCES

BAUMRIND, D. (1986). Sex differences in moral reasoning: Response to Walker's (1984) conclusion that there are none. *Child Development, 57,* 511-521.

BROWN, L., ARGYRIS, D., ATTANUCCI, J., BARDIGE, B., GILLIGAN, C., JOHNSTON, K., MILLER, B., OSBORNE, R., WARD, J., WIGGINS, G., & WILCOX, D. (1987). A guide to reading narratives of moral conflict and choice for self and moral voice. In L. Brown (Ed.), *Mapping the moral domain: A method of inquiry* (pp. 35-140). Monograph #1. Cambridge, MA: The Center for the Study of Gender, Education, and Human Development, Harvard University.

GILLIGAN, C. (1977). In a different voice: Women's conception of self and morality. *Harvard Educational Review, 47* (4), 481-517.

GILLIGAN, C. (1982). *In a different voice: Psychological theory and women's development.* Cambridge, MA: Harvard University Press.

GILLIGAN, C., & BELENKY, M. (1980). A naturalistic study of abortion decision. In R. Selman & R. Yando (Eds.), *Clinical-developmental psychology* (pp. 69-90). San Francisco: Jossey-Bass.

GILLIGAN, C., LANGDALE, C., LYONS, N., & MURPHY, M. (1982). *The contribution of women's thought to developmental theory.* Final report submitted to National Institute of Education.

GILLIGAN, C., & MURPHY, J. (1979). Development from adolescence to adulthood: The philosopher and the dilemma of the fact. In D. Kuhn (Ed.), *Intellectual development beyond childhood* (pp. 85-99). San Francisco: Jossey-Bass.

HAAN, N. (1978). Two moralities in action contexts: Relationships to thought, ego regulation and development. *Journal of Personality and Social Psychology, 36,* 286-305.

HAAN, N. (1985). *Gender differences in moral development.* Paper presented at the American Psychological Association meetings, Los Angeles, CA.

JOHNSTON, K. (1985). *Two moral orientations—Two problem-solving strategies: Adolescents' solutions to dilemmas in fables.* Unpublished doctoral dissertation, Harvard University, Cambridge, MA.

KOHLBERG, L. (1969). Stage and sequence: The cognitive-developmental approach to socialization. In D. A. Goslin (Ed.), *Handbook of socialization theory and research* (pp. 347-480). Chicago: Rand McNally.

KOHLBERG, L. (1984). *The psychology of moral development, Vol. 2.* San Francisco: Harper & Row.

LYONS, N. (1982). *Conceptions of self and morality and modes of moral choice: Identifying justice and care in judgments of actual moral dilemmas.* Unpublished doctoral dissertation, Harvard University, Cambridge, MA.

LYONS, N. (1983). Two perspectives: On self, relationships, and morality. *Harvard Educational Review, 53,* 125-145.

MISHLER, E. (1986). *Research interviewing: Context and narrative.* Cambridge, MA: Harvard University Press.

PIAGET, J. (1965). *The moral judgment of the child.* New York: Free Press. (Original work published 1932)

WALKER, L. J. (1984). Sex differences in the development of moral reasoning: A critical review. *Child Development, 55,* 677–691.

WALKER, L. J. (1986). Sex differences in the development of moral reasoning: A rejoinder to Baumrind. *Child Development, 57,* 522–526.

YOUNISS, J. (1980). *Parents and peers in social development.* Chicago: University of Chicago Press.

When Is a Moral Problem Not a Moral Problem?
Morality, Identity, and Female Adolescence

LYN MIKEL BROWN

Feminist thinkers must self-consciously and critically confront various traditions of political discourse, feminist and nonfeminist. There are among us, for example, those who seek solutions to our public and private dilemmas by depriving us of a grammar of moral discourse and forcing all of life under a set of terms denuded of a critical edge. In so doing, they would deprive the human object, female and male, of the capacity to think, to judge, to question, and to act, for all these activities are importantly constituted by an everyday, ordinary language infused with moral terms. —J. B. Elshtain, "Feminist Discourse and Its Discontents"

Jean, seventeen years old, in her third year of the Dodge Study at Emma Willard describes the following real-life conflict in response to the question, Could you describe to me a situation where you had to make a decision and you weren't sure what was the right thing to do?

A girl who just recently left this school—she is, was, a freshman here, and she was thirteen years old, and she had a lot of problems at home. And she was having a lot of problems here . . . trying to cover it all up by being really loud and obnoxious. . . . She said once to me that [when] she came here, the thing that she wanted more than anything was to be accepted. But she was doing everything in her power to not be accepted. . . . And so she was getting really unhappy here . . . and everybody ragged on her. Plus the fact that she was doing poorly in school and there was a lot of threats at home about if you don't get A's and B's . . . and she was really unhappy. And last Tuesday she was sitting in front rocking back and forth hugging herself and saying I can't stand it here. She was talking about how she just wanted to kill herself and she just couldn't handle it anymore. And all I could think about was what if this little thirteen-year-old-girl really tries to jump out a window, how will I feel after that? And my immediate answer was I'd just feel like garbage. So the next day I said, Well, even if [she] gets mad at me and never wants to speak to me again, I'd rather she be alive and never want to speak to me than be dead and not have the chance. So I went and told the counselor. . . . And so I said, 'I have a friend, a real friend, who is not very happy and who is really seriously considering suicide.' And as soon as I said 'suicide,' she just said, 'what!?' And I said, 'Yes.'

(When you were trying to decide what to do, what was the conflict in this situation?) It was between, well, doing what I knew positively was the best thing for [her] and what I was thinking, the whole thing. Well, she told me something as a friend, and in private and . . . she could have just been pulling my leg and being very upset and didn't really mean it. And should I really go, and maybe I'll be wasting [the counselor's] time. And then I thought . . . I considered just trying to talk to [her] myself and just listen and be a friend.

(Without bringing in the counselor?) Without bringing in the counselor and just listening to her and trying as hard as I could to be [the counselor], be like [the counselor], without [her] presence.

Jean struggles between the imperative she felt to help her friend, the possibility that she may not have the full or accurate story, and the realization that revealing her friend's situation may sever their relationship. Acknowledging her doubts, she acts. She cannot risk her friend's life. Surprisingly, when Jean was asked if she considered the situation she described a "moral" problem, she responds:

No, it was just a question of what was best for [my friend], and I realized getting her out of school was the best for her because she would have had a breakdown or something. Thirteen is really kind of young to have a breakdown at a boarding school.

For Jean morality is:

Kind of the rules, rules you grow up with and what you internalize from what your parents tell you and what you get from your environment, which is something you decide you want to live by— your rules you live by, that you will stick to and change with the situation, not change, like if the weather is bad I will change my

139

morals, but something where it is a difficult situation and you realize that your morals don't really fit the situation.

(What makes something a moral problem for you?) If it really doesn't fit in. Right now a moral problem is something that although it might agree with what I think—what fits with my ideal, kind of my formed idea of morals—but violently contrasts with my mother's ideas of morals and the morals that I have to live with at Emma Willard, because all three have to work themselves out inside of me before I can decide to do what's right. And so it's difficult combining the three because although they have some common points, they have very, very different points also. So I have to decide whose morals I should use and it depends.

Jean's response poses an intriguing question: How does one make sense of the discrepancy between Jean's struggle, her use of prescriptive moral language, her felt imperative to respond to her friend, and the value she places on their friendship, on the one hand; and her contention, on the other, that for her, this situation did not create a moral problem? The apparent discrepancy in Jean's case is not an isolated example but typifies a pattern that appears in nearly 30 percent of the interviews in the third year of the study at Emma Willard.

It has been suggested repeatedly that female development may not fit neatly into the traditional developmental models in psychology exemplified by such theorists as Freud and Erikson, or Piaget and Kohlberg (Chodorow 1978; Douvan and Adelson 1966; Erikson 1968; Gilligan 1982; Lyons 1983; Miller 1976). The value placed on separation and individuation as developmental endpoints have resulted in a lack of attention to the centrality of attachment and relationship for healthy psychological development. Those who have begun to attend to the voices of girls and women find that female identity development may challenge such established definitions of the nature of self and relationship (Belenky et al. 1986; Gilligan 1982, 1987; Josselson 1987).

By examining the moral conflicts generated by four adolescent girls and their subsequent responses to questions about morality and responsibility, this chapter considers these observations while addressing two central questions: (1) What does it mean that the responses of conflict and responsibility these young women express are not labeled "moral" responses, either by themselves or by the existing theoretical paradigms charting the development of "moral reasoning"? and (2) What does a description and analysis of these cases suggest about the relationship between female identity development in adolescence and the nature of morality?

Four stories of conflict

An analysis of cases similar to Jean's reveals a number of patterns or themes. First, in these narratives the conflict, though described in various contexts and situations, takes a similar form. The manifest content of the narratives has to do with personal relationships; they are stories centrally concerned with attachment and with dialogue. The struggle or conflict focuses on an imperative to act or respond in a manner they describe as good, right, or best. This imperative results from knowledge of the other's particular situation or knowledge of the interdependence of relationship. In other words, the imperative to act arises from the experience of relationship and the belief that to turn away from a person in need, particularly a friend, is wrong (Gilligan 1982; Gilligan and Attanucci 1988).

Jean's case clearly illustrates this pattern. Her need to act in a way that is "best" for her friend arises from an understanding of the particularities of her friend's situation. The story she tells clearly indicates she knew the pressures impinging upon her young friend and that she knew them through shared experiences and communication with her. This knowledge of her friend's feelings creates an imperative to respond, and Jean does so in the face of doubt and ambiguity. She is uncertain both of her assessment of the situation and of the consequences should she act—that is, would her action ultimately threaten the friendship.

Kate, also seventeen, describes a similar imperative, although the context of her conflict (and its immediacy) is much different from that of Jean's. Kate struggles to decide whether or not she and a friend ought to speak to the school administration to express dissatisfaction with a teacher, when she was not personally having trouble with the teacher's style. She says:

> It was a hard decision for me whether or not I should go. I don't know, for me everything was fine, because when I was interested I could go and talk to the teacher. I certainly had no problem going and doing my own research, making my own assignments. I work best that way. *But I had to think from this perspective* [emphasis added]. I can see how this is a problem for the other people, and

it is not fair for all of them to be having this. They aren't getting what they should be out of this course and they need someone. Everyone talked about it. Someone had to go and talk, and it was, you know, it was a question of *would it be selfish of me* not to do it, because things were fine for me, but I knew there was a problem [emphasis added]. So I went and talked, with this other girl, to the [administration].

For Kate the difficulty centers on whether and how to act given her knowledge of the members of the class who were experiencing difficulty and, as she discusses later in the interview, her understanding of the potential repercussions of her action for the teacher and the class. She explains to the interviewer, "But I had to think from this perspective." By knowing that she knows—knowing by stepping out of her perspective and seeing that, for the others, from their point of view, there was a problem—not speaking on their behalf would be seen by her as a "selfish" choice. For Kate, then, "selfish" refers to deliberate inattention. It means being self-centered, looking out for herself alone when she could be responsive to others, turning away when it is clear to her that "they need someone" and that from *their* perspective they "were really, really upset." Kate understands that it is precisely because she and her friend are *not* having a difficult time with the teacher that they *should* be the ones to speak up. She explains why:

Everyone was really frustrated with it and because this friend of mine and I weren't having real problems with the material, we didn't have the same kind of frustration. We didn't have the same resentment. We just felt that something maybe should just be said so that the situation should be corrected . . . the hardest thing was that we didn't want it to be malicious or something . . . because we didn't feel that way at all. It was both of us, I guess for the obvious reasons. We like her [the teacher] very much and we didn't want to hurt her feelings, and we weren't saying the way she was teaching the class was wrong. It was just that . . . students weren't advanced enough to handle the kind of classroom situation.

It is important to Kate that the teacher understand the spirit in which she and her friend act—that she understand their intent and the complexity with which they view the situation. She and her friend worry about the consequences of misunderstanding—tension in the classroom, hurting the teacher's feelings, and the potential for tension between the teacher and the administration. Though Kate acknowledges issues of fairness—"it is not fair . . . they aren't getting what they should be out of this course"—she also recognizes her act as a response to need—"they need someone."

Kate, like Jean, makes a choice to speak in spite of her uncertainty. Within the boundaries of a particular story, each story highlights responsiveness; each emphasizes knowledge of the other(s), of their particular situations, of their particular needs.

Faye also illustrates this pattern. As editor-in-chief of the yearbook, she must decide whether or not to confront a girl who is not doing her job. She says:

> It's like I kept feeling torn between should I get someone new and say you are fired, or should I just keep waiting. . . . I guess my conflict was I didn't really want to confront her, but I knew I had to. . . . I wasn't really sure if I was being reasonable in the things I was asking her to do. Part of me wanted to go yell at her, and when I would see her upset *about the things that were going on in her life* or just other things that she was busy with, I couldn't just go and say, you know, Why aren't you doing this? *I felt I couldn't just look at my situation*, that this is the most important thing, because I realized there were other things going on . . . but . . . it was getting to be too much work for other people [emphasis added].

Faye finds that she cannot simply act on what first appears to be a clear-cut violation of expectations—that her classmate is not doing her job. The classmate's perspective, when taken into account, makes the issue more complicated. Faye acknowledges that in order to attend to the needs of all involved in the situation, she must recognize that not only is her own work and the work of others increasing because this person is not doing her job—which justifies firing her—but she must include the possibility that she may have been asking too much, or that perhaps there were other things happening in the classmate's life that may be affecting her work. She recognizes clearly that "I couldn't just look at my situation."

As mentioned earlier, these girls do not describe their real-life dilemmas as "moral" dilemmas or problems. Although their rationale takes various forms, there are similarities that appear to be key to understanding "morality" from their perspective. For some of these young women, morality is defined much like developmental psychologists concerned with morality would expect it to be defined, that is, as rules, standards, principles that guide the self, protect relationships, or order the social world (Colby and Kohlberg 1987; Kohlberg 1984; Piaget 1932). Moreover, "morality" framed in this way is described as something taught in school, by parents, or, more generally, by "society." Frequently it has a quality of being outside themselves, as prior to themselves. Defined in this way it is, in Piagetian (1932) terms, "heteronomous" morality, or in Kohlbergian (1984) terms, "conventional" morality. As such, since it is defined by others or by the external situation, it can be, and frequently is, manipulated or changed depending on the situation.

As Jean stated earlier, morality is "the kind of rules you grow up with and what you internalize from what your parents tell you and what you get from your environment, which is something you decide you want to live by—your rules you live by, that you will stick to and change with the situation." Rules, then, are chosen and "stuck to," yet they are also flexible and contingent on her environment. For Jean a moral problem is something that contrasts her morals with her mother's or those of Emma Willard School. She knows three moral points of view, each equally viable, similar in quality. The difficulty for her is in "combining the three" or deciding *whose* morals to use. Yet Jean's struggle to solve the conflict she experiences with her friend does not reflect a morality defined as "the rules you live by." Her conflict reflects a struggle to sort out what her friend "really" needs and who she is or ought to be in relation to her friend. Rather than an externalized or "internalized rule," Jean's conflict highlights responsiveness to relationship. She is concerned about the welfare of a friend she has observed closely. She is concerned about the veracity of her observations. And she is concerned about the consequences of her action—for her friend, for their relationship, and, as importantly, for a definition of herself as a moral person. Rather than a choice among various a priori moral points of view, Jean's choice will have implications for her own moral identity.

Kate's discussion of "morality" has a similar quality to Jean's. Like Jean she does not consider her situation to be a "moral" problem. The interviewer asks, Would you describe the situation that you just described as a moral problem? and Kate answers:

It's really hard to say what's moral and what's not. I have—at any given point in time—I have certain sets of maybe principles that I have never really sat and defined. They aren't—morals frequently have religious connotations and things like that . . . I don't have morals that are just for the sake of morals: Someone says this is how it is. I have principles of my own *that shift as I get older*. But I am always, you know, I live according to . . . *But they are flexible*. I would weigh any given situation and . . . it is never a black-and-white, right-and-wrong situation [emphasis added].

(Would this situation you described, be within the realm of a moral problem?) In the sense that I just mentioned, if you call that a moral decision, yes. But it wasn't. In a way it wasn't really, because I never questioned what I was doing, as really right or wrong. I felt I was doing the right thing, but I felt badly about it.

(Why?) Afraid that it would be misinterpreted or harmful or. . . . *(To whom?)* The faculty member, the head of the [administration]. It might make a tension there. It might make the class worse. It might, there were all kinds of things, you know.

(You started describing morality and what morals were. Do you want to elaborate on what you said?) I think that is really all. It is never something I think of as moral. Because in my mind I think of morals as being very structured, binding kind of—*and the principles I have for myself aren't that way, so I never really call them morals* [emphasis added].

(What do you base those principles on?) Oh, I really don't know. All kinds of things. What I have learned, you know, social influences and things like that. *(Can you give me an example of one that is presently important?)* I don't know, I don't ever really think about them. They just happen. I can't deny the fact that there are guiding things in my life like that, because, you know, society just has them. But I never really sit down and think about them. So it's hard to know where and what they are just because they are such an integral part of my actions and my everything.

Kate makes a distinction in her description of morality that Jean does not. When discussing what morality means to her, she distinguishes between morality that is given a priori in the social world, such as religious beliefs, and those she considers to be her own moral principles. She describes those in the external world as "morals for the sake of morals, someone says this is how it is"; a morality in which things are "black and white, right and wrong." Her own moral principles, much like Jean's, are "flexible," not like the "structured, binding" kinds of principles in the world. She does not, in fact, refer to them as moral principles; she doesn't really think about them. "They just happen." Yet, they are the guiding things in her life; things that are integral to her action and, as she says, "to my everything." In the same way, Kate's real-life dilemma does not fit the definitions of morality she describes as structured and binding principles. Her experience of conflict does not raise questions framed in dichotomous terms—right or wrong, black or white. Her moral conflict emerges when, as she says, "I felt I was doing the right thing, but I felt badly about it." For Kate, the conflict is neither dichotomous nor defined a priori. It is an experience more closely aligned with her feelings and knowledge. Moral issues in a given situation are "weighed," but the personal struggle arises from acknowledging her responsibility for the web of feeling and relationship that could potentially fracture as a consequence of any action she might take. Whatever she chooses to do, someone is potentially hurt or "misinterpreted," and as a result she feels "badly," although she believes she was "right" to have acted the way she did.

Ann, also in her third year of the study, responding to a painful and complex dilemma about whether to speak with her best friend who was not being communicative, also illustrates this pattern. She describes her conflict:

> My friend sort of went through this period when we were not communicating with each other, and I saw myself as having to make a choice. Was I going to continue to be her friend, or was I going to totally wipe her out? Not really wipe her out, but erase her as one of my social friends, until she came around to me and said, 'What's the matter?'

While struggling to decide whether or not to speak, Ann considers how much she needs her friend, especially at that time of "transition" in her life. She explains, "If she got angry with me she would divorce herself from our friendship. At that point I knew I wouldn't be able to handle such an emotional thing. Such a break in a relationship that had been strong for so long." Ann also realizes that her initial decision not to speak up may have been self-serving:

I mean my action not to talk with her was basically very selfish.

(What do you mean by selfish?) I was thinking of myself. I wasn't thinking of her. I wasn't thinking that she needed to prove something to herself, that she had to show herself that she could survive.

In contrast to this experience with her friend, Ann defines a "moral problem" as "whether to go out and get drunk or not." When asked what morality means to her she states:

When I think of moral I think of a defined right and a defined wrong, and there is no way of falling in between . . . morality tells me my values. *This had nothing to do with my values. It just had to do with life, my friendship with somebody* [emphasis added].

(What does morality mean to you?) Morality means what's right and what's wrong. You have a set of moral things: you know, don't smoke, don't have sex before you get married, don't drink, don't drive fast. Those are values that I think society in general and your upbringing gives you and your parents reinforce. Morality in my mind is I have a certain set of beliefs—honesty, trust—and morality is whether I am going to stay with them. . . . It [this situation] was sort of like my feelings . . . and your feelings are connected with your morality. Your feelings sort of control what you think is right or wrong, depending on the situation. But in this way I don't think it was a moral decision. It was my feelings.

Ann struggles with how to integrate feelings—so central to her conflict with her friend—and morality. She distinguishes between inside—her feelings—and outside—a set of beliefs she has taken from society or her upbringing, and this distinction causes her confusion. "Morality," itself, is something distanced from herself and her feelings; it is something that tells her what to value, yet has nothing to do with "life, my friendship with somebody." She and the conflict she experiences with her friend are detached from the realm of morality as defined by the world around her, except perhaps for some vague notion she has that her feelings somehow impact what she values. Ann reiterates a list of "don'ts" that she acknowledges are both societal and parental but not apparently examined or personally owned. Morals are things that she takes on or discards. In contrast, Ann locates the problem with her friend around the issue of perspective. She realizes that both she and her friend had reason to act the way they did, and as a result it was selfish of her not to allow her friend room "to prove something to herself." Knowing what she, herself, needed and attending to what her friend knows and feels, she experiences a conflict that threatens their relationship. She feels a personal responsibility for the way she thinks about, feels, and acts with regard to her friend.

Kate's narrative exemplifies a third prevalent theme heard in these cases: There is a clear and readily available language with which to talk about an "impartial" morality (Blum 1987)—that is, a rights or justice-based morality (Gilligan 1982; Kohlberg 1984; Lyons 1983)—since it is a morality defined and transmitted by the culture. But these girls struggle and appear confused when they attempt to apply the terms of this morality to their situations of moral conflict. An impartial morality does not capture the complexity of their conflicts, yet they have no other language in which to speak if they wish their thoughts to be understood and legitimatized. A corollary to this theme is the tendency for these young women to de-emphasize, in some cases to devalue, their "particularized" (Blum 1987) knowledge of relationship—a knowledge derived from their observations, feelings, and personal experience. Early in her interview-narrative, as Kate struggles to clarify how she perceives the conflict, she says:

> It's difficult to know when you are being fair in any kind of judgment on a teacher. *(What do you mean by fair?)* It's hard to know from . . . the teacher in a class has a very good perspective on things and could be, you know, the teacher's method could be leaning toward certain things that I don't know. I hadn't talked to the teacher, that kind of thing. *(So fairness would be?)* I don't really mean fair or unfair. It was a situation where I didn't know if I was—I felt that someone should represent the other students by talking to the [administration]—but I felt personally, I felt badly that I would, that I was doing this, because I myself didn't really have any complaints, except that I felt that other students weren't satisfied and that there literally was a problem.

Kate discards fairness as the construct she would use to explain the situation as she perceives it. It is not a situation that can appeal to justice for the right resolution, but one that appeals to understanding and knowing as a way to avoid harm. Later in the interview she struggles with definitions of the words "responsibility," "respect," and "honor." She says, finally:

> These are issues that are very hard to talk about without using the words that are, that mean things other than I really intend them to mean. . . . I am trying hard not to use respect or right or wrong. But it is hard to describe something like this without it. *(The words that come up are honor and respect?)* Just because I can't think of anything else, but I don't even really use those. It is more of an instinctive feeling.

Again, these words—fairness, honesty, respect—do not explain what she means, do not feel true to her experience. Kate clearly struggles with a way to understand and talk about her experiences. The words that she might use are inadequate. As a result she appears frustrated and moves from attempts at explication to a sort of vacuous generalization—her experiences become "instinctive feelings." To hear only this attempt and not the rich description of her real-life conflict that precedes it would make Kate's reflection on her experiences seem vague or confused. Yet, listening to the care and thoughtful attention with which she reflects on her decision and the complexity of feeling she attributes to herself and others, it becomes more difficult to dismiss her as someone confused. On the contrary, it becomes more obvious why she cannot reduce an emotionally and intellectually complex problem to one general concept—that is, to simply an issue of fairness or honesty. To do so would not be accurate or represent the reality of the situation as she perceives it. It would, in a sense, remove her from a stance of observer and knower.

Kate's struggle to find a way to talk about her experiences reflects the complexity of her dilemma. It is a struggle that recurs in the other interviews. As a result, these adolescents may either express what their experiences *were not* in an attempt to clarify what they *were* or they may subtly de-emphasize or devalue them. Thus, Jean replies that it wasn't a question of morality: "It was *just* a question of what was best for her . . . doing what I positively knew was the best for [my friend]. . . ." And Kate relegates her perspective to "instinctive feelings." In a similar vein, recall Ann's statement of her real-life dilemma: "It had nothing to do with my values. It *just* had to do with life, my friendship with somebody . . . my feelings . . . I don't think it was a moral decision. It was my feelings." In addition, Faye, whose role as editor-in-chief of the yearbook put her in a position to consider the complicated practical and emotional difficulties of firing a classmate, said, "it was *just* me being able to say 'no'." In fact, saying "no" entailed a time-consuming and painful struggle to include the classmate's perspective and feelings, the feelings of co-workers who were affected, and her own perspective.

Jean, Kate, Faye, and Ann exemplify a relational complexity in their interview-narratives of conflict. Each acknowledges and attends to a variety of people and issues in their process of decision making; each explains a way of knowing that involves moving from their perspective to understanding another's, a process that displays not only an awareness and appreciation of the other's point of view, but also an ability to reflect critically on the self's thoughts, feelings, and actions. This complexity and capacity to take a critical perspective in the stories they tell seems absent from their definitions of morality as a priori standards or rules for behavior externally defined by parents or society. Also absent is a sense of a participating, autonomous, freely choosing self—they talk about morality as something imposed on them, as something they must learn, a code they should obey. In their real-life dilemmas, however, they struggle with the complexity of the situations, with what they know of those involved; they take on the risks of action, acknowledging what they do not or can not know.

When is a moral problem not a moral problem?

The discrepancy between the way in which these young women have discussed their real-life conflicts and their definitions of "morality" remains to be explored. Three possible interpretations emerge, depending on how the question—"Do you consider the situation you described to be a moral problem?"—may have been heard and understood in the dialogue between interviewer and interviewee. First, it may have been the case that the young women selected out and responded to the word "problem," that is, their response may indicate that they perceived the dilemmas they described to be "moral," but perhaps not moral "problems." Second, it is possible that they focused on the word "moral," that is, their response might indicate that their dilemmas were indeed problems, but they would not consider them to be "moral" problems. Third, they may have heard the following question: "Do you consider the situation you described to be a 'moral problem'?"—emphasizing "moral problem" as a single term. In this case, the response, No, it was not a 'moral problem,' may be interpreted as, Yes, the situation was moral; yes, the situation was a problem; but, the difficulty or the conflict I experienced was not with the 'moral problem,' but with some other aspect of the experience. The interpretive task, therefore, is to determine which of the three possible alternatives best explains the intended meaning of the responses given by each of these young women. This is an important task because understanding the responses of these female adolescents to this particular question tells much about how they understand and define morality—and how they perceive and experience the interface between their definitions and those of the wider culture.

In order to determine which of the three questions these young women heard, it is important to return to the interview texts—to the conversation between the interviewer and the interviewee. In other words, the response to this question cannot be isolated from the overall conversation or dialogue in which the question is embedded. A close examination of the text of the interviews reveals that the first possible interpretation, that the young women in this sample felt their real-life dilemmas were not "problems" for them, seems unlikely. Consider the struggle and psychological ambivalence they described while making or coming to terms with their decisions: Jean is uncertain even though she knows she must protect her friend. Kate's statement, "It was a hard decision for me whether or not to go," and Faye's, "I kept feeling torn between should I get someone new and say you're fired, or should I keep waiting," illustrate the problematic, or, conflictual nature of the real-life dilemmas they discuss. Consequently, it is relatively easy to refute this first possible interpretation.

The second and third interpretations, however, are not so easily dismissed. The second, that these young women perceived their real-life dilemmas as problems but not problems within the category of "moral" problems, seems more viable. Each girl distinguishes between, on the one hand, a morality of "right and wrong," "black and white," or, on the other, a morality in which she must sort out standards held by herself from those held by authority figures or institutions, such as school or church, and the conflicts in the real-life moral dilemmas she experienced and described. They use moral language to describe their real-life dilemmas—that is, prescriptive statements about what they ought to do in such a situation—yet, they do not rely on general rules of behavior or impartial standards of right and wrong. *If* morality is defined as standards for behavior or role obligations, then these young women seem accurate in their observations that the dilemmas they describe are not "moral" problems.

151

The stories these young women tell indicate that what matters most to them, what they care for and show concern for—in essence, then, what they value—has little to do with such definitions of morality. Recall Ann's assertion that "It had nothing to do with my values. It just had to do with my life, my friendship with somebody . . . my feelings. . . . I don't think it was a moral decision. It was my feelings." Ann distinguishes "values" from the feelings of conflict she experienced in her dilemma. For Ann, decisions about life, feelings, friendship do not fall under the same rubric as those "values that I think society in general and your upbringing give you and your parents reinforce." Yet, clearly, she cares for her friendships, her life, and attends to her feelings in her story of conflict. What sense can be made of this?

At least one answer to this discrepancy is to consider growing theoretical and empirical evidence for the idea that there are two different conceptions of morality or two ways in which one might come to know the moral world: one that relies on impartial rules or role obligations, another that focuses on particular attachments, relies on attention to the specific context of a dilemma and the special needs of all involved, often including the self (Blum 1987; Gilligan 1982, 1986, 1987; Lyons 1983). Gilligan and Attanucci (1988) describe dimensions of human relationships that provide different ways of organizing social and moral reality:

> The distinction between justice and care orientations pertains to the ways in which moral problems are conceived and reflects different dimensions of human relationships that give rise to moral concern. The justice perspective draws attention to problems of inequality and oppression and holds up an ideal of reciprocity and equal respect. The care perspective draws attention to problems of detachment and abandonment and holds up an ideal of attention and response to need. Two moral injunctions—not to treat others unfairly and not to turn away from someone in need—capture these different concerns.

The idea that a morality of rights and a morality of response represent different dimensions of relationship that move along different developmental paths suggests the possibility that the young women represented in this paper tell their stories of moral conflict in a care voice. Their dilemmas draw attention to detachment and abandonment, rather than to inequality and oppression. Jean cannot turn away from her thirteen-year-old friend who is contemplating suicide. Kate cannot abandon her classmates in their confusion. She says, "Someone had to go and talk and it was, you know, it was a question would it be selfish of me not to do it, because things were fine for me, but I knew there was a problem." In this case, the split between "morality" and feelings, or standards of behavior and care and concern for others, has to do with the simple fact that "morality" has a specific and rather narrow meaning in this culture. It is a word of power, carefully and specifically defined and legitimized by Western culture as having to do with concerns for justice and excluding the concerns for care and attention to others that pervade the stories told by these adolescent girls. In other words, the values and concerns expressed by these girls in their dilemmas are not moral problems as morality has been defined for them by those in authority in this society.

If, in fact, there are two moral voices, two frameworks within which two ways of speaking about the moral world can be discerned, the girls in this small sample choose to speak in a care voice. This choice may clarify why their stories of relationship reveal reflective, complex thinking, while their references to societal rules and roles remain either simplistic or opaque. Their capacity for reflection and perspective—and for autonomous action—is less obvious in their discussion of an impartial morality of rights, because their experience does not easily translate to this language. Only by acknowledging and attending to a morality of response is it possible to appreciate the capacity of these young women for autonomous choice and critical perspective. These girls struggle to find a solution that would integrate the needs of all involved in their complex real-life dilemmas. They are aware of the painful consequences someone might have to experience as a result of their choice. The failure to find one "right" solution sustains the experience of real moral dilemma that cannot be easily solved by reliance on a hierarchy of principles or standards (Gilligan 1982; see also Nussbaum 1986 for an elaboration of this point). What is remarkable is the ability of each of these young women to act while acknowledging the inevitable consequences: that is, that someone will experience some hurt regardless of what she chooses to do.

While the notion of two conceptions of morality, or two moral voices, sheds light on the above cases and provides a powerful theoretical rationale for the distinction between the descriptions of real-life dilemmas provided by these girls and a more traditional definition of morality, there is still a third possible interpretation—one that may, in fact, go hand-in-hand with the second. As stated above, perhaps these girls perceive their dilemmas both as problems and as moral; but the concern or the real difficulty they feel or experience is with neither. There is some evidence that for these young women there is yet another dimension to the difficulty they experience; one that has more to do with their feelings about others and themselves as moral actors than with the rubric under which they would place their actions. Consider, for example, Kate's assertion that "I felt I was doing the right thing, but I felt badly about it." What seems to make Kate feel bad is the realization that whatever she chooses to do, ultimately someone—either the teacher or the students—could be hurt. Recall that she is unsure about a number of things: "Maybe the students weren't advanced enough to handle the kind of classroom situation," she wonders. But also, maybe she doesn't know enough about the teacher's motives: "It's hard to know . . . the teacher in a class has a very good perspective on things and could be, the teacher's method could be leaning toward certain things that I don't know. . . ." Kate is troubled by the nature of her involvement and the feelings that emerge for her as she acts. She realizes there are things she may not know, or cannot know fully, and that to act under such circumstances feels bad. Her perception of her responsibility for knowing arises by virtue of the relationship she has with her classmates and with the teacher. She cares that they learn and understand but also that her teacher not be hurt unnecessarily. To act as she does is right. But the real problem for her has to do with what it means to make such a choice and to face a loss knowingly, to claim her perspective and to act on her best assessment of the situation, given what she knows she cannot know and the risk that entails. This interpretation of the implications of action and her felt responsibility to the others in her dilemma hinges on Kate's question, Would it be selfish of me not to do it?

Consider, in addition, Jean's case: For Jean, doing what she considers to be the right thing in the situation involves her in an action in which she feels uncomfortable because it causes her to betray her relationship with her friend; that is, to tell the counselor about her friend's plans, when she told her friend she would not. The "moral" choice is clear (". . . even if [she] gets mad at me and never wants to speak to me again, I'd rather she be alive and speak to me than dead and never have the chance . . ."), but the tension or pull she experiences ("between . . . doing what I knew positively was the best thing for [her]") surfaces as a result of her involvement and relationship with her friend. Paradoxically, by virtue of this interdependence, she perceives herself as a responsible knower and chooser and yet as someone who cannot fully know but who must act because she cares. Jean's way of knowing focuses her attention on potential consequences for those involved—to her friend, to the counselor, to herself—and puts her in a position of responsibility for the consequences; therefore, she must be accurate in her perceptions of the situation. Yet given what she knows of her friend and her situation, Jean is not sure what is the way best to care for her. She is uncertain, not of the moral thing to do, but of her perceptions, her construction of the situation. The problem is in failing the relationship and therefore in failing herself, her personal responsibility. Her choice is right, but she feels badly about the potential for loss, the result of betrayal or misunderstanding.

Faye also illustrates the difficulty of choosing, claiming her perspective in spite of what she does not know and who she may hurt. She struggles as she considers what she doesn't know about her classmate's situation: "And it was also a conflict that I wasn't really sure if I was being unreasonable in the things I was asking her to do. . . . And I was conflicted about it because I thought maybe I didn't make it clear to her the things that I need to do. . . . I couldn't just look at my situation, that this is the most important thing because I realized that there were other things going on. . . ." Faye knows she cannot fully know. Her task is to claim the power of her perspective, to trust that she has enough information to choose. Her difficulty has, in part, to do with her realization that to act raises questions about herself as a knower and accurate perceiver. To act in ways that one feels are good or right is to bring one's perspective into the world; it is to claim a public space, a "moral identity" (Blasi 1983). This is a task these young women find extremely difficult. Their response—No, the situation was not a 'moral problem'—may indicate the struggle they experience has more to do with claiming a moral stance, with acting in the face of potential loss or in the face of the risks of not knowing.

Blasi's (1984) notion that "a morality that actually works, not only in this or that action but also in one's life in general, must be rooted in some form of identity" (p. 136) is central to this way of understanding and interpreting these cases:

> From this perspective, the central moral issue, also for psychologists, concerns one's responsibility for knowing and in using knowledge. The core of immorality is not wanting to know, blinding oneself, acting against one's knowledge. The ultimate sin, if one can use in this context an old-fashioned and unscientific term, is the sin against the light and the spirit. It should be said, incidentally, that the very

155

idea of responsibility for knowledge is alien, not only to noncognitive theories but also to Piagetian cognitivism. From a different angle, responsibility to what one knows—about right and wrong, about others and oneself—is integrity. Integrity acquires, then, a more precise meaning: It is not logical consistency, nor consistency among personality traits, not the resolution of dissonance between cognition and action, when it is the need to reduce one's anxiety; it is, instead, a responsible actualization of what one knows to be right and true. (Blasi 1983, 206)

This responsibility "for knowing" and "using knowledge," a function of claiming a "moral identity," is what seems most problematic for these young women. Jean, for example, knows a great deal—about her suicidal friend, about their relationship—yet, she acknowledges there are things about her friend she does not know. Does she know enough to make the best choice? Will her choice be "a responsible actualization of what [she] knows to be right and true;" will it have integrity?

Blasi's (1984) notion of responsibility for knowledge and for the self as moral actor acknowledges the centrality of perspective as key to understanding the interview-narratives of these girls. Referring to Erikson's (1968) notion of fidelity as "the human virtue that is intimately associated with the development of identity" (P. 130), Blasi ties moral identity to moral action. Thus moral action becomes a question of self-consistency, of personal integrity. Blasi states:

From my perspective, moral identity is directly related to moral action, providing one of its truly moral motives. As already mentioned, one aspect of fidelity, the basic virtue that Erikson considers as inherently tied to the development of identity, consists of a concern with being authentic and true to one's self in action. In my self mode [Blasi 1980, 1983], the connection between moral identity and action is expressed through the concepts of responsibility (in the strict obligation to act according to one's judgment) and integrity. These two concepts are closely related and derive their meaning from a view of moral action as an extension of the essential self into the domain of the possible, of what is not but needs to be, if the agent has to remain true to himself or herself. Responsibility, in this sense, stresses the self as the source of "moral compulsion." Integrity, instead, emphasizes the idea of moral self-consistency, of intactness and wholeness—all essential connotations of the self as a psychological organization. (1984, 132)

Jean knows what she knows through communication, through dialogue in relationship, and struggles to use that knowledge responsibly. Her uncertainty, although it does not immobilize her, creates a problem. Given that theories of female development highlight the importance of sustaining relationship for the development of the self, Blasi's concept of responsibility provides a lens through which the struggle of these female adolescents can be seen to have integrity. The moral reasoning, moral feelings, and moral action in which these young women engage are given coherence by a moral identity achieved through and defined by relationship. In Blasi's sense, their acts have integrity—in their "moral-consistency," their "intactness and wholeness."

The fact that the young women chosen for analysis in this paper did *not* consider their real-life dilemmas to be moral problems has placed the definition of "morality" in tension throughout this paper. The analysis of these cases restates the question of discrepancy as a question of perspective—not which perspective is the better or more correct in its description of morality, but how one is to understand each in its own terms.

These cases illustrate that the struggle to engage actively in a decision that affects another, to care and to attend to another, is a worthy one for these girls. Standards and role obligations are terms that do not accurately describe their experiences, yet they *are* often terms that describe parental, religious, and societal notions of morality. These cases, therefore, illustrate how a culture and a psychology that recognize and value a narrow vision of morality may exclude the moral significance of the experiences of these young women.

Their narratives, however, also illustrate a more complicated point. If, as Blasi contends, the connection between moral identity and action is expressed through responsibility to one's judgment and the self's integrity, for these young women the discrepancy between their relational understanding of morality and the view of morality legitimized in this culture suggests the integrity of the self may be at risk. In other words, if what is morally imperative for them, or what defines and sustains their "moral identity," is not valued or considered truly "moral" by the culture at large, one would expect a loss of trust in the self's perspective and judgment and the self's moral integrity; a loss revealed in these interview narratives as the difficulty these young women have in calling a moral problem a "moral problem."

Thus evidence of insecurity and self-doubt in describing their relational dilemmas as well as difficulty framing their real-life conflicts in a traditional moral language—one that appears not to fit their experience—can, in fact, be heard in these cases. The loss may be of a sense of self as a moral, caring self and of trust in a logic of interdependence and responsiveness derived from personal experience. These cases suggest that evidence of this loss may be found in females during adolescence, a time when, as Gilligan (1987) argues, young women come face to face with cultural traditions and social conventions that may not legitimize their understanding of themselves or their perspectives on the world.

Sources

Belenky, M., B. Clinchy, N. Goldberger, and J. Tarule. 1986. *Women's Ways of Knowing: The Development of Self, Voice, and Mind*. New York: Basic Books.

Blasi, A. 1980. Bridging moral cognition and moral action: A critical review of the literature. *Psychological Bulletin* 88:1–45.

———. 1983. Moral cognition and moral action: A theoretical perspective. *Developmental Review* 3:178–210.

———. 1984. Moral identity: Its role in moral functioning. In *Morality, Moral Behavior, and Moral Development*, edited by W. Kurtines and J. Gewirtz. New York: John Wiley.

Blum, L. 1987. Particularity and responsiveness. In *The Emergence of Morality in Young Children*, edited by J. Kagan and S. Lamb. Chicago: University of Chicago Press.

Chodorow, N. 1978. *The Reproduction of Mothering: Psychoanalysis and the Sociology of Mothering*. Berkeley: University of California Press.

Colby, A., and L. Kohlberg 1987. *The Measurement of Moral Judgment*. New York: Cambridge University Press.

Douvan, E., and J. Adelson. 1966. *The Adolescent Experience*. New York: John Wiley.

Erikson, E. 1968. *Identity: Youth and Crisis*. New York: W. W. Norton.

Gilligan, C. 1982. *In a Different Voice*. Cambridge: Harvard University Press.

―――. 1986. "Exit-Voice Dilemmas in Adolescent Development." In *Development, Democracy, and the Art of Trespassing: Essays in Honor of Albert O. Hirschman*, edited by A. Foxley, M. McPherson, and G. O'Donnell. Notre Dame, Ind.: University of Notre Dame Press.

―――. 1987. "Adolescent development reconsidered." In *New Directions for Child Development, No. 37: Adolescent Social Behavior and Health*, edited by C. Irwin. San Francisco: Jossey-Bass.

―――. 1987. "Remapping the Moral Domain: New Images of the Self in Relationship." In *Reconstructing Individualism: Autonomy, Individuality, and the Self in Western Thought*, edited by T. C. Heller, M. Sosna, and D. Wellber. Stanford, Calif.: Stanford University Press.

Gilligan, C., and J. Attanucci. July 1988. Two moral orientations: Implications for developmental theory and assessment. *Merrill-Palmer Quarterly* 34:223–44.

Johnston, K. 1985. Two moral orientations—Two problem-solving strategies: Adolescents' Solutions to Dilemmas in Fables. Ph.D. diss., Harvard University.

Josselson, R. 1987. *Finding Herself: Pathways to Identity Development in Women*. San Francisco: Jossey-Bass.

Kohlberg, L. 1984. *Essays in Moral Development*. Vol. 2 of *The Psychology of Moral Development*. San Francisco: Harper and Row.

Lyons, N. 1983. Two perspectives: On self, relationship, and morality. *Harvard Educational Review* 49(1).

Miller, J. 1976. *Toward a New Psychology of Women*. Boston: Beacon Press.

Nussbaum, M. 1986. *The Fragility of Goodness*. Cambridge: Cambridge University Press.

Piaget, J. 1965 (Orig. 1932). *The Moral Judgment of the Child*. New York: The Free Press.

CHAPTER 5

Reading for Self and Moral Voice:
A Method for Interpreting Narratives
of Real-Life Moral Conflict and Choice

LYN M. BROWN, MARK B. TAPPAN, CAROL GILLIGAN,
BARBARA A. MILLER, AND DIANNE E. ARGYRIS[1]

Our aim in this chapter is to describe an interpretive method that we have developed as a guide to reading interview narratives of moral conflict and choice. Central to this effort is our belief in the possibility of different perspectives on moral problems, and the potential for conflict among them. In fact, we believe that tension between differing moral voices, and conflict between opposing values, is essential to the moral life; that, as Martha Nussbaum (1986) states "a conflict-free life would be lacking in value and beauty next to a life in which it is possible for conflict to arise" (p. 81). We embrace, then, both the possibility of creative resolutions to moral conflict, and the potential for tragedy. We chose to examine narratives of moral conflict that people have experienced because we believe this method illuminates the complexity of moral voice, while not overlooking the power of silence.

We claim a place from which to stand, to look, and to listen; hence we struggle with questions of interpretation. The method we will describe in this chapter represents our attempt to bring an explicitly hermeneutic approach to the psychological study of morality and moral development. As such it also provides an alternative approach to more traditional methods that have been used in research on moral development (see Colby & Kohlberg 1987; Gibbs & Widaman 1982; Rest 1979).

Our presentation will unfold as follows: We will turn first to a brief consideration of the theoretical and methodological foundations on which we base our present work. We will discuss: 1) our ongoing work (Gilligan 1977, 1982, 1983, 1986, 1987; Gilligan & Wiggins 1987) on distinguishing two moral voices and the description of differences between a "justice" and a "care" orientation or ethic; 2) recent work on narrative analysis, specifically that of Mishler (1986); and 3) classic work on both hermeneutic theory and interpretive method, specifically that of Dilthey (1900/1976) and Ricoeur (1979). Second, we will outline our "Guide to Reading Narratives of Real-Life Moral Conflict and Choice for Self and Moral Voice" (see Brown, Argyris, Attanucci, Bardige, Gilligan, Johnston, Miller, Osborne, Ward, Wiggins, & Wilcox 1987) which describes our interpretive method. Third, we will present one way we have devised to summarize our reading of narratives of moral conflict, using what we have called "Narrative Types" or "Narrative Strategies." Fourth, we will present and discuss the initial data we have gathered concerning the reliability and validity of this approach. And finally, we will conclude by briefly reflecting on some of the implications, for both theory and research, that stem from our work on this method.

Theoretical and Methodological Foundations

The work we report in this chapter grew out of our efforts to create a theoretical framework that would encompass both equality and attachment as dimensions of human relationship and thus explain the recurrence in life history and history of two moral "voices" or "orientations": "justice" and "care" (see Gilligan, 1977, 1982, 1983, 1986, 1987; Gilligan & Wiggins 1987). The distinction between justice and care as different moral voices and relational perspectives is empirically based, following from the observation that when people shift the focus of their attention from concerns about justice to concerns about care, their definition of what constitutes a moral problem changes; and, consequently, a situation may be seen in a different way. Theoretically, our distinction between justice and care cuts across the familiar divisions between thinking and feeling, egoism and altruism, and theoretical and practical reasoning by reconstructing the meaning of these terms. The moral voices of justice and care call attention to the fact that *all* human relationships, public and private, can be spoken of *both* in terms of equality and in terms of attachment, and that both inequality and detachment constitute grounds for moral concern. We believe that since everyone, by virtue of being human, is vulnerable both to oppression and to abandonment, two moral visions—one of justice and one of care—will always characterize human culture.

Our distinction between justice and care as moral voices thus pertains to the ways in which people conceive and/or define moral problems, and it reflects two different dimensions of human relationships that give rise to moral concern. A justice perspective draws attention to problems of inequality and oppression by holding up an ideal of reciprocity and equal respect between persons. A care perspective draws attention to problems of attachment and abandonment by holding up an ideal of attention and responsiveness in relationships. Two moral injunctions—not to treat others unfairly and not to turn away from someone in need—capture these different concerns.

This theoretical foundation forms the basis from which we have been working to develop a method that can be used by researchers interested in studying the moral voices of justice and care and understanding the experience of self in relation to others. Because the data source for our ongoing work has been open-ended, semi-clinical interviews, we found support for our effort in the similar work of Elliot Mishler (1986).

Mishler helped us clarify a number of crucial aspects of the method we present below. Most importantly, his work on interview narratives helped us see clearly the narrative structure of our data: In our effort to discover and describe peoples' moral voices, when we ask an individual, in an open-ended interview, to talk about a situation of real-life moral conflict and choice that she or he has recently faced, what she or he frequently responds with is a narrative—i.e., a story. Mishler observes that:

> Telling stories is far from unusual in everyday conversation and it is apparently no more unusual for interviewees to respond to questions with narratives if they are given some room to speak. ... In general, researchers in the mainstream tradition either have not recognized the pervasiveness of stories because, as I have already remarked, the standard survey interview "suppresses" them, or have treated stories as a problem because they are difficult to code and quantify. We are more likely to find stories reported in studies using relatively unstructured interviews where respondents are invited to speak in their own voices, allowed to control the introduction and flow of topics, and encouraged to extend their responses. Nonetheless respondents may also tell stories in response to direct, specific questions if they are not interrupted by interviewers trying to keep them to the "point." (Mishler 1986, 69)

A second aspect of our approach to which Mishler's (1986) work has brought clarity is the crucial role that context plays in the interpretation of any interview narrative (see also Mishler 1979). Meaning, argues Mishler, is always "contextually grounded—inherently and irremediably" (p. 3). It follows that in order to understand the meaning of an individual's response to an interview question (let alone the full narrative that he or she provides) the researcher must have some understanding of the context from which both the interview and the interviewee have come, as well as the context of their encounter—i.e., the interview relationship itself and the setting in which it occurs. We have tried to remain sensitive to such contextual issues in developing the method we describe below.

In our effort to clarify the interpretive (or hermeneutic) nature of our "Reading Guide," we also found the work of Wilhelm Dilthey (1900/1976) and Paul Ricoeur (1979) to be quite helpful.

Dilthey's concept of the hermeneutic circle points to the fact that complex human phenomena (e.g., interview narratives) can only be understood in a somewhat paradoxical fashion that involves a circular consideration of both the whole and its parts:

> Here we encounter the general difficulty of all interpretation. The whole of a work must be understood from individual words and their combination but full understanding of an individual part presupposes understanding of the whole. . . . [Thus] the whole must be understood in terms of its individual parts, individual parts in terms of the whole. . . . Such a comparative procedure allows one to understand every individual work, indeed, every individual sentence, more profoundly than we did before. So understanding of the whole, and of the parts, are interdependent. (Dilthey 1900/1976, 259, 262)

Our Reading Guide offers one way of operationalizing, in a systematic and deliberate manner, the paradoxical hermeneutic circle. As we will describe in detail below, the method involves "building" an interpretation of a whole interview narrative out of its constituent parts. The difficulty is, however, that an understanding of those parts is not possible without some understanding of the whole narrative. Thus the interpretive procedure is a fundamentally circular one, because while the whole can only be understood in terms of its parts, by the same token the parts only acquire their proper meaning within the context of the whole.[2]

Finally, the work of Ricoeur (1979) helped us extend the insights of Dilthey. Ricoeur argues for what he calls the "paradigm of the text," and then shows how "meaningful human action" as the object of the human (social) sciences conforms to the paradigm of the text:

> The human sciences may be said to be hermeneutical (1) inasmuch as their *object* displays some of the features constitutive of a text as text, and (2) inasmuch as their *methodology* develops the same kind of procedures as those of *Auslegung* or text-interpretation. (p. 73)

Ricoeur (1979) proposes that the process of reading represents the appropriate analogy to the interpretive methodology employed by the human sciences. This is because, says Ricoeur, reading manifests the dialectical relationship between *Verstehen* (understanding, comprehension) and *Erklaren* (explanation) that perplexed and preoccupied Dilthey. Dilthey ultimately argued that understanding was the only interpretive method appropriate for the human studies, and that explanation was inappropriate because it was imported from the natural sciences. Ricoeur, however, rejects this view, and instead sees the dialectic between understanding and explanation, as it is manifest in the process of reading a text, as the key to contemporary methodological problems in the human studies.[3] As such, he argues that it is the "balance between the genius of *guessing* and the scientific character of *validation* which constitutes the modern complement of the dialectic between *Verstehen* and *Erklaren*" (p. 91).

Unfortunately, our purposes here do not allow us to discuss all the complex and complicated issues that stem from Ricoeur's argument. Instead, we simply want to acknowledge Ricoeur's analogy between the procedures employed in reading and interpreting texts, and the procedures employed in interpreting meaningful human action in the social sciences. In the method we describe below we have attempted to make that connection explicit—that is, we have developed a method of interpreting human action (i.e., engaging in social scientific research) that involves reading texts of interview narratives in which such action is represented and described.[4]

The Reading Guide

An Overview

As we have said above, our purpose in creating this method was to develop a way of reading and interpreting complex narratives of real-life moral conflict and choice. We have come to see through reading such interviews that how a person constructs a moral conflict—how she or he defines or interprets the situation, and what she or he focuses on as relevant to the problem—is related to what actions she or he describes and the thoughts and feelings that follow from or accompany this description. In a given situation, people differ in what they consider to be the central *moral* problem, and what they consider to be the best (or better) way to respond to that problem.

The way in which a moral problem is constructed, however, also depends on the context, e.g., who is involved, the relationships between the persons involved—their relative power vis-a-vis each other as well as the strength of the connection between them—where the situation takes place, what role the narrator plays in the conflict, and the personal and cultural history of the narrator. We have observed that when different elements of context and different aspects or qualities of relationship are defined and represented as salient in similar conflicts, what is seen as the central moral issue in a situation may shift, and different actions may be defined as moral and immoral, as right or wrong (see Gilligan 1987; Johnston 1985).

The two moral voices of justice and care can be distinguished in part by a shift in the conception of what is relevant to the moral domain. The method presented here picks up on that shift and is designed for use in interpreting narratives of moral conflict and choice, including narratives systematically collected in the course of formal research.

As an interpretive enterprise, then, this method is not a "Coding Manual" that allows a "coder" to match responses to a predetermined set of criteria (see, for example, Colby and Kohlberg 1987). Instead, it is a way of reading—a Reader's Guide. As such, it is a procedure for teaching others to read a text of a real-life moral conflict to identify what we consider "voice-relevant" aspects of a person's narrative.

The distinction between a Coding Manual and a Reading Guide is an important one. It has to do with both our methodological premises and the nature of our data. Our choice of an open-ended clinical interview method (see Table 1 for a copy of our interview questions) yields complex real-life narratives. Such narratives reflect situational, personal, and cultural factors, including issues of language, perspective, and the relationship between the reader's and the narrator's language and perspective. To develop a method that highlights the interpretive nature of the reading process we have tried to create and describe a way of working where we claim both a theoretical and a methodological stance.

Table 1

Real-Life Moral Conflict and Choice Interview

All people have had the experience of being in a situation where they had to make a decision, but weren't sure of what they should do. Would you describe a situation when you faced a moral conflict and you had to make a decision, but weren't sure what you should do?

1. What was the situation? (Be sure you get a full elaboration of the story).

2. What was the conflict for you in that situation? Why was it a conflict?

3. In thinking about what to do, what did you consider? Why? Anything else you considered?

4. What did you decide to do? What happened?

5. Do you think it was the right thing to do? Why/why not?

6. What was at stake for you in this dilemma? What was at stake for others? In general, what was at stake?

7. How did you feel about it? How did you feel about it for the other(s) involved?

8. Is there another way to see the problem (other than the way you described it?)

9. When you think back over the conflict you described, do you think you learned anything from it?

10. Do you consider the situation you described a moral problem? Why/why not?

11. What does morality mean to you? What makes something a moral problem for you?

**Note to Interviewers:* Questions should follow references to judgments about the, situation. Follow any references to feelings that are mentioned—e.g., Why did you feel mad or angry? Also follow moral language, i.e., should, ought. Questions should focus on: In whose terms judgments are made. Try to understand the terms of the self and the self's perspective on the terms of the other.

Reading an interview text in this way, we enter the hermeneutic circle and build an interpretation of that text—an interpretation that moves from the words on the page, toward an understanding of how, and an explanation of why, a narrator structures his/her experience of relationships and how s/he organizes or "frames" the moral conflict, and back again—in terms of self and the two moral voices of justice and care. These voices are not identified by any key code words or phrases, but rather by the framework or perspective provided by the narrator, and illuminated by the reader.

In constructing this Reading Guide we proceeded from evidence that persons know (and can represent) two moral voices or perspectives in discussing moral conflicts, even though they may indicate a preference for one over the other (see, for example, Johnston 1985). From evidence of the ability to switch perspectives, we assume that the "narrative self" is, in some sense, involved in choice. In reading texts, therefore, we view persons as "moral agents" with respect to the standpoint they take and the concerns they voice or keep silent.

Tracking the "voice" of the narrative self draws our attention to the narrator's perspective (both expressed and preferred) in a particular story of moral conflict. This approach has made it possible for us to investigate empirically what understanding of justice and care a person brings to bear on a particular problem, and also what relationship exists between these two moral voices or perspectives in a particular narrative.

Perhaps it is important to emphasize here that we do not conceive of the moral voices of justice and care as either dichotomous or mutually exclusive. Rather, we consider justice and care as visions of relationship that reflect the vulnerabilities of people in relationships—their liability to oppression and to abandonment, indifference, and neglect. These two perspectives on moral problems may shift over time, but each voice is defined in its own terms. In other words, although some of the criteria used to identify a care idea may have counterparts that may identify a justice idea, others will not. Each voice has as its central tenet a dimension of relationship that gives rise to moral concern, from which certain assumptions about self and other are made, and from which a certain view of the moral world is constructed. Thus, each voice has its own psychological "logic," its own psychic legitimacy and organization that can be followed in narratives of moral conflict and choice. We are ultimately most interested in the narrative strategies people use in describing the realm of moral conflict—the choice of moral orientations and the orchestration of moral voices telling human stories.

This way of reading, therefore, takes as its starting point the premise that a person, represented in the interview text by a speaking voice telling a narrative or story, experiences relationships both in terms of attachment and in terms of equality. We are interested in how a person tells a story about his or her experiences of conflict in relationship. Justice and care voices are characterized by the telling of different narratives about relationship. A care voice describes relationships in terms of attachment/detachment, connection or disconnection. *Care narratives,* consequently, focus on the vulnerability of people to isolation and abandonment, and are concerned with the complexities of creating and sustaining human connection. A justice voice describes relationship in terms of inequality/equality, reciprocity, or lack of respect. *Justice narratives* thus focus on the vulnerability of people to oppression, and are centrally concerned with standards or principles of fairness. Reading in this way we track these two relational "voices" and seek to specify the way in which a person orchestrates or chooses between them.

Interpretive Procedures

As a guide to interpreting texts of real-life moral conflict and choice the goal of the Reading Guide is to present a theoretical perspective and to teach those interested to read interview texts using a specific set of referents defined by this perspective. Thus the interpreter (i.e., reader) is first helped to locate a narrative of real-life moral conflict in a larger interview text and then to read this story a total of *four* different times. Each reading serves to identify a different aspect of the narrative deemed relevant in locating self and ascertaining moral voice.

The multiple readings are necessary because each reading approaches the narrative from a different standpoint. The first reading is designed simply to establish the story told by the narrator. Once this is done, the narrative is read using three different interpretive lenses to locate self and the moral voices of care and justice. In the second reading ("Locating Self") the interpreter reads for the active "self", the narrator (the speaking voice) as an agent telling a story in which he or she appears as an actor in a drama of moral conflict and choice. In the third reading ("Reading for Care") the interpreter reads to track the "care voice." And finally, in the fourth reading ("Reading for Justice") the interpreter reads to track the "justice voice."

To extend the metaphor, each lens brings into focus different aspects of the narrative; to switch metaphors, each reading amplifies different voices. A given statement may have different meanings depending on the lens, and a meaning may become apparent with one lens that is hidden from view by another. Again, our goal is to be able to identify when justice and care, as we have described them, are articulated, and to understand the experience of self in relationship as filtered through each of these moral perspectives.

The first time the interpreter reads through the conflict his or her attention is focused on the narrator's story as he or she presents it. The goal is to understand the context, the drama (the who, what, where, when, and why of the story); to listen, to attempt to "hear" as clearly as possible the narrator's voice in the story about him/herself, and about morality and moral conflict, that he or she is telling.

The next three readings entail a two step process. First, the reader uses colored pencils to mark passages that represent self (green), care (red), and justice (blue) in the interview text. We have found that this visual technique attunes the reader to the specific languages or voices of the narrator without losing sight of the larger story and context of the conflict.

Second, after reading (and underlining) for self, care, and justice, the reader is asked to fill in summary Worksheets (see Table 2). While the Reading Guide explains the interpretive procedure, the Worksheets provide a place for the reader to document relevant pieces of the text and to make observations and interpretive remarks. The Worksheets are designed to highlight the critical move from the narrator's actual words to a reader's interpretation or summary of them, since they require the reader to substantiate his or her interpretation with quotes from the interview text itself. As such, the Worksheets stand between the Reading Guide (and the reader) and the interview text; hence they provide the tool with which the hermeneutic circle is built.

Table 2

Excerpts from Summary Worksheets

III. THIRD READING—CARE   Summary/Interpretation

    A. Is the Care Orientation articulated?
         How would you characterize care?

    B. If Care is not (clearly) articulated?
         What would constitute care in this conflict?

    C. Does self align with Care? How do you know?
         Is the alignment explicit or implicit?

IV. <u>FOURTH READING—JUSTICE</u>   Summary/Interpretation

    A. <u>Is the Justice Orientation articulated?</u>
       How would you characterize justice?

    B. <u>If Justice is not (clearly) articulated?</u>
       What would constitute justice in this conflict?

    C. <u>Does self align with Justice? How do you know?</u>
       Is the alignment explicit or implicit?

    The final step in the reading process requires the reader to answer a series of summary Coding Questions about his or her understanding of self and the two moral voices in the interview narrative (see Table 3). These questions are used in the summary determination of what we have called "Narrative Types" or "Narrative Strategies," which are described in detail below.

Table 3

Summary Coding Questions

I.   The two moral orientations and how they are represented: (check two)

    1. Is the justice orientation articulated? yes _____   no _____

    2. Is the care orientation articulated? yes _____   no _____

II. The relationship between the two moral orientations: (check one)

    1. Justice predominates _____

    2. Care predominates _____

    3. Both justice and care present, neither predominates _____

III. The Narrative Self:

    1. Does the narrative self express an "alignment" in the conflict? (Consider whether or not the narrator comes down on one side of his or her own values. Does the narrator perceive the values of justice or care in relation to his or her own integrity—so that compromising that set of values would be seen as losing a basic or central sense of self? Finally, this "alignment" can be determined by the narrative self rejecting the values of another.)
       yes _____   no _____

    2. What terms/orientation does the narrator use to frame this "alignment" in the conflict?
       justice _____   care _____   both _____

This Reading Guide assumes that the story of a real-life conflict told by the interviewee can be heard and understood by a careful reader. In our open-ended interview format we have partially assured the coherence of the story by training interviewers to ask the narrator clarifying or activating questions, in addition to standard interview questions about his or her construction of the dilemma, resolution of the problem, and evaluation of his or her decision (see Table 1). We *assume* the possibility of understanding the narrator's story because each person has access to experiences of justice and injustice, care and carelessness. We also assume the importance of these experiences in structuring the experience of self (including self-esteem, self-concept, identity) and the ways people act in relation to one another.

An Illustrative Example

In this section we want to briefly illustrate this method using an excerpt of a narrative from an adolescent girl, Tanya. That interview is reproduced in Table 4; in order to approximate the effect of the three color-coded readings (and markings) we have used CAPITAL LETTERING to indicate "self" (green), *underlining* to indicate "care" (red), and boldface to indicate "justice" (blue).

Table 4

Excerpt from Sample Interview Narrative

I: Can you tell me about a situation where you faced a moral conflict, you had to make a decision, but you weren't sure what was the right thing to do?

R: . . . . when we were at camp, I went to camp with my sister and my cousin, <u>and he was really young, he was like maybe seven, and he got really, really homesick.</u> It was over-night. <u>And he was like, always crying at night and stuff.</u> And we had this camp guide who was really tough and I WAS REALLY AFRAID OF HIM, it was like two years ago and I WAS REALLY AFRAID OF HIM. **And he said, "nobody is allowed to use the phone,"** and so my cousin really wanted to call his parents, (Yeah) and it was kind of up to me to go ask the guy if he could. So, EITHER LIKE I GOT BAWLED OUT BY THIS GUY AND ASKED, OR I DIDN'T DO ANYTHING ABOUT IT, <u>**AND HE WAS MY COUSIN, SO I HAD TO HELP HIM,**</u> SO I WENT AND ASKED THE GUY IF HE COULD USE THE PHONE and he started giving me this lecture about **how there shouldn't be homesickness in the camp.** AND I SAID, "SORRY BUT HE'S ONLY SEVEN." (Yeah!) <u>**And he was really young and so he finally got to use the phone,**</u> so he used the phone. And then we had a camp meeting, and um, and the guy started saying, **"Any kid here who gets homesick shouldn't be here,"** and he didn't say my cousin's name, but like, he was like, almost in tears.

I: Oh, and your cousin was there when he said that? Oh, that wasn't very nice.

R: Yah. It was really mean.

I: When you were in this situation . . . . what kinds of things did you consider in thinking about what to do?

R: WELL, MOSTLY, FIRST OF ALL, WHAT WAS RIGHT AND WRONG. AND THE RIGHT THING TO DO WAS TO GO BECAUSE IT WAS MY COUSIN'S GOOD YOU KNOW. (um, hum) And he wasn't going to die or anything, but, you know, he's afraid to go to camp now, because he's like 9 now (yah), and he doesn't want to go back, and SO I SAID, "THIS GUY CAN INTIMIDATE ME, BUT HE CAN'T BEAT ME UP OR ANYTHING." (Yah) I'LL REALIZE THAT THAT'S JUST THE WAY HE IS, BUT I HAVE TO DO THIS, SO. I mean, he might say no, but it can't hurt asking.

Key:

CAPS = "self"
underline = "care"
bold = "justice"

Tanya, a seventh grader, tells a story about being at camp with her younger cousin who becomes homesick and wishes to talk to his mother.[5] Tanya, struggling with her fear of the counselor and her felt sense of responsibility to act on behalf of her cousin, decides to approach the counselor. In response to the interviewer's question about what she considered when thinking about what to do, she shares what appears to be an internal dialogue about the limits to the counselor's actions. These considerations, feelings, actions, and spoken or internalized thoughts, highlighted by green underlining (here by capitalization) help the reader to locate the "narrative self"; that is, the person as actor in the story of conflict she tells.

After locating self in the narrative, the reader moves through the interview a third time attending to the care voice only. Having read the interview twice already at this point, the reader is aware of the drama and the intentions, thoughts, feelings, and actions of the narrator. Reading for care is not meant to blind the interpreter to these aspects of the drama, but to attune him or her to any evidence that the story told may be one in which care concerns play an active part. That is, the reader actively looks for any evidence that will allow him or her to build an interpretation of the story as one concerned with care.

In this example, Tanya describes the distress suffered by her cousin. From a care perspective this perceived suffering on the part of her cousin explains the imperative Tanya felt to respond—in this case to talk with a counselor regardless of her own fear which she expresses twice, as though for emphasis. She is able to place her cousin's response in perspective ("He wasn't going to die or anything") but remains concerned, and justifies her concern with the fact that he remains afraid of camp a full two years later. The focus on her own fears and the concern for her cousin are gathered as evidence that a care orientation is present in her story.

Finally, the reader moves through the interview a fourth time in an attempt to trace the justice voice. The reader seeks evidence that justice concerns are understood and used. This means that she or he must begin again, since the goal is to gather evidence for a different interpretation of the text.

In this example, Tanya expresses difficulty with the counselor's belief that there should be no homesickness in the camp—clearly an inadequate belief given her cousin's situation. In addition, she is not willing to accept without question the rule that "nobody is allowed to use the phone." Her dismissal of the counselor's rules and beliefs because they do not account for her cousin's particular situation provides evidence for an understanding of justice, but also for its rejection in this form. Tanya's alignment with care becomes more explicit later in the interview, when she states why she felt her choice to act was the right one: "It might not be for you or somebody else, but it's helping out my cousin. And that camp director, it was a rule, but people are more important than rules, you know."

This process—reading with one interpretive lens and then another, rather than with both simultaneously—is a key element of the procedure employed when using the Reading Guide. It reflects evidence that the two moral voices are distinct moral perspectives and that what a reader uses as evidence depends in part on the lens he or she takes to the story. Thus, the same idea may be used as evidence for both a justice reading and a care reading; that is, it may reflect both justice and care concerns. A case in point are Tanya's statements "he was my cousin, so I had to help him," and, "I said, 'Sorry, he's only 7!'" Reading for care, one could assume that these statements reflect her observation of her cousin's pain, and the necessity she felt to respond given the nature of their relationship (in fact, later in the interview she talks about their closeness), or a belief that he was too young to control his fear. On the other hand, reading for justice, Tanya's statements may indicate that she feels she has an obligation, either because she is a cousin or because she is older, to watch over her cousin. Both interpretations are viable and make sense within the parameters of the story told. Yet, since much of the story focuses on Tanya's closeness to her cousin and her understanding of his fear, the care interpretation appears to be a more adequate representation of her experience.[6]

Narrative Types

In attempting to move from a reading of a particular interview narrative of moral conflict and choice, to an extensive summary of that reading recorded on the summary Worksheets, to a final representation of the way in which self and moral voice are manifest and articulated in that narrative, we have developed a coding typology that we have called Narrative Types. These categorical types distinguish between narratives with respect to the ways in which the moral voices of justice and care are represented.

Narrative Types are determined as follows: The Summary Coding Questions sheet (see Table 3) is clearly divided into three sections. A one-digit numerical code[7] is assigned to each of the three sections, depending upon how the reader answers the series of questions in that section. In Section I, which identifies the "Presence" of the two moral voices in the narrative, the reader is asked to answer both questions 1 and 2; hence there are four possible responses that a reader could make to that section, and four corresponding numerical codes:

1 = Both justice and care are present in the narrative.
2 = Care is present in the narrative; justice is not.
3 = Justice is present in the narrative; care is not.
4 = Neither justice nor care is present in the narrative; i.e., the narrative is "uncodable."

In Section II, the reader is asked to answer one of the three questions asked regarding the "Predominance" of the two moral voices in the narrative. "Predominance" in this sense refers to the voice that is most salient in the interview narrative—i.e., the voice that is most fully elaborated. Consequently, three codes are possible for Section II:

1 = The justice voice predominates in the narrative.
2 = The care voice predominates in the narrative.
3 = Neither voice predominates in the narrative, although both are present.

And finally, in Section III, the reader is asked to answer questions relating to the "Alignment" that the "narrative self" expresses vis-à-vis the two moral voices in the interview. "Alignment" in this sense refers to the voice that is most central to self as it is represented in the narrative. The reader is asked to answer question 1 first and, if the answer is "yes," then to go on to question 2. Consequently, four codes are possible for Section III:

1 = Self aligns with justice.
2 = Self aligns with care.
3 = Self aligns with both justice and care.
4 = Self does not express an alignment with either voice in the narrative (i.e., the answer to question 1 is "no").

Table 5 presents the numerical codes associated with each of the three sections on the Summary Coding Questions sheet.

Table 5

The Three Coding Dimensions

I. PRESENCE

	JY	JN
CY	1	2
CN	3	4

II. PREDOMINANCE

1. Justice Predominant	1
2. Care Predominant	2
3. Neither Predominant	3

III. ALIGNMENT

1. Justice Alignment	1
2. Care Alignment	2
3. Align. with both	3
4. No Alignment	4

Thus the overall Narrative Type that summarizes a particular narrative of moral conflict and choice is actually composed of three separate but related dimensions: Presence, Predominance, and Alignment. Each narrative receives a one-digit code for each dimension; hence the overall narrative type is a three-digit code composed of the individual codes for each dimension. There are 17 possible Narrative Types, listed and identified in Table 6.

In sum, then, these Narrative Types provide a simplified tool for data description and analysis. They allow us to represent, in the form of a categorical typology, some of the aspects of narratives of moral conflict and choice relevant to self and the two moral voices, justice and care. As such they allow us to compare groups of narratives—comparisons that would be unwieldy at best, and impossible at worst, using only the summary Worksheets obtained from a reader's use of the Reading Guide. We want to stress, however, that these types are by no means the only way to move from the Worksheets to a representation of the data captured by the reader. But they do provide a useful way to generate and explore interesting hypotheses regarding the ways in which self and moral voice are manifest in narratives of moral conflict and choice.

Table 6

Narrative Types

Both Justice and Care Present	"Pure" Care	"Pure" Justice	Uncodable
111	222	311	400
112	224	314	
113			
114			
121			
122			
123			
124			
131			
132			
133			
134			

Reliability and Validity

Our interest in this method has led us to begin to explore both the reliability and the validity of the Reading Guide and the Narrative Types. However, traditional psychometric conceptions of the reliability and validity of psychological tests and measures (see Anastasi 1976; Chronbach 1949) are based on assumptions which render them inappropriate for interpretive approaches such as the one we outline in this chapter (see also Mishler 1986; Packer 1985). The interest in interpretive methodologies among psychologists at present calls for a redefinition, in hermeneutic terms, of these basic notions of research practice—a rethinking of what reliability and validity mean and what concerns these concepts address (see Rogers 1987; Tappan 1987). We can not claim to offer such a redefinition here. We do hope, however, that our preliminary struggles with these issues will be of interest to others doing similar work, and that they represent a helpful step in the right direction.

The determination of *reliability,* meaning here the ability of two or more different interpreters to agree on their interpretation and understanding of a particular interview narrative, is obviously crucial if an interpretive method such as the one we have described above is to be useful to other researchers and practitioners. The establishment of such agreement among interpreters (i.e., "interpretive agreement") creates a common ground for conversing about the data in question; it assumes that, within acceptable limits, both are reading the text in the same way, or interpreting the same text (see Hirsch 1967).

With respect to the method we have developed, we have thought about such interpretive agreement in two related ways. The first, and most general, focuses on agreement in "reading" (cf. Ricoeur 1979). At this level we feel it is important to determine if two readers (i.e., interpreters), using the Reading Guide, do in fact read the same interview narrative of real-life moral conflict and choice in more or less the same way.

Such agreement can be determined by considering three different pieces of information: 1) the degree to which both readers *underline* the same parts of the interview text for self, justice, and care as they read through the narrative of moral conflict and choice; 2) the degree to which both readers agree in their respective *summaries* of that narrative, as those summaries are captured by the Worksheets; and 3) the degree to which both readers express a similar *interpretation* of the narrative, specifically with respect to how self and the two moral voices are orchestrated or represented, as they discuss their readings of that narrative in conference.

In practice, the first and second kinds of agreement, above, provide specific procedures and techniques that facilitate the attainment of the third kind of agreement. And, in fact, while we have not "measured" levels of agreement in each of these three ways, our experience indicates that among the research team that has developed and used the Reading Guide such agreement is consistently high.

The second, and more precise way in which we have determined interpretive agreement among readers using this method is based on the Narrative Types described above. Because the determination of Narrative Type yields categorical representations on several different dimensions of interest, simple percent agreement figures can be computed between readers with respect to the codes that each records for a given set of interviews. Thus, traditional "inter-judge" reliability assessments can be made.

We have ascertained such percent agreement figures for several different readers, based on a set of "reliability cases"—interviews with adolescents, both males and females, taken from both private suburban high schools and public inner-city high schools. Table 7 presents these figures. Readers 1 (Brown), 2 (Miller), and 3 (Argyris) are all considered "expert" readers (all are authors of the Reading Guide); their reliability figures are based on a set of 14 interviews. Readers 4 and 5 are two female graduate students who were trained to use the Reading Guide over the course of a six-week training session conducted by Miller; their reliability figures are based on a set of 10 interviews. As Table 7 indicates, all of the percent agreement figures, when adjusted for chance using Cohen's (1960) *Kappa* statistic, represent levels of "fair" to "almost perfect" agreement beyond chance (Landis & Koch 1977).

Table 7

Agreement between Readers on Coding Dimensions and Narrative Types (%)

Readers	Presence	Predominance	Alignment	Narrative Type
Expert				
1 and 2	.86 (.62)	.93 (.88)	.79 (.71)	.71 (.67)
1 and 3	.64 (.33)	.79 (.65)	.86 (.81)	.64 (.55)
2 and 3	.79 (.63)	.79 (.76)	.79 (.58)	.64 (.58)
Trained				
4 and 5	.90 (0.0)*	.70 (.42)	.80 (.73)	.50 (.42)
1 and 4	.80 (0.0)*	.90 (.83)	.70 (.59)	.60 (.53)
1 and 5	.90 (.63)	.70 (.52)	.80 (.73)	.70 (.63)

Note: Figures in parentheses are Cohen's (1960) *Kappa* coefficients.
*when $p_o = p_e$, *kappa* $= 0.0$

Given these figures, we are confident that the method we have described can be used "reliably" by different readers using the Narrative Typologies to summarize their interpretations of the same set of narratives. It must be stressed, however, that such reliability figures are of a very different sort than those obtained by using other ostensibly interpretive coding manuals (e.g., Colby & Kohlberg, 1987, Loevinger & Wessler 1970). As we have described above, in the Reading Guide there are no prototypical statements that can be "matched" to statements from the interview text (cf. the "Criterion Judgments" employed by Colby & Kohlberg 1987). Rather, the Reading Guide simply provides a framework that the reader uses to guide him or herself through four different readings of a narrative, as he or she enters the hermeneutic circle by "building" an interpretation of that narrative. The Narrative Types on which the above reliability figures are based entail the most basic and simplified summary of that interpretation—a summary that we believe captures important aspects of the way self and the two moral voices are represented in the narrative, but which clearly can not represent the full complexity of the reader's interpretation and understanding of that narrative.

Turning now to a brief consideration of the *validity* of the interpretive method we have described above, again we are faced with the difficulty of both using traditional terms and categories, and using them in new ways. For example, *construct validity* (see Chronbach & Meehl 1955/1973) is crucial if we are to claim that the information our method yields about a narrative and its narrator is germane to the constructs of self and moral voice, and if differences in Narrative Types make any difference with respect to the way individuals feel, think, and act in real life. Thus our validation efforts have focused exclusively on gathering preliminary information about the construct validity of the Reading Guide.

Chronbach and Meehl (1955/1973) argue that the process of construct valdiation is essentially the same as the general scientific procedure used for developing and confirming (or disconfirming) theories. Thus "a construct is defined implicitly by a network of associations or propositions in which it occurs," (the "nomological net") and "construct validation is possible only when some of the statements in the network lead to predicted relations among variables" (p. 30). One of the central validation procedures for testing hypotheses relating to such constructs is the examination of group differences: "If our understanding of a construct leads us to expect two groups to differ on the test [sic], this expectation may be tested directly" (p. 12).

Thus the first source to which we have turned in assessing the construct validity of our method is a comparison of group differences between adolescent males and females with respect to self and moral voice. While Gilligan has been clear to argue that the justice and care voices are not gender specific, she does hypothesize that they are gender related (Gilligan & Wiggins 1987; see also Gilligan 1977, 1982). Hence our hypothesis was that while a majority of both males and females would show evidence of using and understanding both justice and care in their interview narratives, the justice orientation would predominate among males and the care orientation would predominate among females.

Subjects for this study came from the freshman and sophomore classes of a private independent high school in the Northeast (see Gilligan, Johnston, & Miller 1988). The sample consisted of 37 male and 43 female adolescents, aged 14-16. While data on IQ and SES were not obtained for this sample it is reasonable to assume that the two groups were evenly matched on such variables, since the school is characterized by a high degree of selectivity and status, and hence it draws from a very homogeneous population.

The real-life moral conflict and choice interview narratives from this sample were read by Miller and Argyris. The frequency and percentage of

Narrative Types for both males and females are presented in Table 8. The comparison based on the Presence dimension suggests that, as we expected, the majority of both males and females articulate both the justice and care voices in their narratives, and hence there is no significant difference between males and females vis-à-vis this dimension. There is a significant difference, however, with respect to the Predominance dimension, in support of our initial hypothesis.

Finally, we find the virtually identical distribution in the Alignment dimension particularly interesting. Recall that Alignment indicates the voice that is most central to self as it is represented in the narrative of moral conflict. Thus, the fact that both males and females in the sample align similarly—despite differences in predominance—suggests to us that context may play an important role in determining at least one aspect of moral voice.

The school from which this sample was drawn was, until 10 years ago, all male. It has not, however, changed significantly in philosophy or environment since the decision to admit female students. Consequently, we would characterize the atmosphere of the school as primarily "justice focused," and we would suggest that it may be the power of this kind of context that leads to the similarity in Alignment that these data indicate.[8]

Admittedly these are very preliminary findings and interpretations. They do suggest, however, that the Reading Guide and the Narrative Types illuminate both a gender difference, and a context effect, in the representation of self, justice, and care in these adolescent narratives of real-life moral conflict and choice. Consequently, we would argue that these data provide one piece of evidence that we can use in building our case for the construct validity of the Reading Guide.

Before we conclude this discussion we want to take the opportunity to raise an issue related to the validity of this method that, while related to concerns about construct validity, actually comes *prior* to any such concern. This issue is best captured by the term "interpretive validity." In short, we believe that the information that this method yields is not so much focused on a specific construct (although self and the justice and care voices do, to a certain extent, function as constructs) as it is focused on the construction of a particular interpretation of a narrative—an interpretation that is built on the reader's view of how self and the two moral voices are represented in that narrative.

The issue of validity in interpretation has always been of major concern to both hermeneutic theorists and practitioners (see, for example, Bleicher 1980; Hirsch 1967, 1978; Juhl 1980; Palmer 1969; Spence 1982). It is again the work of Ricoeur (1979), however, that has been of most help to us in thinking through these difficult issues.

Table 8

Frequency of Presence, Predominance, and Alignment Scores for Adolescent Co-ed Sample (Age 13-16)

I. PRESENCE

	1	2	3	
Males	24 (.65)	2 (.05)	11 (.30)	37
Females	32 (.74)	6 (.14)	5 (.12)	43
	56	8	16	80

Note: $X^2 (2, N = 80) = 4.97, p\ .10$

II. PREDOMINANCE

	1	2	3	
Males	26 (.70)	10 (.27)	1 (.03)	37
Females	17 (.40)	17 (.40)	9 (.20)	43
	43	27	10	80

Note: $X^2 (2, N = 80) = 9.69, p\ .01$

III. ALIGNMENT

	1	2	3	4	
Males	11 (.30)	6 (.16)	2 (.05)	18 (.49)	37
Females	11 (.26)	10 (.23)	2 (.04)	20 (.47)	43
	22	16	4	38	80

Note: $X^2 (2, N = 80) = 0.66, p\ .90$

Recall that Ricoeur (1979) argues that the modern-day synonym for *Verstehen* is "guessing," and for *Erklaren* it is "validation": both are involved, he claims, in the process of reading. Hence striving for validity in interpretation necessarily involves taking seriously the dialectic between guessing and validation. In fact, argues Ricoeur, this is precisely what the "hermeneutic circle" entails from the start:

> We are [now] prepared to give an acceptable meaning to the famous concept of a *hermeneutical circle*. Guess and validation are in a sense circularly related as subjective and objective approaches to the text. But this circle is not a vicious circularity. It would be a cage if we were unable to escape the kind of "self-confirmability" which, according to Hirsch (1967), threatens this relation between guess and validation. To the procedures of validation also belong procedures of invalidation similar to the criteria of falsifiability emphasized by Karl Popper (1959) ... The role of falsification is played here by the conflict between competing interpretations. An interpretation must not only be probable, but more probable than another. There are criteria of relative superiority which may easily be derived from the logic of subjective probability.
>
> In conclusion, if it is true that there is always more than one way of construing a text, it is not that all interpretations are equal and may be assimilated to so-called "rules of thumb." The text is a limited field of possible constructions. The logic of validation allows us to move between the two limits of dogmatism and skepticism. It is always possible to argue for or against an interpretation, to confront interpretations, to arbitrate between them, and to seek for an agreement, even if this agreement remains beyond our reach. (Ricoeur 1979, 91)

In practice, the "logic of validation" is operationalized most clearly when readers are able to discuss their respective interpretations of the same interview text. Ample opportunity exists at that point for alternative interpretations to be entertained, and for the relative probabilities of each to be considered. In fact, we would recommend that whenever the Reading Guide is used in empirical research at least two readers should read each narrative. Once each has read the interview then it can be discussed between them and differences in interpretation can be addressed. At this point, ways of choosing between them or reconciling them in terms of a new interpretation can be considered or created. Only in this way can the dialectic between guess and validation that Ricoeur (1979) emphasizes be fully maintained.

Discussion and Conclusion

The goal of this chapter has been to outline the interpretive method we have developed for reading complex narratives of moral conflict and choice; a method that represents both equality and attachment as dimensions of human relationship. Given that we continue to face the challenge of developing and refining such a method, we will conclude by discussing some of the implications that we believe flow from this effort—some of which will provide the direction for our ongoing work.

First, our interest in questions of interpretive validity suggests to us the need to create a format for synthesizing the interpretations recorded on the Worksheets in order that more of the richness and complexity of the narrative can be included, while at the same time allowing for a comparison of both different narratives and different interpretations of the same narrative. We are exploring the idea that readers would write a "narrative paragraph" summarizing a given interview, the construction of which might be guided by a set of questions that would be both theoretically derived, and informed by our experience in discovering what questions facilitate "better" (i.e., more valid) interpretations.

A second implication is related to this issue. As we have indicated, it is in practice, and in dialogue, that we make judgments about valid and invalid interpretations. One way for us to further develop our methodology is to reflect on that practice itself by, for example, taping our conference discussions about individual interviews. This would allow us to make our validity *criteria* not only more explicit, but also to subject them to the same kind of scrutiny to which we subject our *interpretations*.[9]

A third implication of this method, as we have argued, is that it allows us to avoid the confining and confusing dualities of traditional theory and research on moral development. Thus, for example, we have tried to avoid the rigid opposition of egoism to altruism, thought to feeling, and justice to care. In addition, we believe that this method allows us to avoid the traditional distinction between moral judgment and moral action.

When we first began interviewing people about their real-life moral conflicts, we obtained more information about how interviewees reasoned about their conflicts than we did about the unfolding narrative of the conflict itself. We found those interviews to be long on interviewees' interpretations but short on the descriptions of the events they were interpreting. In turn, we found it difficult to build interpretations that we could connect to the interviewees' real-life experience. It was as though we had asked the interviewee to perform a monologue, with only very lightly sketched supporting characters, and very little information about what they, or any one else, actually *did*.

Consequently, we redesigned our interview questions (see Table 1). We now ask interviewees to be more specific about the situation in which they experienced themselves in conflict and the actions they took when faced with that situation. In short, we have asked our interviewees to become more elaborate storytellers—to draw richer portraits of both themselves and the other characters in the conflict and—this is crucial—to recount *actual dialogue* from the situation. In a sense we are asking interviewees to *reenact* their conflict in the interview setting.

This has led us to a number of important insights regarding the nature of moral action. First, the stories and dialogues we have obtained vividly illustrate that very few people face or solve moral conflicts in a vacuum. Rather, the person appears to function in an everyday, ongoing context of relationships.

Second, moral action and interaction is much more complex than it has been portrayed in the literature on moral judgment and moral action (see, for example, Kohlberg 1984). We find that people act in at least two contexts that are crucial to our understanding of their moral conflicts, and hence to our interpretation of their moral voice. One is an information-gathering context— moral voice is often revealed by what people feel they need to know from others to solve a conflict and how they go about obtaining that information.

The other is the context in which people implement their decisions in the face of a moral conflict. Both contexts involve a complex series of actions. At times we find that the dialogues people have with themselves and with each other are highly skilled, yet paradoxical and contradictory. For example, people facing difficult, complex moral choices often act in ways that produce the very consequences they wished to avoid in the first place (Argyris 1987).

These findings challenge us to create frameworks that can be used to describe the complex, frequently paradoxical and ironic, nature of moral action. They also challenge us to produce knowledge that is of use to other human beings, not only in generating new insight, but also in helping people to *act* differently. For, as John Macmurray (1957) argues, "we should substitute the 'I do' for the 'I think' as our starting-point and centre of reference; and do our thinking from the standpoint of action" (p. 84).

Thus, in the last analysis, our hope for this method is that it enables and facilitates research that does not sacrifice complexity to duality, usefulness to precision, and action to judgment.

Chapter 5

Notes

1. The first two authors shared primary responsibility for the preparation of this chapter. They are listed in alphabetical order.

The work reported here was supported in part by grants from the Cleveland Foundation, the Bardige Foundation, and the Joseph S. Klingenstein Foundation.

Thanks to Martin Packer and Annie Rogers for their helpful comments on earlier versions of this manuscript.

2. In a similar sense we have emphasized, following Mishler (1986), the importance of considering the context from which the interview has come. Specifically, we would argue that while an individual interview can only be understood in terms of the whole context of which it is part, at the same time a full understanding of that context can only be grasped by understanding the meaning it holds for individual interviewees.

3. Specifically the problem of "validity in interpretation," which we will consider briefly later in this chapter.

4. After this chapter was written we discovered two recent and very insightful treatments of Ricoeur's work with respect to the psychological and developmental interpretation of interview texts—pieces that, in many respects, are quite similar to our own reading of his work (see Freeman 1985; Honey 1987).

5. Because the first reading (reading for the story or the plot) requires a full text, and because space limitation prevents us from presenting and analyzing Tanya's complete narrative, we move directly to the second reading—reading for self.

6. See Gilligan, Brown and Rogers (in press) for a more complete analysis and interpretation of this case.

7. A note on the use of the term "code" here: In developing data analysis techniques based on these "Narrative Types" we have used numerical "codes" to summarize and represent the interpretation of the reader. The term "code" thus refers only to this kind of categorical summary and representation—not to the process of interpreting and analyzing the narrative as a whole.

8. We have evidence from other studies in progress that provide additional support for our hunch that the Alignment dimension may be especially sensitive to context. In particular, when adolescent girls attending an all-girls school are compared with the adolescent girls attending the coed school, there is a significant difference in the Alignment distribution. That is, the girls from the all-girls school show significantly more alignment with care than the girls from the coed school (54% vs. 23%, X^2 [3 $\underline{N}$ = 89] = 20.8 $\underline{p} < .001$). Given our knowledge of, and experience with these two schools, we interpret this difference as indicating that the context of the all-girls school may be more "care focused" than the context of the coed school.

9. We are indebted to Martin Packer for this recommendation.

References

Anastasi, A. 1976. *Psychological testing* (4th ed.). New York: MacMillan.

Argyris, D. 1987. *Exploring moral practice.* Unpublished manuscript, Harvard University.

Bleicher, J. 1980. *Contemporary hermeneutics.* London: Routledge & Kegan Paul.

Brown, L., Argyris, D., Attanucci, J., Bardige, B., Gilligan, C., Johnston, K., Miller, B., Osborne, R., Ward, J., Wiggins, G., & Wilcox, D. 1987. *A guide to reading narratives of moral conflict and choice for self and moral voice.* Cambridge: The Center for the Study of Gender, Education, and Human Development, Harvard University (Monograph #1).

Chronbach, L. 1949. *Essentials of psychological testing* (3rd ed.). New York: Harper & Row.

Chronbach, L. & Meehl, P. 1973. Construct validity in psychological tests. In P. Meehl, *Psychodiagnosis: Selected papers.* New York: W.W. Norton. (Original work published 1955)

Cohen, J. 1960. A coefficient of agreement for nominal scales. *Educational and Psychological Measurement, 20,* 37-46.

Colby, A. & Kohlberg, L. 1987. *The measurement of moral judgment.* New York: Cambridge University Press.

Dilthey, W. 1900/1976. The development of hermeneutics. In W. Dilthey, *Selected writings* (H. Rickman, Ed. & Trans.). Cambridge: Cambridge University Press.

Freeman, M. 1985. Paul Ricoeur on interpretation: The model of the text and the idea of development. *Human Development, 28,* 295-312.

Gadamer, H. 1975. *Truth and method.* New York: Crossroad.

Gadamer, H. 1976. *Philosophical hermeneutics* (D. Linge, Ed. & Trans.). Berkeley: University of California Press.

Gibbs, J. & Widaman, K. 1982. *Social intelligence: Measuring the development of sociomoral reflection.* Englewood-Cliffs: Prentice-Hall.

Gilligan, C. 1977. In a different voice: Women's conceptions of self and of morality. *Harvard Educational Review,* 47, 481-517.

Gilligan, C. 1982. *In a different voice: Psychological theory and women's development.* Cambridge: Harvard University Press.

Gilligan, C. 1983. Do the social sciences have an adequate theory of moral development? In N. Haan, R. Bellah, P. Rabinow, & W. Sullivan (Eds.), *Social science as moral inquiry.* New York: Columbia University Press.

Gilligan, C. 1986. Remapping the moral domain: New images of self in relationship. In T. Heller, M. Sosna, & D. Wellber (Eds.), *Reconstructing individualism: Autonomy, individualism, and the self in Western thought.* Stanford: Stanford University Press.

Gilligan, C. 1987. Moral orientation and moral development. In E. Kittay & D. Meyers (Eds.), *Women and moral theory.* New York: Rowman & Littlefield.

Gilligan, C., & Wiggins, G. 1987. The origins of morality in early childhood relationships. In J. Kagan & S. Lamb (Eds.), *The emergence of morality in young children.* Chicago: The University of Chicago Press.

Gilligan, C., Brown, L., & Rogers, A. (in press). Psyche embedded: A place for body, relationships, and culture in personality theory. In A. Rabin (Ed.), *Studying persons and lives.* New York: Springer-Verlag.

Gilligan, C., Johnston, D.K., & Miller, B. 1988. *Moral voice, adolescent development, and secondary education: A study at the Green River School.* Cambridge: The Center for the Study of Gender, Education, and Human Development, Harvard University (Monograph #3).

Hirsch, E. 1967. *Validity in interpretation.* New Haven: Yale University Press.

Hirsch, E. 1978. *The aims of interpretation.* Chicago: The University of Chicago Press.

Honey, M. 1987. The interview as text: Hermeneutics considered as a model for analyzing the clinically informed research interview. *Human Development,* 30, 69-82.

Johnston, K. 1985. *Two moral orientations—Two problem-solving strategies: Adolescents' solutions to dilemmas in fables.* Unpublished doctoral dissertation, Harvard University.

Juhl, P. 1980. *Interpretation: An essay in the philosophy of literary criticism.* Princeton: Princeton University Press.

Kohlberg, L. 1984. *Essays in moral development, Volume II: The psychology of moral development.* San Francisco: Harper & Row.

Landis, J.R., & Koch, G. 1977. The measurement of observer agreement for categorical data. *Biometrics*, 33, 159-174.

Loevinger, J. & Wessler, R. 1970. *Measuring ego development: Construction and use of a sentence completion test*. San Francisco: Jossey-Bass.

Macmurray, J. 1957. *The self as agent*. Atlantic Highlands, NJ: Humanities Press.

Mishler, E. 1979. Meaning in context: Is there any other kind? *Harvard Educational Review*, 53, 125-145.

Mishler, E. 1986. *Research interviewing: Context and narrative*. Cambridge, MA: Harvard University Press.

Nussbaum, M. 1986. *The fragility of goodness*. Cambridge: Cambridge University Press.

Packer, M. 1985. Hermeneutic inquiry in the study of human conduct. *American Psychologist*, 40, 1081-1093.

Palmer, R. 1969. *Hermeneutics: Interpretation theory in Schleiermacher, Dilthey, Heidegger, and Gadamer*. Evanston: Northwestern University Press.

Popper, K. 1959. *The logic of scientific discovery*. New York: Basic Books.

Rest, J. 1979. *Development in judging moral issues*. Minneapolis: The University of Minnesota Press.

Ricoeur, P. 1979. The model of a text: Meaningful action considered as a text. In P. Rabinow & W. Sullivan (Eds.), *Interpretive social science: A reader*. Berkeley: University of California Press.

Rogers, A. 1987. *Gender differences in moral thinking: A validity study of two moral orientations*. Unpublished doctoral dissertation, Washington University.

Spence, D. 1982.*Narrative truth and historical truth: Meaning and interpretation in psychoanalysis*. New York: Norton.

Tappan, M. 1987. *Hermeneutics and moral development: A developmental analysis of short-term change in moral functioning during late adolescence*. Unpublished doctoral dissertation, Harvard University.

Taylor, C. 1979. Interpretation and the sciences of man. In P. Rabinow & W. Sullivan (Eds.), *Interpretive social science: A reader*. Berkeley: University of California Press.

JOURNAL OF SOCIAL ISSUES
VOLUME 28, NUMBER 2, 1972

Sex-Role Stereotypes: A Current Appraisal[1]

Inge K. Broverman

Worcester State Hospital

Susan Raymond Vogel

Brandeis University Mental Health Center

Donald M. Broverman

Worcester State Hospital

Frank E. Clarkson

Worcester State Hospital

Paul S. Rosenkrantz

College of the Holy Cross

Consensus about the differing characteristics of men and women exists across groups differing in sex, age, marital status, and educa-

[1]This work was in part supported by Contract No. N I H - 71 - 2038 with the National Institutes of Health, Department of Health, Education and Welfare.

tion. Masculine characteristics are positively valued more often than feminine characteristics. Positively-valued masculine traits form a cluster entailing competence; positively-valued feminine traits reflect warmth-expressiveness. Sex-role definitions are incorporated into the self-concepts of both men and women; moreover, these sex-role differences are considered desirable by college students and healthy by mental health professionals. Individual differences in sex related self-concepts are related to sex-role relevant behaviors such as achieved and ideal family size. Sex-role perceptions also vary as a function of maternal employment.

Sex-role standards can be defined as the sum of socially designated behaviors that differentiate between men and women. Traditionally, psychologists have uncritically accepted sex roles as essential to personality, development and function. Thus psychopathologists have considered gender identity to be a crucial factor in personal adjustment, with disturbances in adjustment often attributed to inadequate gender identity. Developmentalists tend to focus upon the conditions and processes which facilitate successful internalization of appropriate sex-role standards. The positive values of sex-role standards have rarely been questioned.

Recently, however, investigators have expressed concern over possible detrimental effects of sex-role standards upon the full development of capabilities of men and women (Blake, 1968; Davis, 1967; Hartley, 1961; Horner, 1969; Maccoby, 1963; Rossi, 1964). Traditional sex-role patterns are also being challenged by the new feminist movement. During such a period of revaluation, there is need for a close systematic scrutiny of the actual content of sex-role standards and an examination of the influence that these standards have upon individual behaviors. For the past six years we have been engaged in programmatic research examining the nature and effects of sex-role standards in our contemporary society. As psychologists with varying theoretical backgrounds, we share the conviction that existing sex-role standards exert real pressures upon individuals to behave in prescribed ways; we share also a strong curiosity as to what these standards consist of, how they develop, and what their consequences are.

It appeared in the mid 1960s that traditional sex-role patterns were in a state of flux, and we anticipated that a corresponding fluidity would appear in definitions of sex roles. As a first step toward determining these definitions, we devised a questionnaire that assesses individual perceptions of "typical" masculine and feminine behavior (Rosenkrantz, Vogel, Bee, Broverman, & Broverman, 1968). This questionnaire has now been administered to almost a thousand subjects, providing normative indices of the   content   of sex-role standards. In addition, individual differences in sex-role perception have been related to a number of independent variables, thus providing some tentative answers to questions about the antecedents and consequents of varying perceptions of sex roles.

Our findings, culled from a number of studies, lead to the following broad conclusions:

1. A strong consensus about the differing characteristics of men and women exists across groups which differ in sex, age, religion, marital status, and educational level.

2. Characteristics ascribed to men are positively valued more often than characteristics ascribed to women. The positively-valued masculine traits form a cluster of related behaviors which entail competence, rationality, and assertion; the positively-valued feminine traits form a cluster which reflect warmth and expressiveness.

3. The sex-role definitions are implicitly and uncritically accepted to the extent that they are incorporated into the self-concepts of both men and women. Moreover, these sex-role differences are considered desirable by college students, healthy by mental health professionals, and are even seen as ideal by both men and women.

4. Individual differences in sex-role self-concepts are associated with (a) certain sex-role relevant behaviors and attitudes such as actual and desired family size, and (b) certain antecedent conditions such as mother's employment history.

These findings will be discussed in detail following a description of our instrument and its development.

DEVELOPMENT OF THE SEX-ROLE QUESTIONNAIRE

Since our concern was with measuring current sex-role perceptions, we rejected traditional masculinity-feminity scales such as the California Psychological Inventory (CPI)(Gough, 1957) precisely because these scales are based on traditional notions of sex-appropriate behaviors and interests, which we suspected might no longer be relevant. Our concern was with the traits and behaviors currently assigned to men and women. Hence we developed our own instrument. Approximately 100 men and women enrolled in three undergraduate psychology classes were asked to list all the characteristics, attributes, and behaviors on which they thought men and women differed. From these listings, all of the items which occurred at least twice ($N =$ 122) were selected for inclusion in the questionnaire. These items span a wide range of content, e.g., interpersonal sensitivity, emotionality, aggressiveness, dependence-independence, maturity, intelligence, activity level, gregariousness.

Many of the earlier studies demonstrating the existence of sex-role stereotypes required subjects to select from a list those traits which characterize men and those which characterize women (Fernberger, 1948; Sherriffs & Jarrett, 1953; Sherriffs & McKee, 1957). In contrast, we conceptualized sex roles as the degree to which men and women are perceived to possess any particular trait. Therefore the 122 items were put into bipolar form with the two poles separated by 60 points.

Men and women subjects in various other samples were then given the questionnaire with instructions to indicate the extent to which each item characterized an adult man (masculinity response), an adult woman (femininity response), and themselves (self response). The order of presentation of masculinity and femininity instructions was reversed for approximately half the Ss within each sample; however, the self instructions were always given last in order to obtain self-descriptions within a masculinity-femininity context.

Scoring the Sex-Role Questionnaire

The scoring procedure for the instrument, developed in our first study, was based upon responses from 74 college men and 80 college women (Rosenkrantz et al., 1968). The concept of sex-role stereotype implies extensive agreement among people as to the characteristic differences between men and women. Therefore, those items on which at least 75% agreement existed among Ss of each sex as to which pole was more descriptive of the average man than the average woman, or vice versa, were termed "stereotypic." Forty-one items met this criterion. To determine the extent of the perceived difference, correlated t tests were computed between the masculinity response (average response to the male instructions) and the femininity response to each of the items; on each of the 41 stereotypic items the difference between these two responses was significant ($p <$ .001) in both the samples of men and women. The sterotypic items are listed in Table 1.

Forty-eight of the remaining items had differences between the average masculinity response and the average femininity response that were significant beyond the .05 level of confidence in each sample, but the agreement as to the direction of the differences was less than 75%. These items were termed "dif-

TABLE 1
STEREOTYPIC SEX-ROLE ITEMS
(RESPONSES FROM 74 COLLEGE MEN AND 80 COLLEGE WOMEN)

Competency Cluster: Masculine pole is more desirable

Feminine	Masculine
Not at all aggressive	Very aggressive
Not at all independent	Very independent
Very emotional	Not at all emotional
Does not hide emotions at all	Almost always hides emotions
Very subjective	Very objective
Very easily influenced	Not at all easily influenced
Very submissive	Very dominant
Dislikes math and science very much	Likes math and science very much
Very excitable in a minor crisis	Not at all excitable in a minor crisis
Very passive	Very active
Not at all competitive	Very competitive
Very illogical	Very logical
Very home oriented	Very worldly
Not at all skilled in business	Very skilled in business
Very sneaky	Very direct
Does not know the way of the world	Knows the way of the world
Feelings easily hurt	Feelings not easily hurt
Not at all adventurous	Very adventurous
Has difficulty making decisions	Can make decisions easily
Cries very easily	Never cries
Almost never acts as a leader	Almost always acts as a leader
Not at all self-confident	Very self-confident
Very uncomfortable about being aggressive	Not at all uncomfortable about being aggressive
Not at all ambitious	Very ambitious
Unable to separate feelings from ideas	Easily able to separate feelings from ideas
Very dependent	Not at all dependent
Very conceited about appearance	Never conceited about appearance
Thinks women are always superior to men	Thinks men are always superior to women
Does not talk freely about sex with men	Talks freely about sex with men

Warmth-Expressiveness Cluster: Feminine pole is more desirable

Feminine	Masculine
Doesn't use harsh language at all	Uses very harsh language
Very talkative	Not at all talkative
Very tactful	Very blunt
Very gentle	Very rough
Very aware of feelings of others	Not at all aware of feelings of others
Very religious	Not at all religious
Very interested in own appearance	Not at all interested in own appearance
Very neat in habits	Very sloppy in habits
Very quiet	Very loud
Very strong need for security	Very little need for security
Enjoys art and literature	Does not enjoy art and literature at all
Easily expresses tender feelings	Does not express tender feelings at all easily

ferentiating" items. The remaining 33 items were termed "non-differentiating."

PERVASIVENESS OF SEX-ROLE STEREOTYPES

Numerous investigators have noted the existence of sex-role stereotypes, i.e., consensual beliefs about the differing characteristics of men and women. These stereotypes are widely held (Lunneborg, 1970; Seward, 1946), persistent (Fernberger, 1948), and highly traditional (Komarovsky, 1950; McKee & Sherriffs, 1959). Despite the apparent fluidity of sex-role definition in contemporary society as contrasted with the previous decades, our own findings to date confirm the existence of pervasive and persistent sex-role stereotypes.

In our initial study (Rosenkrantz et al., 1968) Ss were drawn from a variety of New England institutions of higher learning, e.g., a two-year community college, a four-year city college, women's and men's schools, and parochial schools. Although the subsamples clearly differed with respect to religion and social class, our analyses indicated that they did not differ substantially from each other with respect to sex-role perceptions. Furthermore, the average masculinity responses (responses to "adult man" instructions) given by the male subjects to the 122 items correlated nearly perfectly with the average masculinity responses given by the female subjects ($r = .96$). The mean femininity responses (responses to "adult woman" instructions) given by the men and those given by women were also highly correlated ($r = .95$). In addition, the means of the masculinity responses given by men and women were almost identical, as were the mean femininity responses given by the two groups. Thus, we must conclude that sex-role stereotypes cut across the sex, socioeconomic class, and religion of the respondents, at least in individuals who seek education beyond the high school level.

Responses to the sex-role questionnaire have now been obtained from 599 men and 383 women, both married and single, who range in age from 17 to 60 years and in education from the elementary school level to the advanced graduate degree level. These subjects were divided by sex and into three age groups, 17–24 years, 25–44 years, 45–56 years, making a total of six groups. Educational level varied considerably in the four older groups, while it was relatively homogeneous within the two youngest. Marital status also varied among the age groups;

the oldest groups were comprised predominantly of married individuals (most frequently, parents of college students), the middle age groups consisted of both married and single individuals (including priests and nuns), while most subjects in the youngest age groups were single.

Within each of these six groups, the proportion of subjects agreeing that a given pole was more characteristic of men, or of women, was calculated for each item. All items on which agreement differed significantly from chance at the .02 level of confidence or better were noted. Seventy-four of the items met the criterion in at least four of the six different groups; 47 of the items were significant in all six groups. Thus, although some variation exists from group to group, high consensuality about the differing characteristics of men and women was found on a considerable number of items, and this was independent of age, sex, religion, education level, or marital status.

SOCIAL DESIRABILITY OF THE STEREOTYPIC ITEMS

The literature indicates that men and masculine characteristics are more highly valued in our society than are women and feminine characteristics (Dinitz, Dynes, & Clarke, 1954; Fernberger, 1948; Kitay, 1940; Lynn, 1959; McKee & Sherriffs, 1957, 1959; Sherriffs & Jarrett, 1953; Sherriffs & McKee, 1957; Smith, 1939; White, 1950). Moreover, both boys and girls between 6 and 10 years express greater preference for masculine things and activities than for feminine activities (Brown, 1958); similarly between 5 to 12 times as many women than men recall having wished they were of the opposite sex (Gallup, 1955; Terman, 1938). Sears, Maccoby, and Levin (1957) report that mothers of daughters only are happier about a new pregnancy than are mothers of sons. Investigators have also found that the interval between the birth of the first child and conception of the second is longer when the first child is a boy than when it is a girl; and that the likelihood of having a third child is greater if the first two children are both girls than both boys (Pohlman, 1969).

The valuation, or social desirability, of the characteristics designated as masculine or feminine by the questionnaire responses follows this same pattern: The masculine poles of the various items were more often considered to be socially desirable than the feminine poles. This differential valuation of sex-related characteristics was observed in several different studies. For instance, two different samples of students, one from a Catholic liberal arts college for men and one from an Eastern women's college, indicated the pole of each item that they considered to be the more socially desirable behavior for the population at large (Rosenkrantz et. al., 1968). Of the 41 items defined as stereotypic, 29 had the masculine pole chosen as more desirable by a majority of each sample. We have termed these "male-valued" items; the remaining 12 items are termed "female-valued." Moreover, the men and women showed high agreement about which poles were socially desirable (r between men and women = .96).

Additional samples of men and women were given the questionnaire with instructions to indicate that point on each item scale which they considered most desirable for an adult, sex unspecified. The average response was computed for each item for the sexes separately. The point most desirable for an adult was found to be closer to the masculine pole on the same 29 stereotypic items on which the masculine pole was considered more socially desirable by the previous samples. Also, men and women once more showed high agreement about the point on each stereotypic item that was most socially desirable for an adult.

Content of the Sex-Role Stereotypes

To explore further the dimensions reflected by the stereotypic items, factor analyses were performed separately on the masculinity and feminity responses in both a sample of men and a sample of women. Each analysis produced two initial factors accounting, on the average, for 61% of the total extractable communality. The two factors in all four analyses divided the stereotypic items into those on which the male pole is more socially desirable versus those on which the female pole is more socially desirable. These results indicated that the stereotypic items consist of two orthogonal domains, i.e., male-valued items and female-valued items.

The male-valued items seem to us to reflect a "competency" cluster. Included in this cluster are attributes such as being independent, objective, active, competitive, logical, skilled in business, worldly, adventurous, able to make decisions easily, self-confident, always acting as a leader, ambitious. A relative *absence* of these traits characterizes the stereotypic perception of women; that is, relative to men, women are perceived to be dependent, subjective, passive, noncompetitive, illogical, etc.

The female-valued stereotypic items, on the other hand, consist of attributes such as gentle, sensitive to the feelings of others, tactful, religious, neat, quiet, interested in art and literature, able to express tender feelings. These items will be referred to as the "warmth and expressiveness" cluster. Men are stereotypically perceived as lacking in these characteristics, relative to women.

SELF-CONCEPTS AND SEX-ROLE STEREOTYPES

These factorial distinctions between the male-valued and female-valued components of the sex-role stereotypes have important implications for the self-concepts of men and women.

The social desirability of an item is known to increase the likelihood of that item's being reported as self-descriptive on personality tests (Edwards, 1957). This tendency to align one's self with socially desirable behaviors, together with the fact that the feminine stereotype entails many characteristics that are less socially desirable than those of the masculine stereotype, implies that women ought to reject the negatively-valued feminine characteristics in their self-reports. However, our findings indicate that women incorporate the negative aspects of femininity (relative incompetence, irrationality, passivity, etc.) into their self-concepts along with the positive feminine aspects (warmth and expressiveness).

In a study of college men and women (Rosenkrantz et al., 1968), the mean self-concept scores of the men over the 41 stereotypic items were significantly different from the mean self-concept scores of the women ($p < .001$), indicating that male and female Ss clearly perceived themselves as differing along a dimension of stereotypic sex differences. However, the women's self-concepts were also significantly less feminine than their perceptions of women in general. Similarly, the self-concepts of the men were significantly less masculine than their perceptions of the "average" man.

IDEAL SEX-ROLES

Our evidence and that of others (Elman, Press, & Rosenkrantz, 1970; Fernberger, 1948; McKee & Sherriffs, 1959) suggest that the existing stereotypic differences between men and women are approved of and even idealized by large segments of our society. One hundred thirty-seven college men were given the questionnaire with instructions to indicate that point for each item which is most desirable for an adult man, and that point which is most desirable for an adult woman. The number of Ss who agreed that a particular pole of each item is more desirable for men or women was first computed. On 71 of the 122 items agreement was significantly different from chance ($p < .001$). The masculine pole was judged more desirable ($p < .01$) for men than women on 28 of the 29 male-valued stereotypic items (competency cluster); similar agreement reaches the .07 level of confidence on the remaining stereotypic items. These data indicate that college men feel that it is desirable for women to be less independent, less rational, less ambitious, etc., than men.

The 12 stereotypic female-valued items (warmth-expressiveness cluster), however, present a different picture. On only 7 of the 12 items was there significant agreement ($p < .01$) that the feminine pole is more socially desirable for women than for men; on one item, the agreement reaches the $p < .07$ level; on the remaining 4 items there is no significant agreement, i.e., the socially desirable adult pole is rated desirable as often for men as for women. Thus these male Ss appear to reserve for men those masculine traits which are socially desirable for adults in general, and also to consider 40% of the desirable feminine characteristics as equally desirable for men.

Again it is important to know not only the extent of agreement among Ss as to whether a trait is more desirable for men or for women, but also whether there is a significant difference between the amount of each trait assigned to men and women. Hence, the mean point at which each trait was considered most desirable for men and women, respectively, was computed for each of the stereotypic items. On the 29 male-valued traits, the difference between the means was 9.82; on the female-valued characteristics, the mean difference was 4.94. The t test between these two differences was significant ($p < .01$). This sample of college men, then, perceives male-valued traits as significantly less desirable for women than are female-valued traits for men.

Elman et al. (1970) investigated ideal sex-role concepts of both men and women. Using a shortened version of our questionnaire which included 10 male-valued and 10 female-valued stereotypic items, they asked both men and women to indicate that point on each item which is ideal for men and for women, respectively. Their results indicate that the concepts of the ideal man and the ideal woman in both men and women subjects closely parallel the male and female sex-role stereotypes. The ideal woman is perceived as significantly less aggressive, less independent, less dominant, less active, more emotional, having greater difficulty in making decisions, etc., than the ideal man; the ideal man is perceived as significantly less religious, less neat, less gentle, less aware of the feelings of others, less expressive, etc., than the ideal woman. Both greater competence in men than in women, and greater warmth and expressiveness in women than in men, then, are apparently desirable in our contemporary society. Furthermore, Elman et. al. and our own results suggest that the college population, a group which tends to be critical of traditional social norms and conventions, nonetheless believes that the existing sex-role stereotypes are desirable.

Sex-Role Stereotypes and Judgments of Mental Health

The literature consistently points to a positive relationship between the social desirability of behaviors and clinical ratings of the same behaviors in terms of normality-abnormality (Cowen, Staiman, & Wolitzky, 1961), adjustment (Wiener, Blumberg, Segman, & Cooper, 1959); and health-sickness (Kogan, Quinn, Ax, & Ripley, 1957). Given the relationship existing between masculine versus feminine characteristics and social desirability, on the one hand, and social desirability and mental health on the other, we expected that clinicians would maintain distinctions in their concepts of healthy behavior in men and women paralleling stereotypic sex differences. Secondly, we predicted that behavioral attributes which are regarded as healthy for an adult, sex unspecified, and presumably indicative of an ideal health pattern will more often be considered by clinicians as healthy for men than for women. This latter prediction was derived from the assumption that an abstract notion of health (adult, sex unspecified) will tend to be more influenced by the greater social desirability of masculine stereotypic characteristics than by the lesser desirability of feminine stereotypic traits (Broverman, Broverman, Clarkson, Rosenkrantz, & Vogel, 1970).

The sample in this study consisted of 79 practicing mental health clinicians: clinical psychologists, psychiatrists, and psychiatric social workers. There were 46 men, 31 of whom held PhD or MD degrees, and 33 women, 18 with doctoral degrees. Their ages ranged from 23 to 55 years, and their experience from an internship to extensive professional practice. The clinicians were given the sex-role questionnaire with one of three sets of instructions: *male* instructions asked respondents to "think of normal, adult men, and then indicate on each item that pole to which a mature, healthy, socially competent adult man would be closer"; *female* instructions were to describe "a mature, healthy, socially competent adult woman"; finally *adult* instructions asked for the description of "a healthy, mature, socially competent adult person." Ss were asked to think of the poles of each item in terms of direction, rather than in terms of extremes of behavior.

The results of this study, concerning the stereotypic items, indicated that men and women clinicians did not differ from each other in their descriptions of adults, women, and men, respectively. Furthermore, within each set of instructions there was high agreement as to which pole reflected the more healthy behavior, indicating that these clinicians did have generalized concepts of mental health. We also found high agreement between the pole judged as more healthy for an adult by the clinicians and the pole chosen as more desirable for adults by college students ($\chi^2 = 23.64$; $p < .01$). This confirms the positive relationship between professional concepts of mental health and conceptions of social desirability held by lay people which has been reported by other investigators (Cowen et al., 1961; Kogan et al., 1957; Wiener et al., 1959).

Comparisons of the clinicians' judgments of the healthy men and the healthy women on the competency cluster indicated that the desirable masculine pole was ascribed to the healthy man significantly more often than to the healthy woman (on 25 out of 27 items). However, only about half of the socially desirable feminine characteristics (warmth-expressiveness cluster) were ascribed more often to women than to men (7 out of 11 items). On the face of it, the finding that clinicians tend to ascribe the male-valued, competency cluster traits more often to healthy men than to healthy women may seem trite. However, a consideration of the content of these items reveals a powerful, negative assessment of women. In effect, clinicians are suggesting that healthy women differ from healthy men by being more submissive, less independent, less adventurous, less objective, more easily influenced, less aggressive, less competitive, more excitable in minor crises, more emotional, more conceited about their appearance, and having their feelings more easily hurt.

The clinicians' ratings of a healthy adult and a healthy man did not differ from each other. However, a significant difference did exist between the ratings of the healthy adult and the healthy woman. Our hypothesis that a double standard of health exists for men and women was thus confirmed: the general standard of health (adult, sex-unspecified) is actually applied to men only, while healthy women are perceived as significantly *less* healthy by adult standards.

Essentially similar findings were reported by Neulinger (1968), who asked psychiatrists, psychologists, and social workers to rank 20 paragraphs descriptive of Henry Murray's manifest needs according to how descriptive they were of the Optimally Integrated Personality (OIP), i.e., the mentally healthy person. Each of his Ss completed the rankings once for the male OIP, once for the female OIP. His results showed that, although the two rankings were highly correlated, there were significant differences in the mean rankings of male and female OIP on 18 of the 20 paragraphs, 14 of them at the $p < .001$ level. Neulinger's Ss ranked dominance, achievement, autonomy, counteraction, aggression, etc., as more indicative of mental health in men than in women; sentience, nurturance, play, succorance, deference, abasement, etc., were rated as higher for the female OIP than the male OIP. These findings are strikingly similar to ours. Neulinger interprets his findings as indicating that different conceptions of mental health exist for males and females, and that "the sex orientation of this society is not only shared, but also promoted by its clinical personnel." He believes that these rankings reflect an ideal rather than an optimally functioning person, judging by the female OIP, namely: "an affiliative, nurturant, sensuous playmate who clings to the strong, supporting male [Neulinger, 1968, p. 554]."

BEHAVIORAL CORRELATES OF SEX-ROLE STEREOTYPES

Family Size

Davis (1967) and Blake (1969) have proposed that a critical psychological factor affecting the number of children a woman has is her acceptance or rejection of the feminine social role prevalent in our society. Blake (1969) has argued that most societies hold "pronatalistic" attitudes which prescribe for women the role of childbearer and rearer. Effective functioning in this feminine role encourages childbearing and earns social approval, while acceptance of an alternative role, such as gainful employment outside of the home, tends to reduce childbearing and earn social disapproval. Several studies have reported that working women do indeed desire (Ridley, 1959) and have (Pratt & Whelpton, 1958) fewer children than do nonworking women.

Certainly the sex-role stereotypes delineated by our research appear to be pronatalistic. Women who are perceived and perceive themselves as relatively incompetent might well feel inadequate to the challenges and stresses of employment. A less anxiety-provoking course of action would be to focus one's energies on home and family for which societal approval is certain, regardless of one's effectiveness in this role. Accordingly, we investigated the relationship between self-perception in the context of stereotypic sex roles and the number of children a woman has (Clarkson, Vogel, Broverman, Broverman, & Rosenkrantz, 1970).

Sixty Catholic mothers of male college students were studied. Their ages, 45 to 59 years, permitted the assumption that their families were completed. Only women with two or more children were included, thus excluding women with possible fertility problems. Education ranged from seven grades completed to doctoral degrees, with the median at 12 grades; the number of years employed outside the home since completion of formal education ranged from 0 to 29 years, with the median at 7.5 years.

Mothers with high competency self-concepts, as measured by our sex-role questionnaire, were found to have significantly fewer children than mothers who perceived themselves to be low on the competency items (3.12 versus 3.93 children, $p < .025$). Number of years worked was inversely related to number of children as expected, but did not reach statistical significance ($p < .10$).

Incorporation of male-valued stereotypic traits into the self-concepts of women should not be interpreted as a shift away from the positively valued characteristics of the female stereotype. The correlation between the self-concept score based on the competency cluster and the self-concept score based on the warmth-expressiveness cluster is low and not significant. Moreover, the self-concept scores on the warmth-expressiveness cluster were not related to family size. Thus, the self-concepts of mothers with relatively fewer children differed from the self-concepts of mothers with relatively more children only with respect to the negatively valued aspects of the feminine stereotype, i.e., the competency cluster, but do not differ with respect to the positively valued feminine traits, i.e., the warmth-expressiveness cluster.

Interpretation of these findings is not without ambiguity. It is not clear whether women who perceive themselves as relatively more competent chose to have fewer children; or whether a woman's estimation of her own competency diminishes as a function of her preoccupation with home and family. Preliminary analyses of new data from unmarried women attending a Catholic women's college suggest, however, that self-concept may be primary. College women with relatively high competency self-concepts perceive their ideal future family size as significantly smaller (4.16 children) than college women who see themselves as relatively less competent (4.89 children). Furthermore, those women who perceive themselves as more competent indicate that they plan to combine employment with childrearing, while women who perceive themselves as relatively less competent indicate that they plan to stop working when they become mothers. Self-concept in the context of stereotypic sex roles is thus related not only to the number of children a woman has once her family is completed, but apparently influences the plans of young women concerning their future sex roles.

These data clearly demonstrate a predictable and systematic relationship between sex-role attitudes—specifically, self-concept in a sex-role context—and concrete sex-role behaviors.

Maternal Employment

We have conceptualized sex-role stereotypes very broadly as attitudinal variables which intervene between particular antecedent conditions and sex-role behaviors. The following study demonstrates the relationship between sex-role attitudes and the specific antecedent condition of maternal employment.

We reasoned that a person's perception of societal sex roles, and of the self in this context, may be influenced by the degree of actual role differentiation that one experiences in one's own family. Maternal employment status appears to be central to the role differentiation that occurs between parents. If the father is employed outside the home while the mother remains a full-time homemaker, their roles tend to be clearly polarized for the child. But if both parents are employed outside the home, their roles are more likely to be perceived as similar—not only because the mother is employed, but also because the father is more likely to share childrearing and other family-related activities with the mother. Evidence exists that husbands of working wives share more in household tasks (Hoffman, 1963) and decisions (Blood, 1963; Heer, 1963) than husbands of wives remaining at home. Moreover, a number of studies suggest that the mother's employment history and status do in fact minimize a daughter's perception of sex-role related behavioral differences (Hartley, 1964), increase the likelihood of her expectation to combine marriage and a career (Riley, 1963), and make her more likely to actually pursue a career (Graham, 1970).

Accordingly, we examined the relationship between mother's employment status and sex-role perceptions of college students (Vogel, Broverman, Broverman, Clarkson, & Rosenkrantz, 1970). The sex-role questionnaire was administered under standard instructions to 24 men and 23 women whose mothers had never been employed, and to 35 men and 38 women whose mothers were currently employed. For each S the mean masculinity, femininity, and self-response scores were computed, separately for the male-valued (competency) items and for the female-valued (warmth-expressiveness) items.

As expected, daughters of employed mothers perceived significantly smaller differences between men and women than did daughters of homemaker mothers, on both the competency cluster and the warmth-expressiveness cluster. Sons of employed mothers perceived a significantly smaller difference between women and men on the warmth-expressiveness cluster than did sons of homemaker mothers. However, the perceptions of the two groups of male Ss did not differ significantly on the competency cluster. Further analysis uncovered another significant difference: Daughters of employed mothers perceived women less negatively on the competency characteristics than did daughters of homemaker mothers. Thus, while the two groups did not differ in their perceptions of women with respect to the characteristics usually valued in women (warmth-expressiveness), daughters of employed mothers did perceive women to be more competent than did the daughters of homemaker mothers.

No significant differences were found between the mean self responses of Ss with employed mothers compared to Ss with homemaker mothers for either men or women. The self responses fall between the masculinity and the feminity responses for all Ss. However, since the difference between the masculinity and the feminity responses is significantly smaller in Ss whose mothers are employed compared to Ss with homemaker mothers, the meaning of the self-concepts of the two groups may differ as a function of the different contexts in which they occur.

The results of this study suggest that the stereotypic conceptions of sex roles are not immutable. Insofar as perceptions of sex roles are subject to variation as a function of the individual's experience, then societal sex-role stereotypes may also be subject to change.

SUMMARY AND CONCLUSIONS

Our research demonstrates the contemporary existence of clearly defined sex-role stereotypes for men and women contrary to the phenomenon of "unisex" currently touted in the media (Bowers, 1971). Women are perceived as relatively less competent, less independent, less objective, and less logical than men; men are perceived as lacking interpersonal sensitivity, warmth, and expressiveness in comparison to women. Moreover, stereotypically masculine traits are more often perceived to be desirable than are stereotypically feminine characteristics. Most importantly, both men and women incorporate both the positive and negative traits of the appropriate stereotype into their self-concepts. Since more feminine traits are negatively valued than are masculine traits, women tend to have more negative self-concepts than do men. The tendency for women to denigrate themselves in this manner can be seen as evidence of the powerful social pressures to conform to the sex-role standards of the society.

The stereotypic differences between men and women described above appear to be accepted by a large segment of our society. Thus college students portray the ideal woman as less competent than the ideal man, and mental health professionals tend to see mature healthy women as more submissive, less independent, etc., than either mature healthy men, or adults, sex unspecified. To the extent that these results reflect societal standards of sex-role behavior, women are clearly put in a double bind by the fact that different standards exist for women than for adults. If women adopt the behaviors specified as desirable for adults, they risk censure for their failure to be appropriately feminine; but if they adopt the behaviors that are designated as feminine, they are necessarily deficient with respect to the general standards for adult behavior.

While many individuals are aware of the prejudicial effects

of sex-role stereotypes both from personal experience and hear-say, evidence from systematic empirical studies gives added weight to this fact. The finding that sex-role stereotypes continue to be held by large and relatively varied samples of the population and furthermore are incorporated into the self-concepts of both men and women indicates how deeply ingrained these attitudes are in our society. The magnitude of the phenomenon with which individuals striving for change must cope is well delineated.

On the other hand, the finding that antecedent conditions are associated with individual differences in stereotypic sex-role perceptions offers encouragement that change is possible and points to one manner in which change can be achieved. Finally, the finding that stereotypic sex-role self-concepts correlate with actual and desired family size testifies to the central role in behavior that these concepts play. One can speculate that eventual change in sex-role concepts will in fact be associated with far reaching changes in the life styles of both women and men.

REFERENCES

Blake, J. Are babies consumer durables? *Population Studies*, 1968, **22**, 5–25.

Blake, J. Population policy for Americans: Is the government being mislead? *Science*, 1969, **164**, 522–529.

Blood, R. O., Jr. The husband-wife relationship. In F. I. Nye and L. W. Hoffman (Eds.), *The employed mother in America*. Chicago: Rand McNally, 1963.

Bowers, F. The sexes: Getting it all together. *Saturday Review*, 1971, **54**, 16–19.

Broverman, I. K., Broverman, D. M., Clarkson, F. E., Rosenkrantz, P., & Vogel, S. R. Sex-role sterotypes and clinical judgments of mental health. *Journal of Consulting Psychology*, 1970, **34**, 1–7.

Brown, D. G. Sex role development in a changing culture. *Psychological Bulletin*, 1958, **55**, 232–242.

Clarkson, F. E., Vogel, S. R., Broverman, I. K., Broverman, D. M., & Rosenkrantz, P. S. Family size and sex-role stereotypes. *Science*, 1970, **167**, 390–392.

Cowen, E. L., Staiman, M. G., & Wolitzky, D. L. The social desirability of trait descriptive terms: Applications to a schizophrenic sample. *Journal of Social Psychology*, 1961, **54**, 37–45.

Davis, K. Population policy: Will current programs succeed? *Science*, 1967, **158**, 730–739.

Dinitz, S., Dynes, R. R., & Clarke, A. C. Preference for male or female children: Traditional or affectional. *Marriage and Family Living*, 1954, **16**, 128–130.

Edwards, A. L. *The social desirability variable in personality assessment and research.* New York: Dryden, 1957.

Elman, J. B., Press, A., & Rosenkrantz, P. S. Sex-roles and self-concepts: Real and ideal. Paper presented at the meeting of the American Psychological Association, Miami, August 1970.

Fernberger, S. W. Persistence of stereotypes concerning sex dfferences. *Journal of Abnormal and Social Psychology,* 1948, **43,** 97–101.

Gallup, G. *Gallup poll.* Princeton: Audience Research Inc., 1955.

Gough, H. G. *California Psychological Inventory Manual.* Palo Alto: Consulting Psychologists Press, 1957.

Graham, P. A. Women in academe. *Science,* 1970, **169,** 1284–1290.

Hartley, R. E. Current patterns in sex roles: Children's perspectives. *Journal of the National Association of Women Deans and Counselors,* 1961, **25,** 3–13.

Hartley, R. E. A developmental view of female sex-role defintion and identification. *Merrill-Palmer Quarterly of Behavior and Development,* 1964, **10,** 3–16.

Heer, D. M. Dominance and the working wife. In F. I. Nye and L. W. Hoffman (Eds.), *The employed mother in America.* Chicago: Rand McNally, 1963.

Hoffman, L. W. Parental power relations and the divsion of household tasks. In F. I. Nye and L. W. Hoffman (Eds.), *The employed mother in America.* Chicago: Rand McNally, 1963.

Horner, M. Fail: Bright woman. *Psychology Today,* 1969, **3.**

Kitay, P. M. A comparison of the sexes in their attitudes and beliefs about women. *Sociometry,* 1940, **34,** 399–407.

Kogan, W. S., Quinn, R., Ax, A. F., & Ripley, H. S. Some methodological problems in the quantification of clinical assessment by Q array. *Journal of Consulting Psychology,* 1957, **21,** 57–62.

Komarovsky, M. Functional analysis of sex roles. *American Sociological Review,* 1950, **15,** 508–516.

Lunneborg, P. W. Stereotypic aspects in masculinity-femininity measurement. *Journal of Consulting and Clinical Psychology,* 1970, **34,** 113–118.

Lynn, D. B. A note on sex differences in the development of masculine and feminine identification. *Psychological Review,* 1959, **66,** 126–135.

Maccoby, E. Woman's intellect. In S. M. Farber and R. H. Wilson (Eds.), *The potential of women.* New York: McGraw-Hill, 1963.

McKee, J. P., & Sherriffs, A. C. The differential evaluation of males and females. *Journal of Personality,* 1957, **25,** 356–371.

McKee, J. P., & Sherriffs, A. C. Men's and women's beliefs, ideals, and self-concepts. *American Journal of Sociology,* 1959, **64,** 356–363.

Neulinger, J. Perceptions of the optimally integrated person: A redefinition of mental health. *Proceedings of the 76th Annual Convention of the American Psychological Association,* 1968, 553–554.

Pohlman, E. *The psychology of birth planning.* Cambridge, Mass.: Schenkman, 1969.

Pratt, L., & Whelpton, P. K. Extra-familial participation of wives in relation to interest in and liking for children, fertility planning and actual and desired family size. In P. K. Whelpton and C. V. Kiser (Eds.),

Social and psychological factors affecting fertility. Vol. 5. New York: Milbank Memorial Fund, 1958.

Ridley, J. Number of children expected in relation to nonfamilial activities of the wife. *Milbank Memorial Fund Quarterly,* 1959, **37,** 277–296.

Riley, M., Johnson, M., & Boocock, S. Womans changing occupational role: A research report. *The American Behavioral Scientist,* 1963, **6,** 33–37.

Rosenkrantz, P. S., Vogel, S. R., Bee, H., Broverman, I.K., & Broverman, D. M. Sex-role stereotypes and self-concepts in college students. *Journal of Consulting and Clinical Psychology,* 1968, **32,** 287–295.

Rossi, A. S. Equality between the sexes: An immodest proposal. *Daedalus,* 1964, **93,** 607–652.

Sears, R. R., Maccoby, E. E., & Levin, H. *Patterns of child rearing.* New York: Row, Peterson, 1957.

Seward, G. H. *Sex and the social order.* New York: McGraw-Hill, 1946.

Sherriffs, A. C., & Jarrett, R. F. Sex differences in attitudes about sex differences. *Journal of Psychology,* 1953, **35,** 161–168.

Sherriffs, A. C., & McKee, J. P. Qualitative aspects of beliefs about men and women. *Journal of Personality,* 1957, **25,** 451–464.

Smith, S. Age and sex differences in children's opinions concerning sex differences. *Journal of Genetic Psychology,* 1939, **54,** 17–25.

Terman, L. M. *Psychological factors in marital happiness.* New York: McGraw-Hill, 1938.

Vogel, S. R., Broverman, I. K., Broverman, D. M., Clarkson, F. E., & Rosenkrantz, P. S. Maternal employment and perception of sex-roles among college students. *Developmental Psychology,* 1970, **3,** 384–391.

White, L., Jr. *Educating our daughters.* New York: Harper, 1950.

Wiener, M., Blumberg, A., Segman, S., & Cooper, A. A judgment of adjustment by psychologists, psychiatric social workers, and college students, and its relationship to social desirability. *Journal of Abnormal and Social Psychology,* 1959, **59,** 315–321.

9

Women's Rationality and Men's Virtues: A Critique of Gender Dualism in Gilligan's Theory of Moral Development

John M. Broughton

> I have a great mother complex. I want to help people and be kind to them. I was told to work on that stuff—be more aggressive and more full. And it all depends on how you look at it. I am sort of happy with the way that I am. I am fairly good looking. And I am intelligent. And I think I am a pretty nice person. . . . I really enjoy being with other people and getting close to people. That is possibly the most meaningful thing for myself right now, just being close to people. I guess I really like to communicate with people and get feedback from people on a deep level. . . . (What makes you feel committed?) The fact that I know them really well and are getting close to them and know what some of their needs are, and some of their wishes and some of their fears, as they do for me. I feel committed when I get close to somebody. (What obligations do you feel towards these people?) To be honest with them, not to do anything which would hurt them.
>
> —Gilligan's Subject #15

Moral versus Cognitive Sex Differences

It may not be purely accidental that discussions of psychological differences between men and women customarily have the same point of departure in the domain of the specifically *moral* aspects of the psyche. In these discussions, it is often Freud's (1925/1961, 1931/1961) notorious observations concerning the relative degrees of morality in men and women that are used to motivate closer examination of the issues.

It may be reasonable to argue that it is the peculiarly contentious nature of Freud's observations that makes his distinction between the sexes so salient. However, it seems possible that it is his particular use of *moral* attributes as features distinctive of sex, and his assumption, following Weininger (Millett 1970), that they could be transmitted only by *fathers,* that gives his

---

Reprinted by permission from *Social Research* 50, no. 3: 597–642. Copyright © 1983 by the journal.

remarks their edge. Generally speaking, where the psychological differences between men and women have been explained in terms of contrasting cognitive attributes (e.g., Strong 1943; MacKinnon 1962; Witkin et al. 1962; Maccoby 1966), there has been less outcry and fewer accusations of sexism. To some extent, any explicit statement of sex differences is controversial and, especially in recent years, is likely to have come under intense critical scrutiny. However, the suggestion that men and women are cognitively different typically seems to be experienced as less disturbing or threatening than the intimation that they are morally different.

This situation may have something to do with the fact that within our positivistic culture, claims about cognitive differences are more, easily seen as free from value-judgments. This would appear to be so for three reasons. First, cognition itself is usually seen as being oriented to fact rather than value. Second, assessments of individuals' different moralities are more easily perceived as attempts to establish differences in these individuals' moral *worth*. Third, the assessment of cognitive differences seems to be more amenable to established scientific procedures of objective measurement. Thus, the fact that Freud's observations about sex differences were not based on traditional scientific methods and were nonmetric in character is often used to discredit them.

However, this common-sense contrast between "scientific," cognitive, value-free assessments and "speculative," moral, value-laden interpretations has been obscured by Lawrence Kohlberg. Kohlberg has used rigorous scientific methods of measurement (see Colby et al. 1983) to establish a theory of moral development parallel to Piaget's cognitive stage theory. Furthermore, he has claimed that research reveals a pattern of sex differences in moral judgments, with the majority of adult women reasoning at "conformist" stage 3 while adult men typically reason at "legalistic" stage 4 (Kohlberg & Kramer 1969).

Kohlberg's position could not be dismissed as biologistic, as Freud's had been, since Kohlberg had explicitly contrasted his "interactionist" assumptions about development with Freud's "maturationist" ones. The sex differences were not innate or learned but "developed." Genetics was supplanted by genesis, but without abandoning the concept of human nature (Blasi 1976), thus advancing the progressivist trend away from biological versions of medieval substances and essences. This combination of qualities in Kohlberg's theory has elevated moral psychology to the level of a postreligious system which appears to prove once and for all on scientific and humanistic grounds Eve's lesser moral worth than Adam's. The hierarchical ordering of stages implicit in the developmental nature of the theory seems to make it quite clear that men are morally superior to women, not just different from them. There is a certain irony to this since, in an earlier work, Kohlberg replaced Freud's asymmetrical treatment of boys' and girls' awareness of

their sex with a more egalitarian developmental concept of symmetrical gender identities (Kohlberg 1966). This cognitive alternative to Freud became
one of the mainstays of Chodorow's more recent and influential rejection of
the traditional psychoanalytic theory of gender (Chodorow 1978).

"Fish Gotta Swim, Bird Gotta Fly": Gilligan's Sex-specific Psychology

The finding of male superiority on Piagetian measures of "formal operations" (Neimark 1975; Modgil & Modgil 1976) has received hardly any
attention at all. But the findings on Kohlberg's measure of "moral maturity"
have stirred up considerable debate. Perhaps the most dramatic outcome of
this controversy is the work of Carol Gilligan (1977, 1979, 1982a; Dulit
1983). Much as various psychoanalytic theorists, most of them women, had
criticized the Freudian "sexual phallic monism" that made girls' development a function of a felt penis-lack (Chasseguet-Smirgel 1976), Gilligan has
aimed to undermine Kohlberg's "sexual moral monism" that made women's
moral development into a stage 4 lack. She does so by arguing—along the
lines first suggested by Virginia Woolf's concept of "gynocentrism" and later
developed more fully in a psychological direction by feminist writers such as
Jean Baker Miller (1976), Evelyn Keller (1978), and Susan Griffin (1978)—
that there is a double rather than a single human nature: there is a qualitatively different set of stages in women's moral development. These stages
represent the progressive emergence of an orientation to affective qualities
of sympathy, caring, and tolerance of ambiguity which ground an ethical
focus on responsibility and nonviolence, "the ideals of human relationships—that everyone will be treated with equal respect and that no one will
be left alone or hurt" (Gilligan 1981, 66). Following Gutmann (1965),
Bakan (1966), and Chodorow (1978), she claims that underlying this moral
vision is a concept of self as "connected" rather than "separate," subject
#15's comments at the start of this paper being a classic example.

Gilligan aspires to an "ethics of ambiguity" in which abstract features of
moral decision-making are contextualized in terms of immediate situational
factors, especially those originating in the specificity of interpersonal relationships. Gilligan's dimorphism resembles the common opposition drawn
between Gestalt psychology and early structural psychology. Like gestal-
tists, women have a synthetic sensibility, focusing on wholes and the texture
of relations and configurations, rather than analyzing things in terms of
parts, elements, or boundaries. They are sensitive to and dependent upon
context, and this is the reason for their ability to see ambiguities. Their
understanding is more "perceptual," more immediately "experiential," and
less ordered in terms of cognitive or logical abstractions from—or representations of—experience. They cross boundaries and see unexpected similari-

ties. Their intelligence exhibits what Guilford described as "divergent" rather than "convergent" qualities (Guilford 1957).

This divergent, synthetic, contextual mental configuration, Gilligan argues, is and should be normative for women. It would appear that only a woman who fully embraces such a moral orientation, to the exclusion of other ethical positions, reasonably can be called a fully developed woman.

Kohlberg's claim that development is essentially a step-by-step movement toward formal principles of justice concerning rights and duties Gilligan sees as holding only for men. She argues that women appeared to be reasoning at a lower moral level than men because they were being evaluated with respect to a male criterion that was inappropriately applied to women. For example, if subject #15's style of discourse excerpted at the beginning of this article were to be applied to the relational feelings and commitments of the characters in the "Heinz dilemma," #15 would be scored "stage 3" or "interpersonal conformist." In addition, she stresses that the use of hypothetical dilemmas as the basis of Kohlberg's measurement instrument leads to a systematic and discriminatory underestimation of women's moral potential. That potential, she argues, can be realized only in relation to the context of personal life problems that are located in relation to a concrete self and other, that require action, and that occur in areas where women have the power to choose, such as in the situation of having to decide whether or not to have an abortion (Gilligan & Belenky 1980). Paradoxically, in this latter study, administration of the Kohlberg instrument was a central part of the procedure, and the findings from it were a central part of the reported results. The selective retention of the Kohlberg instrument, despite its supposed nonvalidity for women, remains to be explained.

Gilligan's alternative moral vision carries with it the clear implication that men harbor an illusory reality. She sees men as guilty of what Hampshire (1959, 1978) has called "false individuation," the illegitimate reduction of the complex ongoing flow of everyday moral situations and behavior to a definite grid of discrete actions and fixed elements which fail to reflect the true difficulties and nuances of the ethical life. The feminist sociologist Jessica Benjamin (1987) has referred to men's illusory autonomy as "false differentiation," and has linked it to an instrumental rationality. Gilligan too sees men's morality as instrumental and, like Parsons (Parsons & Bales 1955), opposes to it female "expressiveness."

The Empirical Validity of Gilligan's Theory

To what degree does Gilligan's account really fit the empirical facts? How much of an interview can be interpreted adequately in terms of the descriptions she presents? In order to assess this most fairly, an analysis was made of one of Gilligan's own interviews, in fact, one of her favorites—subject

#63. Gilligan has been wont to use this rich and satisfying thirty-five-page transcript to typify the phenomena that her theory appeals to. This is an interview with a young, educated, unmarried, white, middle-class woman who had had an abortion and whose interests had since turned to medicine.

It must be acknowledged that almost all of the values and beliefs central to Gilligan's theory of women are to be found in this interview. Nevertheless, almost all of the "rational" concepts that she attributes to men are to be found there too! There are repeated affirmations of "independence," "self-control," "conserving your energy," "not splitting [your]self" (i.e., self-consistency), and other notions that would appear to be more compatible with the idea of a "separated" male self rather than a "connected" female self. This orientation is well captured in #63's recommendation of "arguments that protect individual freedom. . . . What's important is individual freedom and decision . . . individual determination." She stresses as a central guide the capacity for individual decisiveness: "Your life force or some life force given to you by God . . . does sustain. That is enough to make you very hard." Furthermore, many of her statements reflect a concern for the "overall good," to be understood as morally specifiable in terms of a person's "not impinging on somebody else." This rather liberal conception of morality, defined individualistically and privatistically, seems much closer to that view which Gilligan attributes to the typical male (e.g., Gilligan 1982a, 19).

In addition, #63 appears to be rather fluent in the supposedly "male" language of rights. "What right has the state to lock up anybody?" she inquires. In connection with the American Medical Association's opposition to Medicaid, she becomes an explicit proponent of the "rights" orientation: "You have a right to say something about somebody's actions and you don't have a right to mess with their psychological and moral beliefs. . . . I think of a lot of things you should be crying 'Rights!' " Gilligan correctly predicts that, as a woman, #63 will be concerned with people's suffering. However, even that concern is voiced by #63 in terms of rights: "Where do you have the right to cause human suffering?" she asks rhetorically. Gilligan stresses the primacy of the "responsibility orientation" over the "rights orientation" in women. However, #63 argues explicitly that responsibilities are grounded in rights: "People suffer, and that gives them certain rights, and that gives you a certain responsibility."

On the issue of moral obligation, Gilligan again turns out to be correct. In conformity with the womanly voice, #63 does reject the notion of obligation. But on closer inspection we find that this is only because she assumes that duty is to be equated with external coercion: "I don't like the idea of duty. [It's like someone] told you to do it." Thus, she can hardly be said to have rejected any concept of moral obligation in terms of conscience, or an internal sense of necessity.

From Gilligan's point of view, #63 reflects the "female" concern with human relationships. However, a careful examination of the text reveals that the subject thinks of relationships in an impersonal way rather than a personal one. In the famous "Heinz dilemma" of Kohlberg, she says that Heinz should respect his relationship to his wife because "he owes her something" for what she has done for him previously. Elsewhere, she describes the ideal relationship as one where there is a "giving of realistic information." For #63, therefore, human relatedness is cognitive, not affective, and is based upon a relatively mechanistic principle of concrete exchange. #63 also passes beyond the boundaries of Gilligan's description of women's personalized understanding of social relations to emphasize in a rather "masculine" manner the extrapersonal aspects of morality. Defining morality, she asserts that "there is a personal and sociological aspect to it, and beneath that are both these in making moral decisions." Under "sociological," she includes "economics" and "class structure."

All but one of the excerpts cited so far are from the unstructured, autobiographical part of Gilligan's interview. However, when Gilligan comes to the part where she employs the dilemmas from Kohlberg's instrument, #63 becomes even more "masculine" in her responses. First, she appeals to a notion of "justice": "You can break laws because the laws are not too just." Her opinion is, "I think he should do it" (i.e., steal the drug to save his dying wife). Since she does not believe in moral obligation, on account of its coerciveness, she retreats to the position that "You do the best you can." However, she elevates that homily to the level of what she calls a "principle." She says, "It would be living out his principles, in a sense, to do it." In contrast to Gilligan's claim that women's morality is affective and personal in orientation, #63 insists that "politically, it doesn't make a damn bit of a difference how you feel about the other people involved. It is the *principle* involved." That this is not merely a casual use of words, concealing an otherwise situationally relativistic ethics, is suggested by the way in which she goes on to explain her underlying reasoning:

> The principle is you have the duty to go about doing positive action to prevent death. . . . I think it is a universal value. . . . It was a natural thing. "Do it this way." I generally feel there are universal considerations. That is part of the natural system and order of things. . . . It is kind of the values that come from life situations. But then again, those are universal. . . . Since they [values] are not relative, I assume they are natural. . . . Considerations about what is just and what isn't I think have to develop after you're born. . . . Morality is sort of a philosophical consideration.

Contrary to Gilligan's wish, and much to the horror of the interviewer, this favored female subject insists upon restating, more or less, the basic tenets of the Kohlbergian theory of moral development! This is all the more impressive, since at the beginning of the interview #63 had firmly rejected Kohlberg's theory, about which she claimed to know a good deal.

Due to his sex role, the present author decided that it would be only fair to look at one of the interviews that Gilligan uses to illustrate the "male" form of moral reasoning, a subject referred to affectionately, yet noncontextually, as "#32." Again, to some extent, Gilligan's predictions are borne out. This young man (also white and middle class, unmarried, yet living with a woman) says that Heinz is "morally obligated" to steal the drug and that "it is objectively right to do so, because of the priority of the woman's life over his [the druggist's] right to get money." He defines morality as "an appeal to reason."

Nevertheless, with a slight shift of questioning from "should one" to "would one"—a common elision in a Gilliganian interview—he explains where the sense of obligation originates:

> In the immediate situation, that is where it came from. When you say "wife," I sort of get a feeling of love and tenderness, that in his situation that is probably where—. It wouldn't strike me in that situation, if I were doing it for my wife. I wouldn't feel as though it were my obligation to steal it. It is something that I would obviously want to do, and as though a part of me would be dying if I didn't do it.

He emphasizes the importance of being "put in a situation where I can help," and admits that "I don't feel sort of called on to help people on the other side of the world." When he is asked "What is morality or ethics?" he replies:

> Generally, it means to me acting in a way not to hurt . . . being decent to other people. And by "decent" what do I mean? Something like, well, not taking advantage of other people, not hurting them. . . . And, I mean, I think that morality does include the feeling that I should help people when I am in a position to help somebody.

Here, #32 appears to espouse an ethic of responsibility. In so doing, he conforms to Helen Weinreich Haste's (1981) finding, in a reanalysis of Kohlberg's data, that moral orientations to responsibilities are commonly found in male subjects (e.g., Kohlberg's case 42, described by Haste [1983]).

#32 goes on to elaborate his view of the moral.

> (What does it mean to you to say that something is morally right or morally wrong?) It means that relates to what a person does or

has done in that situation, involving people, interaction. . . . It somehow arises from the situation. . . . Somehow, morality is more what happens between people. . . . Morality has to do with the way one acts towards other people. . . . You would want to be able to make other people feel comfortable. . . . I am having trouble thinking in completely abstract terms, and I can't quite think off-hand of situations to put myself in. . . . I don't always feel that something can be objectively right or wrong. . . . In the case of abortion, I would say that is more a personal value.

The fact that such examples are not isolated instances is confirmed in an ironic way by Gilligan herself. In her article with Murphy (Murphy & Gilligan 1980) she presents material from two subjects to document the existence of thinking that is clearly and consistently "contextual relativism." On inspection of this paper, it turns out that both these subjects are male! What is more impressive is Murphy and Gilligan's observation that these men moved *out of* the formalistic "male" mode of thinking *into* the contextual "female" mode, which the authors construe as an irreversible developmental transformation! Of course, Gilligan could defend herself by pointing out that the psychological dimorphism which she has described, rather than being an absolute one, reflects only differential *tendencies* in men's and women's thinking. Although the complete crossover in the case of these two men would still be very hard to account for, it must be admitted that she has offered us in her book some strong examples of her typical "male" and "female" tendencies appearing respectively in men and women. What more graphic illustration of her point could there be than #15's comments which head the present essay? Isn't this a convincing illustration of the Chodorowian "connected self" central to Gilligan's theory? The example becomes even more compelling in the following additional excerpt from the interview with #15, which reveals the thrill and risk of transcending boundaries and barriers:

It is hard to describe, but you know when the level of communication is taking place just by how it makes you feel. It is just the self . . . being touched by somebody else without all the crust around it to protect it from being touched, with that stuff all stripped away. The deeper self. . . . When I get more in contact with this deeper universal stuff, somehow some of these distinctions and divisions fall away and there is more of a union. . . . I have been told that one of my problems is I get almost smotheringly close to people and show my real self. People tell me they get smothered and feel like they lose their identity and they become merged in some insep-arable hold, which is scary. And I guess I am looking for some love affair which takes the mystical "two are now one" sort of thing. But that frightens a lot of people I have run into. Just getting too close in the effort to show real selves. But you start losing selves sometimes, and you lose separate identities.

Only one problem: #15 was a man!

The Vanishing Sex Difference between Gilligan's and Kohlberg's Theories

The upshot of the previous section is that Gilligan does not demonstrate convincingly that women's reasoning fits her three-stage description. In the Kohlbergian style, she presents only short excerpts from her interviews, leaving us unclear as to whether or not the moral discourse that remains in the rest of the interviews can be accounted for adequately under one or another of her three levels. There is no assurance of the representativeness of the excerpts she gives us. Since she does not report the kind of heterogeneity that I have been able to identify in her own interviews, a special kind of selectivity seems to have occurred in her interview analysis. Even in the case of the excerpts that she does present, her interpretations and paraphrases appear not to do total justice to what her subjects were saying. For example, the interviewees often appeal to notions of equality in a way that fits her scheme no more than it does Kohlberg's (Parsons 1979). Conversely, it appears that the interview material that she presents underdetermines the interpretation that it is supposed to establish. For example, why should we take the statement of Gilligan's nineteen-year-old who is facing her second abortion and does not know whose role to take as the dilemma of "the feminine identification of goodness with self-sacrifice" (Gilligan 1982a, 496) rather than as a classic instance of the intractable contradictions of the simple "empathic" role-taker described by Kohlberg's stage 3?

Gilligan tries to distinguish her sequence as one of increasingly sympathetic and harmonious relations between "self and other," but this is hardly much of a contrast to Kohlberg's notion of increasingly equilibrated relations of "role-taking." "Sympathy" and "role-taking" would appear to be related in some way, and how "harmony" and "equilibrium" could be distinguished conceptually is not at all self-evident. Similarly, she tends to treat equality, caring, responsibility, nonviolence, etc., as though they were principles of general validity, not just values possessing local usefulness. In this respect, her view approximates that of Frankena (1973), according to whom principles of justice are rationally compatible with principles of beneficence.

Moreover, Gilligan's "stages" are not very different from Kohlberg's. Her first level of "selfishness and survival" appears to be more or less identical with Kohlberg's "preconventional" morality. Her second level, at which the need for approval and the desire to help others converge in a "self-sacrificial goodness," is easily confused with Kohlberg's third stage, as we have just seen. Kohlberg's stage 3 "interpersonal concordance" morality includes concerns for love and caring as well as a concern for the fulfillment of role expectations.

Even Gilligan's third level, which we might expect to reveal the contrast best, is similar in many ways to Kohlberg's postconventional level. True, the idea of self-other interdependence is more general and less specifically moral than Kohlberg's notion of decentered role-taking. However, the two constructs seem quite compatible. Gilligan tends to make them appear opposites by contrasting women's "responsibility orientation" with men's emphasis on abstract and absolute rules, rights, duties, and principles. There are at least six features of this supposed antinomy indicating that she may have exaggerated the opposition.

First, Kohlberg is careful to distinguish rights from rules; the latter are central only in conventional morality. Second, rights (and their correlative duties) are not abstract or decontextualized (Kohlberg 1982). Even in law, the very business of judgment is a complex decision concerning the contextual appropriateness of applying general notions of rights to particular, concrete situations (Levi 1948).

Third, Gilligan asserts that "the morality of rights differs from the morality of responsibility in its emphasis on separation rather than attachment, in its consideration of the individual rather than the relationship as primary" (Gilligan 1979). However, rights and duties are concerned precisely with social relatedness, and the very reciprocity of a right and a duty captures that concern. This is not to deny that individualism and privatism are central to Western legal and moral systems. They certainly are, and so pervasive are they that Gilligan herself does not escape them. For example, she studies her subjects as separate, thinking minds abstracted from their sensuous, ongoing life context and relationships; she encourages women's quest for independence, autonomy and self-sufficiency; and, especially noteworthy, she talks about an abortion as entirely the concern of the pregnant woman. Nor does emphasizing the interpersonal make one less of an individualist; the very idea of interindividual relationships has always been at the heart of individualism (Waterman 1981).

Fourth, rights and duties are not absolute (Dworkin 1977). Only at the conventional level could they be so construed. Even within the utilitarian or social-contract orientation of Kohlberg's stage 5, what is morally right and what moral rights are to be upheld are always relative to particular systems of utilities or consensual social ideas. Once it is granted that rights and duties are not absolute, then the "flexible," "relative" virtues that Gilligan espouses appear less unlike rights and duties. For example, Gilligan and her subjects seem to presuppose something like "the right of all to respect as a person," "the right to be treated sympathetically and as an equal," and "the duty to respect and not to hurt others." It is certainly not the presence or absence of prescriptivity that distinguishes Gilligan and Kohlberg. For example, as can be seen in the quotation from Gilligan (1981) in the second section of this article, she speaks of the "ideals of human relationships." Given that she is so uncompromising about what these ideals are, it is difficult to see in what way she is not here recommending more or less binding rights and duties or perhaps even "principles" of personal welfare and benevolent concern. We may conclude that, by Gilligan's own standards, insofar as women treat sympathy, equality, and nonviolence as optional choices dependent on situational factors they depart from being moral *and* from being women.

Although, at best, Gilligan's third level resembles Kohlberg's postconventional level, at worse it resembles the upper half of his conventional level, stage 4. By confounding rights with fixed and absolute rules, she confuses postconventional with conventional moral judgment. This may account for her tendency to select as female "virtues" qualities conventionally or traditionally attributed to women, and her tendency to see development as progressive adaptation to these stereotypical norms. At other times, she succeeds in distinguishing postconventional from conventional but truncates Kohlberg's theory at the fifth stage, making him appear to be either a legal positivist or a social-contract utilitarian. If this were the case, then her criticisms of him for subordinating welfare to justice would be inappropriate, since that distinction can be made clearly only beyond stage 5. It is precisely Kohlberg's notion of universalizable principles of justice based on ideal role-taking that is designed to protect morality from a narrow legalistic or absolutistic interpretation, to criticize utilitarian welfare concerns compatible with social Darwinism, and to prescribe the right thing to do even in areas of life experience where there are no relevant specified rights. Thus, a fifth caveat to Gilligan is: "Principles are not the same as rights." In fact, it is via moral principles that any given system of rights and duties is evaluated; principles serve to legitimize ethically adequate moral and legal systems and to delegitimize inadequate systems (Kohlberg 1973; Habermas 1975; Dworkin 1977). Gilligan appears not to realize that Kohlberg's metaethical position is strictly deontological and cannot be reduced to the teleological metaethics grounding stage 5.

Finally, Kohlberg's sixth stage of morality incorporates self, responsibility, nonviolence, and even a kind of caring in a way what makes the Kohlberg/Gilligan contrast seem less extreme. The final stage reintroduces the self as equal in a manner quite similar to Gilligan's transition from "self-sacrificial" to "interdependent" morality. It also includes notions of responsibility along with its conception of universal moral obligation. Responsibility, like affectional relation, is one of the content areas for all the Kohlberg stages, and, thanks to Blasi (1981) as much as to Gilligan, it has been elevated recently to a more formal role in the theory (Kohlberg 1982). While Kohlberg has not incorporated communitarian ethics explicitly in his final stage, principles of nonviolent resistance would appear to be part of the universalizable content of that stage. He refers to the example of Gandhi as much as Gilligan does, although in doing so he pays more attention to acts of resistance and civil disobedience in the face of an unjust state. Gilligan does not seem very concerned with societal transformation, given her desire to imbed women even more deeply in the domestic and personal aspects of welfare in civil society.

It is this confinement that leads Gilligan to split caring from justice, failing to see that, while justice requires abstraction, it is intended as the abstract form that caring takes when respect is maintained and responsibility assumed for people whom one does not know personally and may never come to know. Therefore, Gilligan does not seem to acknowledge the importance of respect or responsibility in the relationship of a government to its nation's citizens, or nation-states to each other, or of states, governments, and citizens to past or future generations. "Caring" is limited as the basis of an ethical orientation unless it can overcome the parochiality that its association with friends and family tends to convey (cf. Rustin 1982). It may be true that Kohlberg's claim that "love is a local form of justice" is an inadequate attempt to generalize concepts from the public and judicial sphere of morality to the intimate domain and, at best, works only in atypical cases of interpersonal life, like Kohlberg's dilemma of "Joe and his father." Nevertheless, Gilligan appears equally unrealistic in wishing that all social phenomena be based on concrete affectional ties. To limit and privatize the moral domain by inflating the Judeo-Christian concept of goodness and love leads to the problems described by Sidgwick (1893, 105–15, 238–48) and Frankena (1973, 56–57, 79–94). As the latter says, "The life of pure love . . . is not the moral life. . . . Love by itself gives us no way of choosing between different ways of distributing good and evil" (Frankena 1973, 56–57). A principle of help or care does not work in situations where helping one agent harms another. Even in the Heinz dilemma this is a problem; shouldn't Heinz "care" for the druggist too? More dramatically, this undifferentiated humanistic ethic of care can lead to tragedies like Vietnam: the rationale given for the intervention in Southeast Asia was one of altruistic concern to help a suffering ally. Similarly, unqualified nonviolence is insupportable, as we can infer from the contradictions that Gandhi embodied, especially in his attitude toward the Nazi slaughter of the Jews (Erikson 1969).

The egalitarian ethic that Gilligan recommends to us is part of liberalism, yet a part forgetful that, within the liberal tradition, equality must be balanced with *liberty*. Nowhere in Gilligan's ethic is the need for freedom voiced. In particular, it would appear that women do not need to be free in order to reach the maximum of their developmental potential. The liberation of women is not necessary to reach Gilligan's level 3, much as it is dispensable in reaching Kohlberg's stage 6. For cognitive-developmental theorists, issues surrounding oppressive asymmetrical relations of illegitimate authority and the abuse of power do not have to be engaged because the mind, in the full course of its development, rises above mere concrete relations of oppression by envisaging the perfect mutuality and reciprocity of symmetrical human relationships from which unwarranted power differentials and the corruption of authority have been eliminated. Gilligan's women are doubly free, since they subvert men's rational mastery by constructing a different worldview, a view of a world in which mastery has no place.

The Dubious Empirical Status of Sex Differences in Moral Development

A decade ago, Maccoby and Jacklin's (1974) review of research on childhood exposed the myth of pervasive psychological sex differences. They showed that, contrary to stereotypical norms, there is no clear evidence that girls are more passive, dependent, compliant, anxious, timid, withdrawn, self-effacing, suggestible, impulsive, nurturant, or social than boys; nor are they less analytic (including field independent), decontextualized, active, competitive, achievement oriented, organized, or planful.

Although Gilligan announces that "the differences between the sexes are being rediscovered in the social sciences" (Gilligan 1979, 432) and others seem to be in agreement (e.g., Golding & Laidlaw 1979–80; Flanagan 1982; Kegan 1982), it is still far from clear that the existence of such differences with respect to moral development has been established. The debate over the existence or nonexistence of sex differences in moral judgment scores was triggered by an early study that found sex differences in favor of men (Haan et al. 1968). At that time, Kohlberg and Kramer (1969) explained the findings as follows: "Stage 3 interpersonal concordance morality is a functional morality for housewives and mothers; it is not for businessmen and professionals." This interpretation is peculiar, given that most of the subjects in the Haan study were students, among whom one might expect to find relatively few housewives and mothers or businessmen and professionals.

Since then, Keasey (1972); Blatt and Kohlberg (1975); Turiel (1976); Holstein (1976); Levine (1976); Haan, Langer, and Kohlberg (Haan et al. 1976); Erickson et al. (1978); and Gibbs, Widaman, and Colby (1982) found no sex difference in childhood or adolescence; and Weisbroth (1970); Berkowitz et al. (1980); and Gibbs, Widaman, and Colby (1982) found no sex difference in early adulthood. However, Fishkin, Keniston and MacKinnon (1973) found one for adults, Erickson et al. (1978) and Bussey and

Maughan (1982) found a sex difference for young adults, Haan, Langer and Kohlberg (Haan et al. 1976) found one in early and middle adulthood, Kuhn et al. (1977) found one in middle adulthood, and Holstein (1976) found a transitory difference in middle adulthood. Like Kohlberg and Kramer, Erickson et al. (1978, 3) concluded that the differences could be attributed to social role-taking opportunities: "Late adolescent and adult males in our society are afforded greater opportunities to take on roles of responsibility having societal import, and . . . females' sex role socialization has discouraged such activity for women."

Undaunted by her own finding of no sex differences in a study of students that was controlled for educational privilege (Murphy & Gilligan 1980), Gilligan reanalyzed these and other data, and in the process brought to light some sex differences in means and distributions of scores. In opposition to Kohlberg and Kramer, and Erickson et al., Gilligan, Langdale, and Lyons (1982, 83–93) argued that, given the educational parity of their male and female subjects, such differences could not be attributed to social role-taking opportunities but must instead be attributed to a sex bias in the Kohlberg theory and scoring system.

In a review of cross-cultural tests of Kohlberg's theory, Blasi and Broughton (in press) found several instances of sex differences. Admittedly, there was a tendency for the sex differences to be a little larger in cases where the difference was in favor of men. In addition, there was a tendency for men to exhibit a wider range of stages of reasoning. However, where sex differences were found, they were equally often in favor of women (e.g., in the Bahamas) as they were in favor of men (e.g., in Israel). Furthermore, in the U.S. and cross-cultural longitudinal studies, the rates of development over time were commensurate for male and female subjects, with a tendency for females to advance more rapidly.

Overall, the findings indicate that the existence of a sex difference in moral development, at least of the Kohlbergian variety, is still open to question, especially for the age groups prior to adulthood.

The findings that perhaps contradict Gilligan's claims most directly are those reported by Norma Haan (1978). Haan identified what she calls an "interpersonal morality" that contrasts with the "formal morality" described by Kohlberg. Much as Gilligan has suggested, despite its greater internal inconsistency, subjects were found to prefer this interpersonal morality in action situations, while there was a trend toward greater use of formal morality in dealing with hypothetical dilemmas. Formal reasoning, in fact, was found to be a liability in action situations, subserving mental processes of defensive isolation and intellectualization and tending to paralyze action. In this and another (1975) study Haan found that reasoning level was higher regarding a real-action situation than it was regarding a hypothetical one. Furthermore, she found that interpersonal moral reasoning diverges increasingly from the formal type with development. Again in concordance with Gilligan, Haan found that ego processes play an important role in interpersonal morality but not in formal morality. However, *no sex difference was found in the use of these two moralities*; both female and male subjects tended to prefer to use interpersonal moral reasoning in the action situations. Moreover, the experience of the action situations was found to advance both kinds of morality equally, suggesting a common developmental mechanism.

Other empirical findings cast doubt upon the dichotomy of moralities that Gilligan describes. For example, men's capacity for moral commitment based on sympathetic caring, a desire for social harmony, and a dedication to nonviolence, despite their simultaneous penchant for rationality, is testified to by several studies. Keniston's *Young Radicals* comes first to mind (1968). Keniston's in-depth examination of the moral character, development, and politics of the male activists revealed that their status was postconventional on Kohlberg's scale, while exhibiting all the virtues of responsibility, sympathy, caring, etc., that are supposed by Gilligan to be incompatible with that status. Furthermore, departing from Chodorow's characterization, Keniston revealed through an extensive clinical procedure that these young men's beliefs and activities were grounded in a warm, personal relationship to their mothers, one that had not been rejected but had continued into adulthood as a source of identity. A parallel finding appears in Zahaykevich's (1982) research on Russian dissidents (all male). All the subjects were found to be postconventional according to Kohlberg's scheme. She identified three types of dissenter, only one of which, the "abstract rationalist" type, was characterized by an emphasis on reason as a moral guide. The other types—"heroic romantic" and "carnivalesque historicist"—eschewed abstract rationality and emphasized community, relationship, and personal solidarity as the bases of morality and political action. They saw cultural, spiritual, and aesthetic values as central to ethics. All the dissidents studied were committed to nonviolent resistance, and none evinced the kinds of fantasies of violence that Pollak and Gilligan (1982) find in their male subjects.

Concerning Gilligan's claims about the "separate" and "connected" self, there is one study in particular that supports the dualistic view (Carlson 1971), although Gilligan herself does not cite it. However, several phenomenological studies of the structure of self find the same kind of dividedness into public and private in both sexes (Laing 1960; Winnicott 1965; Broughton 1981). Gilligan claims that there is a sex difference in Eriksonian ego-identity development, but a recent review by Weiss shows that the findings are quite mixed, with many showing similar trajectories for men and women (Weiss 1983). Several other studies of the development of the ego reveal very similar patterns for male and female subjects. Perry's (1968) scheme for intellectual-ethical development applies to both men and women (cf. Parker 1978). Fowler (1981) found that his stage of religious identity applied equally to men and women. Basseches' (1980) levels in the development of "dialectical thinking" applied equally to his male and female subjects. In a study of ten samples of men totaling five hundred subjects between the ages of eleven and fifty-one, Loevinger and colleagues found the same stages of ego development as in women (Redmore et al. 1970). In Broughton's (1978) study of developmental levels in child, adolescent, and young-adult world-views, male subjects exhibited no differences from female subjects. Of particular note is the fact that rationalist and irrationalist philosophies appeared as a function of age and developmental status, not as a function of gender. Following Freire's and Gilligan's interview method of allowing subjects to define their own problems and issues, Golden (1983) identified in high-school students four sequential developmental cycles in which norms of achievement and affiliation were first established and then relativized, contextualized, and criticized. In longitudinal and cross-sectional studies, both male and female students were found to pass through these phases of value change; there were no sex differences in development.

All six of these investigations are particularly relevant to Gilligan's claims, since all six developmental schemes involve a hierarchy of increasing "contextuality" and decreasing "absoluteness." Indeed, it was from Perry's scheme (developed on male subjects) that some of Gilligan's understanding of women's contextual relativism was derived. This comes as no surprise to the psychologists of cognitive style who have known for a long time that boys exhibited both "convergent" and "divergent" forms of mental activity (Getzels & Jackson 1962; Hudson 1968), and that supposed sex differences in analytic reasoning (e.g., field independence) were hard to substantiate (Maccoby & Jacklin 1974). In addition, in the study conducted by Kuhn et al. (1977) both tolerance of ambiguity and empathy were found to be a function of moral level and not of gender.

Womanhood as a Moral Concept

Gilligan's alternative to Kohlberg "doubles up" on it, preserving a parallel with it rather than replacing it. Without her always realizing it, this doubling up or paralleling strategy has the consequence of challenging many of the assumptions upon which Kohlberg's approach originally was founded. For example, Gilligan implicitly has shifted the metaethical ground of the psychology of normative ethics, supplanting Kohlberg's "deontological" approach to morality with an "aretaic" one that is oriented to *virtues* (Frankena 1973; cf. MacIntyre 1982) and that describes qualities of the ideal person and the good life rather than prescribing the rights and obligations that comprise a just society. Gilligan's view is similar in many respects to

Aristotle's account of the different virtues appropriate for men and women in the first book of his *Politics*.

An important aspect of this metaethical shift, not less significant on account of its obviousness, is that the step from Kohlberg to Gilligan entails a rearrangement of human psychology such that moral development is now seen as fused with the development of gender itself. As Kohlberg (1966) had suggested a decade earlier, sex-role is not what the social-learning theorists tried to convince us it was. Rather, it can be conceived in terms of "gender identity," a rational cognitive construction which is not learned but undergoes successive developmental transformations via a process of self-socialization. In this sense, sex is no longer to be seen as a matter of "roles" imposed from without. Gilligan's theory aspires to synthesize these two parts of cognitive-developmental theory that Kohlberg had kept separate, at the same time undermining his claims, first, that the process of gender formation was essentially the same for both sexes, and, second, that it was purely a matter of identity. Instead, much the same way Freud appeared to do, Gilligan makes gender a specifically moral issue. Despite a certain kinship with Erikson, she does not attach herself primarily to his theory of identity formation. Neither does she draw her ideas from the gender identity paradigm of Kohlberg's earlier paper. Furthermore, she does not entertain the possibility of sex differences in cognitive development. Psychological sex dimorphism is confined to moral development. Thus, womanhood is defined as a specifically moral status. Given the developmental dimension, gender is not a given; one can only gradually *become* a woman. In de Beauvoir's words, "Woman is a becoming" (1953, 30). However, in Gilligan's book, one cannot become a woman without developing specific, circumscribed values and commitments in the moral domain, including stipulated metaethical commitments to an aretaic or virtues orientation rather than a deontological or justice orientation. Thus, some female people never really become properly gendered. Those whose development ceases at the second level of self-sacrificial morality are to be conceived not only as not fully moral but also as not fully women. To be a "moral" person, in the strict sense of the term, one must attain the fullness of one's potential as a gendered individual.

Women Do Not Develop

There are other ways in which Gilligan's claims undermine the Kohlbergian paradigm. For example, she challenges the primacy of structural form. The morality that she recommends (for women, at least) is relatively *content*-oriented, in the sense that it is the particulars of concrete selves and their actual ongoing personal relationships to concrete others that ground moral decision-making and action. Sometimes it appears as though it is not the *actual* relational contents that are crucial but rather the *way* in which such concreteness is taken into account. To the extent that this is what Gilligan intends, we might say that it is not content itself that grounds moral decision-making but rather the general form of content, the manner of its being cognized and employed in ways of social behaving. Thus, content is almost raised to the level of form in this interpretation.

This is perhaps why Gilligan looks more like a theorist of "personality traits" than a moral developmentalist. The differentiae used to distinguish women and men look very much like the stock bipolar traits of individual-differences psychologists: field-dependence/independence, tolerance/intolerance of ambiguity, open/closed-mindedness, impulsiveness/reflectiveness, flexibility/rigidity, etc. (Cattell 1965). In a sense, she borrows what she would call a "male" style here, preferring congeries of abstract psychic elements over the relational concept of "structure." Gilligan thus embodies the unfortunate tendency of all psychologists of sex differences to gravitate toward a psychology of traits (Sherif 1979).

Comprehending exactly what Gilligan intends is complicated by the fact that, at times, she does not seem to be elevating content above structure so much as raising *action* above thought. In the latter case, then, we would say that women's morality inheres in a way of behaving rather than a way of dealing with the concrete particulars of personal relationships and commitments. Perhaps another way of saying the same thing is that she wishes to elevate *function* above structure, in which case it is not so much a dispensing with thought but emphasizing its functional value in practice, in its capacity to inform commitments and guide activity in the complex nexus of interpersonal relatedness. Such a functional approach tries to compensate for the excessive intellectualism of the structural approach by giving a salient role to *experience,* not in the abstract sense of assimilation and accommodation of conceptual schemes but in the sense of what it feels like to grapple with specific relational events such as those involved in an abortion decision. It is argued that women's moral experience is qualitatively different from men's (Gilligan, Langdale & Lyons 1982).

Paradoxically, however, Gilligan fails to question the original oppositions between form and content, thought and action, structure and function, concept and experience, abstract and concrete. She leaves women in almost the same position that Aristotle left them, representing matter while men represent form, the form that is given to matter (Whitbeck 1976).

While the attempt to resuscitate the concepts of concreteness, content, action, practicality, function, and experience, which structural approaches have tended to suffocate, is well intentioned, running them all together into an undifferentiated mass tends to lead to a crude romanticism that rejects rationality uncritically, often using as the basis of the argument precisely those principles of rationality (e.g., noncontradiction) that are being rejected. This kind of romanticism is typical of attempts to "feminize" logocentric psychological theories and is not specifically feminist in any way (Broughton 1984). Since such attempts conform to the very dichotomies presupposed by the logocentric theories in the first place rather than calling them into question, they tend to perpetuate the status quo, to affirm the established division of labor, and to foreclose the possibility of radical transformation. Intractable duality offers only the appearance of liberation from a "male" monism. In fact, it leaves us with little more than its mirror image. In this, Gilligan's rebellion exemplifies what Barrington Moore (1968) calls "conservative solidarity" and Richard Sennett (1981) terms "disobedient dependence." Gilligan repeats the pragmatists' attempt to secede from positivism, and in so doing joins the pragmatist illusion that the problems of formalism can be solved by returning to functional concepts of action-based inquiry and context-sensitive problem-solving.

A disturbing consequence of the revolt against structure is that it implies that women do not develop. As I have tried to demonstrate elsewhere (Broughton 1982), the concept of "development" in modern Western thought is tied to a model of hierarchically ordered structural systems. Insofar as Gilligan rejects the formal, abstract quality of such systems, and (at least for women) abandons the distinction of competence and performance that they require, she perforce gives up the possibility that women's consciousness undergoes systematic transformation through an equilibration process. This is tantamount to being unable to explain the movement from one stage to another. Indeed, it is tantamount to dispensing with the whole notion of "stage." This radical step is foreshadowed in the way that Murphy and Gilligan rejected both differentiation-integration and sequential transformation as criteria of more morally-developed positions (Murphy & Gilligan 1980, 97–100).

Strictly speaking, then, Gilligan's reinterpretation implies that only men develop, while women pass through "phases," "types," or "positions." This may account for the fact that, as she reports, her female subjects can proceed through her levels relatively rapidly (Gilligan & Belenky 1980). Indeed, the process of making an abortion decision sometimes appears more like a Wernerian "microgenesis" than a set of structural transformations. Thus passage through the levels is a kind of functional adaptation, akin to moving through the phases of problem-solving, task-performance, or "coping" as described in the literature of popular psychology. This kind of movement looks much more like something "produced" than something developing, as Lasch (1976, 7–8) has pointed out. Gilligan's account of femininity therefore approximates traditional feminist social-learning views within which it is construed as an artificial sex-role manufactured to fit particular social needs and requirements. Masculinity, on the other hand, would seem to be less a product of society than an autonomously evolving, transcultural developmental outcome.

Dimorphism is more infectious than Gilligan realizes. Despite her attempts to confine it to the content of male and female development, it tends to spread to the level of the form of life itself, making the transformational experiences of men and women different in kind. Men develop; women are produced.

Trait Psychology and Ethical Relativism: Are There More Than Two Genders?

What Piaget and Kohlberg achieved for psychology was the replacement of intellectual "factors" and personality "traits," defined arbitrarily in terms of age norms, by developmental differences ordered and evaluated in terms of their relation to a final telos or end-point which was explicitly and rationally justified on philosophical grounds (Elkind 1969; Kohlberg & de Vries 1971). Gilligan's attempt to retain the evaluative order and telos, without the philosophical justification of why movement through the order is to be construed as a rational progress, leaves her in a precariously inconsistent position. It is not unlike the position in which Jane Loevinger finds herself (Broughton & Zahaykevich 1977, 1980), indeterminate between a logically ordered developmental stage hierarchy and a relativistically defined set of types or trait clusters. This kind of inconsistency can be accommodated only by giving up one of the two conflicting metatheoretical assumptions—developmental or type/trait—or by transcending both in a new synthesis, a theoretical innovation. Coincidentally, Noam, Kohlberg, and Snarey have recently attempted such a maneuver themselves, although without a great deal of success (Noam et al. 1983; cf. Broughton 1983a).

Insofar as Gilligan dismisses Kohlberg's competence measure (the hypothetical dilemmas and the corresponding structural scoring system) and looks only at everyday moral-affective functioning, she gives up on the possibility of distinguishing potentiality from actuality, moral capability from moral performance. While this distinction is itself problematic in a variety of ways, she fails to acknowledge its complexities and so lapses into a kind of situational or contextual relativism (Frankena 1973). This is in addition to her "gender relativism." In general, her conceptual apparatus is much more conducive to a thoroughgoing relativism, including cultural and ethical relativism, than to any kind of universalist account (see, especially, Murphy & Gilligan 1980).

Relativism leads to all kinds of paradoxes, not the least of which is that to be consistent a relativist must be a nonrelativist about relativism, since its opposite (nonrelativism) is not considered even relatively valid. A parallel problem arises with "tolerance of ambiguity." Is one to be tolerant even of intolerance of ambiguity? If Gilligan were to embody genuinely the contextual relativism and tolerance of ambiguity that she holds as the highest virtues of womanhood, then she would have to be accepting, not rejecting, of structure, principles, and formal reasoning and would have to give up the specific qualities that she has so unambiguously attributed to women! Even were we to grant that women have the qualities that she attributes to them, those qualities would be bound to conflict and interfere with each other, since they have no rational consistency with one another. For example, women are required to be tolerant of ambiguity and simultaneously to be unambiguously caring and responsible. A similar problem arises for women who aspire to subjective "field dependence" without acknowledging that the latter logically requires the existence of a field that is objectively distinct from that which is dependent on it. The ambiguity between field dependence and field independence is presumably one which is not to be tolerated by the field-dependent woman. Such conceptual paradoxes are not confined to Gilligan's theory. For example, they appear earlier in Loevinger's theory of ego development in women (Broughton & Zahaykevich 1980).

In supplanting rational ethical rights and obligations with concrete commitments based on contextual and interpersonal sensitivity, Gilligan conflates the moral with the social and both with the practical. Here she is in agreement with her above mentioned subject #63, who summarizes her response to the Heinz dilemma by saying, "It is kind of more practical considerations than moral." Gilligan refers to her ethics as one of "best fit," where the "actual consequences of choice" become central in evaluating the morality of that choice. The possibility of moral objectivity is given up as a rationalist's pipe dream (Murphy & Gilligan 1980, 83). Thus Gilligan conforms to the greater pragmatism of the female voice that she documents empirically in her 1979 paper (435, 444). Her relativism extends and exaggerates this dispersion of the ethical; it has as its ultimate consequence the admission that it is no longer possible to say what morality is or to give any clear rational ground for it—what she calls the "ineluctable uncertainty of moral choice" (Murphy & Gilligan 1980, 83). The positivists rub their hands in glee as "philosophical speculation" is banished, so that ethics can then be absorbed easily into the world of facts. Moral problems are nothing but "dilemmas of fact," in Murphy and Gilligan's felicitous phrasing. "Ought" is thus reduced to "is" and prescriptive to descriptive, just as philosophical moralists from Dewey (Dewey & Tufts 1932) to Kohlberg (1971) had warned. Under Gilligan's interpretation, morality becomes simply the diversity of forms that it is found to take, or the diversity of things which are taken to be morality. Women's morality, and therefore also their very gender itself, becomes reducible to the "is," the order of more or less contingent "personality" factors, which in turn can be rendered empirically as psychological and social traits or processes observed at particular points in time and space. Generalizations from such observations become entirely dubitable, in tune with Gilligan's exhortations to women that they eschew the general in favor of the particular. (Presumably men would tend to make such generalizations, but women would not understand or believe them!)

Arguably, to the same degree, it follows from Gilligan's account that there ceases to be any particular thing called "gender." If the sexes are mutually exclusive, then "gender" denotes nothing in particular, serving only as a nominal rubric under which fall two specific forms of transformational psychological system. If men and women are nonoverlapping forms of mental life, "gender" is reducible without loss to "male plus female" and degenerates to the point of serving only a purely descriptive function. Since there is nothing to assure us that these two transformational systems cumulatively exhaust all psychological possibilities, there is no a priori reason why one might not discover a third gender, or a fourth, perhaps corresponding to nondeontological and nonaretaic metaethical systems.

The Denial of Self-Deception, Desire, and Being

In psychology, the notion that males and females exhibit different kinds of "self" can be traced to David Gutmann's (1965) paper on women and ego-strength and David Bakan's (1966) book on "agency" and "communion," both authors having been influenced primarily by psychoanalytic theory. Thus, Gilligan's dualism could be said to have its roots in the psychoanalytic tradition. Although she does not acknowledge the work of either Gutmann or Bakan, she does link her dualism to Chodorow's sociological "object relations" approach. However, there is something peculiar about this liaison, given that the assumptions of the cognitive-developmental approach are fundamentally incompatible with psychoanalytic theory. In fact, in both Piaget and Kohlberg, the developmental-stage idea was formulated in explicit opposition to Freudian theory, rejecting the concepts of primary process, repression, and the conflict-ridden dynamic unconscious, and discounting the centrality of sexuality and aggression, the significance of concrete attachments or objects-choices, and the formation of self and morality through processes of introjection and identification. By positing each "stage" as a complete replacement of the prior stage, the developmental approach eliminates the role of memory. Moreover, by extending the process of gender formation and moral development from childhood into adolescence and early adulthood, the formative role of early experience is further erased.

Despite her sensed affinity for Chodorow, Gilligan actively subscribes to all these departures from the psychoanalytic tradition. In particular, by limiting women's morality to the conscious, conflict-free sphere of the developing ego, she denies the possibility of self-deception. She ignores the Freudian revelation that we have an interest in not knowing ourselves and so hides from sight women's collusion in their own oppression (the later being "projected" into the male morality of mastery). As long as Gilligan asks her subjects only what they think of themselves, and accepts what they say at face value, she cannot distinguish insightfulness from defensiveness, knowledge from wishful thinking, or fact from fantasy. In trying to restore the subject to cognitive structuralism, she has collapsed subjectivity and objectivity into a flat, one-dimensional psychology. It is an idealist psychology in which self and self-concept are assumed to be identical. Small wonder then that Gilligan's women offer little resistance to traditional views of what women are and what their place is. Much as her interview offers them no way to penetrate their own self-mystifications, it offers them no way to penetrate the cultural mystifications of femininity. They are left without reason or desire for emancipation.

In Gilligan's Cartesian framework, knowledge is split from interest as mind is from body and reason from emotion. When gender is equated with cognitive style, it is severed from sexuality. The central iconography of abortion potentiates the fantasy of the total mastery of women's bodies by women's minds. Perhaps an even more contentious segregation of pure consciousness from the psychosomatic is attempted when Pollak and Gilligan (1982) interpret projective-test data cognitively rather than clinically in order to show that women are naturally nonaggressive. Gilligan's answer to Freud's question "What do women want?" seems to be "They don't want anything!" When a cognitive self and a moral worldview rule the psyche, desire, either sexual or aggressive, is largely irrelevant. What is there left, then, for women to do but to accept their nature, adjust to their social location, and retreat into the comfort of their "difference"? There is no sense in desiring another or in "aggressively" resisting oppression when life's travails are all in the mind.

The net result of this inexorable mentalism is that thinking is elevated to the point of its divorce from being. In actuality, Gilligan is not looking for evidence that her subjects are sympathetic, caring, responsible, or nonviolent. She is satisfied as soon as these qualities are manifested as espoused values in speech. It is enough that the "voice" or narrative style are different. Development is thus close to learning to talk in a certain way.

This, in turn, predisposes Gilligan's view to class and ideological biases. There is, in fact, a strong resemblance between her level 3 and what Bernstein (1975) has described as "new middle-class" discourse, or Reisman has termed the "other-directed" style of the modernized white-collar world. Carlson's 1971 paper, otherwise quite sympathetic with Gilligan's position, contains a literature review showing that the different cognitive styles which Gilligan describes are not to be found in nonwhite or nonmodernized groups and, furthermore, are subject to major historical alterations.

Conclusion

It is not the purpose of this critique to deny the contribution that Carol Gilligan has made to our understanding of the psychology of either gender or moral development. In drawing attention to the multiplicity of metaethical assumptive frameworks, she has offset any Kohlbergian tendencies to theoretical imperialism. In suggesting that women's experience is different from men's, she has reminded us that even the charismatic authority of the monolithic term "development" cannot distract us from the reality of human differences. In arguing for the salience of love, care, and commitment, she has restored to the focus of our vision the complex opposition between private and public morality.

Neither is it the purpose of this essay, in questioning the sharp distinction that Gilligan has drawn between herself and Kohlberg, to defend the latter's theory, which is surely subject to a number of serious criticisms (Broughton 1978b, 1983a). In fact, Kohlberg *accepts* much of Gilligan's theory (e.g., Kohlberg & Power 1981) and, insofar as he does so, the current critique takes issue with both theorists and their *folie à deux*.

Neither is it the purpose of this review to deny the existence of differences in general between the sexes or the reality of psychological gender differences in particular. Rather, in an attempt at a dialectical treatise on difference, I have sought to reveal some of the various contradictions that arise when a vision of gender is constructed in terms of a dualistic psychology. For example, Gilligan's separation and sharp contrast of "male" and "female" normative ethics and metaethics seems, in her own terms, extremely "masculine" in its emphasis on difference and boundary, its abstraction of the mind from life, and its tendency to essentialize gender, removing it from the context of relationships, discourse, culture, societal structure, and processes of historical formation. She subscribes to the very decontextualized binary logic that elsewhere she eschews as the false consciousness of a mystifying male moiety (Chodorow 1979).

How, then, can Gilligan account for the crossovers documented above even in her own interviews? At times, following other gender dualists like Daly (1978) and Ruddick (1980, 1984b), she covers herself by saying that the two forms of consciousness are not always mutually exclusive. Thus, sometimes, she backs off from the dual typology to a trait theory (e.g., Gilligan 1982a, 2), admitting that there are moments when men speak in the female voice and women speak in the male voice. However, as in Ruddick and Daly, such concessions are made infrequently and rarely with conviction. The reason for this is that to dwell on the overlap of genders undermines the whole explanatory framework. Is a man speaking in the feminine voice at that moment a woman? Or is he merely a female impersonator? At least at the intuitive level of "Who is female and who is male?" gender is a relatively clear distinction, and when slippage is permitted between gender and "voice" the latter loses its power to serve as either an explanation or an illumination of the former. Like "hysterical versus obsessive," "extroverted versus introverted," or "flexible versus rigid," the notion of "connected versus separated" voice then assumes the stature of a mere personality dimension. Such is the cost of backing down from a "type psychology" to a "trait psychology" (Cattell 1965, 54–55).

It is one of Gilligan's assumptions, following Virginia Woolf, that women's voice may be suppressed in a male-dominated culture, with the consequence that women's only alternative to silence may be to imitate male reasoning. As Lanser and Beck (1979) have put it, "Such a masculinization of women's minds is a patriarchal commonplace." They describe how this process tends to produce a "double voiced" discourse. This certainly could account for the appearance of the language of individualism, separation, rights, and justice in women's discourse. In addition, one of the things that Gilligan is pointing out about women is their contextual relativism, which allows them to appreciate different "voices."

However, the reverse case, the appearance of the female voice in men's discourse, cannot be explained along either of these lines. Since men are not oppressed by women, men are not the victims of "matriarchal feminization." Also, if the natural male tendency is to accentuate separation and boundary, and to be intolerant of ambiguity or plurality, then it should be most unnatural for men to appreciate or borrow the female voice. Thus, either an additional explanatory principle must be invoked or the thesis of "patriarchal masculinization" needs to be repealed and some substitute interpretation located to account for the symmetrical crossing over of voices exposed by empirical observation.

There is a sense in which gender is not indispensable to Gilligan's account. That is, she appears to be engaged in a broad metaphysical and epistemological task, a revival of liberal romantic idealism and mentalism requiring the collapse of some standard distinctions (e.g., subjectivity/objectivity and ideology/reality) and the erection or resurrection of others (e.g., cognition/affect, knowledge/interest, and mind/body). Such a philosophical task tends to take on a life of its own, apart from the additional considerations of whether or how such oppositions might be aligned with "male/female." One might also regret the strategic error of tying such oppositions to gender, since any synthesis of opposed terms then appears to undermine the distinctness of the sexes. As we have seen, her philosophical polarizations do not work. In fact, their revival of a thoroughgoing Cartesianism flies in the face of two centuries of philosophical critique (Cocks; McMillan 1982). Worse, as Flax (1980) has so interestingly shown, Descartes' dualisms themselves reflect a traditionally macho rejection of anything symbolizing the feminine. Thus, the empirically observable crossing over of voices is matched by the failure of Gilligan's conceptual polarizations.

However, the failure of these oppositions need not imply a retreat to androgyny, with its strange language of "masculine femininity" and "feminine masculinity." Admittedly, as writers from Hegel to the structuralists and critical theorists have pointed out, there are general social conditions of work, class, ideology, discourse, and mass culture that tend to homogenize men and women, making them in the same general image. Yet within that sameness, polarization may be introduced at any point where it might stabilize structures or modulate conflict. Gilligan's dualism appears to be one such surface polarization, constructed within the interests of a liberal individualism that can only benefit from more deeply inscribing the pseudoantinomies of rationality and irrationality that constitute its ideological foundation. In generating more talk about gender—indeed, in rendering gender itself as a form of speech or "voice"—developmental psychology augments the circulation of individualistic discourse and intensifies the flow of power that permeates its various surfaces, including the psychosomatic interiors of its various interlocutors.

The critical possibilities that emerge from Gilligan's undertaking arise at the point of opposition to Kohlberg's rationalism. However, in the absence of a grounded understanding of rationality or a dialectical vision of relation, the critical moment slips away. First, Gilligan mistakenly assumes that to reject Kohlberg's theory is to dispense with rationality as a basis for moral judgment, at least for women. In other words, she assumes that Kohlberg's account of "rationality" is an adequate one. A more parsimonious approach would be to work at the necessary task of examining Kohlberg's theory critically, while reserving the right for women to be rational under some description of reason less narrow than Kohlberg's.

Second, in confounding rationality with dogmatism, obsessive formality, and intellectualization, Gilligan's critique approximates a romantic position of direct opposition to judgment, limitation, and separation. On the rebound, she moves to an emphasis on the Dionysiac crossing and dissolution of boundaries. Such a counterposition entails two problems. On the one hand, it suggests an eternal return to a point psychologically prior to gender, which would preempt the desired distinction of women's consciousness from men's. On the other hand, it tends to support a psychodynamically regressive tendency toward infantile fusion with the mother. Such a romanticism has difficulty sustaining a distinction between a critique of false individuation and an argument for infantilization. As Benjamin's Hegelian analysis has pointed out, psychological development requires not a return to infantile connectedness but a dialectical reconstruction of dependence, in which individuation is reconciled with the need to have one's subjectivity recognized (Benjamin 1987). Gilligan misinterprets Chodorow's view of women. Chodorow (1978) characterized women's psychological structure not in terms of a simple tendency to connect but in terms of a complex and fragile preservation of the tension between merger and individuation.

There are echoes here of the classic Freud-Jung debate (see, e.g., Freud 1914/1963). Freud warned against a mystical developmentalism that undermined the basic psychoanalytic concept of unconscious wish. He saw in Jung an attempt to view gender as a duplication (Elektra as double of Oedipus), to render as complementary polarities achieving balance through development what were, in reality, the components of critical contradictions that only analytic insight and sublimation could modulate. In Gilligan's polarized developmental construction of gender on the basis of mirror-image traits, there is a return to the notion of symmetrical male-female complementarity. Early on, under the pressure of theoretical as well as clinical considerations, Freud gave up on the idea of gender symmetry. Although he proposed the notion of negative or "shadow" Oedipal complexes underlying the bisexuality of men and women, he was opposed to Jung's "animus/ anima" conception (later adapted by Winnicott) on account of its implications of symmetry.

Augmenting Freud's insight, Lacan has pointed to the social origins in humanistic ideology of the idea that genders are symmetrical complementaries (Mitchell & Rose 1982). He interprets the persistence of this antidialectical distortion as psychodynamically rooted in the infantile illusion that desire is reducible to satisfiable need, and that male and female be mutually the exclusive objects of that satisfaction. This symmetrical pseudomutuality is reproduced in Gilligan's rational-affective dualism, and also at her highest stage where asymmetry of desire, power, or communication is precluded a priori by the assumption of a natural tendency to harmonious self-other equality.

What's lacking in Lacan? Admittedly, his structuralist presuppositions leave him with crippling difficulties in understanding object relations, internalization, and fantasy, in explaining the way in which boys and girls assume the garb of their respective genders, in accounting for the personal rather than societal dimension of sexism, and in permitting any constructive departure from gender norms. Nevertheless, his clinical and conceptual struggles with gender leave us with some helpful directions for thinking the issue through from a point of view that is both psychodynamic and hermeneutic. First, his Hegelian unfolding of "being" provides a developmental perspective that is neither liberal individualist nor cognitivist. It therefore allows us to see the political struggle involved in gender identity, to distinguish gender from sex-role or self-interpretation, and to recuperate the existential significance that sex and gender have to us. Second, only the introduction of some asymmetry into both gender and cross-gender relations can preserve sexual distinction from a precipitous collapse into the blended voices of androgyny. At the same time, the basis of this asymmetry in the paradoxical nature of desire provides a way of understanding the important, tense, and yet variable link that gender has to sexuality. It is this connection to mutual sexual desire that works as a guarantee against androgynous unisexuality.

Third, *pace* Gilligan, gender is fundamentally a symbolic issue. The power of the masculine and feminine inheres to a significant degree in what they symbolize to men and women. This helps us to grasp the importance of discursive interaction, and the power relations that it mediates, in the never-ending negotiation of gender relations. It helps us to understand the sensuous, aesthetic quality of the relations between gendered individuals. It further helps in highlighting the liability of male and female, the degree to which they are subject to gradual or sudden changes of meaning, even to the point that they may turn dialectically into each other in the mutual permeation of interlocutors' being. Not least of the advantages of an appreciation of variability is that the tension between heterosexuality and homosexuality is not excluded.

Fourth, dwelling upon symbolism and significance implies both continuity and discontinuity. On the one hand, there is a symbolic tradition of masculinity and femininity borne by culture that is a constant reminder of the origins of present sex and sexuality in the activities and experiences of previous generations. On the other hand, the requirement that the symbolism of gender and sexuality be interpreted anew in each generation, even in each relationship, introduces a space for subjective will and objective novelty. This encourages a sensitivity to the ways in which gender and sexuality are both culturally diverse and historically formed and projected, while still presenting an insolubly rich field of discourse and struggle for each new pairing and each new social group.

These ontological, asymmetrical, sexual, symbolic, historical, cultural, hermeneutic, and intersubjective qualities of gender cry out for a vision more complex and with greater descriptive scope than a dualistic psychology of development has yet been able to offer. Gender and sexuality are phenomena that are in a relation of friction with superimposed cultural or ideological stereotypes and individual self-interpretations. It is the recognition and continuation of that friction which helps to make being gendered simultaneously entertaining and poignant. If we fail to recognize that friction, for whatever reason, we anesthetize ourselves to the sensuous texture and creative possibilities of being female or male.

Ethical Sensitivity and Moral Reasoning among Men and Women in the Professions

Muriel J. Bebeau and Mary Brabeck

The view that males and females differ in essential traits has been used to argue that men and women should be assigned to different societal roles (Lewin 1984; Rosenberg 1982). Historically, the perceptions that women lack the masculine traits of instrumentality, assertiveness, logical reasoning, detachment, and autonomy have been viewed as barriers to a woman's success in male-dominated fields (e.g. medicine, law, dentistry, higher level management) (Kaufman 1984). Historically, characteristics such as caring, sensitivity to others' needs, empathy, and concern about relationships have been viewed as "feminine" virtues by philosophers and "feminine" traits by psychologists. It has been argued that these characteristics especially equip women for the maternal role (Cancian 1987; Shields 1975; 1984) and certain professional roles (e.g., nursing and teaching, roles that involve nurturing and care) (Ehrenreich and English 1978).

Recently, however, some writers (e.g., Friedman 1988; Levine 1970) have suggested that feminine traits are especially valuable in male-dominated professions such as medicine and dentistry. The belief that women would enhance these professions through their relationship-oriented qualities (Levine 1970) suggests that women ought to be encouraged to enter male-dominated professions. This view is buttressed by Gilligan (1982) and other feminist theorists (Chodorow 1978; Lyons 1983; this volume; Martin 1985; this volume; Miller 1976; Noddings 1984; this volume). These writers do not challenge the belief that males and females differ in virtues and morality. Rather, they argue that theories of moral reasoning, and related test instruments, should put more value on "feminine" qualities and concerns. Reminiscent of Jane Addam's (1902) claim at the turn of the century that social progress depended on the unique moral insights of women, Gilligan (1982, 1986) has argued that an adequate moral theory is revealed by attending to "a different [feminine] voice."

There is evidence of the ubiquity of these stereotypes regarding masculine and feminine virtues and abilities (Bem 1974; Broverman et al., 1972; Chafetz 1978). Such gender differences, if they in fact exist, would have important implications for the education of people in the professions, as both relationship-oriented qualities and impartial, principled reasoning abilities are important for professionalism. However, recent suggestions (Gilligan 1982) that women score lower on tests of moral reasoning such as Kohlberg's, which emphasizes abstract reasoning and appeals to principles of justice at higher levels, is problematic because moral reasoning has been shown to be an important correlate of clinical performance (Sheehan et al. 1980).

What is the evidence to support the existence of gender differences? How can such differences be characterized? What evidence is there that moral theories and related test instruments are biased because they fail to attend to the different voice Gilligan identifies as an ethic of care? In this chapter we will review the literature that examines these questions. We will describe a recent four-component theoretical model of moral development (Rest 1983) that led us to investigate gender differences in an aspect of morality that is separate from moral reasoning. Specifically, we examined gender differences in situation-embedded ethical sensitivity among students aspiring to the dental profession. We will describe the instrument used to measure ethical sensitivity among dental students, the Dental Ethical Sensitivity Scale (Bebeau and Rest 1982) and present the results of our empirical work. Finally, we will argue that our empirical results suggest a reinterpretation of Gilligan's gender-related theory, an explanation for the conflicting results in other studies of male and female differences in moral development, and productive new directions for educators and for future research on the ethic of care.

REVIEW OF LITERATURE

People do believe that males and females differ in morality. Girls and women have a reputation among teachers, peers, and parents for being more helpful and empathic (Block 1984; Hoffman 1977; Shigetomi, Hartmann, and Gelfand 1981) and females report themselves to be more empathic and altruistic than males (Eisenberg and Lennon 1983; Eisenberg, Fabes, and Shea, this volume). Moreover, males expect females to make moral decisions from a more emotional perspective while seeing male morality as based on law and order reasoning (Bussey and Maughan 1982) and both male and female students classify care morality as "feminine" and justice morality as "masculine" (Ford and Lowery 1986). While self perceptions are not necessarily associated with overt behavior, the stereotype suggesting "a splitting of love and work that relegates expressive capacities to women while placing instrumental abilities in the masculine domain" (Gilligan 1982, p. 17) persists.

These views regarding male and female differences were carried into expectations of females entering the professions. In the early 1970s it was argued that the entrance of women into male-dominated professions would enhance the professions, principally because women would bring "feminine" qualities that would make the professions more person-oriented (Levine 1970). However, studies of successful academic psychologists (Helmreich et al. 1980) and of aspiring dentists (Bebeau and Loupe 1984) suggest that men and women with the qualifications to enter the professions are very similar to each other in perceptions of instrumentality and expressiveness, and do not describe themselves in the stereotypic ways observed in the general population. Women who aspire to the professions describe themselves as more instrumental than women in the general population, and men describe themselves as more expressive than do men in the general population (Bebeau and Loupe 1984).

Gilligan suggests that the expressive capacities of women influence the ways women reason about moral issues. She criticizes Kohlberg's (1969) theory because, she says, at the highest levels of his model the moral concern of females, the ethic of care, is omitted. She argues that women who have a greater concern with maintaining relationships are more likely to be scored at stage 3, the stage of mutual interpersonal expectations, relationships and conformity; males' concern with issues of justice would lead them to score at stage 4, the social system and conscience maintenance stage. Further, Gilligan asserts that hypothetical dilemmas assess logic and abstract reasoning which are more characteristic of male reasoning. Females, she argues, are excluded from the highest stages of the model because their reasoning is more particularistic and contextual.

There is evidence that logic, analytic ability and abstract reasoning are perceived as masculine traits (Broverman et al. 1972; Chafetz 1978; Lloyd 1983). However, evidence from observations of behavior does not support the stereotype (cf., Maccoby and Jacklin 1974; Linn and Petersen, 1985; Sherman 1978). If Gilligan's claim that females' contextual reasoning results in deflated scores on moral reasoning tests that assess abstract thought, we would find women scoring lower than males on the two measures of moral reasoning most commonly used, the Moral Judgment Interview (MJI) (Colby, Kohlberg, Gibbs, and Lieberman 1983) and the Defining Issues test (DIT) (Rest 1979).

To date, the literature examining gender differences in moral reasoning as defined by Kohlberg's theory do not support Gilligan's claim. Walker (1984; 1986; Walker and deVries 1985; Walker, deVries, and Trevethan 1987) has conducted a series of studies using meta-analysis to determine the effect of gender on MJI scores. He has consistently reported small effect sizes. In a recent report of a meta-analysis of 80 studies with a total of 152 samples, involving 10,637 subjects given the MJI, Walker (1986) reported that males did not score significantly higher than females. The Cohen's *d* to assess the mean effect size revealed that gender accounted for one twentieth of 1 percent of the variance in moral reasoning (r^2 = .0005). Baumrind (1986), a critic of Walker's work, also reported that when the effects of education are controlled, findings of gender differences in MJI scores are eliminated.

Meta-analysis (Thoma 1986) of 56 samples of over 6,000 male and female subjects who responded to the DIT yielded similar results. Thoma reported that at every age and educational level, females scored significantly higher than males, but less than half of 1 percent of the variance in DIT scores could be attributed to gender. Further, he found that education was 500 times more powerful in predicting moral judgment level than gender. These results have been supported by narrative reviews (Brabeck 1983) and by longitudinal studies that have reported that females are as likely as males to advance in the sequential order of development predicted from Kohlberg's theory (Snarey, Reimer, and Kohlberg 1985; Walker, 1989).

These results indicate that females use concepts of justice in making moral judgments as often as their male counterparts. Females are as likely as males to resolve moral issues in which individuals have competing claims, by appealing to abstract principles of justice. However, it has been argued that these studies do not necessarily undermine Gilligan's claim that Kohlberg's theory of moral reasoning is biased, because of flaws in the scoring schemes and design of the stimulus materials. With respect to the scoring scheme, Smetana (1984) argued that the Kohlbergian scoring schemes, in particular the MJI, do not include an ethic of care at all stages, thus one could not expect to find gender differences. The assumption made here is that care and justice are two distinct and separate moralities. In contrast, Kohlberg (Kohlberg, Levine, and Hewer 1983) has claimed that care is included in justice reasoning. A careful review of the MJI scoring criteria, that have been in use since 1978 (Colby et al. 1983) show that levels of relationship, caring, and interpersonal trust are considered norms and elements that are applied at each stage of the MJI scoring scheme. With respect to bias in stimulus materials, Walker (1989) showed that the ethic of care has been reliably identified and scored in studies using the dilemmas from the Kohlberg measure. It remains for future investigators to assess Kohlberg's claim that care and justice are indivisible (see also, Higgins, this volume). Nevertheless, researchers have attempted to design new measures and modify existing measures to examine care and justice as separate orientations as described by Gilligan. Studies examining claims about gender differences in the care/justice moral orientations must be interpreted cautiously since these studies are few, often employ small samples, and use different measures of moral orientation. However, there is a body of literature available that suggests the following conclusions.

First, the ethic of care can be identified in people's responses. The ethic of care has been identified and reliably scored in response to both real-life dilemmas (i.e., when subjects identify a personally experienced dilemma and discuss it) and hypothetical dilemmas (i.e., when subjects discuss a hypothetical story dilemma, such as whether or not Heinz should steal a drug to save his wife's life) (Langdale 1986; Lyons 1983; Pratt, Golding, and Hunter 1984; Rothbart, Hanley, and Albert 1986; Walker et al. 1987; Walker 1989). This suggests that the ethic of care identified by Gilligan is an identifiable aspect of people's moral responses.

Second, most studies indicate the majority of people, both males and females, use both the care and justice orientation (Gilligan and Attanucci 1988; Rothbart, Hanley, and Albert 1986; Walker et al. 1987). Thus, both males and females have been found to be concerned about the potential pain others might suffer, and to consider human relationships important moral considerations.

Third, studies examining the hypothesis that moral orientation is gender related yield inconsistent findings. Some studies that posed hypothetical moral dilemmas report no significant differences between males' and females' moral orientations (Rothbart, Hanley, and Albert 1986; Walker et al. 1987); other studies report females more likely to use a care orientation and males to use a justice orientation (Langdale 1986). Two studies that scored care-response and justice-rights responses on versions of the DIT that were modified to include care issues (Friedman, Robinson, and Friedman 1987; Pratt and Royer 1982), failed to support Gilligan's claims that males are more concerned with individual rights and women with care and concern for relationships. Furthermore, Ford and Lowery (1986) found no gender differences in students' ratings of the extent to which they used the response (care) and rights (justice) orientations. Interpretation of these studies is made difficult by the diverse ways in which care and justice orientations are measured. It must also be noted that it has not yet been empirically demonstrated that the "rights-justice" orientation measured in these studies are valid measures of Kohlberg's construct of justice moral reasoning.

Fourth, use of moral orientation appears to be related to the type of moral dilemmas being resolved. This conclusion is drawn from reviewing the studies that have used the Lyons' (1983) standardized scoring scheme to examine moral orientation by asking subjects to identify a personally experienced moral dilemma and to describe how they resolved it (Gilligan and Attanucci 1988; Lyons 1983; Langdale 1986; Rothbart et al. 1986; Walker et al. 1987). While there is inconsistency among these studies (e.g., Walker et al. 1987, did not find gender differences in moral orientation), and while most males and females used both orientations, females showed a preference for the care orientation and males for justice in self-identified moral dilemmas.

However, some researchers (Higgins, Power, and Kohlberg 1984; Nunner-Winkler 1984; Rothbart et al. 1986) report that the choice of orientation is related not to the gender of the respondent but to the type of dilemma discussed. For example, Higgins et al. (1984) report that a dilemma concerning helping another student is likely to elicit a care orientation; a dilemma about a theft is associated with justice considerations. Furthermore, Walker et al. (1987) report that while there were no gender differences in the types of "real life" moral dilemmas children identified, women reported more "personal" moral dilemmas and men more "impersonal" dilemmas. Women were more likely to raise family-related issues than men; men were more likely to raise work-related issues. These results may be due to differences in what males and females focus on as critical in defining a situation as a moral issue. The focus of moral concerns may be influenced by the activities and roles that are central in a person's life at any given time (e.g., Ruddick 1984).

Our literature review revealed that there is little difference in the ways males and females reason about the moral ideal; both principles of justice and principles of care are invoked in deciding what one ought to do to resolve a hypothetical moral dilemma. However, the differences we found in studies of self-defined moral conflicts suggest that males and females may be focusing on different issues. In a related study, Brabeck and Weisgerber (1988) asked male and female college students to describe their responses to the same real-life event, the explosion of the Challenger spacecraft. They found that while males and females did not differ in level or type of affective response, they focused on different aspects of the event. Women reported spontaneously focusing on more of the person-centered aspects of the tragedy while men reported the technological aspects were more salient. However, Brabeck and Weisgerber did not measure moral reasoning. Ford and Lowery (1986) suggest that to examine whether or not females focus on issues of relationship, responsibility, and care in defining a conflict as moral, "it seems necessary to return to a standardized . . . format." In order to examine whether males and females differ in their focus on care or justice in defining a conflict as moral, we used a standardized test (described later) to examine gender differences in situation-embedded ethical sensitivity. Rest's (1983) recently described theory of the components of morality offered a theoretical model for testing our hypothesis.

A NEW PERSPECTIVE ON MORAL DEVELOPMENT: ETHICAL SENSITIVITY

Rather than arguing that the Rawlsian concept of justice as fairness exemplified by Kohlberg's stage theory excludes concern for care, connectedness, and harmony, one might search for the presence or absence of care, as it relates to other components of morality. Rest (1983) has described ethical sensitivity as the first of a four component model of morality. Ethical sensitivity (Component 1) is the identification of the salient ethical aspects of a dilemma. The processes of Component 1 are used prior to (Component

2) formulating a morally defensible course of action, for example, appealing to principles of justice. These processes are followed by Component 3, distinguishing between moral and nonmoral values and committing to the moral value, and Component 4, executing and implementing a plan of action that resolves the moral problem effectively.

According to Rest, ethical sensitivity (Component 1) can be distinguished from principled moral reasoning (Component 2). While the latter involves "determining what course of action would best fulfill a moral ideal, what *ought* to be done in the situation" (Rest 1983, p. 561) the former involves interpreting the situation and identifying "possible courses of action in a situation that affect the welfare of someone else" (p. 559). Moral sensitivity includes making inferences from individuals' verbal and nonverbal behaviors, identifying what others want or need, anticipating their reactions to one's attempt to help, and responding with appropriate affect.

NEW MEASURE OF MORAL SENSITIVITY: DESCRIPTION AND SUMMARY OF STUDIES OF VALIDITY AND RELIABILITY

Bebeau and Rest (1982) have developed a measure of ethical sensitivity (Rest's Component 1) to assess the ability of dentists to identify and interpret typical ethical problems that arise in dental practice. Four dramas, based on a study of the recurrent ethical problems in the practice of dentistry (Bebeau, Reifel, and Speidel 1981) are presented in the Dental Ethical Sensitivity Test (DEST).

Synopsis of DEST Dramas

The Judy Radiwich Case. Dr. Oldham is about to retire. He plans to sell his practice to Dr. Young, a recent graduate. Dr. Oldham observes Dr. Young as he considers a treatment for Judy Radiwich, a young woman from a prominent family in the community. They have been patients of Dr. Oldham's practice for years. As they discuss the treatment, a difference of opinion develops on what treatment should be recommended. Dr. Oldham insists that Dr. Young follow his advice.

The Jim Lohman Case. Jim Lohman has a toothache that requires endodontic treatment. He needs much other work, but has little money. Several options are presented, but he has difficulty making a decision.

The Margaret Herrington Case. Ms. Herrington has recently moved to a new city. Her new dentist notices advanced periodontal disease and traumatic occlusion on the crown of a molar, and moderate periodontal disease around five other crowns. Upon inquiry, the dentist is informed that the crowns were placed about two years ago. Margaret appears to be unaware of the periodontal disease. The dentist believes the crowns cannot be salvaged; they must be replaced. Margaret does not have dental insurance.

The Sandy Johnson Case. Sandy Johnson is a young woman with serious dental and oral health problems. She is extremely thin. She is interested in improving her appearance as she believes she is getting a new job. She resists any discussion of nutrition and describes her annoyance with her mother who is, as she describes it, constantly nagging her about eating.

The dramatizations consist of dialogues between a dentist and client, such as might occur in a dental office. These tape-recorded dramas serve as stimulus materials that subjects hear. Subjects are tested on what they identify as the problems presented. This is accomplished by having subjects enter into a dialogue with a drama character. The subject's dialogue and subsequent responses to interview questions, which ask about the assumptions and perspectives underlying the student's responses, are tape recorded.

The interviews are transcribed and scored for the degree of sensitivity to several characteristics of the patient and sensitivity to the responsibilities of the dentist. The four interviews are scored by assigning ratings from one to three to indicate the degree of recognition of each of 34 criteria (seven to ten criteria per drama). Summing across the four dramas yields a minimum score of 34 and a maximum of 102 points.

It is noteworthy that the scoring criteria were developed in collaboration with practicing dentists and moral philosophers. We believe that both issues of fairness (justice) and concerns for harmony, connectedness, and nonviolence (care) are reflected in the criteria. In fact, it was the practicing dentists who most clearly articulated the ethic of care. Examples include: concerns for giving information about the status of health in a way that will cause the least hurt; concerns that giving bad news about standard care could so undermine trust in the profession that the individual may stop seeking care, and thus be doubly harmed; and, an overriding concern for resolving problems in a way that maintains relationships between dentists and patients, and between patients and the profession.

DEST Reliability

The reliability of the DEST is reported in several studies, most recently summarized in Rest, Bebeau, and Volker (1986). Item agreement averaged 86.5 percent in one study, and 89.9 percent in another. Agreement between raters, that is, correlations calculated for drama subscores, averaged .87 for the four dramas. Test-retest correlations over several weeks averaged .68 at the individual drama level, and by the Spearman-Brown formula is estimated at .90 for the test as a whole.

The Validity of Moral Sensitivity as a Theoretical Construct

Research exploring the properties of measures of moral sensitivity in professional situations is still underway. However, findings from Volker's (1984) study of moral sensitivity, using a measure designed for counseling psychologists, and studies of dental students' moral sensitivity using the DEST (see Rest et al. 1986), indicate the following:

1. The content validity of both measures is well established, and the scoring criteria are sufficiently well defined to produce adequate interrater reliability.

2. Moral sensitivity correlates only moderately with DIT scores (in the .2 to .5 range), which indicates that Component 1 processes are separate from Component 2 processes. Thus, morality is not a single, unitary process. It is possible for a person to be skilled at interpreting the ethical issues in a situation (Component 1), but unskilled at working out a balanced view of a moral solution (Component 2), and vice versa.

3. There is evidence for both convergent and divergent validity. Both Bebeau and Volker asked experienced clinicians to rate transcripts of subject responses on moral sensitivity without knowledge of their respective scoring schemes. These ratings were compared to scores produced by the scoring system. Volker reported a correlation of .95, indicating agreement between his formalized measure of moral sensitivity and the more intuitive judgments of experienced clinicians, thus demonstrating convergent validity. He also offered evidence of divergent validity in that moral sensitivity scores were negatively ($-.52$) correlated with verbosity. DEST scores correlated .69 with the practitioner's intuitive rankings of moral sensitivity and only correlated in the .20 to .40 range with measures of verbal fluency, technical knowledge, and word count of subjects' responses.

4. Data collected from a sample of counseling psychologists and from several samples of dental students indicate that individuals vary greatly in moral sensitivity. Further, moral sensitivity, as measured by the DEST, has been shown to improve with deliberate instruction (Zimney 1986).

5. Although each DEST drama contributes specific variability in moral sensitivity, evidence of the degree of internal consistency of the measures is high enough (Cronbach alphas ranging from .70 to .78) to enable us to study moral sensitivity as a construct.

EMPIRICAL INVESTIGATION OF MORAL REASONING AND ETHICAL SENSITIVITY

Our examination of Rest's Component 2, the moral reasoning (DIT scores) and Component 1, moral sensitivity (DEST score) among male and female dental students draw upon data from a number of on-going studies of professional ethical development. We expected that women dental students would be more sensitive to the potential hurt experienced by the dental patient, more concerned about the affective state of the patient, and more aware of the interpersonal issues. Thus, we predicted that females would identify more ethical aspects of dilemmas that professionals face when treating dental patients than would males. Research has shown that differential socialization (e.g., Block 1984) has led women to place greater emphasis on interpersonal relationships. Females have also been found to be more accurate than males in decoding nonverbal cues about another person's affective state (Eisenberg and Lennon 1983; Eisenberg et al., this volume) and more likely to appeal to empathic role taking to justify stage 3 moral reasoning (Gibbs, Arnold, and Burkhart 1984). Thus, we hypothesized that while males and females would not differ in their reasoning after a moral dilemma had been defined (Component 2), they would differ in sensitivity to ethical issues (Component 1). Research described earlier, which found that differences in moral orientation were related to the type of situation subjects identified as moral dilemmas, supports our prediction.

The advantage of studying gender differences in this professional school context using the DEST are as follows: 1) extensive data on background variables are available, so the equivalency of the male and female groups can be established, and 2) the DEST is a well-validated measure that, though not specifically designed to test Gilligan's conceptions of different moral orientations, makes extensive use of these concepts in assessing an ability which is thought to be an essential component of moral behavior. The DEST scoring scheme provides an overall indication of sensitivity and specific items assess recognition of issues of care and issues of justice. Both relationship and justice issues are contained in all the DEST dramas, but two dramas present situations in which there is a high degree of tension between care and justice. Analysis of specific items in these dramas seemed particularly appropriate for determining gender preferences for these issues.

Analysis of data from several data sets enabled us to 1) compare male and female dental students' moral reasoning; 2) examine gender differences in ethical sensitivity, particularly the ability to identify ethical problems which are embedded in situations frequently encountered by dentists; 3) analyze whether male dental students are more likely to recognize justice issues and female students more likely to identify care issues as salient; 4) examine differences between males and females in the priority assigned care and justice issues; and 5) determine whether students can integrate both care and justice issues in their responses to ethical problems after training.

To determine whether women would attend to care issues more than men, we selected a subset of the existing DEST scoring criteria where issues of care and justice seemed to be in tension (see DEST Scoring Manual [Bebeau and Rest 1982], items 11.C. and 11.D. of the Radiwich Case, and items I.E. and I.F. of the Herrington Case). The Radiwich and Herrington dramas (described earlier) presented clues to a conflict between relationship and justice in a way that expert clinicians find difficult to resolve (Bebeau, Reifel, and Speidel 1981). By applying existing criteria, it is possible to assess the degree to which students attended to each issue. For example: In the Judy Radiwich drama, technical clues about Judy Radiwich's dentition, combined with Judy's expressed concern for aesthetics ought to alert the student to recommend a treatment alternative that is contrary to the wishes of Dr. Oldham. A tension develops between the young dentist's duty to give priority to the patient's rights (the fairness issue) and his wish to maintain harmony with Dr. Oldham, a colleague, elderly man, and a person from whom he hopes to purchase the practice (the care issue). In the Margaret Herrington drama, clues are presented that ought to alert the listener to the fairness issue: Margaret should not have to pay again for work that does not meet professional standards and appears to have caused harm to her periodontal health. Likewise, the dialog ought to alert the listener to the care issue: because Margaret's previous dentist helped her overcome her apprehension (she liked and trusted him), and because she cares deeply about her oral health, news about her health status and the previous inferior dental work is likely to be upsetting and may interfere with her confidence in both the old and new dentist and could influence her decision to continue with dental care.

The selected items from the Radiwich and Herrington dramas were scored for the degree to which students recognized each issue. The scoring manual includes discrete descriptions for a three-point scale, where 3 = clear recognition and 1 = no recognition. Judges are permitted to use a 1.5 and 2.5 category for responses that fall short of the next criterion. Then, responses were examined to see whether men and women students had a tendency to prioritize care over justice or vice versa. Responses to each drama were classified into one of the following categories: Clearly recognized both issues (e.g., scores a 2.5 or 3 on care, and 2.5 or 3 on justice); Shows some, but equal, recognition of both issues; Prioritizes justice over care; Recognizes justice/ignores care (e.g., scores a 3 on justice, a 1 on care); Prioritizes care over justice; Recognizes care/ignores justice; Ignores both issues. See Moen (1987) for exact coding rules.

University of Minnesota dental students complete the DIT and the DEST as part of course requirements for the curriculum in professional ethics. The DIT was first administered in 1979, and data are currently available for all entering freshmen and several advanced level groups. DEST scores were first obtained in 1981 and protocols have been collected for 145 beginning and over 500 advanced level students. Typically, protocols are scored by a cadre of practicing dentists who use the Scoring Manual (Bebeau and Rest 1982), and provide individual feedback to students.

In addition to DEST and DIT scores, data are available on undergraduate GPA, scores on the Dental Aptitude Test, dental school GPA, clinical performance ratings, and other demographic variables. Clinical performance ratings, assigned by clinic directors and codirectors at the end of the senior year, were selected for gender comparison because the scale includes assessment of interpersonal skills, personal characteristics, and professional abilities that are relevant to Gilligan's theoretical claims. The 20 item six-point Likert scale used at Minnesota is similar to scales used in medical schools, but Minnesota faculty achieve remarkably high interrater reliability when compared with other studies of the reliability of such measures (Meetz, Bebeau, and Thoma 1988). Further, clinical performance ratings of Minnesota students predict timely completion of dental school requirements, a criterion faculty believe is an important predictor of success in practice. Clinical ratings are not related to preadmissions criteria nor to dental school GPA.

We conducted a number of analyses to investigate gender differences in ethical sensitivity (Component 1), measured by the DEST and moral reasoning (Component 2), measured by the DIT. (These results and additional discussion can be found in Bebeau and Brabeck 1987). A summary of the results follows.

A meta-analysis of seven groups of male and female dental students (first year and third year) who took the DIT prior to implementing an ethics curriculum, indicated effect sizes (Cohen's d) that varied from $-.45$ to $.53$ across the samples. Collapsing across the seven samples indicated a mean of 47.20, $SD = 12.64$ for 593 males, and a mean of 47.60, $SD = 12.97$ for 184 females, with an effect size of $d = .03$. This difference is lower than the average effect size ($d = .21$) reported by Thoma (1986), suggesting that men and women dental students are very similar in moral reasoning ability.

Since educational factors have been shown to account for differences in moral judgment (Thoma 1986), we needed to determine the equivalency of the 196 male and 44 female students before analyzing gender differences in ethical sensitivity. No significant differences were observed on undergraduate GPA (Males $M = 3.21$, $SD = .36$; Females $M = 3.23$, $SD = .35$); Dental Aptitude Scores (Males $M = 4.85$, $SD = 1.47$; Females $M = 4.50$, $SD = 1.36$); or, Clinical Performance Ratings (Males $M = 90.14$, $SD = 15.33$; Females $M = 89.81$, $SD = 14.57$). On the two clinical performance subscales, where we thought gender differences might appear, that is, personal attributes and interpersonal abilities, women achieved slightly higher scores (mean differences of .5 and 1.00 point respectively), but the differences were not significant.

Our meta-analysis replicates previous reports (Thoma 1986) that gender differences in the ability to resolve hypothetical dilemmas, using principles of justice as measured by the DIT, are small. Females and males do not differ in their ability to reason abstractly about moral issues (Component 2).

Next, we examined gender differences in ethical sensitivity (Component 1). Transcripts of 196 men and 44 women (class of 1985 and 1986) who took the DEST in the spring of their junior year were analyzed by two raters, both dentists, who established their interrater reliability following the procedures described in Bebeau, Rest, and Yamoor (1985). Agreement ranged from 78 percent to 91 percent, with an average of 86 percent across the 34 items. Interrater reliability, calculated for the total score for each drama, ranged from .78 to .91, with an average reliability of .83. The mean DEST score for 44 women in the two classes was significantly higher $p < .002$ than for the 196 men. An estimate of the effect size (Cohen's d) indicates a moderate effect, $d = .51$ overall, and analysis of differences at the drama level indicates that each drama is contributing to the overall effect. Item analysis indicates that women scored significantly higher than men on only four of the 34 items, equal to or somewhat higher than men on 23 items, somewhat lower than men on six items, and significantly lower on one item. Thus, the observed gender differences resulted from a cumulative effect that was not attributable to any identifiable cluster of items.

One possible explanation for the greater ethical sensitivity of women might be attributed to prior experience or training within the profession. Equivalency of males and females on clinical performance and attitudes, academic achievement, and previous professional experience was established prior to testing for gender differences in DEST scores. However, Coombs (1976) reported that prior experience in dentistry was a determining factor in career choice for 58 percent of the women entering dental school in the early 1970s. Therefore, a comparison of DEST scores of the 20 women who had such prior experience or training with those who did not was made; it was not significant, $p < .67$.

Women dental students showed significantly greater sensitivity to the ethical issues contained in professional dilemmas than did their male colleagues. These differences cannot be attributed to differences in clinical performance, academic achievement or prior experience in the profession, or to prior training or experience in the related professions, dental hygiene, nursing or dental assisting. Thus, there appears to be a gender difference in what Rest has identified as Component 1, the ability to identify the ethical issues of a dilemma.

To further investigate gender differences in ethical sensitivity, we compared mean recognition scores by gender for the care and justice items and examined how the men and women prioritized the care and justice issues in each of the two cases from the DEST. Complete transcripts were available for 87 women who completed the DEST as juniors between 1981 and 1985. An equal number of men from each class was randomly selected for the gender comparison. Analyses of recognition of care and justice issues in the two DEST dramas were conducted by a dental student who practiced rating items and comparing ratings with the test developer until 80 percent agreement was consistently achieved. Samples selected to test interrater reliabilities achieved 90 percent agreement. Comparison of mean recognition scores by gender for care and justice items indicated one significant finding. The women achieved significantly higher scores ($M = 2.26$, $S.D. = .77$) than the men ($M = 2.02$, $S.D. = .85$) on recognition of the justice issue in the Radiwich case. Cohen's d estimate of the effect size, indicated a small to moderate effect (.36) favoring women. A chi-square revealed that women did not prioritize care over justice issues more frequently than men, nor did men prioritize justice over care issues more frequently than women. In fact, trends were not even in the expected direction, as 36 percent of the men compared with 29 percent of the women recognized care but ignored the justice issue (see Table 8.1). Based on the item analysis described earlier and the prioritization of care and justice concerns differences in ethical sensitivity appear to

Table 8.1
Prioritization of Care and Justice Issues by Gender for Two Dramas

Number of Responses Per Category

Prioritization Categories	Men (N=87)			Women (N=87)		
	Judy Radiwich	Margaret Herrington	Cases Combined	Judy Radiwich	Margaret Herrington	Cases Combined
Complete Integration	16	2	18 (10%)	10	4	14 (8%)
Some Integration	16	10	26 (15%)	14	6	20 (11%)
Care over Justice	4	3	7 (4%)	4	1	5 (3%)
Care Ignore Justice	13	38	51 (29%)	25	38	62 (36%)
Justice over Care	23	6	29 (17%)	20	9	29 (17%)
Justice Ignore Care	9	3	12 (7%)	9	5	14 (8%)
Ignores both Issues	6	25	31 (18%)	5	24	29 (17%)

result from greater sensitivity to a wide range of patient characteristics and professional responsibilities rather than to a greater propensity on the part of women to attend to issues of care.

Consistent with the literature we reviewed on gender differences in moral reasoning (Component 2), women who were at the same educational level as their male counterparts did not give greater priority to issues of care, nor were there differences in the ability of males and females to integrate care and justice issues. A concern to educators is the fact that only about one-fourth of the students give equal recognition to both issues and 17.5 percent of the students failed to recognize either issue. Since this integration is necessary for adequate identification of the moral aspects of a professional dilemma, these results suggest a need for training and led us to examine significant changes in ethical sensitivity following completion of a professional ethics course.

Forty juniors (38 males and 2 females) who completed the DEST before and after a five week course in Professional Problem Solving were selected from Zimney's (1986) sample and categorized according to preference for care and justice issues in the Herrington and Radiwich cases. We examined changes in subjects' integration of care and justice issues following instruction. The chi-square ($df = 6$) was 19.31, $p < .001$, ($N = 40$) and significant changes occurred in two categories: 1) the proportion of students who integrated care and justice after instruction was significantly greater, and 2) the number of students who no longer ignored both care and justice issues was greatly reduced (see Table 8.2). Zimney's (1986) study showing significant change in DEST scores following instruction indicates that moral sensitivity is an ability that can be developed. Our results confirm that higher levels of integration of care and justice can be achieved following instruction.

The DEST was designed to measure ethical sensitivity in a dental context, but we believe it could be used to explore gender differences with other populations. Technical knowledge of dentistry is prerequisite to a full understanding of the complexity of the ethical issues, but the measure has been used successfully to assess sensitivity of entering freshmen (Bebeau, Rest, and Yamoor 1985), who presumably lacked technical knowledge. Alternatively, the methodology employed in the DEST could be used to develop profession-specific tests to study ethical sensitivity among males and females in other professions.

This line of research also suggests that much may be gained by understanding morality as multi-faceted. The findings of researchers that women are socialized to be more empathic, altruistic, and nurturing (Block 1984; Eisenberg et al., this issue) may be useful in examining the source of the gender difference we observed. Other fruitful areas of study may be to explore gender differences in commitment to moral values (Component 3), or the ability to effectively execute moral intentions (Component 4 in Rest's

Table 8.2
Percent of Students (N = 40) Integrating Care and Justice Issues Before and After Instruction
Number of Responses Per Category

Prioritization Categories	Before Instruction			After Instruction		
	Judy Radiwich	Margaret Herrington	Cases Combined	Judy Radiwich	Margaret Herrington	Cases Combined
Complete Integration	1	6	7 (9%)	2	11	13 (16%)
Some Integration	0	1	1 (1%)	2	5	7 (9%)
Care over Justice	1	2	3 (4%)	0	1	1 (1%)
Care Ignore Justice	4	20	24 (30%)	3	14	17 (21%)
Justice over Care	8	3	11 (14%)	10	5	15 (19%)
Justice Ignore Care	13	0	13 (16%)	20	1	21 (26%)
Ignores both Issues	13	8	21 (26%)	3	3	6 (8%)
Total			80 (100%)			80 (100%)

255

[1983] system). Clearly, those engaged in the education and development of professionals need to examine how students are being trained to attend to the care and justice issues in moral dilemmas they will confront within their profession.

REFERENCES

Addams, J. (1902). *Democracy and social ethics*. New York: Macmillan and Co.

Baumrind, D. (1986). Sex differences in moral reasoning: Response to Walker's (1984) conclusion that there are none. *Child Development* 57: 511–21.

Bebeau, M. J., and Brabeck, M. M. (1987). Integrating care and justice issues in professional moral education: A gender perspective. *Journal of Moral Education* 16: 189–203.

Bebeau, M. J., and Loupe, M. (1984). Masculine and feminine personality attributes of dental students and their attitudes toward women's roles in society. *Journal of Dental Education* 48: 309–14.

Bebeau, M. J., and Rest, J. R. (1982). *The dental ethical sensitivity test*. Center for the Study of Ethical Development, Burton Hall, University of Minnesota.

Bebeau, M. J., Rest J. R., and Yamoor, C. M. (1985). Measuring dental students ethical sensitivity. *Journal of Dental Education* 49: 225–35.

Bebeau, M. J., Reifel, N. M., and Speidel, T. M. (1981). Measuring the type and frequency of professional dilemmas in dentistry. *Journal of Dental Research* 60 (Abstract #891) 532.

Bem, S. L. (1974). The measurement of psychological androgyny. *Journal of Consulting and Clinical Psychology* 43: 155–162.

Block, J. H. (1984). *Sex role identity and ego development*. San Francisco: Jossey-Bass.

Brabeck, M. (1983). Moral judgment. Theory and research on differences between males and females. *Developmental Review* 3: 274–91.

Brabeck, M., and Weisgerber, K. (1988). Responses to the Challenger tragedy: Subtle and significant gender differences. *Sex Roles* 19: 639–50.

Broverman, I. K., Vogel, S. R., Broverman, D. M., Clarkson, F. E., and Rosenkrantz, P. S. (1972). Sex-role stereotypes: A current appraisal. *Journal of Social Issues* 28: 59–78.

Bussey, K., and Maughan, B. (1982). Gender differences in moral reasoning. *Journal of Personality and Social Psychology* 42: 701–6.

Cancian, F. (1987). *Love in America: Gender and self-development*. Cambridge, MA: Cambridge University Press.

Chafetz, J. S. (1978). *Masculine feminine or human*. Itasca, IL: F. E. Peacock Publishers.

Chodorow, N. (1978). *The reproduction of mothering: Psychoanalysis and the sociology of gender*. Berkeley, CA: University of California Press.

Colby, A., Kohlberg, L., Gibbs, J., and Lieberman, M. (1983). A longitudinal study of moral judgment. *Monographs of the Society of Research in Child Development* 48: (1–2, Serial No. 200).

Coombs, J. A. (1976). Factors associated with career choice among women dental students. *Journal of Dental Education* 40: 724–32.

Ehrenreich, B., and English, D. (1978). *For her own good: 150 years of the experts' advice to women*. Garden City, NY: Anchor Press/Doubleday.

Eisenberg, N., and Lennon, R. (1983). Sex differences in empathy and related capacities. *Psychological Bulletin* 94: 100–31.

Ford, M. R. and Lowery, C. R. (1986). Gender differences in moral reasoning: A comparison of the use of justice and care orientations. *Journal of Personality and Social Psychology* 50: 777–83.

Friedman, E. (1988). Changing the ranks of medicine:Women MDs. *Medical World News*, April 25, pp. 57–68.

Friedman, W. J., Robinson, A. B., and Friedman, B. L. (1987). Sex differences in moral judgments? A test of Gilligan's theory. *Psychology of Women Quarterly* 11: 37–46.

Gibbs, J. C., Arnold, K. D., and Burkhart, J. E. (1984). Sex differences in expression of moral judgment. *Child Development* 55:1,040–43.

Gilligan, C. (1982). *In a different voice: Psychological theory and women's development*. Cambridge, MA: Harvard University Press.

_____ . (1986). Reply by Carol Gilligan. *Signs: Journal of Women in Culture and Society* 11: 324–33.

Gilligan, C. and Attanucci, J. (1988). Two moral orientations: Gender differences and similarities. *Merrill-Palmer Quarterly* 34: 223–37.

Helmreich, R. C., Spence, J. T., Beane, W. E., Lucker, G. W., and Matthews, K. A. (1980). Making it in academic psychology: Demographic and personality correlates of attainment. *Journal of Personality and Social Psychology* 39: 869–908.

Higgins, A., Power, C., and Kohlberg, L. (1984). The relationship of moral atmosphere to judgments of responsibility. In *Morality, moral behavior and moral development*, eds W. M. Kurtines and J. L. Gewirtz. New York: John Wiley and Sons.

Hoffman, M. L. (1977). Sex differences in empathy and related behavior. *Psychological Bulletin* 84: 712–22.

Kaufman, D. R. (1984). Professional women: How real are the recent gains? In *Women: A feminist perspective*, ed. J. Freeman. Mountain View, CA: Mayfield Publishing Co.

Kohlberg, L. (1969). Stage and sequence: The cognitive-developmental approach to socialization. In *Handbook of socialization theory and research*, ed. D. A. Goslin. Chicago: Rand McNally.

Kohlberg, L., Levine, C., and Hewer, A. (1983). *Moral stages: A current formulation and a response*. Basel: Karger.

Langdale, S. (1986). A re-vision of structural-developmental theory. In *Handbook of moral development*, ed. G. L. Sapp. Birmingham, AL: Religious Education Press.

Levine, P. T. (1970). Distaff dentists. *Journal of Dental Education*, 34: 352–57.

Lewin, M. (1984). *In the shadow of the past: Psychology portrays the sexes*. New York: Columbia University Press.

Linn, M. C., and Petersen, A. C. (1985). Facts and assumptions about the nature of sex differences. In *Handbook for achieving sex equity through education*, ed. S. S. Klein. Baltimore: The Johns Hopkins University Press.

Lloyd, G. (1983). Reason, gender and morality in the history of philosophy. *Social Research* 50: 490–513.

Lyons, N. (1983). Two perspectives: On self, relationships, and morality. *Harvard Educational Review* 53: 125–45.

Maccoby, E. E., and Jacklin, C. N. (1974). *The psychology of sex differences.* Stanford, CA: Stanford University Press.

Martin, J. R. (1985). *Reclaiming a conversation.* New Haven, CT: Yale University Press.

Meetz, H.K., Bebeau, M. J., and Thoma, S. J. (1988). The validity and reliability of a clinical performance rating scale. *Journal of Dental Education* 52: 290–97.

Miller, J. B. (1976). *Toward a new psychology of women.* Boston: Beacon Press.

Moen, T. K. (1987). Gender differences in dental students' ability to recognize ethical issues. Unpublished manuscript, University of Minnesota, School of Dentistry.

Noddings, N. (1984). *Caring: A feminine approach to ethics and moral education.* Berkeley, CA: University of California Press.

Nunner-Winkler, G. (1984). Two moralities? A critical discussion of an ethic of care and responsibility versus an ethic of rights and justice. In *Morality, moral behavior and moral development*, eds. W. M. Kurtines and J. L. Gewirtz. New York: John Wiley and Sons.

Pratt, M. W., Golding, G., and Hunter, W. J. (1984). Does morality have a gender? Sex, sex role, and moral judgment relationships across the adult life span. *Merrill-Palmer Quarterly* 30: 321–40.

Pratt, M. W., and Royer, J. M. (1982). When rights and responsibilities don't mix. Sex and sex-role patterns in moral judgment orientation. *Canadian Journal of Behavioral Science* 14: 190–204.

Rest, J.R. (1979). *Development in judging moral issues.* Minneapolis: University of Minnesota Press.

_____ . (1983). Morality. In *Carmichael's Manual of Child Psychology, Volume 3: Cognitive Development*, ed. P. Mussen. (556–629), New York: John Wiley and Sons.

Rest, J. R., Bebeau, M. J., and Volker, J. (1986). An overview of the psychology of morality. In *Moral development: Advances in research and theory*, ed. J. R. Rest. New York: Praeger Publishers.

Rosenberg, R. (1982). *Beyond separate spheres: Intellectual origins of modern feminism.* New Haven, CT: Yale University Press.

Rothbart, M. K., Hanley, D., and Albert, M. (1986). Gender differences in moral reasoning. *Sex Roles: A Journal of Research* 15: 645–53.

Ruddick, S. (1984). Maternal thinking. In *Mothering: Essays in feminist theory*, ed. J. Trebilcot. Totowa, NJ: Rowman & Allanheld Pub.

Sheehan, T. J., Hustad, S. D., Candee, D., Cook, C. D., and Bergen, M. (1980). Moral judgment as a predictor of clinical performance. *Evaluation in the Health Professions* 3: 393–404.

Sherman, J. (1978). *Sex-related cognitive differences.* Springfield, IL: C. C. Thomas.

Shields, S. (1975). Functionalism, Darwinism, and the psychology of women: A study in social myth. *American Psychologist* 30: 739–54.

_____ . (1984). "To pet, coddle and do 'do for'" Caretaking and the concept of maternal instinct. In *In the Shadow of the past: Psychology portrays the sexes*, ed. M. Lewin. NY: Columbia University Press.

Shigetomi, C. C., Hartmann, D. P., and Gelfand, D. M. (1981). Sex differences in children's altruistic behavior and reputations for helpfulness. *Developmental Psychology* 17: 434–37.

Smetana, J. (1984). Morality and Gender: A Commentary on Pratt, Golding, and Hunter. *Merrill-Palmer Quarterly* 30: 341–48.

Snarey, J., Reimer, J., and Kohlberg, L. (1985). The development of socio-moral reasoning among kibbutz adolescents: A longitudinal cross-cultural study. *Developmental Psychology* 21: 3–17.

Thoma, S. (1986). Estimating gender differences in the comprehension and preference of moral issues. *Developmental Review* 6: 165–80.

Volker, J. M. (1984). Counseling experiences, moral judgment, awareness of consequences, and moral sensitivity in counseling practice. Ph.D. diss., University of Minnesota.

Walker, L. J. (1989). A longitudinal study of moral reasoning. *Child Development* 60: 157–166.

_____ . (1986). Sex differences in the development of moral reasoning: A rejoinder to Baumrind. *Child Development* 57: 522–26.

_____ . (1984). Sex differences in the development of moral reasoning: A critical review. *Child Development* 55: 677–91.

Walker, L. J., and deVries, B. (1985). Moral stages/moral orientations: Do the sexes really differ? In C. Blake (Chair), Gender difference research in moral development, Symposium conducted at the meeting of the American Psychological Association, Los Angeles.

Walker, L. J., deVries, B., and Trevethan, S. D. (1987). Moral stages and moral orientations in real life and hypothetical dilemmas. *Child Development* 58 (3): 842–58.

Zimney, L. (1986). Unpublished Data. University of Minnesota.

CHAPTER 19

Two Moralities? A Critical Discussion of an Ethic of Care and Responsibility versus an Ethic of Rights and Justice

GERTRUD NUNNER-WINKLER

This chapter reinterprets Gilligan's assumption of two moralities. It attempts to show the following: First, some of the sex-specific differences noted are not differences in moral orientation but concern conceptions of the good life. Second, morally relevant differences are differences not in ethical positions but in emphasis of one against the other of two types of moral duties (positive versus negative duties), which both belong to morality. Third, the consideration of situational particularities does not discriminate between the two moral approaches. Finally, some data that do not support the assumption of sex-specific moral judgments are presented.

Gilligan (1977, Note 1; see also Murphy & Gilligan, 1980; Langdale & Gilligan, Note 2) has recently claimed that there are two contrasting approaches to morality: an ethic of care and responsibility and an ethic of justice and rights. The first approach, more typical for females, corresponds to the experience of the self as part of relationships, as "connected self"; moral judgments consider specific details of concrete situations and are guided by an interest in minimizing the overall harm done. The justice orientation, more characteristic of males, on the other hand, is an expression of an autonomous, independent, "individuated" self; moral judgments follow principles defining rights and duties without "due" consideration of specific circumstances and costs implied. Gilligan accuses Lawrence Kohlberg of stating the justice orientation as the only valid moral orientation, thus neglecting the contribution of the other approach to morality.

In this chapter I shall try to reinterpret Gilligan's position. First, differences noted between the "male" and the "female" approach, as far as they are

---

I am indebted to E. Tugendhat for valuable suggestions and criticisms.

moral, I take to be differences not in ethical position but in emphasis of one against the other of two types of moral duties. Second, the consideration of situational particularities does not discriminate between the two moral orientations. Third, a considerable part of the sex-specific differences are not moral differences: Gilligan's description of an ethic of care and responsibility includes questions concerning the conception of the good life that do not belong to morality proper. In the last part of the chapter I shall attempt to derive several hypotheses about sex-specific moral preferences formulated in terms of theoretical distinctions introduced in the first part and shall test them against empirical data collected in a study on adolescent development.

THE DISTINCTION BETWEEN PERFECT AND IMPERFECT DUTIES

For theoretical clarification I consider a distinction that was introduced by Kant in his *Metaphysik der Sitten* (1977) and later elaborated especially by B. Gert in his *The Moral Rules* (1973), namely, the distinction between perfect and imperfect duties. Perfect duties are *negative* duties, that is, duties of omission (e.g., do not kill, do not cheat, etc.); imperfect duties are *positive* duties, duties of commission, which, however, do not prescribe specific acts but only formulate a maxim to guide action (e.g., practice charity). This maxim thus delineates a broad set of recommendable courses of action some of which the actor realizes by, at the same time, applying pragmatic rules and taking into account concrete conditions, such as individual preferences, contingencies of location in space and time, and so on.

Perfect duties, because they require only *not* to act, can, at least in non-conflictual cases, be followed strictly by everybody at any time and location and with regard to everybody (Gert, 1973). Imperfect duties, on the other hand, can never be observed completely: It is impossible to practice charity all the time and with regard to everybody. Positive maxims do not define limits of their application, do not specify which and how many good deeds have to be performed and whom they are to benefit so that the maxim can be said to have been followed. Due to this latitude, the following of maxims requires what Kant calls power of judgment (*Urteilskraft*). The asymmetry between perfect and imperfect duties is also reflected in the differential reactions to transgression. The failure to meet perfect duties is considered a vice (*Laster*), the failure to meet imperfect duties is lack of virtue (*Untugend*).

THE ETHIC OF CARE AND RESPONSIBILITY AS AN ETHIC OF IMPERFECT DUTIES; THE ETHIC OF RIGHTS AND JUSTICE AS AN ETHIC OF PERFECT DUTIES

The characteristics Gilligan (1977) enumerates show the ethic of care and responsibility to be primarily an orientation to imperfect duties, the ethic of rights and justice to be primarily an orientation to perfect duties. Thus, the most eminent goals of the ethic of care are the wish to care for and help others, to meet obligations and responsibilities, a concern for others and feelings of compassion, a responsibility to discern and alleviate trouble in this world (p. 511). This orientation to imperfect duties finds its most concise expression in one woman's statement in the interview: "Is it right to spend money on a pair of shoes, when I have a pair of shoes and other people are shoeless?" (p. 510). The very form this reflection takes, the interrogative, is proof of its being derived from an imperfect duty, namely, the principle of charity, which does not define its own form of application, its own limits, and the degree to which it is binding.

The ethic of rights and justice, on the other hand, is depicted as being mainly concerned with rights of individuals and their protection, that is, ways of ensuring that rights of individuals will not be interfered with by others. Such rights, it seems, are conceived to be invulnerable, absolute rights valid at all times and places and for all persons; they are conceived as rights corresponding to perfect duties. No one would deny that both kinds of duties are considered part of one morality, the unity of which is constituted through adherence to some universalizing procedure. How, then, is Gilligan's claim that it is still a question of contrasting moral approaches to be understood. I think it can be interpreted to mean that females (1) feel more obliged to fulfill imperfect duties than males, and (2) in cases of conflict will more likely opt for the fulfillment of imperfect duties, whereas males will insist more rigidly on having the perfect duties respected. The first part of the statement, I think, is more adequately construed as a difference in moral action and moral character and not as a difference in ethical position, for the latitude of imperfect duties per definition requires that individuals make use of their moral understanding to derive concrete action decisions. This kind of difference in interpersonal orientation parallels the distinction between diffuse and specific role relationships that Talcott Parsons (1964, pp. 65f., pp. 153ff.) notes: In diffuse relationships, that is, relations between relatives, friends, neighbors, it is assumed that one may ask for any kind of support, and the burden of proof rests with the role partner who withholds help. In specific relationships, on the contrary, the kind of help that may legitimately be asked for is clearly specified and limited, and the burden of proof rests with the partner demanding support. The hypothesized sex-difference in orientation might thus be a consequence of the fact that traditionally females are much more exclusively involved in diffuse relationships than are men and therefore feel bound to meet any need arising, whereas men are much more used to specific relationships and tend first to question the other person's "right to demand help." This hypothesis I shall take up in the last part of the chapter.

The interpretation that in cases of conflict females opt for fulfilling imperfect duties, and males perfect duties, implies a difference in ethical positions insofar as females might be assumed to reverse the male order of priority of perfect over imperfect duties. Yet this interpretation is implausible, for Gilligan

(1977) ascribes to the ethic of care an orientation to contextual particularities—"It is the reconstruction of a moral dilemma in its contextual particularity which allows an understanding . . . and thus engages the compassion and tolerance considered previously to qualify the feminine sense of justice" (p. 511)—which is incompatible with an a priori strict ordering of one set of rules over the other. In fact, it is precisely this consideration of contextual particularities that Gilligan (Note 1) sees as lacking in the ethic of rights and justice—"Kohlberg retains his conception that principles of justice are context free" (p. 83). This differential awareness of situational specifics marks one of the main differences between the two ethics.

The plausibility of this implied equation between an orientation to imperfect duties and contextual particularity, respectively, to perfect duties and their contextual independence will be discussed in the following passages. I want to show that this equation holds true only for a very specific aspect of Kant's moral position that is shared by scarcely anyone, namely, that perfect duties allow no exceptions. It does not hold true for Kohlberg, even though he presents his construction of rights in such a misleading way that it does provoke the kind of criticism Gilligan voices.

THE ROLE OF SITUATION-SPECIFIC KNOWLEDGE IN MORAL JUDGMENT

In the nonconflictual case, the following of perfect duties presupposes scarcely any knowledge of situational specifics. As all that is required is *not* to act in a specified way at any time or location and with regard to everybody, all one needs to know are some general empirical facts valid for *all* situations (e.g., what substances are poisonous, giving strong enough poisons to a human being will kill him or her, etc.) or at best some narrowly limited specific facts (e.g., if that person does not receive a specific medicine now, he or she will die) or truth values for specific statements (e.g., it is true that X happened). Yet the range of concrete facts one might need to know is clearly confinable and can deductively be determined: only those facts are relevant that pertain immediately to the rule in question; that is, for the rule do not kill, relevant facts are all potential risks to life; for the rule do not lie, only the empirical truth of statements asked is relevant.

Imperfect duties, on the other hand, require situation-specific knowledge, for they demand contextually situated decisions in regard to when and where to act and in regard to whom. Thus, Gilligan's proposition that the ethic of care takes situational details into account, whereas the ethic of rights does not, seems plausible: Imperfect duties require by their logical characteristics a concrete specification that perfect duties do not. Yet the picture gets more complicated as soon as one considers cases where duties collide. Only if one assumes that there are rules without exceptions can there be any moral judgments that can be made without taking note of situational specifics. This actually is Kant's position. Kant (1959) maintains that perfect duties enjoy absolute priority over imperfect duties, that is, allow for no exceptions. Thus, he explicitly states that even if lying to a murderer might save a friend's life, it cannot be justified, for "truthfulness . . . is a *perfect duty valid under all circumstances* (p. 205).[1]

This position is extreme, however, and is shared by scarcely anyone. In the modern discussion the justifiability of exceptions to rules is widely accepted. It finds a clear expression in the differentiation between actual duties and prima facie duties that W. D. Ross (1930, pp. 8–31, 61f.) introduced: Rules are valid only prima facie, that is, under normal circumstances, when there are no other moral considerations that bear on the decision. In Gert's (1973) exposition, the "except" clause plays the same role. Thus Gilligan's claim that the ethic of care is oriented to situational particularities that the ethic of rights will neglect is valid only at first sight. For even to observe perfect duties requires—if exceptions are deemed justifiable—that the question of consequences of different courses of action in a specific situation has to be examined: For it might well be that the imperfect duty to prevent harm may in a concrete case legitimately override obligations following from a perfect duty. Therefore I think one cannot very well hold context orientation to be a feature that constitutes contrasting approaches to morality. Context orientation is a prerequisite for *all actual moral judgments.*

One problem still remains open: how moral decision is to be reached in such cases of conflicting duties. Moral choice in dilemmas is based on a process of reflection on the potential universalizability of the specific solution, found by taking all particulars of the concrete situation into account. It is this compatibility of universalism with an orientation to situational particularities that has often been overlooked. Hare (1963) makes this point very lucidly in his distinction between universality and generality: "The thesis of universalizability does not require moral judgments to be made on the basis of highly general moral principles. . . . Moral development . . . consists in the main in making our moral principles more and more specific by writing into them exceptions and qualifications to cover kinds of cases of which we have had experience" (p. 40).

It may very well be true that people will come up with different solutions: People will differ in the weight they will give to various considerations. As Gert (1973) puts it: "One man might publicly advocate killing one man in order to save ten others. . . . Another man might not publicly advocate violation in this situation. He might feel that a significant decrease in the protection from violations of the rule plus general anxiety due to added uncertainty more than offsets the possible benefit" (p. 99). This is true because

---

[1] Cf. "It cannot be that opposing rules are simultaneously obliging: if it is [strict] duty to act according to one rule, then it is not only not duty to act according to a contrary one, but it is even undutiful. Thus a collision of duties and obligations is unthinkable. It can be, though, that two reasons of obligations collide. . . . [In that case] it is not the stronger obligation but the stronger reason of obligation that dominates" (1977, p. 330).

"evils are ranked in too many diverse ways" (p. 126). It might also be true that sex-specific differences in the ranking of evils might show up; thus, for instance, I would assume, in accordance with the hypothesis put forward earlier, that females might weigh consequences on the level of the social system as less grave than consequences on the level of interpersonal relations. Yet this could be taken to be a sex-specific filling in of a latitude that is conceded within the limits of morality, whereby morality is understood as constituted through an obligation to some universalizing procedure, that is, to impartiality.

One minor point may still be noted pertaining to the question of methodology. Gilligan (Note 1) tends to see Kohlberg's use of hypothetical dilemma as another indication of the abstraction of moral problems from the "contingencies of human social existence" she criticizes in him:

> While the analytic logic of justice is consonant with rational social and ethical theories and can be traced through the resolution of hypothetical dilemmas, the ethic of care depends on the contextual understanding of relationships. . . . While the analytic logic of justice can be traced through the deductive resolution of *hypothetical* dilemmas and the understanding of systems of rules, the ethic of care is manifested through the understanding of *actual* situations of moral conflict and choice. [pp. 9–10]

I think this is a misunderstanding. If exceptions are allowed, concrete circumstances have to be taken into account in solving a moral conflict—be it a hypothetical or an actual conflict. There is a difference, namely, that in actual dilemmas one can never be sure whether facts are correctly perceived. Yet this difference lies on the level of empirical truth of descriptive statements, not on the level of normative judgment.

KOHLBERG'S POSITION

The main criticism Gilligan (Note 1) directs against Kohlberg is that he neglects situational particularities in making moral judgments: "Kohlberg built a theory of moral development on a unitary moral conception of fairness and justice. . . . Thus the social concept of moral decision was replaced by the structures of formal thought which provided a rational system for decision that was autonomous and *independent of time and place*" (p. 7). Kohlberg's "principles of justice [are] *context-free* and [can] generate *objectively right* solutions to moral problems" (Murphy & Gilligan 1980, p. 83). Yet by the logic of his own moral convictions Kohlberg by necessity must orient his moral judgments to concrete situational circumstances. This is because in a conflict between perfect and imperfect duties he not only maintains—unlike Kant—that the perfect duty *may* be violated but almost requires that it *must* be violated; that is, Kohlberg adopts a radical female position, however ironic this may sound. Thus, for instance, in the Heinz dilemma the issue is whether

Heinz may break into the druggist's store to steal a drug to save his wife's life. In terms of the distinctions introduced earlier, the Heinz dilemma depicts a conflict between a perfect duty (not to steal) and an imperfect duty (to prevent evil, namely, the death of the sick woman). Kant would have denied that Heinz may break into the store: If one may not lie in order to save a life, one may not steal either. Kant (1959) gives another example that proves the same point: A man has been entrusted with a large sum of money. The owner dies without the heirs knowing anything of the deposit. The man, a charitable and philanthropic person, lost all his fortune without any fault of his own; his wife and children are starving. The heirs, however, are unkind, rich, and wasteful, and "it were just as well that the additional wealth were to be thrown into the ocean" (p. 82). Even in this extreme situation the man may not keep the money to feed his wife and children, for "it is wrong, it contradicts duty" (ibid.)—that is, it is wrong under all circumstances, context free.

Kohlberg, quite on the contrary, demands that Heinz steal the drug "because the right to life supercedes or transcends the right to property" (Colby, Gibbs, Kohlberg, Speicher-Dubin, & Candee, Note 3, p. 80). This justification rests on the assumption of a clear hierarchy of differentially binding duties and obligations. Yet whereas in Kant the hierarchical ordering of duties is based on their formal characteristics (perfect duties, as they are negative duties, which can be followed and are to be followed under all circumstances and with regard to everybody, are superordinate to imperfect duties, which only formulate maxims that can never be completely followed), Kohlberg seems to posit the hierarchy of rights by content: "There is a hierarchy of rights and values. Stealing is justified as serving a universal right to or value of life which is prior to laws" (ibid.). Because of its utmost priority, this universal right to life is henceforth treated as if it were a perfect right corresponding to a perfect duty in Kant's sense: It is a right that must be granted universally; that is, it implies seemingly perfect duties regardless of concrete circumstances or of personal ties. Thus, for Kohlberg it is as much a duty to steal for a stranger as it is to steal for one's own wife: "It would be right to steal for a stranger because the right to life should be accorded universally to all men whose lives can be saved regardless of personal ties" (ibid., p. 82). The problem with this position is that "saving life" by its structural characteristics is an imperfect duty, which does not specify its own limits: A universally accorded right to life implies the universal duty to save "all men whose lives can be saved regardless of personal ties," even if that would require violation of property rights. Thus we all are not only required to give away all the money we own but also justified—in fact, maybe even obliged— to rob all banks as well as all members of our society who own more than they need to feed themselves so as to be able to save the starving children in the third world, whose sad fate is well known to all of us.[2]

I assume Kohlberg would not support such a revolutionary Robin Hood

---

[2] Langdale and Gilligan (Note 2, pp. 52–53) also point out this difficulty in Kohlberg.

strategy. If this were correct, it follows that, for Kohlberg as well, decisions in moral dilemma hinge on concrete circumstances: Thus, it may be justifiable to rob for one's own wife or even a stranger one has met, but it may be less justifiable to rob with the intent to send the money to India. Yet in Kohlberg's own justifications, the factual dependency of moral judgments on a consideration of concrete circumstances is veiled; thus Gilligan rightly denounces the neglect of situational contingencies on Kohlberg's part. This neglect, though, I take—in contrast to Gilligan—not to be characteristic of a certain type of morality, the morality of rights and justice; rather, it is because Kohlberg has not clearly recognized the logical structure of imperfect duties. This can be seen from the misleading formulation he uses. He speaks of a universal right to life, which seems to imply a universal, hence perfect, duty to save life. Perfect duties, however, can be formulated only in the negative: All one can say is that every human being has a right *not* to be killed, disabled, deprived of freedom by others.

MORALITY VERSUS QUESTIONS OF THE GOOD LIFE

Thus far only part of Gilligan's position has been discussed: the assumption that an orientation to care can be juxtaposed to an orientation to rights, whereby only the former takes situational particularities into account, whereas the latter denies their relevance. The second half of this assumption has been refuted: Consideration of concrete situational details is indispensable for *all* moral judgments (if exceptions are allowed). The first part has been reformulated: Females feel more obliged to fulfill imperfect duties of charity, whereas males adhere more strictly to the perfect duties of noninterference, although both types of duty belong to morality.

Yet Gilligan's conceptualization of the two approaches to morality is more encompassing than has hitherto been stated. Gilligan sees them as emanating from different experiences of the self in the world: "The principle of nonviolence and an ethic of care . . . informs the world of the connected self, the principle of fairness and an ethic of justice . . . informs the world of the separate self" (Langdale & Gilligan, Note 2, pp. 42–43). The experience of the self in the world is itself a process of development, described for the ethic of care as the unfolding of the concept of responsibility. I think that in this conceptualization of the "connected self" and of stages of responsibility, moral orientation and development is mixed with aspects of ego development and with questions of the good life. To substantiate this claim I will analyze two examples. In the first, concerning ways of conflict resolution in child play, "social connectedness" is interpreted by Langdale and Gilligan as the basis of a specific moral orientation, although it might well be simply an expression of specific ego interests. The second example concerns reflections about life plans at pregnancy; in the decision of this issue questions of the good life are confounded with moral problems.

In the first example, two 6-year-olds respond to the dilemma "created when, in playing with a friend, they discover that they and their friend want to play a different game." Characteristic of the little girl are the following statements: *"We don't have a real fight"* and "we agree what we should do" and "we should play one . . . , then the other"; while the little boy starts out by stating: "I wanted to stay outside—he wanted to go in" and ends with the statement *"I would do what I want—he would do what he wants."* The italicized statements are pointed out by the authors as especially good exemplifications of the contrasting principles of care versus fairness. As long as it is so described, however, this dilemma is not a moral dilemma, but the inner conflict of an individual choosing among his or her own conflicting needs. Each child has two desires: the desire to play a specific game and the desire to play with a specific friend. The little girl forgoes the chance to play the preferred game (at least for some time) yet in return maintains the chance to play with the friend. The little boy, on the other hand, proves to be more interested in playing the preferred game, and be it alone, than in playing with his friend. Thus far each child may have chosen among different needs that proved not to be simultaneously satisfiable. There is nothing moral about this choice: It is well known that females are more interested in relationships and males more in things (objects).[3] Neither one or the other of these preferences is morally more recommendable. Gilligan might consider this very construction of the dilemma to be a male version while she sees it as a moral dilemma, that is, not as an intraindividual choice among one's own conflicting needs but as an interindividual choice between satisfying one's own needs or the needs of others. Yet I do not think that it really is a moral question. Adequately satisfying each other's needs is what a good relationship means. If a relationship is not good, that is, if both partners cannot find satisfaction and enrichment in sharing alter's interests, separating and searching for a more congenial partner might—so long as no other considerations must be considered, such as marriage and children—be better than a permanent pseudo-moral adoption to alien interests.

Once the friendship dilemma comes to be seen as a moral dilemma of conflicting needs of ego and alter, however, the central issue of imperfect duties arises immediately: how far to go in fulfilling the needs of alter. It is this issue around which Gilligan presents the female moral development as revolving. Different levels of the conceptualization of responsibility formulate different answers: On the first level, responsibility centers on the self and on relationships that are self-serving; on the second level, responsibility orients to the needs of others such that the satisfaction of one's own needs is considered selfish and self-sacrifice is deemed as "good"; on the last level, the focus of responsibility

---

[3] This difference in interests also is reflected in career choices. In our study, for example, 27% of the girls but only 5% of the boys mentioned "contact with other people" as one of the most important criteria in selecting among different careers. On the other hand, 25% of the boys and only 12% of the girls report specific factual interests that they want to follow up in a career, such as interest in cars and in natural sciences.

is shifted to the relationship itself, the stability of which is comprehended as depending on the fulfillment of the needs of self *and* other. This developmental sequence, although it answers a central problem of imperfect duties, is too narrowly conceived as moral development: It is a more encompassing learning process; it is a process of the development of self as an autonomous person, as a competent actor. Thus on the third level the insight is developed that the second-level understanding of goodness as self-sacrifice is a welcome device to avoid taking upon oneself the responsibility for one's own actions. And it is only on the third level that the individual can clearly recognize his or her own needs and interests and separate them from externally obtruded ones and becomes willing to assume the responsibility for the consequences that the following of one's own needs may entail. This competence is a prerequisite for all life choices (career, partner, world view, political conviction, etc.), of which moral decisions make up only one part.

Gilligan, I think, unduly treats this general process of ego development as moral development and treats as moral choices what in reality are decisions about ways of life. This can be seen very clearly in the way Gilligan (1977) presents her interviews on abortion. The women questioned answer not the issue of whether an abortion is morally justifiable but rather questions of the "good life": namely, What kind of person do I want to be? What kind of life do I want to lead? This claim may seem unjustified, for most of the women do start off the discussion with formulating moral considerations, such as, "I don't believe in abortion. Who can say when life begins" (p. 497), or even "It is taking a life" (p. 499). Yet in fact these considerations do not enter the decision process; the question of abortion is dealt with as a choice between different ways of life. This can be seen if one examines the kind of reasons that are put forward by the same woman who considers abortion as taking life. Among the reasons she lists for having an abortion are the fear of losing a good job, losing independence, difficulties in handling the relationship with the father of the child; among the reasons against having an abortion she mentions enjoying more home life, being admired by others for bringing up a child alone; having less feelings of guilt. Another woman is quoted as comprehending through pregnancy her own "inner conflict between the wish to be a college president and to be making pottery and flowers, having kids and staying home" (p. 508).

I do not want to deny that morally relevant considerations do sometimes enter into the question of life choice. Thus, for instance, the woman quoted earlier hesitates about a professional career for fear of losing her compassion on the way up. Yet most considerations mentioned concern for morally neutral ego goals, such as a desire for a fulfilling occupation or the desire to avoid internal conflicts of priority between family and job, and the decision seems mainly to involve a morally neutral balancing out of different ego interests.

To summarize, I tend to think that not all the differences Gilligan sees as constitutive for two contrasting approaches to morality are really differences in moral orientation. Social connectedness is largely a result of greater social-than task-oriented interests; stages of responsibility describe a process of disentangling self from conformity expectations, which is a general process of ego development in as much as conformity expectations extend to many non-moral issues. It may still be true that females feel more obliged than males to fulfill imperfect duties, to answer to concrete needs of others, even at their own costs. It also seems plausible that this characteristic is, as Gilligan suggests, a consequence of women's greater social involvement. It might also be, however, merely a consequence of an inability to recognize and stand up to one's own needs, that is, a consequence of lack of ego strength, of an inability to say no. If this is true, the status of a "female" approach to morality would be very ambiguous, indeed.

SOME DATA CONCERNING SEX DIFFERENCES IN MORAL JUDGMENT

In this last section I employ the data Rainer Döbert and I have collected. We interviewed 112 male and female adolescents in the age range of 16–22 years and of different socioeconomic backgrounds. The interview covered intensity of adolescent crisis, moral judgment, coping and defense styles, parental patterns of conflict resolution and child rearing, political socialization, and so on. It was not designed specifically to test sex-specific morality, yet some of the results may serve to test the following hypotheses derived from the assumptions of an ethic of care and responsibility:

1.   Females feel more bound by imperfect duties than do males; that is, in a conflict between a perfect and an imperfect duty females will more likely opt for transgression of the perfect duty.
2.   In moral decisions females will take more situational details into account.

To test these hypotheses, a subsample of 98 subjects was drawn from the original study, that matched male and female subjects on educational background and, as far as possible, on age as well. The subjects are distributed as shown in Table 19.1.

TABLE 19.1.   Distribution of the sample over the variables age, education, and sex

Variable	Male			Female		
	High	Medium	Low	High	Medium	Low
Education						
Number of subjects	15	17	17	15	17	17
Average age	18.5	17.1	16.2	19	16.8	16.5

To test the first hypothesis, three different morally relevant decisions will be used. The first concerns the decision in Kohlberg's mercy-killing dilemma: A woman who is incurably ill and suffers unbearable pain asks the doctor for an extra dose of morphine to make her die. Should the doctor give it to her or refuse it? This story depicts a conflict between a perfect duty, do not kill, and an imperfect duty, relieve pain. The action decision was classified into four categories:

> The doctor should give the drug, notwithstanding the law, because the woman suffers so much and should be allowed to decide for herself (active mercy killing).
>
> The doctor should not give the drug, because the law is legitimate; at most he may stop excessive medical support (passive mercy killing).
>
> The doctor should not give the drug so as not to risk punishment.
>
> Undecided: the doctor should, because of pain, yet should not, because of punishment.

The subjects responses are distributed over these four categories as is shown in Table 19.2.

The data show that in this dilemma females do not feel more bound by the imperfect duty to relieve pain. If anything at all, females more eagerly seek to avoid punishment. This finding might be taken as proof of the female tendency to consider consequences in making moral decisions, yet the moral ambiguity of this tendency is that it is not specified how consequences for the different persons involved are to be balanced. Any procedure balancing costs to ego versus benefits to alter would, I assume, have to make use of some universalizing procedure.

In the second morally relevant decision, subjects were asked to pass a moral judgment on the following action: A person talks an old-age pensioner into ordering a useless journal. The judgment could take the following form: I find this action very bad (3), pretty bad (2), not particularly bad (1). From the "female" point of view, this action might be interpreted as exploitation of a weak or poor elderly person by a skillful salesperson who simply tries to maximize his or her own profits at all costs. From the "male" point of view,

TABLE 19.2.   Distribution of Answers to the Mercy-Killing Dilemma

Response	Male	Female
Doctor should—pain	30	24
Doctor should not—law	7	8
Doctor should not—punishment	11	14
Undecided	1	3

one might defend this action as a legitimate pursuit of business interests, based on the assumption that all market partners can take care of themselves and look out for their own interests. Thus, one might expect females to condemn this action more than males. This is not the case, however: The average evaluation of this action by males and females is identical; both find it pretty bad (2.0).

For the third morally relevant decision, the same format was used for an evaluation of the following action: A person does not want to lend some money to a friend and therefore pretends not to have any money. Again, females might be expected to deny help less readily when asked for it, and therefore to condemn this action more strongly. Again, the data do not bear out this expectation: Males and females alike judge this action as not particularly bad (males 1.4, females 1.3).

To test the hypothesis that in moral decisions females will take more situational details into account, responses to the following dilemma (taken from Gleser Ihilevich, 1969) depicting an interpersonal conflict were analyzed. "You live with your aunt and uncle, who have taken care of you since your parents were killed in an accident when you were only five years old. One stormy night you have a date with a friend, but your aunt and uncle will not let you go out because it is late and the weather is bad. You are about to leave anyhow when your uncle issues the order: 'You stay at home because I said so.'" No situa- ational details were considered to have been taken into account in responses such as these: "I'd go anyhow"; "That's none of his business"; I'd be furious and leave." Situational details were considered to have been taken into account in these: "I would go, if the date was very important to me, if not, I'd stay"; "If I'd accepted them as parents, I would stay, because I respect them"; "It depends how they handle conflicts in other situations—if they forbid everything, I'd go"; "If we were meeting in a group and it was only 8 o'clock, I'd go, if we were meeting alone and it was 10 o'clock I'd stay at home."

Of the subjects, 14 of the males and 12 of the females considered concrete situational particularities when making their decisions on how to act in this interpersonal conflict. Those taking situational details into account are slightly older (.35 years) and of higher socioeconomic background (of the lowest edu- cational level, only 16%, of the two higher levels, 42% consider concrete circumstances).

Certainly one could not hold the analysis of these few data to be an ade- quate test of sex differences in moral judgment. Still, it should be noted that the data presented do not lend support to the assumption that females (at least in the age range tested) observe imperfect duties more closely than do males or give more consideration to contextual particularities.

REFERENCES

Gert, B. *The moral rules.* New York: Harper & Row, 1973.

Gilligan, C. In a different voice: Women's conceptions of the self and of morality. *Harvard Educational Review,* 1977, *47*(4), 481–517.

Gleser, G. C., & Ihilevich, D. An objective instrument for measuring defense mechanisms. Journal of Consulting and Clinical Psychology, 1969, 33(1), 51–60.

Hare, R. M. *Freedom and reason.* New York: Oxford University Press, 1963.

Kant, I. Über den Gemeinspruch: Das mag in der Theorie richtig sein, taugt aber nicht für die Praxis (1793). In *Kleinere Schriften zu Geschichtsphilosophie, Ethik and Politik.* Hamburg: Felix Meiner Verlag, 1959.

Kant, I. *Die Metaphysik der Sitten.* Frankfurt: Suhrkamp, 1977. (originally 1797)

Kant, I. Über ein vermeintliches Recht, aus Menschenliebe zu lügen. ibid. pp. 199–206.

Murphy, J. M., & Gilligan, C. Moral development in late adolescence and adulthood: A critique and reconstruction of Kohlberg's theory. *Human Development,* 1980, *23,* 77–104.

Parsons, T. The social system. New York: Free Press, 1964.

Ross, W. D. The right and the good. Oxford: The Clarendon Press, 1930.

REFERENCE NOTES

1. Gilligan, C. *Do the social sciences have an adequate theory of moral development?* Unpublished manuscript, Harvard University, 1980.

2. Langdale, S., & Gilligan, C. *The contribution of women's thought to developmental theory: The elimination of sex bias in moral development research and education.* Interim Report submitted to: National Institute of Education.

3. Colby, A., Gibbs, J., Kohlberg, L., Speicher-Dubin, B., & Candee, D. *Standard form scoring manual.* Unpublished manuscript, Center for Moral Education, Harvard University, 1979.

Book Reviews

LISTENING TO A DIFFERENT VOICE:
A REVIEW OF GILLIGAN'S *IN A DIFFERENT VOICE*

Anne Colby
Radcliffe College
William Damon
Clark University

In a Different Voice: Psychological Theory and Women's Development. Carol Gilligan. Cambridge: Harvard University Press, 1982. Pp. 184. $15.00 hardcover; $5.95 paperback.

Gilligan makes bold claims in her book, *In a Different Voice:* first, that women differ from men in their basic life orientations; and second, that developmental theories, in particular, devalue the feminine orientation. This review is an evaluation of the book's accuracy in relation to psychological research. It is concluded that research evidence does not support a generalized distinction between men and women in their orientations, and that Gilligan's allegation of gender bias in developmental theory, specifically Kohlberg's moral development theory, is unwarranted. The most important contribution of the book is Gilligan's extension of moral development theory.

This book has created an unusual excitement within and beyond the field of psychology, no doubt because it is full of exciting ideas. Gilligan writes with force and elegance. Her characterizations of male and female psychological perspectives are intriguing as well as intuitively appealing. The book stimulates thought and discussion about some of the most profound issues of human development, and does not shy away from controversy. These reasons alone make it worthwhile reading.

Nevertheless, the book also must be assessed objectively for its contribution to psychological theory and research. How accurate are its claims concerning the prior literature? How sound are the new data

Requests for reprints should be sent to Anne Colby, Henry A. Murray Research Center, Radcliffe College, 10 Garden St., Cambridge, MA 02138.

Merrill-Palmer Quarterly, October 1983, Vol. 29, No. 4, pp. 473–481.

that are presented? How original is the view that it presents, and how fruitful is the direction that it marks out? Although the book has been widely reviewed in both the psychological and mass media, it has not been examined with these questions in mind. Instead, most reviews have focused on the ideological implications of Gilligan's statement. In the current review, we shall discuss the scholarly value of this work, giving particular attention to its potential contribution to developmental psychology.

The most striking feature of Gilligan's book is its boldness. It offers no less than a sweeping critique of all major developmental theories on the grounds that they are biased against women. Included in the culpable network are Freud, Piaget, Bettelheim, Levinson, McClelland, Kohlberg, and Erikson, as well as a host of their followers. If Gilligan's charges are justified, developmental psychology must return to the drawing board, since it has misrepresented a majority of the human race.

Gilligan stakes her argument on two main assertions: first, that women are typically different from men in their basic orientations to life; and, second, that many existing psychological theories, in particular developmental theories, devalue the feminine orientation. For the sake of examining Gilligan's position, it is useful to separate the two assertions and to scrutinize Gilligan's defense of each.

The Feminine Orientation toward Relationships

Gilligan claims that there is a very general psychological sex difference that distinguishes women from men throughout life, beginning in infancy. Women, she writes, are oriented toward attachment and "connectedness" to others, whereas men are oriented toward individuation and "separateness' from others. The feminine orientation predisposes women toward interest in human relationships, while the male orientation predisposes men toward interest in individual achievement. One consequence of this difference in orientation is that women find it easier than men to establish intimate relationships. Another is that women's personal identities are likely to be grounded upon their intimate relationships, whereas men's are likely to be grounded upon their occupational choices.

To explain the origin of the differences between male and female psychological orientations, Gilligan adopts the position put forth by Chodorow in her feminist revision of psychoanalytic theory (Chodorow, 1978). According to this position, distinctly male and female orientations are formed early, and irreversibly, with the mother-child relation. Because women are almost universally responsible for early child care, male children discover themselves through the contrast between themselves and an opposite-sex parent, whereas female children discover themselves through the similarity between themselves and a same-sex parent. Before long, boys have developed the notion that they are essentially different from significant others in their lives; in contrast, girls experience a fundamental similarity between themselves and others. Gilligan quotes Chodorow's (1978) remark that "Girls emerge with a stronger basis for experiencing another's needs and feelings as one's own" (p. 167). Boys, on the other hand, tend toward a "more emphatic individuation" which curtails "their primary love and sense of empathic tie" (p. 150). Gilligan (1982) credits Chodorow's position with replacing psychoanalytic theory's "negative and derivative description of female psychology with a positive and direct account" (p. 8).

Is Gilligan on firm ground in her distinction between typical male and female orientations to life? In order to answer this question, it is necessary to decompose Gilligan's synthetic concept of global masculine and feminine orientations. That is, Gilligan has synthesized research and theory on sex differences in a number of quite different domains of development, claiming that they form a coherent whole, with a common root in the connectedness-separateness difference. A careful review of the literature, however, reveals that some of the differences to which Gilligan refers are better substantiated than others. Furthermore, the implications for Gilligan's thesis of those differences that have been shown to exist are not always clear.

On the positive side, it is true that boys and girls often play differently. Boys tend to prefer organized games with elaborate systems of rules; girls prefer dyadic intimate exchanges and turn-taking games with relatively few players (Maccoby & Jacklin, 1974; Luria & Herzog, Note 1). This difference may indicate a sex-linked difference in children's social interactions, with possible implications for the development of moral judgment or identity formation.

It is also clear that differential stereotypes of males and females are widely held, as has been documented by Broverman, Vogel, Broverman, Clarkson, and Rosenkrantz (1972) and others. Males are commonly viewed as more independent, objective, ambitious, and the like, while females are seen as more aware of others' feelings, and more tactful and expressive. But the evidence that these stereotypes reflect reality is much less convincing. For example, there is very little support in the psychological literature for the notion that girls are more aware of others' feelings or are more altruistic than boys. Sex differences in empathy are inconsistently found and are generally very small when they are reported (Hoffman, 1977; Mussen & Eisenberg-Berg, 1977; Staub, 1978). The findings on the applicability of Erikson's identity construct to girls and women are also mixed. Marcia (1980), for example, reports some differences in women's versus men's responses to questions concerning occupational identity. But a recent comprehensive review (Waterman, 1982) of research on Erikson's identity theory concludes that "males and females are more similar than different in their use of developmental processes," and, for the great majority of persons, "males and females undergo similar patterns of identity development" (p. 315). There have been few, if any, sex differences reported for measures derived from Piagetian cognitive developmental theory.

Thus, it must be concluded that evidence in support of Gilligan's distinction between orientations is mixed. Sex differences have been found in some aspects of social behavior, achievement motivation, occupational choices, and so on, and have been described by several theorists and researchers prior to Gilligan (e.g., Bakan, 1966; Deutsch, 1944; Dweck & Bush, 1976; Gutmann, 1965; Horner, 1972; Wyatt, 1967). But there are also a number of areas in which differences are slight or nonexistent, such as many aspects of prosocial and cognitive development. The available research data, therefore, do not reveal a clear picture of a global dichotomy between the life orientations of men and women.

Certainly the male-female distinction that Gilligan advances has some intuitive appeal, as both her literary citations and anecdotal material indicate. This intuitive appeal should not be discounted lightly, since the point of Gilligan's critique is that one must look beyond social scientific research to appreciate fully this difference. If it is true that social science fails to account for women's experience, this may be why Gilligan is able to provide only sporadic scientific documentation for her claim that men and women have distinct orientations to life. The scarcity of consistent data on this issue could be seen as neither surprising nor damaging to Gilligan's thesis, for we could not expect a flawed science to provide an accurate view of reality.

The Claim of Antifeminine Bias in Developmental Theory

Although Gilligan makes a broad indictment in her introduction, her focus on this issue is restricted to moral development. Gilligan believes that men's moral sensibilities reflect a concern for justice, whereas women's reflect a concern for care. This difference is because, Gilligan claims, men begin with an orientation toward separateness, and women toward connectedness. From a separateness perspective, socialized living requires an intricate moral system of rules and rights in order to resolve persons' competing claims to justice. Such a morality is needed to create links between persons, who are assumed to be fundamentally in conflict regarding their rights. In contrast, an orientation toward connectedness requires no such system. All that is needed is a sensitivity to the needs of others and a benevolent attitude, both of which are dominant in the feminine preference for the morality of care.

Gilligan's main argument with contemporary theories of moral development derives from her belief that, when faced with a hypothetical moral dilemma of the Kohlbergian sort, girls and women are at a disadvantage when compared with boys and men. This is because Kohlberg's hypothetical dilemmas pose conflicts of justice, in which the rights of different persons come into conflict. Since women see morality as a problem in care rather than in justice, they are ill-prepared to reason about the focal issues under investigation. Further, Kohlberg's scoring system is calibrated on a sequence of justice values. Women, who value care and responsibility, inevitably will score lower than men when assessed by this justice-bound system. To make matters worse, Gilligan asserts, hypothetical moral dilemmas tap processes of rationalization and logical deduction. Gilligan suggests that such skills come more naturally to men than to women (though, as noted previously, there is no evidence to support this suggestion).

A final problem of Kohlberg's system, writes Gilligan, is its tendency to score all care and responsibility responses as Stage 3. Since Stage 3 is considered a low-normal score for adults within most populations, this scoring bias relegates adult women to a moral status that is somewhat lower than that of men.

Gilligan uses a number of strategies to make her case. First, she quotes some girls' and boys' reasoning about Kohlberg's Heinz dilemma, and draws contrasts between their orientations. For example, 11-year-old Amy is set against 11-year-old Jake: Amy sees the story as a "narrative of relationships" whereas Jake sees it as "a math problem with humans." This, Gilligan claims, is a characteristic difference between boys and girls, and the developmental scoring system rewards the boys. Gilligan tells us that Jake would score an entire stage higher than Amy because of his more logical approach to the problem.

Gilligan then goes on to present her own research as further indication of how inadequately Kohlberg's system represents women. Some of the research involves open-ended questions about the self and morality. For example, Gilligan asks males and females questions like, "If you had to say what morality meant to you, how would you sum it up?" and "How would you describe yourself to yourself?" Gilligan uses subjects' answers in an anecdotal manner, selecting cases that illustrate her overall claim that women are more interpersonally oriented, but no less sophisticated, than men. Her consistent implication is that Kohlbergian scoring would undervalue the intellectual and moral worth of the women's statements that she quotes. Gilligan does not attempt, however, to score these quotes herself, either by Kohlberg's scheme or by any replacement system. Nor does she present any empirical data regarding her interview studies.

The more ambitious and intriguing research that Gilligan presents goes beyond the interview technique to study real-life moral decisions of women in crisis. The particular crisis of Gilligan's subjects is unwanted pregnancy. Gilligan extensively questioned 21 women who faced the decision of whether or not to have an abortion. The questions focus on the women's choices, and their views of their own lives. Gilligan demonstrates, through extensive quotes from these women, a "caring" orientation to the moral problems entailed in abortion decisions. Unfortunately for the sake of her main thesis, Gilligan did not collect any comparative data in this study. Ideally, the women in Gilligan's study should have been compared with men faced with the same dilemma. For example, the fathers of the unborn children could have been questioned and their responses compared to those of the mothers. Then it could have been ascertained whether women are uniquely caring in response to abortion-type decisions, or whether men also share this orientation when faced with such decisions.

Because of this methodological limitation in Gilligan's abortion study, it is impossible to tell whether or not women differ from men in how they frame moral issues. In fact, research by Smetana (1981) casts doubt on whether people necessarily see moral issues as the primary considerations in deciding whether or not to have an abortion; many women and men think of abortion as a personal or social-conventional dilemma, and act accordingly. Although Gilligan's abortion interviews yield some interesting data on real-life decision-making processes, they do not provide support for her thesis of sex bias in Kohlberg's theory.

Only the question of sex differences in developmental stage scores on Kohlberg's measure bears directly on Gilligan's charge that Kohlberg's theory is sex biased. That is, Kohlberg's system cannot be said to be biased against women unless they score lower than men. In fact, the data on this issue are clear-cut, and quite different than Gilligan's representations of them. Two recent reviews of the literature report that if educational and occupational backgrounds of subjects are controlled, there are no sex differences in moral judgment stage scores (Rest, in press; Walker, in press). This finding applies both to Kohlberg's measure and to Rest's Defining Issues Test. The few studies that have found sex differences favoring men have not established statistical controls for education and work experience, variables that correlate significantly with moral judgment within each sex. Such differences disappear entirely when proper controls are established. Furthermore, several recent longitudinal studies of moral judgment (Erickson, 1980; Snarey, 1982) have found that girls' and women's moral judgment develops through the same developmental sequence in the same order as does male subjects' moral reasoning.

As for the particular issue of whether a caring perspective is confused in Kohlberg's system with Stage 3, one must distinguish between Kohlberg's early scoring procedures in which form and content did tend to be confounded, and his current system in which they have been more fully differentiated. In the early procedures, concern with loving relationships and interpersonal trust was indeed scored as indicative of Stage 3. In the current procedures, the issues of affiliation, trust, and social harmony (under the manual headings of "Norms" and "Elements") are represented at every stage, from the first to the last. The current procedures have been in use since 1978. Levels of relationship, caring, and interpersonal trust that are both more and less developmentally advanced than Stage 3 are built into the current Kohlberg scoring system (Colby, Kohlberg, Gibbs, Candee, Speicher-Dubin, Hewer, Kauffman, & Power, in press).

Issues relating to the greater relativity and diffidence of women and their supposed unwillingness to accept the abstractness of Kohlberg's hypothetical dilemmas have not been systematically investigated. Another, more important, question is whether the rights and response orientations represent two qualitatively different organizations of thought with different sequences of development, or whether they can both be subsumed within Kohlberg's stage sequence. It is not yet possible to determine whether moral judgment is best described by a single underlying sequence or by two different sequences, since Gilligan has not yet developed empirical criteria by which to code developmentally the judgments in the responsibility mode, and Kohlberg's scoring criteria have not been extended for use with real-life dilemmas.

In summary, Gilligan's arguments are questionable in some respects. While her portrayal of general, sex-linked life orientations is intuitively appealing, the research evidence at this point does not support such a generalized distinction. Further, to the extent that differences of this sort do exist, there is no evidence whatsoever that they are due to early and irreversible emotional experiences between mother and child.

As for moral development specifically, there may be preliminary indications that men and women emphasize different aspects of morality and frame spontaneously-chosen dilemmas somewhat differently. But it is just as likely that all men and women use both orientations, and that the type of dilemma being discussed is as influential in determining a person's orientation as is the person's gender.

Because sex differences in moral stage disappear when occupation and education are controlled, and because girls and women pass through the same stages in the same order as men, Gilligan's allegation of gender bias against Kohlberg's theory is unwarranted. Women's thinking in response to Kohlberg's dilemmas cannot be said to be devalued by his stage scheme, because women's judgments consistently are scored as developmentally equivalent to men's.

We must conclude, then, that Gilligan's most important contribution is not her widely acclaimed critique of existing developmental theories, but rather her preliminary extension of moral development theory and method. Her use of situations in which real moral decisions are made could constitute an advance over the use of hypothetical moral dilemmas. It is only through such investigation that the complex processes that characterize actual moral judgment can be identified, and the relation of moral judgment to moral conduct can be illuminated. A description of multiple styles, orientations, and dimensions of moral judgment would enrich our conception of moral development.

A review of this book would be incomplete without some discussion of the ideological position it represents. Gilligan has taken a new perspective on feminine psychological characteristics that have been assumed to reflect women's oppression—their deference, their self-doubt, their dependence—and has chosen to see these characteristics as representing strengths rather than weaknesses. This is, of course, an ideological position rather than an empirically verifiable, social-scientific claim. The argument has been made somewhat differently by others along the following lines: Although there are obvious disadvantageous psychological consequences to being socially subordinate, outside the dominant system, and relatively powerless, there are also some advantages. Outsiders may escape some of the dominant group's weaknesses, and may even be able to develop special strengths and insights by virtue of their subordinate position. In questioning some of Gilligan's methods and specific conclusions, we do not mean to diminish the importance of identifying and describing the development of certain traditionally feminine characteristics that have been devalued illegitimately. On the other hand, it is equally important to guard against reinforcing gender stereotypes that in themselves contribute to the maintenance of women's oppression.

REFERENCE NOTE

1. LURIA, Z., & HERZOG, E. *Gender segregation and play groups.* Paper presented at the meeting of the Society for Research in Child Development, Detroit, April 1983.

REFERENCES

BAKAN, D. *The duality of human existence.* Boston: Beacon Press, 1966.

BROVERMAN, I., VOGEL, S., BROVERMAN, D., CLARKSON, F., & ROSENKRANTZ, P. Sex-role stereotypes: A current appraisal. *Journal of Social Issues,* 1972, *28,* 59–78.

CHODOROW, N. *The reproduction of mothering.* Berkeley: University of California Press, 1978.

COLBY, A., KOHLBERG, L., GIBBS, J., CANDEE, D., SPEICHER-DUBIN, B., HEWER, A., KAUFFMAN, K., & POWER, C. *The measurement of moral judgment.* New York: Cambridge University Press, in press.

DEUTSCH, H. *The psychology of women: A psychoanalytic interpretation.* New York: Grune & Stratton, 1944.

DWECK, C. E., & BUSH, E. S. Sex differences in learned helplessness: Differential debilitation with peer and adult evaluators. *Developmental Psychology,* 1976, *12,* 147–156.

ERICKSON, V. L. The case study method in the evaluation of developmental programs. In L. Kuhmerker, M. Mentkowski, & L. V. Erickson (Eds.), *Evaluating moral development.* New York: Character Research Press, 1980.

GILLIGAN, C. *In a different voice: Psychological theory and women's development.* Cambridge: Harvard University Press, 1982.

GUTMANN, D. L. Women and the conception of ego strength. *Merrill-Palmer Quarterly,* 1965, *11,* 229–240.

HOFFMAN, M. Sex differences in empathy and related behaviors. *Psychological Bulletin,* 1977, *84,* 712–722.

HORNER, M. Toward an understanding of achievement-related conflicts in women. *Journal of Social Issues,* 1972, *28,* 157–176.

MACCOBY, E., & JACKLIN, C. N. *The psychology of sex differences.* Stanford: Stanford University Press, 1974.

MARCIA, J. E. Identity in adolescence. In J. B. Adelson (Ed.), *Handbook of adolescent psychology.* New York: Wiley, 1980.

MUSSEN, P., & EISENBERG-BERG, N. *Roots of caring, sharing, and helping: The development of prosocial behavior in children.* San Francisco: Freeman, 1977.

REST, J. Morality. In J. H. Flavell, & E. Markmas (Eds.), *Cognitive development.* New York: Wiley, in press.

SMETANA, J. Reasoning in the personal and moral domains: Adolescent and young adult women's decision-making regarding abortion. *Journal of Applied Developmental Psychology,* 1981, *2,* 211–226.

SNAREY, J. The moral development of Kibbutz founders and Sabras: A cross-sectional and ten year longitudinal cross-cultural study. Unpublished doctoral dissertation. Harvard University, 1982.

STAUB, E. *Positive social behavior and morality.* New York: Academic Press, 1978.

WALKER, L. Sex differences in the development of moral reasoning: A critical review of the literature. *Child Development,* in press.

WATERMAN, A. S. Identity development from adolescence to adulthood: An extension of theory and a review of research. *Developmental Psychology,* 1982, *18,* 341–358.

WYATT, F. Clinical notes on the motives of reproduction. *Journal of Social Issues,* 1967, *23,* 29–56.

Psychology of Women Quarterly, 1987, 11, 37–46. Printed in the United States of America.

SEX DIFFERENCES IN MORAL JUDGMENTS? A TEST OF GILLIGAN'S THEORY

William J. Friedman, Amy B. Robinson, and Britt L. Friedman
Oberlin College

This study was designed to test Gilligan's (1982) claim that men and women differ in moral judgments. One hundred and one college students read four traditional moral dilemmas and rated the importance of 12 considerations for deciding how the protagonist should respond. Six of the statements were derived from the description by Kohlberg et al. (1978) of post-conventional moral reasoning, and six were derived from Gilligan's description of women's style of moral reasoning. Subjects also rated themselves on a measure of sex-typed personality attributes. There were no reliable sex differences on either of the types of moral reasoning, and confidence intervals allowed the rejection of all but negligible differences in the directions predicted by Gilligan's model. Furthermore, men and women showed highly similar rank orders of the items for each dilemma. The personality measures also failed to predict individual differences in moral judgments.

In several recent publications, including her influential book of 1982, Gilligan has claimed that there are sex differences in the nature of moral reasoning (1977, 1979). She specified a number of distinctive qualities of women's moral judgments and argued that these qualities are inadequately assessed by the scoring system used to measure an individual's status in Kohlberg's stages of moral development. In her view women are more likely than men to base their moral decisions on the consequences for the individuals involved and on obligations to care for and avoid hurting others. Men are more likely than women to view moral conflicts as abstract, logical problems concerning rights and rules.

As Walker (1984) has pointed out, Gilligan failed to provide acceptable empirical support for her model. So far the main evidence that bears on her claims comes from studies using traditional measures of moral reasoning

Author's address: Department of Psychology, Oberlin College, Oberlin, Ohio 44074
We wish to thank Dr. Mark McKinley for his assistance in obtaining subjects.

37

such as Kohlberg's interview procedures and Rest's Defining Issues Test (DIT). Two reviews of this literature (Rest, 1979a; Walker, 1984) provide little support for Gilligan's prediction that scoring procedures based on Kohlberg's theory will lead to the assignment of women to lower stages of moral development.

While traditional measures apparently do not assign women to lower stages than men, it is still possible that women prefer different bases of justification. For example, if Gilligan is correct, one could imagine two separate dimensions of moral justification, one reflecting the style she attributes to men and the other reflecting the style she attributes to women. Presumably, the first dimension is assessed by the usual measures of Kohlberg's stages. The second dimension, however, might require new measures based on Gilligan's description of women's style of justification. Gilligan's theory seems to imply that men would receive higher scores on the first type of measure and that women would receive higher scores on the second type of measure. The first implication appears to be incorrect, but the second remains to be tested.

In the present study we attempted to test both aspects of Gilligan's (1977, 1979, 1982) claims concerning sex differences in moral reasoning. Subjects evaluated the importance of each of a series of considerations for deciding how to respond to a moral dilemma. Half of these dimensions were derived from Gilligan's (1982) description of women's style of moral reasoning (which for convenience we will call *care based*). The other half were adapted from the description of post–conventional moral reasoning in Kohlberg, Colby, Gibbs and Speicher–Dubin's (1978) scoring manual (which we will call *justice based*). Post-conventional reasoning should be common among college populations (Rest, 1979b), and it is the stage that appears most consistent with Gilligan's description of men's style of moral justification. Gilligan's model implies that women should rate the first set as more important than men do, and that men should rate the second set as more important than women do.

We chose a rating measure rather than a production measure, because we believed that it would be more sensitive to the weights that individuals place on multiple bases of justification. Production measures may reveal information about only a subset of the dimensions the individual could consider because of attempts to maintain self consistency during the interview and because attentional and memory limitations may constrain the number of types of justifications that can be considered. Rating measures allow individuals to evaluate each of a number of justifications in turn. Rating measures also make it easier to conduct correlational analyses which can be used to investigate the psychological reality of hypothesized dimensions.

In addition to examining sex differences in the two hypothesized bases of moral justification, we also tested whether individuals' agreement with them could be better predicted by sex–typed personality measures than by sex alone. Research on the relationship between gender and personality typically shows significant differences on a number of self-rated attributes, along with large individual variation within each sex (e.g., Bem, 1974; Spence & Helmreich, 1978). Some of these attributes, such as sensitivity to others and nurturance, are particularly relevant to Gilligan's model because empathy is thought to form part of the bases for women's moral reasoning. It may be that women who score high on "feminine" scales may show Gilligan's predicted style of moral reasoning but that women who are low on these items will prefer Kohlberg's post-conventional justifications. We administered Spence and Helmreich's (1978) Personal Attributes Questionnaire (PAQ), which allows the computation of a Masculinity Scale (M), a Femininity Scale (F) and a third MF scale. The M and F scales are comprised of attributes that are considered socially desirable for both sexes but on which the corresponding sex tends to receive higher scores. The MF scale includes items on which social desirability varies substantially as a function of sex. It is computed in such a way that men tend to receive higher scores.

METHOD

Subjects

One hundred and one introductory psychology students, 47 men and 54 women, participated in the study. Seventy-eight were students at a liberal arts college and 23 were students at a community college.

Instruments

In the PAQ subjects rate themselves on a five-point scale (0–4) indicating the extent to which each of 24 attributes describes them. M, F and MF scores, based on the sum of the eight relevant items, range from 0–32.

The measure of moral reasoning was adapted from Rest's DIT (1979b). Three of the four dilemmas used (Heinz, the escaped prisoner, and the newspaper) were taken directly from his instrument. The fourth (the doctor's dilemma) also belongs to the DIT, but the wording was that of the corresponding dilemma in Kohlberg et al. (1978). Also taken from the DIT were the instructions and the format for rating the importance of individual items.

The main difference between this measure and the DIT was the 12 items for each dilemma that are rated by importance. In the DIT, each item corresponds to one of Kohlberg's stages or is a meaningless catch item. In our instrument, six of the items were based on Gilligan's (1982) description of women's moral reasoning and six were based on Kohlberg et al.'s (1978) stage criteria. Items were interspersed in a fixed random order. In both the DIT and our measure, subjects rate the importance of each item in making a decision about the dilemma. These judgments are reported on a five-point scale with points labelled *great, much, some, little* and *no* importance. In addition, subjects choose the first, second, third and fourth most important of the 12 items. The five-point ratings allow the assessment of the importance given to items more or less independently of one another, since there is not a forced distribution. The choice of the most important items does have a forced distribution, so item ratings are partially correlated.

For each dilemma the six items derived from Gilligan (1982) (G items) were generated by applying each of six aspects of her description to the content of the dilemma. These six aspects are (a) considering the actual consequences for the people involved, (p. 95); (b) considering the effects on specific relationships (pp. 28, 74); (c) considering the particular context and/ or the nature of the people involved (pp. 58, 100, 101); (d) considering the actor's willingness to sacrifice versus selfishness (pp. 101, 103); (e) considering the obligation to exercise care in relationships (pp. 16, 73, 74); and (f) considering the obligation to avoid hurt (pp. 73, 95).

The six items from Kohlberg et al.'s (1978) manual (K items) were generated from the following aspects; (a) considering whether there is a moral principle at stake to which all individuals should adhere (Part I, pp. 17, 20–22); (b) considering whether there is a rational standard that applies to the situation (I, pp. 17, 20; IV, 150, 156, 327); (c) considering that some values are more fundamental than others (I, p. 27; III, p. 70); (d) considering that certain human rights are more fundamental than the law (I, pp. 17, 28; III, p. 70; IV, pp. 261, 506); (e) considering the rights of the *individuals* involved (I, p. 31; III, pp. 116, 217; IV, p. 214); and (f) considering the right of the individual to make autonomous value decisions (III, pp. 283, 298, 352; IV, p. 61).

Following are examples of these 12 item types, all taken from the Heinz dilemma, in the order listed above.

G Items.
Is Heinz likely to risk getting shot as a burglar or going to jail for the chance that stealing the drug might help?
Is this likely to weaken or strengthen the relationship between Heinz and his wife?
How old are Heinz and his wife, and do they have children who could help them raise money?
Heinz's willingness to substitute himself for his wife and bear the brunt of society's laws.
Does Heinz have a responsibility to care for his wife?
Which outcome will cause the least hurt for all of the people involved?

K Items.
Whether there is a moral code to which all individuals should adhere.
What values are going to be the consistent basis for governing how people act towards each other?
The relative weights of life and property.
Whether the value of life and the equality of human rights are prior to law.

Whether the druggist, in exercising his individual rights, infringes on the rights of others.

Whether Heinz has a right to make a decision based on his own system of values.

The five-point importance ratings (0–4) for G items and K items were summed to form G and K scales (0–24) for each dilemma. These were also summed to form overall G and K scores (0–96). Similar composites were computed using the subjects' selection of the four most important items. Each item was assigned a 1 if it was the first or second most important item and a 0 otherwise. The sums, designated GHi and KHi, ranged from 0 to 2. Overall GHi and KHi scores could range from 0 to 8. Missing values for individual items led to the coding of composites as missing in the case of each scale.

Procedure

Testing took place in group sessions of approximately 45 minutes. Subjects were told that they were participating in separate studies concerning personality, opinions about social problems, and time concepts. The time concept questions were administered last and will not be discussed here. Subjects recorded the date, their sex, and answers to the PAQ and moral judgment instrument on computer-scorable forms.

In addition to the main study, an independent group of 8 male and 12 female introductory psychology students from the liberal arts college were tested for their ability to assign individual G and K items to descriptions of the two systems. Subjects were told that they were participating in a study of social judgments. They were given a sheet listing each of the six aspects used in generating the G items (see Instruments section; page numbers were deleted) under the heading *System A* and the six aspects used in generating the K items under the heading *System B*. Subjects were asked to read carefully the descriptions of the "two systems for deciding how to act" and to keep the sheet handy and refer to it as they rated individual items. Next they were given a packet containing the four dilemmas and items used in the main study, with the difference that an A and B were placed next to each item instead of the importance scales. Subjects were asked to read a dilemma and then decide whether each of the 12 items best matched System A or B.

RESULTS

PAQ

Male and female means for the M scale were 20.20 (SD = 4.20) and 19.08 (4.09); F scale: 23.09 (4.33) and 24.17 (4.03); and MF: 16.04 (3.99) and 13.73

Table 1
Correlations between the G and K scores of each dilemma

		Heinz		Doctor		Prisoner		Newspaper	
Scale		K	G	K	G	K	G	K	G
Dilemma	Scale								
Heinz									
	K								
	G	.10							
Doctor									
	K	.45***	.25**						
	G	.28**	.30**	.18*					
Prisoner									
	K	.41***	.30***	.67***	.26**				
	G	.21*	.37***	.32***	.46***	.29**			
Newspaper									
	K	.50***	.16	.56***	.22*	.51***	.27***		
	G	.17	.28**	.16	.62***	.27**	.51***	.09	

* $p<.05$
** $p<.01$
*** $p<.001$

(4.31), respectively. All three differences were in the expected direction, but only MF showed a significant sex difference, $t(91) = 2.70$, $p<.01$, two-tailed. None of the six means differed by more than 1.5 points from the same-sex groups in Spence and Helmreich's (1978) University of Texas sample, suggesting that our subjects were not an exceptional group among undergraduates on these dimensions.

Construct Validity of G and K Scales

The Pearson correlations between the G and K scales for each dilemma provided support for convergent and divergent validity of the two dimensions (see Table 1). The mean correlation between pairs of K scales from the four different dilemmas was $r = .52$, and that between pairs of G scales was $r = .42$. Alphas for G and K were .78 and .85, respectively. The mean of the between–dilemma, between G and K correlations was $r = .24$.

External Validity of G and K Items

The independent sample was very accurate in assigning individual items to the descriptions of the two systems. The mean proportion of assignments to the intended system was .92.

Sex Differences in Moral Judgment Indices

Sex differences were sought at the level of cross–dilemma composites, at the level of scales for each dilemma and at the level of individual items. The most sensitive test of Gilligan's model should be the comparison of male and female means on overall G and K scores. The mean overall K score for males was 63.60 and for females 66.46, $t(84) = -1.06$, n.s. The failure to show a significant difference, of course, does not justify the acceptance of the null hypothesis even when the mean difference is in the opposite direction. But 95% confidence limits on the mean difference allow us to reject a difference favoring males of more than 2.49. This corresponds to a difference of .10 on the 0–4 scales of individual items. The mean overall G score was 55.22 for males and 53.19 for females, $t(73) = -.83$, n.s. Confidence limits on the difference allow us to reject a difference favoring females of more than 2.81 or .12 units on individual items. A similar analysis based on the highest rated items from each dilemma also failed to support predictions from Gilligan's model. Women received higher overall KHi scores than men, $t(89) = -1.16$, n.s., and men showed higher overall GHi scores than women, $t(94) = -2.10$, $p < .04$.

None of the K or G scales for individual dilemmas showed significant sex differences and, on all but one of the eight, the differences were in the opposite direction of that expected from the sex difference model. Of the comparable KHi and GHi scores, only two of these showed significant sex differences, but both were inconsistent with the model. Women received higher KHi scores, $t(99) = -2.09$, $p < .04$, and men higher GHi scores, $t(99) = -2.61$, $p < .02$, on the newspaper dilemma.

Tests for sex differences at the level of individual items (using both types of importance ratings) showed that only five out of the possible 96 differences were significant at the .05 level. Three of these were in the opposite direction of that predicted. It should be noted that the failure to find sex differences was not an artifact of including such poorly written G items as to cause a "ceiling effect." For each of the dilemmas, at least one of the G items received one of the four highest means on the five-point importance rating scale.

One final way of evaluating the sex difference claim, and one in which the statistical analysis poses between–sex *similarity* as the alternative to the null hypothesis, is to correlate the mean item ratings of men and women for each dilemma. Correlations for the five point scale importance ratings showed r's (10) of .95, .96, .92 and .97 ($ps < .001$). This shows that the rank order of mean item scores was highly similar for men and women.

Correlations between PAQ and Moral Judgment Indices

The next analysis was conducted to determine whether the two styles of moral justification could be better predicted by individual differences in sex–

typed personality measures. For each sex we computed correlations between M, F and MF; and K, G, KHi and GHi. Of the 24 correlation coefficients, only one was significant (for males MF was correlated with K, $r(41) = -.25$, $p < .05$), and it was in the wrong direction. Of the 24 coefficients, only 12 were in a direction showing that higher K scores were associated with higher M or MF scores or higher G scores were associated with higher F scores.

A separate set of analyses compared K, G, KHi and GHi scores among four groups defined by subjects' conjoint status as above or below the sample means on M and F. (For example, one group was above the M mean and below the F mean.) Between-group ANOVA's for both sexes combined failed to show significant group differences on any of the variables. Separate analyses for each sex also failed to produce significant group effects.

DISCUSSION

The results indicate that neither gender nor sex-differentiated personality attributes are reliably associated with the type of moral judgments that individuals make. The composites based on the two dimensions that we deduced from Gilligan's theory are very unlikely to have differed by more than a trivial amount as a function of sex. Very few of the 48 individual items showed sex differences and most were in a direction inconsistent with the theory. Furthermore, men and women showed highly similar patterns in rating the importance of individual items in each dilemma. Taken together with previous studies using Kohlberg's procedure and the DIT (Rest, 1979a; Walker, 1984), these findings seem to cast doubt on the validity of Gilligan's (1977, 1979, 1982) claims.

Before accepting this conclusion it is important to consider a number of ways in which the present study may be limited in testing Gilligan's theory. First, it is possible that the items that we used are not valid measures of the hypothesized dimensions. We attempted to define the six aspects for each dimension by working closely with the sources and to derive appropriate items to fit the dilemmas, but the items were not validated against conventionally accepted measures. (In the case of the care basis, there is no obvious standard against which to validate our items.) However, naive subjects were very accurate in assigning our items to descriptions of the two systems which were derived from the published sources. Thus, to the extent that the descriptions given in the Method section are faithful to the theories, our items seem to be externally valid. It should also be noted that the correlational analyses supported the convergent and divergent validity of the two dimensions. Finally, it seems reasonable to suppose that at least *some* of our items would correspond to the theoretical dimensions. Given our sample size we should have had considerable power to detect sex differences at the level of individual items. Yet only two of 96 comparisons supported Gilligan's model and these are most reasonably ascribed to chance in light of the low significance levels (*ps* < .04 and .05) and the three significant item differences in the opposite direction.

Second, it is possible that special demographic or ideological characteristics of our sample preclude generalizations to other groups. The PAQ data offer some measure of protection against this problem, at least if we assume that group differences would also be reflected in sex–differentiated personality attributes. As previously noted, the sample in this study did not differ substantially from Spence and Helmreich's (1978) University of Texas sample on M, F or MF for either sex, suggesting the possibility of generalizing the results to other undergraduate populations. In addition, while our community college sample was too small to allow much power to detect subsample differences, there was some indication that liberal arts college women have higher K scores than community college women, $t(17) = 2.34$, $p<.04$, but that the two groups did not differ on G scores, $t(15) = .50$, n.s. The first difference would be expected given the usual positive correlation between intelligence and Kohlberg's stages of moral development. The apparent similarity of the two groups on G suggests that our results for this dimension may have some generality across demographic groups. Generalization to non–college populations may seem riskier, especially since moral reasoning is related to level of education (e.g., Rest 1979a). However, it is not obvious why the sex differences that Gilligan predicts would interact with education.

A third possible limitation is the use of a rating measure rather than a production measure. We chose a rating measure for reasons explained earlier, but it is worth noting that Gilligan's original research used women's spontaneous productions. Colby and Kohlberg (1984) have argued that rating methods, which assess comprehension and preference, may lead to different patterns of results than methods which use spontaneous productions. Attempts to correlate the two sorts of measures of Kohlberg's stages have produced somewhat inconsistent results (e.g., Froming & McColgan, 1979; Gibbs, Arnold, Morgan, Schwartz, Gavaghan, & Tappan, 1984; Rest, 1979a), and it remains unclear whether our method choice limits our ability to evaluate Gilligan's theory.

Perhaps the most serious challenge to the conclusion would be that the distinctive qualities of women's moral reasoning cannot be detected using traditional moral dilemmas. Gilligan (1982) states that a theory of women's morality must be based on "frequently occurring real life dilemmas of empathic interpersonal concerns" (p. 70). In light of this claim, further tests of her model using dilemmas that seem to meet these criteria may be warranted. However, the fact that Gilligan (1982) is able to give examples of women's distinctive approach to Kohlberg's dilemmas suggests that the dilemmas are not irrelevant to women's moral concerns. In the present study it is not easy to see why, if the theory is correct, women should not give greater importance than men to Heinz's responsibility to care for his wife or to the doctor's consideration of which decision will cause the least hurt to the people involved.

Finally, while this study fails to support Gilligan's (1977, 1979, 1982) claims for sex differences, it does provide preliminary evidence for the reality of a basis of moral judgments that is distinct from Kohlberg's. The correlations indicating some convergent and divergent validity of the G scale and the considerable importance accorded many G items would all seem to justify further research on care-based judgments. It appears that such a dimension would be important for understanding the moral reasoning of both women and men.

REFERENCES

Bem, S. L. (1974). The measurement of psychological androgyny. *Journal of Consulting and Clinical Psychology, 42,* 155–162.

Colby, A. & Kohlberg, L. (1984). Invariant sequence and internal consistency in moral judgment states. In W. M. Kurtines and J. L. Gewirtz (Eds.), *Morality, moral behavior and moral development* (pp. 41–51). New York: Wiley.

Froming, W. J. & McColgan, E. B. (1979). Comparing the Defining Issues Test with the Moral Dilemma Interview. *Developmental Psychology, 15,* 658–659.

Gibbs, J. C., Arnold, K. D., Morgan, R. L., Schwartz, E. S., Gavaghan, M. P., & Tappan, M. B. (1984). Construction and validation of a multiple choice measure of moral reasoning. *Child Development, 55,* 527–536.

Gilligan, C. (1977). In a different voice: Women's conception of the self and of morality. *Harvard Educational Review, 47,* 481–517.

Gilligan, C. (1979). Woman's place in man's life cycle. *Harvard Educational Review, 49,* 431–446.

Gilligan, C. (1982). *In a different voice: Psychological theory and women's development.* Cambridge, MA: Harvard University Press.

Kohlberg, L., Colby, A., Gibbs, J., & Speicher–Dubin, B. (1978). *Standard form scoring manual.* Cambridge, MA: Center for Moral Education, Harvard University.

Rest, J. R. (1979a). *Development in judging moral issues.* Minneapolis: University of Minnesota Press.

Rest, J. R. (1979b). *Revised manual for the Defining Issues Test, an objective test of moral judgment development.* Minneapolis: Minnesota Moral Research Project.

Spence, J. T., & Helmreich, R. L. (1978). *Masculinity and femininity: Their psychological dimensions, correlates, and antecedents.* Austin: University of Texas Press.

Walker, L. J. (1984). Sex differences in the development of moral reasoning: A critical review. *Child Development, 55,* 677–691.

First draft received: November 19, 1985
Final draft received: February 17, 1986

Kohlberg's 1966 challenge to the dominant theories concerning gender development influences current research in the field.

The Role of Gender Identity and Gender Constancy in Sex-Differentiated Development

Eleanor E. Maccoby

Upon rereading Kohlberg's 1966 paper on children's sex-role concepts and attitudes, I am struck by how well it stands the test of time. From today's perspective, it is difficult to realize how revolutionary the paper was for its time. In the early sixties, when it was written, there were two dominant theories about the gender aspects of development. Versions of learning theory stemming from Hull or Skinner probably had the strongest following. Learning theory was just beginning to be transformed into *social* learning theory through the added emphasis on observational learning or imitation, but the framework lacked the cognitive emphasis it has since acquired. Psychoanalytic theory was learning theory's main competitor. Kohlberg presented a theory that explicitly departed from both of the dominant views at that time.

Kohlberg in 1966: Departure From Then-Current Themes

Let us recall some of Kohlberg's statements in that remarkable 1966 paper. He argued that children's gender concepts are constructed, not directly taught. He claimed that fairly universal body imagery contributed to core gender schemas, but he parted company with the Freudians in his belief that the relevant images were not genital in nature but rather derived from adult gender differences in size and strength. He believed that gender concepts change in orderly ways over a considerable developmental time

NEW DIRECTIONS FOR CHILD DEVELOPMENT, no. 47, Spring 1990 © Jossey-Bass Inc., Publishers span, and that these changes are linked to general cognitive growth. While he noted that individual children differ in their rate of progress through the series of developmental steps, he did not think that different children took essentially different paths. Thus, he did not believe that variations among families in the degree and kind of sex-role socialization pressures they imposed had much power to shape children's sex role acquisitions differentially, at least not in comparison to the power of developmental forces impinging on all children. He distinguished gender identity from other aspects of children's understandings about the sex-linked characteristics of self and others. He viewed the formation of gender schemas, particularly identity schemas, as prior processes that motivate children to imitate same-sex others and to value and adopt whatever activities are deemed sex-appropriate in their respective cultures.

One of the most controversial points of this work dealt with the role of reinforcement. Social learning theorists argued that reinforcement and punishment were basic processes whereby children acquired sex-typed behavior, and that differential development of boys and girls could be traced to their having been reinforced or punished for different things. Kohlberg turned this process around, claiming that gender identity was a cognitive categorizing of the self and that this self-concept, once formed, then determined what would be rewarding to a child. Thus, for Kohlberg even reinforcement became to some degree a consequence rather than a cause of sex typing. Specifically, he claimed that the establishment of a firm gender identity would make children more susceptible to reinforcement by same-sex others. Thus, he anticipated by more than twenty years a paper by Fagot (1985) in which boys' behavior was shown to be influenced by the "reinforcements" provided by other boys, not by those provided by girls or by teachers, whereas girls' behavior was influenced by the reactions of teachers and of other girls, not by those of boys.

While nowadays there is by no means general agreement with all of these ideas that Kohlberg enunciated nearly twenty-five years ago, it is safe to say that some of them are now widely taken for granted. Gender schema theories now have a wide currency (for example, Bem, 1981), and as the cognitive revolution has spread through all walks of academic psychology, Kohlberg's writings seem central to the discipline, not peripheral as they once did. It is true that support for the hard version of stage theory has waned, and most current scholars no doubt believe in a greater degree of domain specificity in cognitive development than Kohlberg espoused. But a good deal of evidence has accumulated to support several aspects of Kohlberg's account.

Gender Constancy

Kohlberg's work on gender constancy has probably excited more attention and controversy than any other aspect of his theory. He said, "The child's gender identity can provide a stable organizer of the child's psychosexual attitudes only when he is categorically certain of its unchangeability" (1966, p. 95). He also said that children acquire gender constancy at about the same age as that identified by Piaget as typical for acquiring constancy (conservation) of such properties of physical objects as their mass, weight, and number. With DeVries (1969), Kohlberg conducted a study of "species constancy" and found that four-year-olds believed that a cat could change into a dog if its whiskers were cut off or if it wore a dog mask, whereas by age six or seven, they did not believe the cat's species identity could be changed in this way. Kohlberg saw the achievement of species constancy and gender constancy as closely linked: "The process of forming a constant gender identity is not a unique process determined by instinctual wishes and identifications, but a part of the general process of conceptual growth" (p. 98).

Kohlberg was not very clear about the age at which gender identity is sufficiently established to become the basis for sex typing. He cited DeLucia's (1963) work on toy preference with children of kindergarten age—who were thus at the lower bound for establishment of gender constancy—and noted that toy preferences were firmly established by this age. He referred to the work of Money, Hampson, and Hampson (1957) and agreed with them that gender identity becomes firmly established relatively early in life, and thereafter becomes very difficult to change. He did not agree, however, with their view that this process reflects a critical period for sexual imprinting in humans, analogous to critical periods in birds: "Rearing a person as a member of one sex rather than the other does not mean that there will be a difference in exposure to parents or other love objects; there will be, however, a difference in labeling of the self. Such labeling is perhaps irreversible because basic cognitive categorizations are irreversible" (p. 87). He then discussed Smedslund's (1961) work showing that while cognitive categorizations achieved before the age of cognitive constancies are easy to change, they are difficult to change after this age. But in this discussion Kohlberg overlooked the fact that Money and Hampson claimed that gender identity was difficult to change after the age of three, whereas Smedslund was talking about cognitive developmental steps normally taken at about the age of six. Kohlberg varied considerably with respect to which age or cognitive developmental level should be critical for children's achievement of gender constancy. As discussed later here, the range within which he varied (ages four to seven) is central to a developmental account of sex typing. However, the main import of Kohlberg's account is his placement of the acquisition of gender constancy at the same age as the shift to operational thought, at about five to seven years of age.

In the years following the publication of Kohlberg's 1966 paper, several writers became interested in the implications of gender constancy for imitation of same-sex models. This issue was important because social learning theorists were saying that imitation of same-sex models was a central process whereby children became sex-typed, whereas Kohlberg was arguing that the imitation of same-sex models was a consequence, rather than a cause, of the acquisition of gender schemas. He said that observational learning is "selective and internally organized by relational schemata" (Kohlberg, 1966, p. 83). With respect to the selective imitation of the same-sex parent, he argued that this should occur only after children had developed gender schemas that enabled them to know and value sex-appropriate activity. He thought that "effectance" or competence motivation would ensure that children would value the activities and characteristics appropriate for their own gender, once they understood what the gender-relevant attributes were. Kohlberg thought it was obvious that "a boy who desires to engage in masculine activities will prefer a male teacher or model to a female" (p. 127). Taking these two ideas together—that gender schemas only become firm organizing forces for behavior when gender constancy has been achieved, and that gender schemas provide the impetus for same-sex imitation—an obvious hypothesis was that such imitation should be more likely among children who were able to demonstrate gender constancy. It would also follow that same-sex imitation should not be common among children younger than the criterial age for gender constancy: somewhere between ages five and seven.

Maccoby and Jacklin (1974) reviewed the literature on imitation of same-sex models. In a series of studies in which children aged six or younger had been offered the opportunity to imitate either a single same-sex model or a single cross-sex model, the large majority of studies found no preferential imitation of the same-sex model. Over the age of six, there appeared to be an increased likelihood of same-sex imitation. These results seemed to fit nicely with the view that a child's motivation to seek out and utilize gender-appropriate information is enhanced by the achievement of gender constancy.

This view was also supported by other research. Ruble, Balaban, and Cooper (1981) found that children's utilization of information about the gender appropriateness of toys depended on their acquisition of gender constancy. In a study by Slaby and Frey (1975), with a group of children ranging in age from two to nearly six years, the children who had achieved gender constancy were more likely to selectively attend to same-sex models than were children who were not gender-constant. This was true even when chronological age had been controlled statistically. In this study, the measure used to reflect children's selective interest in same-sex models was the amount of time spent watching each of the two models. However, we know that observation of another person can reflect a variety of motives. It is worth noting that at low levels of gender constancy, girls actually spent somewhat more time watching male models than did boys, while at the higher levels the reverse was true. In the light of more recent work, the behavior of young girls might reflect wariness of, rather than identification with, males. In any case, the relationship of same-sex watching with gender constancy is the main point of interest.

Slaby and Frey (1975) raised an important point for subsequent work. They showed that the attainment of gender constancy is not an all-or-nothing phenomenon but rather a sequence of steps that form a Guttman scale. The ability to classify the self and others as to gender comes first, usually by age four. The next achievement is the understanding that one's gender is temporally stable: one always has been, and always will be, the same sex. And the final step is the understanding that gender is not affected by changes in hair style, clothing, or gender-typed activities. A boy can wear a dress or play with dolls and still be a boy. This last step, which Slaby and Frey call "gender consistency," follows fairly closely on the heels of temporal stability, both being achieved by the age of four-and-one-half years. This is surprisingly early. Emmerich and colleagues (Emmerich, Goldman, Kirsh, and Sharabany, 1977) found that among a large number of underprivileged children, the usual age for achieving gender constancy was considerably later, closer to age seven. Recent work by Wehren and DeLisi (1983) also pinpoints the age between five and seven years old as the usual time when children learn to maintain their gender designations in the face of changes in the gender appropriateness of a child's appearance or activities. They also found, however, that questions about temporal stability were answered correctly at an earlier age, commonly by age five. There is evidence that children's success in answering questions about gender constancy depends in part on the order and the way questions are asked (Siegal and Robinson, 1987) and whether pictorial aids or only verbal methods are used (Martin and Halverson, 1983). To the extent that the age of achieving gender constancy varies according to the aspect of constancy tested and the experimental procedure used, we are on slippery ground in trying to specify the age at which children should display a positive motivation to adopt behaviors appropriate to their sex.

The questions that Kohlberg and his supporters raised about the role of imitation in the acquisition of sex-typed behavior of young children soon drew a response from social learning theorists. In an elegantly designed study, Perry and Bussey (1979) exposed children to multiple models of both sexes. In one condition, four male models chose one activity, and four female models chose another. In another condition, the ratio of male-to-female choices of a given activity was three to one. In addition, there was a condition where equal numbers of male and female models chose an activity, and also a no-model control condition. In the first condition of high within-sex consensus among models, children consistently imitated the same-sex models. In the second condition of only moderate within-sex consensus, there was less same-sex imitation, but it was greater than chance. In the third condition of absence of model consensus, and in the no-model control condition, the children's activity choices were not sex-typed. In a second experiment, Perry and Bussey showed that children did not preferentially imitate a same-sex model if that model had previously been shown behaving sex-inappropriately. The authors concluded that imitation is alive and well as a process whereby sex-typed behavior is acquired, and they argued that social learning theory had been vindicated.

It is curious that Perry and Bussey's study was viewed as a refutation of cognitive developmental theory. First, the children who were subjects in the study were eight years old. Thus, they were old enough to easily fulfill the cognitive developmental requirement that children should have well-stabilized gender concepts and gender identity before they can be expected to imitate same-sex models selectively. Second, the fact that consensus among multiple models of the same sex fostered same-sex imitation indicates that children were forming abstractions or schemas on the basis of what they saw—abstractions concerning which behaviors are appropriate for males, which for females. To my knowledge, no cognitive developmental theorist has doubted that children learn a great deal about what activities are appropriate for the two sexes from observing male and female persons in real life and on television, and from reading about them in books. The issue has been whether, once aware of how people of a given sex behave, an observer will behave likewise. An observer who has many exemplars could learn a great deal about the distinctive behavior of the !Kung Bushmen without adopting the behavior. In short, the Perry and Bussey experiments left open the problem of an observer's motivation for imitating. This was the question that Kohlberg tried to answer through his emphasis on gender identity and sex constancy.

One could interpret the Perry and Bussey experiment as presenting a more serious challenge to psychoanalytic theory than to cognitive developmental theory. It indicated that children were unlikely to conclude from the behavior of a single model that the modeled behavior was relevant to sex typing. The child had to know that the model was a good exemplar of a gender class. This prerequisite has implications for the role of the same-sex parent as a prime source of sex typing. A girl who sees her mother both driving a car and wearing lipstick would not be able to tell which activity represents "feminine" behavior until she observes enough women and men to determine which behaviors distinguish the two sexes and which do not. The need for multiple models clearly called into question the idea that sex typing is based on identification with the same-sex parent.

A more serious challenge to cognitive developmental theory was presented by Bussey and Bandura (1984) in their study of a small group of privileged preschoolers ranging in age from twenty-nine to sixty-eight months. Once again multiple models were used, and in this study gender constancy was assessed. Subjects were selected so that there were equal numbers of subjects at each of three of Slaby and Frey's (1975) gender constancy levels. For both boys and girls, the mean number of imitative responses was nearly twice as great for the same-sex as for the cross-sex models. Both the amount of imitation and the levels of gender constancy increased with age, and age and gender constancy were highly correlated (.76 for boys, .82 for girls). Not surprisingly, when age was controlled statistically, gender constancy did not account for any additional variance in imitation. In this study, the number of subjects was small. In the model-exposed group, there were only three subjects of each sex at each of the three levels of gender constancy. Readers interested in the question of whether children who had not achieved any degree of gender constancy would selectively imitate must look for a significant difference in the choice of models between three very young girls and three very young boys. The data that would enable us to do this are not given in the published report, but the difference would have to be very large indeed to reach significance with these sample sizes. In a sample in which age and gender constancy are so heavily confounded, statistical controls will not succeed in pulling them apart. No doubt the authors could have just as easily reported that after controlling for gender constancy, there was no predictive power left for age.

The Bussey and Bandura study does provide clear evidence that children under the age of six will imitate same-sex models when multiple models are used and the actions that the models perform are perfectly correlated with their sex. As noted above, the test of the relevance of gender constancy is less clear. In their conclusion, the authors say that same-sex imitation "seems to involve relying on classifying males and females into distinct groups, recognizing personal similarity to one group of models, and tagging that group's behavior patterns in memory as the ones to be used as a guide to behavior" (1984, p. 1297). One can see here the evolution of social learning theory into cognitive social learning theory. The authors' conclusion is very much the same as what cognitive developmental theorists have been saying all along: imitation depends on the formation of gender schemas, and on the consonance of incoming information with an already formed gender identity. As other authors have noted (for example, Perry, White, and Perry, 1984), cognitive developmental theory and cognitive social learning theory no longer differ with respect to these elements in their accounts of sex typing. They both emphasize "self-socialization," to use the Maccoby and Jacklin (1974) term.

Gender Identity and Gender Cognition

What conditions did Bussey and Bandura think would lead an observer to "tag a behavior pattern in memory as a guide to behavior"? They believed they had demonstrated that gender constancy was not necessary. Citing Huston (1983), they say that "sex labeling and differential structuring of social experiences teach children to use the sex of the model as a guide for action" (1984, p. 1297). Based on evidence that children as young as six months of age can distinguish male from female faces, they imply that labeling must be a very early acquisition. However, discrimination and labeling are two different things: animals and infants can discriminate many things that they cannot label. Probably, accurate labeling of self and others as to gender is usually acquired toward the end of the third year. From this age on, gender identity takes on additional structure as children learn about the temporal stability of gender and its ability to survive changes in appearance and activities. Bussey and Bandura argue that simple labeling of self and other, along with some knowledge about the differential characteristics of the two sexes, is enough to motivate children to adopt sex-appropriate behavior. The issue seems to boil down to whether any greater coherence or stability of the gender self-concept, other than simple labeling, is needed for this motivation to be present and serve as a guide for children's behavior.

In thinking about this issue, we can glean insight into the nature of identity schemas from a recent study by Gelman, Collman, and Maccoby (1986). This study dealt with gender inferences. Preschool-age children were asked questions about a series of picture sets such as presented in Figure 1. For each set, children were given either familiar or unfamiliar information about the boy and girl pictured on the top row. For example, for one set, the experimenter said, pointing to the boy, "this boy has little seeds inside"; then, pointing to the girl, "this girl has little eggs inside." Next, pointing to the third child (dressed like the girl above), the experimenter asked one of two different questions: (1) "This child has seeds inside. Is this a boy or a girl?" or (2) "This child is a boy. Does he have seeds or eggs inside?" Questions of the second kind were much easier for the children to understand and were usually answered correctly by four-year-olds. The same children did not do better than chance on the first question. In other words, young children easily made inferences about gender properties once they were told the core gender category to which someone belonged; they could not make the reverse inference, however, from property to category.

In this same study, the children were given a standard gender constancy test. Their performance on these questions was at a chance level. It can be seen that most of the items on measures of gender constancy

Figure 1. Sample Picture Set Used in the Classification, Property Inference, and Control Conditions

require an inference from property to category. Children are asked, "if this boy wears a dress, or does girl things, is he a boy or a girl?" Those of preschool age usually cannot answer correctly, even though they know full well that if the boy were a boy, he would not wear a dress or do "girl things."

These findings can be put into the context of some recent work on identity constancy in natural kinds (Gelman and Markman, 1987; Keil, 1986). Keil presented young children with a task very similar to the species constancy problem used by Kohlberg (1966) and DeVries (1969). Starting with a picture of a racoon, Keil showed its hair being cut short, a stripe being painted down its back, and a little bag of smelly material being placed under its tail, so that it looked and smelled like a skunk. The question was whether the animal was still a racoon. Did it still have racoon blood? Would it have racoon babies or skunk babies? Alternatively, children were presented with changes in an artifact: a pitcher being transformed into a vase by having its spout and handle taken away. Many children preserved the identity of the racoon while readily agreeing that the pitcher had been changed into a vase. The claim is that there are certain kinds of categories that have a core identity from which children readily induce hidden properties. Younger children may not know what defining characteristics an adult would use to classify an exemplar into a category, but, nevertheless, once they have decided that an exemplar *is* a member of a natural-kind category, children as young as age three will readily infer that it has additional hidden properties. Children make inferences on the basis of category membership that they are unwilling to make on the basis of perceptual similarity.

The relevance of this work for issues of gender identity seems to be as follows. The categories male and female are natural kinds. That is, they are rather like species categories and unlike artifacts such as pitchers. Children are likely to entertain wide-ranging, deep theories about the properties male or female creatures might have. Once children are either provided with a gender label or else produce the label themselves on the basis of a person's name, appearance, or activities, the label becomes a basis for attributing to that person a whole cluster of characteristics associated with gender. The label becomes a kind of magnet, attracting new information about gender characteristics. As Hough, Hoffman, and Cowan (1980) have shown, if three-year-olds are told that a given child is a boy, they will claim that the child is smart, big, strong, mad, fast, loud, and mean; and if that child is a girl, they will claim that the child is dumb, weak, soft, little, scared, slow, quiet, and nice. The research cited above suggests that children make such inferences from a natural-kind category such as gender, while they are unlikely to do so for other categories or artifacts.

Stereotypes around natural-kind categories form quickly and early. This does not mean, however, that a young child understands the defining criteria for placing an exemplar in the category. Just as young children may not know that an island is defined as a body of land entirely surrounded by water, rather than as a body of land with palm trees or beaches, they may not know that human gender is defined by primary and secondary sex characteristics. Even if they are aware of the defining attributes at an early age, their selection of and reliance on these attributes as crucial for categorization comes considerably later. The switch to utilization of defining attributes does not come all at once; it is domain specific. Hence we cannot point to a specific age at which children should come to base their gender judgments on adultlike criteria. No doubt this development varies from child to child, depending in part on the information available to each child. It may be that the switch to a reliance on defining attributes makes a child less vulnerable to a belief that people's gender can change, if the defining attributes are themselves stable. Yet clearly children can believe their gender is stable without knowing its defining attributes.

We know that children who are too young to pass the usual gender constancy test nevertheless display clear sex typing in their behavior. The Bussey and Bandura experiment discussed earlier indicates that if the information about gender is made clear through convergent information from multiple models, children will imitate same-sex others at a young age—younger than the age at which we might expect them to understand the consistency of gender through a series of transformations. Do these facts mean that Kohlberg was wrong and that a firm, stable gender identity is not needed for sex typing to occur? Or does it mean that Kohlberg was right about the importance of the gender self-schema for sex typing, but children develop a firm, stable gender identity earlier than Kohlberg thought?

There is good reason to favor the latter view. It is instructive to consider a phenomenon observed by Marcus and Overton (1978) when they contrasted a pictorial version of the gender constancy test with one in which live children were used as models. A classmate of the subject stood behind a wooden frame so that overlays could be used to change the child's hairstyle and clothing. Marcus and Overton noted that in the live-model condition their subjects became acutely uncomfortable as they observed these changes, so much so that their performance was disrupted. The children's discomfort appears to reflect a strong conviction that such changes really could not and should not be occurring. Marcus and Overton also found that nearly all of their youngest subjects (kindergarten age) said that they and other children could not change their gender if they wanted to. In other words, they really believed that their gender was constant, even though they failed other gender constancy tests.

Appearance-reality distinctions are important in this domain of questioning, and Trautner (1985) reports that children who have difficulty making appearance-reality distinctions are also likely to be confused on the gender constancy questions. In other words, when asked whether gender changes when a child wears cross-gender clothes or hairstyles, some children may not be sure whether the experimenter is asking whether the child has *really* changed sex or only appears to have done so. Some of the gender constancy questions appear to invite children to adopt a playful or phantasizing judgmental set. As Martin and Halverson (1983) have shown, children who adopt a "pretend" set are more likely to fail gender constancy items. Siegal and Robinson (1987) report that four-year-olds, when told about another child who said that a little girl would become a boy if she played boys' games, frequently explain the other child's answer in ways that indicate they are just pretending in order to please the experimenter.

It seems clear that Kohlberg, and some of the rest of us, were misled by the gender constancy test. As the study by Gelman and colleagues shows, this test calls for a kind of inference that is difficult for young children to make. Furthermore, it appears to require that children adopt a small set of defining attributes for gender and avoid taking a pretend rather than a reality judgmental set. These modes are often not characteristic of the way young children categorize. A four-year-old's failure to pass the test probably does not mean that the child lacks a firm, stable gender identity, or even that the child is often in doubt about the gender of other persons. Gender is one of the most overdetermined elements of identity. We use gender-specific personal pronouns and proper names. To these we add indicators in the way of clothing and hairstyles. It may be, too, that such culturally specific indicators are merged with more universally available cues to gender. Whatever the cluster of cues children use, the point is that it would be very difficult for a child to be in doubt about his or her gender after the age of three or four, or to believe that one's gender is really subject to change.

Does this mean that gender concepts are not, after all, connected to general cognitive growth? Not at all. The hundreds of studies of conservation conducted after Piaget's original work have indicated that the achievement of conservation is not an all-or-nothing structural change, and that aspects of conservation are available much earlier than Piaget thought, if assessment methods are appropriately geared to children's productive capacities. Thus, the achievement of gender constancy at age four would not be out of synchrony with early levels of constancy in other domains.

In short, one could take the position that none of the research done in the years since the publication of Kohlberg's 1966 paper invalidates the idea that a firm and stable gender identity schema is a necessary condition for motivating children to match their own behavior to what they understand to be sex-appropriate characteristics. The existing research does not definitively *validate* the Kohlbergian hypothesis either. The important questions simply remain open. And we should be aware that even if Kohlberg was right about the motivation that underlies self-socialization for sex typing, it would still be possible for some degree of early sex-differentiation (that is, any occurring in the first two or three years of life) to be present as a result of factors other than gender identity schemas—factors such as biologically prepared behavior patterns that differ by sex, or early differential conditioning.

The above analysis suggests that the essential elements of gender constancy are usually in place by about age four. Furthermore, this stable self-concept can be present, and can motivate children's adoption of sex-typed behavior, even though at this age children do not understand the defining attributes of gender. The question of defining attributes is an important one, and one that Kohlberg struggled with. He cited an example of a boy, just turning six years of age, who when he saw his father carrying his mother's purse said, "Why are you carrying the purse, dad?

Are you a lady or something? You must be a lady; men don't carry purses" (Kohlberg, 1966, p. 116). Kohlberg suggested that children have a strong need to maintain their gender identity: "Until the child, at around age seven, establishes an abstract, constant definition of gender based on anatomy, his gender self-categorization is related to every possible sex-typed attribute" (1966, p. 116). He thought that this condition was temporary, however, and that with increasing anatomical knowledge children would become "more discriminating and less compulsive" in their use of sex-typed traits for making judgments about gender identity.

Gender Flexibility

Kohlberg appears to have enunciated two rather incompatible principles. On the one hand, there was the claim we have been discussing: once children know that their sex is a stable personal attribute, then they will value sex-appropriate activities and will become especially interested in same-sex others because of their similarity to the self. In particular, the child will begin to take the same-sex parent, and presumably other same-sex persons, as preferred models and will become more strongly tied emotionally to same-sex others. Thus, processes are set in motion by the achievement of gender constancy, which strengthens sex typing. Kohlberg's countervailing theme, on the other hand, was that the achievement of gender constancy makes sex typing more flexible (weaker?). Children who know that their gender identity will not change no longer need to worry about conforming to all the attributes of their gender for fear of changing into the other sex.

Kohlberg's hypothesis about gender flexibility has been strongly revived in more recent writings. Huston (1983, p. 407) says, "a full understanding of gender constancy marks a turning point that permits (but does not guarantee) a decrease in rigidity and an increase in flexibility of children's concepts about sex-typing." Serbin and Sprafkin (1986) studied children at each year of age between three and seven and found that while gender knowledge was increasing sharply during this time, and affiliation toward same-sex others also increased, gender salience diminished. Children in this study were asked to group pictures of people according to which seemed to go together; gender was a possible basis, but the pictures could also be classified on the basis of the activities in which the pictured people were engaged. Young children most often classified by gender, older children by activity. Of course, from this finding we do not know whether gender had become less salient or activity more so as children approached age seven.

A decrease in gender salience at about age six or seven is certainly a possible explanation for the Serbin and Sprafkin results. However, it is difficult to believe that gender is not salient for six- and seven-year-olds, or that their gender concepts are flexible, even for those who do have a stable gender identity. We may recall Damon's (1977) interviews with children from age four to age ten, in which he found that children aged six and seven were intensely sexist; for example, they believed that it was morally wrong for a boy to wear a dress. Older children were more flexible, in that they believed such a boy might be stupid but not naughty. In a review of work on gender segregation and related phenomena, Maccoby (1988) reports that gender segregation is powerfully maintained by children, even (perhaps especially) in the absence of adult pressure, up to at least age ten.

I suggest that the achievement of gender constancy does not make children more flexible with respect to sex typing. Gender constancy has to do with identity judgments, not with the stereotypes that surround a gender category once an identity judgment is made. A boy of seven or eight years of age may know that he will not turn into a girl if he carries his mother's purse. Nevertheless, he would be acutely embarrassed if another boy saw him doing so and would avoid such an action. After children understand about the temporal stability of their gender, all the powerful forces for adopting sex-typed behavior that Kohlberg pointed to—affiliation with same-sex others, the need for cognitive and personal consistency, and so on—are still in place and still motivate children to adopt sex-typed behavior and attitudes. If children become more flexible in some respects by, say, age nine or ten, I argue that this has nothing to do with gender constancy, which we now believe is achieved much earlier (at around age four). Rather, the flexibility probably reflects increasing information about how tight the connection is between gender and a range of activities. For most activities, there is not complete model consensus, and children amass information about exceptions as they grow older. They learn which inferences from category membership can be widely generalized and which cannot. In the experiment by Gelman, Collman, and Maccoby (1986), four-year-olds appeared ready to make a very wide range of inferences about a child once they knew the child's sex. Given that a child was a boy, they were ready to believe that he had seeds rather than eggs inside, that he had andro rather than estro in his blood, and so on. Older children, with their greater knowledge about exceptions, might not be so willing to make such broad inferences about unfamiliar qualities; certainly, they would hesitate to make inferences that ran contrary to generalizations based on their own prior knowledge.

Sex-role flexibility grows in another way that again may have nothing to do with gender constancy. Children learn to discriminate among situations in terms of how relevant gender is to each situation. Gender will always be relevant, and hence salient, when people are dating or otherwise involved in mate selection. Gender is more relevant on the school playground than in the classroom, at least in coeducational schools. Gender schemas are always available, but as several writers have noted (for example, Deaux and Major, 1987; Bem, 1981) they are not always called into play. Kohlberg would probably have thought of gender as so central a part of self-identity that we never divest ourselves of it nor function with gender in abeyance. Recent thinkers about gender salience imply that we can and do function without regard to gender under some circumstances. The central question is what are the conditions that determine when and whether our gender schemas will be activated? Current issues, then, take us away from the ground Kohlberg charted. Nevertheless, our thinking about gender can never be the same as it would have been had Kohlberg not written about it.

References

Bem, S. L. "Gender Schema Theory: A Cognitive Account of Sex-Typing." *Psychological Review*, 1981, *88*, 354–364.

Bussey, K., and Bandura, A. "Influence of Gender Constancy and Social Power on Sex-Linked Modeling." *Journal of Personality and Social Psychology*, 1984, *47*, 1292–1302.

Damon, W. M. *The Social World of the Child*. San Francisco: Jossey-Bass, 1977.

Deaux, K., and Major, B. "Putting Gender into Context: An Interactive Model of Gender-Related Behavior." *Psychological Review*, 1987, *94*, 369–389.

DeLucia, L. A. "The Toy Preference Test: A Measure of Sex-Role Identification." *Child Development*, 1963, *34*, 107–117.

DeVries, R. "Constancy of Generic Identity in the Years Three to Six." *Monographs of the Society for Research in Child Development*, 1969, *34*. (Serial no. 127.)

Emmerich, W., Goldman, K. S., Kirsh, B., and Sharabany, R. "Evidence for a Transitional Phase in the Development of Gender Constancy." *Child Development*, 1977, *48*, 930–936.

Fagot, B. I. "Beyond the Reinforcement Principle: Another Step Toward Understanding Sex Roles." *Developmental Psychology*, 1985, *21*, 1097–1104.

Gelman, S. A., Collman, P., and Maccoby, E. E. "Inferring Properties from Categories Versus Inferring Categories from Properties: The Case of Gender." *Child Development*, 1986, *57*, 396–404.

Gelman, S. A., and Markman, E. "Young Children's Inductions from Natural Kinds: The Role of Categories and Appearances." *Child Development*, 1987, *58*, 1532–1541.

Haugh, S. S., Hoffman, C. D., and Cowan, G. "The Age of the Very Young Beholder: Sex Typing of Infants by Very Young Children." *Child Development*, 1980, *51*, 598–600.

Huston, A. "Sex Typing." In P. H. Mussen (ed.), *Handbook of Child Psychology*. (4th ed.) Vol. 4. New York: Wiley, 1983.

Keil, F. C. "The Acquisition of Natural Kinds and Artifact Terms." In W. Demopoulos and A. Marras (eds.), *Language Learning and Concept Acquisition*. Norwood, N.J.: Ablex, 1986.

Kohlberg, L. "A Cognitive-Developmental Analysis of Children's Sex-Role Concepts and Attitudes." In E. E. Maccoby (ed.), *The Development of Sex Differences*. Stanford, Calif.: Stanford University Press, 1966.

Maccoby, E. E. "Gender as a Social Category." *Developmental Psychology,* 1988, *24,* 755-765.

Maccoby, E. E., and Jacklin, C. N. *The Psychology of Sex Differences.* Stanford, Calif.: Stanford University Press, 1974.

Marcus, D. E., and Overton, W. F. "The Development of Cognitive Gender Constancy and Sex-Role Preferences." *Child Development,* 1978, *49,* 434-444.

Martin, C. L., and Halverson, C. F., Jr. "Gender Constancy: A Methodological and Theoretical Analysis." *Sex Roles,* 1983, *9,* 775-790.

Money, J., Hampson, J. G., and Hampson, J. L. "Imprinting and the Establishment of Gender Role." *Archives of Neurological Psychiatry,* 1957, *77,* 333-336.

Perry, D. G., and Bussey, K. "The Social Learning Theory of Sex Differences: Initiation Is Alive and Well." *Journal of Personality and Social Psychology,* 1979, *37,* 1699-1712.

Perry, D. G., White, A. V., and Perry, L. C. "Is Early Sex-Typing Due to Children's Attempts to Match Their Behavior to Sex-Role Stereotypes?" *Child Development,* 1984, *55,* 2114-2121.

Ruble, D. N., Balaban, T., and Cooper, J. "Gender Constancy and the Effects of Sex-Typed Televised Toy Commercials." *Child Development,* 1981, *52,* 667-673.

Serbin, L. A., and Sprafkin, C. "The Salience of Gender and the Process of Sex Typing in Three- to Seven-Year-Old Children." *Child Development,* 1986, *57,* 1188-1199.

Siegal, M., and Robinson, J. "Order Effects in Children's Gender-Constancy Responses." *Developmental Psychology, 23* (2), 283-286.

Slaby, R. G., and Frey, K. S. "Development of Gender Constancy and Selective Attribution to Same-Sex Models." *Child Development,* 1975, *46,* 849-856.

Smedslund, J. "The Acquisition of Conservation of Substance and Weight in Children. III: Extinction of Conservation of Weight Acquired Normally and by Means of Empirical Controls on a Balance." *Scandinavian Journal of Psychology,* 1961, *2,* 1-3.

Trautner, H. M. "The Significance of the Appearance-Reality Distinction for the Development of Gender Constancy." Paper presented at the biennial meeting of the Society for Research in Child Development, Toronto, Ontario, Canada, April 1985.

Wehren, A., and DeLisi, R. "The Development of Gender Understanding: Judgments and Explanations." *Child Development,* 1983, *54,* 1568-1578.

*Eleanor E. Maccoby is emeritus professor of psychology,
Stanford University. She is the author of numerous articles and
several books, including* Social Development: Psychological
Growth and the Parent-Child Relationship *(1980) and, with
Carol Jacklin,* The Psychology of Sex Differences *(1974).*

How Different Is the "Different Voice"?

Catherine G. Greeno and Eleanor E. Maccoby

Gilligan's book *In a Different Voice* was intended to right a wrong. In 1965 Jean Piaget wrote, "The most superficial observation is sufficient to show that in the main the legal sense is far less developed in little girls than in boys." Several studies using Lawrence Kohlberg's moral development scale also reported sex differences (and male superiority) in the level of moral reasoning employed in response to hypothetical moral dilemmas.[7] Gilligan argues that these supposed deficiencies of female development result from an injustice inherent in the research. She notes that the research paradigm, and the analyses of moral "levels," have been based primarily on the study of male subjects. As a result, psychologists have fallen into an observational bias; by "implicitly adopting the male life as the norm, they have tried to fashion women out of a masculine cloth" (p. 6), and women's particular moral development "falls through the sieve" (p. 31) of an androcentric research tradition. Gilligan's view is that with a less biased approach to moral thinking, one would find that women's thinking was somewhat different from men's, but not less mature. Psychologists have erred, not in believing that women are different from men, but that they are inferior to men; because women develop along a moral path that is distinct from that followed by men, existing research paradigms have failed them.

Because Gilligan addresses Kohlberg's paradigm primarily, it is well

7. Jean Piaget, *The Moral Judgment of the Child* (New York: Free Press, 1965), p. 77; Henry Alker and Paul J. Poppen, "Ideology in University Students," *Journal of Personality* 41, no. 4 (December 1973): 653–71.

to be aware of certain features of his work, as well as some of the recent advances in theory, method, and findings.[8] The major goal of Kohlberg and his colleagues has been to trace developmental change in moral reasoning. While Kohlberg originally thought he could distinguish six such levels, more recent work indicates that there are four that can be applied to the large majority of children and adults. These four levels form a clear developmental progression. That is, individuals move from one to the next as they grow older, and there is evidence for the claim that the four levels have validity for individuals from a variety of cultural backgrounds. The transition from level 3 to level 4 is of the greatest interest for our purposes. Level 3 is considered to be the first stage of adult reasoning. Some studies using Kohlberg's rating system found that women tended to remain scored there, while men more consistently matured to level 4.[9] Level 3 reasoning involves a concern with maintaining bonds of trust with others. The individual strives to be—and to be seen by others as—a "good" or "nice" person. The "good" or "right" action is that which will not hurt those with whom one has valued relationships. Shared feelings and agreements take priority over individual interests. The move to level 4 involves what might be called a move to a societal level of thought, where moral issues are considered in terms of a system of law or justice that must be maintained for the good of society. The higher level does not supersede or supplant the lower—persons who can think in societal terms about moral issues also can continue to think about the effects of their actions on other persons with whom they have relationships—but a new progression in thought has occurred. There can be no doubt that level 4 considerations do appear in an individual's thinking later than level 3 considerations. In this sense, the societal level is more mature.

Here Gilligan makes her primary departure from the work that precedes her. She argues that although the androcentric coding system used for Kohlberg's dilemmas shows women remaining at level 3 more often than do men, women are not in fact fixed at this relatively immature level but progress along a path different from that followed by men. Specifically, she believes that women move from an exclusive orientation toward serving others' interests to a greater emphasis on self-

---

8. Lawrence Kohlberg, *The Philosophy of Moral Development: Moral Stages and the Idea of Justice* (New York: Harper & Row, 1981); Anne Colby et al., "A Longitudinal Study of Moral Judgment," *Monographs for the Society for Research in Child Development* 48, nos. 1–2, whole no. 200 (Chicago: University of Chicago Press, 1983).

9. James Fishkin, Kenneth Keniston, and Catharine MacKinnon, "Moral Reasoning and Political Ideology," *Journal of Personality and Social Psychology* 27, no. 1 (July 1973): 109–19; Norma Haan, M. Brewster Smith, and Jeanne Block, "Moral Reasoning of Young Adults: Political-social Behavior, Family Background, and Personality Correlates," *Journal of Personality and Social Psychology* 10, no. 3 (November 1968): 183–201.

actualization. Thus the "different construction of the moral problem by women may be seen as the reason for their failure to develop within the constraints of Kohlberg's system" (p. 19).

Current work reveals, however, that Gilligan has been attacking a straw man. In a comprehensive review paper, Lawrence Walker considers sixty-one studies in which the Kohlberg paradigm is used to score moral reasoning for subjects of both sexes. These show that in childhood and adolescence, there is no trend whatever for males to score at higher levels than females on Kohlberg's scales. In adulthood, the large majority of comparisons reveal no sex differences. In the studies that do show sex differences, the women were less well educated than the men, and it appears that education, not gender, accounts for women's seeming lesser maturity. Throughout this large body of research, there is no indication whatever that the two sexes take different developmental paths with respect to moral thought about abstract, hypothetical issues.[10]

Because Gilligan's own writings do not include data on how girls and women change their moral thinking as they grow older, we do not know whether a different scoring system, based on Gilligan's formulations, would show differences in the sequence of developmental steps. For two reasons we think it highly doubtful that such differences will emerge if and when the necessary comparisons are made: (1) the number of men and the number of women who reach the different Kohlberg levels at successive ages are highly similar, which suggests that the sexes follow the same developmental path; and (2) thinking about moral issues is closely linked to, though not identical with, general cognitive development, and we know that the sexes do not differ in the average rate at which they climb the ladder of cognitive growth.

Of course, thinking about hypothetical moral issues is not all there is to morality. In retrospect, it is unfortunate that Gilligan focused her attack primarily on the Kohlberg paradigm. Gilligan has other points to make about morality, and in the long run, her greatest contribution may be her work on these other aspects of moral decision making. Women, Gilligan believes, are bound into a network of intimate interpersonal ties. Compared with men, they are more empathic and compassionate, more concerned lest they fail to respond to others' needs, and made more anxious by the threat of separation from their loved ones. All these things could be true even if the sexes did not differ in their thinking about abstract moral issues.

Gilligan is not the only writer to point to sex differences in the capacity for intimate interpersonal relationships. The claim that women are more oriented toward interpersonal relations has a well-established

10. Lawrence Walker, "Sex Differences in the Development of Moral Reasoning: A Critical Review," *Child Development* 55, no. 3 (June 1984): 667–91.

history in many forums of discussion. Women's predominance in the nurturance and care of young children is an accepted and cross-culturally universal fact. Theorists have used women's presumably greater interpersonal orientation to "explain" a wide variety of sex-linked phenomena, ranging from differences in mathematical or spatial ability to differences in the nature of the roles assigned to women in most societies. Talcott Parsons and R. F. Bales's distinction between the instrumental (masculine) and the expressive (feminine) functions in family organization provides an early example. The more recent work of Sandra Bem and of Janet Spence, Robert Helmreich, and Joy Stapp makes similar distinctions.[11]

Research has indicated that there are indeed some robust sex differences that relate to Gilligan's concerns. For example, empathy and altruism have been frequently examined for sex differences.[12] Self-report scores on these qualities are particularly striking: in each of the sixteen self-report studies reported by Nancy Eisenberg and Roger Lennon, women rate themselves as more empathic than do men. These sex differences are sometimes very large statistically. Also, it has been found that when observers, such as teachers or peers, are asked to rate qualities of people they know, females are rated as more empathic and altruistic than males.[13] The stereotype of women's greater empathy and altruism is very strong, and, as Martin Hoffman points out in his review of empathy, "The relevant theorizing in the literature is in essential agreement with this stereotype. . . . There appear to have been no theorists who contradict [it]."[14]

It is clear that women have a greater *reputation* for altruism and empathy than do men, and that women accept its validity. Whether the reputation is deserved is a more complicated question. There are many studies in which people are unobtrusively observed while confronting an opportunity to help others. In general, these studies do not show that women are any more likely than men to offer help. However, most of these studies involve situations in which the person to be helped is a

11. Talcott Parsons and Robert F. Bales, *Family, Socialization and Interaction Process* (Glencoe, Ill.: Free Press, 1955); Sandra L. Bem, "The Measurement of Psychological Androgyny," *Journal of Consulting and Clinical Psychology* 42, no. 2 (April 1974): 155–62; Janet T. Spence, Robert Helmreich, and Joy Stapp, "Ratings of Self and Peers on Sex Role Attributes and Their Relation to Self-Esteem and Conceptions of Masculinity and Femininity," *Journal of Personality and Social Psychology* 32, no. 1 (July 1975): 29–39.

12. For a useful review, see Nancy Eisenberg and Roger Lennon, "Sex Differences in Empathy and Related Capacities," *Psychological Bulletin* 94, no. 1 (July 1983): 100–131.

13. Douglas B. Sawin et al., "Empathy and Altruism" (Department of Psychology, University of Texas at Austin, 1979, mimeographed).

14. Martin L. Hoffman, "Sex Differences in Empathy and Related Behaviors," *Psychological Bulletin* 84, no. 4 (July 1977): 712–22.

stranger. It has become clear that an individual's helpfulness to strangers depends on a complex set of factors that may or may not be related to gender. Thus, a person's readiness to offer help depends on the sex of the person in need, on perceived risks entailed in helping, and on the helper's beliefs about whether he or she has the skills needed to be an effective resource (e.g., a man is more likely to offer to change a tire, a woman, to soothe a child). It should be noted that in real life most altruistic acts are performed for the benefit of persons close to us. We suspect that if a real sex difference in altruism emerges, it will be found with respect to helpful acts directed toward friends and intimates, not toward strangers. But this work remains to be done; so far a sex difference can be neither confirmed nor refuted.

Recent work on children's play groups indicates that even at a very early age males and females show decidedly different styles in social interactions.[15] This research provides some evidence supporting an "agentive/expressive" distinction, similar to the one proposed by Parsons and Bales, but at a preadult phase of development. Girls' groups are smaller, most often a dyad or triad of "best friends" whose interactions are based on shared confidences. Boys' groups are larger and more task-oriented; that is, play tends to center on some goal-directed game or activity. These differences appear fairly early in childhood and are persistent. It is possible that some of the gender differences postulated in areas such as empathy and altruism stem from these early tendencies and preferences. An interesting parallel is, in fact, found in the literature on intimacy among adults. Women's relationships tend to focus on self-disclosure, and "liking" among women is highly correlated to the amount of self-disclosure that goes on in a relationship. For men the correlation between liking and self-disclosure is very low.[16] Self-disclosure tends to be a feature of intimacy and may be connected to the kind of network of interpersonal ties that Gilligan perceives. A great deal of work is left to be done on the exact nature of intimate relationships and possible gender differences therein.

When we read Gilligan, it is easy to be impressed by the elegance of her style and by the historical, philosophical depth of what she has to say. In these respects, her writing is very refreshing compared to the dry fact citing of much of social science. It seems almost philistine to challenge the nature of her evidence. Many women readers find that the comments by

15. For a review, see Eleanor Maccoby, "Social Groupings in Childhood: Their Relationship to Prosocial and Antisocial Behavior in Boys and Girls," in *Development of Antisocial and Prosocial Behavior: Theories, Research and Issues*, ed. Dan Olwens, Jack Block, and Marian Radke-Yarrow (San Diego: Academic Press, 1985).

16. Zick Rubin and Stephen Schenker, "Friendship, Proximity, and Self-Disclosure," *Journal of Personality* 46, no. 1 (March 1978): 1–22.

women quoted in Gilligan's book resonate so thoroughly with their own experience that they do not need any further demonstration of the truth of what is being said. The fact remains, however, that Gilligan claims that the views expressed by women in her book represent a *different* voice— different, that is, from men. This assertion demands quantitative, as well as qualitative, research. There is no sphere of human thought, action, or feeling in which the two sexes are entirely distinct. Reproductive activity is the area in which behaviors come closest to being truly dimorphic, but apart from this, the male and female distributions overlap greatly, and in most respects, men and women are more alike than they are different. A claim that the two sexes speak in different voices amounts to a claim that there are more women than men who think, feel, or behave in a given way. Simply quoting how some women feel is not enough proof. We need to know whether what is being said is distinctively *female*, or simply human. We believe that no researcher who makes assertions such as Gilligan's can escape the obligation to demonstrate a quantitative differ- ence in the proportion of the two sexes who show the characteristic in question. Here, Gilligan's research, as cited in the book, is unsatisfying. One study on abortion decisions was understandably confined to women subjects, and we consequently cannot compare how women and men think about this issue. Another study by Susan Pollak and Gilligan, after comparing the responses of men and women to a set of pictured scenes, maintained that women are made more anxious than men by the isolation that is involved in achievement, while men are made anxious by intimacy. However, a recent attempt to replicate that study raises serious questions about the way the pictures were classified to elicit the sex differences. Other classification systems reveal no tendency for the sexes to differ in their anxiety about intimacy or separation.[17] Finally, Gilligan has not yet provided any evidence that boys and girls follow different developmental courses in their thinking about morality. The book's only evidence con- cerning children's responses to moral issues consists of quotations from two eight-year-olds and two eleven-year-olds. These quotations fit our stereotypes about boys and girls, and intuitively we may feel that Gilligan must be right. But can we remain satisfied with this level of evidence?

We can only sound a warning: women have been trapped for genera- tions by people's willingness to accept their own intuitions about the truth of gender stereotypes. To us, there seems no alternative to the slow,

17. Susan Pollak and Carol Gilligan, "Images of Violence in Thematic Apperception Test Stories," *Journal of Personality and Social Psychology* 42, no. 1 (January 1982): 159–67; Kay Bussey and Betty Maugham, "Gender Differences in Moral Reasoning," ibid., 42, no. 4 (April 1982): 701–6; Cynthia J. Benton et al., "Is Hostility Linked with Affiliation among Males and with Achievement in Females? A Critique of Pollak and Gilligan," ibid., 45, no. 5 (November 1983): 1167–71.

painful, and sometimes dull accumulation of quantitative data to show whether the almost infinite variations in the way human beings think, feel, and act are actually linked to gender. Let us hasten to say that we are not arguing that the sexes do not differ in important respects. We only urge that claims about what these differences are should be subjected to the empirical tests that are the basis of social science.

Department of Psychology
Stanford University

A Methodological Critique

Zella Luria

In a Different Voice has had a predictably wide audience among women. Indeed the six story-filled essays have an intuitive fit with how many women see themselves, especially in relation to men. Given the potential influence of this work in characterizing women's thinking, it becomes imperative to scrutinize the bases of its arguments and to ask whether the evidence is yet sufficient to warrant Gilligan's conclusions. If the evidence is found insufficient, what further research might be needed for a more rigorous test of the book's intriguing assertions?

Gilligan's work demonstrates her immersion in the field of adolescent development and the influence on her of psychoanalytic theory. In research (as well as in popular thought) on the psychology of adolescence, Sigmund Freud and Erik Erikson are critical figures; the theories and methodologies of both turn up repeatedly in all of Gilligan's writing here and elsewhere. The weaving of literary examples (presumably as metaphors), theoretical proposal, and loosely defined empirical research can be a winning but seductive design; occasionally Gilligan does not draw a clear line between theoretical speculation and discussion of data and slips from hunch, example, or metaphor to "proven fact." The structure of her work, to use a metaphor myself, is built of solid bricks intermixed with some of cardboard.

In Gilligan's interview work, for instance, the nature of the evidence is sometimes unclear. Although psychological work on adolescents has been criticized for relying too heavily on the single method of the semi-structured interview that is favored by Gilligan, that method *can* be a useful technique if certain requirements of rigorous research are fulfilled. First, good samples must be carefully characterized by age, social class, education, and method of recruitment so that readers can securely apply the findings to similar groups. In general, Gilligan's sample specification is inadequate to justify her group characterizations. For example, eight males and eight females at different ages do not make up a number sufficient to characterize all males and females. Then, too, samples drawn from classes on moral development at Harvard University are dubious exemplars of students generally. Questionable, moreover, is the match within this sample itself between male and female students. Such matching does not occur in the central study of attitudes toward abortion. Twenty-nine women considering abortions in Boston may provide an important example of decision making, but they cannot provide data on how men and women differ in such thinking.[18] None of this rules out the possibility that adequate, well-specified samples for interview could be studied. Gilligan, however, has not yet done it.

Second, interviews that yield discursive data such as explanations, personal histories, and discussion of abstract questions require objective rules that categorize the respondents' texts. The rules for categorizing—X is a caring answer, Y is a rationalization and is also an abstract answer, Z is an abstract answer with caring, and so on—must be specified to ensure that all investigators make the same decisions about what particular responses mean, regardless of the theory under study. If the measuring system is reliable, investigators who may not share biases or views should, by careful rule application, agree nonetheless on the categorization of interview answers. Since the group working with Kohlberg on the studies of moral development central to Gilligan's critique has had three coding schemes and since Gilligan tells little of her own, no reader can know if this second requirement—the reliable objective scoring system—has been met. Thus the reader cannot make a personal judgment on the author's understanding of a particular answer or on the way in which answers are classified.

Third, Gilligan's juxtapositions of disparate samples pose problems about combination rules. Even if all subjects were asked about Kohlberg's dilemma on Heinz and the pharmacist, what was the rationale for considering abortion candidates and Harvard students as combined sources for data on two gender voices? The interviews of the twenty-nine pregnant women in the abortion study covered many questions necessarily absent from the Harvard students' interviews. After all, the family planning agency from which Gilligan recruited subjects expected her to talk about more than Heinz and the Kohlberg moral dilemmas. One is left with the sense that the combination of the data does not conform to the usual rules of psychological procedure—shared sampling, shared procedure, shared scoring—but is the result of a somewhat impressionistic

18. This sample is also unlike one of women who refuse to consider abortion, as can be seen in Kristin Luker's *Abortion and the Politics of Motherhood* (Berkeley and Los Angeles: University of California Press, 1984).

grouping of the stories Gilligan's subjects told. Obviously no psychologist would object to such a technique for deriving hypotheses, but Gilligan seems, at least, to be proferring it as a basis for proof.

It is highly likely that Gilligan is concerned with these issues of methodology. However, the book lacks any careful statement on them. One is left with the knowledge that there were some studies involving women and sometimes men and that women were somehow sampled and somehow interviewed on some issues as well as on the Kohlberg stories. Somehow the data were sifted and somehow yielded a clear impression that women could be powerfully characterized as caring and interrelated. This is an exceedingly intriguing proposal but it is not yet substantiated as a research conclusion. The interesting answers to queries liberally sprinkled along with the case studies through the volume cannot substitute for objectively derived data.

Gilligan's hypothesis, moreover, gives rise to another question, Does she truly believe that we need one psychology for women and another for men? At the 1983 meeting of the Society for Research in Child Development, her response was no, but her book suggests that her answer is yes. She gives no evidence of the extent of overlap between male and female responses to the Kohlberg moral dilemmas, as if the data consist of two virtually nonoverlapping curves. If there is one statement to be clearly and loudly stated to the public by students of sex differences, it is that overlap of scores by males and females is always far greater than the differences in those scores, particularly on psychological measures. We are not two species; we are two sexes.

It appears, then, that to yield so strong a theory as that which structures *In a Different Voice*, Gilligan has to some degree oversimplified the case and overinterpreted the data. Yet we might still ask whether her conclusions seem plausible when placed in the context of overall evidence. The lead review by Lawrence Walker in the June 1984 issue of *Child Development* details the evidence on sex differences found in studies using the Kohlberg moral reasoning measure. No sex differences that can be measured in replicable, developmentally orderly, and statistically significant ways are cited in the review. Of the nineteen adult studies reported there, fourteen yield no significant sex differences and five find men ahead in measures of moral reasoning. When usual summary techniques are applied to add all the studies together, the data do not support any finding of a statistically significant sex difference. In the review's last table, however, there is a footnote citing results by Gilligan et al. in an unpublished 1982 manuscript. Four samples of sixteen subjects—made up, one gathers, of eight men and eight women in each of four different age groups—were tested and showed no difference in average scores of men and women. A footnote suggests that "more men than women displayed at least one instance of postconventional (a higher stage) reasoning."[19] Are thirty-two men and thirty-two women the data base for Gilligan's different voices?

A recent doctoral thesis by Betsy Speicher-Dubin helps us to understand why some interpretations of sex differences may have been derived from older data. When social class is truly controlled, that is, by determining a married woman's class by her own education and work history rather than by her spouse's, sex differences do not appear. Results from the University of California Institute of Human Development at Berkeley based on archival data from the Oakland study—whose design was described by Harold Jones in 1939 and whose results relevant to this discussion were described by Speicher-Dubin in 1982[20]—showed women coming out slightly ahead on the Kohlberg measure. As the match between male and female class and education becomes more equitable, it might be reasonable to expect that male and female scores may not be very different. The relevant literature is replete with instances of presumed sex differences (we call some of them stereotypes) that disappear when better controls are used. On the other hand, if one wants to find sex differences, as Gilligan apparently does, one can get them simply by not controlling for class and education. One further related point: a 1979 review of work on a Kohlberg-like test—the Defining Issues Test developed by J. R. Rest—concluded that sex differences are rarely significant among students at the junior high, senior high, college, or graduate level or among adults. It is not even true, therefore, that at one stage in life one sex has an advantage which the other assumes at a later stage.[21] This evidence has not since been disputed.

Curiously, all of this discussion began just as Kohlberg and his colleagues took a new scoring manual to press. A previous publication by that group includes an example in an appendix of how responses demonstrating care of others can be coded at all stages.[22] Still, we cannot know whether Gilligan used such a method because her book contains no statement describing her interview and scoring criteria. Another recent review concludes that Gilligan's theory has been given wide scholarly

19. Carol Gilligan et al., "The Contribution of Women's Thought to Developmental Theory: The Elimination of Sex Bias in Moral Development Research and Education," cited in Walker (n. 10 above), p. 686.

20. Harold E. Jones, "The Adolescent Growth Study, I. Principles and Methods," and "The Adolescent Growth Study, II. Procedures," *Journal of Consulting Psychology* 3 (1939): 157–59, 177–80; Betsy Speicher-Dubin, "Relationships between Parent Moral Judgment, Child Moral Judgment, and Family Interaction: A Correlational Study" (Ph.D. diss., Harvard Graduate School of Education, 1982).

21. Mary Brabeck, "Moral Judgment: Theory and Research on Differences between Males and Females," *Developmental Review* 3, no. 3 (September 1983): 274–91.

22. Anne Colby et al., *Assessing Moral Stages: A Manual* (New York: Cambridge University Press, 1984); Colby et al. (n. 8 above).

attention, but "empirical evidence in support of her assertions is less available."[23] I welcome the research that will test those assertions.

*   *   *

What is it that we want today as women and as feminists? That is not a question about evidence but about goals. Do we truly gain by returning to a modern cult of true womanhood? Do we gain by the assertion that women think or reason in one voice and men in another? Gilligan's view focuses on characteristics of the person; the situation is only a vehicle for the expression of the reasoning personality, whether that be caring or abstract. The same rationale has often been used to shunt people into the "appropriate" job. Social psychologists during the last decade have been struggling to free psychology of these views of personality produced in the 1950s for the good reason that people are not, in fact, all that predictable in different circumstances. People differ in how they size up situations and then in their behavioral responses.[24] Actually, Gilligan's tie to the Kohlberg method does not give her—or Kohlberg—a sound basis for talking about people's behavior, only for analyzing what they say, alas!

A reasonable goal seems to me to make women—and men—able to choose when to be caring and related and when to be concerned with abstract issues. (While I do not view abstraction and ability to care as opposites, for the sake of the argument let us assume that they are nonoverlapping ways of thinking or behaving.) Modern women will need *not* to be always caring and interrelated, if indeed they ever were constantly so. And they are also in situations where being abstract and rights oriented is a necessity. My purpose as a feminist is to train women to choose their actions sensibly and flexibly depending on the situations they confront.

Some of my students are frightened. All around them are striving women. Many of my students are feminists but are also somewhat timid, traditionally feminine, and unsure of their ability to manage the real overload of work and family. They are horrified by real life competition for graduate school, for jobs, for men. How can we help such women deal with society today while trying to change it in productive ways? That seems to me to be the task. The world will not stop to let off those caring

23. Brabeck, pp. 275, 277.

24. Daryl Bem and David C. Funder, "Predicting More of the People More of the Time: Assessing the Personality of Situations," *Psychology Review* 85 (1978): 485–501; Jack Block and Jeanne H. Block, "Studying Situational Dimensions: A Grand Perspective and Some Limited Empiricism," in *The Situation: An Interactional Perspective*, ed. David Magnusson (Hillsdale, N.J.: Lawrence Erlbaum Associates, 1980); David Magnusson and Norman S. Endler, eds., *Personality at the Crossroads: Current Issues in Interactional Psychology* (Hillsdale, N.J.: Lawrence Erlbaum Associates, 1977).

women whose fears and repugnance keep them from learning new choices. Surely Gilligan and I want one voice that allows both men and women a variety of differentiated responses. Anything else is a step backward.

Department of Psychology
Tufts University

Sex Differences in the Development of Moral Reasoning: A Critical Review

Lawrence J. Walker
University of British Columbia

WALKER, LAWRENCE J. *Sex Differences in the Development of Moral Reasoning: A Critical Review.* CHILD DEVELOPMENT, 1984, **55**, 677–691. In this article the bases for recent allegations of sex bias in Kohlberg's theory of moral development are discussed. Studies comparing the development of moral reasoning between the sexes are then reviewed. Only a few inconsistent sex differences have been found in childhood and adolescence. Some studies indicate that, in adulthood, males evidence higher moral development than females, but in these studies sex differences are confounded with differences in level of education and occupation. A metaanalysis (a statistical procedure for combining findings) supported the conclusion that the overall pattern is one of nonsignificant sex differences in moral reasoning. Discussion focused on implications for moral development theory and research.

Kohlberg's (1969, 1976, 1981) theory of moral reasoning development has been criticized as being biased against women (e.g., Gilligan, 1977, 1982a; Haan, 1977; Holstein, 1976). The allegation of sex bias is a serious charge against any psychological theory and is even more controversial when leveled against a theory of moral development. The minimal foundation for such an interpretive claim against a theory would be evidence indicating greater moral maturity for males than for females. For this reason it seems appropriate to review the existing research literature to determine whether consistent sex differences in reasoning about moral dilemmas have been found and, if so, what explanations might account for these differences. Such a review is necessary since the assertions regarding sex bias and sex differences in moral reasoning are becoming bolder and more frequent and are found not only in scholarly writing but also in textbooks and the popular press (e.g., Gilligan, 1982c; Saxton, 1981). Although the current controversy revolves around a contemporary theory of moral development, the issue is not new; historically, women have often been

regarded as morally inferior to men (e.g., Freud, 1927).

The charge of sex bias might be warranted for two reasons. First, a theorist could explicitly advocate or popularize a poorly founded claim that the sexes are fundamentally different in rate and end point of moral development. For example, Freud (1927) asserted that women lack moral maturity because of deficiencies in same-sex parental identification. Second, a theorist might offer no such opinion, but define and/or measure moral maturity in ways that inadvertently favor one sex or the other and thus create a false impression of real differences in moral maturity. The allegations of sex bias against Kohlberg's theory have been based primarily on the latter reason.

Gilligan (1977, 1979, 1982a, 1982b) has been the most articulate critic alleging sex bias in Kohlberg's theory. She contends that Kohlberg's theory and scoring system are insensitive to characteristically feminine concerns for welfare, caring, and responsibility, and that Kohlberg, in failing to recognize the principled nature of these concerns, has de-

Portions of this paper were presented at the meeting of the Canadian Psychological Association, Montreal, June 1982. Many thanks to Sandra L. Bichard for her help in the preparation of this paper, and to Michael Boyes, Merry Bullock, C. Ann Cameron, Michael Chandler, Brian de Vries, Robert Leahy, Tannis MacBeth Williams, and three anonymous reviewers for their helpful comments. Requests for reprints should be sent to Lawrence J. Walker, Department of Psychology, University of British Columbia, Vancouver, British Columbia, Canada V6T 1Y7.

nigrated such thought to lower stages. She argues that Kohlberg's conception of morality is androcentric in that there is an emphasis (particularly at the higher stages) on traditionally masculine values such as rationality, individuality, abstraction, detachment, and impersonality—an emphasis that is reflected by the assertion that justice is the universal principle of morality.

Kohlberg's Theory

A brief description of Kohlberg's theory (1969, 1976, 1981) may be helpful at this point. He has postulated six stages in the development of moral reasoning. The initial two stages form the preconventional level. People at this level (primarily children) conceive of rules and social expectations as being external to the self. In Stage 1—punishment and obedience—right is defined by literal obedience to authority and the avoidance of punishment and physical damage. In Stage 2—individualism, instrumental purpose, and exchange—right is defined as serving one's own interests and desires and as letting others do likewise; cooperative interaction is based on terms of simple exchange. The conventional level subsumes Stages 3 and 4. People at this level (primarily late adolescents and adults) identify with, or have internalized, the rules and social expectations of others, including authorities. In Stage 3—mutual interpersonal expectations, relationships, and conformity—right is defined as concern for shared feelings, expectations, and agreements that take primacy over individual interests. In Stage 4—social system and conscience maintenance—focus is on the maintenance of the social order and the welfare of society or the group by obeying the law and doing one's duty. Stages 5 and 6 form the postconventional and principled level. At this level, people (a small minority of adults) differentiate themselves from the rules and expectations of others and think in terms of self-chosen principles. Stage 5—prior rights and social contract or utility—has utilitarian overtones in that right is defined by mutual standards that have been agreed upon by the whole society and by basic rights and values. In Stage 6—universal ethical principles—right is defined as accordance with self-chosen, logically consistent principles that are abstract and ethical and that all humanity should follow. It should be noted that Stage 6 has been dropped except as a theoretical construct because of its absence in Kohlberg's longitudinal data (Colby, Kohlberg, Gibbs, & Lieberman, 1983).

In Kohlberg's approach, moral development is assessed by responses to a number of hypothetical moral dilemmas that currently entail the following issues: life, law, morality and conscience, punishment, contract, and authority. Scoring of these responses according to Kohlberg's manual (Colby, Kohlberg, Gibbs, Candee, Hewer, Kaufman, Lieberman, Power, & Speicher-Dubin, in press) can yield two measures: a global stage score and a moral maturity score. The global stage score is determined by the modal stage of reasoning, with a minor stage being included if the second most frequent stage has 25% or more of the scored responses. The moral maturity score (MMS), a more quantitative measure, is given by the sum of the products of the percentage of usage at each stage multiplied by the number of that stage; it can range from 100 to 500.

Kohlberg (1976) claimed that the order of the stages is invariant, but he predicted variability in rate and eventual end point of development. There are two main determinants of rate of moral development: (1) attainment of appropriate levels of cognitive development, and (2) exposure to appropriate sociomoral experiences. Kohlberg (1973, 1976) has hypothesized that cognitive development is a necessary but not sufficient condition (i.e., a prerequisite) for the development of moral reasoning. This claim has been supported by studies (e.g., Kuhn, Langer, Kohlberg, & Haan, 1977; Walker, 1980) that indicate that attainment of a moral stage requires the prior or concomitant attainment of the parallel cognitive stage.

Level of moral development is influenced not only by cognitive prerequisites but also by exposure to sociomoral experiences (Kohlberg, 1969, 1973). The essential feature of these social experiences for moral development is the provision of role-taking opportunities in conflict situations. These experiences arise both through interpersonal relationships with family and friends and through real participation in the economic, political, and legal institutions of society. The effect of these experiences is thought to be a function not only of their quantity but of their quality in terms of the degree to which they afford opportunities for leadership, communication, decision making, and responsibility. Both of these determinants of rate of moral development (cognitive prerequisites and sociomoral experiences) may be useful in explaining variability in moral reasoning between groups (e.g., socioeconomic classes, cultural groups, the sexes).

The Issue of Sex Bias

Kohlberg's philosophical defense of his model of moral reasoning development (e.g., Kohlberg, 1981) may seem to reinforce the view expressed by Gilligan and others that he considers thinking at the higher stages to be detached, disinterested, and unmindful of the concrete realities of interpersonal relationships. However, there are two problems with that conclusion. First, it fails to recognize the self-limiting scope of Kohlberg's approach to moral development. His theory is a *cognitive* theory that deals with the adequacy of justifications for solutions to moral conflicts. It does not speak directly to the issues of moral emotions and behaviors, although Kohlberg (1978) has admitted the necessity and desirability of going beyond "cognition." Second, this criticism fails to recognize the contextual basis of principled moral judgment in action (vs. abstract descriptions). Kohlberg (1982) argues that there is no conflict between using moral principles and being contextually relative in moral judgment. Principled moral reasoning is contextually relative since it can be sensitive to aspects of a given situation in ways that rule-bound moral reasoning cannot. Boyd's (1979) interpretation of principled moral reasoning in terms of its accompanying "psychological postures" demonstrates the concrete aspects underlying such reasoning. For example, central to Kohlberg's conception of mature moral reasoning is the attitude of mutual "respect for persons" as ends, not means (Boyd, 1983). It should be remembered in this context that principled moral thinking is not the exclusive domain of moral philosophers but has also been used by activists such as Martin Luther King and Mother Teresa of Calcutta (Kohlberg, 1981).

Gilligan's (1977) response to the bias she saw inherent in Kohlberg's theory was to postulate an alternative stage sequence for the development of women's moral reasoning. These stages were derived from interviews with 29 women who were considering having an abortion. In the first level that Gilligan described, the orientation is to individual survival in that the self is the sole object of concern. The following transitional level represents a movement from this self-centered orientation toward responsibility that entails an attachment to others. In the second level, goodness is seen as self-sacrificial caring for others in order to gain their acceptance. The second transitional level represents an attempt to be responsible to self as well as to others and is based on notions of honesty and fairness. In the third level, the orientation is to a morality of nonviolence, and caring is seen as a universal obligation. Unfortunately, the only data that have been presented as yet to support this proposed stage sequence have been anecdotal (Gilligan, 1982a). None of the usual types of evidence for a stage sequence (i.e., longitudinal, cross-sectional, or experimental) has been reported. Nor has she provided an explanation as to why males and females may develop different orientations to moral judgment. Despite this lack of empirical support, her claim that the sexes follow different developmental pathways is, nevertheless, intended as a major challenge to the cognitive-developmental assumption of the universality of stage sequences (Gilligan, 1982b).

If there is sex bias in Kohlberg's approach, how could it have arisen? A trite response is that, because Kohlberg is a man, he has taken a masculine point of view in theorizing about moral development. An equally trite rejoinder would be to point out that Kohlberg has had a number of female colleagues, including the senior author of the recent editions of the scoring manual (Colby et al., in press). A second and much more serious possible source of bias is that the stage sequence has been constructed from the longitudinal data provided by an exclusively male sample (Colby et al., 1983). This lack of representativeness is a real threat to the generalizability of the model and could easily be a source of sex bias, but to date, no data have been presented to show that females do not follow Kohlberg's sequence of stages. Nonetheless, it is impossible to determine whether the same stages and sequence would have been derived if females had been studied originally. A third potential source of bias is the predominance of male protagonists in the moral dilemmas used as stimulus materials in eliciting reasoning. Females may have difficulty relating to these male protagonists and thus exhibit artifactually lower levels of moral reasoning. The effect of protagonists' sex on moral reasoning has been examined in a number of studies. Bussey and Maughan (1982) found more advanced reasoning with same-sex protagonists (for male subjects only). Freeman and Giebink (1979) also found more advanced reasoning with same-sex protagonists (for female subjects only).

On the other hand, Orchowsky and Jenkins (1979) found more advanced reasoning with opposite-sex protagonists, and Garwood, Levine, and Ewing (1980) found no evidence of differential responding when protagonist sex was varied. Thus, the data are equivocal regarding this potential source of bias.

To summarize, it is possible that sex bias exists in Kohlberg's theory, in particular because of his reliance on a male sample, but this remains to be determined. This review was undertaken to examine the consistency of sex differences in moral reasoning.

Sex Differences in Moral Reasoning

This review of the literature covered all studies using Kohlberg's measure in which sex differences in development of moral reasoning were examined. A study was excluded (a) if only one sex was assessed, (b) if there was no report or analysis of sex differences, (c) if age and sex were confounded (e.g., comparing mothers and their sons), (d) if subjects were selected according to stage, (e) if the data had been reported previously in another study (e.g., Kuhn et al. [1977] and Haan, Weiss, & Johnson [1982] both reported data that had been previously reported by Haan, Langer, & Kohlberg [1976]), or (f) if some objective measure of moral reasoning (such as the Defining Issues Test [DIT]) was used instead of Kohlberg's interview measure. There were several reasons for excluding studies using the DIT and similar measures: It is not appropriate for children and early adolescents; it does not stage-type (instead it yields continuous indexes, the "P" or "D" scores); it relies on stage definitions that differ somewhat from Kohlberg's (cf. Kohlberg, 1981; Rest, 1979); and Rest (1979) has already provided a brief review of DIT research on sex differences. He found that DIT studies were fairly consistent in failing to reveal significant sex differences.

It is important to note that the exclusion from this review of studies that did not examine sex differences implies that the review probably overestimates the incidence of sex differences in research on moral development. It is reasonable to assume that most of the researchers who did not report a sex difference found the sexes to be similar. The fact that differences are more likely to get published exacerbates the problem and makes Type I error more likely (what Rosenthal [1979] labeled the "file-drawer problem").

Since the concerns regarding sex bias in Kohlberg's theory have focused primarily on the conventional and principled stages (e.g., Gilligan, 1977), it is possible that sex differences would only become apparent in adulthood, when such moral reasoning is predominant. To clarify this issue, a developmental analysis of sex differences in moral reasoning seems appropriate. Therefore, the studies to be reviewed are presented in three tables that divide the life span into the somewhat arbitrary periods: (a) childhood and early adolescence, (b) late adolescence and youth, and (c) adulthood. A finding for each sample within a study is provided if there were separate analyses or a nonsignificant interaction between sample and sex. Unless otherwise noted, a nonsignificant finding indicates that both the main effect of sex and any interactions with sex were not significant; that includes studies involving repeated measures, which are designated "experimental design" or "longitudinal design," as appropriate. A number of researchers who did not analyze sex differences did present enough data (e.g., the number of males and females at each moral stage) to allow me to do such an analysis (typically conducting a Kolmogorov-Smirnov test for ordinal data; Siegel, 1956), and that is noted.

Childhood and early adolescence.—The results of research in which sex differences in moral reasoning in childhood and early adolescence were examined are summarized in Table 1. There were 31 such studies, involving a total of 2,879 subjects who ranged in age from about 5 years to 17 years. The pattern revealed is that sex differences in moral reasoning in childhood and early adolescence are infrequent; for the 41 samples, only six significant differences were reported.

One of these differences (White, 1975) cannot be taken at face value since the reported statistical analysis is actually not significant, contrary to the author's conclusion. This leaves five significant findings. Biaggio (1976) found that girls in her Brazilian sample of 10-, 13-, and 16-year-olds were more advanced in moral reasoning than the boys (MMS = 275 vs. 235). Blatt and Kohlberg (1975, Study 2) found pretest differences among their 15–16-year-olds that favored girls (316 vs. 275). Krebs and Gillmore (1982) found that the girls in their sample of 5–14-year-olds evidenced slightly more advanced moral reasoning than the boys. Turiel (1976) found differences favoring girls for 10–11-year-olds (268 vs. 254) and 12–14-year-olds (308 vs. 279). Finally, Saltzstein, Diamond, and Belenky (1972) found that girls tended to be classified at Stage 3, whereas boys tended to be classified primarily at Stages 1–2, but also at Stages 4–5 (these stages were collapsed for analyses). It should be noted that one-third of this sample was classified at Stages 4–5. Such high scoring for young subjects seems anomalous, especially according to current scoring procedures. (Revisions in scoring and stage definitions will be discussed in a later section.)

To summarize, sex differences in moral reasoning apparently are rare early in the life span and, when they occur, indicate more mature development for females, although even these infrequent differences are relatively small.

Late adolescence and youth.—The results of research in which sex differences in moral reasoning in late adolescence and youth were examined are summarized in Table 2. There were 35 such studies, involving a total of 3,901 subjects who were mostly high school and university students. As was found earlier in the life span, sex differences in moral reasoning in late adolescence and youth are infrequent: only 10 of the 46 samples yielded significant sex differences.

Three of these sex differences are of dubious relevance, as the researchers either failed to provide appropriate statistics to substantiate their claims (Alker & Poppen, 1973; Fishkin, Keniston, & MacKinnon, 1973) or conducted highly questionable analyses (Lockwood [1975] used incorrect error terms in his analysis of variance).

Two other researchers found that, although there were no overall sex differences, sex did interact with other variables. Arbuthnot (1975) found an interaction between sex and sex role identity that indicated that both women and men with nontraditional sex role identities had higher moral reasoning Levine (1976) found that women used more Stage 3 reasoning than men did on the standard dilemmas involving fictitious characters, whereas there were no sex differences on modified dilemmas involving primary others (i.e., one's own mother or best friend).

Five additional findings indicating significant sex differences in late adolescence and youth remain to be discussed. Arbuthnot (1983) found that women in his uni-versity sample evidenced more advanced moral reasoning than men (by about one-third of a stage). Bar-Yam, Kohlberg, and Naame (1980) reported two significant differences in a study of Israeli high school students. In both the Moslem-Arab and Youth-Aliyah samples, boys had higher levels of moral reasoning than girls (296 vs. 249, and 376 vs. 350, respectively). Both samples were drawn from ethnic groups where the status of women has traditionally been low, with few opportunities for decision making within the family and society and with typically low levels of education. It is interesting to note that no differences were found in the kibbutz and Christian samples, in which attitudes could be expected to be more egalitarian.

Bussey and Maughan (1982) found that men in their university sample evidenced more advanced moral reasoning than women. My analysis of data presented by Haan, Smith, and Block (1968) for their study of university students indicated that women were overrepresented at Stage 3. This study may involve some misscoring of stage of moral development (a possibility that Haan [1971] has noted). There are two bases for this suggestion. First, subjects responded to the dilemmas in questionnaire format rather than the recommended interview format (Colby et al., in press), which would result in more ambiguous responses and hence less reliable scoring. Second, moral stage definitions have been significantly altered since that study was conducted, in part because of the anomalous scoring of many subjects in their university sample as being preconventional.

To summarize, sex differences in moral reasoning in late adolescence and youth are rare, as was the case earlier in development. In contrast to the data from childhood and early adolescence, however, most studies in which sex differences were obtained indicate more mature development for males, although the differences, once again, were small (i.e., less than half a stage).

Adulthood.—The results of research in which sex differences in moral reasoning in adulthood were examined are summarized in Table 3. There were 13 such studies, involving a total of 1,223 subjects who ranged in age from 21 years to over 65 years. Sex differences in moral reasoning in adulthood are slightly more frequent than earlier in the life span; or, alternately, sex differences are more frequent in this generation than in later generations. (It is impossible to separate de-

TABLE 1

STUDIES EXAMINING SEX DIFFERENCES IN MORAL REASONING IN CHILDHOOD AND EARLY ADOLESCENCE

Study	Sample	Findings	Comments
Baumrind, Note 1	9 years ($N = 164$)	N.S.	finding based on data obtained from author & calculated by me via the Kolmogorov-Smirnov test; for a description of this study see Baumrind (1982)
Bear & Richards, 1981	11–13 years ($N = 60$)	N.S.	
Biaggio, 1976	10 years ($N = 30$); 13 years ($N = 30$); 16 years ($N = 30$)	girls > boys	Brazilian sample
Bielby & Papalia, 1975	10–14 years ($N = 12$)	N.S.	
Blatt & Kohlberg, 1975 (Study 2)	11–12 years ($N = 66$); 15–16 years ($N = 66$)	apparently N.S. for the younger group; girls > boys for the older group	experimental design; an age × sex interaction was found, but no analysis of the simple main effects was reported
Davidson, 1976	7–13 years ($N = 176$)	N.S.	
Gibbs, Widaman, & Colby, 1982.	4th grade ≈ 10 years ($N = 26$)	N.S.	
	5th grade ≈ 10 years ($N = 30$)	N.S.	
	7th grade ≈ 12 years ($N = 23$)	N.S.	
	7th grade ≈ 12 years ($N = 35$)	N.S.	
	9th grade ≈ 14 years ($N = 18$)	N.S.	
Gilligan, Langdale, Lyons, & Murphy, Note 2	8 years ($N = 16$)	N.S.	
	12 years ($N = 16$)	N.S.	
	15 years ($N = 16$)	N.S.	
Haan, 1978	13–17 years ($N = 56$)	N.S.	
Haan, Langer, & Kohlberg, 1976.	10–15 years ($N = 42$)	N.S.	
Holstein, 1976	initially 13 years ($N = 53$)	N.S.	3-year longitudinal design
Kavanagh, 1977	14–15 years ($N = 48$)	N.S.	experimental design
Keasey, 1972	6th grade ≈ 12 years ($N = 155$)	N.S.	
Krebs, 1967	6th grade ≈ 12 years ($N = 123$)	N.S.	no analysis by author; finding based on data from his Table 3 and calculated by me via the Kolmogorov-Smirnov test
Krebs & Gillmore, 1982	5–14 years ($N = 51$)	girls > boys	
Kuhn, Note 3	K–2d grade ≈ 5–7 years ($N = 68$)	N.S.	
Leming, 1978	7th grade ≈ 13 years ($N = 30$)	N.S.	
Parikh, 1980	12–13 years ($N = 20$); 15–16 years ($N = 19$)	N.S.	Indian sample; age × sex interaction not examined

TABLE 1 (*Continued*)

Study	Sample	Findings	Comments
Saltzstein, Diamond, & Belenky, 1972	7th grade≈13 years (N = 63)	girls tended to be at Stage 3, while boys tended to cluster at lower stages	
Selman, 1971 (Study 1)	8–10 years (N = 60)	N.S.	
Simon & Ward, 1973	11–12 years (N = 60)	N.S.	British sample
Sullivan, McCullough, & Stager, 1970	12 years (N = 40)	N.S.	
	14 years (N = 40)	N.S.	
Taylor & Achenbach, 1975 . .	K–2d grade≈5–7 years (N = 30); retardates matched for MA (N = 30)	N.S.	
Timm, 1980	5th grade≈11 years (N = 80)	N.S.	
Turiel, 1976	10–11 years (N = 63); 12–14 years (N = 62); 15–17 years (N = 85)	girls > boys for the two younger groups; girls≈boys for the older group	an age × sex interaction was found, but no analysis of the simple main effects was reported
Walker, 1980	9–13 years (N = 101)	N.S.	experimental design; no relevant analysis by author; finding based on data of initial sample and calculated by me via the t test
Walker, 1982	10–13 years (N = 50)	N.S.	experimental design
Walker, 1983	10–12 years (N = 60)	N.S.	experimental design
Walker, de Vries, & Bichard, in press	13–14 years (N = 16)	N.S.	
White, 1975	7–8 years (N = 15)	N.S.	Bahamian samples
	9–10 years (N = 42)	N.S.	
	11–12 years (N = 54)	N.S.	
	13–14 years (N = 23)	claims boys > girls	the validity of the analysis is suspect since the t value reported is actually n.s.
White, Bushnell, & Regnemer, 1978	8–17 years (N = 426)	N.S. (except for data previously reported by White [1975])	Bahamian samples; cross-sectional, longitudinal, and sequential designs

velopmental and cohort differences with these data.) For the 21 samples considered, four significant differences were reported, all favoring men.

Unlike previously discussed studies that involved rather homogeneous samples of school and university students, in the studies of adults that revealed differences in moral reasoning, sex was often confounded with educational and/or occupational differences. Haan et al. (1976) found that men scored higher than women in both their 21–

30-year-old sample and their 47–50-year-old sample (parents of the younger group). According to Haan (1977), the older women in this study were mostly housewives. The occupational status of the younger women was not described.

In the two remaining studies that revealed differences, sex was similarly confounded with occupational differences. Holstein (1976) found differences favoring men (409 vs. 366) on her first test but not on the retest. Nearly all the men in her sample

TABLE 2

STUDIES EXAMINING SEX DIFFERENCES IN MORAL REASONING IN LATE ADOLESCENCE AND YOUTH

Study	Sample	Findings	Comments
Alker & Poppen, 1973	undergraduates (N = 192)	men were more likely to be at the preconventional or principled levels	no descriptive statistics and no statistical analyses provided
Arbuthnot, 1975	undergraduates (N = 78)	N.S. main effect of sex, but interaction with sex role identity	nontraditional sex role identities were associated with higher moral reasoning for both sexes
Arbuthnot, 1983	undergraduates (N = 207)	women > men	
Bar-Yam, Kohlberg, & Naame, 1980	kibbutz-born 15–17 years (N = 19)	N.S.	Israeli samples
	Christian-Arab 15–17 years (N = 37)	N.S.	
	Moslem-Arab 15–17 years (N = 25)	boys > girls	
	Youth-Aliyah 15–17 years (N = 12?)	boys > girls	Youth-Aliyah were disadvantaged immigrants who were sent to kibbutzim
Berkowitz, Gibbs, & Broughton, 1980	undergraduates (N = 82)	N.S.	experimental design
Bielby & Papalia, 1975	15–19 years (N = 12)	N.S.	
	20–34 years (N = 12)	N.S.	
Bush & Balik, 1977	undergraduates (N = 40)	N.S.	experimental design
Bussey & Maughan, 1982 . . .	undergraduates (N = 40)	men > women, also interaction with sex of protagonists in dilemmas	Australian sample
D'Augelli & Cross, 1975	undergraduates (N = 133)	N.S.	no analysis by authors; finding based on data from their Table 4 and calculated by me via the Kolmogorov-Smirnov test
Edwards, 1978	16–21 years (N = 40)	N.S.	Kenyan samples
	undergraduates (N = 52)	N.S.	
Evans, 1982	high school students (N = 81)	N.S.	experimental design
Fishkin, Keniston, & Mac-Kinnon, 1973	undergraduates (N = 75)	women tended to be Stage 3; men tended to be Stage 4	no descriptive statistics and no statistical analyses provided
Froming, 1978	undergraduates (N = 200)	N.S.	
Gibbs, Arnold, Ahlborn, & Cheesman, in press	14–18 years (N = 60)	N.S.	experimental design; sample composed of delinquents
Gibbs, Arnold, & Buckhart, in this issue	11–21 years (N = 177)	N.S.	
Gibbs, Widaman, & Colby, 1982	14–17 years (N = 165)	N.S.	experimental design
	10th grade≈16 years (N = 34)	N.S.	

684

TABLE 2 (*Continued*)

Study	Sample	Findings	Comments
	10th and 11th grades≈15 years (N = 23)	N.S.	
	undergraduates≈19 years (N = 51)	N.S.	
	undergraduates≈19 years (N = 38)	N.S.	
Gilligan, Kohlberg, Lerner, & Belenky, 1971	high school≈15–17 years (N = 50)	N.S.?	boys and girls differed by only 11 MMS points, but no analysis was reported
Gilligan, Langdale, Lyons, & Murphy, Note 2	19 years (N = 16)	N.S.	
Haan, 1975	undergraduates (N = 310)	N.S.	
Haan, Langer, & Kohlberg, 1976	16–20 years (N = 78)	N.S.	
Haan, Smith, & Block, 1968	university students and Peace Corps volunteers (N = 510)	more women than men were at Stage 3 (41% vs. 23%); no apparent differences at other stages	no analysis by authors; finding based on data from their Table 2 and calculated by me via the Kolmogorov-Smirnov test
Haan, Stroud, & Holstein, 1973	16–35 years (N = 58)	N.S.	sample composed of "hippies"
Haier, 1977	undergraduates (N = 112)	N.S.?	men and women differed by only 7 MMS points, but no analysis was reported
Kahn, 1982	12–19 years (N = 30)	N.S.	Irish sample; finding based on analysis provided by Kahn (Note 4)
Kavanagh, 1977	17–18 years (N = 48)	N.S.	experimental design
Leming, 1978	11th grade≈17 years (N = 30)	N.S.	
Levine, 1976	undergraduates (N = 300)	N.S. main effect of sex, but interaction with content of dilemma	
Lockwood, 1975	8th grade≈14 years (N = 30); 11th grade≈17 years (N = 28)	claims boys > girls	the validity of the analysis is suspect since incorrect error terms were used (see his Table 3)
Maqsud, 1980a	16–19 years (N = 57)	N.S.	Nigerian samples
	17–19 years (N = 56)	N.S.	
Maqsud, 1980b	14–17 years (N = 97)	N.S.	Nigerian sample
Murphy & Gilligan, 1980 . . .	initially undergraduates (N = 26)	N.S.	longitudinal design
Simon & Ward, 1973	14–16 years (N = 60)	N.S.	British sample
Small, 1974	undergraduates (N = 48)	N.S.	experimental design
Sullivan, McCullough, & Stager, 1970	17 years (N = 40)	N.S.	
Walker, de Vries, & Bichard, in press	15–17 years (N = 16)	N.S.	
	undergraduates 17–24 years (N = 16)	N.S.	

685

335

TABLE 3

STUDIES EXAMINING SEX DIFFERENCES IN MORAL REASONING IN ADULTHOOD

Study	Sample	Findings	Comments
Baumrind, Note 1[a]	parents of 9-year-olds, ages not provided (N = 284)	N.S.	finding based on data obtained from author and calculated by me via the Kolmogorov-Smirnov test; for a description of this study, see Baumrind (1982); sample composed of married couples
Bielby & Papalia, 1975 ..	35–49 years (N = 12)	N.S.	
	50–64 years (N = 12)	N.S.	
	65 years + (N = 12)	N.S.	
Buck, Walsh, & Rothman, 1981	parents of preadolescents, ages not provided (N = 60)	N.S.	sample composed of married couples; no analysis by authors; finding based on data from their Table 1 and calculated by me via the Kolmogorov-Smirnov test
Gibbs, Widaman, & Colby, 1982	mostly parents of undergraduates, mean age was 38 years (N = 30)	N.S.	
Gilligan, Langdale, Lyons, & Murphy, Note 2[b]	22 years (N = 16)	N.S.	
	27 years (N = 16)	N.S.	
	36 years (N = 16)	N.S.	
	46 years (N = 16)	N.S.	
Haan, 1974	Peace Corps volunteers, initially mean age was 23 years (N = 70)	N.S. for both 1st and 2d test	longitudinal design; no analysis by author; finding based on data from her Table 4 and calculated by me via the Kolmogorov-Smirnov test
Haan, Langer, & Kohlberg, 1976	21–30 years (N = 83)	men > women	
	47–50 years (N = 179)	men > women	sample composed of married couples
Holstein, 1976	initially mean age was early 40s (N = 106)	men > women on 1st test; N.S. on 2d test	3-year longitudinal design; sample composed of married couples
Nassi, 1981	former Free Speech Movement arrestees (N = 26)	N.S.	no direct analysis by author; finding based on data from her Table 2 and calculated by me
	former student government leaders (N = 28)	N.S.	via Fisher's test for each sample of subjects; average age of all three samples is 34 years
	random sample of former students (N = 23)	N.S.	
Parikh, 1980	parents of teenagers, ages not provided (N = 78)	men > women	Indian sample; sample composed of married couples
Walker, Note 5	23–84 years (N = 62)	N.S.	sample composed of university employees
Walker, de Vries, & Bichard, in press	graduate students 21–52 years (N = 16)	N.S.	
Weisbroth, 1970	21–39 years (N = 78)	N.S.	

[a] It should be noted that, although my analysis revealed no significant difference between men and women, Baumrind (1982) did report a difference favoring men. Her finding was not included in this table because it was based on a subsample of the data provided by Baumrind (Note 1).

[b] Although Gilligan et al. (Note 2) found no differences in their analysis of MMSs, they did report a subsidiary analysis that indicated that more men than women displayed at least one instance of postconventional reasoning. However, the relevant data as presented in their Figure 2 indicates the opposite pattern. Thus, the appropriate interpretation of this analysis remains unclear.

had careers in business, management, or the professions, whereas only 6% of the women were employed. Similarly, Parikh (1980) found that men in her Indian sample scored higher than women (326 vs. 280). The men were all self-employed professionals, whereas most of the women were housewives. All of the remaining studies summarized in Table 3 seem to have entailed more homogeneous samples and have not yielded significant sex differences. The Weisbroth (1970) study, for example, involved doctoral students and professional or semiprofessional employees in universities or teaching hospitals and revealed no differences. The men and women in the Buck, Walsh, and Rothman (1981) study, Gilligan, Langdale, Lyons, and Murphy (Note 2) study, and Walker (Note 5) study were comparable in education and occupational levels, and no differences in moral reasoning were found. Several other studies (Bielby & Papalia, 1975; Buck et al., 1981; Haan et al., 1968; Holstein, 1972; Keasey, 1971; Parikh, 1980) have provided direct evidence regarding the relation between moral development and a variety of social experiences (e.g., family discussions, education, occupation, political and social activity).

A widely shared assumption (initially stated by Kohlberg & Kramer, 1969) is that women fixate at Stage 3, whereas men progress to Stage 4, or, as alleged by Gilligan (1982a, p. 70), "the thinking of women is often classified with that of children." Even among the studies that yielded some evidence of sex differences, there is no evidence, in adulthood, for such a claim. The modal stage for both men and women in the Holstein (1976) study and Haan et al. (1976) study (as reported by Haan et al. [1982] for a large subsample of their 47–50-year-old subjects) was Stage 4, and the modal stage for both sexes in the Parikh (1980) study was Stage 3. Thus, although sex differences may be reported in some studies, they tend not to be of the magnitude that has been suggested.

To summarize, it is apparent that sex differences in moral reasoning in adulthood are revealed only in a minority of studies, and even in those studies the differences tend to be small.

Metaanalysis

The conclusion indicated by this review is that the moral reasoning of males and females is more similar than different. However, this traditional method of literature review has been criticized as being suscepti-ble to biases and ignoring valuable information available in research reports. Meta-analytic procedures that enable reviewers to combine statistically the results of a series of studies are viewed as a more powerful and objective method than summary impression (Cooper & Rosenthal, 1980) and therefore were used as an adjunct to the traditional review described above.

Rosenthal (1978) has provided a comprehensive discussion of metaanalytic procedures, which need not be duplicated here. One of the more powerful, yet simple and routinely applicable, methods is the Stouffer method. Briefly, the steps in this method are (a) compute the exact one-tailed p of the test statistic reported, (b) compute the Z score (the standard normal deviate) associated with each p value, (c) sum these Z scores and divide by the square root of the number of findings being combined, and (d) compute the appropriate p value for this overall Z score, which indicates the probability level for the observed pattern of findings. Step a requires that a test statistic with degrees of freedom be provided. However, since sex differences were often of secondary interest to researchers, many failed to report the statistics on which they made inferences of no differences or reported statistics without indicating direction. The solution adopted for this review, but one that may increase distortion, was to assume an exact finding of no difference and use $p = .50$.

This metaanalysis of the studies reported earlier in this paper tested the hypothesis that males are more advanced than females in moral reasoning development, and, although the trend was in the predicted direction, this pattern was not significant, $Z = +.73$, $p = .23$, one-tailed. Even this finding probably overestimates the incidence of sex differences, given the reporting and publishing biases discussed earlier. Thus, the conclusion yielded by the metaanalysis is consistent with that of the traditional review.

It is also important to note that Kohlberg has introduced both conceptual and procedural revisions to his theory in an attempt to account more adequately for his longitudinal data (Colby et al., 1983). The preconventional stages have undergone little revision, but the more advanced conventional and principled stages—the level of moral reasoning common to adulthood—have been significantly redefined. The extent of these changes is reflected in the low correlation (.39) between the scores yielded by the original and current scoring manuals (Carroll & Rest, 1982). Revisions in scoring procedures (Colby, 1978; Kohlberg, 1976) have been twofold: (1) in the definition of the unit of analysis, and (2) in better differentiation of content from structure. Colby (1978) claimed that these revisions should eliminate the tendency to underestimate the reasoning of females because of particular content (e.g., focus on relationships, love, and caring).

Earlier studies, in particular, may have involved considerable misscoring (as was previously argued for the Haan et al. [1968] and Saltzstein et al. [1972] studies) that may account for some of the reported sex differences Thus, it is interesting to note that all but two (Arbuthnot, 1983; Bussey & Maughan, 1982) of the research teams that found significant sex differences used early versions of Kohlberg's scoring manual: the 1958 version (Turiel, 1976), the 1963 version (Saltzstein et al., 1972), the 1968 version (Haan et al., 1976), the 1971 version (Bar-Yam et al., 1980; Biaggio, 1976), and the 1972 version (Blatt & Kohlberg, 1975; Holstein, 1976; Parikh, 1980). The version used by Haan et al. (1968) was not reported. It is unlikely that this pattern is coincidental, but fortunately there is more direct evidence regarding the effects of changes in scoring. Holstein (1976) rescored data previously presented in a preliminary report (Holstein, 1972). The modal stage for men according to both scoring methods was Stage 4, but the modal stage for women changed from Stage 3 with the older scoring method to Stage 4 with the newer scoring method. Thus, some of the reported sex differences in early studies may, in fact, represent measurement artifacts.

Conclusions

The allegation that Kohlberg's theory is biased against the moral reasoning of women has become more vehement and more frequently expressed. The primary basis for this claim is that Kohlberg relied solely on the data from his longitudinal sample of males to derive and validate his description of moral development. This review and metaanalysis of the research literature indicates that, contrary to the prevailing stereotype, very few sex differences in moral development have been found. Of the 108 samples summarized in Tables 1–3, only eight clearly indicated significant differences favoring males. Furthermore, sev-

eral of these studies yielding sex differences favoring men were methodologically flawed, primarily because sex and occupational/educational differences were confounded. In addition, most studies reporting sex differences relied on early stage definitions and scoring procedures.

Support for the null hypothesis (i.e., that there are no sex differences in stage of moral reasoning), such has been amassed here, is usually not of any particular significance; but given the persistent belief that there are sex differences, this review may provide a heuristic perspective on a difficult issue. At the same time it is important to realize, as Kohlberg (1982) has noted, that the lack of stage disparity in moral reasoning between males and females does not preclude the possibility of sex differences in content within a stage (e.g., reliance on particular norms) or in the preferential use of various orientations in the making of moral judgments.

Rather than arguing over the extent to which sex bias is inherent in Kohlberg's theory of moral development, it might be more appropriate to ask why the myth that males are more advanced in moral reasoning than females persists in light of so little evidence. This review of the literature should make it clear that the moral reasoning of men and women is remarkably similar, especially given publication and reporting biases that make differences more likely to be reported. Perhaps it is time to focus our attention on other concerns, such as the questions of the role of cognitive prerequisites and sociomoral experiences in facilitating moral development and of the relationship of moral reasoning to moral emotions and behaviors.

Reference Notes

1. Baumrind, D. Personal communication, March 3, 1982.
2. Gilligan, C., Langdale, S., Lyons, N., & Murphy, J. M. *The contribution of women's thought to developmental theory: The elimination of sex bias in moral development research and education.* Unpublished manuscript, 1982. (Available from the Center for Moral Education, Harvard University, Cambridge, Massachusetts 02138.)
3. Kuhn, D. *Role-taking abilities underlying the development of moral judgment.* Unpublished manuscript, 1972. (Available from D. Kuhn, Graduate School of Education, Harvard University, Cambridge, Massachusetts 02138.)

4. Kahn, J. V. Personal communication, November 22, 1982.
5. Walker, L. J. *Social experiences and moral development in adulthood.* Paper presented at the biennial meeting of the Society for Research in Child Development, Detroit, April 1983.

References

Alker, H. A., & Poppen, P. J. Personality and ideology in university students. *Journal of Personality,* 1973, **41,** 653–671.

Arbuthnot, J. Level of moral judgment as a function of sex and sex role identity. *Journal of Social Psychology,* 1975, **97,** 297–298.

Arbuthnot, J. Attributions of responsibility by simulated jurors: Stage of moral reasoning and guilt by association. *Psychological Reports,* 1983, **52,** 287–298.

Bar-Yam, M., Kohlberg, L., & Naame, A. Moral reasoning of students in different cultural, social, and educational settings. *American Journal of Education,* 1980, **88,** 345–362.

Baumrind, D. Are androgynous individuals more effective persons and parents? *Child Development,* 1982, **53,** 44–75.

Bear, G. G., & Richards, H. C. Moral reasoning and conduct problems in the classroom. *Journal of Educational Psychology,* 1981, **73,** 664–670.

Berkowitz, M. W., Gibbs, J. C., & Broughton, J. M. The relation of moral judgment stage disparity to developmental effects of peer dialogues. *Merrill-Palmer Quarterly,* 1980, **26,** 341–357.

Biaggio, A. M. B. A developmental study of moral judgment of Brazilian children and adolescents. *Interamerican Journal of Psychology,* 1976, **10,** 71–78.

Bielby, D. D., & Papalia, D. E. Moral development and perceptual role-taking egocentrism: Their development and interrelationship across the life-span. *International Journal of Aging and Human Development,* 1975, **6,** 293–308.

Blatt, M. M., & Kohlberg, L. The effects of classroom moral discussion upon children's level of moral judgment. *Journal of Moral Education,* 1975, **4,** 129–161.

Boyd, D. R. An interpretation of principled morality. *Journal of Moral Education,* 1979, **8,** 110–123.

Boyd, D. R. Careful justice or just caring: A response to Gilligan. *Proceedings of the Philosophy of Education Society,* 1983, **38,** 63–69.

Buck, L. Z., Walsh, W. F., & Rothman, G. Relationship between parental moral judgment and socialization. *Youth and Society,* 1981, **13,** 91–116.

Bush, D. F., & Balik, B. Factors contributing to moral stage change in adolescence and adulthood: Presenting and discussion of moral dilemmas. *Social Science Forum: An Interdisciplinary Journal,* 1977, **1,** 14–24.

Bussey, K., & Maughan, B. Gender differences in moral reasoning. *Journal of Personality and Social Psychology,* 1982, **42,** 701–706.

Carroll, J., & Rest, J. Moral development. In B. Wolman & G. Stricker (Eds.), *Handbook of developmental psychology.* Englewood Cliffs, N.J.: Prentice-Hall, 1982.

Colby, A. Evolution of a moral-developmental theory. In W. Damon (Ed.)., *New directions for child development: Moral development* (No. 2). San Francisco: Jossey-Bass, 1978.

Colby, A., Kohlberg, L., Gibbs, J. C., Candee, D., Hewer, R., Kaufman, K., Lieberman, M., Power, C., & Speicher-Dubin, B. *Assessing moral stages: A manual.* New York: Cambridge University Press, in press.

Colby, A., Kohlberg, L., Gibbs, J., & Lieberman, M. A longitudinal study of moral judgment. *Monographs of the Society for Research in Child Development,* 1983, **48**(1–2, Serial No. 200).

Cooper, H. M., & Rosenthal, R. Statistical versus traditional procedures for summarizing research findings. *Psychological Bulletin,* 1980, **87,** 442–449.

D'Augelli, J. F., & Cross, H. J. Relationship of sex guilt and moral reasoning to premarital sex in college women and in couples. *Journal of Consulting and Clinical Psychology,* 1975, **43,** 40–47.

Davidson, F. H. Ability to respect persons compared to ethnic prejudice in childhood. *Journal of Personality and Social Psychology,* 1976, **34,** 1256–1267.

Edwards, C. P. Social experience and moral judgment in East African young adults. *Journal of Genetic Psychology,* 1978, **133,** 19–29.

Evans, C. S. Moral stage development and knowledge of Kohlberg's theory. *Journal of Experimental Education,* 1982, **51,** 14–17.

Fishkin, J., Keniston, K., & MacKinnon, C. Moral reasoning and political ideology. *Journal of Personality and Social Psychology,* 1973, **27,** 109–119.

Freeman, S. J. M., & Giebink, J. W. Moral judgment as a function of age, sex, and stimulus. *Journal of Psychology,* 1979, **102,** 43–47.

Freud, S. Some psychological consequences of the anatomical distinction between the sexes. *International Journal of Psycho-analysis,* 1927, **8,** 133–142.

Froming, W. J. The relationship of moral judgment, self-awareness, and sex to compliance behavior. *Journal of Research in Personality,* 1978, **12,** 396–409.

Garwood, S. G., Levine, D. W., & Ewing, L. Effect of protagonist's sex on assessing gender differences in moral reasoning. *Developmental Psychology*, 1980, **16**, 677–678.

Gibbs, J. C., Arnold, K. D., Ahlborn, H. H., & Cheesman, F. L. Facilitation of sociomoral reasoning in delinquents. *Journal of Consulting and Clinical Psychology*, in press.

Gibbs, J. C., Arnold, K. D., & Burkhart, J. E. Sex differences in the expression of moral judgment. *Child Development*, in this issue.

Gibbs, J. C., Widaman, K. F., & Colby, A. Construction and validation of a simplified, group-administerable equivalent to the moral judgment interview. *Child Development*, 1982, **53**, 895–910.

Gilligan, C. In a different voice: Women's conception of the self and of morality. *Harvard Educational Review*, 1977, **47**, 481–517.

Gilligan, C. Woman's place in man's life cycle. *Harvard Educational Review*, 1979, **49**, 431–446.

Gilligan, C. *In a different voice: Psychological theory and women's development.* Cambridge, Mass.: Harvard University Press, 1982. (a)

Gilligan, C. New maps of development: New visions of maturity. *American Journal of Orthopsychiatry*, 1982, **52**, 199–212. (b)

Gilligan, C. Why should a woman be more like a man? *Psychology Today*, June 1982, pp. 68–77. (c)

Gilligan, C., Kohlberg, L., Lerner, J., & Belenky, M. Moral reasoning about sexual dilemmas: The development of an interview and scoring system. *Technical report of the commission on obscenity and pornography* (Vol. 1). Washington, D.C.: Government Printing Office, 1971.

Haan, N. Moral redefinition in families as the critical aspect of the generational gap. *Youth and Society*, 1971, **2**, 259–283.

Haan, N. Changes in young adults after Peace Corps experiences: Political-social views, moral reasoning, and perceptions of self and parents. *Journal of Youth and Adolescence*, 1974, **3**, 177–194.

Haan, N. Hypothetical and actual moral reasoning in a situation of civil disobedience. *Journal of Personality and Social Psychology*, 1975, **32**, 255–270.

Haan, N. *Coping and defending: Processes of self-environment organization.* New York: Academic Press, 1977.

Haan, N. Two moralities in action contexts: Relationships to thought, ego regulation, and development. *Journal of Personality and Social Psychology*, 1978, **36**, 286–305.

Haan, N., Langer, J., & Kohlberg, L. Family patterns of moral reasoning. *Child Development*, 1976, **47**, 1204–1206.

Haan, N., Smith, M. B., & Block, J. Moral reasoning of young adults: Political-social behavior, family background, and personality correlates. *Journal of Personality and Social Psychology*, 1968, **10**, 183–201.

Haan, N., Stroud, J., & Holstein, C. Moral and ego stages in relationship to ego processes: A study of "hippies." *Journal of Personality*, 1973, **41**, 596–612.

Haan, N., Weiss, R., & Johnson, V. The role of logic in moral reasoning and development. *Developmental Psychology*, 1982, **18**, 245–256.

Haier, R. J. Moral reasoning and moral character: Relationships between the Kohlberg and the Hogan models. *Psychological Reports*, 1977, **40**, 215–226.

Holstein, C. B. The relation of children's moral judgment level to that of their parents and to communication patterns in the family. In R. C. Smart & M. S. Smart (Eds.), *Readings in child development and relationships.* New York: Macmillan, 1972.

Holstein, C. B. Irreversible, stepwise sequence in the development of moral judgment: A longitudinal study of males and females. *Child Development*, 1976, **47**, 51–61.

Kahn, J. V. Moral reasoning in Irish children and adolescents as measured by the Defining Issues Test. *Irish Journal of Psychology*, 1982, **5**, 96–108.

Kavanagh, H. B. Moral education: Relevance, goals and strategies. *Journal of Moral Education*, 1977, **6**, 121–130.

Keasey, C. B. Social participation as a factor in the moral development of preadolescents. *Developmental Psychology*, 1971, **5**, 216–220.

Keasey, C. B. The lack of sex differences in the moral judgment of preadolescents. *Journal of Social Psychology*, 1972, **86**, 157–158.

Kohlberg, L. Stage and sequence: The cognitive-developmental approach to socialization. In D. A. Goslin (Ed.), *Handbook of socialization theory and research.* Chicago: Rand McNally, 1969.

Kohlberg, L. Continuities in childhood and adult moral development revisited. In P. B. Baltes & K. W. Schaie (Eds.), *Life-span developmental psychology: Personality and socialization.* New York: Academic, 1973.

Kohlberg, L. Moral stages and moralization: The cognitive-developmental approach. In T. Lickona (Ed.), *Moral development and behavior: Theory, research, and social issues.* New York: Holt, Rinehart & Winston, 1976.

Kohlberg, L. Moral education reappraised. *Humanist*, 1978, **38**(6), 13–15.

Kohlberg, L. *Essays on moral development: The philosophy of moral development* (Vol. 1). San Francisco: Harper & Row, 1981.

Kohlberg, L. A reply to Owen Flanagan and some

comments on the Puka-Goodpaster exchange. *Ethics*, 1982, **92**, 513–528.

Kohlberg, L., & Kramer, R. Continuities and discontinuities in childhood and adult moral development. *Human Development*, 1969, **12**, 93–120.

Krebs, D., & Gillmore, J. The relationship among the first stages of cognitive development, role-taking abilities, and moral development. *Child Development*, 1982, **53**, 877–886.

Krebs, R. L. *Some relationships between moral judgment, attention, and resistance to temptation.* Unpublished doctoral dissertation, University of Chicago, 1967.

Kuhn, D., Langer, J., Kohlberg, L., & Haan, N. S. The development of formal operations in logical and moral judgment. *Genetic Psychology Monographs*, 1977, **95**, 97–188.

Leming, J. S. Intrapersonal variations in stage of moral reasoning among adolescents as a function of situational context. *Journal of Youth and Adolescence*, 1978, **7**, 405–416.

Levine, C. Role-taking standpoint and adolescent usage of Kohlberg's conventional stages of moral reasoning. *Journal of Personality and Social Psychology*, 1976, **34**, 41–46.

Lockwood, A. L. Stage of moral development and students' reasoning on public policy issues. *Journal of Moral Education*, 1975, **5**, 51–61.

Maqsud, M. Locus of control and stages of moral reasoning. *Psychological Reports*, 1980, **46**, 1243–1248. (a)

Maqsud, M. Relationships between personal control, moral reasoning, and socioeconomic status of Nigerian Hausa adolescents. *Journal of Youth and Adolescence*, 1980, **9**, 281–288. (b)

Murphy, J. M., & Gilligan, C. Moral development in late adolescence and adulthood: A critique and reconstruction of Kohlberg's theory. *Human Development*, 1980, **23**, 77–104.

Nassi, A. J. Survivors of the sixties: Comparative psychosocial and political development of former Berkeley student activists. *American Psychologist*, 1981, **36**, 753–761.

Orchowsky, S. J., & Jenkins, L. R. Sex biases in the measurement of moral judgment. *Psychological Reports*, 1979, **44**, 1040.

Parikh, B. Development of moral judgment and its relation to family environmental factors in Indian and American families. *Child Development*, 1980, **51**, 1030–1039.

Rest, J. R. *Development in judging moral issues.* Minneapolis: University of Minnesota Press, 1979.

Rosenthal, R. Combining results of independent studies. *Psychological Bulletin*, 1978, **85**, 185–193.

Rosenthal, R. The "file-drawer problem" and tolerance for null results. *Psychological Bulletin*, 1979, **86**, 638–641.

Saltzstein, H. D., Diamond, R. M., & Belenky, M. Moral judgment level and conformity behavior. *Developmental Psychology*, 1972, **7**, 327–336.

Saxton, M. Are women more moral than men? An interview with psychologist Carol Gilligan. *Ms.*, December 1981, pp. 63–66.

Selman, R. The relation of role taking to the development of moral judgment in children. *Child Development*, 1971, **42**, 79–91.

Siegel, S. *Nonparametric statistics for the behavioral sciences.* New York: McGraw-Hill, 1956.

Simon, A., & Ward, L. O. Variables influencing pupils' responses on the Kohlberg schema of moral development. *Journal of Moral Education*, 1973, **2**, 283–286.

Small, L. Effects of discrimination training on stage of moral judgment. *Personality and Social Psychology Bulletin*, 1974, **1**, 423–425.

Sullivan, E. V., McCullough, G., & Stager, M. A developmental study of the relationship between conceptual, ego, and moral development. *Child Development*, 1970, **41**, 399–411.

Taylor, J. J., & Achenbach, T. M. Moral and cognitive development in retarded and non-retarded children. *American Journal of Mental Deficiency*, 1975, **80**, 43–50.

Timm, J. T. Group care of children and the development of moral judgment. *Child Welfare*, 1980, **59**, 323–333.

Turiel, E. A comparative analysis of moral knowledge and moral judgment in males and females. *Journal of Personality*, 1976, **44**, 195–208.

Walker, L. J. Cognitive and perspective-taking prerequisites for moral development. *Child Development*, 1980, **51**, 131–139.

Walker, L. J. The sequentiality of Kohlberg's stages of moral development. *Child Development*, 1982, **53**, 1330–1336.

Walker, L. J. Sources of cognitive conflict for stage transition in moral development. *Developmental Psychology*, 1983, **19**, 103–110.

Walker, L. J., de Vries, B., & Bichard, S. L. The hierarchical nature of stages of moral development. *Developmental Psychology*, in press.

Weisbroth, S. Moral judgment, sex, and parental identification in adults. *Developmental Psychology*, 1970, **2**, 396–402.

White, C. B. Moral development in Bahamian school children: A cross-cultural examination of Kohlberg's stages of moral reasoning. *Developmental Psychology*, 1975, **11**, 535–536.

White, C. B., Bushnell, N., & Regnemer, J. L. Moral development in Bahamian school children: A 3-year examination of Kohlberg's stages of moral development. *Developmental Psychology*, 1978, **14**, 58–65.

Moral Stages and Moral Orientations in Real-Life and Hypothetical Dilemmas

Lawrence J. Walker, Brian de Vries, and Shelley D. Trevethan

University of British Columbia

WALKER, LAWRENCE J.; DE VRIES, BRIAN; and TREVETHAN, SHELLEY D. *Moral Stages and Moral Orientations in Real-Life and Hypothetical Dilemmas.* CHILD DEVELOPMENT, 1987, **58**, 842–858. We examined 2 influential theories of moral reasoning: Kohlberg's moral stage model and Gilligan's moral orientation model. 3 issues were of particular interest: (*a*) the relation between reasoning about hypothetical and real-life dilemmas, (*b*) the validity of Gilligan's notion of sex-related moral orientations (response vs. rights), and (*c*) the relation of moral orientation to moral stage. Participants were 80 family triads (mother, father, and child, total *N* = 240), with children drawn from grades 1, 4, 7, and 10. In individual interviews, they discussed hypothetical dilemmas and a personally generated real-life dilemma, which were scored for both moral stage and moral orientation. Content analyses were also conducted for the real-life dilemmas. Results indicated consistency in moral stage between responses to hypothetical and real-life dilemmas, supporting the notion that stages are holistic structures. However, few individuals showed consistent use of a single moral orientation. The evidence regarding the relation between sex and orientation was inconsistent. Among other results, sex differences were evident in dilemma content but were not evident in orientations when dilemma content was controlled. The sexes did not differ in stage of moral development; however, there were moral stage differences as a function of moral orientation.

Although research in the area of moral psychology has been extensive over the last 2 decades, a number of unresolved issues remain—some of which are addressed by the present study. Specifically, what is the relation between individuals' reasoning about hypothetical moral dilemmas and personally generated real-life dilemmas? How valid is Gilligan's (1982) claim that there are two moral orientations (response and rights)? What is the nature and extent of sex differences in moral stages and orientations? What is the relation between moral stage development and moral orientations? These issues will be discussed in turn.

Hypothetical versus Real-Life Moral Reasoning

The dominant research paradigm in assessing moral development is to present individuals with a series of hypothetical dilemmas (e.g., Should Heinz steal an overpriced drug in order to save his wife's life?) and to ask them to respond to probing questions (Colby & Kohlberg, in press). Many of these dilemmas are classics, drawn from literature and moral philosophy. Kohlberg believes that such dilemmas are best for eliciting the highest level of competence—for "testing the limits"—since most individuals find them conflictual and they allow reflection without interference from preconceptions. However, some critics (e.g., Baumrind, 1978; Haan, 1977) have decried the exclusive use of hypothetical dilemmas, arguing that this approach has limited generalizability. The concern is that these dilemmas focus on issues that may be unfamiliar or irrelevant and, as such, may minimize the individual's identification and emotional involvement with the task. Baumrind (1978) argued that a more appropriate paradigm would be to "focus on so-

Portions of this research were reported at the meeting of the Canadian Psychological Association, Halifax, June 1985, and at the meeting of the American Psychological Association, Washington, DC, August 1986. This research was supported by a grant to Lawrence J. Walker from the Social Sciences and Humanities Research Council of Canada (no. 498-83-0010). We wish to acknowledge the competent work of our research assistants and typists—Michael Boyes, Gloria Baker-Brown, Sue Branson, Debbie Butler, Karen Flello, Tina Glasier, Judy McLean, Tom Moran, Cydney Smith, Liz Surowiec, and Joyce Wijeratne—and to express our gratitude to Rosemarie Sampson of Mount Saint Vincent University for her reliability scoring. The families who participated in this project did so with good-hearted cooperation and interest, and we are indebted to them. We wish to thank the anonymous reviewers for their helpful questions and comments. Correspondence concerning this article should be sent to Lawrence J. Walker, Department of Psychology, University of British Columbia, Vancouver, BC, Canada V6T 1Y7.

[*Child Development*, 1987, **58**, 842–858. © 1987 by the Society for Research in Child Development, Inc. All rights reserved. 0009-3920/87/5803-0001$01.00]

cial situations that implicate the respondent" (p. 75).

There has been some research comparing reasoning about hypothetical versus real-life dilemmas. Kohlberg, Scharf, and Hickey (1971), for example, examined the levels of moral reasoning evidenced by 34 prison inmates on the standard dilemmas as compared to "prison" dilemmas and found that the latter elicited significantly lower scores. This disparity was attributed to the coercive and exploitive moral atmosphere of the prison. Similarly, Higgins, Power, and Kohlberg (1984) compared the levels of moral reasoning evidenced by 61 high school students on the standard dilemmas versus "school" dilemmas. Their preliminary analyses indicated that school dilemmas elicited lower levels of reasoning than the standard dilemmas for regular high school students, but that there was no disparity for students in alternative "democratic" schools.

Two studies have compared women's reasoning about standard dilemmas and reasoning about their problem pregnancies. Gilligan and Belenky (1980), with a sample of 20 women, found that 45% scored higher on their real-life dilemmas than on the standard dilemmas, 15% were lower, and 40% were at the same level. Smetana (1982), with a sample of 70 women, reported that reasoning on the two types of dilemmas was highly related ($r = .70$), with all differences occurring within one adjacent stage.

The most comprehensive study regarding this issue was reported by Haan (1975), who compared the moral reasoning of 310 University of California (Berkeley) students on the standard dilemmas versus the Free Speech Movement (FSM) issue. She found that 42.9% of the students scored higher on the FSM dilemma than on the standard dilemmas, 22.3% were lower, and 34.8% were at the same level. These students were scored at Stages 2–6. However, when Kohlberg and Candee (1984) rescored these data according to the revised moral scoring system (Colby & Kohlberg, in press), no subjects were found at Stages 2, 5, or 6. Thus, given the reduction in range of moral stage scores, the extent of the disparity may not be as great as initially reported. An additional concern regarding this study is that many students may have been superficially imitating the rhetoric of FSM leaders without adequate comprehension—a possibility that should not be discounted, since students completed a questionnaire rather than the recommended oral interview.

Common to all these studies is the problem that the real-life dilemma was always one raised as an issue by the researchers, not the subjects, and so these dilemmas may not be as relevant as has been implied. Indeed, many subjects do not regard student protest and abortion as moral issues at all (Haan, 1975; Smetana, 1982). This suggests that it would be more appropriate to have subjects discuss their own real-life moral dilemmas and to compare such reasoning with reasoning about hypothetical dilemmas.

Relatively little is known about the kinds of moral problems and issues that people confront in everyday living. A description of such real-life dilemmas may provide some indication of the representativeness of the hypothetical dilemmas used in the standard interview. Some previous research is relevant: Rybash, Roodin, and Hoyer (1983) asked older adults to describe a moral problem they had encountered and then classified their problems as involving either family (advice-giving and -taking, caregiving and living arrangements, financial matters), friends and neighbors (sexual- and alcohol-related activities, unwanted involvement in another's affairs, and another's personal welfare), or societal/legal expectations (occupational decisions, lawful behaviors). Yussen (1977) asked adolescents to write a realistic moral dilemma (note that the dilemma need not have been one from their own experience), and then classified their dilemmas as involving alcohol, civil rights, drugs, interpersonal relations, physical safety, sexual relations, smoking, stealing, and working. Not much else is known. Thus, one objective of our study was to describe the moral problems that individuals recall and to assess how these might differ across ages and between sexes.

Both Gilligan and Belenky (1980) and Haan (1975) found that over 40% of their subjects evidenced higher moral reasoning on the real-life dilemma than the hypothetical dilemmas (vs. 15%–22% lower). They argued that this pattern was indicative of developmental transition, but it implies that the use of hypothetical dilemmas is not adequate to capture the highest level of competence for many individuals. Kohlberg's strict moral stage model (see Walker, 1986a) posits that each stage represents a holistic structure, implying that individuals should be relatively consistent in their moral reasoning across varying contents and contexts (including hypothetical and real-life dilemmas). Thus, another objective of this study was to compare the levels and patterns of moral reasoning regarding standard hypothetical dilemmas versus personally generated ones.

Moral Orientations

Gilligan (1982; also see Langdale, 1986; Lyons, 1983; and Noddings, 1984) proposed that males and females differ in their basic life orientation, particularly in conceptions of morality. A moral orientation represents a conceptually distinct framework or perspective for organizing and understanding the moral domain. Gilligan believes that males typically have a justice or rights orientation because of their individualistic and separate conceptions of self, their detached objectivity, and their proclivity for abstract and impartial principles. Thus, she holds that males view morality as involving issues of conflicting rights. On the other hand, Gilligan believes that females typically have a care or response orientation because of their perception of the self as connected to and interdependent with others, their sensitivity not to endanger or hurt, their concern for the well-being and care of self and others, and for harmonious relationships in concrete situations. Thus, she holds that females view morality as involving issues of conflicting responsibilities. It is important to note that Gilligan believes these orientations to be sex-related, but not sex-specific. She has not yet posited the origins of these orientations in either biology or social experience.

In addition to proposing these sex-related moral orientations (rights vs. response), Gilligan has also claimed that contemporary theories of moral development (especially Kohlberg's) are insensitive to females' moral thinking—primarily because these approaches have empirical roots in exclusively male samples. The bias and limited perspective on morality that Gilligan believed was inherent in Kohlberg's approach led her to conclude that females' moral development was being down-scored in his sytem. However, Walker's (1984, 1986c) review and meta-analysis of the research literature indicated that the overall pattern was one of nonsignificant sex differences in moral reasoning. The present study provides additional data on this issue with a large sample (N = 240) representing a wide portion of the life span (5–63 years) for both hypothetical and real-life dilemmas.

The issue of whether or not sex differences are obtained when Kohlberg's approach is used is separable from Gilligan's other claim of sex-related moral orientations. Several critics have provided theoretical commentaries on Gilligan's views (e.g., Boyd,

1983; Brabeck, 1983; Broughton, 1983; Kohlberg, 1984; Nails, 1983; Sichel, 1985) that will not be duplicated here. What is of concern here is the empirical validity of her claim. The evidence is currently quite limited, and many issues remain to be addressed. For example, only anecdotal data were included in Gilligan's (1982) well-known book, and her original study of moral orientations (1977) was limited to women and a single-context dilemma (i.e., abortion). Furthermore, Ford and Lowery (1986) failed to find sex differences among undergraduate students who were asked to describe a moral conflict, read a paragraph outlining the response and rights orientations, and then rate the extent to which they had used these orientations in thinking about their conflict. However, Lyons (1983) conducted open-ended interviews with 30 individuals (8–60+ years), asking them to discuss their own real-life moral dilemmas. These interviews were analyzed for considerations of rights and response in three components of their reasoning: construction (What is the problem?), resolution (What should be done about it?), and evaluation (Is it the right thing to do?). The results supported Gilligan's claim of sex-related moral orientations: response considerations were predominant for 75% of the females, whereas rights considerations were predominant for 79% of the males. Pratt (1985) replicated this pattern of sex-related moral orientations with a sample of 62 adults (18–75 years). He found that 53.6% of the women had a response orientation, whereas 73.5% of the men had a rights orientation.

In both Lyons's (1983) and Pratt's (1985) studies, participants simply recounted one of their own moral problems. This suggests the possibility that their findings may be an artifact of the differing moral problems that the sexes encounter or choose to relate, rather than a basic difference in orientation in solving moral problems (Ford & Lowery, 1986; Walker, 1986b). In this regard, Pratt conducted a content analysis of his participants' dilemmas, categorizing them as either relational or nonrelational. He found that women reported more relational dilemmas than did men and that men reported more nonrelational dilemmas than women. Nonrelational dilemmas were almost always scored as reflecting the rights orientation, whereas relational dilemmas elicited both orientations.

As previously noted, Gilligan (1982) describes the care and response orientation as entailing a concern for maintenance of personal relationships. Kohlberg (1984) similarly holds that this orientation is "directed primarily to relations of special obligations to family, friends, and group members, relations which often include or presuppose general obligations of respect, fairness, and contract" (p. 349). In the present study, we attempted to examine such suggestions by conducting a content analysis that would identify the nature of the relationship in the real-life conflict as either personal or impersonal. In this way it could be determined whether or not there are sex differences in the type of dilemma recalled, whether or not there is a relation between orientation and dilemma content, and whether or not there are sex differences in orientations within types of dilemmas.

If the sex difference in moral orientations is as pervasive and basic as Gilligan's (1982) theorizing implies, then it should also be evident in responses to standard moral dilmas, not only in idiosyncratic real-life dilemmas. Langdale (1986) analyzed moral orientations expressed in response to Kohlberg's Heinz dilemma and a hypothetical abortion dilemma, finding that the sex difference in orientation was still evident. It should be noted, though, that Langdale's analysis was only for the resolution component of her participants' reasoning and not for the construction and evaluation components. Furthermore, Gilligan, Langdale, Lyons, and Murphy (1982) argued that the use of hypothetical dilemmas may obscure moral orientations because the moral problem has been preconstructed by the researcher, in contrast to real-life dilemmas in which subjects construct the problem as well as evaluate its resolution. For example, they argued that Kohlberg's dilemmas are typically constructed as conflicts of rights, with other issues ignored. In this regard, Langdale (1986) reported that the hypothetical Heinz and abortion dilemmas elicited more rights considerations than did real-life dilemmas (Lyons's, 1983, data). It would seem that the appropriate solution would be to compare responses between real-life and hypothetical dilemmas, allowing participants to construct the problem in the hypothetical dilemmas and with questioning more open-ended, along the lines of questioning for the real-life dilemmas (as suggested by Gilligan et al., 1982).

Gilligan (1986, p. 10) has summarized her claims regarding moral orientations as follows: "(1) that justice and care are distinct moral orientations—i.e., two frameworks that organize thinking about what constitutes a moral problem and how to resolve it, (2) that

most people in describing a moral problem and its resolution focus on one orientation and minimally represent the other, and (3) that the direction of focus is associated with gender." We understand these claims to mean that individuals will be consistent in the use of a single orientation. Langdale (1986) interprets Gilligan's claims similarly, arguing that a moral orientation is characterized as a traditionally defined structured whole, having a consistent inner logic. "Structured wholeness implies that, at a given point in time, most of an individual's moral reasoning will reflect a single underlying structure of thought both within and across situations" (p. 31). Thus, in our view, it is important to determine whether individuals are consistent in their orientation across dilemmas or whether particular dilemmas elicit certain considerations, and furthermore, whether or not sex differences in orientations are pervasive.

Another issue concerning moral orientations is whether or not they entail any developmental patterns. Are adults more mature than children in terms of moral orientations? How is moral maturity defined within Gilligan's framework (Sichel, 1985)? Is the sex-related pattern in moral orientations evidenced across the life span? Gilligan et al. (1982) reported that moral orientations in real-life dilemmas were evident across the life span, but the sample (from Lyons, 1983) was small (i.e., 6 children, 11 adolescents, and 13 adults). Langdale (1986) reported a similar pattern for the Heinz dilemma with a larger sample ($N = 137$). The present study will provide more extensive data regarding this issue of developmental trends in moral orientations for both real-life and hypothetical dilemmas and with a large sample representing a wide portion of the life span.

Moral Stages and Moral Orientations

A final issue concerns the relation between moral stage and moral orientation. Gilligan holds that Kohlberg's approach tends to undervalue the response orientation, identifying such reasoning with lower stages of moral thought. Langdale's (1986) data supported this claim since she found that individuals with a response orientation scored significantly lower in moral reasoning development than did those with a rights orientation (recall that her data were restricted to the Heinz dilemma only). Since the present study assessed both moral reasoning development and moral orientations, using both Kohlberg's standard dilemmas and individuals' real-life dilemmas, it provides relatively comprehensive data regarding the empirical relation between moral stage and orientation.

Method

Participants

The sample was composed of 80 family triads (mother, father, and child)[1] for a total N of 240 individuals. Only intact families were recruited and no other siblings were involved. The children were drawn from four age groups (with 10 boys and 10 girls in each group): grade 1 (M = 6.8 years, SD = .47), grade 4 (M = 9.8, SD = .52), grade 7 (M = 12.4, SD = .49), and grade 10 (M = 15.7, SD = .34). As might be expected in our society, fathers were slightly older than mothers (fathers' M = 41.3 years, SD = 5.8, range = 29–63, vs. mothers' M = 39.6 years, SD = 4.4, range = 30–51), $t(158)$ = 2.05, p < .05. Fathers also had more education than mothers (fathers' M = 16.6 years, SD = 3.1, range = 8–23, vs. mothers' M = 15.3 years, SD = 3.0, range = 10–26), $t(158)$ = 2.61, p < .01. Parents similarly differed in occupational status, according to the Standard International Occupational Prestige Scale (Treiman, 1977), which provides popular evaluations of occupations (fathers' M = 56.5, SD = 14.7, range = 28–86, vs. mothers' M = 48.5, SD = 9.4, range = 31–78), $t(158)$ = 4.08, p < .001. Parents were employed in diverse occupations, except for one father and 31 mothers who were homemakers and for three mothers who were college or university students. The families volunteered to participate in the study in response to a letter sent home with students. These families resided in a large Canadian city and each was offered $25 for its participation.

Procedure

Families came to the university, typically in the evening or on the weekend, to participate in the study. After providing explanations and obtaining consent, each family member was taken to a small office for an individual interview conducted by a research assistant. These interviews typically took 45–90 min and were tape-recorded for later transcription and scoring.

The interview had two parts: the hypothetical dilemmas and the real-life dilemma. Since there are three alternate forms of Kohlberg's interview (each consisting of three dilemmas), the form used with each family was randomly chosen (and so all members of a family responded to the same set of hypothetical dilemmas). Since the intent was to allow participants to construct the conflict in each hypothetical dilemma, the standard issue was not initially made explicit (by omitting summary sentences such as "So having tried every legal means, Heinz gets desperate and considers breaking into the man's store to steal the drug for his wife. Should Heinz steal the drug?"). Rather, after presenting the "facts" of each dilemma, the interviewer first asked a series of non-orientation-specific questions (as suggested by Gilligan et al., 1982) that allowed participants to construct, resolve, and evaluate the solution for the conflict (i.e., What is the problem? What are the considerations? What should be done and is it the right thing to do?). These questions were then followed by the standard and other interviewer-determined probe questions. After the three hypothetical dilemmas, each participant was asked to discuss her or his conception of morality and to recall a recent real-life moral dilemma from his or her own experience. The interviewer probed regarding the participant's construction, resolution, and evaluation of this dilemma (following Lyons, 1982), typically asking these questions: "Have you ever been in a situation of moral conflict where you had to make a decision about what was right but you weren't sure what to do? Could you describe the situation? What was the conflict for you in that situation? In thinking about what to do, what did you consider? What did you do? Do you think it was the right thing to do? How do you know?" If necessary, the interviewer continued probing until each participant revealed a real-life dilemma. Although some readers may not recognize all of these issues or problems as "classical" moral dilemmas (to be described later—see Table 2), the participants did identify them as conflictual situations involving a decision about right and wrong—they were moral dilemmas for them—and reasoning regarding all these real-life dilemmas was scorable for both moral stages and orientations.

Scoring

Content analyses of real-life dilemmas.—Two separate content analyses were conducted for the real-life dilemmas: the first was a descriptive analysis of the *moral issue* that was the focus of the dilemma, and the second was an analysis of each dilemma in terms of the nature of the *relationship* that it entailed. The categories for both typologies were established after the authors had read all the dilemmas, being blind to the identity of

---

[1] The findings regarding intrafamilial patterns in moral reasoning will be reported in another article.

the subjects. The derivation of these categories and the classification of dilemmas into categories was through discussion among the authors until all disagreements were resolved. The first typology was an attempt to summarize the moral issue or concern that was most salient for the dilemma. In some sense each dilemma is unique, but 30 categories were derived (see Table 2), each containing more than one dilemma (a thirty-first category, "other," included a small number of single dilemmas that could not be otherwise classified). The second typology refers to the nature of the relationship that each dilemma entailed—either personal or impersonal. A "personal" moral conflict was interpreted as one involving a specific person or group of people with whom the subject has a significant relationship, defined generally as one of a continuing nature (e.g., a family member, friend, close neighbor, colleague, associate, partner). An "impersonal" moral conflict was interpreted as one involving a person or group of people whom the subject does not know well (a stranger or acquaintance) or is not specified or is generalized (e.g., students, clients), or as one involving institutions (e.g., police), or involving an issue primarily intrinsic to self. Examples of a personal moral conflict include: whether or not to put father in a nursing home against his wishes, and whether or not to tell a friend that her or his spouse was having an affair. Examples of an impersonal moral conflict include: whether or not to correct a clerk's error in failing to charge for an item, and whether to absorb business loss (as an employer) or cut employees' wages.

Interrater reliability for these content analyses was determined with a second rater who independently classified all 240 real-life dilemmas, being provided only with the categories. For the moral-issue typology there was 92.1% agreement, and for the relationship typology there was 93.3% agreement.

Moral development.—The scoring of the hypothetical dilemmas for moral reasoning development followed the procedures described in Colby and Kohlberg's (in press) manual, and was done by the first author. This scoring was conducted blindly and by each dilemma separately across subjects (i.e., without knowing the subject's identity or scores on other dilemmas). Scores were assigned for each moral judgment in the interview that matched a criterion judgment in the appropriate section of the manual. These scores were combined to provide the percent usage at each stage for the interview. Since the manual

is keyed to particular dilemmas and issues and since few of the real-life dilemmas were exactly represented in the manual, the scoring of the real-life dilemmas required a slight adaptation of the standard scoring procedure. The lack of explicit criterion judgments for real-life dilemmas meant that the scorer had to rely more on the general stage structure definitions for each criterion judgment than on particular critical indicators (that are dilemma specific). Thus, scores were assigned for every moral judgment that matched a stage structure definition for a criterion judgment anywhere in the manual (regardless of the dilemma or issue). These scores were used to determine the percent usage at each stage.

Level of moral development was calculated both for the hypothetical dilemmas and for the real-life dilemma. Although level of moral development can be expressed in various ways, it is always determined on the basis of the pattern of percent stage usage. An overall score that includes information regarding usage at all stages is the *weighted average score* (WAS), which is given by the sum of the products of the percent usage at each stage multiplied by the number of that stage, and can range from 100 to 500. Such a measure derived from stage percentages allows the use of parametric statistics, and such statistics have been widely used on WASs. A more qualitative measure of moral development for which nonparametric statistics are appropriate is provided by the *global stage score* (GSS), which can be expressed in two levels of differentiation: a 5- or 9-point scale. The 5-point GSS is simply determined by the modal stage of reasoning: Stage 1, 2, . . . , 5. The 9-point GSS is determined by the modal stage of reasoning (if only one stage has 25% or more of the scores) or by the two most frequent stages (if each has 25% or more of the scores): Stage 1, 1/2, 2, 2/3, . . . , 5. Thus, the 9-point GSS consists of pure and mixed stage scores. WASs and GSSs were calculated for both the hypothetical dilemmas and the real-life dilemma.

The choice of the measure of moral development is dependent upon the purpose of the analysis (Walker, 1986c). For testing certain theoretical predictions of the moral stage model, such as the sequentiality of the stages, only modal stage scores (i.e., 5-point GSSs) are relevant since change must always be the next higher modal stage, and other information (e.g., shifts in the distribution of responses at adjacent stages) is ignored. However, when assessing individuals' level of development, more sensitive measures are appropriate, such as the 9-point GSS and the WAS. If only modal stage scores were examined, then it would be unnecessarily difficult to detect many meaningful developmental changes or differences.

Interrater reliability was determined by a second rater who independently scored 24 randomly selected interviews. For the hypothetical dilemmas, there was 87.5% exact agreement in GSSs (9-point scale) and $r = .94$ for WASs. For the real-life dilemmas, there was 75.0% exact agreement in GSSs and $r = .90$ for WASs.

Moral orientations.—The scoring of the dilemmas for moral orientations followed the procedures described in Lyons's (1982) manual, and was done by the first author. This scoring was conducted blindly and by each dilemma separately (across subjects). Although the manual focuses on responses to real-life dilemmas, Lyons (1982, p. 168) stated that it could be applied to standard hypothetical dilemmas, and Langdale (1986) reported that she successfully did so. In scoring the hypothetical dilemmas, only responses to the non-orientation-specific questions were considered, not responses to the standard Kohlbergian probes since it is possible that a particular line of questioning might elicit reasoning representing one orientation or the other. A related issue that should be noted is whether the description of hypothetical dilemmas may similarly "pull" particular types of reasoning. If that is the case, then significant differences in orientations should be evidenced across different dilemmas.

Each consideration (i.e., thought unit) presented by the participant in the construction, resolution, and evaluation of the dilemma was categorized as reflecting either the response or rights orientation, following guidelines in the manual. The relative number of considerations within each orientation determined the *modal orientation* for each dilemma ("rights," "response," or "split" if there was an equal number for each orientation). A more sensitive score, the *percent response score*, was also calculated as the percentage of all considerations that reflected the response orientation. (Although Gilligan et al., 1982, and Lyons, 1982, 1983, described the derivation of such a score, they failed to report any relevant analyses. A percent rights score would be complementary to the percent response score and analyses would, therefore, be redundant.) Percent response scores were determined for each hypothetical dilemma separately and overall the hypothetical dilemmas (by summing the number of consider-

ations for each orientation over the three dilemmas), as well as for the real-life dilemma.

Interrater reliability for scoring rights and response considerations was determined by a second rater who independently scored 24 randomly selected interviews. For the hypothetical dilemmas, reliability was .77; and for the real-life dilemmas, .79. As a further check on the validity of the scoring, 16 randomly selected real-life dilemmas were independently scored by another rater who had been directly trained by Nona Lyons, the author of the scoring manual. In this case, reliability was found to be .77. Although these reliabilities are within acceptable limits, they are not strong—possibly reflecting the fact that the scoring system is in preliminary form and under revision (N. P. Lyons, personal communication, March 9, 1984).

Results

Hypothetical versus Real-Life Moral Reasoning

The first issue addressed by this study was the relation between reasoning about standard hypothetical moral dilemmas and personally generated real-life ones. Table 1 provides frequency distributions for the GSSs as a function of age, sex, and type of dilemma, as well as data for the WASs. The issue was examined by conducting a 5 (age: grades 1, 4, 7, 10, and adults) $\times$ 2 (sex) $\times$ 2 (type of dilemma: hypothetical, real-life) analysis of variance (ANOVA) with repeated measures on the last factor, using the WAS as the dependent variable. (A Box's M test supported the assumption of homogeneity of variance.) The main effect of sex and all interactions with sex were not significant. The ANOVA revealed a highly significant effect of age, $F(4, 230) = 134.00$, $p < .001$ (see Table 1), and an effect for type of dilemma, $F(1,230) = 4.76$, $p = .03$; the hypothetical dilemmas elicited a slightly higher level of reasoning than the real-life dilemma (mean WASs = 308.3 vs. 296.6). The correlation between the WASs for the two types of dilemmas was strong and highly significant, $r = .83$, $p < .001$.

Since some researchers, such as Baumrind (1986), believe that sex differences are more appropriately examined in terms of GSSs, Mann-Whitney tests were conducted for both hypothetical and real-life dilemmas using this score. Congruent with the finding of the ANOVA with WASs, there were no significant sex differences, z's = 1.60 and .87, respectively.

TABLE 1

MORAL DEVELOPMENT AS A FUNCTION OF AGE AND SEX FOR BOTH DILEMMA TYPES

| | FREQUENCY OF GSSs | | | | | | | | | WAS | |
GROUP	1	1/2	2	2/3	3	3/4	4	4/5	5	M	SD
Hypothetical dilemmas:											
Grade 1:											
Males	1	6	2	1	...	...	...	...	...	163.3	37.5
Females	1	8	1	...	...	...	...	...	...	155.2	24.4
Grade 4:											
Males	...	2	3	5	...	...	...	...	...	210.9	27.0
Females	...	3	5	2	...	...	...	...	...	195.6	25.6
Grade 7:											
Males	...	...	3	5	2	...	...	...	...	245.7	32.3
Females	...	...	...	7	3	...	...	...	...	267.3	25.5
Grade 10:											
Males	...	...	...	3	7	...	...	...	...	292.3	22.3
Females	...	...	...	5	4	1	...	...	...	279.5	27.5
Adults:											
Males	...	...	...	1	8	52	15	4	...	358.7	31.5
Females	...	...	...	1	16	60	2	1	...	340.0	24.7
Real-life dilemmas:											
Grade 1:											
Males	1	6	3	...	...	...	...	...	...	160.0	33.7
Females	3	3	4	...	...	...	...	...	...	155.0	43.8
Grade 4:											
Males	1	2	7	...	...	...	...	...	...	180.0	35.0
Females	...	3	2	4	1	...	...	...	...	210.0	56.8
Grade 7:											
Males	...	2	2	5	1	...	...	...	...	220.0	42.2
Females	...	1	...	8	1	...	...	...	...	247.1	39.8
Grade 10:											
Males	...	...	...	2	6	1	1	...	...	302.5	47.8
Females	...	...	...	4	6	...	...	...	...	278.8	27.6
Adults:											
Males	...	...	...	2	32	28	14	2	2	342.5	51.3
Females	...	...	...	3	38	29	7	3	...	328.2	40.4

An alternate approach to examining this issue is to analyze the extent and pattern of differences in GSSs (this is the approach taken by previous researchers). In terms of 5-point GSSs, 62.1% of the participants evidenced the same modal stage for both types of dilemmas, 20.4% were higher on the hypothetical dilemmas than the real-life dilemma, whereas 17.5% were lower. A binomial test indicated no significant difference in the number of participants evidencing either pattern of disparity between types of dilemmas.

The notion that each stage represents a holistic structure implies that individuals should be relatively consistent in their reasoning between types of dilemmas. Again, GSSs were examined for the extent of consistency. Even on the more differentiated 9-point GSS scale, there was substantial consistency, with 91.3% of the participants evidenc-

ing the same or adjacent level (e.g., Stage 3 and 3/4) in their reasoning on the two dilemma types. (Recall that dilemmas were scored independently.) These patterns confirm the structural integrity of the stages across differing contexts and contents.

Also of interest are the kinds of moral issues that are of concern in the real-life dilemmas. The moral-issue content analysis yielded the typology provided in Table 2. This table indicates the frequency of each category of moral issue and the percentage of children and adults of both sexes who reported such dilemmas. The small number of dilemmas in each category precluded statistical analyses, but inspection of the table allows for some observations. Children's moral dilemmas clustered in categories 12–19 (e.g., issues concerning friendship, honesty, theft, and fighting), whereas fewer adults reported such dilemmas (76.3% vs. 30.6%). Adults' di-

TABLE 2

CONTENT ANALYSIS OF THE MORAL ISSUES IN REAL-LIFE DILEMMAS

		PERCENTAGE FOR EACH GROUP			
MORAL ISSUE	FREQUENCY	Boys[a]	Girls[a]	Men[b]	Women[b]
1. Marital relationship	6	...	...	1.3	6.3
2. Parental control/discipline	12	...	...	7.5	7.5
3. Obedience to parents	5	5.0	7.5	...	...
4. Sibling relationship	2	...	...	...	2.5
5. Nursing care for parents	5	...	...	1.3	5.0
6. Dealing with dying relatives	4	...	...	...	5.0
7. Work versus family	6	...	...	5.0	2.5
8. Work performance	17	...	...	17.5	3.8
9. Work relationship	10	...	...	11.3	1.3
10. Evaluating students	4	...	...	3.8	1.3
11. Obedience to teachers	2	2.5	2.5	...	...
12. Friendship	21	25.0	22.5	2.5	...
13. Promises	7	7.5	7.5	1.3	...
14. Confidences	11	5.0	5.0	5.0	3.8
15. Apologies/confessions	7	5.0	...	1.3	5.0
16. Honesty/cheating/fraud	27	2.5	15.0	13.8	11.3
17. Theft	19	10.0	15.0	7.5	3.8
18. Mischief	7	10.0	...	1.3	2.5
19. Fighting/nastiness	11	12.5	10.0	...	2.5
20. Sexual abuse	4	...	...	...	5.0
21. Protest	3	...	...	1.3	2.5
22. Religious beliefs	2	...	...	1.3	1.3
23. Racism/discrimination	3	2.5	...	...	2.5
24. Animal welfare	4	5.0	...	...	2.5
25. Life preservation	4	...	...	1.3	3.8
26. Birth control	3	...	...	1.3	2.5
27. Abortion	6	...	...	2.5	5.0
28. Inequitable wills	2	...	...	1.3	1.3
29. Substance use	7	2.5	5.0	2.5	2.5
30. Choosing objects/activities	9	2.5	7.5	5.0	1.3
31. Other	10	2.5	2.5	3.8	6.3
Total	240	100.0	100.0	100.7[c]	100.6[c]

[a] N = 40.
[b] N = 80.
[c] Figures do not sum to 100 because of rounding.

lemmas clustered in categories 1–6 (family-related issues), category 7 (work vs. family), and categories 8–10 (work-related issues). Here there is an apparent sex difference: Women were more likely to raise family-related issues than men (26.3% vs. 10.0%), whereas men were more likely than women to raise work-related issues (32.5% vs. 6.3%). Recall in this context that the sample included one male but 31 females who were homemakers. However, females who were employed outside the home were more likely to discuss family-related issues than were homemakers (32.7% vs. 16.1%).

Moral Orientations

As noted earlier, Gilligan (1986, p. 10) holds that "most people focus on one orienta-tion and minimally represent the other"; that is, a substantial proportion of the reasoning should reflect one orientation with relatively little reasoning reflecting the other. Thus, it is important to determine whether or not most individuals are sufficiently consistent in rea-soning within one orientation or the other to warrant such a claim. To examine this issue, a score was calculated to represent the percent-age of all considerations reflecting the *modal* moral orientation (rights or response) over the four dilemmas (three hypothetical and one real-life). What level of consistency should the concept imply? Since 50% represents the minimum possible (i.e., both orientations equal) and 100% represents perfect consis-tency (i.e., one orientation exclusively), a cri-terion of 75% or greater was adopted. Using this criterion, only 40 of 240 participants (16.7%) were consistent in the use of a single orientation. Although there were no sex differences in the extent of consistency, $\chi^2(1, N = 240) = 2.43$, N.S., children evidenced greater exclusivity than adults, $\chi^2(1, N = 240) = 9.00$, $p < .005$ (see Table 3); that is, adults were more likely than children to use a mix of both orientations. Using an even more liberal criterion (66% or greater), only 37.5% of the participants were consistent (age differences using this criterion did not reach significance).

Even when examining the single real-life dilemma (see Table 3), the extent of consistency was not great: only about one-half of the participants (53.3%) used one orientation 75% or more of the time. The same age difference was evidenced on the real-life dilemma using the 75% criterion, $\chi^2(1, N = 240) = 5.88$, $p < .02$, but did not reach significance using the 66% criterion, $\chi^2(1, N = 240) = 3.01$, $p = .08$.

An alternate approach in assessing consistency in orientation use between the different types of dilemmas (hypothetical vs. real-life) would be to calculate the correlation in percent response scores. This relation was found to be significant, although weak, $r = .14$, $p < .02$ (cf. the correlation between dilemma types in WASs, $r = .83$). These data indicate that most individuals use both orientations to a significant degree, and that analyses based only on modal orientation should be interpreted with caution.

An especially sensitive and appropriate measure of moral orientations is the percent

response score (as argued in the Method section). To examine age and sex differences in the two types of dilemmas, a 5 (age) × 2 (sex) × 2 (type of dilemma: hypothetical, real-life) ANOVA was conducted, with repeated measures on the last factor and using the percent response score as the dependent variable. (A Box's M test supported the assumption of homogeneity of variance.) This analysis yielded a significant effect for age, $F(4,230) = 6.61$, $p < .001$, which was qualified by an interaction between age and sex, $F(4,230) = 2.73$, $p = .03$; and by an interaction between age and type of dilemma, $F(4,230) = 5.40$, $p < .001$. Note that this analysis yielded no other significant effects. In particular, and contrary to Gilligan's (1982) claims, there was no main effect of sex—females, in general, did not use response considerations more than males; nor was there a main effect of type of dilemma—real-life dilemmas did not, in general, elicit more response considerations than did hypothetical dilemmas. However, both of these factors (sex and type of dilemma) did interact with age (see Figs. 1 and 2). The loci of these interactions were determined by analyses of simple main effects. Tests of the simple main effect of sex for each age group indicated that there were no differences at grades 1, 4, or 7; however, grade 10 boys had higher response scores than girls (53.0% vs. 36.7%), contrary to Gilligan's claims; whereas, among adults, women had higher response scores than men (52.7% vs. 44.1%), as she would predict.

The interaction between age and type of dilemma was also examined by analyses of simple main effects. Tests of the simple main effect of type of dilemma for each age group indicated that there were no differences at grades 4, 7, or 10; grade 1 children, however, had much higher response scores with hypothetical dilemmas than the real-life dilemma (37.7% vs. 9.2%), while adults showed the opposite pattern—somewhat higher response scores with the real-life dilemma than the hypothetical dilemmas (53.1% vs. 43.6%).

It had been suggested earlier that use of a particular moral orientation might be a function of the content of the dilemma, thus it is important to examine the standard dilemmas in order to determine whether or not they elicit variability in responding. To examine this notion, a 3 (form: A, B, C) × 3 (dilemma: 1st, 2d, 3d) ANOVA was conducted using the percent response score as the dependent variable (recall that each of the three interview forms has three dilemmas). This analysis revealed an interaction between form and di-

TABLE 3

NUMBER OF SUBJECTS EVIDENCING CONSISTENCY IN MORAL ORIENTATIONS

AGE GROUP	CRITERION	
	75% +	66% +
All dilemmas:		
Children ...	22 (27.5%)	34 (42.5%)
Adults	18 (11.3%)	56 (35.0%)
Total	40 (16.7%)	90 (37.5%)
Real-life dilemma:		
Children ...	52 (65.0%)	62 (77.5%)
Adults	76 (47.5%)	105 (65.6%)
Total	128 (53.3%)	167 (69.6%)

NOTE.—Criteria represent the percentage of all considerations reflecting the modal moral orientation (either rights or response).

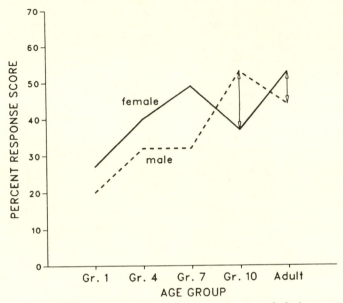

FIG. 1.—Mean percent response scores across age groups for both sexes

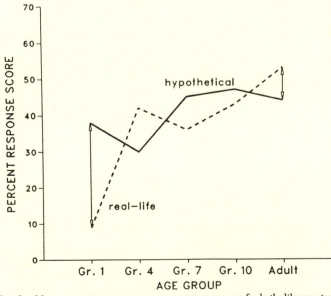

FIG. 2.—Mean percent response scores across age groups for both dilemma types

352

lemma, $F(4,474) = 4.376$, $p < .002$, indicating significant differences in orientation usage as a function of dilemma content. The loci of this interaction were determined by subsequent analyses of simple main effects and Scheffé multiple comparison tests ($\alpha = .05$). On Form A, it was found that the Heinz dilemma (Should Heinz steal to save his wife?) elicited higher response scores than either the judge dilemma (Should Heinz be punished for stealing?) or the Joe dilemma (Should Joe refuse to give his father the money that he had earned to go to camp?) (means = 53.1% vs. 39.3% and 32.8%). There were no differences in response scores across dilemmas on Form B. However, on Form C, the Marines dilemma (Should a captain order a soldier to go on a suicide mission?) and the Valjean dilemma (Should Valjean be punished further for stealing food for his family after he had escaped from prison?) elicited higher response scores than the brothers dilemma (Is it worse to cheat or to steal?) (means = 46.6% and 44.6% vs. 26.7%). Thus, the content of a dilemma elicited a significant pull on the orientation that individuals evidenced.

In order to examine sex differences on the standard dilemmas, analyses were conducted for each of the nine hypothetical dilemmas. Significant sex differences were found for only two: Heinz (Should Heinz steal to save his wife?) and judge (Should the doctor who commits euthanasia be punished?), t's(79) = 2.27 and 3.10, respectively, p's < .05. For both dilemmas, females had higher response scores than males (Heinz: 60.3% vs. 46.3%; judge: 47.2% vs. 25.8%). These dilemmas, perhaps more so than the others, raise sociolegal issues (e.g., life vs. law).

To further examine the notion that use of a particular moral orientation might be a function of the content of the dilemma, a content analysis of the real-life dilemmas was conducted in terms of the nature of the relationship that each moral conflict entailed—either personal or impersonal. An examination of age and sex differences in dilemma content indicated no sex differences overall, $\chi^2(1, N = 240) = 2.40$, N.S., but children were more likely to report personal dilemmas, and adults, impersonal ones, $\chi^2(1, N = 240) = 5.00$, $p < .05$. As shown in Table 4, there were no sex differences in dilemma content among children, $\chi^2(1, N = 80) = 0$, N.S., but among adults, women were more likely to report personal dilemmas, whereas men tended to report impersonal ones, $\chi^2(1, N = 160) = 4.27$, $p < .05$.

TABLE 4

CONTENT ANALYSIS OF THE NATURE OF THE RELATIONSHIP IN REAL-LIFE DILEMMAS AS A FUNCTION OF AGE AND SEX

| | NATURE OF RELATIONSHIP | |
SEX	Personal	Impersonal
Children:		
Male	25 (62.5%)	15 (37.5%)
Female ...	24 (60.0%)	16 (40.0%)
Adults:		
Male	29 (36.3%)	51 (63.8%)
Female ...	43 (53.8%)	37 (46.3%)
Total ...	121 (50.4%)	119 (49.6%)

The consistency data for moral orientations presented previously in this section indicated that relatively few individuals clearly preferred one orientation to the other. As such, data describing modal moral orientations may be misleading. Nevertheless, in order to allow comparisons with previous research and to facilitate analyses of the relation between dilemma content and orientation, Table 5 presents frequencies of modal moral orientations for both sexes as a function of content in the real-life dilemma. Analysis of the relation between sex and moral orientation (over dilemma content) indicated that males were more likely to have a rights orientation (46.7%), and females, a response orientation (44.2%), congruent with Gilligan's predictions, $\chi^2(2, N = 240) = 9.99$, $p < .01$. In order to examine developmental patterns in the relation between sex and moral orientation, chi-square analyses were conducted for adults and children separately (the relatively small number of children at each age precluded separate analyses for each age group). These analyses indicated that, for children, there was no relation between sex and moral orientation, $\chi^2(2, N = 80) = 1.33$, N.S., whereas for adults there was, $\chi^2(2, N = 160) = 9.76$, $p < .01$.

Analysis of the relation between moral orientation and dilemma content (see Table 5) revealed that, as predicted, dilemmas focusing on a personal relationship were more likely to elicit a response orientation (44.6%), whereas dilemmas that focused on an impersonal relationship were more likely to elicit a rights orientation (47.1%), $\chi^2(2, N = 240) = 11.14$, $p < .005$. However, within either type of dilemma content, sex differences were not significant (see Table 5), $\chi^2(2, N = 121) = 5.31$, for the personal-

TABLE 5

Modal Moral Orientation for Both Sexes as a Function of the
Nature of the Relationship in Real-Life Dilemmas

Sex	Moral Orientation		
	Response	Rights	Split
Personal relation- ship:			
Male	18 (33.3%)	22 (40.7%)	14 (25.9%)
Female	36 (53.7%)	17 (25.4%)	14 (20.9%)
Total	54 (44.6%)	39 (32.2%)	28 (23.1%)
Impersonal relation- ship:			
Male	12 (18.2%)	34 (51.5%)	20 (30.3%)
Female	17 (32.1%)	22 (41.5%)	14 (26.4%)
Total	29 (24.4%)	56 (47.1%)	34 (28.6%)

relationship dilemmas and $\chi^2(2, N = 119) = 3.11$, for the impersonal-relationship dilemmas. (Similarly, there were no sex differences for either children or adults within dilemma content.) Thus, when dilemma content was held constant, sex differences in moral orientations were no longer apparent.

Moral Stages and Moral Orientations

The final issue to be addressed is the relation between moral reasoning development and moral orientation. According to Gilligan (1982), Kohlberg's approach undervalues the response orientation, and thus individuals with that orientation should be lower in moral development than those with a rights orientation. To examine this suggestion for the hypothetical dilemmas, a 3 (orientation: response, rights, split) × 2 (sex) ANOVA was conducted, with the WAS as the dependent variable. (Age was not included as a factor in this ANOVA since its inclusion with orientation and sex produces empty cells. Analyses reported in a previous section indicated strong age trends in WASs, but no interaction between age and either sex or dilemma type.) This analysis for the hypothetical dilemmas yielded no significant effects. To examine Gilligan's suggestion for the real-life dilemmas, a 3 (orientation) × 2 (sex) × 2 (relationship: personal, impersonal) ANOVA was conducted, with the WAS as the dependent variable. (Age was not included as a factor in this ANOVA for the reason noted above. The nature of the relationship in the real-life dilemma was included as a factor in order to determine moral stage differences as a function of dilemma content and to examine any interactions between this factor and both

orientation and sex.) This ANOVA revealed two significant effects. First, there was an effect for the nature of the relationship in the dilemma, $F(1,228) = 12.39$, $p < .001$, which indicated that impersonal dilemmas elicited a higher level of moral reasoning than did personal dilemmas (mean WASs = 310.0 vs. 283.5). Second, there was a significant orientation effect, $F(2,228) = 15.22$, $p < .001$; and a subsequent Scheffé multiple comparison test ($\alpha = .05$) indicated that individuals with either a response or split orientation evidenced a *higher* level of moral development than did those with a rights orientation (mean WASs = 311.6 and 319.4 vs. 268.6, a difference of about half a stage). A correlational analysis similarly indicated a significant relation between WASs and percent response scores for the real-life dilemma, $r = .28$, $p < .001$. These findings are illustrated in Table 6, which presents frequencies at each moral orientation as a function of modal GSS. This table reveals that lower-stage individuals (Stages 1 and 2) predominantly had a rights orientation, Stage 3 and 4 individuals were fairly evenly distributed between orientations (although a response orientation is modal at Stage 3 and a rights orientation at Stage 4), whereas the most mature (Stage 5) individuals tended to use both orientations.

Discussion

This study examined several issues arising from two differing approaches to morality—Kohlberg's (1984) theory of moral reasoning development and Gilligan's (1982) theory of moral orientations. For both of these approaches, an important issue is the relation

TABLE 6

MODAL MORAL ORIENTATION AS A FUNCTION OF MORAL GLOBAL STAGE
SCORE IN REAL-LIFE DILEMMAS

| | MORAL ORIENTATION | | |
MORAL STAGE	Response	Rights	Split
1	. . .	6 (85.7%)	1 (14.3%)
2	6 (14.0%)	31 (72.1%)	6 (14.0%)
3	58 (47.2%)	34 (27.6%)	31 (25.2%)
4	19 (31.1%)	23 (37.7%)	19 (31.1%)
5	. . .	1 (16.7%)	5 (83.3%)

between reasoning about hypothetical moral problems versus real-life ones. Does the structural integrity of Kohlberg's moral stages hold when extended to real-life dilemmas, and are Gilligan's sex-related moral orientations evidenced in standard dilemmas? Another issue characterizing these two approaches is that of sex differences and sex bias, with Gilligan claiming that Kohlberg's theory has not heard "the different voice" of females and is insensitive to their response orientation. Finally, while age trends have been well established for moral development, they have not been examined as yet for moral orientations.

Kohlberg's approach has been critiqued for its exclusive reliance on hypothetical moral dilemmas—dilemmas that may seem, to many individuals, to be irrelevant, unfamiliar, and constrained. Much of the previous research has indicated sizable disparities between scores yielded by the standard dilemmas and by real-life ones; for example, Kohlberg et al. (1971) found that hypothetical dilemmas elicited higher moral reasoning than prison dilemmas, whereas Gilligan and Belenky (1980) found higher reasoning with abortion dilemmas and Haan (1975) found higher reasoning on the FSM issue. These researchers, although using real-life dilemmas, did not use ones personally generated by participants, and so these dilemmas may not have been perceived as morally relevant. In the present study, participants were asked to recall and discuss a real-life moral problem from their own experience. This was done in an attempt to examine the generalizability of the model when the assessment procedure deviated from the typical and recommended use of hypothetical dilemmas.

The real-life dilemmas frequently differed from those used in the standard interview. The moral issues raised by subjects were wide-ranging and revealed marked age differences and some apparent sex differ-

ences among adults. The results also indicated that the standard dilemmas elicited a slightly higher level of moral reasoning than did the real-life dilemmas (by 12 WAS points). This finding supports Kohlberg's claim that the standard hypothetical dilemmas are adequate for capturing individuals' best level of moral reasoning competence. The results also indicated little disparity between scores yielded by the different types of dilemmas, with 91.3% of the participants obtaining the same or adjacent level on the 9-point GSS scale and with $r = .83$. These data provide further support for Kohlberg's strict moral stage model that demands consistency in moral reasoning across varying contents and contexts (Walker, 1986a).

Gilligan (1982) and Noddings (1984) have proposed that there are two moral orientations: a rights orientation (based on an individualistic conception of self and a justice conception of morality) and a response orientation (based on an interdependent conception of self and a care conception of morality). One of the issues addressed in this study concerned intraindividual consistency in the use of these orientations. If each moral orientation represents a distinctive framework for understanding morality and is as basic to our functioning as has been proposed, then individuals should show a clear preference for one or the other that generalizes across moral problems, be they real-life or hypothetical. However, if most people use both orientations to a significant degree, then the validity of this notion of consistency as such is suspect, just as the moral stage concept would be invalid if most people used all stages in their reasoning. The findings indicated low levels of intraindividual consistency in both real-life and standard dilemmas. Apparently, most individuals use a considerable mix of both orientations—with no clear preference or focus. As such, the classification of individuals simply on the basis of modal moral orientation may be misleading and inaccurate, and the use of the term "orientation" inappropriate. Note, however, that although Gilligan claims that most people focus on one orientation, she (1985) has also stated that everyone "knows" and "understands" both. It is not yet clear what this means empirically or what it implies for the concept of orientation.

Although Gilligan argued against the use of hypothetical dilemmas because of their depersonalized nature, it is important to determine whether or not orientations are evidenced with standard stimulus materials—just as it was important to determine the applicability of Kohlberg's stage model to real-life dilemmas. In this study, both orientations were evident in the hypothetical dilemmas which had been adapted to allow participants to construct the problem and to respond to non-orientation-specific questions. In general, responses to real-life and hypothetical dilemmas were similar (contrary to Langdale's, 1986, finding with more limited data), although the youngest children used response considerations less with real-life dilemmas than with hypothetical ones, and adults, more. Developmentally, there was an increase with age in response scores—a phenomenon not apparent in previous research with small samples. Younger children often conceptualized and resolved moral problems egocentrically, in terms of "effects to self," which, according to Lyons (1982), is characteristic of the rights orientation. Gilligan (1977) originally proposed developmental stages in the response orientation but, as yet, no scoring system has been developed to assess such a developmental sequence and no supportive data have been presented.

In relation to Gilligan's (1982) proposal that these orientations are sex-related, the data of this study are inconsistent. Specifically, there was no difference between the sexes in response scores among younger children, and high school boys had higher scores than girls, contrary to Gilligan's claims. However, congruent with her notions, women had higher scores than men. Also, a sex-related pattern in orientations was not found for most of the standard dilemmas, although females had higher response scores than males on two of nine dilemmas. In terms of modal moral orientations for the real-life dilemma, a significant relation between sex and orientation was found, although only for adults. Thus, the evidence regarding the relation between sex and orientation is mixed.

When the content of these dilemmas was analyzed in terms of the nature of the relationship they entailed, it was found that females reported more personal-relationship conflicts and males more impersonal-relationship conflicts. This is a novel finding that requires further exploration. However, within each type of dilemma content, sex differences in moral orientations were not evidenced. Also, it was found that personal-relationship dilemmas elicited a response orientation, whereas impersonal-relationship dilemmas elicited a rights orientation regardless of the subject's sex. Thus, differences in moral orientations can be just as well attributed to the type of moral dilemma that subjects discuss as to their sex. These findings raise the question of whether or not the sex difference that is sometimes evident in moral orientation is due to the differing types of moral conflicts that females and males encounter. This is not to deny that the choice and construal of a dilemma may reflect one's orientation. However, the social experiences of males and females differ in everyday life and may explain the nature of the moral dilemmas they relate.

In addition to claiming that there are sex-related moral orientations, Gilligan also holds that Kohlberg's theory (among others) is biased against females and the response orientation since his theory focuses on justice and was derived from the responses of an exclusively male sample. The minimal (though not sufficient) empirical foundation for this claim would be evidence that females and/or individuals with a response orientation are down-scored in his system. The results of this study indicated no sex differences in stage of moral reasoning development—a finding consistent with the conclusion of earlier reviews and meta-analyses (Walker, 1984, 1986c). This study also determined the pattern of differences in moral development among individuals with different orientations. No differences were found with the hypothetical dilemmas (contrary to Langdale's, 1986, finding based on analysis of a single dilemma); however, with the real-life dilemma, individuals with a rights orientation evidenced lower levels of moral development (by about half a stage) than those with a response or split orientation, contrary to Gilligan's claims. These findings fail to support the notion that Kohlberg's theory and scoring system are biased against the "female" response orientation.

Indeed, one of the intriguing findings of this study (albeit one based on a small N) was that individuals at a high level of moral development tended to be split in their orientations—to evidence substantial amounts of both response and rights reasoning. This suggests that Kohlberg's conceptualization of mature moral thinking entails a coordination or integration of these two orientations. Lyons's (1982) scoring system for these orientations, however, is a disjunctive one wherein considerations are scored as reflecting *either* a rights or a response perspective and cannot be scored as coordinated. There is no reason to assume that the rights and response orientations are mutually exclusive. Certainly the data of this study indicate that Kohlberg's theory is not simply reflected by the rights orientation.

References

Baumrind, D. (1978). A dialectical materialist's perspective on knowing social reality. In W. Damon (Ed.), *New directions for child development: Moral development* (No. 2, pp. 61–82). San Francisco: Jossey-Bass.

Baumrind, D. (1986). Sex differences in moral reasoning: Response to Walker's (1984) conclusion that there are none. *Child Development, 57,* 511–521.

Boyd, D. (1983). Careful justice or just caring: A response to Gilligan. *Proceedings of the Philosophy of Education Society, 38,* 63–69.

Brabeck, M. (1983). Moral judgment: Theory and research on differences between males and females. *Developmental Review, 3,* 274–291.

Broughton, J. M. (1983). Women's rationality and men's virtues: A critique of gender dualism in Gilligan's theory of moral development. *Social Research, 50,* 597–642.

Colby, A., & Kohlberg, L. (Eds.). (in press). *The measurement of moral judgment* (Vols. 1–2). New York: Cambridge University Press.

Ford, M. R., & Lowery, C. R. (1986). Gender differences in moral reasoning: A comparison of the use of justice and care orientations. *Journal of Personality and Social Psychology, 50,* 777–783.

Gilligan, C. (1977). In a different voice: Women's conception of the self and of morality. *Harvard Educational Review, 47,* 481–517.

Gilligan, C. (1982). *In a different voice: Psychological theory and women's development.* Cambridge, MA: Harvard University Press.

Gilligan, C. (1985, November). *Two moral orientations: Implications for thinking about moral development and moral education of women and men.* Paper presented at the meeting of the Association for Moral Education, Toronto.

Gilligan, C. (1986, Spring). [Letter to D. Baumrind]. *Newsletter of the APA Division on Developmental Psychology,* pp. 10–13.

Gilligan, C., & Belenky, M. F. (1980). A naturalistic study of abortion decisions. In R. L. Selman & R. Yando (Eds.), *New directions for child development: Clinical-developmental psychology* (No. 7, pp. 69–90). San Francisco: Jossey-Bass.

Gilligan, C., Langdale, S., Lyons, N., & Murphy, J. M. (1982). *The contribution of women's thought to developmental theory: The elimination of sex bias in moral development research and education.* Unpublished manuscript, Harvard University, Cambridge, MA.

Haan, N. (1975). Hypothetical and actual moral reasoning in a situation of civil disobedience. *Journal of Personality and Social Psychology, 32,* 255–270.

Haan, N. (1977). *Coping and defending: Processes of self-environment organization.* New York: Academic Press.

Higgins, A., Power, C., & Kohlberg, L. (1984). The relationship of moral atmosphere to judgments of responsibility. In W. M. Kurtines & J. L. Gewirtz (Eds.), *Morality, moral behavior, and moral development* (pp. 74–106). New York: Wiley.

Kohlberg, L. (1984). *Essays on moral development: Vol. 2. The psychology of moral development.* San Francisco: Harper & Row.

Kohlberg, L., & Candee, D. (1984). The relationship of moral judgment to moral action. In L. Kohlberg, *Essays on moral development: Vol. 2. The psychology of moral development* (pp. 498–581). San Francisco: Harper & Row.

Kohlberg, L., Scharf, P., & Hickey, J. (1971). The justice structure of the prison—a theory and an intervention. *Prison Journal, 51*(2), 3–14.

Langdale, C. J. (1986). A re-vision of structural-developmental theory. In G. L. Sapp (Ed.), *Handbook of moral development: Models, processes, techniques, and research* (pp. 15–54). Birmingham, AL: Religious Education Press.

Lyons, N. P. (1982). *Conceptions of self and morality and modes of moral choice: Identifying justice and care in judgments of actual moral dilemmas.* Unpublished doctoral dissertation, Harvard University, Cambridge, MA.

Lyons, N. P. (1983). Two perspectives: On self, relationships, and morality. *Harvard Educational Review, 53,* 125–145.

Nails, D. (1983). Social-scientific sexism: Gilligan's mismeasure of man. *Social Research, 50,* 643–664.

Noddings, N. (1984). *Caring: A feminine approach to ethics and moral education.* Berkeley: University of California Press.

Pratt, M. W. (1985, August). Sex differences in moral orientations in personal and hypothetical dilemmas? Don't forget those old outcasts of content and process. In C. Blake (Chair), *Gender difference research in moral development.* Symposium conducted at the meeting of the American Psychological Association, Los Angeles.

Rybash, J. M., Roodin, P. A., & Hoyer, W. J. (1983).

Expressions of moral thought in later adulthood. *Gerontologist*, **23**, 254–260.

Sichel, B. A. (1985). Women's moral development in search of philosophical assumptions. *Journal of Moral Education*, **14**, 149–161.

Smetana, J. G. (1982). *Concepts of self and morality*. New York: Praeger.

Treiman, D. J. (1977). *Occupational prestige in comparative perspective*. New York: Academic Press.

Walker, L. J. (1984). Sex differences in the development of moral reasoning: A critical review. *Child Development*, **55**, 677–691.

Walker, L. J. (1986a). Cognitive processes in moral development. In G. L. Sapp (Ed.), *Handbook of moral development: Models, processes, techniques, and research* (pp. 109–145). Birmingham, AL: Religious Education Press.

Walker, L. J. (1986b). Experiential and cognitive sources of moral development in adulthood. *Human Development*, **29**, 113–124.

Walker, L. J. (1986c). Sex differences in the development of moral reasoning: A rejoinder to Baumrind. *Child Development*, **57**, 522–526.

Yussen, S. R. (1977). Characteristics of moral dilemmas written by adolescents. *Developmental Psychology*, **13**, 162–163.

Reply by Carol Gilligan

Among his many astute observations, William James noted that when a new idea is introduced, the first response is to say that it is so obviously false, it is hard to see how anyone could believe it; the second is to say that it is not original, and everyone has always known it to be true.[32] My critics are making both statements, but in doing so they introduce a central confusion. I am saying that the study of women calls attention to a different way of constituting the self and morality; they are focusing on the issue of sex differences as measured by standards derived from one sex only. In other words, my critics take the ideas of self and morality for granted as these ideas have been defined in the patriarchal or male-dominated tradition. I call these concepts in question by giving examples of women who constitute these ideas differently and hence tell a different story about human experience. My critics say that this story seems "intuitively" right to many women but is at odds with the findings of psychological research. This is precisely the point I am making and exactly the difference I was exploring: the dissonance between psychological theory and women's experience.

The sex difference issue was raised in a curiously unacknowledged way by those psychologists who chose all-male research samples, since the choice of a single-sex sample reflects an implicit premise of gender difference. But a sex-difference hypothesis cannot be tested adequately unless the standards of assessment are derived from studies of women as well as from studies of men. Otherwise, the questions being asked are, How much are women like men? Or, how much do women deviate from a male-defined standard?

It was in an effort to ask a different question that I wrote the book under discussion, seeking to discover whether something had been missed by the practice of leaving out girls and women at the theory-building stage of research in developmental psychology—that is, whether Piaget's and Kohlberg's descriptions of moral development, Erikson's description of identity development, Offer's description of adolescent development, Levinson's and Vaillant's descriptions of adult development, as well as more general accounts of human personality and motivation, contained a consistent conceptual and observational bias, reflected in and extended by their choice of all-male research samples.[33]

---

32. William James, *Pragmatism* (New York: New American Library, 1907), p. 131.

33. Piaget (n. 7 above); Lawrence Kohlberg, "Stage and Sequence: The Cognitive-Developmental Approach to Socialization," in *Handbook of Socialization*, ed. David A. Goslin (New York: Rand McNally, 1909). Erikson began his work on identity with returning war veterans in the 1950s and advanced it further in *Young Man Luther* (New York: W. W. Norton & Co., 1958). Daniel Offer, *The Psychological World of the Teenager: A Study of 175 Boys* (New York: Basic Books, 1969); Daniel Levinson, *The Seasons of a Man's Life* (New York: Ballantine Books, 1978); George Vaillant, *Adaptation to Life* (Boston: Little, Brown & Co., 1977). For a discussion of psychological norms based on studies of males, see David McClelland, *Power: The Inner Experience* (New York: Irvington, Halsted-Wiley, 1975); Joseph Adelson, ed., *Handbook of Adolescent Psychology* (New York: John Wiley & Sons, 1980), esp. Joseph Adelson and Margery Doehrman, "The Psychodynamic Approach to Adolescence."

The "different voice" hypothesis was an answer to this question. What had been missed by leaving out women was a different way of constituting the idea of the self and the idea of what is moral. Rather than seeing to what extent women exemplify what generally is taken to be self and morality, I saw in women's thinking the lines of a different conception, grounded in different images of relationship and implying a different interpretive framework. Attention to women's thinking thus raised a new set of questions about both male and female development and explained a series of observations that previously had not made sense. Discrepant data on girls and women, commonly interpreted as evidence of female deficiency, pointed instead to a problem in psychological theory.

That this problem affected women differently from the way it affected men seemed clear. Since women's voices were heard though a filter that rendered them confused and incoherent, it was difficult for men to understand women and for women to listen to themselves. In my book, I sought to clarify two related sets of problems, put forth in my subtitle: problems in psychological theory and problems in women's development. The argument was not statistical—that is, not based on the representativeness of the women studied or on the generality of the data presented to a larger population of women or men. Rather, the argument was interpretive and hinged on the demonstration that the examples presented illustrated a different way of seeing.

In defining a shift in perspective that changes the meaning of the key terms of moral discourse—such as the concept of self, the idea of relationship, and the notion of responsibility—I described an ethic of care and response that I contrasted with an ethic of justice and rights. I also cited as an empirical observation the prominence of the care perspective in women's moral thinking and used literary examples to amplify and extend the voices in my interview texts. My critics cannot make up their minds whether it is naive or self-serving to think of women as caring or whether this is a fact so obvious that it does not need repeating. But as they elaborate these contentions, it becomes increasingly apparent that the book they are discussing is different from the book which I have written.

They speak of the nineteenth-century ideal of pure womanhood and the romanticizing of female care: I portray twentieth-century women choosing to have abortions, as well as women college students, lawyers, and physicians reconsidering what is meant by care in light of their recognition that acts inspired by conventions of selfless feminine care have led to hurt, betrayal, and isolation. My critics equate care with feelings, which they oppose to thought, and imagine caring as passive or confined to some separate sphere. I describe care and justice as two moral perspectives that organize both thinking and feelings and empower the self to take different kinds of action in public as well as private life. Thus, in contrast to the paralyzing image of the "angel in the house," I describe a critical ethical perspective that calls into question the traditional equation of care with self-sacrifice.

The title of my book was deliberate; it reads, "in a *different* voice," not "in a *woman's* voice." In my introduction, I explain that this voice is identified not by gender but by theme. Noting as an empirical observation the association of this voice with women, I caution the reader that "this association is not absolute, and the contrasts between male and female voices are presented here to highlight a distinction between two modes of thought and to focus a problem of interpretation rather than to represent a generalization about either sex." In tracing development, I "point to the interplay of these voices within each sex and suggest that their convergence marks times of crisis and change." No claims, I state, are made about the origins of these voices or their distribution in a wider population, across cultures or time (p. 2). Thus, the care perspective in my rendition is neither biologically determined nor unique to women. It is, however, a moral perspective different from that currently embedded in psychological theories and measures, and it is a perspective that was defined by listening to both women and men describe their own experience.

The most puzzling aspect of my critics' position is their dissociation of women's experience from women's thinking—as if experiences common to women leave no psychological trace. Thus Greeno and Maccoby cite examples of sex differences in their references to "women's predominance in the nurturance and care of young children [as] an accepted and cross-culturally universal fact" (p. 313 above); to recent research indicating "that even at a very early age males and females show decidedly different styles in social interactions" (p. 314); and to findings of sex differences "in the literature on intimacy among adults" (p. 314). Kerber observes that "it seems well established that little boys face a psychic task of separation that little girls do not" (p. 309 above). Yet in endorsing the position of no sex differences, they appear to believe that nothing of significance for moral or self development is learned from these activities and experiences. The burden of proof would seem to rest with my critics to give a psychologically coherent explanation of why the sex differences they mention make no difference to moral development or self-concept. To say that social class and education contribute to moral development while experiences typically associated with gender are essentially irrelevant may say more about the way development is being measured than it does about morality or gender.

In replying to my critics, I wish to address three issues they raise: the issue of method, the issue of theory or interpretation, and the issue of goals or education. The first question is what constitutes data and what data are sufficient to support the claims I have made. To claim that there is a voice different from those which psychologists have represented, I need only one example—one voice whose coherence is not recognized within existing interpretive schemes. To claim that common themes recur in women's conceptions of self and morality, I need a series of illustrations. In counterposing women's conceptions of self and morality to the conceptions embedded in psychological theories, I assume that a psychology literature filled with men's voices exemplifies men's experience. Therefore, in listening to women, I sought to separate their descriptions of their experience from standard forms of psychological interpretation and to rely on a close textual analysis of language and logic to define the terms of women's thinking.

Like all psychological research, my work is limited by the nature and context of my observations and reflects my own interpretive frame. There are no data independent of theory, no observations not made from a perspective. Data alone do not tell us anything; they do not speak, but are interpreted by people. I chose to listen to women's descriptions of experiences of moral conflict and choice, to attend to the ways that women describe themselves in relation to others, and to observe changes in thinking over time. On the basis of these observations and my reading of psychology, I made a series of inferences about the nature of sex differences, about women's development, about the concept of self, and about the nature of moral experience.

Seizing on the Walker article recently published in *Child Development*, my critics claim that there are no sex differences in moral development because there are no sex differences on the Kohlberg scale.[34] Thus they completely miss my point. My work focuses on the difference between two moral orientations—a justice and a care perspective rather than on the question of whether women and men differ on Kohlberg's stages of justice reasoning. On two occasions, I have reported no sex differences on Kohlberg's measure.[35] But the fact that educated women are capable of high levels of justice reasoning has no bearing on the question of whether they would spontaneously choose to frame moral problems in this way. My interest in the way people *define* moral problems is reflected in my research methods, which have centered on first-person accounts of moral conflict.[36]

34. Walker (n. 10 above).

35. John Michael Murphy and Carol Gilligan, "Moral Development in Late Adolescence and Adulthood," *Human Development* 23, no. 2 (1980): 77–104; Gilligan et al. (n. 19 above).

36. Carol Gilligan and John Michael Murphy, "Development from Adolescence to Adulthood: The Philosopher and 'The Dilemma of the Fact,'" in *Intellectual Development beyond Childhood*, ed. Deanna Kuhn (San Francisco: Jossey-Bass, 1979), pp. 85–99; Carol Gilligan and Mary Belenky, "A Naturalistic Study of Abortion Decisions," in *Clinical-Developmental Psychology*, ed. Robert L. Selman and Regina Yando (San Francisco: Jossey-Bass, 1980), pp. 69–90.

My critics are unaware that Walker's conclusions and use of statistics have been seriously challenged by two of the researchers on whose findings he most heavily relies. In replies submitted to *Child Development*, Norma Haan reports significant sex differences on the Kohlberg test, even when controlling for social class and education and using the new scoring method; Diana Baumrind notes that the most highly educated women in her sample were less likely than other women or men to score at Kohlberg's postconventional stages because they were less likely to frame moral problems in terms of abstract principles of justice.[37] Thus lower scores on the Kohlberg measure do not necessarily reflect lower levels of moral development but may signify a shift in moral perspective or orientation.

The example in my book of eleven-year-old Amy illustrates how a care perspective is rendered incomprehensible by the Kohlberg frame. This point is extended by interviews conducted with Amy and Jake when they were fifteen. At fifteen, both children introduce both moral perspectives in thinking about the Heinz dilemma, although the order of introduction is not the same. Amy's ability to solve the problem within the justice framework leads her to advance a full stage on Kohlberg's scale, but Jake's introduction of the care perspective signifies no advance in moral development, according to Kohlberg's measure. The Kohlberg test, in its equation of moral development with justice reasoning, does not adequately represent either Amy's or Jake's moral thinking. Amy's own terms remain at fifteen the terms of the care perspective, and from this standpoint she sees moral problems in the justice construction. To equate her moral development with her ability to reason within this framework is to ignore her perceptions; but it is also to encourage her, in the name of development, to accept a construction of reality and morality that she identifies as problematic. For Jake, the equation of moral judgment with the logic of justice reasoning encourages him to take the position that anyone disagreeing with his judgment has "the wrong set of priorities." He takes this stand at first when asked about the druggist's refusal to relinquish his profit but then abandons it in the recognition that there is another way to think about this problem. At eleven, Jake saw the Heinz dilemma as "sort of like a math problem with humans"; at fifteen he recasts it as a story about two people whose actions can be interpreted differently, depending on the constraints of their situation, and whose feelings, when elaborated, evoke understanding and compassion. What

---

37. For a more extensive discussion of Amy's and Jake's moral reasoning at age fifteen, see Carol Gilligan, "Remapping Development: The Power of Divergent Data," in *Value Presuppositions in Theories of Human Development*, ed. Leonard Cirillo and Seymour Wapner (Hillside, N. J.: Lawrence Erlbaum Associates, in press).

had seemed a simple exercise in moral logic thus becomes a more complex moral problem.[38]

If my critics had pursued their questions about method and evidence, they would have discovered that in 1983 Nona Lyons reported a systematic procedure for identifying justice and care considerations in people's descriptions of real life dilemmas, and Sharry Langdale, in a doctoral dissertation, demonstrated that Lyons's method could be adapted for coding responses to hypothetical dilemmas.[39] With a cross-sectional, life-cycle sample of 144 males and females who were matched for social class and education, Langdale found significant sex differences in the use of justice and care considerations. My critics also could have learned that Kay Johnston, in a recently completed dissertation, created a standard method (using Aesop's fables) for assessing moral orientation use and preference. Johnston demonstrated that sixty eleven- and fifteen-year-old girls and boys from a middle-class suburban community were able to understand the logic of both the justice and care orientations, to use both strategies of reasoning in solving the problems posed by the fables, and to explain why one or the other orientation provided a better solution. She also found consistent sex differences in orientation use and preference, as well as variation across fables.[40]

These studies and others confirm and refine the "different voice" hypothesis by demonstrating that (1) the justice and care perspectives are distinct orientations that organize people's thinking about moral problems in different ways; (2) boys and men who resemble those most studied by developmental psychologists tend to define and resolve moral problems within the justice framework, although they introduce considerations of care; and (3) the focus on care in moral reasoning, although not characteristic of all women, is characteristically a female phenomenon in the advantaged populations that have been studied. These findings provide an empirical explanation for the equation of moral judgment with

38. Norma Haan, "With Regard to Walker (1984) on Sex 'Differences' in Moral Reasoning" (University of California, Berkeley, Institute of Human Development, 1985, mimeographed); Diana Baumrind, "Sex Differences in Moral Reasoning: Response to Walker's (1984) Conclusion That There Are None," *Child Development* (in press).

39. Nona Lyons, "Two Perspectives: On Self, Relationships, and Morality," *Harvard Education Review* 53, no. 2 (1983): 125–46, and "Conceptions of Self and Morality and Modes of Moral Choice: Identifying Justice and Care in Judgments of Actual Moral Dilemmas" (Ed.D. diss., Harvard Graduate School of Education, 1982); Sharry Langdale, "Moral Orientations and Moral Development: The Analysis of Care and Justice Reasoning across Different Dilemmas jn Females and Males from Childhood through Adulthood" (Ed.D. diss., Harvard Graduate School of Education, 1983).

40. Kay Johnston, "Two Moral Orientations—Two Problem-solving Strategies: Adolescents' Solutions to Dilemmas in Fables" (Ed.D. diss., Harvard Graduate School of Education, 1985).

justice reasoning in theories derived from studies of males; but they also explain why the study of women's moral thinking changes the definition of the moral domain.

My critics' readiness to dismiss findings of sex differences is evident as well in the fact that they cite the Benton et al. critique of Susan Pollak's and my study of images of violence but overlook the three articles that followed in its wake: our reply, "Differing about Differences"; their response, "Compounding the Error"; and our rejoinder, "Killing the Messenger."[41] Pollak and I agree with Benton et al. that a priori classification of Thematic Apperception Test (TAT) pictures poses a serious problem in motivation research, but we see no exception to this problem in the classification they propose. Our study, however, relied on a content analysis of the violent stories written by women and men, an analysis that our critics ignore. This analysis revealed that, within the texts of the stories written (considered independently of the pictures), violence was associated with intimacy in stories written by men and with isolation in stories written by women. The report by Benton and her associates of sex differences in the incidence and location of violence are not inconsistent with our conclusions; however, their failure to conduct a content analysis suggests that their study was not a serious attempt at replication.[42]

If the Walker article implies that questions about sex differences in moral development can be reduced to an issue of Kohlberg test scores, the Benton et al. critique suggests that questions about sex differences in violent fantasies can be reduced to an issue of picture classification. Given that researchers repeatedly find significant sex differences in the incidence of both violent fantasies and violent behavior, the rush to dismiss the exploration of these differences on the basis of picture classification seems like an attempt to paper over a huge social problem with a methodological quibble. My critics are concerned about stereotypes that portray women as lacking in anger and aggression; but they do not consider the lower incidence of violence in women's fantasies and behavior to be a sex difference worth exploring. Thus my critics essentially accept the psychology I call into question—the psychology that has equated male with human in defining human nature and thus has construed evidence of sex differences as a sign of female deficiency, a psychology that, for all the talk about research design and methods, has failed to see all-male research samples as a methodological problem.

41. Pollak and Gilligan (n. 17 above); Benton et al. (n. 17 above); Susan Pollak and Carol Gilligan, "Differences about Differences: The Interpretation of Violent Fantasies in Women and Men," *Journal of Personality and Social Psychology* 45, no. 5 (1983): 1172–75; Bernard Weiner et al., "Compounding the Error: A Reply to Pollak and Gilligan," ibid., pp. 1176–78; Susan Pollak and Carol Gilligan, "Killing the Messenger," ibid. 48, no. 2 (1985): 374–75.
42. Pollak and Gilligan, "Killing the Messenger," pp. 374–75.

My work offers a different perspective, on psychology and on women. It calls into question the values placed on detachment and separation in developmental theories and measures, values that create a false sense of objectivity and render female development problematic. My studies of women locate the problem in female development not in the values of care and connection or in the relational definition of self, but in the tendency for women, in the name of virtue, to give care only to others and to consider it "selfish" to care for themselves. The inclusion of women's experience dispels the view of care as selfless and passive and reveals the activities that constitute care and lead to responsiveness in human relationships. In studies conducted by myself and my students, women who defined themselves in their own terms—as indicated by the use of active, first-person constructions—generally articulated the value of care and affirmed their own relational concerns. In thinking about choices in their lives, these women were able to adopt a critical perspective on societal values of separation and independence and to reject confusing images of women, such as "supermother" or "superwoman," that are at odds with women's knowledge about relationships and about themselves. Women's ability to act on this knowledge was associated in several doctoral dissertations with invulnerability to eating disorders, recovery from depression, and the absence of depressive symptoms in mothers of young children.[43] But if my characterization is accurate, there is no question that this knowledge brings women into conflict with current societal arrangements and often confronts them with painful and difficult choices.

My critics and I share a common concern about the education of our women students, as well as, I assume, a more general concern about the future of life on this planet. In light of these considerations, how best might we approach the education of both women and men students? To label women's concerns about conflicts between achievement and care as a sign of weakness is to render women frightened and fearful. This approach only reinforces the impression that women's fears are groundless. Women need to engage the problems created by the overload of work and family because these conflicts fall most heavily on women. But it is a disservice to both women and men to imply that these are women's problems.

---

43. Catherine Steiner-Adair, "The Body Politic: Normal Female Adolescent Development and the Development of Eating Disorders" (Ed.D. diss., Harvard Graduate School of Education, 1984); Dana Crowley Jack, "Clinical Depression in Women: Cognitive Schemas of Self, Care, and Relationships in a Longitudinal Study" (Ed.D. diss., Harvard Graduate School of Education, 1984); Ann Kinsella Willard, "Self, Situation and Script: A Psychological Study of Decisions about Employment in Mothers of One Year Olds" (Ed.D. diss., Harvard Graduate School of Education, 1985). See also Jane Stoodt Attanucci, "Mothers in Their Own Terms: A Developmental Perspective on Self and Role" (Ed.D. diss., Harvard Graduate School of Education, 1984).

That developmental psychology has been built largely from the study of men's lives is not my invention. While we may disagree about the particular nature of the problems in this representation, as women we do ourselves an immense disservice to say that there is no problem. Since morality is closely tied to the problem of aggression—an area where sex differences are uncontested—it may be of particular interest at this time for both sexes to explore whether women's experience illuminates the psychology of nonviolent strategies for resolving conflicts. I am well aware that reports of sex differences can be used to rationalize oppression, and I deplore any use of my work for this purpose. But I do not see it as empowering to encourage women to put aside their own concerns and perceptions and to rely on a psychology largely defined by men's perceptions in thinking about what is of value and what constitutes human development.[44]

Graduate School of Education
Harvard University

44. The research described in this paper was supported by a generous gift from Marilyn Brachman Hoffman, and by grants from the William F. Milton Fund, the small grants section of NIMH, the Spencer Foundation grants to Harvard junior faculty, the National Institute of Education, and the Carnegie Corporation and the Bunting Institute of Radcliffe College. I owe a particular debt of gratitude to Jane Attanucci, Lyn Mikel Brown, Kay Johnston, and Bernard Kaplan.

Commentaries

Editor's Note

Developmental and individual differences in moral reasoning have been controversial topics in developmental psychology for nearly a generation. In 1984, Lawrence Walker reviewed the literature and concluded that there was no consistent evidence indicating sex differences in moral development. Diana Baumrind, in the first of the present articles, takes issue with Walker's conclusion, on statistical and conceptual grounds. Walker was invited to reply to these criticisms and defends his original conclusion. This exchange could obviously be extended, but we believe this trio of articles well illustrates some of the key statistical, conceptual, and philosophical disagreements currently marking the study of moral development.

Sex Differences in Moral Reasoning: Response to Walker's (1984) Conclusion That There Are None

Diana Baumrind

University of California, Berkeley

BAUMRIND, DIANA. *Sex Differences in Moral Reasoning: Response to Walker's (1984) Conclusion That There Are None.* CHILD DEVELOPMENT, 1986, **57**, 511–521. Data from the Family Socialization and Developmental Competence Project are used to probe Walker's conclusion that there are no sex differences in moral reasoning. Ordinal and nominal nonparametric statistics result in a complex but theoretically meaningful network of relationships among sex, educational level, and Kohlberg stage score level, with the presence and direction of sex differences in stage score level dependent on educational level. The effects on stage score level of educational level and working status are also shown to differ for men and women. Reasons are considered for not accepting Walker's dismissal of studies that use (a) a pre-1983 scoring manual, or (b) fail to control for education. The problems presented to Kohlberg's theory by the significant relationship between educational and stage score levels in the general population are discussed, particularly as these apply to the postconventional level of moral reasoning.

In a recent review of some 50 studies, Walker (1984) concluded that there are no consistent sex differences or biases in Kohlberg's theory or measure of moral development. However, I will attempt to show that certain of the decisions Walker made were not well-suited to the theory he was testing and resulted in a bias favoring findings of no sex differences. Therefore, research findings included in his review do not warrant the conclusion that there are no sex differences but suggest instead that the source and specific nature of these differences have yet to be established.

Understanding these differences is important because sex bias may be but one manifestation of a more pervasive cultural bias re-

The research reported here was supported by grants from the W. T. Grant Foundation, National Institute of Child Health and Human Development Grant no. HD-02228, National Institute on Drug Abuse Grant no. DA/HD-01919, and National Science Foundation Grant no. BNS-8010666. While completing this manuscript, the author was supported by a Research Scientist Award from the National Institute of Mental Health Grant no. KO5-MH00485. Continuing work on this longitudinal program of research is supported in part by National Institute of Mental Health Grant no. RO1-MH-38343. I wish to thank Dr. Steven Pulos for his assistance with data analyses, and his comments. Requests for reprints should be sent to Diana Baumrind, Institute of Human Development, 1203 Edward Chace Tolman Hall, University of California, Berkeley, CA 94720.

sulting from Kohlberg's restriction ot the meaning of morality to universal cognitive judgments about justice as fairness. The presence of sexual or cultural bias in his definition of morality would limit the scope of Kohlberg's theory and recommend against universal adoption of his restrictive definition of morality, especially when applied to females, or citizens of Second and Third World countries.

This article includes three parts. In the first I demonstrate some of the shortcomings with Walker's (1984) analyses. In the second, I present additional analyses of data from the Family Socialization Project (FSP). In the third, I relate Walker's analyses and the FSP data to more general issues concerning moral development.

Shortcomings of Walker's Analyses

In his review and meta-analysis, Walker includes data on three age periods: childhood, youth, and adulthood. Only the data on adulthood, however, are relevant to the controversy on sex differences, since the allegation of bias arises from the presence of sex differences in the attainment of the highest level of moral reasoning and not in differential rate of development. The differences favoring girls throughout childhood and early adolescence are easily explained by their accelerated general development. However, the finding of sex differences favoring adult men in so highly valued a personal attribute as moral maturity would be of great social concern. Fortunately for Kohlberg's theory, Walker concluded that only four of the 21 adult samples he considered showed significant sex differences (all favoring men). Unfortunately, Walker's analysis was flawed.

Walker included in the studies that did *not* show sex differences data on 9-year-old children and their parents from the FSP (Baumrind, 1982). However, I reported a sex difference favoring fathers over mothers with the same data from the FSP. The purpose of the FSP study in which sex differences were reported was to determine whether the Bem Sex Role Inventory gender classification had predictive power over and above knowledge of biological sex on 20 child-rearing and personal measures. Among the significant effects of biological sex was that on Kohlberg stage scores. Hierarchical analyses of variance were used to test the effect on all dependent measures. However, Kohlberg stage scores, unlike the other 19 dependent measures in that study, are discrete values intended to assess discontinuous theoretical entities. Therefore,

the use of analysis of variance, while expedient in order to treat all 20 dependent measures similarly, was not appropriate.

Moral Development Is a Discontinuous Variable

Kohlberg, following Piaget, regards stages not as a measurement device but rather as the true nature of moral development. Therefore, it is not theoretically meaningful to treat stage scores as continuous in testing the hypothesis of sex differences. The Kolmogorov-Smirnov test used by Walker to test sex differences in moral reasoning on some of the largest samples in his review (including the FSP sample) assumes a continuous distribution and is inappropriate for the same reason as the use of analysis of variance in the Baumrind study. Because stages are discrete, and different stages or levels have different meanings, it is more appropriate to examine differences in frequency of men and women within a stage or stages than to compare the difference between mean stage scores of men and women. That is, the assumption of a continuous distribution leads to the question, Is there a sex difference in moral reasoning? rather than to the more specific and theoretically cogent question, Is there a sex difference at a given stage in moral reasoning? Thus one might argue that, as a consequence of women's focus on issues of caring, they would be over-represented at Stage 3 and under-represented at the postconventional formal level of reasoning in the Kohlberg system. Practically, a general search for sex differences across stages may lead to the conclusion of no sex differences or only minimal sex differences, when in fact the possibility remains that a significant sex difference does exist at a particular stage or level but not across all stages or levels.

Proneness to Type II Errors

Walker has attempted to amass support for the null hypothesis, to argue that there are no sex differences in Kohlberg's stage system scoring. Apart from the logical impossibility of proving the null hypothesis, the method of analysis selected by Walker biased his results in favor of the null hypothesis he favored in three ways.

First, in reanalyzing other investigators' data (including data from the FSP) Walker chose to use the Kolmogorov-Smirnov test. That test, used under the conditions that Walker used it, is excessively prone to Type II errors, that is, it will fail to detect a (sex) difference when such a difference exists. The Kolmogorov-Smirnov test assumes a continuous distribution, which cannot contain ties (identical scores). But a stage theory contains six prototypic scores, of which only five are typically used, and requires by theory the presence of ties. The Kolmogorov-Smirnov test becomes increasingly conservative as the number of ties increases, and Walker introduced no correction for ties (personal communication to Steven Pulos, November 27, 1984).

Second, sex differences favoring males are found more frequently in the adult studies. However, Walker combined all studies cited in his first three tables into a single meta-analysis, even though only the adult data in his Table 3 are crucial to the issue of whether sex differences in level of moral development exist, and the adult data comprise only 16% of the studies cited in his meta-analysis. In so doing, he increased the probability of failing to find sex differences favoring males.

Third, Walker did not take into account differences in sample size among the studies cited. With increasing sample size the power of the Kolmogorov-Smirnov test increases less rapidly relative to that of the t test or the Mann-Whitney test (Siegel, 1956), making it more subject to Type II errors with sample sizes greater than 30. All studies with a sample size of 30 or less failed to find significant sex differences, whereas four of the 11 studies with a sample size greater than 30 found significant differences. Another four of the 11 large sample studies were examined with the Kolmogorov-Smirnov test, which is inappropriately conservative for the reasons just cited. One of these (FSP), as we will show, does reveal sex differences favoring males at the highest educational level.

Discounting Studies in Which the 1983 Manual Was Not Used

Walker argued that studies that do show sex differences can be discounted if they did not use the new conventions established by the 1983 scoring manual. FSP protocols were scored by the conventions established by the 1971 manual. However, FSP findings cannot be discounted on that account unless all studies using earlier manuals are discounted on the basis that the new manual represents Kohlberg's theory, and prior manuals do not. But the new scoring manual has already been criticized for questionable construct validity and ambiguously defined scoring standards (Cortese, 1984).

Of particular concern is the absence of an empirical terminal stage. According to Walker

(p. 678), Kohlberg dropped Stage 6 because it was absent from his longitudinal sample. Although Stage 6 reasoning has been dropped from the scoring manual, it is evident from the numerous references to Stage 6 in Kohlberg's newest collection of essays on moral development that it has not been dropped as *the* pivotal metaphysical ideal in the Kohlberg system (e.g., Kohlberg & Elfenbein, 1981). In a structural theory of moral development such as Kohlberg's, the entire stage sequence, and each stage within the sequence, is teleologically determined by the ideal terminal stage. Kohlberg's Stage 6 embodies Rawls's (1971) model of justice. According to Kohlberg, it was selected to assure a "hard" structural theory of stages that could "characterize the domain of justice in interpersonal interactions, just as notions of equilibrium and reversibility characterize the domain of logico-mathematical and physical reasoning" (Kohlberg, Levine, & Hewer, 1983, p. 62). This terminal or ideal stage anchors Kohlberg's claim to having achieved rational consensus on the content of the right in conflicts about justice, "analogous to norms of scientific rationality in the philosophy of science" (Kohlberg et al., 1983, p. 62). The absence of an *empirically* defined ideal stage compromises the construct validity of the five preceding stages. By eliminating Stage 6 as an empirical entity, Kohlberg has decapitated the corpus of his theory rather than merely doffed its empirical hat from its metaethical head.

It is indeed a matter of some concern that the correlation is only ".39 between the scores yielded by the original and current scoring manuals" (Walker, pp. 687–688). This correlation between two operational definitions of the "same" theory is strikingly low, resulting in less than 16% of shared variance between the scores obtained using the original and the current manuals. However, impartiality requires that if, on the basis of this low relationship, one rejects any, one rejects *all* findings using the pre-1983 scoring manual, including, of course, the findings that there are no sex differences in level of moral judgment.

At this point in time, it is difficult to know what to make of the conceptual and procedural revisions that have recently been offered by Kohlberg and his colleagues (Colby, Kohlberg, Gibbs, & Lieberman, 1983; Kohlberg, 1981, 1984; Kohlberg et al., 1983) to the stage theory of moral development. The 1983 scoring manual is different from the previous ones; it is not yet clear that it is better.

Discounting Studies Because the Significance of Sex Differences Is Nullified by Controlling for Education

Walker's second major challenge to the studies that showed sex differences favoring adult males is that these differences were confounded with social status. But if (*a*) stage score level and educational level are systematically interdependent in the real world, and (*b*) both are determined by social status, then eliminating sex differences by statistically controlling for educational level obscures rather than clarifies the challenge to Kohlberg's theory presented by the dependence in the real world of Kohlberg's stage score level on sex and social status.

Neither Walker nor Kohlberg have acknowledged that the highly significant relationship between Kohlberg sociomoral level and social status variables (including education) in the general population represents a serious challenge to a theory of moral development. According to Walker, Kohlberg explains the relationship by saying that postconventional reasoning requires, in addition to a certain level of cognitive development, exposure to appropriate sociomoral experiences. Walker indicates that "These experiences arise both through interpersonal relationships with family and friends and through real participation in the economic, political, and legal institutions of society" (p. 678). However, neither Kohlberg nor Walker state the nature or the magnitude of the expected relationship between these two quite different kinds of qualifying experiences and Kohlberg stage score level, or whether one kind can substitute entirely for the other kind. Does the theory suggest a linear relationship between variables such as years of education or social status and stage score level, or is there instead a necessary threshold for each stage? If (as seems more consonant with the theory) the latter, what threshold is posited for each stage?

Of particular interest is the relationship between amount and quality of education and postconventional and, specifically, Stage 6 reasoning. Kohlberg constructed his "theoretical definition of a sixth stage from the writings of a small elite sample; elite in the sense of its formal philosophic training and in the sense of its ability for and commitment to moral leadership" (Kohlberg et al., 1983, p. 60). It was also a male sample. Kohlberg observes that postconventional reasoning almost never occurs in pre-industrial societies "because of their relatively simple degree of social-structural complexity and because their populations have little or no formal education" (Kohlberg et al., 1983, p. 113). However, Kohlberg does not specify what level of complexity and amount of formal education suffice to permit truly moral (i.e., Stage 5 or Stage 6) reasoning to germinate. Similarly, although the relationship between education and stage score level is known to be highly significant for men, less is known about the relationship for women. Further, it is not known whether the sex difference in stage score level favoring men exists uniformly at all educational levels. Although the data from the Family Socialization Project cannot address these questions for the population at large, they can do so for a socially and educationally advantaged group of mature, married couples. This sample is ideal for examining the interrelationships among sex, professional status, and postconventional reasoning, because it is skewed in the direction of higher educational and therefore higher Kohlberg stage score levels. Stage 6 reasoning typifies 21 of the 303 adults in the FSP sample.

Reanalysis of Data from the FSP

The reanalysis of the FSP data presented in this article takes the stage theory seriously by employing statistical techniques that treat the stages as discrete. These data will be used to probe Walker's conclusion that there are no sex differences in adult moral judgment level using Kohlberg's scale.

Method

Subjects.—Subjects in the Family Socialization Project are middle-class, well-educated Caucasian individuals residing in the San Francisco Bay area, and consist of 164 9-year-old children (78 girls, 86 boys) and most of their parents (158 mothers, 145 fathers), whose median ages were 38 (mothers) and 41 (fathers).

Data.—As part of the second wave of data collection in a longitudinal study of the impact of family socialization practices on the social competence of children and adolescents, four Kohlberg dilemmas were administered to parents in interview form. The interviews consisted of four Kohlberg stories (Joe and his father, Son tells a lie, Heinz and the druggist, Wife wants euthanasia).

The interviews were scored by one rater using Kohlberg's 1971 scoring manual. Prior to scoring the rest of the protocols, the rater achieved 90% agreement in major score or major/minor reversal score with Constance Holstein (Holstein was trained by Kohlberg, e.g., Holstein, 1976) on 20 cases, 10 training material cases and 10 actual protocols. Following the conventions established by the 1971 manual, the transcribed interview is unitized and the central issue in each unit is identified. A single stage score is assigned to each unitized issue. "Global issue scores" representing modal characteristics of the subject's reasoning on a given issue across a range of questions or stories are then determined for each story and across all stories. A single "major" stage score is assigned if 50% or more of the global issue scores reflect this stage. A "minor" stage score is assigned if > 25% but < 50% of the global issue weighted scores reflect a stage. The *Typical* moral stage score is the major stage score for the entire protocol. The *Maximum* moral stage score is the highest major or minor stage score obtained at least twice by the respondent for any of the four individual stories. A *Typical/Maximum* score was constructed to include information from both the Typical and Maximum scores in order to have a finer-grained classification of subjects and to avoid problems inherent in data with the restricted range of the Typical and Maximum scores. The Typical/Maximum score is the Typical moral stage score with sublevels corresponding to the Maximum score. For example, persons with a Typical score of 4 and a Maximum of 6 were assigned a score of 4,6; and persons with a Typical score of 4 and a Maximum score of 5 were assigned a score of 4,5. This scale is, of course, only ordinal.

The Typical and Maximum scores are used only when the frequency distribution of subjects is examined. When the relationship between moral reasoning and another variable, for example, education, is examined, then the Typical/Maximum score is used. If the analysis reported for the Typical/Maximum is conducted with the Typical score, the same results are found, but to a lesser degree, due to the greater sensitivity of the Typical/Maximum score. In all but one case the results are significant ($p < .05$) for both the Typical/Maximum score and the Typical score. The one exception is the Mann-Whitney comparison within educational levels 1 + 2 (Table 3), where the z for the Typical score is 1.89, $p = .059$.

A variation of the Hollingshead and Redlich (1958) education scale, described in Table 3, was used because it differentiates at the higher educational levels which are overrepresented in the FSP sample.

Results

Results to be presented demonstrate: (*a*) the presence of sex differences across stage score levels only when education is not controlled, (*b*) the presence of sex differences favoring men only at the postconventional level, and finally (*c*) the presence of sex-differentiated effects of educational level and employment status on stage score level.

Sex differences across stage score levels.—If, in order to probe Walker's conclusions, equal interval levels and a continuous distribution for the scale are assumed, an analysis of variance for adults reveals significant effects favoring men, $F(1,302) = 5.42$, $p < .02$. With analysis of covariance, in which amount of education is the covariate, the effect of sex is no longer significant. However, such an analysis is based on the assumption that the relation between education and moral development scores is the same for men and women. Later in this section I show that this assumption is unwarranted for the FSP data.

I have argued that statistics such as analysis of variance or t tests are inappropriate because the construct of moral reasoning is theoretically discontinuous and the intervals between stages cannot be assumed to be equal. Therefore, for all the analyses that follow, ordinal and nominal level nonparametric statistics were selected.

Using the Mann-Whitney test, there was a significant difference favoring males ($z = 2.80$, $p < .01$). Thus, when education is not controlled, significant sex differences are found using ANOVA or the Mann-Whitney test, whereas none were found by Walker (1984) using the Kolmogorov-Smirnov test.

Sex differences within stage score levels.—I have argued further that the most theoretically cogent analyses are conducted within rather than across stage score levels. Gilligan (1982) has suggested that, characteristically, women are concerned with welfare, caring, and responsibility more than they are with abstract, universalistic justice. Accordingly, within the Kohlberg system, more adult women than men should be represented at the conventional level (Stages 3 and 4, but particularly at Stage 3) and fewer should be represented at the higher, postconventional levels (Stages 5 and 6, but particularly at Stage 6).

This hypothesis was examined using prediction analysis (Froman & Hubert, 1980; Hildebrand, Laing, & Rosenthal, 1977) in which the adequacy of a model is assessed by determining the error cells in a contingency table—those cells that represent types of subjects that should not occur according to the theory—and then computing values of K (the proportion of subjects *observed* in all of the error cells) and U (the proportion of subjects *expected* in the error cells, given the marginal frequencies). An overall measure of a model's prediction success is given by $\nabla = 1 - K/U$. ∇ can be directly interpreted as the proportionate reduction of errors that is achieved by the theoretical predictions over the hypothesis of statistical independence. A test of statistical significance on ∇ can be performed to investigate whether the error reduction is significantly greater than zero or greater than the reduction occurring in another model. The results (Table 1) do not support the hypothesis (Kohlberg & Kramer, 1969) that women "fixate" at Stage 3. However, more women were found at Stage 4, the other conventional stage, as measured by both the Typical and the Maximum scores. The prediction of fewer women at postconventional stages was supported at Stage 5 for the Typical score and at Stage 6 for the Maximum score.

Sex differences in the effect on stage score level of educational level and employment status.—Based on data obtained primarily from men, Kohlberg and his colleagues have assumed that education and employment status are equally important determinants of stage score level for women. For example, Walker offers the nonemployed status of women as an explanation for their lower level of reasoning in Haan et al.'s sample

TABLE 1

RESULT OF THE PREDICTION ANALYSIS WITH NUMBER OF MALES AND FEMALES AT EACH KOHLBERG STAGE SCORE LEVEL

Stage	Females	Males	∇
Typical moral reasoning:			
2	11	4	. . .[a]
3	14	14	0
4	52	33	.19*
5	72	82	.10*
6	9	12	.18
N	158	145	. . .
Maximum moral reasoning:			
3	4	3	0
4	36	19	.28*
5	92	83	0
6	26	40	.25*
N	158	145	. . .

[a] No prediction concerning sex difference was made for preconventional stages, hence no analysis was conducted.

* $p < .05$.

(Haan, Langer, & Kohlberg, 1976). If he were correct, the moral level of employed women should be higher than that of nonemployed women. In fact, the 59 FSP women who were not employed did not differ significantly in stage score level from their employed peers (Mann-Whitney, $z = .58$, $p = .56$). Further, the correlation between stage score level and educational level was significant for men (tau $= .19$, $p < .01$) but not for women (tau $= .05$). Thus, for women, in contrast to men (in this highly educated sample), neither educational level nor employment per se are important determinants of level of moral judgment.

Similarly, the impact of postgraduate education on Stage 6 reasoning differs by sex. For males, but not for females, postgraduate education appears to be a necessary (although not sufficient) condition for Stage 6 reasoning; of the 12 males at Stage 6, 11 had at least a Master's degree, whereas this was true of only one of the nine Stage 6 women, $\chi^2(1, N = 21) = 10.54$, $p < .001$.

Sex differences in stage score level within educational level.—The educational level in men is much higher than that of women in the well-educated FSP sample (Mann-Whitney, $z = 8.33$, $p < .001$) as well as in the general population. As can be seen in Table 2, the sex difference favoring men in educational level is significant for every stage represented, except for Stage 2.

The final analysis was designed to ascertain if the higher stage score level of men exists at all educational levels, or instead exists only at the higher educational levels where men predominate. Mann-Whitney tests for sex differences in stage score within levels of education were calculated. For this analysis, educational levels 1 and 2 were combined, as were educational levels 6 and 7, to increase the number of women at the highest (MA and above) and men at the lowest (2 years or less of college) levels of education: At the high end, only three women were assigned to level 1, whereas 54 men were; all 10 parents at level 7 were women. It can be seen in Table 3 that the direction of significant sex differences in moral reasoning is reversed at the lowest and highest educational levels: At the highest educational level (1 and 2), men obtain a higher moral level than women, as expected; but at the lowest educational level (6 and 7), women obtain a higher moral level than men.

Discussion

In this sample of well-educated husbands and wives, sex differences in Kohlberg

TABLE 2

SEX DIFFERENCES IN EDUCATION LEVEL BY KOHLBERG STAGE SCORE LEVELS

KOHLBERG STAGE	FEMALES			MALES			MANN-WHITNEY
	Mdn	Q	N	Mdn	Q	N	Z
2	4	3–4	11	2	1–3	4	1.53
3	3	2–4	14	2	1–3	14	1.98*
4	4	3–5	52	3	2–3	33	3.11**
5	3	2–5	72	2	1–3	81	6.20***
6	3	3–4	9	2	1–2	12	2.87**

NOTE.—Medians (Mdn) and Interquartile Ranges (Q) are based on the interval that contains the 50th, 25th, and 75th percentiles, respectively. Due to the assumed ordinal nature of the construct, the interpolation method was not employed. One father at Stage 5 had a missing response on the education variable and is therefore not included in this analysis.
* $p < .05$.
** $p < .01$.
*** $p < .001$.

stage score levels are found when either analysis of variance or more appropriate ordinal or nominal level nonparametric statistics are used. When educational level is not controlled, more women are found at Stage 4 and more men at the postconventional level. Educational level and employment status are significantly related to men's but not to women's stage score level. For men, but not for women, postgraduate education appears to be a necessary (although not sufficient) condition for Stage 6 reasoning to occur. In this sample, the difference favoring males is found only at the higher educational levels, where men predominate. When men and women with 2 years or less of college are compared, the stage score level of women is higher. These data demonstrate that the presence and direction of the sex difference in stage score level depend on the educational level of the population studied.

In the remainder of this article, I discuss two issues: (a) the presence or absence of sex differences as a function of educational level of the sample studied, and (b) the cultural bias in Kohlberg's theory and constructs (in contradistinction to his measure).

The Relationship of Educational Level to Sex and Stage Score Level

The presence of sex differences in stage score level depends on the educational level of the population studied. The inconsistency of sex differences across the studies reviewed by Walker may be explained by variations in educational level among the samples studied. If men and women are equated for educational level and the educational range is mid-level, no sex difference in Kohlberg stage score is likely to be found. At the educational extremes, sex differences emerge, but in opposite directions.

TABLE 3

SEX DIFFERENCES IN TYPICAL/MAXIMUM STAGE BY LEVEL OF EDUCATION

EDUCATION LEVEL[a]	FEMALES			MALES			MANN-WHITNEY
	Mdn	Q	N	Mdn	Q	N	Z
1 + 2	5,5	4,5–5,5	41	5,5	4,6–5,6	92	2.10*
3	5,5	4,4–5,5	38	5,5	4,5–5,5	27	.35
4	4,4	3,4–5,5	36	5,5	4,4–5,5	15	1.85
5	5,5	4,4–5,5	15	5,5	5,5–5,5	4	.85
6 + 7	5,5	4,4–5,5	28	4,4	4,4–4,4	6	2.88**

NOTE.—Medians (Mdn) and Interquartile Ranges (Q) are based on the interval that contains the 50th, 25th, and 75th percentiles, respectively. Due to the assumed ordinal nature of the construct, the interpolation method was not employed.
[a] Education Levels: 1 = Ph.D., M.D., or J.D.; 2 = M.A.; 3 = B.A.+; 4 = B.A.; 5 = 3 years college; 6 = A.A. or 2 years college; 7 = 1 or fewer years of college.
* $p < .05$.
** $p < .01$.

The finding that, among individuals with a high school education but with 2 years of college or less, women score at a higher level than men, and indeed higher than other women with more education, has not (to my knowledge) been noted before. The reason for the finding may simply be that the high level of intelligence associated with postconventional reasoning guarantees more men than women that they will obtain a higher education. Alternatively, more women than men may take advantage of opportunities to resolve social conflicts at a high cognitive level in their interpersonal encounters, whereas more men than women may require the formal cognitive training provided by university education in order to apply principled reasoning to social-cognitive dilemmas. The finding that at the highest level of education more men than women use postconventional reasoning is consistent with results from almost all studies that do report a sex difference in adult stage score levels.

Kohlberg and Walker assume that when a control for education nullifies the sex difference in stage score level, it follows that the sex difference is spurious. However, educational level does not assess merely academic skills or knowledge of subject matter. It is in fact the best single index of social niche, indicating at its higher levels acculturation into the dominant values of the intelligentsia in Western society. Therefore, controlling for education begs the question in a dispute about the presence of sexual/cultural bias in Kohlberg's system. To the extent that sexual/cultural niche is controlled (by controlling for educational level), we must fail to find evidence of a sexual/cultural bias across stages.

It would be useful for Kohlberg or Walker to: (a) specify an educational threshold for each stage, (b) explain the sex difference in the "suitable" conditions necessary for postconventional reasoning to occur, (c) explain why postgraduate education is necessary for Stage 6 reasoning to occur in men but not in women, and (d) explain why full moral development requires a college degree in any society.

Sexual/Cultural Difference versus Deficit

The presence of a strong educational effect (above a theoretically justifiable threshold) raises the troubling issue of cultural elitism, which may be manifested as an apparent sex bias, in the event that more women than men are excluded from the "right kind" of educational experiences either by discrimination or by their own choice.

Kohlberg defends his system against the long-standing allegation of cultural elitism and ideological bias (e.g., Baumrind, 1978; Reid, 1984; Sampson, 1981; Schweder, 1982; Simpson, 1974; Sullivan, 1977) by attempting to distinguish between the intrinsic worth of persons and the value placed on their actions or judgments. As a Stage 6 thinker, Kohlberg claims that he and his system hold that all persons are of equal worth. However, the logic of Kohlberg's position leads to the contrary, and commonsense, position that a person's moral worth *is* judged by his or her actions, and these actions in turn are dependent upon the quality of the moral judgments that guide them. Kohlberg implicitly agrees, because he regards moral development, defined as a change toward greater differentiation, integration, and adaptation as measured by "higher" stages on the Kohlberg scale, as *the* primary objective of a "truly democratic educational process" (Kohlberg, 1981, p. 96). He also holds that there is a necessary, although complex, relation between moral judgment level and moral action, and that the relation is highest at the postconventional level, particularly at Stage 6. Clearly, then, individuals differ in their moral worth, and, in the Kohlberg system, their moral worth is measured by stage score level.

The charge of sexual or cultural *bias* in Kohlberg's theory arises from his claim in "From *Is* to *Ought*" (Kohlberg, 1981) that a developmentally advanced mode of reasoning about social issues, in particular, postconventional reasoning, is *morally* more mature than a developmentally prior mode, in particular, conventional reasoning. Were he to have claimed merely that conventional reasoning about such issues was more mature morally than preconventional reasoning he would have aroused little opposition, since in all societies children are socialized to internalize the mores of their society, and adults who reason about social issues at a preconventional level are regarded as socially immature. It is Kohlberg's claim that postconventional and, in particular, Stage 6 reasoning is *morally* superior to conventional reasoning because it meets the criterion of universality that opens him to the charge of sexual/cultural bias. Postconventional reasoning occurs less frequently in Eastern cultures and in Second and Third World countries and in women's thinking than in the reasoning of males with postgraduate educations. Yet Kohlberg claims "that there is a universalistically valid form of rational moral thought process which all persons could articulate assuming social and cultural conditions suitable to cognitive-moral stage development" (Kohlberg et al., 1983, p. 75). With equal access to such conditions, Kohlberg claims that no sex differences or cultural differences in moral level would be found. But in assuming that with equal access, all cultures would choose such conditions Kohlberg equates differences in the value placed on the universality criterion with deficits in orientation about morality.

Kohlberg chose to equate morality with justice because a justice orientation:

best renders our view of morality as universal. It restricts morality to a central minimal core, striving for universal agreement in the face of more relativist conceptions of the good.

Another reason for focusing upon justice is our concern for a cognitive or "rational" approach to morality. . . . Possibly the most important reason for focusing upon justice is that it is the most structural feature of moral judgment. . . . Justice "operations" of reciprocity and equality in interaction parallel logical operations or relations of equality and reciprocity in the non-moral cognitive domain. [Kohlberg et al., 1983, p. 93].

But Kohlberg's preference for reasoning about the logical priority of a principle such as life over an alternative principle such as property rights represents the peculiar bias of Western industrialized society (Reid, 1984; Sampson, 1981), particularly, of its male members. Moral leaders in non-Western societies do not appear to share Kohlberg's moral orientation. For example, in their study of African community leaders, Harkness, Edwards, and Super (1981) failed to find any instances of Stage 5 or 6 reasoning. Similarly, some "postconventional" reasoners (such as kibbutz members) who share Western values but emphasize communal and collective moral principles rather than individualistic ones are partially missed or misunderstood by Kohlberg's model (Snarey, Reimer, & Kohlberg, 1985). Indeed, as Emler (1983) suggests, Kohlberg's higher stages may constitute secular humanist values couched in the abstract language of individual rights, reciprocity, distributive justice, and equity (Simpson, 1974). Gilligan (1982) claims that Kohlberg's notion presents an incomplete picture, and that there is a fundamentally dialectical tension between justice conceived as impartiality and justice conceived as compassionate concern. The latter expresses a *preference* for concrete, particularistic thinking shown by more of the highly educated women than men in the FSP study.

Morality has signified much more to philosophers throughout the ages than the "central minimal core" Kohlberg chooses to study. The kinds of phenomena Kohlberg's "minimal core" fails to encompass include: (a) judgments about what constitutes a good and meaningful life, (b) acts of social responsibility that go beyond rights and duties to a commitment to transform society in accord with one's social ideal, and (c) special obligations to friends and family that arise from ingroup identity. These omissions are central to alternative perspectives on morality.

For example, Buddhists and Marxists, so different in most ways, share an understanding of individuals as socially embedded from conception, so that as individuals mature they become able to conceive of nature as their own real body; physical nature constitutes human beings' inorganic flesh and the social environment their organic flesh. Alienation is a consequence of separating oneself from the physical and social environment in which one is naturally embedded. This view of the individual as socially embedded rather than as autonomous and self-centered, and this emphasis on the importance of practical wisdom, are commonly thought to characterize more women than men and more individuals in Second and Third World countries than our own. It should generate a perspective on morality as practical, transformational, and concerned with concrete, particular persons and contexts.

By contrast, Kohlberg, in common with Kant, restricts the term "moral" to the formulation of universal, rational principles of objective and impartial treatment with the emphasis entirely on speculative wisdom (or sophia). Practical wisdom or praxis is relegated to the preconventional or conventional levels. Praxis is a term rooted in Judeo-Christian tradition that refers to the individual's and the community's commitment to realize the Good in ritual, custom, and ethical action. It was adopted by Marx to refer to the transformational, by contrast with the interpretive, function of human thought and action. Sexual/cultural differences emerge in studies that restrict morality to Kohlberg's minimal core because of its partiality toward a form of formal, abstract reasoning that is functionally ill-suited to the circumstances of individuals who occupy nonprofessional niches in any society, or who embrace collectivist objectives.

I agree with Kohlberg that a conception of ideal moral judgment should rest on an adequate conception of what it is. I affirm further that an adequate conception of ideal moral judgment should not rest on what it is not and cannot be. Were Stages 5 and 6 equally distributed among both sexes, and all peoples, there could be no charge of sexual/cultural bias against the Kohlberg system (although the system could still be viewed as insufficient). But Stages 5 and 6 are not equally distributed, and so the charge of bias cannot be dismissed as a myth. Further, some persons capable of universalistic moral reasoning reject it as an orientation because it is an idealized notion of morality that substitutes conformity of judgment to an ideal for conformity of action to judgment, and thus justifies not conforming one's morally relevant actions to one's moral judgments.

Ethical universalism neither is nor ought to be. Cultural pluralism, including ethical diversity, is beneficial to the survival of the human species, provided that all parties to a dispute are able to decentrate from their contradictory moral orientations and agree upon procedures for resolving practical disputes that arise from their differences about how life should be lived.

Those of us who want to investigate "moral" phenomena now speak in many different voices, precluding the use of the term "moral" for any one voice. Kohlberg and his colleagues have chosen to study the development of universal principles concerning justice as fairness. Other researchers have elected to study quite different phenomena within the moral domain. I recommend, therefore, that each of us select an operationally well-defined term with minimal surplus meaning to describe the theoretical construct we claim to have measured, and that we all agree to reserve the term "moral" for the domain.

References

Baumrind, D. (1978). A dialectical materialist's perspective on knowing social reality. In W. Damon (Ed.), *New directions for child development: No. 2. Moral development* (pp. 61–82). San Francisco: Jossey-Bass.

Baumrind, D. (1982). Are androgynous individuals more effective persons and parents? *Child Development, 53,* 44–75.

Colby, A., Kohlberg, L., Gibbs, J., & Lieberman, M. (1983). A longitudinal study of moral judgment. *Monographs of the Society for Research in Child Development, 48*(1–2, Serial No. 200).

Cortese, A. J. (1984). Standard issue scoring of moral reasoning: A critique. *Merrill-Palmer Quarterly, 30,* 227–246.

Emler, N. (1983). Moral character. In H. Weinreich-Haste & D. Locke (Eds.), *Morality in the making* (pp. 47–71). New York: Wiley.

Froman, T., & Hubert, L. J. (1980). Application of prediction analysis to developmental priority. *Psychological Bulletin, 87,* 136–146.

Gilligan, C. (1982). *In a different voice: Psychological theory and women's development.* Cambridge, MA: Harvard University Press.

Haan, N., Langer, J., & Kohlberg, L. (1976). Family patterns of moral reasoning. *Child Development, 47,* 1204–1206.

Harkness, S., Edwards, C. P., & Super, C. M. (1981). Social roles and moral reasoning: A case study in a rural African community. *Developmental Psychology, 17,* 595–603.

Hildebrand, D., Laing, M., & Rosenthal, A. (1977). *Prediction analysis of cross classifications.* New York: Wiley.

Hollingshead, A. B., & Redlich, F. C. (1958). *Social class and mental illness.* New York: Wiley.

Holstein, C. (1976). Development of moral judgment: A longitudinal study of males and females. *Child Development, 47,* 51–61.

Kohlberg, L. (1981). *Essays on moral development: Vol. 1. The philosophy of moral development: Moral stages and the idea of justice.* San Francisco: Harper & Row.

Kohlberg, L. (1984). *Essays on moral development: Vol. 2. The psychology of moral development: The nature and validity of moral stages.* San Francisco: Harper & Row.

Kohlberg, L., & Elfenbein, D. (1981). Capital punishment, moral development, and the constitution. In L. Kohlberg (Ed.), *The philosophy of moral development* (pp. 243–293). San Francisco: Harper & Row.

Kohlberg, L., & Kramer, R. (1969). Continuities and discontinuities in childhood and adult moral development. *Human Development, 12,* 93–120.

Kohlberg, L., Levine, C., & Hewer, A. (1983). *Moral stages: A current formulation and a response to critics.* Basel: S. Karger.

Rawls, J. (1971). *A theory of justice.* Cambridge, MA: Harvard University, Belknap Press.

Reid, B. V. (1984). An anthropological reinterpretation of Kohlberg's stages of moral development. *Human Development, 27,* 56–74.

Sampson, E. E. (1981). Cognitive psychology as ideology. *American Psychologist, 36,* 730–743.

Schweder, R. A. (1982). Liberalism as destiny [Review of *Essays on moral development: Vol. 1. The philosophy of moral development: Moral stages and the idea of justice*]. *Contemporary Psychology, 27,* 421–424.

Siegel, S. (1956). *Nonparametric statistics for the behavioral sciences.* New York: McGraw-Hill.

Simpson, E. L. (1974). Moral development research. *Human Development, 17,* 81–106.

Snarey, J. R., Reimer, J., & Kohlberg, L. (1985). Development of social-moral reasoning among Kibbutz adolescents: A longitudinal cross-cultural study. *Developmental Psychologist, 21,* 3–17.

Sullivan, E. V. (1977). A study of Kohlberg's structural theory of moral development: A critique of liberal social science ideology. *Human Development, 20,* 353–376.

Walker, L. J. (1984). Sex differences in the development of moral reasoning: A critical review. *Child Development, 55,* 677–691.

New Ideas in Psychol. Vol. 7, No. 3, pp. 295–314, 1989
Printed in Great Britain

0732–118X/89 $3.00 + 0.00

CARING — IN AN INTERPRETIVE VOICE

BILL PUKA

Department of Philosophy, Rensselaer Polytechnic Institute, Troy, NY 12180–3590, U.S.A.

Abstract—What is implied by offering an interpretive account in social science, rather than a statistical one? This question is pursued in the context of Carol Gilligan's reflections on her own work, on *In A Different Voice* and the account of care and gender it presents. In particular, consideration is given to the relation of statistical findings to theoretical inferences, and the interpretive problems faced in criticizing "patriarchal" views of moral development, such as Kohlberg's stage theory.

Carol Gilligan's Response to Critics (1986) reveals the underlying approach to theory that shapes her influential view of caring and women's development. Her brief reflections on method should substantially alter how her substantial audience views this vision. But, more broadly, these reflections should inform our understanding of other influential writings in gender studies and critical theory [Chodorow (1978) and Miller (1976) are chief examples]. Such accounts share Gilligan's attempt to utilize empirical observations without being determined by their statistical significance or extent.

The main points of Gilligan's Response form the following outline:

(1) Critics mistakenly view *In a Different Voice* (Gilligan, 1982) as a statistical argument for sex differences in moral development. They then rebut this argument with evidence of no sex differences in justice development, as measured by the Kohlberg scale. The Walker (1984) study is cited especially.

(2) This rebuttal misinterprets the "different voice hypothesis" and the insights it has yielded. Its argument is interpretive and its empirical citations merely illustrative. It claims that since current theories of moral development are based primarily on male experience and male needs, studying women will likely reveal a different moral perspective.

(3) In fact attending to "what had been missed by leaving out women" has revealed "a different way of constituting the idea of self and the idea of what is moral." It has defined "a shift in perspective that changes the key terms of moral discourse such as the concept of self, the idea of relationship."

(4) To reveal this shift, the voice of responsible caring has been contrasted with an ethics of rights and justice. Where care promotes empathy, relationality, responsiveness in context, and also avoiding hurt and rendering aid, justice stresses legalistic protection for individual autonomy, for all people and situations alike.

(5) Since the Kohlberg scale assumes patriarchal conceptions of self, other, and morality, women will score well on it, or not, depending on how studiously they practice male competences, how seriously they play male games. Sometimes they may do this well, usually not as well, one would expect. But such gender differences do not show spontaneous moral preferences and perspectives. They do not reveal differences in competence with gender-dominant moral themes.

383

(6) Last, critics show no awareness of recent research showing sex differences *by moral theme* reported by Lyons (1983), Langdale (1984) and Johnston (1985). They also seem unaware of criticisms by Haan (1985) and Baumrind and Pulos (1985) of Walker's literature review claiming no significant sex differences.

In this essay I will think through Gilligan's distinction between a statistical and interpretive account of care, or gender development, tracing out its surprising implications. (Some of these may be sobering for her supporters as well as her critics.) Several key aims will be pursued: The first is to affirm and elaborate the significance of Gilligan's claim that her type of view has been fundamentally misassessed by empirical critics. The so-called Kohlberg/Gilligan debate must be framed on a very different, interpretive level. The second is to suggest that the nature of an interpretive account is more complex than it would appear; it has unrecognized, unwelcome implications for Gilligan's own view, as well as Kohlberg's. Since this sort of account is so encompassing and holistic, it actually diffuses the significance of Gilligan's bias claims—the significance of gender bias and theme bias in Kohlberg's theory. It also diffuses the apparent force of any new or future evidence for care as a constructive alternative.

The third aim is to suggest, therefore, that we are far from having enough empirical data or interpretive accounting to begin a serious comparison of Kohlberg's and Gilligan's views. Thus we should wonder at the prominent belief that Gilligan's gender analysis, by its fundamental nature, substantially decides the Kohlberg/Gilligan debate. This possibility is undermined by the holistic nature of interpretive analysis, which Gilligan committedly chooses. Likewise, we should wonder at the belief that Kohlberg's decades of methodological refinement, empirical findings, and theoretical justifications simply overwhelm Gilligan's sparse interpretations. This view is undermined by Kohlberg's faiiure to address whole levels of analysis that are crucial to Gilligan's interpretive account. In an interpretive account, robust theoretical analysis at some levels (e.g., in structural aspects of cognition or meta-ethics) may not compensate for missing analyses at other levels (e.g., in gender formation and self concept).

Finally, this discussion hopes to illustrate that an "interpretive account" is by far the most serious and appropriate theoretical model for moral development. In part this is because the field places special emphasis on qualitative research and holistic (cross-disciplinary) theory. Moreover, I suggest, this interpretive approach actually embodies the logic of mature care, thereby further illustrating care's strength. Mature caring approaches problems of observation and understanding mindful of their vast complexities and holistic interrelations. It recognizes the need to become involved in long-term cognitive struggle that will not likely admit of neat, categorial solutions. (Among such solutions would be a .05 level of statistical significance in certain empirical results, or demonstrated bias in certain methods of research and conceptual analysis.)

The difficulty in pursuing these aims is not in the logic of analysis, which will seem deceptively simply here. Rather it involves driving home the force of what is obvious and what it obviously implies. Thus my method will be to ruminate, focus, call to attention, rather than to assert and argue points. I will address how observers see (and might see) conceptions of moral development, as much as what these conceptions themselves maintain.*

THE STATISTICAL RESPONSE

Gilligan's main point of clarification on her view (outlined above) should have a powerful impact on the current response to care. Most of Gilligan's critics within the research community have viewed her position as empirically derived, or at least aspiring to be. They have taken her critique of bias in moral development research, in Kohlberg's research especially, as focused on research design. Gilligan seems to challenge Kohlberg's statistical claims from such a perspective. This is the impression created, for example, when Gilligan faults the hypothetical (artificial) nature of Kohlberg's research dilemmas, with their forced-choice format, and when she warns of the biasing effects of his all-male sampling. If these biases were confirmed, by using alternative research methods and showing significantly different results, the case would be closed in their eyes. If not, Gilligan's case would be closed.

Critics also have interpreted Gilligan's reliance on several studies in her book as revealing the research evidence from which her theoretical claims arose (see above, pp. 1–2). Response protocols from these studies are cited in each chapter. Seemingly they provide the research basis for each position taken, for each component of care and each contrast with justice. Moreover, when Gilligan speaks of an "association" between the care theme and female gender development ("its association is an empirical observation"), critics hear claims of "empirical correlation" in the normal (statistical) sense (see above, p. 1). They

---

*Devotees of both Kohlberg's and Gilligan's approach in moral development have perceived drafts of this essay as veiled apologies for "the other side." In this polarized climate it is important that the reader at least entertain the hypothesis that the essay speaks to both sides, as its stated aims indicate. Also, given the perspectival focus of our discussion it is important that readers take several perspectives on the views advanced, especially when they seem shallow and faulty on first glance. (This would constitute a fair hearing or sympathetic reading of the essay, as befits the preferred ethic of each perspective being discussed.) Those who side strongly with Gilligan in the Kohlberg/Gilligan debate, will more naturally find this essay biased toward Kohlberg. Its major claim is that an interpretive account is encompassing and holistic, and must be assessed in terms of its overall balance of pros and cons. Issues of moral theme or gender outlook, including bias in these areas, are merely components in this account. Since Kohlberg's research has almost a 30 year headstart on Gilligan's, it is understandable that it has filled in more components of the required account. Since it is much more complete, and has many strong points, it is likely to be a more credible view, despite its flaws. Still, I believe that Gilligan's formative analysis proceeds at a deeper level than Kohlberg's in key ways. Thus it is more challenging to Kohlberg's theory than may be apparent to some. Some devotees of Kohlberg's approach find this assumption too generous to Gilligan. Moral development is a field of social science primarily, in which hard data hold more sway than interpretive speculations on bias. I believe, however, that the critical tradition and critical feminism in particular have shown otherwise. Of course, in looking at conflicts between Kohlberg's and Gilligan's views, we should keep in mind the many ways their positions are compatible and even complementary.

assume that Gilligan's empirical studies have found empirical sex differences in moral development. The actual numbers showing significance will be forthcoming.

It was from this perspective, clearly, that the critics Gilligan responds to concentrated on evidence for no sex differences. But it is also on such bases that many rigorous researchers simply dismissed Gilligan's 'Different Voice' from the outset. (On similar bases, many of the writings in gender studies have been passed by in this arena.) Gilligan's book, critics notice, offers no quantitatvie findings or statistical analyses. It cites only the most exploratory pilot research to support claims. The research interviews used in Gilligan's studies were neither standardized nor validated in any rigorous way, nor was a standardized coding or scoring system used to evaluate results. Even today, the scoring system used by Lyons (1983) to verify Gilligan's claims remains under major construction. More importantly, it has never coded for *levels* of care, though such levels are what place Gilligan's view in the field of moral development. It is the developmental psychologies of Freud, Piaget, Kohlberg, and Erikson that Gilligan criticizes, and contrasts with care. Gilligan's references to bias in Kohlberg's research methods, as critics see it, are not amply rigorous. They are not empirically demonstrated.

Gilligan's 'Response to Critics' holds that these bases of criticism are misguided. Though empirical evidence and methodological analysis are hardly beside the point, they do not *define* Gilligan's position as critics assume. They merely figure into that position, and often in a secondary way. For example, while Kohlberg's forced-choice dilemmas may pull for certain lines of moral judgment, their bias rests more heavily on two conceptual assumptions underlying them: (1) adequate moral reasoning solves all problems, and does so decisively; (2) moral judgment is, by definition, a form of conflict resolution. Thus even when research respondents resist the pull of Kohlberg's dilemmas, when they try to skirt conflicts of interest, their response is evaluated relative to the problems these dilemmas want solved. Their reluctance on the way to decision is not counted, though it should be. In this way, then, the methodological pull problem is conceptually based and interpretively uncovered. It is not shown by the empirical frequency of ultimately decisive conflict resolutions Kohlberg records, though this evidence can sometimes bolster the interpretive point.

If Gilligan's self-descriptions are correct, and such descriptions seem easy to substantiate, her empirical critics are guilty of the most fundamental and pervasive sort of error. This could hardly be more important to care's reputation or status among researchers.

Many of Gilligan's legion supporters mistakenly view care in this same overly empirical light. When Gilligan claimed that by attending to "what had been missed by leaving out women" she had uncovered "a different way of constituting the idea of self and the idea of what is moral," and when Gilligan described the compassionate, relational features of caring, some supporters assumed she was directly reporting new and substantial data on sex differences. She was describing significant evidence of a divergent developmental track uncovered in her studies. Many assumed, apparently, that this evidence rivaled that of "patriarchal" researchers, statistically or otherwise. After all, it was being used to criticize their evidence and pose a similar sort of alternative view. It was derived from research methods that built upon, and were designed explicitly to transcend, those of Piaget and Kohlberg.

Many supporters now assume, apparently, that Gilligan's empirical research has basically discredited Kohlberg's, by showing bias in his empirical methods and by producing reliably discrepant data. The only research task left open, it now seems, is to amass more and more data of a harder and harder (statistical) sort, to finish the job.

Gilligan's interpretation of her work undermines this supportive response as well. The strength of Gilligan's account, in her view, cannot be assessed primarily by the strength of her own formative findings, nor by her methodological criticisms. These may provide clues and initial grounds for interpretive criticism. They may suggest alternative visions to dominant views, but they do not contend directly with rival positions. In the same way, even the harder statistical findings of rival views cannot decide their case, according to Gilligan. Nor can these data contend directly with care. This is the more important point which may take a bit longer to sink in. Let us consider it.

The prevailing ideology of research psychology favors statistical significance above all. It views matters of conceptual bias or interpretive dispute as troublesome side-issues. They often can be handled, it is assumed, without substantially altering the evidence. Under this assumption, and assuming Kohlberg's initially soft data are now hardened sufficiently, Gilligan's project simply makes no sense. It should never have been launched in the first place, given her sparse and soft data. The same can be said for most leading accounts in gender studies or critical theory that generate sweeping empirical generalizations from meager clinical observations. Indeed, many empirical researchers see no point to them. How can their prescientific approach be taken seriously in the present research era?

From the interpretive point of view, however, interpretation and critical analysis *create* the evidence. They decide, above all, that findings of a sort are evidence of care in particular, or of justice reasoning and not care, or of development as opposed to mere change. Interpretation determines when statistical significance is significant. And from this broader perspective it is the rigorous researcher, significant data in hand, that seems a babe-in-the-woods at the .05 level.

Of course, Piaget and Kohlberg also distinguish themselves as researchers by emphasizing the *qualitative* aspects of their data. Moral judgment is not merely verbal behavior, nor judgment about "morals." Rather it is reasoning that meets certain justified criteria of moral relevance and adequacy. It is *interpreted* data in that respect. However, Gilligan's sense of "interpretive account" goes well beyond this, as we will see.

UNDER INTERPRETATION

In Gilligan's eyes, her position stands on its ability to interpret all types of germane evidence accurately ("coherently") and insightfully—more accurately and insightfully than "the opposition." Coherence and insight are gained by uncovering the relations among varied types of evidence and their contexts of observation. From this interpretive perspective, Gilligan's empirical case is Kohlberg's empirical case, as well as the empirical case of Piaget and the other patriarchal researchers combined. It is both sex differences and no sex differences, theme differences and similarities. The point of contention, at the interpretive level, is over what both types of results show. Do they show human development of gender bias, moral adequacy or legalism? To get at this "empirical" question, one must go beyond the so-called data, qualitative or otherwise.

In Gilligan's interpretive account, the manner in which patriachal theorists define their research domain, or base research methods on those definitions, or rely on philosophical principles to reconstruct findings, constitute "data." Even the primarily speculative processes by which Freud or Erikson evolved a vision of moral development count as data. These assumptions, doctrines and methods, as well as how they are related, is what Gilligan observes when she observes context, when she observes bias. Yet what sort of statistic can analyze these phenomena and relationships significantly?

Notice that on this interpretation of care, Gilligan need not have conducted any research of her own to launch her account. Her case against "male"-oriented justice is made, for the most part, through reinterpreting Kohlberg's findings. Even Gilligan's positive case for care may have been derived by reinterpreting the alleged inadequacies of Kohlberg's lower stages as strengths, and promoting the subsidiary virtues of his higher stages to prominence. After all, as Gilligan notes, Kohlberg's stage 3 justice is founded on empathy and trust, on maintaining close relationships and talking problems out, on avoiding hurt and offering generous help to others. Likewise, stages 4, 5 and 6 contain subsidiary prescriptions to aid others and cater to group welfare. Thus while Gilligan's empirical studies extend, detail, and illustrate the case better, they are not that case. This shows how far off Gilligan's empiricist critics are, under her self-interpretation.

To many of Gilligan's most reflective supporters, the workings of this interpretive logic were obvious in her work all along. It is the empirical researcher's mistake to see interpretive method as an empirical hedge, as a way to compensate for soft or missing data with conceptual argument. To the contrary, interpretive method takes a broader and deeper perspective on its empirical phenomenon than does empirical research. It tries to get a truer assessment of the weight that various sorts of data, across the board, should have on our beliefs.

Yet there is a direct and far reaching implication of interpretive logic that supporters also must keep in mind. Just as the overall strength of patriarchal positions cannot be assessed by the statistical significance of their empirical results, so future Gilligan research which might show sex differences or moral theme differences cannot decide care's case. We cannot have it both ways. When Gilligan's 'Response' cites three studies showing sex differences (Langdale, 1984; Lyons, 1983; Johnston, 1985) it seems that their existence alone had significance.

But on Gilligan's logic, their findings might not even strengthen care's case. Everything depends on how well such studies, along with any other evidence in the empirical portion of care, can be figured into the care position overall. A key to this interpretive problem, which Gilligan does not try to turn here, involves interpreting the evidence as evidence for care *in particular*. Other interpretations are always possible, even plausible, and other plausible interpretations surely will be forthcoming from "rival" human development camps.

It is for this very reason that the seemingly decisive Walker review, showing no substantial sex differences in justice development, can only add weight to Kohlberg's position. Whether it does, and how much it does, depends on the competition between two views: Kohlberg's view that "no differences" show human (cross-gender) development, and Gilligan's view that "no differences" match spontaneous male development with female learning of male competences. Even if the Walker review were methodologically flawless (as Gilligan doubts) it would be little more than food for interpretive thought in this sense.*

Of course, the interpretive competition between Gilligan and Kohlberg may seem asymmetrical in a patriarchal research environment. Gilligan's account, like any feminist account, cannot be vulnerable to the strong gender biases and limitations evident in patriarchal views. Thus significant data should play a much stronger role in care's interpretive case as a matter of course. They simply could not be explained away interpretively, as Piaget's and Kohlberg's have been by Gilligan. No doubt, there is some truth to this view. But it does not grasp the sheer magnitude of the interpretive task. Let us consider it.

THE INTERPRETIVE TASK

On the critical side of interpretation, we must be aware of how numerous and wide-ranging the sources of bias are in any account. They are far more numerous and difficult to uncover in interpretive accounts than in statistical ones. (Interpretive accounts must *encompass* statistical accounts, thus compounding the bias problem.) Gilligan's overall tally of conceptual slants and limitations has barely begun to be calculated. Yet it is the presumed end-point of this calculation, and its comparison with Piaget's or Kohlberg's tally, that is crucial interpretively. It is the presumed end-point that allows us to compare the credibility of Kohlberg's and Gilligan's holistic interpretations.

Some of Gilligan's feminist critics sense a class and ethnic bias in caring values and in the developmental path to caring consciousness. At least two of the three studies cited in Gilligan's book seemingly show such a "bias" by sampling affluent, white Harvard students only (Gilligan, 1982, pp. 2–3). These critics also sense an ironic acquiescence to sexist stereotypes in care's virtues of nurturance,

---

*Some critics fault Gilligan's response to critics for internal inconsistency: "She claims that care is not a statistical account on the one hand, then challenges Walker's statistics on the other." By understanding the nature of an interpretive account, we see that both stances have their proper place.

self-sacrifice, and forgiveness. Such critical "intuitions" must be taken seriously at the interpretive level. All such interpretations have a primary power here that would be secondary in empirical accounts. For while Gilligan clearly is aware of the stereotypical and sexist brands of caring, she has yet to offer solid interpretive grounding to distinguish care as cognitive development and competence from care as sexist socialization and noble self-delusion.

Gilligan openly acknowledges that she has not reliably identified the distinctive sources of care. "No claims are made about the origin of the differences described" (Gilligan, 1982, p. 4). While this disclaimer is understandable empirically—it sounds primarily *empirical* unfortunately—it is devastating interpretively. For just as well-supported interpretations are needed here to fend off possible bias charges, they are even more important for constructing the positive case for care as moral development. They are crucial to showing that care *develops,* rather than being learned, and that it is *morally progressive* over time. They are crucial to showing that care is in fact an *organized moral* orientation at all, rather than a set of social mores or value preferences. Interpretive gaps on care's constructive side seem Gilligan's most serious problem. This is especially the case where they compound with biases on the interpretive level to weaken her account overall. It is easy to see why.

The constructive side of Gilligan's interpretive task, as noted, involves winning the data for care. Part of this process is explanatory, and part involves comparative justification. In key respects these must be interwined. To assert that care constitutes a moral theme, a holistic cognitive orientation, and a developing process involves extensive interpretation. As noted, these features of cognition are not merely observations read off descriptively from what people say. But simply having an intrepretive *slant* does not make an interpretive *account*. An account is explicit by nature; it is an explanatory accounting of something. An interpretive account or theory must explain its interpretations, and show why they make sense. Part of this process is comparative and evaluative by nature: Why does this interpretation make more sense than some others?

In Gilligan's case, the comparative process is most salient because she is criticizing other views. She is making a case against justice theory and "human" development, a case for *divergent* care and gender development. Thus she must show that her account of the deep failings of justice is more telling than alternative accounts of its near-complete adequacy. She must show that care truly diverges from justice and that it is a comparably adequate or better ethic. Taking this sort of comparative stance is typical of critical and feminist accounts in general. We do not merely offer one possible or even plausible way to see things, with little to recommend it. Rather, we claim to offer clarification and insight. This means not only that we explain the phenomena glimpsed by patriarchal theories better than they do, but we explain the new phenomena we have uncovered in a better way than they can.

When we listen to a respondent express concern for relationships or a strong reluctance to hurt others, some of us may hear two value commitments being expressed. (The first may not seem morally focused, the second might.) Others may hear two purely personal preferences. On other occasions a respondent may deprecate self-interest as "selfishness" and praise the attempt to talk out problems with friends, in hopes of reaching consensus. These preferences may sound unrelated to the foregoing in some ways, related in others. They may seem interrelated to us as observers but not clearly interrelated to our respondents, as *they* tell it.

When Gilligan listens to these four concerns, and others, she hears strains in a holistic moral theme, strands in an integrated conceptual web. She hears a resounding relationship among these concerns, and still others, such as the need to show compassion and the need to protect oneself. After listening for a long time, and listening apparently to the theorists she criticizes, Gilligan hears the workings of a cognitive *system* beneath these expressed concerns. It is a system that seems so enduring and integrated that it can actually develop. That is, it can undergo drastic transformation, yet remain intact. (For example, care can go from a variant of egoism at Level I to altruism at Level II, and still remain care, as Gilligan hears it.)

Now the interpretive question, for Gilligan as for us, is which is the "different" voice? This must be Gilligan's question in forming her view as well as ours in evaluating it. Which of us hears what is being said, and which is just hearing voices (our own voices)? This is the heart of an interpretive account.

Just as hearing with a certain interpretive bent does not account interpretively for what one hears, so explaining one's bent need not recommend it. Gilligan's account must carefully frame the different ways a voice can be heard and explicitly weigh their relative plausibility, deciding on her intuitive favorite. And the more creatively it "hears" data—the more projectively and distinctively Gilligan interprets them—the more intrepretive grounding is needed. Gilligan must provide this grounding for herself, as well as others.

From the Kohlbergian perspective, "care" sounds like the expression of non-moral concerns, of socialized and non-developing preferences for certain conventional values. It also sounds like component features of justice, in some respects. Such relevant alternative renderings must figure into care's interpretive account, care's interpretive critique. Or they must be ruled out by it. Until they are, the question of whether care is really a different voice at all remains wide open.*

---

*These considerations may seem idle to some, raising undue worry about interpretive improbabilities. The data for care are clear and compelling to many Gilligan supporters, "striking," as Gilligan often puts it. The moral tone and adequacy of these data, and even their female associations, are intuitively obvious. So is their divergence from justice. As a result, the constructive problem for interpretive care is small, as some see it. But this is just the sort of support an interpretive case cannot accept. It is more appropriate, oddly, on the empirical level. Since interpretive accounts are explanations by nature, they can only take intuitions, like statistically significant data, into account. As explanations, interpretive accounts are characteristically variable, also, admitting an array of plausible alternatives. (This variability and the explanatory imperative it creates only increases as interpretations become increasingly inclusive and projective, as they depict cognitive holism and systematic integration beneath surface verbalization.) Suppose we are asked

LEVEL OF INTERPRETATION

Thus far we have considered how an interpretive account differs from a statistical, or primarily data-based account, and the implications of this difference. We will focus now more specifically on the type of interpretive account that Gilligan and most critical theorists attempt.

Gilligan's interpretive edge relative to patriarchal justice theory rests on two main factors. On the constructive side, in the positive case for care, it rests on relating moral judgment to self-concept, and then relating these concepts further to gender. It rests on showing the dependence of moral judgment and adequacy on the way one conceives problems of relationship, the problems to be worked out by moral judgment. Then it involves showing that one's gender identity poses relationships and their problems differently. (Marxian analyses portray the dependence of moral ideology on the politics of class struggle, and on general socio-economic conditions, in similar fashion.) Patriarchal theories of moral development are less complete and accurate than Gilligan's, presumably because they fail to take these relations into account.

On the critical side, Gilligan's interpretive edge rests on showing that empirical evidence for justice development is tainted by its contexts of observation or interpretation. Again, the analysis is founded ultimately on gender identity and relationships. But here their relation to preferences and ideology is more prominent. The deep ideology of individualism and the protection of autonomy is preferred by males because it serves their gender identity needs for individuation. The moral logic of individual rights and merit (just desert) serves this ideology best. Thus it is preferred in both male judgment and the patriarchal development theory that interprets it. Here male preferences are set as objective and universal standards of moral maturity and adequacy for all. As Gilligan (1979) notes, the deep ideology of individualism coheres with other basic ideologies of Western culture and ethnocentrism, as well as socio-economic status and class-ism. Together these ideologies influence the way dominant approaches define research problems, design methodologies to pose them, and theorize about results. Yet these influences have been overlooked by justice theorists, in both their account of moral reasoning as they observe it, and their account of *how* they observe it. In these respects their views are biased as well as limited.

Thus while Gilligan may not account for the moral distinctiveness, cognitive

---

the question, "Did you consider other ways of seeing things, other likely causes of bias in Piaget or Kohlberg that do not reflect gender or moral theme, other ways of seeing empathic or relational responses that are either compatible with justice or not necessarily connected in a developing cognitive system?" We must be able to answer, "Yes, we considered these alternatives very carefully and here is why we decided against them in reaching our conclusions." So far there is little indication that these central interpretive projects have even begun in Gilligan's account. This is testimony to just how difficult a task Gilligan has taken on by choosing to offer an interpretive account rather than a merely empirical or statistical one. It indicates just how far care has to go to become what it aspires to be.

holism, or inherently developmental nature of care, she does interpret both care and justice as pragmatic strategies for preserving identity. She shows us how these orientations may deal with problems of relationship (moral or otherwise) which arise from the way we conceive self and other. Ultimately Gilligan may wish to define moral orientation directly in such terms.

It is from this interpretive perspective, and from a comparison of care and justice as such strategies, that Gilligan can show why justice is *too* clear, decisive and consistent—that is why justice is legalistic, absolutistic and rigid. It is in comparison with the proper amount of concern and compassion care tells us to show—to show even when others do not "deserve" it—that justice appears insensitive and downright punitive. Those trying to express their empathic connection with others find it so, as their (gender) identities beckon them to. By contrast, those whose identities seek to protect autonomy, find the effects of others doing likewise as their just due.

It is important to notice that these two sides of Gilligan's interpretive edge do not concern particular, circumscribed phenomena. They do not identify isolated sources of bias, isolated limitations in patriarchal research. Rather, they extend Gilligan's *levels* of research and analysis beyond those encompassed by the views of moral development that she criticizes. This not only shows that Gilligan's account is interpretive rather than statistical, but indicates the type of interpretive account it is. It shows the level at which it is pitched and the ground it covers. As these levels are very broad and interrelated, so is the ground they cover and so is the depth they achieve. Neither Piaget nor Kohlberg, for example, have a theory of moral self (in Gilligan's sense) or of gender development. They have no research evidence on the relation or lack of relation between self-concept and their moral stages. Neither do they have a theory of ideology and its influence (or lack of it) on their brand of research method and theory. Kohlberg tries to justify his definition of moral, as opposed to nonmoral, reasoning and his ordering of the moral stage sequence, by using philosophical criteria of moral relevance and adequacy. However, Gilligan's ideological level of analysis would underlie and undermine such philosophic justifications, calling their rational objectivity into question. This is what makes her critique so radical, so potentially devastating. This is what makes feminist and critical accounts typically so.*

---

*As noted, there is a strong empirical component to the deeper levels of analysis. The way patriarchal researchers define their research domain and methods, using philosophical principles to interpret observations and order them, counts as "data" in Gilligan's account. Yet these factors obviously do not figure into Piaget's or Kohlberg's account at the empirical level either. Thus even the empirical portion of the patriarchal case is undermined inclusively from below. Ultimately, when working at the interpretive level Gilligan has chosen, this additional sort of empirical evidence and conceptual analysis must be the basis of each competing theory, or it must be explained away. Moreover, as noted, this comparative effort is necessary simply to claim the empirical *existence* of the phenomenon in question—to claim findings of care as care, justice as justice, moral development as development rather than socialization. Gilligan has extended the notion of qualitative data to this broad extent, by offering her sort of interpretive account.

Again, all this may be obvious to Gilligan's most interpretively-minded
supporters, those in gender studies and critical theory especially. But its full
implications for evaluating Gilligan's view, or any feminist or critical view, may
be surprising. We confront extremely difficult problems here of matching levels
of interpretation to each other correctly for comparison across accounts. Their
different strengths must be weighed by level, and by quality of interpretation at
that level. We must also face the problem of making global assessments of
decidedly holistic accounts that do not have the same levels of analysis filled in,
leaving some levels completely blank.

MATCHING AND FILLING IN

As noted, our typical practice in formulating critical accounts is to compare reinterpretations of phenomena at third-order or fourth-order levels of analysis
with the first- and second-order claims of rival views. In doing so, we rarely
consider what rival re-interpretation of claims would look like at our favored
levels of analysis. We rarely imagine how rival theorists would reflect on our
methodology as we reflect on theirs. Rather, we typically assume that our initial
match across levels constitutes "the debate" in question—the Kohlberg/Gilligan
debate, for example. This may turn out to be true, in fact. But it must be argued
interpretively. There is the obvious alternative that our rival views are talking
past each other and that the interpretive connections we draw are ultimately
spurious. The fact that we can think up some ways in which different
phenomena may relate, or cite some apparently functional relations among
them, hardly confirms anything interpretively. It may be a start, but almost any
interpretation can make this start.

On this lack of analysis we often conclude that our side has won the debate in
question, so long as our account is strong. After all, the other side has virtually
no analysis to speak of at our more fundamental level. (What do Piaget or
Kohlberg have to say about ideological preferences and their roots in gender or
even self-concept?) Often the response of rival theorists promotes such a
conclusion. For example, Kohlberg's (1984) response to Gilligan prefigures her
other empirical critics by relying on the Walker study to refute sex differences
claims. On the theoretical side, Kohlberg offers philosophical accounts of
justice—of its moral pedigree and adequacy—while recounting care's lack of
each. Such responses could be used to nudge care into filling out its interpretive
account. But they seem unresponsive to her account in its present form. They do
not address its levels of analysis as they stand. As such, these responses caricature
their own side of the interpretive debate, allowing the other side to make
seemingly fair comparisons between sides, and conclude victory. But making a
fair comparison requires far more interpretive grounding than this. Let us
consider the obvious problems we face.

Relative strength

In general we can be confident that a more fundamental level of analysis
soundly trumps a less fundamental one when their quality at each level is
relatively equal. Yet we obviously cannot be confident, a priori, that any

particular fundamental account will be credible enough to do its job. To the contrary, we can expect more fundamental analysis to be much more difficult going, much more difficult to assess in general. Most feminist and critical analyses are far more integrative and holistic than the accounts they criticize. Some are so inclusive in scope that the minimal amount of information needed to tender them credibly seems beyond anyone's grasp. This is the perennial problem of Marxian accounts, which try to interpret particular events or doctrines or practices in terms of general, socio-economic conditions.

In the present case, Gilligan works from the broad and poorly understood fields of gender identity formation, self-concept, and ideology. However, her account does not survey or assess the "literature" in these areas. Rather Gilligan rests her case on three thin supports. The first consists of unexplicated generalizations from Chodorow's clinical observations on early childrearing (see Gilligan, 1982, pp. 7–8). Since males must separate from mother to become little "boys" and girls need only identify with mother to become little "girls," Gilligan notes, their respective "experience of relationships" and "issues of dependency" will be different in general. Moreover, we will find that "males tend to have difficulty in relationships, while females tend to have problems with individuation" from then on.

Presumably many types of research evidence and interrelated interpretations would be needed to derive such broad and lasting influences from the hard to observe and easy to misinterpret phenomena of infant psychology. These needs are not mentioned, much less fulfilled in Gilligan's account.

Second, Gilligan cites two studies of children's games (pp. 9–10) and one of women's anxiety in the corporate setting (pp. 14–15). These are assumed to show the further continuity and pervading strength of gender outlooks, as well as their moral proclivities. However this assumption is never supported interpretively. The game studies impute individual cognitive competence by observing group *behavior* (Piaget, 1965/1932; Lever, 1976). The corporate study uses projective tests to probe strength of motivation, of whatever kind (Horner, 1972). To show that these types of studies get at the same type of phenomenon that Chodorow considers, or that Gilligan investigates in her self-concept research, requires a good deal of analysis.

Even citing these studies for care initially should involve much more interpretive accounting than Gilligan offers. After all, the authors of these studies do not interpret their own results in this way. Rather, Gilligan wins these data for care by dubbing the conclusions of these authors patriarchal. Then she restates these findings in relational, caring terms (Gilligan, 1982, pp. 9–10, 14–15). But little interpretive rationale is offered for preferring Gilligan's alternative interpretation of results to theirs, or for rejecting theirs.

Lastly, Gilligan offers extremely formative interpretations of her own most formative research with the "Describe Yourself to Yourself" interview. (There has been no developed procedure for conducting, coding, or interpreting results of this interview.) Gilligan's claim that the way people define themselves correlates with their moral purposes and preferences is illustrated here by extremely selective and anecdotal comparisons of a handful of research protocols—only a few sentences from each protocol are typically cited.

Again, it is not surprising that some conceptual correlations can be found between aspects of some types of cognition (self-concept) and others (moral theme). But showing the kind of strong and pervasive correlation that would indicate *causal* connections between gender, self-concept, social outlook and moral sense is an interpretive matter of another kind. Even merely illustrating a connection of this sort must be approached differently. Yet, again, Gilligan's correlations here are not so much accounted for interpretively, as asserted. They are laid before us under a certain description for our intuitive assent. As a result, Gilligan's position is left vulnerable to the sort of critique Broughton (1983) offers. Here, longer passages from the response protocols used to illustrate care, are interpreted from a separational, justice perspective, yielding plausible results. This sort of problem might have been mitigated had Gilligan utilized any established method of interpretation as found in hermeneutics, phenomenology, or even psychoanalysis.

By contrast, Kohlberg's apparently less fundamental levels of research and theory are filled with reams of progressively hard data, and literally volumes of progressively sophisticated theory in psychology and philosophy (Kohlberg, 1969, 1971, 1973, 1984). Scores of confirming Kohlberg studies have been performed over the past three decades not only spanning both genders and a wide range of religious and ethnic groups, but importantly different cultures as well (Kohlberg 1958, 1969; Parikh 1980; Nisan & Kohlberg, 1982; Snarey, Kohlberg, & Noam, 1983). Kohlberg's research methods have been explained, justified, criticized, revised, tested, retested, explained and justified again, in extensive detail. In fact, Kohlberg is one of the few social scientists to develop an explicit methodological rationale ("bootstrapping") for the progressive refinement of his research program over time (Colby, Kohlberg, Gibbs, & Lieberman, 1983). He has justified this rationale, also, relative to prominent Lakatosian theories of social research (Lakatos, 1978). In the important 1983 monograph, Colby, Kohlberg, Gibbs, and Lieberman rigorously validate their detailed scoring system and the results of his central and most controversial longitudinal study, based on this system. These accounts have drawn surprisingly meager challenge, in sharp contrast to the history of methodological Kohlberg criticism.

Moreover, Kohlberg has offered extensive accounts of the developmental and moral assumptions that guided his research and theory. Each of these accounts contains extensive comparative justification and responds to a range of possible and actual criticisms. For example, Kohlberg (1969, 1984, chap. 3) explained and justified his focus on the structure of moral reasoning and on stages of natural development relative to behaviorist and socialization accounts of moral learning as well as psychoanalytic and functionalistic accounts. He explained and justified his conception of cognitive-moral reasoning and adequacy by comparing major ethical traditions on the normative and meta- level. Three interrelated components composed this account. Firstly, Kohlberg offered intuitive moral comparisons of developmental stages that were ordered structurally and chronologically. Increasing moral adequacy here was judged in a largely theory–neutral way, by whether a system of reasoning was internally consistent, able to handle a wide range of cases, and so forth (Kohlberg, 1971). Secondly, Kohlberg rated these intuitive comparisons relative to philosophical criteria drawn from the Kantian, deontological tradition of normative ethics. In the process he argued for the superiority of this tradition relative to its main teleological and areteic alternatives (Kohlberg, 1971, 1973, 1984, chap. 4; Kohlberg and Boyd, 1973). Kohlberg further justified this choice of criteria at a second-order, meta-ethical level, by arguing for formalism against descriptivism and other non-formalist positions. Lastly, Kohlberg rated his intuitive moral comparison of stages relative to more meta-ethical criteria alone, the correlativity criterion especially. Here he argued for the relative superiority of a cognitive-moral system that relates legitimate moral interests or claims with responsibilities to fulfill those claims, symmetrically (Kohlberg, 1973).

Key points in Kohlberg's theory remain significantly flawed, in my opinion. (I have objections to every conceptual component of his account just mentioned.) However, he offers enough of an interpretive account, and of the right comparative sort, to tell where the flaws are and to gauge their gravity. By contrast, as noted, Gilligan offers virtually no competing analysis of care's moral tone, adequacy, or developmental character. Of course this gap is not unlike Kohlberg's lack of showing at the levels of gender, self-concept, and ideology. Thus on the whole, the two accounts may seem on a par. Yet, in addition, Gilligan's interpretive showing at her own favored levels of gender and self-concept seems very weak thus far. This seems especially true relative to how Kohlberg fills levels in. Thus, as we compare these competing accounts across levels, it is unclear that Gilligan's more fundamental line of interpretation makes her account more credible overall.

The right match

In fact, it is unclear how to match different levels when comparing competing accounts. This is our second interpretive problem. We cannot be sure that a critical account in question has compared levels correctly, especially if it offers no interpretive account of how to match levels. Gilligan's levels of gender, self-concept and ideological analysis surely underlie justice and care when these two orientations are interpreted as means to preserve and express one's identity, to solve problems of relationality and individuation prompted by them. But there is still the question of whether care and justice are *moral* orientations in these respects, or in others, as Piaget and Kohlberg argue. Are the distinctively moral functions of these orientations determined by gender identity or other factors? There is a question, indeed, whether the influence of gender identity matters to their moral quality or validity at all.

Preserving and expressing one's sense of identity and solving identity problems may be what morality is all about. At least it may be a good part of morality's purpose. But this would have to be "argued" or accounted for interpretively. Likewise morality may be little more than one's personal conscience, one's personal morals or values.* But suppose moral judgment is

---

*As some critics see it, later chapters of Gilligan's book portray moral orientation in these ways.

primarily about something else. Suppose it is the system of compromises among our private moralities, for example. Then the likelihood that one gender identity, psychological type or cultural ideology favors it is questionable grounds for criticism. It is a questionable basis for interpretive explanation as well. I assume that we feminists would not dismiss the possibility that love and kindness are generally superior among moral ideals or virtues, simply because females may prefer them "constitutionally," or because Nepalese prefer them culturally, or Sufis religiously. It is difficult to think of any ethic that would not be far more accommodating to some psychological or cultural types than others, or that may not favor one or two most.

Thus, suppose Gilligan were correct in her analysis of how gender identity influences justice orientation or care focus and of how a "human development" approach to moral judgment research would likely favor one focus unfairly. This still need not undermine Kohlberg's claims for the superior moral quality and adequacy of "justice" reasoning or structure, and its universal stage development. Further interpretive accounting is needed to match her levels of analysis appropriately to his. Further analysis is needed to show that her views on "moral" focus extend to general structures of moral reasoning in Kohlberg's sense, as claimed.

Empty but filling

Lastly, we face the problem of evaluating currently emply levels of analysis in each account, given their clear potential to be filled in. It is important when comparing Gilligan's account with Piaget's or Kohlberg's that we point out missing elements in each. Yet it is difficult to know how to evaluate incompleteness relative to the degree of strength or credibility of analyses filled in. It would seem grossly unfair, for example, to dismiss care's voice in moral development solely because it has not accounted for its claimed moral status or developmental character. Care typically attends to people's needs, and needs are usually the most morally relevant features of general welfare considerations in ethics. Care also expresses honesty, compassion, and sense of responsibility which are often morally focused virtues and sentiments, even in the philosophical traditions favored by Piaget and Kohlberg. (Of course honesty is often cruel, just as responsibility can be directed toward "fellow thieves.") Indeed there is an explicit benevolence tradition in ethics, albeit a perennially weak one, that overlaps with key elements of care. On the developmental side, also, there are some features of care levels, as described by Gilligan, that are similar to cognitive–developmental structures and processes such as differentiation and hierarchical reintegration (see Gilligan, 1982, pp. 74–103.)

Thus we can forecast in general terms how Gilligan's caring analysis might proceed at these levels. We can forecast its possibilities for success even if we cannot forecast its details reliably, or its relative strength. We also can forecast how it might be germane to those analyses of rival views, already filled in. Likewise, using more developed feminist accounts, we can imagine how Gilligan's analysis of gender identity formation and its influences might be filled in a bit more fully.

It would also seem grossly unfair to simply discount Gilligan's empirical case relative to Kohlberg's, solely because her research is more formative. Kohlberg's (1958) early research was much like Gilligan's is now. It has taken literally decades to develop into a well-coded, statistically reliable system with clearly significant results. While its newfound success may have seemed very unlikely at the outset, as Gilligan's may seem to some now, her evolving research has the advantage of Kohlberg's mistakes and accomplishments from which to learn.

Moving in the other direction, we cannot merely dismiss Kohlberg's account of human development in morality because it offers no analysis or research on gender identity or self-concept in moral reasoning. Nor can we conclude that it is biased or limited as a result. As noted, Kohlberg offers elaborate rationales for pursuing *human* (unisex) development. Kohlberg's structure/content distinction in moral reasoning is designed to buffer his cognitive research focus from likely influences of socialization at the outset, including gender, class, ethnic and religious influences. It is relative to this focus on the bare structure of moral reasoning, rather than on values, virtues and motivations, that Kohlberg's all-male (all Chicagoan) research sampling of culturally universal development must be understood.

In addition, Kohlberg's recent attempts to fill in missing parts of his account, to research responsibility in particular, have uncovered an importantly different voice of caring. Kohlberg, Higgins, and Power (1984) investigated how adolescents deliberate about problems as these problems actually arise in the functioning of relationships. This research not only used real-life rather than hypothetical dilemmas, as Gilligan prefers, but it caught relational thinking while it was relating, in a more relational context than Gilligan's research sampled. (Gilligan sampled respondents individually, as they made moral judgments individually.) In addition, it explicitly looked at the varied range of relationships, not emphasizing intimate, personal relations. Initial findings seem to indicate that "care" speaks only to certain types of dilemmas in certain types of close and role-governed relationships (Kohlberg, 1984, p. 350). This supports Kohlberg's view of care as an "ethic" of "special relations" and special obligations.* Here we see how a missing level of interpretive analysis can be filled in by a rival view, even using methods of the rival position.

Recently, Kohlberg had begun research on self-concept and its effects on moral judgment. Yet unlike Gilligan, he had focused specifically on *moral* self-concept, feeling that this distinctive component of self is key. Kohlberg sought to discover whether identifying one's self as a *moral* self causes one to practice more faithfully what one preaches. Here we see how a rival view can approach the same type of issue, at the same level, in its own distinctive way. We might forecast from this approach the type of results and theoretical claims Kohlbergians might generate on identity orientation and moral preference.

---

*Kohlberg would contrast this with a general, relational orientation, or a general system of moral competence, which his stages chart.

HOLISM AND CARING COMPARISON

As noted, Gilligan's account of care and Kohlberg's account of justice are extremely holistic. Gilligan's analysis argues that Kohlberg's account must become even more holistic. To make a truly fair comparison of them, to have the sort of Kohlberg/Gilligan debate that treats each side with care, we must fill in as many key levels as possible and compare them every which way. This is necessary, at the interpretive level, just for getting the *facts* of care and justice straight. Such a project requires a good deal of interpretive creativity and patience.

If we are going to use reinterpretations of Kohlberg's data and criticisms of his methods to evaluate his view, these should be compared with Kohlbergian *re*interpretations of Gilligan's formative data, as related to her contexts of observation and theory. Here we would pursue the following sorts of questions:

(1) Does Gilligan's care truly share sexist stereotypes, on the female side, paralleling those attributed to Kohlbergian justice on the male side?

(2) Is Gilligan's "female difference" interpretation of alleged sex differences more or less feminist than the Kohlberg/Kramer (1969) hypothesis? (This hypothesis attributes allegedly slower *rates* of female development to institutionalized sexism as it is observed in research.)

(3) Do Gilligan's open-ended interviews merely free up moral thinking (when compared to Kohlberg's forced-choice dilemmas) or do they pull artifactually for certain themes and preferences? For example, do they capture the way we spontaneously *reflect* on moral beliefs and attitudes but not how we spontaneously express or use them to solve problems? Do these interviews reflect the peculiarities of how a particular interview happens to go, peculiarities that are filtered out appropriately by standardized, hypothetical dilemmas?

(4) Does Gilligan's different voice hypothesis, with its focus on what is peculiar to different moral orientations and gender orientations, bias findings against the gender and theme commonalities of so-called "human development" that Kohlberg seeks?

(5) What might the shape of care be after extensive research is performed on it in a wide variety of (cultural) settings, including longitudinal studies using reliable scoring systems?

(6) How will care's moral adequacy claims compare with those of justice once a moral philosophy and meta-ethics for care is worked out?

Yet we should also consider how Kohlberg's and Gilligan's accounts might be independent, along with the phenomena they describe. What else might Kohlberg's stages be than (a) an invariant sequence of general moral development (as Kohlberg sees them) or (b) a two-tier sequence of development (in Gilligan's eyes) charting a male-oriented penchant for individuation at higher stages? Might these stages be a three-tier sequence? Might they chart (1) personal (egoistic) conscience at the first moral level (stages 1 and 2), then (2) moral conventionalism at the second level (stage 3 and part of 4), and last (3) the distinctive morality of law and political institutions at higher stages?*

Also, what else might care be than a general and naturally developing set of cognitive systems? Might it be a set of circumscribed strategies (partially learned/ partially reflective) for coping with oppressive crises or for coping with sexist crises such as those surrounding abortion decisions? Might it be a form of ego development characteristic of one gender, that has some quasi-moral effects in some types of cases? These obvious alternatives should be compared with Gilligan's explicit interpretational challenge to Kohlberg's stages, and also with Kohlberg's own theory of his stages.

With these sorts of analyses under way, we would have the raw materials for a care/justice or Kohlberg/Gilligan debate at the interpretive level.

REFERENCES

Baumrind, D., & Pulos, S. (1985) Sex differences in moral judgment: Critique of Walker's conclusion that there are none. *Human Development,* **57,** 511–521.

Broughton, J. M. (1983). Women's rationality and men's virtues: Gender dualism in Gilligan's theory of moral development. *Social Research,* **50**(3), 597–642.

Chodorow, N. (1978). *The reproduction of mothering.* Berkeley: University of California Press.

Colby, A., Kohlberg, L., Gibbs, J., & Lieberman, M. (1983). A longitudinal study of moral development. *Monographs of the Society For Research In Child Development,* **48**(4).

Gilligan, C., & Murphy, J. M. (1979). Development from adolescence to adulthood: The philosopher and the dilemma of fact. In D. Kuhn (Ed.), *Intellectual development beyond childhood.* San Francisco: Jossey-Bass.

Gilligan, C. (1977). In a different voice: Women's conceptions of the self and morality. *Harvard Educational Review,* **47,** 481–517.

Gilligan, C. (1982). *In a different voice.* Cambridge, MA: Harvard University Press.

Gilligan, C. (1986). Response to critics. *Signs,* **11,** 324–333.

Haan, N. (1985) Hypothetical and actual moral reasoning in a situation of civil disobedience. *Journal of Personality and Social Psychology,* **32,** 255–269.

Holstein, C. (1976). Development of moral judgment: A longitudinal study of males and females. *Child Development,* **47,** 51–61.

Horner, M. (1972) Toward an understanding of achievement-related conflicts in women. *Journal of Social Issues,* **28,** 157–175.

Johnston, K. (1985). *Two moral orientations—Two problem-solving strategies: Adolescents' solutions to dilemmas in fables.* Unpublished doctoral dissertation, Harvard University.

Kohlberg, L. (1958). *The development of modes of moral thinking and choice in the years ten to sixteen.* Unpublished doctoral dissertation, University of Chicago.

Kohlberg, L. (1969). Stage and sequence: The cognitive-developmental approach to socialization. In D. A. Goslin (Ed.), *Handbook of socialization theory and research.* Chicago: Rand McNally.

Kohlberg, L. (1971). From is to ought: How to commit the naturalistic fallacy and get away with it in the study of moral development. In T. Mischel (Ed.), *Cognitive development and epistemology.* New York: Academic.

Kohlberg, L. (1984) *The psychology of moral development.* New York: Harper & Row.

---

*The morality of law and public policy should emphasize individual rights-to-noninterference, for either gender, for at this level our moral claims are primarily against violent law breaking and coercive state power, rather than against each other.

Kohlberg, L. (1973) The claim to the moral adequacy of a highest stage of judgment. *Journal of Philosophy,* **70.**

Kohlberg, L., & Boyd, D. (1973). The is-ought problem: A developmental perspective. *Zygon,* **8.**

Kohlberg, L., & Kramer, R. (1969). Continuities and discontinuities in child and adult moral development. *Human Development,* **12.**

Higgins, A., Power, & Kohlberg, L. (1984). The relation of moral atmosphere to judgments of responsibility. In W. Kurtines & J. Gewirtz (Eds.), *Morality, moral behavior and development.* New York: Wiley.

Lakatos, I. (1978). *The methodology of scientific research programs.* New York: Cambridge University Press.

Langdale, S. (1984). *Moral observations and moral development: The Analysis of care and justice reasoning across different dilemmas in females and males from childhood through adulthood.* Unpublished doctoral dissertation, Harvard Graduate School of Education.

Lever, J. (1976). Sex differences in the games children play. *Social Problems,* **23,** 478–487.

Lyons, N. (1983). Two perspectives: On self, relationships and morality. *Harvard Educational Review,* **53.**

Miller, J. B. (1976). *Toward a new psychology of women.* Boston: Beacon Press.

Murphy, J. M., & Gilligan, C. (1980). Moral development in late adolescence and adulthood: A critique and reconstruction of Kohlberg's theory. *Human Development,* **23.**

Nisan, M., & Kohlberg, L. (1982). Universality and cross-cultural variation in moral development: A longitudinal and cross-sectional study in Turkey. *Child Development,* **53,** 865–876.

Parikh, B. (1980). Moral judgment development and its relation to family enivronmental factors in Indian and American families. *Child Development,* **51,** 1030–1039.

Piaget, J. (1965). *The moral judgment of the child* (1932). New York: Free Press.

Perry, W. (1968). *Forms of intellectual and ethical development in the college years.* New York: Holt, Rinehart, Winston.

Sassen, G. (1980). Success anxiety in women: A constructivist interpretation of its source and its significance. *Harvard Educational Review,* **50.**

Snarey, J. R., Kohlberg, L., & Noam, G. (1983) Ego Development and education: A structural perspective. *Developmental Review,* **3,** 303–338.

Walker, L. J. (1984). Sex differences in the development of moral reasoning: A critical Review. *Child Development,* **55,** 677–691.

RELATED ESSAYS

Puka, B. (1989). The liberation of caring. *Hypatia,* **4,** 11. Reprinted in M. Brabeck (Ed.), *Who cares?* New York: Praeger Press.

Puka, B. (1989) The majesty and mystery of Kohlberg's stage 6. In T. Wren (Ed.), *The moral domain.* Cambridge, MA: MIT Press.

Puka, B. (1989). Toward the redevelopment of Kohlberg's theory: Preserving essential structure, removing controversial content. In W. Kurtines & J. Gewirtz (Eds.), *Handbook of moral behavior and development, Vol. I: Theory.* New York: Erlbaum Associates.

Puka, B. (In press). Interpretive experiments: Probing the care-justice debate in moral development. *Human Development.*

Sex Differences in the Development of Moral Reasoning: A Rejoinder to Baumrind

Lawrence J. Walker

University of British Columbia

WALKER, LAWRENCE J. *Sex Differences in the Development of Moral Reasoning: A Rejoinder to Baumrind.* CHILD DEVELOPMENT, 1986, 57, 522–526. Baumrind criticizes the procedures of my review and meta-analysis of the research literature on sex differences in moral reasoning development and disagrees with my conclusion that the overall pattern is one of nonsignificant differences. This rejoinder addresses these criticisms, discussing issues such as the nature of moral development, the focus on adulthood, the choice of statistics, the effect of differing sample sizes and scoring systems, and the role of social experiences in explaining variability in moral development. Baumrind's data are interpreted in this context. An updated review and meta-analysis of the research literature again support the conclusion that there are no consistent sex differences in moral reasoning development.

Recently, we have witnessed the resurrection of the controversial and difficult, if not intractable, issue of sex differences in moral development and sex bias in theories of morality. Since morality is so fundamental to our existence and so obviously value-laden, it is incumbent upon us to examine and interpret the relevant data carefully.

Baumrind (1986) and others, notably Gilligan (1982), have argued that Kohlberg's (1981, 1984) theory and measure are insensitive to females' "different voice" on moral issues and denigrate females' thought to lower stages, thereby caricaturing them as morally deficient or aberrant. My (Walker, 1984) review and meta-analysis of the research literature indicated, however, that the overall pattern of findings is one of nonsignificant sex differences in moral reasoning development. Baumrind, in her critique, argued that my review procedure was flawed in several respects and reflected a bias against the finding of differences. She questioned the adequacy of Kohlberg's definition of morality and alleged that the theory entails sexual, cultural, and educational biases. In this context, she presented additional analyses of data from her Family Socialization Project (FSP).

Baumrind alleged that I attempted to amass support for the null hypothesis that there are no sex differences in moral reasoning development. She is incorrect. The purpose of my review was to determine whether or not research, in which Kohlberg's measure was used, indicated consistent sex differences in moral reasoning development (see pp. 677, 680). The *conclusion* I came to on the basis of the review and meta-analysis of the extant research literature was that these data do not support the rejection of the null hypothesis. In this rejoinder, I respond to the various criticisms raised by Baumrind.

The Nature of Moral Development

Baumrind is correct that Kohlberg, as a cognitive-developmental theorist, posits a strict moral stage model. This model holds that moral reasoning stages represent holistic structures that develop in an invariant sequence and that constitute a hierarchy. The appropriate analyses for testing the criteria for a stage model differ from those needed for measuring the effects of an intervention or individuals' level of development (Walker, in press–a). For example, one criterion of the model is the sequentiality of the stages. Development is held to be irreversibly progressive, one stage at a time. Change must always be to the next higher *modal* stage. In assessing this claim, only modal stage scores are relevant, and other information (e.g., shifts in the distribution of responses at adjacent stages) is ignored. However, in assessing developmental level, there is no reason to ignore such information, and the most sensitive measure should be used. If only modal stage scores were used, it would be unnecessarily difficult to detect many real developmental changes or differences.

Requests for reprints should be sent to Lawrence J. Walker, Department of Psychology, University of British Columbia, Vancouver, BC, Canada V6T 1Y7.

Secondary Analyses

A few researchers either failed to analyze sex differences in their data (e.g., Haan, Smith, & Block, 1968) or conducted inappropriate analyses (Baumrind, 1982), so I conducted secondary analyses on the data that were available. (Incidentally, Baumrind is incorrect in stating that our differing findings for her FSP are based on the same data: her original analysis had a $N = 225$; my secondary analysis had a $N = 284$; and her present analysis, $N = 303$.) Baumrind argued that my use of the Kolmogorov-Smirnov test for secondary analyses was inappropriate, in part because it is too conservative. On the contrary, it was chosen because it is a test of *all* possible alternatives to the null hypothesis that the distribution of two groups is identical (e.g., in central tendency, dispersion, and skewness). This test is slightly less powerful than the Mann-Whitney test (favored by Baumrind) for detecting differences in central tendency, especially with large sample sizes and many ties (Siegel, 1956). However, the Mann-Whitney test only detects differences in central tendency and is insensitive to any other type of difference. It assumes that the scores represent a distribution that has underlying continuity (Siegel, 1956)—one of Baumrind's criticisms of the Kolmogorov-Smirnov test. In comparison to the Mann-Whitney, the Kolmogorov-Smirnov test is more powerful in detecting differences with small samples and differences other than central tendency (Siegel, 1956). For example, if the distribution of scores was bimodal for one sex (e.g., Stage 1–2 and 4–5 for males) and modal for the other (e.g., Stage 3 for females), the medians for the two sexes would be the same, although the distributions are very different: the Mann-Whitney test would not be significant, whereas the Kolmogorov-Smirnov test would be. Nevertheless, to provide the most liberal test of sex differences in moral reasoning development, I reanalyzed the studies in question using the Mann-Whitney test and found a change in the finding for only one of 11 samples (namely, Baumrind's FSP adults). When I recalculated the meta-analysis, the change was minor (from the original $Z = +.73$ to $+1.06$, one-tailed $p = .14$).

Focus on Adulthood

Baumrind argued that only the data of adults are relevant to the question of sex differences in moral reasoning development, and that I biased the results of the review and meta-analysis by including the data of children and adolescents. This argument is based on the notion that bias in Kohlberg's theory arises from sex differences at the highest level of moral reasoning. However, she did not explain how there is bias at that level but not at lower ones. If the whole approach is biased, as she claimed in her Discussion, then sex differences could occur at any level. Other critics argue that Kohlberg's theory is pervasively biased against the thinking of females of all ages (e.g., Gilligan, 1982, chap. 2). In any event, adults reason at almost all stages (e.g., Baumrind's adults range from Stage 2 to 6). Therefore, Baumrind offered no convincing reasons to focus exclusively on the data of adults.

Baumrind dismissed the findings of differences favoring girls in childhood and adolescence by alluding to their "accelerated general development" but did not cite evidence of this general sex difference. Her belief seems contrary to the available data regarding the consistency and magnitude of sex differences in general (Maccoby & Jacklin, 1974).

Sample Size

Baumrind alleged that I did not take into account the differing sample sizes of the studies I reviewed. This, of course, reflects the limitations of the traditional "box-score" review procedure, and she is correct that, in the review, I did not discount the findings of studies with small samples. She is incorrect, however, in claiming that differing sample sizes were not taken into account. A second analysis, a meta-analysis, was also conducted. Since p level is heavily influenced by sample size and since the meta-analysis was based on the Z scores derived from each study, it did take into account differing sample sizes. The results of the meta-analysis corroborated the conclusion drawn from the review.

It is noteworthy that Baumrind stressed that significant differences tend to be found with large samples. That phenomenon, of course, implies a weak effect. For example, the effect size derived from Baumrind's (1986) analysis of sex differences in moral stage, as expressed by Cohen's d (the standardized mean difference), was $+.27$, one that would be considered small according to Cohen (1977), who described an effect size of .8 as large, .5 moderate, and .2 small.

Scoring Systems

Baumrind alleged, quite mistakenly, that I discounted the findings of studies with significant sex differences that used early versions of Kohlberg's scoring system. She is correct in claiming that *if* I discounted the findings of early studies with differences, then I should have also discounted the findings of early studies without differences. However, she is incorrect in claiming that I discounted findings. My conclusion was based on two sets of analyses, a box-score review and a meta-analysis, and early studies were included in both. I did, however, note Colby's (1978) claim that revisions to moral stage descriptions and scoring procedures should eliminate any tendency to underestimate females' moral reasoning because of particular content; and I did note the pattern that, of the 12 studies reporting differences, 10 used early versions of the scoring system. Unfortunately, the relevant data to address this issue have yet to be reported. No study has directly compared the extent of sex differences in the same data set scored with an early scoring system versus the current Standard Issue Scoring system (Colby & Kohlberg, in press).

Baumrind also argued that the current system is no better than previous ones. The conventional criteria for evaluating the adequacy of a scoring system are validity and reliability. The evidence is clear that data scored according to the current system are more in accord with the predictions of the stage model (structure, sequence, and hierarchy) than were data scored with earlier systems and, furthermore, that scoring reliability also is better with the current system (see Colby, Kohlberg, Gibbs, & Lieberman, 1983; Walker, in press-c).

Baumrind's final criticism of the current scoring system is that its lack of Stage 6 criterion judgments compromises the validity of the preceding stages. The absence of Stage 6 from the manual reflects the empirical rarity of such individuals. Kohlberg and his colleagues have not yet obtained enough Stage 6 reasoning data to provide criterion judgments in the manual. However, Stage 6 remains the developmental end point, and descriptions and interpretations of Stage 6 are widely available (e.g., Kohlberg, 1984). The validity of the theory is not threatened by the absence of Stage 6 from the scoring manual.

The Significance of Social Experiences for Moral Development

Baumrind alleged that I discarded the findings of studies in which sex was confounded with levels of education and/or occupation. I did not discard these findings—they were included in both the review and meta-analysis. The overall pattern was one of nonsignificant sex differences. I did not deny that a few studies with particular samples did yield significant differences; indeed, I highlighted them. The small number of samples in which significant differences were found would be expected by chance. I did not regard these differences as spurious or nullified by controlling for education and/or occupation. That is, I did not attempt to "explain away" those findings, but I did note the confounding of sex with these social experiences in order to illustrate the point that, when differences occurred, they were explicable in terms of the theory's predictions regarding variability in moral development. Thus, the relevant analyses concern whether or not there are differences in moral reasoning development within levels of these social experiential factors that explain variability. Baumrind's (1986) analysis of sex differences in moral reasoning within educational levels, unfortunately, is not that meaningful since it entailed a serious confounding of sex and education at both high and low education levels (the only levels where there were differences). For example, she combined levels 1 and 2 to represent a single level when there were three women and 54 men with doctorate degrees (level 1) and 38 women and 38 men with master's degrees (level 2). There was a similar confounding at levels 6 and 7. It is not appropriate to claim that these women and men were at the same educational levels; and her conclusion that there are sex differences in moral reasoning within educational levels is not warranted on the basis of this analysis.

Baumrind regards the relation between moral development and sociomoral experiences (especially education) as a "serious challenge" to the theory. In contradistinction, I interpret the relation as evidence for the construct validity of the theory. Level of education has been found to correlate with most developmental variables. Of what value is education if it has no impact on moral thought, and what would be the validity of a theory concerned with the development of moral reasoning that did not evidence such a relation?

Baumrind called for a clarification of the role of these experiences for moral development. As I noted previously (Walker, 1984), Kohlberg hypothesized two main determinants of moral development: (*a*) attainment of prerequisite levels of cognitive and perspective-taking development, and (*b*) exposure to appropriate sociomoral experiences. Claims regarding the former determinant are derived from the cognitive-developmental assumption of structural parallelism that implies that isomorphic processes are involved in parallel stages in different domains of cognition. There is now considerable evidence that both cognitive and perspective-taking development place an upper limit on moral development (Walker, in press—a). Claims regarding the latter determinant are derived from the cognitive-developmental assumption that disequilibrium (or cognitive conflict) is the cognitive motivational mechanism that induces development (Walker, in press—a). Thus, the experiences that promote moral development are not only logical, but often are also emotional, personal experiences involving responsibility and decision making—ones that entail cognitive conflict. These experiences stimulate moral reasoning by providing role-taking opportunities in conflict situations. They arise in interpersonal relationships and through education, occupation, and citizenship activities. Kohlberg's theory, of course, does not predict that any particular experiences are necessary for attainment of a given stage. The experiences that will affect moral development are ones that induce rethinking of current modes of moral reasoning. Thus, the number of years someone sits in a classroom is not a direct index of the amount of relevant experience (there is no educational threshold for each stage), and, furthermore, it should be noted that the sexes frequently differ, even within educational level, in the nature of the programs in which they enroll. What is of concern is whether or not life experience, including but not only educational experience, encourages reflection on, and discussion of, social and moral issues. Similarly, whether or not someone is employed is not of much concern (and that was the extent of Baumrind's 1986 analysis). What is of concern is the extent to which the occupation permits responsibility, communication, and decision making. Individuals who are in low-level occupations (which is where more women in the labor force are employed than men) tend to be denied the opportunity for significant moral decision making on the job. In fact, running a household may provide more opportunity for such experiences than many occupations, including some in which men predominate. (See, in this context, my recent study [Walker, in press—b] of both cognitive and experiential influences on moral development with a representative sample of adults.) Incidentally, the empirical rarity of individuals with principled moral reasoning has precluded a thorough examination of the conditions that facilitate its development.

Conclusion

Baumrind's criticisms of my 1984 article are without foundation. I maintain that the review and meta-analysis provided a dispassionate examination of the evidence regarding sex differences in moral reasoning development. Given these criticisms and the widespread, popularized claims about sex differences in moral reasoning, we (Walker & de Vries, 1985) recently reported an updated review that included 80 studies, with a total of 152 samples, involving a total of 10,637 subjects. Of the 152 samples, a nonsignificant sex difference was reported for the vast majority (130, or 85.5%). Females had higher scores in nine samples, whereas males had higher scores in 13 samples. The few differences favoring females tended to occur in homogeneous samples of school and university students, whereas the few differences favoring males tended to occur in heterogeneous samples of adults (in which the sexes differed in levels of education and occupation—a situation, as Baumrind noted, that is typical of our society). Thus, the overall pattern yielded by the review is one of nonsignificant sex differences.

I also conducted a meta-analysis with the studies included in the review using the Stouffer method (Rosenthal, 1984) to test the hypothesis that males are more advanced in moral reasoning than are females. The meta-analysis indicated that, although the pattern was in the predicted direction, it was not significant, $Z = +1.08$, one-tailed $p = .14$. The mean effect size was extremely small, Cohen's $d = +.046$, which means that sex explains only one-twentieth of 1% of the variance in moral reasoning development, $r^2 = .0005$.

Thus, given the effect size and the results of the meta-analysis, one is forced to conclude that no nontrivial relationship exists; the evidence is that males and females are more alike than different in moral reasoning development. There is no empirical support for the claim that Kohlberg's theory down-scores the moral thinking of females. Furthermore, even if differences had been found, they would only indicate bias if they did not accurately reflect reality. For example, males have been found to be heavier than females on average, and Caucasians to be taller than Orientals, but that hardly implies that our systems of weight and height measurement are biased. Demonstrating that a theory is biased requires more than findings of difference among groups. Assuming that the sexes do not differ, the minimal (but certainly not sufficient) basis for an interpretive claim of sex bias against a theory would be consistent evidence indicating greater moral maturity for males than for females. There is no such basis for an allegation of bias.

References

Baumrind, D. (1982). Are androgynous individuals more effective persons and parents? *Child Development, 53*, 44–75.

Baumrind, D. (1986). Sex differences in moral reasoning: Response to Walker's (1984) conclusion that there are none. *Child Development, 57*, 000–000 (in this issue).

Cohen, J. (1977). *Statistical power analysis for the behavioral sciences* (rev. ed.). New York: Academic Press.

Colby, A. (1978). Evolution of a moral-developmental theory. In W. Damon (Ed.), *New directions for child development: Moral development* (No. 2, pp. 89–104). San Francisco: Jossey-Bass.

Colby, A., & Kohlberg, L. (Eds.). (in press). *The measurement of moral judgment* (Vols. 1–2). New York: Cambridge University Press.

Colby, A., Kohlberg, L., Gibbs, J., & Lieberman, M. (1983). A longitudinal study of moral judgment. *Monographs of the Society for Research in Child Development, 48*(1–2, Serial No. 200).

Gilligan, C. (1982). *In a different voice: Psychological theory and women's development.* Cambridge, MA: Harvard University Press.

Haan, N., Smith, M. B., & Block, J. (1968). Moral reasoning of young adults: Political-social behavior, family background, and personality correlates. *Journal of Personality and Social Psychology, 10*, 183–201.

Kohlberg, L. (1981). *Essays on moral development: Vol. 1. The philosophy of moral development.* San Francisco: Harper & Row.

Kohlberg, L. (1984). *Essays on moral development: Vol. 2. The psychology of moral development.* San Francisco: Harper & Row.

Maccoby, E. E., & Jacklin, C. N. (1974). *The psychology of sex differences.* Stanford, CA: Stanford University Press.

Rosenthal, R. (1984). *Meta-analytic procedures for social research.* Beverly Hills, CA: Sage.

Siegel, S. (1956). *Nonparametric statistics for the behavioral sciences.* New York: McGraw-Hill.

Walker, L. J. (1984). Sex differences in the development of moral reasoning: A critical review. *Child Development, 55*, 677–691.

Walker, L. J. (in press–a). Cognitive processes in moral development. In G. L. Sapp (Ed.), *Moral development: Models, processes, and techniques.* Birmingham, AL: Religious Education Press.

Walker, L. J. (in press–b). Experiential and cognitive sources of moral development in adulthood. *Human Development.*

Walker, L. J. (in press–c). The validity of the moral stage model and the reliability of the moral judgment interview. In L. Kohlberg & D. Candee (Eds.), *Research in moral development.* Cambridge, MA: Harvard University Press.

Walker, L. J., & de Vries, B. (1985, August). Moral stages/moral orientations: Do the sexes really differ? In C. Blake (Chair), *Gender difference research in moral development.* Symposium conducted at the meeting of the American Psychological Association, Los Angeles.

Merrill-Palmer Quarterly, Vol. 34, No. 3

Sex Differences in Morality and Moral Orientation: A Discussion of the Gilligan and Attanucci Study

Jyotsna Vasudev

Wayne State University

Gilligan and Attanucci in their study on sex differences in moral orientation (*Merrill-Palmer Quarterly*, July 1988) chose an important topic in need of systematic and substantive research. But the design and sample of their investigation has compromised the significance of their findings. Although questions of the relationships between orientation, age, stage, and sex were not considered in their study, at this juncture of research and theory such relationships should be the very issues in any investigation of Gilligan's ideas.

[*Editor's Note: A reply by Gilligan and Attanucci to this discussion will appear in the next issue of the* Quarterly.]

The goal of this discussion is twofold: First, to review briefly the history of and the current debate on sex differences in morality. Second, to address some important issues raised by Gilligan and Attanucci (1988).

The advent of feminism has rendered most academic disciplines self-conscious. The myriad forms of bias against women in theory and practice across disciplines are beginning to be recognized and questioned. In the crudest form of this bias, women have been seen as structurally inferior to men and therefore less capable of rational thought which is the quintessential dimension of a mature intellect. In lieu of a rational capacity, women have been granted a generous portion of emotion, passion, and intuition which, although inferior to incisive reason, undermine rationality. With some reflective change in attitude, several philosophers have begun to suggest that women are different but perhaps equal to men (e.g., Lloyd, 1983; Nicholson, 1983).

To some extent, the feminist revolution also recapitulates these themes in its philosophical and political agenda. These themes, how-

The author thanks Marlene Devoe for her comments and suggestions on the manuscript. Correspondence should be sent to Jyotsna Vasudev, Department of Psychology, Wayne State University, 71 West Warren Ave., Detroit, MI 48202.

Merrill-Palmer Quarterly, July 1988, Vol. 34, No. 3, pp. 239–244.

ever, reappear as somewhat incompatible goals with equally polarized philosophies. On the one hand, the issue of equality between
the two sexes entails a recognition that there is no difference between women and men. In accord with this position, women are encouraged to perform and achieve like men. On the other hand, it is
argued that a stance of "no difference" devalues women's experience and prerogative and perpetuates the myth that the behavior and
reasoning of men represent exemplary models of maturity. In accord
with this criticism, women are encouraged to legitimize rather than
repudiate their ways of thinking, feeling, and perceiving. Erikson, for
example, encourages women to stand for in public what they have
stood for in private. Both these stances are inherently wise. But with
an increasing polarization of these goals we move further away from
the reality of women's lives which derive meaning from the very tension between these goals rather than from choosing one or the other.

In view of the history and politics of bias against women, sex differences as an area of theory and research in psychology has also become politicized. Given the inheritance of a philosophical and an intellectual tradition rife with bias against women, some psychologists
have examined current theories, methodologies, and research findings for sex bias. Although such a scrutiny is good for the soul of the
discipline, it arouses mixed feelings when research becomes a format
for an ideologically motivated debate. At its best, the politics of the
issue force researchers to consider responsibly the implications of
their findings for informing policies and programs. Researchers are
prompted to examine the convenient rubric of an objective, apolitical, and value-neutral science. At its worst, the overlay of politics
makes it easier to accept, reject, or interpret research findings to serve
an ideology regardless of their "truth" value. This form discourages
dialogue and critical inquiry, and encourages polemical rhetoric.

Against this background, the issue of sex differences in morality
has become controversial as differences in morality are relatively
more amenable to value judgment. Gilligan (1977, 1982), a colleague
of the late Lawrence Kohlberg, has figured prominently in this debate.
She maintains that because they were derived from an all male sample, the theory and stages described by Kohlberg are biased against
women. Specifically, women, as compared to men, have been relegated to Stage 3 which represents an interpersonal morality. Gilligan
believes this relegation to a lower stage stems from Kohlberg's conception of morality as a deontological principle of justice which is formal, abstract, and rational. Compared to men who think formally and
define the moral domain autonomously, women's reasoning is contextual and embedded in relations with others. By confining his crite-

rion of principled morality to respect for rights, Kohlberg gives inadequate attention to moral concerns voiced by women. Gilligan maintains that a disproportionate emphasis on autonomy, in turn, leads to an idealistic conception of adulthood which favors separateness over connections among individuals.

Gilligan has also argued that because Kohlberg's methodology relies on hypothetical dilemmas it fails to account for real-life issues in which judgment and action interact dynamically. Based on her research with women contemplating abortion, Gilligan suggests that women construe moral dilemmas in terms of conflicting responsibilities more than conflicting rights; they are concerned with issues of compassion and care more than abstract notions of equality and rights. Gilligan (1977, 1982) has proposed an alternative scheme of morality which charts the progressive integration and differentiation of women's understanding of conflict between caring for one's own self and the other.

Gilligan's ideas encouraged a serious inquiry of sex bias in Kohlberg's theory and research findings. Recent data on this issue seem to support Kohlberg's contention that when samples are controlled for education, socioeconomic status, and occupation there are no differences between males and females (Gibbs, Arnold, & Burkhart, 1984; Vasudev & Hummel, 1987; Walker, 1984, 1986). Some researchers, however, continue to find and explain sex differences in Kohlberg's theory (Baumrind, 1986).

Gilligan's findings on women also encouraged an expansion of the moral domain to include considerations of care and responsibility (Broughton, 1983; Colby & Damon, 1983; Kohlberg, 1982). Gilligan and Attanucci, in this issue of the *Quarterly*, aim to explicate moral orientations of care and justice and examine how they relate to sex differences in orientation and focus. This issue is topical and important. The general criticism of this study is the hiatus between tenuous data and strong claims made by the researchers. It seems that the most valuable contribution of their investigation consists of suggestions for other researchers and questions which need to be addressed in empirical research. Because these suggestions are tangentially linked with this study, one wonders why they did not guide the research to begin with. Given our keen interest in Gilligan's alternative scheme and expansion of the existing conception of morality, this study offers sparse results.

First, the sample of the study is seriously limited. It consists of small subsamples of three studies and is too haphazard and confounded to substantiate issues of moral orientation and possible gender differences. In Study 1, for example, 21 subjects are spread across three large age groups with just three subjects in one age group. In Study 2 there are 39 subjects with twice as many men as women; these subjects are spread across two age groups and the authors report a high attrition of subjects ($n = 19$) who failed to provide real-life dilemmas. In Study 3, 20 subjects are confined to one age group. The age groups are expansive and the researchers do not even report any statistics on age. Given this confounding of age, sex, attrition, and large age groupings, it is difficult to interpret the meaning and direction of these results. By the time these confounding variables are factored in any interpretation, there is little left to assess with some degree of confidence.

Further, although the relationship between orientation, stage, and age was not a research question of the study, it is crucial to Gilligan's theory. At this juncture of the controversy, the finding that both justice and care perspectives are represented in real-life dilemmas and that people tend to focus on one set of concerns is hardly surprising. Similar findings and ideas have already been discussed by Gilligan and other writers as well (Broughton, 1983; Gibbs, Arnold, & Burkhart, 1984; Gilligan, 1977, 1982; Haan, 1978; Lyons, 1983). What is critical is how these orientations are represented across the life span for males and females; how these orientations change, shift, and mutually transform each other; and how they are related to broader issues of moral reasoning and action. Although no single study is expected to address these questions comprehensively, single studies should at least address one or two of these goals. To this extent, the restricted age groups of adolescents and adults in this study are not informative. In addition, given the broad, unsystematic groupings within this range precludes any explanation of the relationship between orientation and age/stage even for these groups.

Second, this article reiterates Gilligan's contention that hypothetical dilemmas are a poor facsimile of real-life choices in which the demands of reasoning and action are inextricably interwoven. I fully endorse this contention. Research methodologies which focus on one type of dilemma, however, provide partial information. The difference, similarity, and interaction between hypothetical and real-life concerns become palpable when respondents are requested to address both concerns. Such a strategy has a double benefit. On the one hand, the hypothetical dilemma ensures the needed control that all individuals consider the same dilemma. On the other hand, the dilemmas generated by the respondents represent a wide variety of moral issues which impinge on the lives of individuals and also engage the tension between the imperatives of abstract reasoning and moral choices in an imperfect world. Such a methodology may also reveal how, if so, concerns of care and justice provide a single or "bi-focal" approach to real and hypothetical problems; further, how, if so, these concerns interact with gender, age, and type of dilemma.

Third, this study fails to clarify the relationship between moral orientation and moral understanding where the latter includes the other in a part-whole relationship. If moral understanding is our larger goal, then the "focus" and "orientation" in themselves are inadequate explanations of morality. The authors make a pertinent observation that people can adopt both justice and care perspectives, and these, in turn, are susceptible to the interviewer's cues. Examples 1J and 1C in their Table 1 are a case in point. To move the argument beyond labeling the perspective, 1J could be asked "What would happen if your friends did not share the set of standards you value?" Similarly, 1C could be asked "What would happen if your 'real' friends did not accept your decisions?" Such additional questions would test the limits and importance of the chosen or spontaneous perspective. The respondent's ability to consider the other perspective or the continued elaboration along the chosen perspective would elucidate the conceptual linkages between these perspectives in the reasoner's mind.

To conclude, my commentary is a criticism, a hope, and a justified demand for theory-driven research to substantiate Gilligan's theory. The opening summary of the debate on sex differences underscores the political and psychological significance of Gilligan's ideas. Good ideas can shine by their own light, but when coupled with weak data they risk being dismissed as trivial.

REFERENCES

BAUMRIND, D. (1986). Sex differences in moral reasoning: Response to Walker's (1984) conclusion that there are none. *Child Development, 57*, 511–521.

BROUGHTON, J. M. (1983). Women's rationality and men's virtues: A critique of gender dualism in Gilligan's theory of moral development. *Social Research, 50*, 597–642.

COLBY, A., & DAMON, W. (1983). Listening to a different voice: A review of Gilligan's *In a Different Voice. Merrill-Palmer Quarterly, 29*, 473–481.

GIBBS, J. C., ARNOLD, K. D., & BURKHART, J. E. (1984). Sex differences in the expression of moral judgment. *Child Development, 55*, 1040–1043.

GILLIGAN, C. (1977). In a different voice: Women's conception of self and morality. *Harvard Educational Review, 47*, 481–517.

GILLIGAN, C. (1982). *In a different voice: Psychological theory and women's development.* Cambridge, MA: Harvard University Press.

GILLIGAN, C., & ATTANUCCI, J. (1988). Two moral orientations: Gender differences and similarities. *Merrill-Palmer Quarterly, 34*, 223–237.

HAAN, N. (1978). Two moralities in action contexts: Relationships to thought, ego regulation and development. *Journal of Personality and Social Psychology, 36,* 286–305.

KOHLBERG, L. (1982). A reply to Owen Flanagan and some comments on the Puka-Goodpaster exchange. *Ethics, 92,* 513–528.

LLOYD, G. (1983). Reason, gender, and morality in the history of philosophy. *Social Research, 50,* 490–513.

LYONS, N. (1983). Two perspectives: On self, relationships and morality. *Harvard Educational Review, 53,* 125–145.

NICHOLSON, L. J. (1983). Women, morality and history. *Social Research, 50,* 514–536.

VASUDEV, J., & HUMMEL, R. C. (1987). Moral stage sequence and principled reasoning in an Indian sample. *Human Development, 30,* 105–118.

WALKER, L. J. (1984). Sex differences in the development of moral reasoning: A critical review. *Child Development, 55,* 677–691.

WALKER, L. J. (1986). Sex differences in the development of moral reasoning: A rejoinder to Baumrind. *Child Development, 57,* 522–526.

Much Ado About . . . Knowing? Noting? Nothing?
A Reply to Vasudev Concerning Sex Differences and Moral Development

Carol Gilligan and Jane Attanucci

Harvard University

Evidence of moral voice and moral orientation—people speak about both justice and care but tend to focus on one or the other—includes psychologists' choices about how to speak and where to stand. Vasudev (1988) argues from a justice standpoint that we make much ado about nothing; when psychologists control for socioeconomic status, sex differences disappear. Yet women and men are not socioeconomic equals, nor, given sex differences in violence and child-care, are women simply disadvantaged. We have chosen to make much ado about knowing about theories based on all-male research samples and about noting differences in women's moral orientation.

A friendly colleague said to us recently: "But everyone knows there are sex differences." Why then such controversy, we thought. Clearly, one can observe striking sex differences in such morally relevant behavior as the incidence of violent crime, or note the sex differences in the composition of the prison population. One also can notice the sex differences in such morally relevant behavior as taking care of young children. Yet the discussion of sex differences and moral development within the field of psychology often seems premised on the assumption that common knowledge about sex differences is misleading and sociological facts of sex difference are irrelevant to theories about moral reasoning or moral emotions, or to psychological studies of moral development (see for example, Walker, 1984; Eisenberg & Lennon, 1983).

Thus Vasudev (1988), commenting on our recent paper (Gilligan & Attanucci, 1988), makes what she terms the "justified demand" that we join our "good ideas" with "strong" rather than "weak data," so that our ideas will not be dismissed by others as "trivial." In fact, data on sex differences in morally relevant behavior are, as just noted,

---

Correspondence should be sent to Carol Gilligan, Graduate School of Education, Harvard University, Roy E. Larsen, Appian Way, Cambridge, MA 02138.

Merrill-Palmer Quarterly, October 1988, Vol. 34, No. 4, pp. 451–456.

so readily available that they serve to underscore Sandra Scarr's observation that sex, like race, is "so sensitive [an issue in psychological
research] that many investigators try to hide such variation under the
general rubric of research on children or social class or parenting practices, all of which are well-known to vary by race and gender" (1988,
p. 56). Like Scarr, we believe that "ignorance of the importance of racial and gender differences in this society has not served those very
groups that investigators believed they were protecting" (p. 56).

From the study of moral voice and moral orientation in relation to
gender which we reported (1988) in the last issue of the *Quarterly*,
we learned that:

1. The relationship between moral orientation and gender is not
symmetrical, as the work of Lyons (1983) and others as well as some
of our own previous work has implied. Just as justice and care are not
polar opposites or mirror images of one another (with justice uncaring
and care unjust), so women and men are not opposite sexes with respect to moral voice or moral orientation. Our data provide evidence
that educationally advantaged North American males have a strong
tendency to focus on issues of justice when they describe an experience of moral conflict and choice; two thirds of the men in our
studies exhibited a "justice focus." One third of the women we
studied also showed a justice focus. But, one third of the women focused on care, in contrast to only one of the 46 men. From these data,
we conclude that a care focus (or different voice, within the justice
focused framework of moral theory), although not characteristic of all
women, is almost exclusively a female phenomenon in our studies of
educationally advantaged North Americans. Had we left women out
of our samples, care focus in moral reasoning would virtually have dis-
appeared.

2. Similarities between males and females with respect to moral
voice are highlighted by our shift in the method of data analysis. By
replacing Lyons's computation of "predominant moral orientation"
with the more stringent computation of "focus" as a measure of
moral orientation (75% or more considerations in one voice), we find
that one third of both females and males articulate justice and care
concerns with roughly equal frequency. By creating this category
(Care Justice) in addition to our two focus categories (justice focus,
care focus), we represent more clearly that concerns about justice
and concerns about care are common human concerns and not the
province of either sex. Furthermore, our study offered illustrations of
the way that the same decision (whether or not to turn in someone
who is drinking in violation of a medical school rule) is construed differently, depending on whether it is cast as a problem of justice (e.g.,

whether it is justified to show mercy in this case) or whether it is cast as a problem of care (e.g., what is the best way to respond to the problem posed by the drinking). This evidence runs counter to the claim made by Kohlberg (1984) and others (see Walker [1984], for example) that the moral voices of justice and care are domain specific, with justice pertinent to public or institutional dilemmas and care germane to the private or personal conflicts. Instead, our data illustrate how both justice and care voices can and do articulate both public and private concerns, albeit in different terms.

3. The fact that people tend, in describing an experience of moral conflict, to elaborate either justice or care concerns suggests that the psychology of moral development is characterized by a tendency toward loss of voice or perspective. The extent of the focus phenomenon (two thirds of both the women and the men we studied demonstrated the focus phenomenon, i.e., showed a justice or a care orientation) was the surprising finding of our recent research. Furthermore, our data indicate that the tendency to silence one moral voice or to lose sight of one set of moral concerns is a liability that both sexes share.

In these ways, our empirical study enabled us to clarify and refine our basic concepts of moral voice and moral orientation and also to understand better the relationship between moral orientation and gender. First, our data support our description of a "different voice" that is identified not by gender but by theme, specifically, by the focus on care concerns. Second, the evidence that care focus is, with one exception, a female phenomenon in our present data makes it clear why in our previous studies of college students, pregnant women, and educationally advantaged adults and children, it was our attention to women's conceptions of self and morality that led us to describe a different voice, a voice at odds with the definition of morality as a matter of justice. Finally, the tension between psychological theory and women's development is clarified by the observation that one third of the educationally advantaged women in our samples do not fit well into a justice-focused conception of morality. Thus the question arises: Does this lack of good fit signify a problem in women or a problem in theory?

Where we differ from our colleagues engaged in moral development research is not in our observation of sex differences per se but in our interpretation of the differences we observe. Where our colleagues have seen evidence of female deficiency in disparities between women's moral reasoning and psychologists' moral theories (deficiencies which they have attributed to women's position of social and economic disadvantage), we have seen a problem in theory, a problem reflected in the practice of choosing all-male research samples. This once common practice of leaving out women and designating all-male samples as "representative" both revealed and left a residue of different problems for women and men. Taken in itself as an instance of human behavior, the choice of all-male research samples suggests that men in the context of Western culture may have difficulty noticing the omission of women or seeing this omission as significant, whereas women may experience difficulty in noticing or seeing the omission of themselves, or in judging that omission to be nontrivial.

The current disagreement among psychologists over the question of sex differences and moral development bears on the issue that Vasudev (1988) raises concerning the neutrality or objectivity of psychological research. Vasudev objects to the fact that "sex differences as an area of theory and research in psychology has become politicized" (p. 240) and dates this politicization to our criticism of all-male research samples—as if the choice of an all-male sample for research on moral development, or identity development, or adolescent development, was a politically neutral or ideologically vacant act. That such samples were standard practice within a psychology which adopted what Vasudev calls "the convenient rubric of an objective, apolitical and value-neutral science" (p. 240) in itself calls this rubric into question. In our opinion, one of the virtues of the sex difference issue is that it rapidly reveals the impossibility of a disinterested position, or an Archimedean standpoint. In the human sciences, we cannot, as Hannah Arendt noted, "jump over our own shadows."

To remain cognizant of one's shadow, it is important to identify where one stands. In this sense, Vasudev's (1988) claim to assess our research from an objective, or dispassionate, or ideologically neutral position, may encourage her to judge the significance of our work within the framework of Kohlberg's stage theory as if Kohlberg's theory was orientation neutral. The relationship between moral orientation and moral stage, she claims, "should be the very issue in any investigation of Gilligan's ideas" (p. 239). In this criticism, she misses the central point of our work: the identification of moral voice as a characteristic of all moral discourse. To ask about moral voice also draws attention to the questions: Who is speaking about morality and in whose terms?

It is true that we have made much ado about knowing that psychologists have repeatedly left out girls and women in choosing research samples which they have characterized as representative of humans. We saw this omission as revealing, and judged it to be detrimental not only to psychology and to women, but also to men, encouraging men to silence concerns that they often felt deeply and thus to accede to an inadequate representation not only of others but also themselves. If it is easier in the present context for women to voice concerns about care and connection and to label instances of disconnection or detachment as a cause for moral concern, then it becomes especially important for psychologists to amplify women's voices in studying moral behavior. In contrast to Vasudev (1988), who argues in support of "Kohlberg's contention that when samples are controlled for education, socioeconomic status and occupation, there are no differences between males and females," (p. 241) we believe that females in this society cannot be characterized, simply in terms of social and economic deficits. The tendency for women to assume responsibility for the care and nurture of young children is not, in our opinion, a sign of deficiency—although the assumption of this responsibility often places women in a situation of economic dependency and social disadvantage.

Our data, which indicate the capacity of people to speak in terms of both justice and care, point to moral voice and moral standpoint as an important feature of moral development, and of research on moral development. Our suggestion that researchers listen for moral voice and attend to moral orientation in designing their studies as well as in analyzing their data, leads us also to emphasize that knowledge of more than one moral voice and standpoint creates a choice about how to speak and where to stand. Thus we arrive at a new way of thinking about the relationship between self and morality. Rather than following the traditional separation of self from morality, we see evidence of moral voice and moral orientation as providing data on where a person stands in a world which is irreducibly social and relational and therefore one which people tend to imbue with moral concern.

Our disagreement with Vasudev stems from the fact that we observe women and men to stand in different positions within American society and within Western culture and to engage in different activities, which we consider morally germane. If psychological research on moral development does not reflect these sex differences in social and economic situations and in what would seem to be morally relevant behavior, then we would scrutinize the measures rather than reach the conclusion that such differences between males and females are of no psychological consequence and have no moral implications.

REFERENCES

EISENBERG, N., & LENNON, R. (1983). Sex differences in empathy and related capacities. *Psychological Bulletin, 94,* 100–131.

GILLIGAN, C., & ATTANUCCI, J. (1988). Two moral orientations: Gender differences and similarities. *Merrill-Palmer Quarterly, 34,* 223–237.

KOHLBERG, L. (1984). *Psychology of moral development: Essays on moral development.* San Francisco: Harper & Row.

LYONS, N. (1983). Two perspectives: On self, relationships, and morality. *Harvard Educational Review, 53,* 125–145.

SCARR, S. (1988). Race and gender as psychological variables: Social and ethical issues. *American Psychologist, 43,* 56–59.

VASUDEV, J. (1988). Sex differences in morality and moral orientation: A discussion of the Gilligan and Attanucci study. *Merrill-Palmer Quarterly, 34,* 239–244.

WALKER, L. (1984). Sex differences in the development of moral reasoning: A critical review. *Child Development, 55,* 183–201.

Human Development 1991;34:61–80

© 1991 S. Karger AG, Basel
0018–716X/91/0342–0061$2.75/0

Interpretive Experiments:
Probing the Care-Justice Debate in Moral Development

Bill Puka

Rensselaer Polytechnic Institute, Troy, N.Y., USA

Key Words. Bias · Care · Gender · Gilligan · Interpretation · Justice · Kohlberg · Moral development · Patriarchy

Abstract. Two proposals are made: (a) theories of development are developmental phenomena themselves and should be addressed developmentally, and (b) developmental theories are conceptual research programs that should proceed experimentally. The implications of these proposals are traced with respect to the care-justice, or Kohlberg-Gilligan, debate regarding moral judgment and gender role. Various 'different voice' counterhypotheses are posed for the purpose of comparison with Gilligan's 'different voice' of caring and her critique of justice as the basis of moral judgment. Exploration of these counterhypotheses suggests how care's voice and Kohlberg's vision might be nurtured together.

A developmental theory, like the process it depicts, is a process of development. As with any such process, we must address its current stage relative to earlier ones, and to a certain course of evolution. Each stage merits specialized treatment, and the theory-building process should be nurtured in many promising directions.

A crucial feature of Kohlberg's theory of moral development is that it 'conceived itself' developmentally. Colby et al. [1983] have offered an explicit meta-theory of the moral stage theory, tracing its three main stages of development and its three accompanying scoring methods. They also presented a 'bootstrapping method' for theory building that explains how these theory-

stages evolved. With rare exception [Nicolayev and Phillips, 1979], Kohlberg's critics have yet to address his developmental theory from this developmental perspective. The result has been gross distortions in what 'Kohlberg's theory' (as if there were only one) holds and in where its strengths and faults lie [Puka, 1989a]. Most important, dubious developments in Kohlberg's meta-theories have not been distinguished from the steady course of his data-based stage theory.

Developmental theories also constitute conceptual experiments or research programs. They try out certain initially plausible, or creatively implausible, hypotheses to see where they lead. Theory building has its own well-developed research methods and designs, evolved in fields such as philosophy, theology, physics, and literary criticism. These range from constructive methods (hermeneutics, inductive inference, linguistic analysis, parsimonious reduction) through critical methods (Cartesian skepticism, counterfactuals and counterexamples, deconstructions), to supportive ones (comparative justification, application to cases, assessment relative to meta-criteria). This theoretical methodology functions on its own research plane, beside the more empirical aspects of social science. It is a common error, a false wisdom, to assume that social scientific theory should develop only in direct, dialectical relation to data. Neither interpretive accuracy nor explanatory adequacy can be determined by empirical data. Such deep theoretical issues are only resolved by prolonged theoretical analysis.

On this experimental plane of theory, Kohlberg falls as far short as his critics. Indeed, it seems standard practice in research psychology to view theorizing as a crude form of global speculation, sharply divergent from research. As Gilligan [1986] portrays the process, one's 'own conceptual frame' and one's 'general reading of psychology' bring coherence to intuitively striking observations. But clearly such 'theoretical impressionism' will not do in the study of moral development. Here we depend heavily on qualitative, interpretive analysis and complex philosophical views. Nor will theoretical approaches do that are allegedly 'less interpretive' than Gilligan's (or Freud's or Erikson's). Theories simply are not direct stabs at the truth. They are wide-ranging inquiries, characterized by varied purposes and goals. Many of these goals are only remotely tied to accurate description.

Had Kohlberg theorized experimentally, his initial conceptions of morality and maturity would have been mere hypotheses, not grounding assumptions. He would not have concluded at the outset that moral cognition reduces to justice reasoning, then designed his moral judgment interview to test it. He would not have installed liberal egalitarianism as the ideal, a priori endpoint of psychological development. Rather, Kohlberg would have devised a variety of moral judgment interviews, designed to probe different senses of morality and requisite competencies. He would have interpreted interview data in several distinct ways, relative to the range of key ethical ideals. This effort would have generated utilitarian stages, benevolence stages, libertarian, and meritocratic stages of moral judgment. And these alternative interpretations would have been debated comparatively, for all to examine and assess. Also, Kohlberg would have tried various ways of relating moral psychology to philosophy and of defining a developmental sequence on these bases. His respondents' own sense of morality would have figured in as well. The relation between philosophy and psychology is something for a research psychologist to investigate, not assume. And to a psychologist, a respondent's subjective moral sense should have legitimacy apart from its philosophical validity. Perhaps this is the most incontrovertible insight of critics such as Gilligan.

The 'Different Voice': An Extended Invitation

The present analysis of Gilligan's 'different voice' illustrates a developmental and experimental approach to developmental theory – it poses a theoretical research program. According to Gilligan [1982], Kohlberg's theory may reflect an individualistic outlook on human affairs, an outlook that typifies male gender role and identity. As a theory of human development, consequently, it may favor self-interested and self-protective moral norms and goals. This bias is best served by the theme of justice, with its demanding individual rights, restrictive duties, and rigid, legalistic 'social contracts'. Yet, as there is a second half to human identity – the female half – so there is a second theme of moral development. This is responsive caring, reflecting a relational sense of self and other, characteristic of female identity. The relational care theme, with the spontaneous women's development it reflects, has been discriminated against in developmental theory, according to Gilligan. Specifically, it has been underrepresented, undervalued, and distorted within Kohlberg's stages of justice reasoning. A more adequate theory of development would chart the complementary progress of both themes, justice and care, as reflected in the moral perception, conceptualization, and interaction of both females and males.

The potential of Gilligan's hypothesis is easily underestimated unless it is contemplated in the context of the theoretical research traditions with which it is associated. Gilligan's 'different voice' extends the proven research design of critical theory, linking supposedly impartial and universal viewpoints to the partisan interests of a certain social group. It also furthers the powerful feminist research program – first, by exposing the apparent use of male standards in assessing general human abilities and, second, by posing an alternative feminine outlook based on neglected female experience.

Most important, the 'different voice' brings moral development into the central moral debate in human history. This debate concerns the conflicting yet somehow complementary links between just law and benevolent virtue. One finds the essence of this debate in ancient Confucian texts in which 'human heartedness' is the recommended salve for the constrictive moralism of ritual justice. The central tension of the Judeo-Christian tradition rises from the contrary pulls of commandment justice and the heartfelt ethic of love and mercy. Indeed, the conflict between justice and benevolence has been the centerpiece of moral philosophical debate for the past century, pitting Kantians against utilitarians, deontologists against teleologists. Many would argue that political conservatism and liberalism part company on the same ground.

The 'different voice', then, speaks for many. If only as a representative of these traditions, this hypothesis merits long-term theoretical research and development. Gilligan's 'different voice' is especially well-suited for such purposes; it is one of the few psychological views that takes an explicitly developmental and experimental approach to theory itself. Gilligan [1986, p. 325f.] casts the critical voice of her hypothesis to address 'biases at the theoretical level', not biases in research method or data analysis. The constructive voice of Gilligan's hypothesis distinguishes its interpretive conceptions of care and justice from 'statistical' ones, or descriptively simple ones. Thus, it is a mistake to see the 'different voice' merely as an *empirical* research hypothesis.

Gilligan [1986] emphasizes the distinctly interpretive or theoretical nature of her hypothesis in replying to critics. For Gilligan, research surveys [Walker, 1984] showing no significant gender differences on Kohlberg's instrument do not clear away gender bias. Admittedly 'no differences' may be interpreted as parity between naturally developing male and female competence in justice reasoning. But they may also show that females typically learn to simulate male skills. On such an account, the natural competencies of female moral judgment may escape notice. Only how one interprets Kohlberg's findings will tell. The data cannot speak for themselves, and data alone cannot test an interpretive hypothesis [Gilligan, 1986, p. 328]. Indeed, interpreting such data and testing such hypotheses show how one conceives morality itself.

In these respects, and in being carefully dubbed a hypothesis, the 'different voice' can only represent a first stage of theory building. As such it invites further research and development on a distinctively theoretical plane. As an interpretive alternative to the 'dominant voices' in moral development, Gilligan's 'different voice' also models a crucial research strategy – that of comparative theoretical analysis and assessment. And in presenting the 'different voice' for assessment, Gilligan invites us to take part in this comparative research program.

I accept this invitation here by posing 5 interpretive hypotheses – 5 alternative 'different voice' interpretations of Gilligan's observations. These are specifically designed for comparison with Gilligan's own particular 'different voice', to test its interpretive strength.

Following Gilligan's lead, I adopt the approaches of critical and feminist theory, beginning with the crucial three-part distinction among: (a) the intended aims of a theorist in formulating an interpretive account; (b) the subsequent meta-interpretations and

reinterpretations of such accounts relative to these intentions, and (c) the actual content, form, and function of the theorist's position.

Gilligan, for example, recognized Kohlberg's intention to chart human development in moral reasoning in a manner that transcends gender, culture, and class. Kohlberg aspired to support this intention, Gilligan observed, with an objective philosophical justification, an impartial defense of impartial justice. Gilligan's 'different voice' reinterprets Kohlberg's stage theory, hypothesizing that it actually depicts individualistic outlooks and self-protective moral preferences typical of males. These preferences are then supported, as Gilligan sees it, by the patriarchal ideologies of Kantianism.

In like fashion I view Gilligan's hypothesis as a sincere attempt to challenge patriarchal bias and callous individualism in Kohlberg's theory. It provides a sketch of a relational care orientation, preferred by women, that completes the picture of human moral development. Yet, I question the moral adequacy and de facto feminism of care and explore alternative ways that caring may figure in women's lives and thought and may relate to justice. I also question whether Gilligan locates Kohlberg's bias in the right place or demonstrates the relevance of 'care focus' to moral development.

My aim throughout this discussion is to preserve the strengths of both Gilligan's and Kohlberg's views, and the two moral traditions they champion. Gilligan's 'different voice' is challenged only where its own critical challenges have served to undermine Kohlberg's theory. Preserving the strengths of Kohlbergian justice is surprisingly crucial for Gilligan's own account, as her view of moral maturity combines care with justice.

Yet Gilligan's own account of justice points almost exclusively to flaws – rigidity, legalism, impersonality, aloofness, unresponsiveness, callousness, judgmentalism, punitiveness, abstractedness, inattentiveness to detail and context, and uncooperativeness – that make justice an unfit partner for care.

By utilizing theoretical research methods, we can construct 'different voices' that extend Gilligan's interpretive approach, while overcoming its key limitations. Unfortunately, in posing her hypothesis, Gilligan never makes her interpretive methods explicit. She offers virtually no basis for judging her interpretation plausible among possible alternatives, nor does she pose any such alternatives for comparison. Yet the key implication of recognizing that theory is underdetermined by data [Gilligan, 1986] is that one's interpretive method must bear the weight of proof, rendering one's interpretation preferable to alternatives [Puka, 1989b].

Mindful of these limitations, I first identify the assumptions that ground Gilligan's interpretations and then propose counterhypotheses against which these interpretations can be tested. In a sense, these alternative 'voices' will vie for Gilligan's interpretive favor by trying to accommodate the very data from which her own 'different voice' stems.

The Four Assumptions of Gilligan's Web and Five Counterhypotheses

Like her view of relationality in caring, Gilligan's 'different voice' hypothesis represents an interconnected web of mutually dependent relations. In this web, cognitive-moral orientation depends on social orientation and social orientation depends on self-

concept. Self-concept, in turn, depends largely on gender identity, which is a function of early childhood socialization [Gilligan, 1982, chapt. 1]. Crucial relations also exist between the critical and constructive facets of Gilligan's hypothesis, between charges of justice bias and claims to the adequacy of care.

An analysis of these connections shows that Gilligan's web rests on 4 assumptions, each in need of support.

Assumption 1: Gender and Justice Bias. To hold that justice bias is mainly due to gender bias, Gilligan must assume that other causal influences are weaker. This can only be shown by comparative interpretation and analysis of (biasing) causal influences. Such an account has yet to be attempted. Alternatively, to hold that a strong emphasis on justice in Kohlberg's higher stages represents a bias in itself – a bias that serves, but need not reflect, male preferences – Gilligan must assume that this emphasis is illegitimate. It cannot be required by the moral concerns and competencies of those stages. This assumption depends on an analysis of the legitimate moral reasoning requirements of each higher stage, set by its social perspective-taking structure. Likewise, such an analysis has yet to begin.

To test this first assumption, the *politics-of-justice counterhypothesis* is proposed. It suggests that Kohlberg's biases result from a combination of theoretical and methodological factors in his work that cause his higher stages to overemphasize the institutional, political, and legal domains of morality. Once in place, these emphases legitimize further emphasis on rights and justice at higher stages. They also lead to de-emphasis of care and concern, which are prominent at lower stages. But they also downplay various themes of interpersonal fairness and respect that are key to justice. Thus it is not the justice theme itself that is the source of Kohlberg's bias.

Assumption 2: Theme Difference. If focusing on justice in moral cognition underrepresents, undervalues, and distorts care, then the logic of justice cannot accommodate care. But this assumption is difficult to demonstrate. As Gilligan's own critique attests, the basic principles of justice are extremely general and abstract. Once their encompassing implications are traced, respect for autonomy may show powerful links to empathy and relationality. This result is predictable given the heavy reliance on social role taking in Kohlberg's theory. Moreover, nothing in the nature of abstract and universal principles precludes the prescription that we be contextual, particularistic, and situational in showing moral regard.

To test the theme difference assumption, a *care-of-justice counterhypothesis* is proposed. According to this counterhypothesis, Gilligan's account divides the moral themes reflected in Kohlberg's stages into two artificial and polarized components: justice and care. By severing the intimate connection between the fair and benevolent variants of these themes, Gilligan's account underrepresents, undervalues, and distorts the care of justice.

Assumption 3: Comparable Phenomena. To hold that theories of moral development discriminate against care or women's development, Gilligan must assume that justice and care reflect comparable phenomena. If they do not, then the prevalence of one in one domain and the other in another domain does not indicate that accounts in either domain are biased. But more than this, *bias* (toward justice) does not by itself indicate *discrimination* (against care). Additional evidence must be provided of particular biasing effects.

It is unclear whether developmental levels of care exist at all. The scoring system used to provide the major empirical verification of care does not even score for care levels [Lyons, 1983]. Yet in Kohlberg's theory, only that portion of moral cognition that shows development is included in the account of moral reasoning. If care does not show comparable development, it cannot be a comparable phenomenon.

The *separate-realities counterhypothesis* is offered to test this third assumption. It proposes that care and Kohlbergian justice are two different kinds of phenomena. Therefore, accounts of one need not encompass the other, nor can they be criticized for disregarding the other.

The *care-as-liberation counterhypothesis* goes one step further, portraying the separate reality that care may be. Here, reputed care levels of development are recast as psychological coping strategies specifically tailored by women to handle sexism.

Assumption 4: Equal Adequacy. If a justice perspective on moral maturity undervalues care, Gilligan must assume that the moralities of care and justice are of comparable adequacy. This assumption requires a philosophical account comparing the moral strengths and weaknesses of both. Gilligan has provided none.

The *care-off-key counterhypothesis* proposes that care is a seriously inadequate moral theme. Despite its clearly noble ideals, care proves far more limited and problematic than justice in affording basic moral competence, even though there may be serious deficiencies in justice.

Until these 4 crucial assumptions are tested and supported by means of comparative analysis, Gilligan's web hangs suspended in air. In the remainder of the paper, I explore each of the 5 counterhypotheses that have been proposed.

Some ideas examined here have appeared elsewhere, at least piecemeal [Kohlberg et al., 1983; Broughton, 1983]. Indeed, these counterhypotheses encompass the most common arguments in the Kohlberg-Gilligan debate. But I attempt here to transform them from contentious points and counterpoints into useful research hypotheses. Thus, it is incorrect to view these counterhypotheses simply as a critique of Gilligan's proposals. To the contrary, they serve the internal, self-critical development of Gilligan's 'different voice'. Gilligan's [1987, Gilligan and Wiggins, 1988] recent revisionary writings serve a similar function, though they may confound alternative interpretations of care data with meta-interpretations of the 'different voice' hypothesis itself. Of course, since these 'different voices' are theoretical research hypotheses, not components of a view, they are not necessarily consistent with each other. Successful development of some might render others implausible.

The Care-of-Justice Hypothesis

I begin with the care-of-justice hypothesis, which maintains that Gilligan's 'care focus' and 'justice focus' distort Kohlberg's account of moral reasoning. Each (higher) stage in Kohlberg's sequence encompasses an individual liberty component and a group welfare component. Obligations and rights claims at each stage combine the two components structurally and functionally. Gilligan's interpretive stance dissects this interrelational web into two artifical components.

It rends the holistic fabric of 'caring justice' by tearing the due regard for personal autonomy from its supportive context of social concern and responsibility. Only in such isolation does Kohlbergian justice appear individualistic.

In Gilligan's account, justice appears only in its weakest pose. In part, this is because Gilligan ignores Kohlberg's key distinction between the well-integrated structure of justice reasoning and the rigid 'law-and-order' orientation that accompanies certain stage structures [Kohlberg, 1971, 1973, 1984]. Conversely, Gilligan's account virtually ignores the relational, aid-to-others components of Kohlberg's stages. These clearly resonate with the beneficent strains of care and, in some respects, outdo them.

Four main points can be made in support of further research on the care-of-justice hypothesis.

(1) On Gilligan's account, the alleged impersonality and callousness of Kohlbergian justice stem from an emphasis on rules and principles. In Kohlberg's higher stages these rules are allegedly rigid and legalistic, calculating and formulaic. The principles involved are overly general and abstract, and insensitive to context.

In fact, insofar as Kohlberg's system actually scores for rules, it serves to eliminate them. It relegates rule orientations to cognitive type A, rather than the more adequate type B style of cognition [Kohlberg, 1984, pp. 652–683]. Then it excludes cognitive types and styles from stage structure. Moreover, despite avid discussion of general principles and their vices by Kohlberg commentators, only one principle actually graces Kohlberg's stages: the 'golden rule'. It appears at stage 3, which is focused more on caring than justice, and at stage 6, which has been suspended (since 1978) from Kohlberg's system. And, of course, general principles of justice do not occur at stage 4, the main nemesis of care, nor at stage 5. So it is difficult to see how these principles (or rules) foster callousness in justice development.

(2) Gilligan's critique of justice focuses on the individualistic rights and strict law enforcement of stage 4. But she fails to note three mitigating factors in stage structure that provide appropriate moral context. First, stage 4 rights are accorded to individuals to the degree they contribute to the common good. Second, laws and their strict enforcement are prized only as they promote social cohesion and cooperation. (This legal function is especially crucial at institutional levels where intimate relationships cannot suffice.) Third, the toleration of individual differences and of exceptions to laws actually is advocated at stage 4 when this promotes social harmony. (Even in a 'law and order' orientation, laws breeding community disharmony or threats to intimate family ties are opposed.)

(3) Kohlberg's stage 5 upholds individualistic rights to noninterference only in combination with social utilitarian responsibilities. These bid us to relieve need and suffering, and work for the welfare of all. Such responsibilities apply to us relationally, as members of cooperating groups. And they integrate with rights contextually, as care recommends. Hence, no rule, formula, or principle in stage 5 structure suggests how to balance rights and welfare, individual and group.

(4) Kohlberg's stage 6 appears to place overwhelming emphasis on equal respect and reciprocity through individual rights. But clearly its responsibilities entail high degrees of altruism. And if, as both Gilligan and Kohlberg claim, stage 6 logic defines the structure and adequacy of all other stages, significant degrees of altruism should pervade the entire justice sequence. Out of basic respect or fairness at stage 6, we must risk years in jail – even our very lives if necessary – to help total strangers in need. (Kohlberg [1971] makes this clear in resolving his famous Heinz dilemma.) Moreover, it is the right of these strangers to be helped, not merely their plea to our caring compassion. Stage 6 bids that we do favors for people as a matter of course – that we help them whether or not we feel caring toward them, or can relate to them. In short, stage 6 obligations define a do-gooder, aid-to-others ethic. This is the meaning of Kohlberg's claim that, at stage 6 alone, rights and responsibilities are fully correlative.

Before we (or Gilligan) can determine that there exist caring deficiencies in Kohlberg's stages, then, we must address these beneficent implications of justice. We must investigate the holism of moral reasoning as Kohlberg defined it. This task is not easy. Kohlberg's own highly inconsistent accounts of how care relates to justice testify to the difficulties involved. In these accounts [Kohlberg, 1984, chapt. 3, 1986], care is simultaneously: (a) *encompassed* by justice through fellow feeling, role-taking, and a respectful sense of concern; (b) *complementary* to justice as the areteic (virtuous) accompaniment to deontic (obligatory) duties, and (c) *distinct* from justice as a theme of general ethics rather than morality proper.

The Politics-of-Justice Hypothesis

According to this hypothesis, if Kohlberg's higher stages are biased, gender and moral theme are not the chief culprits. Rather, an unhappy interaction of methodological and theoretical factors is to blame, one that leads Kohlberg to de-emphasize interpersonal morality generally, perhaps Kohlberg's most serious mistake.

Five such factors can be suggested. First, the very phenomenon of development requires depictions that emphasize what is *added* at each new stage, not *preserved* from earlier stages. This fact leads Kohlberg to underemphasize lower-stage concerns, with their exclusively interpersonal norms. Second, the scoring of moral judgment requires that stage descriptions emphasize differences, not similarities, among stages. By magnifying these differences to aid in scoring, Kohlberg places unintended emphasis on later-developing competencies. Doing so de-emphasizes interpersonal concerns. Third, because the competence to differentiate large-scale social perspectives is newly added at later stages, these stages overemphasize the institutional, political, and legal domains of morality. (We would predict this result from the first two factors). Fourth, once large-scale social settings are in focus, it is morally appropriate to emphasize rights and justice. The logic of these concepts is tailor-made for such settings. In particular, the exigencies of political and legal institutions call for self-protective powers and fairly applied policies. Thus Kohlberg legitimately emphasizes justice at higher stages. Finally, Kohlberg's stage descriptions tend to blur needed distinctions among the moralities of law, political systems, and nonformal social institutions. This failing plagues social science generally and is the bain of Kohlberg's philosophical writings. Here once again, it causes later stages to favor institutional concerns over interpersonal ones.

Emphasis on institutional, political, and legal domains of morality is associated with a male outlook and preferences. The present hypothesis proposes, however, that it is the preceding factors, rather than 'male bias', that are responsible for this emphasis in Kohlberg's theory. Clearly, the institutional focus of Kohlberg's later stages downplays the role of care in moral judgment. Care is a decidedly interpersonal and pacifistic ethic by nature. Thus, it has little role to play in the threatening and coercive machinations of legal institutions. But this institutional focus also downplays key interpersonal themes of justice and fairness. Thus, Kohlberg's bias is unlikely to derive from a justice theme, and a justice emphasis in moral development is unlikely to be care's chief problem. Surprisingly, then, complementing justice with care will not remedy the problems at hand.

Three main points can be made in support of further research on the politics-of-justice hypothesis.

(1) In formulating stage descriptions Kohlberg faced three main tasks: (a) to accurately reflect his most reliable data; (b) to distinguish among strikingly similar cognitive-moral systems; and (c) to demonstrate the distinct improvements of each stage over its predecessor. These tasks bid Kohlberg to emphasize differences, not similarities, between stages and to focus on what each stage adds, not preserves.

Differentiating stages is central to the moral judgment scoring manual, the source of stage descriptions [Colby and Kohlberg, 1987]. The manual shows that level of social perspective, not moral theme, is the primary determinant of moral stage. Any plausible moral theme expressed at a more differentiated and integrated level of social perspective would betoken a higher moral stage. This fact is clear from the stage descriptions also. The so-called justice theme actually comprises several moral themes, extending from ethical egoism and libertarian rights through social utilitarianism and moral perfectionism ('ideal harmony'). Each is accorded an explicit category in the scoring system [Kohlberg, 1984, p. 406]. Social perspective-taking evolves from exclusively personal and interpersonal levels to include social and institutional ones. Thus, emphasis on what is newly acquired at each stage results in an increasing emphasis on social-institutional morality at higher stages.

(2) Kohlberg's research dilemmas and scoring categories do not distinguish issues of interpersonal, institutional, political, and legal ethics. Questions about breaking the law, or about the appropriate length of criminal sentencing, mix with questions about keeping a promise to a friend. Yet, distinguishing such issues is key to moral reasoning. Their moral logic not only diverges, but often conflicts. Interpersonal morality deals with what is right and good per se, and with showing respect and concern for people. But institutional morality concerns special problems of remote, large-scale cooperation. Thus, it legitimately emphasizes certain otherwise nonmoral issues of social interest and practical feasibility. Political and legal morality concerns what is justifiable – when it is permissible to do what would normally be wrong. Law, even just law, involves enforcement. And enforcement means threat, coercion, and inflicted harm (punishment), to prevent worse harm.

As Kohlberg's research fails to probe for differentiations among these logics, so his stage descriptions fail to mirror those that appear. Kohlberg's claims for the adequacy

of later stages also overlook these differentiations. And similar problems arise when Kohlberg uses theories of political justice [Rawls, 1971] to support his claims of the moral adequacy of higher stages.

(3) By stressing what is added by each new stage, rather than reintegrated from before, Kohlberg steers focus away from morality simpliciter. Higher stages are defined by their differentiation of 'law-maintaining' and 'law-creating' perspectives on social cooperation. At such stages, care's virtues clearly are less useful than those of individual rights and just law. Large-scale social discord cannot be resolved by the interpersonal skills of responsive dialogue and consensus seeking. Natural responses of compassion and empathy also are out of place since intimate relationships or even face-to-face contact are largely precluded here.

Yet, similar constraints characterize the key interpersonal themes of justice. Among these themes are: (a) reciprocating fairly in friendships and family; (b) granting self-determination to our dependents; and (c) recognizing individual merit or demerit. We cannot adequately convey such respectfulness to others in institutionally mediated relations, nor when dealing with large-scale crime and tyranny. (Consider the myth that all members of society can be paid what they deserve for their work.)

The politics-of-justice, like the care-of-justice, hypothesis must be compared with Gilligan's own version of a 'different voice', to assess its plausibility. Once developed, the current hypothesis also must compete with critiques of Kohlberg's theory charging bias by class, culture, or ideology [Simpson, 1974; Sullivan, 1977; Shweder, 1982].

We turn now to hypotheses having more far-reaching implications for the Kohlberg-

Gilligan debate: first, that care orientation and Kohlbergian justice reasoning are independent psychological phenomena, not two versions of the same phenomenon (the *separate-realities hypothesis)*; second, that care levels are quasi-feminist coping strategies for handling sexism, not progressive developments in cognitive-moral competence (the *care-as-liberation hypothesis)*; and third, that care is a deficient moral theme that rightfully ought to be downplayed in Kohlberg's higher stages (the *care-off-key hypothesis)*.

The Separate-Realities Hypothesis

According to the separate-realities hypothesis, Gilligan's care orientation reflects a different sort of cognition than does Kohlberg's moral reasoning. Thus, it is premature to charge Kohlberg's system with discrimination against care or women's development, or to claim that strengths in care focus and weaknesses in justice focus demonstrate limitations in justice reasoning. Likewise, there is little foundation for the prevalent belief that Gilligan's research extends an unduly restricted tradition of moral development research.

It is further proposed that the divide between Kohlberg's and Gilligan's views is best revealed by linking differences in their research approaches to differences in their theoretical accounts. This strategy contrasts sharply with the 'separate realities' approach taken by Kohlberg [1984, chapt. 3, 4]. Here, in response to Gilligan, the 'hard' (formal) structure and duty focus of justice development is distinguished from the 'soft' structure and virtue focus of care. But these distinctions are cut too fine. They admit care too readily to the realms of structural cogni-

tion and morality proper. Such realms are narrow indeed within the broader field of psychology. Therefore, finely distinguished phenomena within them seem mere variants of a single reality – as Gilligan portrays them – not separate realities. The emphasis on 'hard' structure in justice reasoning also fuels charges of excessive formalism in Kohlberg's theory.

To contrast two realities from two variants, or voices, more fundamental distinctions are needed. Thus, I distinguish Kohlberg's research interest in inherent development, basic moral ability, holistic reasoning systems, and shared moral norms, from Gilligan's research focus on moral perception and reflection, learned skills, and relativized value ideologies. These fundamental differences in approach make the incommensurability of Kohlberg's and Gilligan's results quite predictable and comprehensible. They allow us to trace Kohlberg's and Gilligan's accounts to two virtually different fields of inquiry.

Kohlberg seeks a 'common voice' morality that provides shared guidelines for human cooperation and conflict resolution. Different moral voices within society create much of the conflict and lack of sharing that such a morality must address. The 'common voice' responds by adopting a variety of themes as its own – just desert, social welfare, virtue, rights – and by stressing fairness and toleration toward all. The so-called justice or respect theme distinguishes itself from a particular moral theme in this respect. By contrast, Gilligan's research targets distinctive moral voices, relativized to gender identity and social outlook. Such themes are circumscribed by nature and often conflicting. Gilligan also reinterprets Kohlberg's justice as a circumscribed theme – a partisan different voice' claiming to speak for all. But then she does not seek an alternative 'common voice' cleansed of Kohlberg's bias. Had Gilligan's research focused on how all people combine care and justice – had she proposed a different common voice – matters might be different.

Fundamental contrasts between Kohlberg's and Gilligan's approaches support the separate-realities hypothesis. [See Puka, 1989c, for further examination of these contrasts.]

Kohlberg's Focus

(1) Kohlberg's main research tool, the moral judgment interview, poses a variety of difficult hypothetical moral dilemmas. They reflect a search for general moral reasoning ability, across moral tasks. So-called 'real-life' dilemmas, in contrast, are more likely to elicit particularized orientations and choices.

(2) Kohlberg's dilemmas are accompanied by challenging probe questions. These test the limits of moral reasoning competence, and the consistency of response. They help assure that the instrument assesses underlying cognitive systems, not simply surface ideologies or socialized beliefs. Such systems can be said to 'develop' because they are adequately holistic and stable to undergo progressive transformation and yet remain intact. They also are sufficiently self-directed to resist the powerful influences of external forces. Values ideologies are not as self-contained. They are thus less likely to develop systematically.

(3) Probe questions seek to uncover our most basic abilities, rather than refined skills. Only such abilities are likely to be shared, and to uphold a common moral voice. Particular skills and value preferences show individual differences and are more likely to underlie different moral voices.

(4) Kohlberg's [1969] research program has been cross-cultural from the start, and has consistently sustained this emphasis [Reimer, 1977; Parihk, 1980; Snarey, 1982; Nisan and Kohlberg, 1982]. This emphasis reflects Kohlberg's search for a universal, 'common voice' of moral development. Also, Kohlberg has stressed longitudinal research, observing interview respondents at close, regular intervals. One would expect this of a program seeking to identify universal, invariant development.

(5) Kohlberg studied the relation of age to moral stage, and the influence of direct instruction or reinforcement on stage change. His reassuringly negative findings helped to distinguish genuine stage development from social learning [Blatt and Kohlberg, 1975]. Kohlberg also investigated cases of apparent stage regression, which helped to distinguish lowered levels of performance from loss of underlying ability. And by using hypothetical and real-life dilemmas together [Kohlberg et al., 1975], he distinguished underlying cognitive competence from more superficial cognitive skills.

(6) In contrast to Gilligan, Kohlberg examined moral orientations and metacognitions, to distinguish them from development in moral reasoning itself. This metacognitive thought was systematically excluded from the description of stages of moral reasoning.

Gilligan's Focus

(1) Gilligan's [1982, pp. 2, 30, 64] research interviews invite respondents to reflect open-endedly on personal experiences, beliefs, and personal character, which are judged morally relevant by respondents. No

attempt is made to promote a broad-based moral focus in respondents' thinking; deliberation on interpersonal problems is not distinguished from metacognition or socialized opinion. Nor are responses probed, as a means of aiding in the discovery of underlying cognitive systems [p. 2].

(2) Gilligan's main real-life dilemma (used as the basis for charting care levels) is more likely to elicit situational responses than underlying competence. Its focus, abortion, is seen as a severe personal crisis for Gilligan's respondents, and the reactions it incites are termed 'response to crisis' [pp. 72, 107f.]. Obviously, the abortion dilemma elicits distinctly female responses as well – Gilligan chose it for an all-female study, expressly designed to uncover 'women's moral voice' [Gilligan and Belenky, 1980; Gilligan, 1982, pp. 70f, 156].

When almost one-fifth of Gilligan's respondents showed regression in care level, when discussing abortion, Gilligan [1982, p. 108] did not further probe or analyze responses. For her research program, it was not crucial to determine whether a true loss in competence had occurred or merely a functional decline typical of crises.

(3) Unlike Kohlberg's, Gilligan's studies have not been primarily longitudinal or cross-cultural. Thus, they do not focus squarely on the invariant sequence and universality questions. The only longitudinal component of Gilligan's research involved a single follow-up interview administered to 65 of 214 respondents. Only 21 of these 65 interviews were used to derive care levels [Gilligan, 1982, chapt. 3, 4]. Only such longitudinal data can possibly establish care as developmental. Clearly, then, Gilligan's research addresses care as a cognitive orientation, not a developmental phenomenon,

while Kohlberg's work only addresses those aspects of moral reasoning that develop.

(4) In interpreting her data, Gilligan frames no conceptual account of care's moral character. Nor does she argue for care's general adequacy as a common moral voice in human development. To the contrary, Gilligan [1982, pp. 70f., 107f.] specifically categorizes care 'development', under gender orientation. Care's thematic variations of self-protection, approval seeking, self-confrontation, and self-chosen concern for others are categorized in the same way.

(5) In Gilligan's [1982, p. 2] contrast between care and Kohlbergian justice, 'no claims are made about the origins of the differences described or their distribution in a wider population, across cultures or through time'. Thus, Gilligan makes no attempt to distinguish how socialization, maturation, or constructive integration shape care, concerns central to Kohlberg's study of moral development. Without concern, Gilligan acknowledges the influence of nonstructural, nondevelopmental, and even noncognitive factors on the basic shape of care. These include social status and power, traditional mores and gender stereotypes, 'sexual politics,' the 'psychology of passivity', self-confidence and self-deception, loneliness, depression, cycles of repetition, and bad love experiences [pp. 67–71, 79–85, 96, 109–114, 124–126]. To Gilligan, depression, loneliness, and self-deception are key in how one responds to crisis. But it is difficult to see the relevance of these to moral competencies.

(6) Gilligan [1982, pp. 1–6] stresses the causal relation between gender socialization and women's preference for care. Higher levels of care development are portrayed in reflective, metacognitive terms [pp. 90–99], focusing on personal maturity, not structural

adequacy. Moreover, Gilligan [pp. 102–104, 166] buttresses this portrayal with Perry's [1968] levels of intellectual and ethical development. Such metacognitive development, like socialized ideology, is known to shift rapidly. Thus, it is not surprising that 12 of Gilligan's 21 abortion study respondents either developed or regressed in care level within merely a single year interval [p. 108]. By contrast, the minimal time interval observed for structural stage development in Kohlberg's system is 3–5 years [Colby et al., 1983].

The preceding disparities between Kohlberg's and Gilligan's approaches are difficult to explain if we assume that care and justice merely vary a common theme. A vivid indication of care's 'separate reality' comes from Gilligan's self-reflections on method. Replying to critics, Gilligan [1986] argues that how women *reason* in the Kohlberg interview 'has no bearing on the question of whether they would spontaneously frame moral problems in this way ... My interest in the way people define moral responses is reflected in my research method.' The strength of Gilligan's distinction here between moral 'reasoning' and 'defining' or 'framing' undermines the critical relevance of care in Kohlberg's system. Still, Gilligan's meta-interpretations of her 'different voice' are not decisive; other plausible interpretations are possible.

The Care-as-Liberation Hypothesis

If care is not cognitive-moral development, what is it? Care's reputed levels, transitions, and regressions, I propose, are actually loosely related coping strategies. They are tailored to confront sexism (and similar forms of oppression), not moral matters gen-erally. By comparison, care *focus* is primarily a 'service orientation' engendered by patriarchal socialization and maintained by sexist social institutions. Yet Gilligan shows that in some women's minds, this oppressive orientation becomes a tool to cope with, and even resist, the very oppression of which it is a part.

The primary care theme is seen best at Gilligan's [1982, pp. 65, 74, 79] level II, dominated by 'stereotypical feminine virtues' such as 'gentleness' and 'tact' and an overriding desire not to hurt or disappoint anyone. At level II, according to Gilligan, women seek survival by trying to satisfy male expectations; they seek male approval in hopes of garnering male support [pp. 66f., 72, 78]. But to handle crises of hurt, domination, and rejection in relationships, some strategic adjustments are needed to refocus the care focus. (Such crises are normally fermented by males, as Gilligan's studies show [Gilligan and Belenky, 1980; Gilligan, 1982, chapt. 4].)

Within Gilligan's frame of interpretation, the relative effectiveness of these adjustments reflects different levels of care development. But little basis is provided for believing that these care strategies evolve from each other or show any of the other characteristics of cognitive-moral stages. Exhibiting the best of these strategies (care level III), a woman sees through her sexist victimization and servile manner of caring. She then liberates herself by culling care's seemingly true and noble strengths and 'owning' them. Here, for the first time, she learns truly to care for herself. At this level, Gilligan sensitively depicts care's significant strengths.

According to the care-as-liberation hypothesis, however, this newly liberated voice becomes overlegitimized, due to ideological rationalization. Many of the former victimizations of care's 'service orientation' are merely redefined as strengths. Thus level III clears away level II slavishness at a cost. It recasts the imposed limits on women's social power as the personal power to be limited, tentative, selective (contextual), and balanced in the exercise of power. Gilligan's [1982, pp. 54f., 95, 100–102, 165f.] account praises these tempering virtues, thus apparently extending such ideological rationalization to the theoretical level. In these respects, the 'highest level' of care may be morally defective and incompetent, not developmentally adequate or mature. It does not accurately identify the causes of its 'sense of service' in the sexist nature of social institutions and sexual politics. Rather, it falsely personalizes and legitimates responsibility for this orientation as a proper way of 'taking control of one's life' and 'taking responsibility for oneself', or feeling 'adult' and 'good about yourself' [pp. 76–78, 82–85, 91–94]. This problem is compounded, in Gilligan's account, by treating care's 'consciousness raising' as a natural process of development tied to women's very gender identity, and as a matter of personal confidence, psychological self-awareness, and moral self-control.

Support offered for the 'separate-realities' hypothesis serves the present hypothesis as well. Here, I elaborate two previous points relating the 'caring difference' to sexism in socialization and to coping with sexism.

Sexist Socialization

Gilligan [1982, p. 68f.] used the abortion crisis to study the 'politics of sexual relations' in which 'women have traditionally deferred to the judgment of men'. Here, women confront 'problems of passivity and

dependence' that 'have been most problematic' for them [p. 71]. For Gilligan, these problems require resolution of the conflict between conventions of feminity and women's conception of adulthood [pp. 69, 71]. They 'bring to the core of feminine apprehension ... that sense of living one's deepest life underwater' [p. 71]. In short, they confront problems of sexist socialization.

Some respondents in the abortion study reported that they became pregnant in hopes of 'making the baby an ally in the search for male support and protection or, that failing, a companion in male rejection' [p. 72]. Pregnancy was 'the perfect chance to get married and leave home' to 'overcome a sense of powerlessness' [p. 75] or to 'concretize our relationship' [p. 188] or to 'put the relationship to the ultimate test of commitment' [pp. 72, 119]. Likewise, abortion was sought 'to continue the relationship' and not 'drive us apart', because 'since I met him he has been my whole life. I do everything for him' [p. 81].

While Gilligan sees relationality as a general feature of care, her respondents show caring specifically in relations toward males – more specifically, toward sexist male lovers. Likewise, respondents illustrate the so-called common thread of 'not hurting' through concern with not hurting boyfriends. 'I would have jumped out the window not to hurt my boyfriend' [p. 65]. 'I'm afraid I'm heading for a big crisis with my boyfriend ... and he'll be more hurt than I will' [p. 65].

Gilligan's respondents show 'a sense of vulnerability' that stems from 'lack of power' and lack of 'direct participation in society' [p. 66f.]. They defer to 'men on whose protection and support they depend' [p. 67]. One respondent confesses, 'I always felt that [the right to decide] belonged to my father or husband or ... male clergyman ... I never rebelled against it ... I still let things happen to me rather than make them happen' [p. 67]. Gilligan's illustrations of care at level I do not show a general orientation toward self-protection, but selected protectiveness against sexist male rejection [pp. 75–77]. Level II responses do not show a general orientation toward altruism and approval-seeking, but a slavish appeal for male acceptance and support through sexist stereotypes [pp. 69f., 79f.]. [See Puka, 1989d, for further support of these claims.]

Coping and Consciousness

The strategic, coping quality of care is further revealed by level II defense mechanisms. Here, according to Gilligan, women quiet qualms about deferring to males and seeking male approval, by identifying with their own 'martyrdom'. They further rationalize martyrdom as an altruistic virtue [Gilligan, 1982, p. 80f.]. Care's distinctly reflective or metacognitive quality at level III is seen in responses to Gilligan's 'self-interview'. When asked to 'describe yourself to yourself', one respondent remarks, 'I have been thinking about that a lot lately, and it comes up different than what my usual subconscious perception of myself is' [p. 92]. 'I see the way I am and watch the way I make choices' [p. 122]. A second respondent conveys her sense of morality: 'It is part of a self-critical view, part of saying how am I spending my time ... the only way I know is to try to be as awake as possible, to try to know the range of what you feel ... to be as aware as you can of what's going on' [p. 99].

Care 'consciousness raising' is apparent in the same respondents. 'Somewhere in life I got the impression that my needs are secondary to other people's ... going around

serving people' [p. 92f.]. This respondent deals with her lover's needs 'as best I can without compromising my own ... That's a big point for me because the thing in my life to this point has always been compromising. I am not willing to do that anymore' [p. 95].

Yet the distinctly sexist nature of slavish caring is not recognized. Rather, the patriarchal roles of 'sexual politics' are abstracted and generalized until they seem to define interpersonal relations. The main emphasis of the care-as-liberation hypothesis is psychological, not ideological. It concerns the coping character of care and its reaction to oppression. Concerns about lingering sexism in care express a socialist-feminist perspective on morality, but invite liberal or radical feminist analyses as well.

The Care-Off-Key Hypothesis

It is proposed as a final hypothesis that Gilligan assays only the faults of justice and the strengths of mature care. Her account does not offer an overall comparison of themes, before dubbing them 'equally credible'. But once care's pitfalls are added to the analysis, and tempered by justice's strengths, there are strong grounds for rating care below justice in terms of its status in moral development.

Kohlberg [1971, 1982, chapt. 1, 2] often noted the deficiencies of benevolence ethics. These include sanctioning nonmoral values and preferred styles of interpersonal relating, failing to deal effectively with uncaring or abusive people, and expecting infeasible degrees of self-sacrifice in societal contexts. Gilligan offers no response to these criticisms. To further support the care-off-key hypothesis, I suggest 4 additional deficiencies of the ethic of care.

(1) Relationality is a key virtue of care. It counters the individualistic abuses of justice. Yet, while upholding a psychological sense of relationality, care actually may entrench moral individualism. For Gilligan, the central moral problem of care development is a balancing of care for self with care for other. Even at maturity, caring responsibilities to self and to other remain distinct moral perspectives to be balanced differently in different contexts. By contrast, the moral perspective of Kohlbergian justice moves from early-stage egoistic regard to a growing communitarian moral perspective. In later stages, the structure of moral self-concept is organically integrated with the moral (reciprocity) structure of groups – including friendships and peer groups, society, and the human community.

At maturity, taking one's individual perspective on responsibility is ruled out by the impartiality requirements of Kohlberg's moral point of view. As Kohlberg's philosophical interpretations make explicit (Kant's veil of ignorance, Rawls's original position), this point of view pictures only those moral perspectives that we can occupy concurrently. No separable sense of moral self remains to balance with moral others. This is what moral universalization and impersonality mean.

Effective moral decision-making is incomprehensible without such an organic integration of self and other. How one competently 'balances' care for self with care for other is left unresolved in Gilligan's account. That this is so is not surprising. Given how many others there are than oneself, how can one's balance avoid being slavishly altruistic, morally megalomaniacal, or arbitrary?

(2) Contextualism is care's method of choice for making hard caring choices. Balancing care for self and other surely is one of these choices. But contextual response also must resolve conflicts between people we care for, or among the clashing directives of caring responsibilities. For Gilligan, contextual decision-making represents a clear improvement over the rigid and absolutist approach to judgment offered by principles. But, more likely, contextual choice compounds moral problems by getting matters backwards. In moral judgment, care's morality must lead its contextual method, not the reverse. We seek the proper caring decision among the many contextual choices an occasion might pose (caring, just, or prudential). Justice principles have serious shortcomings in prescribing moral choices, but at least they offer *moral* guidance, and often clear guidance. Contextualism may offer no moral guidance at all.

(3) Care's defining features render it helpless or malfunctioning in societal contexts. Yet, here the most egregious problems of need and suffering occur. For Gilligan, care is guided by natural empathic responses. These are shaped in face-to-face encounters with others. But consequent interpersonal skills, in turn, are shaped by tacit conventions that distinguish proper responses to friends, relatives, or acquaintances. Given important differences between societal and interpersonal institutions, caring experience should prove ineffective in nurturing ability to make appropriate social responses.

Still, caring sensibilities 'urge themselves' upon us in social contexts. Care bids that we be ever-attentive to need and suffering. And we often experience similar pangs of compassion for remote and starving masses as for nearby friends in need. Thus, it is tempting to care analogically in social contexts, overpersonalizing their institutional frames. We therefore often approach the political ecology of famine and underdevelopment much as we do next-door hunger and joblessness. But the social reductionism of such caring intentions often results in devastating 'welfare cycles' and unsustainable self-help projects.

Of course, mature and experienced individuals may see that personal helpfulness cannot handle institutionalized deprivation or oppression. But care focus may provide little more, or even a bit less. By contrast, justice principles shine at the institutional level.

(4) Care is, by nature, an expressive ethic. As a benevolence theme, care not only helps and nurtures, but reflects compassion or concern in the process. An expressive ethic holds us responsible for feeling certain ways, for generating certain psychological reactions, and for transforming them into action. But spontaneous emotions like compassion can be hard to purposely nurture and control. Thus, relative to the mere behavioral requirements of justice, care may place sizable burdens on us. For example, care may expect us to feel tenderly toward people we find deeply and enduringly offensive. If we cannot, care may require us to act as if we do.

These responsibilities are especially burdensome for those who have been socialized in emotionally alienating ways. Gilligan claims that males have been socialized in 'callous individualism'. Thus, criticizing their relative lack of compassion in moral judgment, as Gilligan does, seems unfair and uncaring. It discriminates against that 'half of humanity' who are not positively reinforced to 'do what comes naturally' – to show care. Even in expecting both genders to combine care and justice, women are given the far easier task. To become more justice-oriented, women need only revise certain behavior, certain treatment of others. But to become more caring, systematically de-sensitized males must somehow discover how to make compassion flow.

Marshalling additional support for the care-off-key hypothesis invokes extensive philosophical debate. Yet virtually the entire history of ethics testifies to the great difficulties facing intuitionist and communitarian ethics in the benevolence tradition. Indeed, the principles of justice theory were designed to overcome limitations in these ethics.

Conclusions

As the preceding hypotheses are developed, they will be fit for comparison with Gilligan's 'different voice'. The foregoing arguments are meant only to show why these hypotheses are worth pursuing. And as this comparative theoretical research advances, we may finally be in the position to pose a serious Kohlberg-Gilligan debate. I suspect, however, that the research proposed here will detour such conflict, transforming our present conception of caring, women's development, and Kohlberg's theory.

References

Blatt, M., & Kohlberg, L. (1975). The effects of classroom discussion upon children's moral judgment. *Journal of Moral Education, 4,* 129–161.
Broughton, J. (1983). Men's virtue, women's rationality. *Social Research, 50,* 597–624.

Colby, A., & Kohlberg, L. (1987). *The measurement of moral judgment* (Vol. 2). New York: Cambridge University Press.

Colby, A., Kohlberg, L., Gibbs, J., & Lieberman, M. (1983). A longitudinal study of moral judgment. *Monograph of the Society for Research in Child Development, 48* (Serial No. 200).

Gilligan, C., & Murphy, J. (1979). Development from adolescence to adulthood: the philosopher and the dilemma of fact. In D. Kuhn (Vol. ed.), W. Damon (Series ed.), *New directions for child development: Vol. 5. Intellectual development beyond childhood*. San Francisco: Jossey-Bass.

Gilligan, C., & Belenky, M. (1980). A naturalistic study of abortion. In R. Selman & R. Yando (Eds.), *Clinical developmental psychology*. San Francisco: Jossey-Bass.

Gilligan, C. (1982). *In a different voice*. Cambridge MA: Harvard University Press.

Gilligan, C. (1986). Reply to critics. *Signs, 11,* 324–333.

Gilligan, C. (1987). Exit-voice/dilemmas in adolescent development. In A. Foxley, M. McPherson, & G. O'Donell (Eds.), *Development, democracy, and the art of trespassing*. South Bend IN: Notre Dame University Press.

Gilligan, C., & Wiggins, G. (1988). The origins or morality in early childhood relations. In J. Kagan & S. Lamm (Eds.), *The emergence of morality in young children*. Chicago: University of Chicago Press.

Kohlberg, L. (1969). Stage and sequence: the cognitive developmental approach to socialization. In D.A. Goslin (Ed.), *Handbook of socialization theory and research*. Chicago: Rand McNally.

Kohlberg, L. (1971). From is to ought: how to commit the naturalistic fallacy and get away with it in the study of moral development. In T. Mischel (Ed.), *Cognitive development and epistemology*. New York: Academic Press.

Kohlberg, L. (1973). The claim to the moral adequacy of a highest stage of moral judgment. *Journal of Philosophy, 70,* 630–646.

Kohlerg, L. (1976). Moral stages and moralization. In T. Likona (Ed.), *Moral development and behavior*. New York: Holt, Rinehart & Winston.

Kohlberg, L. (1984). *The psychology of moral development*. New York: Harper & Row.

Kohlberg, L., Kaufman, K., Scharf, P., & Hickey, J. (1975). The just community approach to corrections: a theory. *Journal of Moral Education, 4,* 243–260.

Kohlberg, L., Levine, C., & Boyd, D. (1986). The return of stage 6. In W. Edelstein & G. Nunner-Winkler (Eds.), *Zur Bestimmung der Moral.* Frankfurt: Suhrkamp.

Lyons, N. (1983). Two perspectives on self, relationships, and morality. *Harvard Educational Review, 53,* 125–145.

Murphy, J.M., & Gilligan, C. (1980). Moral development in late adolescence and adulthood: a critique and reconstruction of Kohlberg's theory. *Human Development, 23,* 77–104.

Nicolayev, J., & Phillips, D.C. (1979). On assessing Kohlberg's stage theory of moral development. In D.B. Cochrane, C.M. Hamm, & A.C. Kazapides (Eds.), *The domain of moral education.* New York: Paulist Press.

Nisan, M., & Kohlberg, L. (1982). Universality and cross-cultural variation in moral development. *Child Development, 53,* 865–876.

Noddings, N. (1985). *Caring: a feminine approach to ethics and moral education.* Los Angeles: University of California Press.

Nozick, R. (1974). *Anarchy, state, and utopia.* New York: Basic Books.

Parihk, B. (1980). Moral judgment development and its relation to family environmental factors in Indian and American Families. *Child Development, 51,* 1030–1038.

Perry, W. (1968). *Forms of intellectual and ethical development in the college years.* New York: Holt, Rinehart & Winston.

Puka, B. (1989a). Reconstructing Kohlberg's theory: preserving essential structure, removing controversial content. In J. Gewirtz & W. Kurtines (Eds.), *Handbook of moral behavior and development: Theory, research, and application* (Vol. 1). Hillsdale NJ: Erlbaum.

Puka, B. (1989b). Caring – In an interpretive voice. *New Ideas in Psychology, 7,* 295–314.

Puka, B. (1989c). Just regard and caring concern: different voices or separate realities? *MOSAIC Monographs, 4,* 1–49. Bath: University of Bath Press.

Puka, B. (1989d). The liberation of caring. *Hypatia, 4,* 59–82. Reprinted in M. Brabeck (Ed.), *Who cares?* New York: Praeger.

Rawls, J. (1971). *A theory of justice.* Cambridge MA: Harvard University Press.

439

Reimer, J. (1977). A study in the moral development of Kibbutz adolescents. Unpublished doctoral dissertation, Harvard University, Cambridge MA.

Shweder, R. (1982). Review of Lawrence Kohlberg's *Essays in moral development (Vol. I): The philosophy of moral development. Contemporary Psychology, 4.* 421–424.

Simpson, E. (1974). Moral development research: a case study of scientific and cultural bias. *Human Development, 17.* 81–106.

Snarey, J. (1982). The social and moral development of Kibbutz founders and sabras: a cross-sectional and longitudinal study. Unpublished doctoral dissertation, Harvard University, Cambridge MA.

Sullivan, E. (1977). A study of Kohlberg's structural theory of moral development: a critique of liberal social science ideology. *Human Development, 20,* 352–376.

Walker, L. (1984). Sex differences in the development of moral reasoning: A critical review. *Child Development, 55,* 667–691.

Bill Puka
Department of Philosophy
Rensselaer Polytechnic Institute
Troy, NY 12180–3590 (USA)

Human Development 1991;34:81–87

Commentary

Lyn M. Brown, Mark B. Tappan

Harvard University, Cambridge, Mass., USA

Puka has raised a number of interesting issues and questions in his reflections on recent dialogue regarding the work of Gilligan and the work of Kohlberg. Our commentary focuses on what we take to be the most central of these issues and questions, highlighting, in the process, both what we see as the contributions, and the shortcomings, of Puka's efforts.

Two Different Hermeneutics

Perhaps Puka's most important contribution is the degree to which he highlights the fundamentally hermeneutic (i.e., interpretive) nature of both Gilligan's and Kohlberg's work. Both research programs are premised on the assumption that the process of interpretation – what Dilthey [1900/1976] calls 'the process of recognizing [and understanding] a mental state from a sense-given sign by which it is expressed' [p. 248] – entails a fundamental interaction and interrelationship between the interpreter and the text being interpreted. Consequently, both Gilligan and Kohlberg reject the traditional positivist and empiricist assumptions regarding the importance of adopting an objective, value-neutral stance vis-à-vis interview tests. Instead, both acknowledge the essential 'circularity of understanding' [Heidegger, 1927/1962; Packer and Addison, 1989] that characterizes the process of interpretation [Gilligan, 1977, 1982, 1986, 1987; Kohlberg, 1981, 1984; Colby and Kohlberg, 1987].

Yet, in spite of these basic similarities, there are fundamental differences between the hermeneutic assumptions made by Kohlberg and Gilligan – differences that underlie the disagreements and debate between these two approaches, differences, furthermore, that Puka neither acknowledges nor addresses. We would summarize these differences as follows: Kohlberg's approach is based on a 'philosophical' hermeneutics, while Gilligan's is based on a 'psychological' hermeneutics.

Kohlberg's [1984] 'philosophical' hermeneutics is essentially Habermas' [1979, 1983] hermeneutics: the 'rational reconstruction of the ontogenesis of justice reasoning': 'Our theory is a rational reconstruction because it (a) describes the developmental logic inherent in the development of justice reasoning with the aid of (b) the normative criteria of Stage 6 which is held to be the most adequate (i.e., most reversible) stage of justice reasoning' [Kohlberg, 1984, p. 221]. In other words, Kohlberg's process of interpretation (what he calls, following Habermas, 'hermeneutic objectivism') entails identifying the 'deep structure' that governs the way individuals think about issues of justice and fairness in response to hypothetical moral dilemmas, guided by a set of philosophical categories and assumptions that determine what counts as a moral judgment and what does not. Thus, Kohlberg's definition of justice functions in a very specific way in the context of his hermeneutics: It provides the a priori philosophical groundwork for his conception of moral development.

Gilligan's [1982, 1983, 1986, 1987] 'psychological' (or, perhaps, 'literary') hermeneutics, in contrast, focuses on understanding the psychological complexity of individuals' narrative accounts of conflicts and dilemmas in their lives. As such it shares much in common with the way psychoanalysts interpret individual cases – focusing on understanding the meaning of language that expresses and represents the dynamics of relational conflict in the psyche – and with the way literary critics interpret short stories and novels – focusing on understanding the meaning of an author's use of plot, style, character, and form:

> By asking the psychologist's question of how we come to hold moral values and tracing the ontogenesis of values to the experience of human relationships, I ... claim that two moral predispositions inhere in the structure of human connection, given the inequality and the attachment or interdependence of child and parent [Gilligan, 1986, p. 37].

Thus, for Gilligan, the distinction between the moral voices or orientations of justice and care is not a philosophical distinction but a psychological one. That is, it captures two different visions of desirable human relationship that derive from two different lived experiences of the parent-child relationship. The justice voice reflects an ideal vision of equality, reciprocity, and fairness between persons; it derives from childhood experiences of inequality and powerlessness in relation to parents and caretakers. The care voice reflects an ideal vision of responsive relation-

ships, loving and being loved, and listening and being listened to; it derives from childhood experiences of love and connection with parents and caretakers [Gilligan, 1987; Gilligan and Wiggins, 1987].

These two voices and visions, therefore, are the guideposts for a very different kind of hermeneutics than is practiced by Kohlberg and his colleagues. This distinction is clarified in a description of the interpretive method Gilligan and her colleagues [Brown, 1988] have developed to analyze interview texts:

> We have chosen to speak about *reading* for self and moral voice to highlight the interpretive nature of our work. In describing a way of reading, we try to teach not only a way of listening, a way of attending, but also a way of responding. To move away from the framing of moral questions in terms of the contrasts between a unitary view of moral truth and endless moral relativism, we have shifted the focus of attention from abstract moral truths to the observable world of social relationships where people can describe something that happened which they thought was unfair or situations in which someone did not listen. We define two desirable visions of relationship (a vision of justice and a vision of care) and map the social and moral world by the sounds of two voices. Our two-voice method records conflict and tension, as well as harmony and resolution. And because we have two visions, we never lose sight of the fact of perspective. Thus we have worked to develop a method that highlights the interpretive nature of the reading process, and we have tried to operationalize a way of listening, a way of attending to self and moral voice that takes into account both our stance as researchers and the stance of the person speaking within the text [Gilligan et al., 1990, p. 96].

We would argue that Puka's failure to distinguish between Kohlberg's philosophical hermeneutics, on the one hand, and Gilligan's psychological hermeneutics, on the other, leads him to make a number of problematic assumptions and comparisons. Perhaps the most problematic is his assumption that Kohlberg's philosophically informed and derived conception of justice can and should be used as the standard against which to measure Gilligan's conception of the psychologic of care and relationships. For example, Puka claims that because Kohlberg has identified developmental levels in his reconstruction of the ontogenesis of justice reasoning, Gilligan must also document the existence of developmental levels of care, because 'if care does not show comparable development, then it cannot be a comparable phenomenon'. Such a statement implies that there is one 'right' way to speak about or envision development, and that if Gilligan does not accept the Piagetian, structuralist underpinnings of Kohlberg's work, then she is not speaking about development. Yet, in making such a statement, Puka fails not only to consider the current criticism of Piagetian conceptions of development, but also to appreciate the ongoing debate over how the concept of development is and ought to be defined [Cirillo and Wapner, 1986; Harris, 1957; Kagan, 1984; Kaplan, 1967; Lerner, 1983].

Similarly, Puka argues that because Kohlberg 'seeks a "common voice" morality that provides shared guidelines for human cooperation and conflict resolution' (i.e., principles of justice and fairness), Gilligan should seek the same: 'But ... she does not seek an alternative "common voice", cleansed of Kohlberg's bias. Had Gilligan's research focused on how all people combine care and justice – had she proposed a different *common* voice – matters might be different.' Matters might certainly have been different, but, as the history of science has demonstrated again and again, following the lead of the dominant paradigm rarely results in fundamental progress [Kuhn, 1970].

Puka also misrepresents Gilligan's understanding of the justice voice. Puka claims that Gilligan's account of justice points almost exclusively to its negative and problematic aspects: rigidity, legalism, impersonality, aloofness, unresponsiveness, callousness, judgmentalism, punitiveness, abstractness, inattentiveness. Yet, in fact, Gilligan's own representation of the justice voice highlights the power of such a voice to speak out against oppression, domination, discrimination, inequality, or unfairness of treatment in people's lives. Everyone has experienced unfairness and injustice in their lives, just as they have experienced the threat of abandonment and detachment. Thus, according to Gilligan, everyone knows the power of both the justice voice and the care voice:

> Theoretically, the distinction between justice and care cuts across the familiar divisions between thinking and feeling, egoism and altruism, theoretical and practical reasoning. It calls attention to the fact that all human relationships, public and private, can be characterized *both* in terms of equality and in terms of attachment, and that both inequality and detachment constitute grounds for moral concern. Since everyone is vulnerable both to oppression and to abandonment, two moral visions – one of justice and one of care – recur in human experience. Two moral injunctions, not to act unfairly towards others, and not to turn away from someone in need, capture these different concerns [Gilligan, 1987, p. 20].

We would argue, therefore, that Puka misrepresents Gilligan's conception of the justice voice by conflating it with a mixture of Kohlberg's conception of justice and a caricature of a 'callous' and 'impersonal' justice that reflects neither Kohlberg's nor Gilligan's views. Hence Puka has confused and muddled the poles of his comparison. He attempts to clarify what he calls the 'Kohlberg-Gilligan debate' by comparing Kohlberg's conception of justice with Gilligan's conception of care. Yet Puka's comparison, as it stands, is incomplete – and inaccurate – because he leaves out a crucial component of the picture – an accurate representation of Gilligan's conception of justice.

Had he included such a representation, the terms of his comparison would necessarily have shifted. He might then have compared Kohlberg's and Gilligan's respective theoretical and empirical approaches, focusing, perhaps, on the relative merits of adopting a fundamentally philosophical (and structuralist) versus a fundamentally psychological (and poststructuralist) approach to the study of human development. Or he might have explored, from within the framework of Gilligan's two-voice hermeneutic, the tensions, ambiguities, and even tragedies that naturally arise when the demands of justice and the demands of care conflict in human relationships. Either of these approaches would have represented an important contribution to our understanding of the degree to which the dynamics of human moral development are illuminated by the work of Kohlberg and Gilligan.

In short, although we do not accept all of the assertions that Puka makes in his discussion of what he calls the 'separate-realities' hypothesis, we would claim that it most accurately captures the crucial distinctions that exist between Kohlberg's and Gilligan's approaches. We would, however, go one step further, and argue not only that Kohlberg's conception of justice and Gilligan's conception of care represent completely different concepts and phenomena, but also that Kohlberg's conception of justice and Gilligan's conception of justice represent separate and distinct realities. Kohlberg's justice is a philosophical conception of ideal role-taking that defines the endpoint of his devel-

opmental sequence, stage 6, and hence provides the framework for his rational reconstruction of the ontogenesis of justice reasoning. Gilligan's justice, in contrast, like care, is a psychological and 'relational' voice – it assumes that a perspective on relationships underlies any conception of morality, and it draws attention to one set of deeply human concerns about how we ought to live in relation to one another.

Care, Women, and Development

In his discussion of what he calls the 'care-as-liberation' hypothesis, Puka characterizes care as 'primarily a "service orientation" engendered by patriarchal socialization', and he represents Gilligan's view on the development of care as capturing 'loosely related coping strategies...tailored to confront sexism (and similar forms of oppression), not moral matters generally'. Such a view misrepresents and misunderstands the conception of care proposed by Gilligan and her colleagues and, in the process, serves only to devalue and diminish the ethical significance and moral power of women speaking about care and relationships in their lives.

As Puka recalls, Gilligan [1977, 1982] initially addressed the question of how a care voice develops by constructing a developmental sequence based on narratives of adolescent and adult women describing their decisions regarding whether or not to have an abortion. This sequence reflected patterns and presuppositions commonly taken for granted in cognitive-developmental psychology. It consisted of three 'levels' and two 'transitions', essentially reflecting the shifts other developmentalists have traced – a progression from an egocentric position, through a normative or conventional position, to an autonomous, reflective, or critical position. In Gilligan's terms, this sequence entailed a progression in the ways women think about care and relationships, from care of self in order to insure survival ('selfishness'), to care of others in order to be seen as good ('selflessness'), to care of both self and other conceived as interdependent ('nonviolence').

Yet, recent examination of the ways in which school-age versus adolescent girls speak about care and relationships – specifically, mounting evidence that suggests that at adolescence girls may come to not *know* or to not *speak* about what they once knew about care and relationships – has sparked a rethinking and a reconsideration of Gilligan's initial formulation of this developmental sequence [Brown, 1989; Gilligan, 1990; Gilligan et al., 1990]. Consequently, the sequence that Gilligan traced for adolescent and adult women has been reinterpreted not as a maturational or 'natural' process originating in childhood, but rather as a series of specifically female responses to the crises of living in different kinds of social contexts that are heightened during adolescence – that is, to the pressure facing young women coming of age to adapt to androcentric cultural norms, values, and definitions of women.

In other words, the first two positions Gilligan described – 'selfishness', in which women cannot see the necessity of other's needs and terms, and 'selflessness', in which women cannot appreciate and acknowledge their own needs – appear now to reflect particular vulnerabilities in understanding healthy relationships – responses to a culture in which the prevailing conventions of womanhood are still defined by the incapacitating Madonna-whore myth. That is, if a woman is not good, pure, selfless and all-loving, then she is, by definition, bad, tainted, and selfish. The two positions, then, represent an attempt by women to repair or solve, by force of exclusion – i.e., by excluding either themselves or others – a problem of deep confusion about what is happening in the move from childhood to adolescence. The transitions that follow these first two positions, furthermore, mark periods of insight, a gradual appreciation of the importance of including the perspectives and needs of both self and other in order to create and sustain healthy relationships. They reflect the struggles of girls and women to hold on to their perspectives and speak in their own voices as they are pressured to adopt a male-defined, and thus culturally and politically mandated, view of themselves and their relationships to others.

In this sense, a care voice, as Puka suggests, is developed in relation to a dominant world view in which concerns for care are devalued, idealized, or silenced. Thus, attention to this voice in girls and women serves to acknowledge both the androcentric bias of this culture at this time and becomes a lens through which to listen and to understand the psychic consequences of the various forms of oppression women experience, including the development of what feminist scholars have called 'double vision' [Moers, 1976; Showalter, 1985] – the necessity to learn two ways of speaking or two languages, the language of the dominant culture and a language that reflects what they know from experience but is not speakable or valued.

However, what Puka omits in his description of care and its relationship to the male-defined culture in which we live is the power and vision of the female 'outsider' to offer productive critique of the dominant culture, and her capacity, as Rich [1979] says, 'to be a witness for the defense' of those in this culture who struggle to speak about what they know and experience but are still not heard. The ultimate aim of the work in which Gilligan and her colleagues are engaged, therefore, is to give voice to difference and foster resistance to a public world view in which a range of concerns deemed central to women are considered either unspeakable or irrelevant. Thus, in contrast to Puka, we see the intricate and complex relationship among the issues of women, care, and male bias in this culture at this time not as somehow lying outside the moral domain, but rather as matters of deep moral concern for both women and men.

Evidence indicates that, in this culture at this time, girls and women are much more likely to speak about moral problems and concerns in a care voice than are boys and men [Gilligan and Attanucci, 1988]. Yet, despite the gender-relatedness of this voice, it is neither accurate nor helpful to see care simply as a stereotypical feminine response to the demands of a patriarchal and sexist sociocultural environment. Girls and women currently stand in a complex relationship to Western culture, a culture largely established by men. As Showalter [1985] argues, women are neither 'inside' nor 'outside' the male tradition, 'they are inside two traditions, simultaneously, "undercurrents" of the mainstream' [p. 264]. In other words, the undercurrent of female voices and visions has been filtered through a dominant androcentric culture, effectively muting or devaluing female experience [Ardener, 1978; Miller, 1976]. Among the voices that have been subordinated or devalued has been a voice that speaks about caring and concern for others and a vision of connection or attachment between people [Brown, 1989; Gilligan et al., 1990]. We would argue, therefore, that for women to speak about care in this culture, and to insist that this voice be taken seriously as an alternative moral perspective, is not only disruptive, but dangerous – an act of resistance and moral courage.

In the end, then, while we appreciate Puka's attempts to move the field of moral development ahead by offering hypotheses designed to generate further research and clarification, we would argue that to do so on the grounds of a 'Kohlberg-Gilligan debate' seems, upon closer analysis, to be problematic, if not untenable. Characterized by fundamentally different assumptions about what constitutes evidence for moral development, the research programs derived from the insights of Kohlberg and Gilligan are guided by different questions and radically different methods for data collection and analysis. We suggest, therefore, that what will ultimately transform our understanding of women's psychological development and the development of care is not a decontextualized philosophical analysis of the Kohlberg-Gilligan, justice-care 'debate', but rather careful attention to the psychological reality of the voices of girls and women (and boys and men) speaking about care and relationships in their lives, over time, and in different social and cultural contexts.

References

Ardener, S. (Ed.). (1978). *Perceiving women.* New York: Halsted Press.
Brown, L. (Ed.). (1988). *A guide to reading narratives of conflict and choice for self and relational voice.* Monograph No. 1, Project on the Psychology of

Women and the Development of Girls. Harvard University Graduate School of Education.

Brown, L. (1989). *Narratives of relationship: The development of a care voice in girls aged 7 to 16.* Unpublished doctoral dissertation, Harvard University.

Cirillo, L., & Wapner, S. (Eds.). (1986). *Value presuppositions in theories of human development.* Hillsdale NJ: Erlbaum.

Colby, A., & Kohlberg, L. (1987). *The measurement of moral judgment.* New York: Cambridge University Press.

Dilthey, W. (1976). The development of hermeneutics. In H. Rickman (Ed. & Trans.), *Dilthey: Selected writings.* Cambridge: Cambridge University Press. (Original work published 1900).

Habermas, J. (1979). *Communication and the evolution of society* (T. McCarthy, Trans.). Boston: Beacon Press.

Habermas, J. (1983). Interpretive social science vs. hermeneuticism. In N. Haan, R. Bellah, P. Rabinow, & W. Sullivan (Eds.), *Social science as moral inquiry.* New York: Columbia University Press.

Harris, D. (Ed.). (1957). *The concept of development.* Minneapolis: University of Minnesota Press.

Heidegger, M. (1962). *Being and time* (J. Macquarrie & E. Robinson, Trans.). New York: Harper & Row.

Gilligan, C. (1977). In a different voice: Women's conceptions of self and morality. *Harvard Educational Review, 47,* 481–517.

Gilligan, C. (1982). *In a different voice: Psychological theory and women's development.* Cambridge MA: Harvard University Press.

Gilligan, C. (1983). Do the social sciences have an adequate theory of moral development? In N. Haan, R. Bellah, P. Rabinow, & W. Sullivan (Eds.), *Social science as moral inquiry.* New York: Columbia University Press.

Gilligan, C. (1986). Remapping the moral domain: New images of the self in relationship. In T. Heller, M. Sosna, & D. Wellber (Eds.), *Reconstructing individualism: Autonomy, individuality, and the self in western thought.* Stanford: Stanford University Press.

Gilligan, C. (1987). Moral orientation and moral development. In E. Kittay & D. Meyers (Eds.), *Women and moral theory.* Totowa NJ: Rowan & Littlefield.

Gilligan, C. (1990). Teaching Shakespeare's sister. In C. Gilligan, N. Lyons, & T. Hanmer (Eds.), *Making connections: The relational worlds of adolescent girls at Emma Willard School.* Cambridge MA: Harvard University Press.

Gilligan, C., & Attanucci, J. (1988). Two moral orientations: Gender differences and similarities. *Merrill-Palmer Quarterly, 34,* 223–237.

Gilligan, C., Brown, L., & Rogers, A. (1990). Psyche embedded: A place for body, relationships, and culture in personality theory. In A. Rabin, R. Zucker, R. Emmons, & S. Frank (Eds.), *Studying persons and lives.* New York: Springer.

Gilligan, C., & Wiggins, G. (1987). The origins of morality in early childhood relationships. In J. Kagan & S. Lamb (Eds.), *The emergence of morality in young children.* Chicago: University of Chicago Press.

Kagan, J. (1984). *The nature of the child.* New York: Basic Books.

Kaplan, B. (1967). Meditations on genesis. *Human Development, 10,* 65–87.

Kohlberg, L. (1981). *Essays on moral development. Vol. I: The philosophy of moral development.* San Francisco: Harper & Row.

Kohlberg, L. (1984). *Essays on moral development. Vol. II: The psychology of moral development.* San Francisco: Harper & Row.

Kuhn, T. (1970). *The structure of scientific revolutions.* Chicago: University of Chicago Press.

Lerner, R. (Ed.). (1983). *Developmental psychology: Historical and philosophical perspectives.* Hillsdale NJ: Erlbaum.

Miller, J. (1976). *Toward a new psychology of women.* Boston: Beacon Press.

Moers, E. (1976). *Literary women: The great writers.* Garden City NJ: Doubleday.

Packer, M., & Addison, R. (Eds.). (1989). *Entering the circle: Hermeneutic investigation in psychology.* Albany NY: SUNY Press.

Rich, A. (1979). *On lies, secrets, and silence.* New York: Norton.

Showalter, E. (1985). Feminist criticism in the wilderness. In E. Showalter (Ed.), *The new feminist criticism.* New York: Pantheon Books.

Lyn M. Brown
Department of Human Development
Graduate School of Education
Harvard University
Cambridge, MA 02138 (USA)

5

The Character of Moral Development

Dwight Boyd

INTRODUCTION

One of the criticisms that has often been leveled at Lawrence Kohlberg's conception of moral development is that it manifests an impoverished view of human persons, perhaps even one of warped character. Forms of this criticism can be found, either asserted or implied, in intellectually respectable critiques published by a number of our colleagues (Sullivan 1977; Gilligan and Murphy 1979; Murphy and Gilligan 1980) and in the blatantly rhetorical and not so intellectually respectable papers of former U.S. Secretary of Education William Bennett (e.g., Bennett and Delattre 1979). What motivates this chapter is the belief that although there is an important concern underlying this criticism, at least a good part of how it is developed is mistaken. What *can* be taken from the criticism is an encouragement to think more directly and explicitly about how matters of character interact with the theory of moral development as currently expressed in the writings of Kohlberg and his colleagues—which is a major part of the motivation for the dialogue in this volume. On the other hand, the mistake that seems to me quite common is to misinterpret certain aspects of the theory in such a way as to create a straw person, the character of which can then be dismissively caricatured (and along with it, the theory as a whole).

In this paper I will endeavor to articulate a more adequate understanding of Kohlberg's theory, with respect to which the straw-person nature of some lines of criticism can be more clearly seen, and within which some positive claims about character can be illuminated as an integral part of the theory. In order to do this I will cover several different kinds of ground. After I present a more focused statement of the problem, I will first synthesize what I think are some of the most fundamental philosophical assumptions underlying Kohlberg's theory, which the aforementioned criticisms often lose sight of but which must be kept clearly in mind for any full picture of the character of moral development. Then I will work dialectically from correcting some of the common but mistaken character implications of the notion of principled morality to showing what positive picture of character emerges from an appreciation of recent elaborations of the nature of stage six, in the context of the philosophical assumptions already identified. Finally, in order to accomplish the positive task I will also argue that this more adequate interpretation hinges on an understanding of objectivity in morality different from that commonly assumed.

THE PROBLEM REFINED

Using a unique blend of philosophical reflection and empirical study, Kohlberg sought to describe moral learning over the lifespan in developmental terms. As the notion of "development" carries with it not only the notion of change but also the idea of change with regard to some specified dimension *and* in some direction considered to be an improvement, he also needed to articulate his conception of the aim of that development. Kohlberg understood that one's conception of the endpoint of a hierarchically related sequence of developmental stages serves both to draw boundaries around what is to be counted as falling within the domain of this empirical study and to establish criteria by which one can order the data so found into increasing steps of greater adequacy. In addressing this aspect of his theory, Kohlberg repeatedly described a postconventional level of moral reasoning and more specifically, a "stage six" within that level, in terms of the notion of a *principled* interpretation of justice as respect for persons. He has spelled this out in a variety of ways, but a good example for my purposes here is his following description of stage six:

> *The universal-ethical-principle orientation.* Right is defined by the decision of conscience in accord with self-chosen *ethical principles* appealing to logical comprehensiveness, universality, and consistency. These principles are abstract and ethical (the Golden Rule, the categorical imperative); they are not concrete moral rules like the Ten Commandments. At heart, these are universal principles of *justice*, of the *reciprocity* and *equality* of human *rights*, and of respect for the dignity of human beings as *individual persons*. [Kohlberg 1971, p. 165]

A communicative problem arises here: such short content descriptions of complex structures of judgment can be extremely misleading. An analogy for such descriptions of content is that they are like the small, usually dirty windows on the landings of staircases through which, if you are on the outside of a building and *lucky*, you can sometimes get a vague glimpse of people and the direction they are walking on the staircase within the building. Despite Kohlberg's several efforts to articulate the form of stage six more fully, it is certain aspects of such short content descriptions, extrapolated out to their assumed full meaning, that have been generally accepted as constituting an accurate picture of stage six, at least by critics. The problem is, however, that these aspects are taken out of the context of a full understanding of the theory as a whole and the structure of stage six within it. The result is a severely warped, attenuated picture. Moreover, what is important in the context of this chapter is that what gets warped and attenuated is not only stage six as a form of moral judgment, but also, through an oddly intellectualized process of guilt by association, the *person* who might find such a form of moral judgment accommodating. By correcting these misinterpretations of stage six we can lay the groundwork for a more balanced and plausible understanding of the character of moral development implicit in Kohlberg's theory.

Before my main analysis and argument can proceed, however, two further refinements are necessary to clarify the nature of the task; both involve additional problems of communication, in this case not inherent in Kohlberg's writings but in the way the notion of character is being used here. The first is an acknowledgement of the intentional ambiguity in this chapter's title, "The Character of Moral Development." That is, what I intend here is to work *from* the "character of moral development" in the sense of the understanding we currently have about the nature of moral development and the direction it takes (according to Kohlberg's theory) *to* an articulation of the "character of moral development" in the sense of what we might then want to say about the moral character of a person, fully developed according to this view. A shorthand way of saying this is with this question: What moral aspects of the person, of character, would seem best to "fit" our current understanding of stage six in Kohlberg's theory? Having thus asked this, I want to finesse the concern that might reasonably then be raised about the nature of this project—that is to say, what *kind* of "fit" am I presupposing and seeking to uncover? The stages of moral development, as conceived by Kohlberg, are clearly not descriptions of types of persons; nor should they ever be thought of in this way. They are, instead, qualitatively different patterns of interpreting and resolving particular aspects of social interaction among human persons. They are descriptions of a psychological function that persons *engage in*, not descriptions of the moral persons themselves. It is, then, conceptually confused, and in some contexts morally pernicious, to speak in terms such as "the stage two person," or "the stage six person." Thus I want to head off, and reject, any interpretation of my project as simply translating stage descriptions into character talk. On the contrary, this move must be framed more hypothetically, indeed, more speculatively. The question is better understood as follows: If a person had the capacity for stage six moral judgment, and were to be conceived as *using* that capacity to interpret and seek resolution of moral problems, what character traits would we see, given our current understanding of stage six, as congruent with and as facilitating this capacity or use? I realize, of course, that this approach walks immediately into a barrage of conceptual questions having to do with the difference between having a capacity and using that capacity, and this distinction must, in the end, be taken seriously in any thorough consideration of mature moral character. Moreover, there are also quite a number of other empirical questions about the relationship between moral development in terms of stages of moral judgment and in terms of the manifestation of a set of (approved) character traits. I want to acknowledge that these are all crucial questions for us to explore. However, at this time I think we are necessarily at a much grosser level. What we need first, I believe, is a theoretically sound and plausible picture of the categories of concern that will be the basis for such further exploration.

The second refinement is to avoid vagueness in the use of the term "character." That is, to what do I think the notion of moral character refers? This is *not* a notion that has received much attention within mainstream moral development theory ever since Kohlberg (1970) excoriated it with the label "bag of virtues." Of course, some critics of this rejection have repeatedly argued that one cannot get rid of the term so easily (e.g., Hamm 1977; Peters 1972), and it may even be sneaking back into favor in current developmentalist work on the notion of "the moral self." But it is clear that the notion itself is not very clear in any of this; much of the argument and counterargument hinges, I suspect, on different understandings of what character encompasses. In order to avoid adding to these problems of interpretation (especially in the context of the aims of this volume), but without getting into an elaborate conceptual analysis, I will simply assert here as concisely and precisely as possible the outlines of the concept of moral character as I will be using it. In short, I will use "moral character" to mean those enduring aspects of the expression of personhood to which we are inclined to give moral evaluation across different attitudinal and behavioral contexts. Several components of this understanding need emphasizing. (1) Character is the way we express our being *as persons* via attitudinal and behavioral dispositions. (2) These expressions are not just episodic, but must be relatively consistent over time. That is why we often refer to character *traits*. (3) They raise dependable expectations from other persons, regardless of what particular behavior is evidenced—or even regardless of whether this particular behavior is a *successful* expression of the intended aspect of character. (Note that 2 and 3 together allow us to speak of "strong" or "weak" characters.) (4) Some expressions will be nonmoral character traits; others will be clearly moral; and it is possible for some to be both, depending on context. What will determine whether or not something is an instance of *moral* character will be whether it is tied in some way to a particular normative moral orientation. (5) In addition to dividing on the moral/nonmoral description, those traits that *are* moral in this category sense are open to either positive or negative evaluation from a given moral point of view. (This latter point allows us to speak of "good" or "bad" character, as well as "strong" or "weak.")

SOME BASIC STARTING POINTS

For almost thirty years Lawrence Kohlberg endeavored to describe, to measure, and to explore the educational implications of the
development of moral judgment. In doing so he engaged in scores of
empirical studies, using samples from the whole human age span and
a wide variety of cultures. His empirical methodology is now very well
known worldwide and has spawned both hundreds of studies repli-
cating and extending his findings and a large number of critiques
aiming to show that these findings are spurious in some way. His six
stages of moral judgment are now as well known to psychologists as
Campbell's soup is to the American cook. But equally as important as
the empirical methodology and claims are the philosophical dimensions of this theory. Indeed, one of the unique aspects of Kohlberg's
theory of moral development, compared to the rest of mainstream
North American social psychology, is the way that it explicitly integrates into an empirical concern certain understandings of persons
and morality that would normally be solidly located on the philosophical
side of the renowned gap between psychology and philosophy. As I
have argued elsewhere (Boyd 1985), it is this combination of
kinds of claims that has led to one of Kohlberg's more radical, but still
mostly misunderstood, theoretical claims about the "naturalistic
fallacy." Although individually these philosophical starting points of
Kohlberg's theory are undoubtedly well known, a synthesis of them is
warranted here, first, because any thorough dialogue with alternative
approaches to moral experience and growth will in the end revolve
around these starting points, and second, because my eventual claims
about the kind of character that fits stage six are necessarily tied to
these starting assumptions that ground and frame developmental
theory.

The following are what seem to me some of the most basic starting
points of Kohlberg's theory.

1. At the most foundational level is an assumption about the
human self, which is probably drawn from George Herbert Mead.
The assumption is that the psychological self—the sense of "myself"
that we all have—is a social construct. "Self" and "other" are not
metaphysical entities, each standing alone, totally independent. They
are, rather, *correlative categories*, both conceptually and developmentally. One's own self and the self's needs can be delineated only in
reference to an awareness of others as selves and their needs, and vice

versa. We then give moral weight to these divisions via our notion of *person*hood, which recognizes that the welfare of oneself can be both benefited and harmed by others.

2. The second assumption, then, is that the institution of morality is a mode of regulating the interaction of persons with regard to both manners of possible effect on each other. Kohlberg shared with many contemporary philosophers an understanding of morality as a kind of social tool and an understanding of the twin functions this tool is meant to serve. For example, Thomas Nagel has articulated this assumption quite neatly: "The central problem of ethics [is] how the lives, interests, and welfare of others make claims on us and how these claims, of various forms, are to be reconciled with the aim of living our own lives" (Nagel 1986, p. 164). Moral evaluations are then judgments of the appropriateness of some act or pattern of action that might be performed by a (or any) person insofar as it affects the interests of another person or other persons. The type of effect can then be described in terms of persons' benefiting from another's help or care, in terms of their claims to forbearance of another's infringement on their projects or autonomy, or by some combination of these two directions of influence. In short, Kohlberg's psychological theory and findings must always be understood in the context of a particular view of morality; the "moral" in "moral development" has specific and explicitly recognized conceptual boundaries. To put all this in Kohlberg's own terms, let me quote from his response chapter in the recent collection, *Lawrence Kohlberg: Consensus and Controversy*:

> Some philosophic definition of the moral domain is required as a starting point for psychological or empirical study of moral development or morality becomes synonymous with all valuing. Since my thesis I have defined developing morality as involving "a moral point of view" including not only Kant's or Hare's prescriptivity, universalizability and over-ridingness and its implication of judging and acting on principles, but also including impartiality or considering the good of everyone alike and reversibility, which is not quite the same as universalizability. The "moral point of view" is somewhat broader than a concern for distributive, commutative and restorative justice, since it can center on an attitude or principle of beneficence in situations without conflicting claims between two or more others and only involving the self and one other. [Kohlberg 1985, pp. 500-1]

3. A third assumption consists of an integration of the first two; that is, it returns to a view of the person, but now in the context of the interaction of persons and their construction of the mode of mutual

regulation called morality. The assumption is that part of what it means to be a person is the effort to be a *moral* person. Kohlberg rarely acknowledged this assumption in so many words, perhaps because it was so central to his own understanding of his project of identifying stages of moral judgment that he assumed it would be obvious to anyone else. But unfortunately it has remained too much in the background of the common understanding of his theory, with the result, I would suggest, that much of the interpersonal relational flavor of the theory has been missed by both critics and supporters alike. However, it was acknowledged quite explicitly by Kohlberg in a recent reply to some critics. Arguing that he has always avoided any "emotivist" view of the stages (by which he means an interpretation of the stages in terms of different *motives*), Kohlberg points out that, instead, "I have claimed that in some sense there is a primary motivation 'to do the right thing' in the sociomoral world as Piaget assumed a primary adaptation [of] 'truth' motivation for the infant and child's actions toward the physical world" (1985, pp. 498–99). This may be a slightly misfortunate way of putting it because the notion of *doing* the right thing overshadows the notion of *figuring out* what is the right thing to do and tends to eclipse the conceptual point that the latter is necessarily *part of* "doing the right thing." Moreover, I am not sure what kind of action Kohlberg had in mind here, nor the extent to which he wanted to build a behavioral disposition into his conception of the person at this level. However, I think that at the very least—and this is all we need from this assumption—he is claiming that his conception of the human person includes a natural disposition to seek a balance actively between (to use Nagel's words again) "how the lives, interests, and welfare of others make claims on us and how these claims, of various forms, are to be reconciled with the aim of living our own lives." The self of our first assumption does get delineated not just in terms of the other (and vice versa) but *also* in terms of its active attempt to understand, respond to, and *balance* the perceived needs of both the self and others.

4. A fourth step in these starting points of Kolhberg's theory pulls these existing strands together even tighter: the intentionality of morality is assumed and integrated with the developmental nature of the moral person. I have already noted that Kohlberg shared with many contemporary philosophers a view of morality as a social tool constructed by humans to regulate certain aspects of their interaction. However, to say this in this way is to take an external view of that

function, to stand outside the institution of morality and make a descriptive theoretical claim about it. But such an external perspective can never provide more than a partial picture of that institution. The reason for this is that a moral act is an *intentional* act that is tied intrinsically to a particular kind of *reason*. It is not just a piece of behavior that when observed from the outside can be seen to serve a certain social function; instead, it must also be viewed from the inside, from the point of view of the moral agent. And from this perspective a moral act is something a person *does in order to* accomplish some goal or purpose, which is judged to be good and/or obligatory by that person, according to that person's understanding of how the needs of self and other can best be balanced. As Charles Bailey has made this point recently, "Out of the context of reflection and judgment pieces of behavior are neither moral nor immoral but mere happenings: part of the natural world but not of the world of morality" (Bailey 1985, p. 199). Kohlberg often identifies this part of this assumption by referring to his "formalist" meta-ethical position that guides his empirical enquiries. For example, "For the 'formalist' meta-ethical philosophic position I hold, a necessary part of a moral action is guidance or justification by a moral reason, that is, by a judgment of rational and autonomous obligation" (Kohlberg 1985, p. 499).

In addition, the second part of this fourth assumption is that the particular form this "judgment of rational and autonomous obligation" may take in any instance of intentional moral behavior (whether engaged in or contemplated) will depend, at least in part, on the understanding of the notions of moral persons and their interrelation that is currently operative for the person making the judgment. That is, within this theory moral agents are seen as *meaning makers*. They do not more or less successfully just passively absorb and reflect some fixed moral reality that is *a priori* and independent of their efforts; instead, they are continually engaged in the activity of *constructing* that reality through their efforts to "make sense" of their relations to others, who are perceived as like the self but *not* the self. Depending on the experiences a person has had, not the least of which are role-taking opportunities, different coherent patterns of understanding this aspect of the social environment emerge and function as a framework for communication and interaction with other persons. (In short, these are the stages of moral judgment that form the core of Kohlberg's empirical theory.)

5. Finally, a fifth assumption elaborates the interpersonal nature of

this constructive endeavor. It is true that the individual person strives to "make sense" of his or her moral relationships to others and then uses this understanding to frame intentional moral acts. But this further point consists of the recognition that the only meaning that *can* make sense, given the area of concern as defined, is *shared* meaning. This is now the full sense of the notion of morality as a social tool; in short, it is a mode of interpreting human experience that is meaningful only because it is a construction shared by more than one person. Moral concepts of this sort (e.g., trust, equality, care, respect) are the meaning tools that are our preeminent expressions of our recognition of the lived reality of others *and* our claim on their recognition of ours. Moreover, the use of these concepts in the formulation of reasons and rules meant to guide moral action is also necessarily a matter of shared construction. As we have seen from previous assumptions, morality according to this view is our way of balancing the claims arising from the interaction of lives, interests, and welfare. But these very claims are not *given*, not *static*; they emerge from the real interaction of different but connected persons. And they always necessarily have points of view built into them. Thus reasons for action aimed at balance are always essentially contestable, and can only be *aimed* at mutual acceptance. As Kohlberg puts this point, "the function of moral reasoning, judgment and argumentation is to reach agreement where claims or interests conflict, most especially where the conflict is between two or more persons." (Kohlberg 1985, p. 510). In short, moral persons "are not thought of as independent, isolated 'rule followers,' with greater or lesser direct access to moral truth, but rather as rule-followers-in-relation who must construct and continually reconstruct through public dialogue the perspective from which rules governing their interaction have validity" (Boyd 1980, p. 204).

As I have already argued, it is the kind of assumptions just outlined that describe Kohlberg's theory of moral development as much as, or *more than*, the empirical claims that are perhaps more commonly known. These assumptions, quite literally, give the empirical claims meaning; that is, they allow us to interpret what it means to say that people tend to solve moral problems by use of different stages of moral reasoning and tend to go through these stages in a sequential, invariant order, from stage one to stage six. There are probably other such general assumptions we would need to explicate if we were after a comprehensive view of Kohlberg's theory. However, I would argue that any such comprehensive view would have to include, and be anchored in, the assumptions I just articulated. Moreover, I believe they are all we need for my purpose in this chapter, which is to explore the character of moral development in the way I have suggested.

SOME WAYS OF GOING WRONG IN INTERPRETATION OF STAGE SIX (AND THE CHARACTER OF THAT INTERPRETATION)

Given an acceptance of these basic assumptions as philosophical starting points of Kohlberg's theory, I think it is easier to see why some common interpretations of stage six are surely mistakes, mistakes with character implications that are thus avoidable. In identifying some of these mistakes, then, I have the aim of not only correcting them but also illuminating the direction of a more insightful understanding of the character traits that should be thought of as intrinsic to (or at least required by) Kohlberg's theory.

Probably at the bottom of this line of interpretation that I want to deflect is a narrow view of reason that gets exaggerated to the point of caricature by the time stage six is considered. That is, Kohlberg's theory is often characterized as describing increasingly adequate stages of moral *reasoning*. But then, so this misinterpretation goes, if each stage is a stage of reasoning, the lower stages are lower because they have just a little reasoning. As you go up the sequence, you get more reasoning. And this increases until you reach the end, stage six, which is "pure reason," that is, stage six is thought to be *nothing but* reason. But then, a critic will say, what an inhumane notion of moral maturity! Instead of a notion of moral goodness described in human terms of flesh and blood, aspirations and their perversion, affect, will, and strength of character, we get a cold, bloodless, calculating machine, or at least a rigid template for making calculations.

Because this problem raises large issues about theories of rationality and the emotions and about the relationship between the two, I cannot deal completely with it here. However, I believe it is sufficient to avoid this absurd conclusion to point out that it rests on a confusion of the conceptual point about what constitutes a moral act, with the normative criterion that must be appealed to for any "developmental" claim with regard to the increasing adequacy of the stages. As we have already seen, one of Kohlberg's starting points *is* the intentionality of morality, which simply means that (to use Bailey's words again) " to be viewed in a moral dimension at all, a situation and its attendant feelings must always be rationally appraised" (Bailey 1985, p. 203). What counts as appropriate and thorough rational appraisal cannot come from this conceptual point alone. Magnifying the rational side of "rational appraisal" to the image of "cold and calculating" rests on exactly this confusion. That image of stage six begins to lose its influence on us when we realize it depends on this confusion.

It loses even more influence when we realize that to say that something is conceptually tied to rational appraisal is simply to say, at the most basic level, that it is something about which one can or should "stop and think," and without this input (at least in principle), one is engaged in something other than morality, such as anxiety reduction. Finally, it begins to look downright silly when we realize that, contrary to the image of a calculating machine that can only manipulate *a priori* assumptions, any developed form of rational appraisal such as stage six will necessarily be imbued with strong powers of *imagination*. What I mean here can perhaps best be expressed with the words of the Canadian novelist Robertson Davies (via the Oxford lawyer, Pargetter, speaking to Davey Staunton): "When I say imagination I mean capacity to see all sides of a subject and weight all possibilities; I don't mean fantasy and poetry and moonshine; imagination is a good horse to carry you over the ground, not a flying carpet to set you free from probability" (Davies 1972, p. 227).

In this case, the "ground" that needs to be covered has already been formally staked out in the other starting assumptions of Kohlberg's theory identified above. Seeing all sides of a subject and weighting all possibilities is clearly *required* in any mature form of our constructive activity of "making sense" of our social environment—and especially the conflicts within it arising from the different points of view inherent in different persons—in service of balancing the claims arising from the lives, interests, and welfare of both others and self. To reduce this to any narrow sense of calculative reason is simply to miss the rich theoretical context within which the stages exist.

A second characteristic of this line of interpretation that I want to expose and reject probably originates from a shallow understanding of the notion of a moral principle, which, according to the quoted short description of stage six, will be a mainstay of the appropriate rational appraisal. According to this mistaken view, principles are abstract moral rules, "out there," external to but discoverable by human consciousness. They are seen as rigid, inflexible stopping points to our moral deliberation and justification. They are thought to be *sufficient* to dictate answers to concrete moral problems, with the additional power to determine unique answers in all cases. They are, supposedly, by virtue of being blind to context and situational particularities, the way in which we establish consistency in our moral response, even when (especially when?) that consistency is at the expense of perceived complexity and remaining problems. When the notion of moral principles is interpreted in this rigid way, the mind that must find them congenial is to some large extent *closed* (especially in complex moral conflictual situations of the sort stage six is supposed to be able to handle). Further, the character this suggests approaches the caricature of a martinet "goody two-shoes."[1]

Again, I think an adequate response to this view can be made without elaborating a thorough analysis of the nature and role of moral principles in moral deliberation or justification. What we need to see is that the notion of being principled picks out a kind of consistency, but it is not the kind identified by the view at hand; and it can be seen as a kind of virtue, though for entirely the opposite reason from what this mistaken view suggests. In short, we need to keep in mind that principles are not directly related to particular concrete acts, as are moral rules (as in "Do not steal"), but rather serve to compare and evaluate different acts falling under different, often conflicting direct rules. They are, in Dewey's words, "a method and scheme for judging" (1960, p. 136), which exist because we construct them. They are not, then, final stopping points of deliberation or justification but rather flexible attempts to integrate solutions to difficult problems into coherent patterns. A sense of consistency *is* part of the principled picture, but it is consistency in consideration of relevant perspectives, not sameness of answer. When this characteristic of consistency is extended from a logical property of principles to an aspect of personhood, it must then be properly qualified by the quality of *openmindedness*. Principled judgment is dynamic, not static; it is not evidence of a closed mind achieving consistency by ignoring

---

1. A careful synthesis of the implied interpretation of Kohlberg against which Gilligan and Murphy (1979) (and Murphy and Gilligan 1980) offer their critique will adequately support the claim that this is *not* a case of fighting a straw person with another straw person.

things but rather the way in which we strive to keep our minds open in order to *seek* consistency of evaluation.

A third commonly implied, but I think mistaken, characteristic of principled moral judgment could perhaps be developed as part of the second just discussed; however, I believe it is enough of an extension of this mistaken view of principles, and of sufficient importance, to warrant separate treatment. What I have in mind here is what happens when this mistaken view of the logical and functional properties of principles gets extended to more psychological process claims about how principles are thought of as being *used* in moral judgment. Here we run into the common notion of a "principled person" as one who is in a sense flexible in the context of adherence to chosen principles, as one who does not countenance doubt or slippage when it is a case of, or opportunity for, "sticking to one's principles." This is the sense of principle-in-use that is captured by the colloquial notions of "standing on principles" and not budging from a claim with regard to what one sees as "the principle of the matter." There is, of course, an important truth in this view. This truth is that a universalizability requirement is built into our notion of "principle" and the particularly stringent test case for meeting this requirement with regard to some principle that one is claiming to use occurs if one still maintains the principle even when dropping it would somehow favor one's own interests.

However, this truth is only part of the whole picture; it is a serious misrepresentation when taken as all of the picture. What we need to balance it and complete the picture of how principles function might be captured by the notion of a *sense of irony*. That is, it is the flexible perspective on judging, which principled consideration can provide, that gives one room to acknowledge and appreciate incongruities between rule-dictated expectations and what one senses ought to be the case. It is this openness to irony in the face of moral imperatives that provides the superior adaptability of principled judgment and is a necessary antidote to blind persistence of commitment. It is, in short, an essential aspect of attitude for a view that, as we have seen earlier, conceives of moral principles as *interpersonal constructions* of meaning.

This line of argument could be continued for some time, all of it suggesting ways in which we need to be careful in how we conceptualize principled moral judgment. However, I think we already have in front of us enough to facilitate a more direct analysis of what might be at issue between the two views. It should be remembered that my purpose in exposing and correcting these mistaken interpretations is ultimately to approach the question of what kind of character best "fits" our understanding of the stage-six form of moral judgment. What I have done so far, then, is to synthesize one common view that I think takes us in the wrong direction in answering this question, and to suggest what needs to be added in order to correct the view. To summarize, I have noted how the mistaken view tries to paint a picture of a person who is "purely rational," disposed simply to casuistically manipulate known factors; who seeks a sense of consistency through appeal to external abstract rules that simply lay down answers for us; and who has a strong sense of stick-to-it-ive-ness whenever a situation calls a rule into question. I have, then, sought to repaint this picture by noting how appropriate use of reason requires a strong, active imagination, how principles really require consistency of perspective seeking that entails an openmindedness, and how proper *use* of principles promotes ironic adaptability more than inflexibility.

THE STAGE SIX MORAL POINT OF VIEW, OBJECTIVELY SPEAKING

Now these characteristics of persons, as extrapolated from the two different interpretations of stage six, are aspects of personality that could at least in some contexts be considered aspects of character. But, as they stand so far they are what we would have to call nonmoral character traits; neither interpretation is as yet a picture of *moral* character, because all the components of both interpretations can be manifested in clearly nonmoral contexts. As was noted above, such traits can be described as *moral* character traits only when they are manifested in service of a normative moral orientation. The question I want to turn to now is: What are the moral orientations that could convert these two pictures into pictures of *moral* character? I want to show how only the second of the two pictures will be congruent with, and can be seen as traits in service of, the particular moral point of view expressed by stage six. Further, this point of view can be operationally expressed in such a way as to uncover and illuminate heretofore unsuspected dimensions of character that would seem to be required by stage six.

To answer the question of what moral point of view could utilize the two pictures, we have to return to the "starting points" of Kohlberg's theory that I articulated at the outset of this chapter. I have pointed out that Kohlberg's theory starts from a view of morality as a social construction aimed at mutually acceptable regulation of the interaction of persons in terms of how they might benefit from, and avoid harm in, that interaction. Or, as Nagel puts it, morality is the institution that organizes our attempts to solve the problem of "how the lives, interests, and welfare of others make claims on us and how these claims, of various forms, are to be reconciled with the aim of living our own lives" (1986, p. 164). Since the whole point of morality, according to this view, is the achievement of this regulation in some sort of reasonable balance, it cannot be done from solely within the point of view of any particular person's life, interest, and welfare. Instead, it necessitates the construction of an external perspective (one that is "out there") relative to any and all such particular points of view, while at the same time maintaining an appreciation of exactly that particularity in its every instance. But note that what I have just said identifies the concept of *objectivity* as intrinsically connected to the moral project so understood: objectivity is exactly that characteristic of our judgment that somehow is congruent with something "out there" such that error in judgment can be picked out with some confidence and with intersubjective recognition. The "moral point of view" that Kohlberg often refers to (as quoted earlier) is then that point of view within human judgment about acts involving the claims arising from the lives, interests, and welfare of more than one person that *lays claim to objectivity*. What is needed is a better understanding of how a particular view of objectivity shapes the moral point of view at the heart of Kohlberg's theory.

First of all, we need to see that an inadequate view of objectivity permeates the mistaken interpretation of stage six that I have been at pains to avoid. In short, I think that the characteristics I identified as part of the common but mistaken interpretation could be seen as moral character traits *only* by their being conjoined with the interpretation of objectivity inherent in what Kohlberg has described as a "conventional" understanding of morality. That is, on this interpretation what suffices to establish objectivity about moral claims is not any direct reference to the lives, interests, and welfare of persons involved, but rather an appeal to whatever set of abstract role expectations or rules of conduct constitute a particular social system.

It is the existence (or *positing* of the existence) of these role expectations and systemic rules that provides the "out there" perspective relative to the claims inherent within any particular person's point of view. And it is in reference to this conception of morality that the person with a casuistical sense of reason, seeking consistency via clear appeal to rigid rules and simple solutions, not wavering from the task of maintaining allegiance to the rule, is thought to have moral character.

Now if this *were* the interpretation of objectivity inherent in Kohlberg's ideal of stage six principled morality, then we *would* have good reason to express concern, along with the critics, about the concomitant picture of character. But I would argue that this view of objectivity is at fault for leaving the subjectivity of persons—both that of the moral judge and that of the others whose claims need considering—out of the picture, in a way that stage six cannot do. It is a kind of reification of the "out there" that is more appropriately identified, as Max Deutscher (1983) does, as "objecti*vism*": "Objectivism is the view that would have us forget that it is a view; the objectivist is a subject who would forget and have others forget that he is a subject. There is only what is viewed; the viewing of it is passed over" (p. 29). When objectivity is understood in this way it spawns a legitimate complaint that the particularities of real persons and their interaction are eclipsed and seen as secondary in importance to the "objectivity" of impersonal and abstract "principles." That this complaint *cannot* be justifiably directed at Kohlberg can be shown by combining a fuller understanding of the normative core of stage six with the more dynamic sense of objectivity that this stage requires. In the process of doing this, I will also illuminate the essential dimensions of the character of stage six.

First of all, as I have argued elsewhere (Boyd 1980), the normative core of Kohlberg's moral orientation is properly located in the notion of *respect for persons*, not in any narrow view of "justice." It is true that justice has usually been explicitly identified as his focus of attention; and in a few places he has even seemed to equate all of morality with justice. However, this has always turned out to be a very broad notion of justice, one grounded in and seeking to express (in his words) "respect for the dignity of human beings as *individual persons*" (1971, p. 165). Given the conception of persons articulated earlier as one of Kohlberg's basic starting points (that is, persons are relationally defined social selves who have claims on each other both in their need for positive help in fulfilling interests and in their requests for equal consideration of those interests as an expression of autonomy), *respect* for persons does necessitate justice as one dimension. But it is important to keep in mind that this dimension is always contextualized by a more general and diffuse dimension of furthering the other's welfare *as one's own*, that is, of benevolence.

An active, reflexive dealing with these different dimensions of moral experience is now quite clearly articulated by Kohlberg as a necessary aspect of our understanding of stage six. I quote from a recent paper entitled "The Return of Stage 6," coauthored by Kohlberg, myself, and Charles Levine:

> From a Stage 6 standpoint the autonomous moral actor has to consciously coordinate the two attitudes of justice and benevolence in dealing with real moral problems in order to maintain respect for persons. The way of regarding the other which we are calling benevolence views the other and human interaction through the lens of intending to promote good and prevent harm to the other. It is an attitude which presupposes and expresses one's identification and empathic connection with others. . . . Thus, as a mode of interaction between self and others which manifests a Stage 6 conception of respect for persons, benevolence is logically and psychologically prior to what we are calling justice. On the other hand, justice views the other and human interaction through the lens of intending to adjudicate interests, that is, of intending to resolve conflicts of differing and incompatible claims among individuals. Given this adjudicatory lens, justice presupposes a momentary separation of individual wills and cognitively organizes this separation in the service of achieving a fair adjudication through a recognition of equality and reciprocal role-taking. Thus, these two attitudes of benevolence and justice may be experienced in potential tension with each other. . . . We wish to emphasize that although these two attitudes are in tension with each other, they are at the same time mutually supportive and coordinated within a Stage 6 conception of respect for persons. This coordination can be summarized thus: benevolence constrains the momentary concern for justice to remain consistent with the promotion of good for all, while justice constrains benevolence not to be inconsistent with promoting respect for the rights of individuals conceived as autonomous agents. In other words, the aim of the autonomous Stage 6 moral agent is to seek resolution of moral problems in such a way that promoting good for some does not fail to respect the rights of others, and respecting the rights of individuals does not fail to seek promotion of the best for all. As Baier (1965) has succinctly put it, the moral point of view must evaluate "for the good of everyone alike." We think this coordination is what makes the golden rule so compelling and timeless. That is, in its positive interpretation, "Do unto others as you would have them do unto you," it expresses the attitude of benevolence as elaborated in the Christian maxim of "Love thy neighbor as thyself." On the other hand, in its proscriptive interpretation, "Do not do unto others as you would not wish others to do unto you," it expresses the attitude of justice as respecting and not

interfering with the rights and autonomy of others. [Kohlberg, Boyd, and Levine forthcoming]

It is this understanding of respect for persons that must be kept in mind in any analysis of the normative orientation underlying Kohlberg's conception of moral maturity, and thus his whole theory of moral development. Clearly, a thorough exposition of the claims made with regard to this orientation, and particularly how it gets operationalized in terms of psychological processes, is beyond the scope of this chapter. (See Kohlberg, Boyd, and Levine, forthcoming, for further discussion.) However, we already have enough here for us to proceed with the question at hand. The essential point is that the disposition to treat others with *respect* in this general sense will necessarily be at the core of the view of moral character congruent with stage six. The different aspects of the view are then as follows.

Although it is often overlooked, the first point is quite straightforward: both "dimensions" of moral experience—one might even say "poles"—found within the aim of maintaining respect for persons can be expressed in character terms. The attitudes of benevolence and justice are "ways of regarding" others in view of the claims their lives, interests, and welfare make on us. Each of these ways of regarding others can be expressed as a principle of action, resulting in analysis of moral problems from the perspective of principles of justice and beneficence. But in addition, both can also find expression as a disposition state of being, *qua person*. That is, both benevolence and justice can be understood as fundamental moral character traits. Indeed, Frankena (1973) argues, and I agree, that these two are the *only* instances of what he calls "cardinal virtues." What he means by this is that "(1) they cannot be derived from one another and (2) all other moral virtues can be derived from or shown to be forms of them" (p. 64). In short, a character formed primarily of the cardinal virtues of benevolence and justice is clearly congruent with stage six.

Another aspect of this view is the way respect for persons is seen as organizing benevolence and justice in stage six. Frankena also recognizes the potential tension or conflict between the two dimensions or poles (benevolence and justice), but he does not actively deal with it beyond expressing the "hope" that they "are in some sense ultimately consistent" (1973, p. 53). What I want to say about stage six, however, is that it is a form of moral judgment that entails the *active seeking* of the *coordination* of the attitudes of benevolence and justice via the attitude of respect for persons. Stage six does not just view some situations as matters of benevolence and others as matters of justice; rather, it realizes that approaching a situation with either concern may have implications for the other concern. And it is the placing of oneself within the process of coordinating the different pulls of moral action that the active sense of respecting persons captures. Further, what this means for our central question in this chapter is that there must also be aspects of character congruent with this attitude of respectful seeking of coordination of moral response, in an enduring expression of moral personhood.

OBJECTIVITY RECYCLED AND THE CHARACTER TO MAKE IT WORK

Here we have to return to the issue of the nature of objectivity in morality raised earlier. I want to argue that this requirement of conscious coordination of benevolence and justice is inherently tied to a particular, dynamic understanding of objectivity in morality. In the end I want to show that it is through a view of objectivity in moral judgment as "essentially performative" that the centrality of persons to stage six is firmly established and the full nature of respect for persons is operationally captured. Through this analysis we will also see how certain further character traits are not superfluous additions but rather necessary ingredients of a stage-six sense of respect for persons.

I have already noted, very roughly, how the concept of objectivity links the possibility of error in judgment with both some kind of external perspective and the aim of intersubjective agreement. And I have also rejected the particular interpretation of this linkage, found in the common, mistaken view of principled morality, that sees a shared acceptance of a set of definitive, abstract, inflexible moral rules from which any person can derive "*the* correct" answers to moral questions. I have labeled this view "objecti*vism*" because it consists of a reification of moral truth in such a way as to leave the subjective activity of persons constructing that perspective impossible to see. In contrast, to put it more positively, I think we should be looking for a much more constructive understanding of moral truth and error. This has been argued by a number of contemporary philosophers of various persuasions, from Henry David Aiken (1965) to John Rawls

(1980) to J. L. Mackie (1977); and most recently it is the position Thomas Nagel comes to in *The View from Nowhere* (1986), even though he considers himself to be a thoroughgoing realist. Pointing out that "realism about values is different from realism about empirical facts," Nagel argues that the difference amounts to the fact that in the case of morality, "It is not a question of bringing the mind into correspondence with an external reality which acts causally on it, but of reordering the mind itself in accordance with the demands of its own external view of itself" (p. 148).

With this revision of our aim in mind, what we need is some account of *how* objectivity can be understood as providing an external perspective for identifying error, *in such a way that does not lead us into objectivism*. The essentials of such an account are as follows. First of all, I think objectivity needs to be seen as identifying a certain kind of perspective on judgment, when "judgment" is taken in its activity sense, as something that one does or performs. Then, second, this perspective can be loosely expressed as a kind of *detaching* or *decentering*. That is, the objective perspective is in the direction of recognizing, and seeking some kind of reflexive or "reconsiderative" distance on, some aspects of our present understandings or claims. The essential functional point about objectivity, then, is that it consists of whatever kind of *detaching* or decentering best facilitates reflexivity on our own claims—*and* in such a way as to keep open the possibility of the continuation of this reflexive detaching. I think Nagel has captured all the constituent parts of this understanding very precisely in his general interpretation of objectivity.

> Objectivity is a method of understanding. It is belief and attitudes that are objective in the primary sense. Only derivatively do we call objective the truths that can be arrived at in this way. To acquire a more objective understanding of some aspect of life or the world, we step back from our initial view of it and form a new conception which has that view and its relation to the world as its object. In other words, we place ourselves in the world that is to be understood. The old view then comes to be regarded as an appearance, more subjective than the new view, and correctable or confirmable by reference to it. The process can be repeated, yielding a still more objective conception. [Nagel 1986, p. 4]

I need to emphasize several points of this interpretation before exploring what it means in the context of the moral point of view of stage six. The first point that is crucial to keep in mind is that objectivity is primarily connected to inquiry, not answers. Thus in the passage just quoted, Nagel identifies objectivity as a "method of understanding" and notes that only derivatively do we call objective the truths that can be arrived at in this way. What we should be focusing on is not some kind of results or products of understanding, for example, as determined by rigid rules deductively applied, but rather the way or manner in which they are pursued. (In the context of a concern about objectivity in moral *judgment*, it is important to keep in mind that the term "judgment" is often ambiguous: it can refer either to a way or mode of making decisions—a *process*—or to the *result* of particular efforts at decision making—a product. The point here is that the focus of our attention, when we are concerned about objectivity, is properly judgment-as-process rather than judgment-as-product). *Active language* is the appropriate mode of description, as is accurately reflected in Nagel's further description in this passage: "To acquire" it "we step back," "place ourselves," in a "process" that "can be repeated."

The second point I want to emphasize here is a corollary of understanding objectivity as a method of understanding; interpreted in this way, objectivity must always be tied, in some way, to an intentional subject. It is something that *one does*, not something that happens or a state of affairs. The reflexivity that properly modifies the detaching aim of objective thinking can exist *only* if there is a human subject still within the thinking to refer back to, a fact that must be held consciously even when in tension with that direction. As Deutscher (1983) says, "Objectivity is a form, a style, an employment of our subjectivity . . . not its antithesis" (p. 41), and "We can speak of a 'point of view' and say that objectivity is possible only within a point of view and is thus a quality of one's subjectivity" (p. 42). Only an intentional, thinking *subject* can be said to *have* a point of view, and objectivity is the aiming at a particular kind of point of view—one that includes some aspect of that subject or its thinking as part of its object.

The final point important for my purposes here consists of a recognition of the *necessarily* paradoxical flavor of this conception. As Nagel (1986) so clearly sees, the puzzle is that for any pursuit of objectivity,

> its aim is naturally described in terms that, taken literally, are unintelligible: we must get outside of ourselves, and view the world from nowhere within it. Since it is impossible to leave one's own point of view behind entirely without ceasing to exist, the metaphor of getting outside ourselves must have another meaning. We

are to rely less and less on certain individual aspects of our point of view, and more and more on something else, less individual, which is also part of us. [P. 67]

Since we can't literally escape ourselves, any improvement in our beliefs has to result from some kind of self-transformation. And the thing we can do which comes closest to getting outside ourselves is to form a detached idea of the world that includes us, and includes our possession of that conception as part of what it enables us to understand about ourselves. We are then outside ourselves in the sense that we appear inside a conception of the world that we ourselves possess, but that is not tied to our particular point of view. [Pp. 69–70]

Now if we work with *this* notion of objectivity, as opposed to the one I have suggested is inadequate, what then can we say about what this means for our understanding of the stage-six moral point of view? As I have already suggested, and will now try to show, I think this conception of objectivity is what locates persons at the center of the stage-six notion of principled moral judgment, both as intentional moral agents and as objects and subjects of respect. To see this clearly, we must again refer back to Kohlberg's philosophical starting points, which I briefly elaborated at the beginning of this chapter. It will be remembered that the conception of morality underlying Kohlberg's theory is grounded in a view of social selves correlatively defined and then is elaborated as persons trying to "make sense" of their interaction, through their shared endeavor of striving to balance the claims that the lives, interests, and welfare of each make on each other. Then when we take this understanding as the arena within which objectivity, in the sense just articulated, is understood, what we immediately see more clearly is that the plural form ("we") in Nagel's discussion of the basic metaphor of objectivity—"we must get outside ourselves"—cannot always be interpreted as referring to a "royal we" or as referring to all of us, but as referring to persons individually and separately. Within the moral point of view of stage six, however, the "we" that must "get outside ourselves" is truly and necessarily *plural*.[2] Objectivity in *morality* is a method of understanding that simply cannot, in the end, be engaged in by one person alone. On the contrary, it entails two people (or more) aiming at reflexive detaching

---

2. The claim I am making here is my own, not Nagel's. Certainly there is a monological flavor to much of his discussion, at least when he is outlining his *general* conception of objectivity. It is unclear to me whether he would agree with me that this will not do for morality.

or decentering *together*, with respect to each other and self, often at the same time. In regard to this mutual effort, in the context of claims of both benevolence and justice arising from the lived reality of each (or all), the earlier noted characteristics of imagination, openmindedness, and a sense of irony are subordinate moral character traits.

However, other, more central aspects of character also only now become clearly visible. The first of these puts to rest, once and for all, the criticism of stage six as cold and impersonal: an essential aspect of moral objectivity must be the enduring expression and presentation of oneself to the other as *sympathetic*! Mutual decentering hinges directly on this disposition to try to see and feel as the other sees and feels within his or her lived context and understanding of that context. As Frankena puts it, "we must somehow attain and develop an ability to be aware of others as persons, as important to themselves as we are to ourselves, and to have a lively and sympathetic representation in imagination of their interests and of the effects of our actions on their lives" (1973, p. 69). He points out how the need for this has been stressed by Josiah Royce and William James:

> Both men point out how we usually go our own busy and self-concerned ways, with only an external awareness of the presence of others, much as if they were things, and without any realization of their inner and peculiar worlds of personal experience; and both emphasize the need and the possibility of a "higher vision of inner significance" which pierces this "certain blindness in human beings" and enables us to realize the existence of others in a wholly different way, as we do our own. [P. 69]

As James says, "we ought, all of us, to realize each other in this intense, pathetic, and important way" (quoted by Frankena 1973, p. 70). What it requires, as a character expression of moral objectivity, is the enduring disposition to seek an integration of one's understanding and affective appreciation of what the other is *really* like and what the other is *really* feeling, as much as possible independent from both one's own phenomenological situation and one's preconceived understanding and appreciation of the other.

Then, in addition to resting on this kind of basic, mutual sympathetic connection, the kind of objectivity that a stage-six respect for persons seeks also entails a *mutual* reflexivity on understandings and claims. And this requirement has additional, distinct character implications. To see this we must first recall not only that objectivity requires a kind of detaching or decentering (which we have just seen to involve sympathy in the case of moral judgment), but also that this is to be sought in such a way as to facilitate reflexive reconsideration of some present understanding or claim. But, as we have also seen, in morality there is by definition a plurality of points of view from which such understandings and claims arise. Thus there is also a plurality of both subjects and objects of such reflexivity required by objectivity. In short, to put this together, stage-six moral objectivity is expressive of respect for persons through its necessitating a disposition of persons to engage others *performatively* with regard to moral interactions, both those involving benevolence and those involving justice, and especially those requiring an integration of the two attitudes. What this performative engagement requires is, quite simply, the dispositional realization that an individual's understandings of either benevolence or justice claims are potentially (and likely) limited by that individual's particular subjective point of view and that offering these understandings to others with the expectation of their agreement or disagreement, supported by their counterunderstanding from their points of view, is a necessary condition of determining the best understanding. In short, complete reflexivity in matters of moral understandings can be achieved only through *dialogue*.

The additional character implications of this full picture are then, finally, as follows. First of all, as we saw earlier, all of the traditional subordinate character traits, such as courage, patience, loyalty, and the like, should be thought of as derivatives of (or sometimes expressions of) the two cardinal virtues of benevolence and justice. That is, they can be considered *moral* character traits only insofar as they are put into context by the moral point of view framed by benevolence and justice. The connection most commonly seen here is that sometimes in order to *act* benevolently or justly one does need to *be* courageous, patient, loyal, and so on. Undoubtedly this is true. But our understanding of objectivity adds that, in addition and perhaps at a more fundamental level, these other traits are matters of moral character insofar as they make possible and facilitate our performative engagement of each other about what *constitutes* the benevolent or just act.

A more important point is that we can now identify two additional higher-level character traits that seem to be required by our understanding of how a particular view of objectivity interacts with the normative dimensions of stage six. Both of these are on a par with the manifestation of sympathetic connection discussed earlier. The first is *humility*, which is perhaps surprising in the context of the self-righteous flavor often attributed to stage six. One's performative engagement of the other involves making claims of validity for one's current understandings, but it simply cannot function without the conscious realization, expressed in both attitude and behavior, that "*I could be wrong*" about those understandings. Only through *being humble* can a person allow room for other persons and their alternative understandings to be heard and to be considered reflexively by all. Whereas being sympathetic, in the sense outlined above, provides the substantive concerns around which moral judgment revolves—and thus objectivity in moral judgment must accommodate—viewing the validity of one's moral claims and the appropriateness of one's moral actions with humility is required to show respect *for other persons'* sympathetic interpretations and subsequent claims to objectivity in judgment and action.

The other high-level character trait that we can also now see as required by an operative notion of stage-six principled morality consists of a dispositional expression of a *sense of responsibility* for maintaining the conditions of dialogue through which performative engagement can function, and thus objectivity can be sought. As being sympathetic is needed for identifying moral concerns, and being humble is needed to facilitate their common interpretation, being responsible undergirds the whole activity through time. Responsibility is called for in at least two senses. First, one needs to be responsible in the sense of being ready and willing to *respond to* the other. It is not enough merely to be sympathetic and humble; unless one is also prepared and inclined to respond to others' differing perspectives and judgments, one is simply not respecting them as equals in the performative engagement. Second, and in conjunction with this first sense, one also needs to be responsible in the sense of doing everything one can to ensure that the material preconditions of dialogue are in place and maintained adequately. Here we cycle back to our starting point of what morality is all about in the first place. That is, any number of different, concrete acts may be called for by this sense of responsibility—not only because one thinks them to be morally required, but *also* because performing them enhances the possibility that their obligatoriness or worthwhileness will become matters of universal intersubjective agreement. At another level this sense of responsibility may also call for forms of "praxis"—in particular, reflective action aimed at breaking down political barriers of unequal distribution of power and economic barriers of unequal distribution of resources and wealth. Finally, also at this level, being responsible in this sense means taking the next generation seriously enough to educate them. Dialogue with the following generations is an essential aspect of the development of our shared humanity. With this concern in mind, one can then see that "moral education" is a precondition of that particular dialogue if it is to express respect among equals. In short, moral education is an activity of responsible character, located at the intersection of respect for persons and a dynamic search for objectivity in morality.

A CONCLUDING NOTE

It is one thing to call for people of good character and for the education to help them nurture it. It is quite another thing still to do so in a way that goes beyond cliché to a conceptually clear, coherent picture that is theoretically grounded. Kohlberg's theory of moral development is not primarily a theory of moral character. It is a theory about how humans learn to make moral judgments in a psychologically mature way, and it is at the same time a theory that is philosophically rich compared to much of the rest of North American mainstream social psychology. As a *developmental* theory, however, it also necessarily includes a vision of maturity that is not morally neutral. Starting with a different way of focusing its attention, such a theory will naturally see things somewhat differently from those perspectives that view the moral arena primarily in character terms. But in this chapter I have tried to show how an adequate understanding of the moral point of view of stage six, combined with the sense of objectivity that makes this point of view viable, goes some distance toward requiring a vision of good character in addition to a preferred form of moral judgment. It still remains to be worked out how people attain (develop?) such aspects of moral character, how educational efforts might enhance the likelihood of success in this endeavor, and how the aim might need modification to accommodate matters of additional, and perhaps competing, concern with regard to character. From my argument here, however, I hope it is at least clear that there is sufficient ground of common concern and an intersection of kinds of claims to make these tasks worth pursuing.

REFERENCES

Aiken, Henry David. "The Concept of Moral Objectivity." In *Morality and the Language of Conduct*, ed. Hector-Neri Castaneda and George Nakhnikian. Detroit: Wayne State University, 1965.

Baier, Kurt. *The Moral Point of View: A Rational Basis of Ethics*. New York: Random House, 1965.

Bailey, Charles. "Kohlberg on Morality and Feeling." In *Lawrence Kohlberg: Consensus and Controversy*, ed. Sohan Modgil and Celia Modgil. Philadelphia: Falmer Press, 1985.

Bennett, William J., and Delattre, Edwin J. "A Moral Education: Some Thoughts on How Best to Achieve It," *American Educator* 3 (1979): 6–9.

Boyd, Dwight. "The Rawls Connection." In *Moral Development, Moral Education, and Kohlberg: Basic Issues in Philosophy, Psychology, Religion, and Education*, ed. Brenda Munsey. Birmingham, Ala.: Religious Education Press, 1980.

Boyd, Dwight. "The Oughts of Is: Kohlberg at the Interface between Moral Philosophy and Developmental Psychology." In *Lawrence Kohlberg: Consensus and Controversy*, ed. Sohan Modgil and Celia Modgil. Philadelphia: Falmer Press, 1985.

Davies, Robertson. *The Manticore*. New York: Penguin Books, 1972.

Deutscher, Max. *Subjecting and Objecting*. St. Lucia, Queensland, Australia: University of Queensland Press, 1983.

Dewey, John. *Theory of the Moral Life*, 3d ed. New York: Holt, Rinehart and Winston, 1960.

Frankena, William. *Ethics*. Englewood Cliffs, N. J.: Prentice-Hall, 1973.

Gilligan, Carol, and Murphy, John Michael. "Moral Development in Late Adolescence and Adulthood: The Philosopher and the Dilemma of the Fact." In *Intellectual Development beyond Childhood*, ed. D. Kuhn. San Francisco: Jossey-Bass, 1979.

Hamm, Cornel. "The Content of Moral Education, or In Defense of the Bag of Virtues," *School Review* 85 (1977): 219–28.

Kohlberg, Lawrence. "Education for Justice: A Modern Statement of the Platonic View." In *Moral Education*, ed. Nancy F. Sizer and Theodore R. Sizer. Cambridge, Mass.: Harvard University Press, 1970.

Kohlberg, Lawrence. "From Is to Ought: How to Commit the Naturalistic Fallacy and Get Away with It in the Study of Moral Development." In *Cognitive Development and Epistemology*, ed. Theodore Mischel. New York: Academic Press, 1971.

Kohlberg, Lawrence. "A Current Statement on Some Theoretical Issues." In *Lawrence Kohlberg: Consensus and Controversy*, ed. Sohan Modgil and Celia Modgil. Philadelphia: Falmer Press, 1985.

Kohlberg, Lawrence; Boyd, Dwight; and Levine, Charles. "The Return of Stage 6: Its Principle and Moral Point of View." In *The Moral Domain*, ed. Tom Wren. Cambridge, Mass.: MIT Press, forthcoming. Previously published in German as "Wie Wiederkehr der sechsten Stufe: Gerechtigkeit, Wohlwolen und der Standpunkt der Moral." In *Zur Bestimmung der Moral: Philosophische und Sozialwissen-*

schaftliche Beiträge zur Moralforschung, ed. Wolfgang Edelstein and Gertrud Nunner-Winkler. Frankfurt am Main: Suhrkamp, 1986.

Mackie, John Leslie. *Ethics: Inventing Right and Wrong*. New York: Penguin Books, 1977.

Murphy, John Michael, and Gilligan, Carol. "Moral Development in Late Adolescence and Adulthood: A Critique and Reconstruction of Kohlberg's Theory," *Human Development* 23 (1980): 77–104.

Nagel, Thomas. *The View from Nowhere*. New York: Oxford University Press, 1986.

Peters, Richard S. "Moral Development: A Plea for Pluralism." In *Cognitive Development and Epistemology*, ed. Theodore Mischel. New York: Academic Press, 1972.

Rawls, John. "Kantian Constructivism in Moral Theory," *Journal of Philosophy* 77: 9 (1980): 515–72.

Sullivan, Edmund. *Kohlberg's Structuralism: A Critical Appraisal*, Monograph Series #115. Toronto: Ontario Institute for Studies in Education, 1977.

The Liberation of Caring; A Different Voice For Gilligan's "Different Voice"

BILL PUKA

Recent literature portrays caring as a psychological, social, and ethical orientation associated with female gender identity. This essay focuses on Gilligan's influential view that "care" is a broad theme of moral development which is under-represented in dominant theories of human development such as Kohlberg's theory. An alternative hypothesis is proposed portraying care development as a set of circumscribed coping strategies tailored to dealing with sexism. While these strategies are practically effective and partially "liberated," from the moral point of view, they also reflect the debilitating influences of sexist socialization even at the highest level. Gilligan and her colleagues seem to misidentify these inadequacies of mature care. This alternative hypothesis is briefly related to the critical and feminist tradition. Then it is supported with Gilligan's own research and interpretive text.

A compelling vision of "caring" and its role in women's development has evolved in psychology and gender studies (e.g., Miller 1976, Chodorow 1978, Gilligan 1982, Noddings 1985). Gilligan's "different voice" conception of "care" as an ethical orientation and its contrast to the patriarchal preference for individual rights and justice has had a powerful impact on many fields, including philosophy. It has garnered an enthusiastic international following.

Many of Gilligan's supporters, however, are careful to note the formative nature of her account and its potential dangers. As some put it, "Gilligan has helped show that there is some gender difference here, centered around the relational and nurturent orientations of women. Now we must clarify what it is." Gilligan sometimes qualifies her own views similarly (Gilligan 1982, 3, 126). Feminist analysis warns that attempting to distinguish woman's care-taking strengths from her socialized, servile weaknesses flirts with sexism itself. It runs the risk of transforming victimization into virtue by merely saying it is so, of legitimizing subjugation to gender in a misguided attempt at self-affirmation. This seems a typical pitfall for oppressed groups, especially in "personal consciousness-raising" approaches to liberation.

Hypatia vol. 5, no. 1 (Spring 1990) © by Bill Puka

In this essay, I will pose a different voice for Gilligan's "different voice," an alternative hypothesis of what the caring difference might be. On this hypothesis care is not a general course of moral development, primarily, but a set of coping strategies for dealing with sexist oppression in particular. In the spirit of care, this hypothesis is designed to "satisfy everyone," including proponents and critics on each side. Foremost, it seeks to preserve care's strengths and the strengths of women's development. Yet in doing so, it pares back some of care's presumed critical relevance to "justice theories" of development, making room for their virtues while deflecting much unnecessary controversy detrimental to care.[1] The alternative hypothesis also seeks to affirm feminist worries regarding care without threatening Gilligan's main insights or care's research potential.

I

THE TWO ALTERNATIVES

(1) Care As Moral Development: *Gilligan's voice*

Gilligan portrays care as both a general orientation toward moral problems (interpersonal problems) and a track of moral development. As an orientation or focus, care expresses an empathetic sense of connectedness to others, of being in-relation with them, actually or potentially. As a track of development, care evolves from an egocentric form of self-care, through a more conventional sort of do-gooder care. It moves on, finally, to a self-chosen, self-reflective, and self-affirming form of mature caring (Gilligan 1982, Ch. 3 and 4).

At level I of this development, care is self-concerned and self-protective out of a sense of vulnerability. The caring individual seeks above all to avoid hurt and insure psychological survival. With increasing self-confidence and a sense of competence to relate effectively, she sees this protective orientation as selfish and irresponsible. Care then evolves into a more conventional form of caring for others that is socially effective in its adherence to accepted norms. At this second level, the caring person seeks the support and approval of others by living up to their expectations and serving their needs altruistically. On the one hand, this leads to psychological denial and the rationalization of care's slavishness, according to Gilligan. On the other, it breeds a conflicting sense of being put upon and of allowing it to happen, of using the guise of altruism and martyrdom to mask indirect self-interest. With the confidence to face this conflict, and oneself, however, the caring individual moves to level III. Here she recognizes that self-concern is self-responsible, that an adult must balance care for others with care for self as the contexts of her various relationships require.

At both transition points in the care sequence, crises of vulnerability can lead to nihilism and despair, confusion and retreat from care, rather than development. That is, women progress and regress in care, rather than following an invariant, progressive sequence.

Care is defined by theme rather than gender, according to Gilligan (1982, 2). Yet care also is the dominant, spontaneous expression of a "relational social perspective." Since a relational perspective arises spontaneously from the formation of female gender identity and role, care will be the female ethic of choice. (Males characteristically evolve a "separational" or individualistic social perspective, by contrast, and prefer a rights and justice ethic.) In addition, since the most prominent theories of moral development favor the theme of justice, since they "listen to male voices" primarily, these theories tend to discriminate against female development. They under-represent, distort and under-value its "different voice" of caring (Gilligan, 1982, Ch. 3 and 4).

(2) Care as Subjugation and Liberation

The alternative "Care as Liberation" hypothesis portrays care primarily as a sexist service orientation, prominent in the patriarchal socialization, social conventions, and roles of many cultures. This care theme is seen best at Gilligan's level II which is dominated by "stereotypical feminine virtues" such as "gentleness and tact," and an overriding desire "not to hurt" or disappoint anyone, as Gilligan puts it (1982, 76, 65). Here women "seek survival by trying to satisfy male expectations and find male approval in hopes of male support (1982, 66-67, 72, 78).

On the liberation hypothesis, the focus of such a care theme can be adjusted by adult women to handle crisis of hurt, domination, and rejection usually brought on by males in women's daily lives and relationships as clearly reflected in Gilligan's key studies (1982, 2, 3). Such crises engender various responses, each of which has pros and cons. Care "development" or care *levels*, then, actually represent circumscribed coping strategies, of special use to women for facing crises of sexism. While these strategies may be ordered by coping effectiveness, they do not evolve from each other developmentally for the most part. They do not represent general systems of moral competence of the sort that cognitive stages do in classic theories of moral development.

Let us reconsider Gilligan's three levels of care through the lens of this alternative hypothesis. Care at "level I" now becomes primarily a coping strategy for facing hurtful rejection and domination, not for orienting to moral issues generally. It copes with its context, sensibly, by "seeking survival" through self-protection (1982, 75-76, 110-111). Yet the effectiveness of this strategy, its "sense of isolation, aloneness, powerlessness," as Gilligan puts it, can often lead to resuming the conventional, slavish approach of level II care. In Gilligan's research, such coping requires psychological denial and rationalization when used as a strategy adopted by adult women (1982, 80-85). Level II's slavishness is especially difficult to live with if one has reflected at all on one's role and treatment in sexist relationships as Gilligan's respondents have. We would not expect this reflective conflict to arise in the well-socialized girl.

To deal with these inner conflicts of level II coping, while facing additional domination and rejection by men, various strategies recommend themselves. Level III, where the balance between care for others and care for self is struck, is not the obvious alternative. One might revert to "level I," self-protectiveness again. Gilligan describes an assertive mode of this strategy which involves "deliberate isolation." Here one sees oneself as "a loner" who is self-sufficient and unfettered to a degree (1982, 75, 89). This form of self-protection would be especially effective in dealing with "level II" aversion to slavish care and internal "level I" problems of powerlessness and isolation. Yet in addressing these problems in this way, one identifies with one's victimized retreat from care, mistaking it as one's self-affirming strength.

A like strategy of "care" would involve what Gilligan terms "moral nihilism" (1982, 123-126). In its less despairing form, it is a more affirmative approach to self-interest than self-protection is—if nothing is really right or wrong, then "why care?", "why not be selfish?"

Of course, one may not have the self-confidence for such self-affirmation, nor the luck of finding those modes of self-affirmation that "work for you." In this context, one may fall into moral confusion and hopelessness. Gilligan describes this "development" as well—"I'm still in love with him, no matter what he has done, and that really confuses me . . . I can't get him out of my mind" (1982, 124). Such regression in caring can also result from the servile strategy of trying level II "service orientation" over and over again, despite its failure. Gilligan terms these sorts of phenomena "cycles of repetition" and the "psychology of passivity," though she does not apply these descriptions to level II.

When considering the basis of this reinterpretation thus far, three features of Gilligan's account are key. First, care is depicted as progressing and regressing, alternately, not necessarily as evolving in order of levels. Second, Gilligan does not claim, nor offer evidence, that lower levels of care generally occur earlier in development. And finally, Gilligan's studies do not observe any one respondent traversing all three levels of care in order, or otherwise. Therefore, the seemingly undevelopmental disorder or variability of care fits here.

There are, however, more effective coping strategies which care might try. Through the self-confidence gained by surviving abandonments and hurt, and reflectively learning their lessons, women may emerge to "level III" care. In this explicit "consciousness-raising" strategy, a woman seeks the "middle path" between self-protection and slavishness. She balances self care with care for others more evenly. "Level III" care is clearly a more subtle and effective path for the sexist realities a woman faces than "level II" coping. It shows significant insight into the validity of benevolent virtues and compassionate response, along with acknowledgment of their dangers. Here a woman learns where she can exercise her strengths, interests, and commitments within the male power structure and where she would do better to comply with that structure. A delicate contextual balance must be struck to be effective here.

Since this approach carries forward some of the aversive "service orientation" of level II, its internal effectiveness is enhanced by rationalization, as it was at level II. Likewise, since the slavishness of this orientation is now more reflectively recognized than at level II, effective rationalization must take a far more reflective and legitimating form. Thus in this "level III" coping strategy, a woman takes personal responsibility for compliance. She portrays it as adult and self-chosen *in its selectivity*, and even virtuous in this selectivity. Furthermore, she abstracts and generalizes the strategy as a legitimate and even preferred ethic—a carefully balanced, caring-for-others-in-general ethic— from which males could learn much. She distinguishes such a service orientation from slavish level II conventionalism by recasting the *limits* of her social and moral power as the very *power* to be limited, to be tentative, contextual, and morally balanced in her exercise of power. Gilligan emphasizes the peculiar virtues of such contextualism and tentativeness in level III care (1982, 54-55, 95, 100-102, 165-167).

PARTIAL DEVELOPMENTS

As should be apparent, support for this alternative "different voice" will derive from Gilligan's own text. The "care as liberation" hypothesis proposes that Gilligan's observations and *interpretations* of care *may* not best support her overall position that care constitutes moral development. At the least, they lend comparable support to the view that care is primarily a form of coping with sexism. Before we detail this support, a few reflections on the significance of this hypothesis are in order. We will begin with its relation to Gilligan's conception of moral maturity, to possible (sexist) biases in her interpretive theorizing, and to the non-developmental strengths of care she uncovers.

While the highest level for care shows a degree of cognitive liberation from sexist oppression, its "consciousness-raising" may not see through many sexist aspects of its own ethic. In this regard it is morally defective and incomplete rather than mature or adequate. Level III care does not accurately identify the causes of its "sense of service" in the sexist nature of social institutions and sexual politics primarily. Rather it "progressively" personalizes and legitimizes responsibility for this orientation as a desirable form of "taking control of one's life" and "taking responsibility for oneself," of learning to feel "adult" and "good about oneself" (75-78, 82-85, 91-94).

Unfortunately, Gilligan's descriptions of care maturity at level III appear to reflect and legitimate this process. They portray only the effectiveness of care, not the inadequacies of self-alienation involved. These descriptions actually may compound the problem by portraying care's consciousness-raising approach to liberation as a *spontaneous* or *natural* development reflective of female gender. By making this approach dependent on *personal* confidence, psychological *self*-awareness, and on moral *self*-control and *self*-responsibility, Gilligan seemingly weakens the key connection her account draws between relational orientation and female gender identity.

In an account of care's progressive struggle with sexism, level III care might be faulted for its lack of political sense or institutional focus out of which a sense of solidarity with other women and a need for cooperative social action might derive. Care's almost total lack of social-institutional focus at level III certainly raises questions about its general moral adequacy. The attempt to balance serving others with self care at level III does not solve the problem of slavishness. It merely tempers and accommodates to it in a morally questionable way. This accommodation is then intellectualized, especially in Gilligan's descriptions of level III, by portraying it as a necessary complement to "male-oriented" justice (1982, 100). (Marx described a similar tendency of crude communism to *universalize* private (alienated) property, including women as male property, in a misguided hope of moralizing it.) By contrast, a truly liberated ethic for women (and other oppressed groups) might speak in a truly new voice, expressing themes of unfolding, liberated experience. In so doing it might not promote either responsive responsibility or demand for individual rights in themselves or in combination. Hopefully this view of care addresses feminist concerns and those of critical theorists. Obviously it is framed primarily from the perspective of socialist feminism though it hopes to accommodate radical and liberal feminist perspectives as well in the particular context it addresses.

At the same time, there can be no doubt that it is psychologically and morally better for women to cope with oppression in these caring ways than not at all. To be able to handle a circumscribed range of moral problems through a particular set of orientational strategies surely shows moral skill. Coming to certain valid moral beliefs and insights, working out one's caring stance on key interpersonal situations clearly, represents a moral advance in some cognitive-psychological domain. And of course, it is morally better that people see through oppression part way than not at all. This is true even when they deceive themselves when doing so; after all, self-deception is a skill of sorts in certain contexts. When such moral progress is accompanied by increased self-awareness and confidence, learning to take control of one's life and responsibility for oneself, additional moral progress is likely to result. These are all moral developments in women's conceptual orientations which Gilligan has uncovered perceptively and ordered artfully. Gilligan has detailed women's moral *socialization* well also, it appears.

Still, the evolution from somewhat duped and debilitated in some domain to somewhat disabused and functional in that domain differs from steadily progressive development in general competence. In this latter process we primarily move from fairly competent to progressively more so. Circumscribed moral coping skills tailored to gender-specific and oppressive contexts differ from broad systems of cognitive moral competence. Such systems organize and process the fundamentals of social experience for all, at the most basic level, while recognizing that much of our most salient experience is not of this sort.

Theories of human development in moral cognition, such as those of Piaget and Kohlberg, seek to chart the progression of such basic meaning and reasoning systems. As a result, care coping and its struggle for liberation need not be covered by the classic theories of moral development Gilligan criticizes. Nor do these theories discriminate against care when leaving such phenomena out. Likewise, such theories need not, and should not, cover the so-called "justice focus" that Gilligan associates with male gender preferences, nor any other "macho" ethic there may be. This is so even when such orientations primarily speak to male experience and reflect patriarchal competencies in sexist society.

The theories of Piaget, Kohlberg, and especially Freud should be criticized for *bias*, patriarchal and otherwise. However, where justice bias in basic cognitive *structure* is found, it will not likely discriminate against care orientation, as Gilligan describes this phenomenon. And when such biases are removed, such caring is not likely to be better represented in these sorts of human developmental theories.

"Slave Morality" and Other Ideologies

The "Care as Liberation" hypothesis utilizes the speculative conceptual models and political jargon of critical theory for two reasons. First, it seeks to emphasize the uncanny relationship between care maturity, as Gilligan portrays it, and the "slave morality" phenomenon long recognized in this tradition. Second, it seeks to show how Gilligan's own critical approach to exposing patriarchy in classic moral development theory might apply to her own view. It does this, in part, by applying the sort of analysis Gilligan offers of level II caring to her level III of caring.

Gilligan's critique, after all, tries to show how males "rationalize" their gender-identity needs through moral (justice) orientations. They claim such needs as their just due. Patriarchal theories then further "rationalize" this rationalization by abstracting and legitimizing it at its "highest" level as a generally applicable form of moral competence. The "Care as Liberation" hypothesis builds on Gilligan's own observations of how women rationalize their moral victimization at level II. It suggests how care theory may further "rationalize" this circumscribed sort of rationalization by abstracting and legitimating it (at its "highest" level) as a generally applicable form of moral competence. In offering this analysis I do not assume that women or victims of oppression generally suffer more "ideological distortion" *overall* than those who oppress them, far from it. Rather this analysis posits partial distortions of one sort, in relation to one sort of coping, and only to a degree.

The "slave morality" phenomenon, as we know, was identified most vividly in the spread of Christianity among poor and oppressed peoples. As Nietzscheans observed, for example, the Christian message of "love as service" appeals by transforming vices of subservience into virtues of redemption. "Bear your cross, be humble, meek, patient, and long-suffering for His sake. Love and give even to those who abuse you, asking nothing for yourself, and all will be given to you." Such a message appeals even more when it prescribes such virtues and distributes such burdens to all, as is especially notable in Christianity. Marx identified this ideological "opiate" in secular ideals as well, including ideals of communism. As noted, he predicted that proletarians, victimized by private property, would misconceive their liberation in the ideology of equal property, equal distribution of wealth. In this way they would at least share their victimization "after the revolution." For Marx, Nietzsche, and others, truly liberating moral revolution (or development) is not found in such selective validation of servitude as one climbs out of it. It does not consist in balancing or equalizing servitude. Rather, moral adequacy is found in a radical transformation of our understanding of human welfare and mutuality. Of course, this transformation need not overturn enduring virtues of the Feminine, noted by Radical feminists and Gilligan as well.

While the "Care as Liberation" hypothesis is not dependent on such speculative positions, nor the often slanted or over-generalized observations that accompany them, it benefits from what commonsense plausibility they have.[2] (See Nicholson (1983) for a very interesting analysis in a related tradition.)

It is important to recognize, however, that challenges to the moral and psychological adequacy of care and coping, from a critical theory perspective, are somewhat secondary to the intent of this hypothesis. The "slave morality" analysis applies only to one aspect of the "consciousness-raising" component of level III care. The heart of "care as liberation" distinguishes care as socialization and skillful coping from care as general moral development. In this way, as noted, it preserves many of care's psychological strengths while fending off damaging counter-criticisms from classic theories of moral development. There is no dispute, I take it, that Gilligan's contrast between care and justice, female relationality and male individuation, captures gender *socialization* by and large. Nor is there likely to be dispute that effective coping, for either gender, *might* vary these themes in ways that Gilligan's care levels depict. Rather the current Kohlberg-Gilligan dispute, for example, is over whether these levels are "cognitive-developmental." It is over whether they spontaneously evolve in a way that expresses holistic cognitive systems and their inherent processes of constructional self-transformation. Care need not enter this cognitive-developmental domain, nor theoretical controversy, to make its contribution.

It also is important to recognize that the explicitly feminist analysis of care coping I offer, while important in its own right, may be one aspect of a broader view concerning "response to authoritarianism." Care levels bear a strong resemblance to patterns of attitudinal assimilation and accommodation commonly observed among poor and oppressed groups, or in oppressive situational contexts. Taking the levels in order, their "oppression focus" may be rendered in commonsense terms: Level I—Protect yourself against harm from those in power. Ensure your psychological survival in the face of ongoing domination through strategies of self-protection and self-concern. Level II—To overcome ongoing powerlessness, play the roles those in power set for you. Serve and sacrifice to gain their approval and support thereby participating in their power and avoid harm. Be circumspect in pursuing your true interests, or even in recognizing them. And maintain a sense of fulfillment and self-esteem in expressing the competencies of pragmatic service. Level III—With the partial success of strategy II, and where otherwise possible, acknowledge your (non-threatening) true interests. Ferret out spheres of power for pursuing these interests within the gaps of the established power structure. Embrace the competencies of those oppressed roles one cannot avoid. Identify with them and use them with one's "true" competencies as a source of evolving strength and pride.

Social scientists have observed this sort of pattern in the orientation of inmates in prison camps as associated with a related phenomenon, "identification with the aggressor" (Bettleheim 1943; A. Freud 1946; Sanford 1955), Kohlberg has observed it in the prison communities he has studied (Kohlberg, et al 1975; Jennings, et al 1983, 1983a). There also are anecdotal accounts (novels, films, documentaries) of this pattern in blue collar orientations toward authoritarian management and in "third world" orientations toward the "economic imperialism" of industrialized nations.

In this context, it is notable that Gilligan portrayed care levels only in the responses of women facing the oppressive machinations of sexist institutions and relationships (1982, 71-72, 107-108). In particular, Gilligan's respondents faced threats of male rejection and abandonment in love relationships due to unexpected pregnancies. They consciously saw their abortion decisions as severe crises for these relationships and themselves.

Again, the "Care as Liberation" hypothesis is not dependent on the sorts of global and anecdotal observations cited above, though it benefits from their strongest and most shared insights. This hypothesis can and will be supported from Gilligan's own account of care and its relation to the field of moral development.

II

WORKING HYPOTHESIS

Since "care as liberation" is a working hypothesis designed for comparison with Gilligan's "different voice," its supporting case must be framed relative to Gilligan's as well. It must "argue" that Gilligan studies (a) socialization, reflective consciousness-raising, and coping more than moral development, (b) gender-based coping more than a care theme of coping which women happen to prefer, and (c) coping with oppression and especially sexism rather than more general coping with moral issues. The fact that this hypothesis derives its case from Gilligan's own text reflects Gilligan's own acknowledgment that care is influenced by socialization and coping with sexism. As noted, however, her account opts for the dominance of moral developmental processes in care's evolution, viewing other factors as secondary. This may be a function of the Kohlbergian framework from which her work stems. The "Care as Liberation" hypothesis questions this interpretation based on the nature of Gilligan's reported observations and research methods. Thus, while it poses different themes for care, it does so in Gilligan's own voice. (It is best thought of as part of an internal debate which Gilligan might have with herself, or which supporters might have among themselves, regarding how to voice the caring they hear.) We begin with points (b) and (c) above.

Women and Sexism

It is easy to misunderstand Gilligan's claim that the "different voice" is characterized by theme, not gender (1982, 2). Care is not a theme that all women must prefer, or that all women have been observed preferring. Neither is it a theme males cannot adopt. However, it is the theme that Gilligan considers characteristic of women, not men. This is so, in the first instance, because Gilligan claims to have found an "empirical association" of this sort. But more important, it is so because Gilligan claims to have identified the apparent cause of this association, the relational orientation built into female gender-identity. Gilligan's research is aimed at uncovering this distinctively gender-based causal relation. Likewise, her research with colleagues and students is focused on the gender difference issue (Lyons 1982, Langdale 1983, Johnston 1985).

> The different voice I describe is characterized not by gender but theme. Its association with women is an empirical observation; and it is primarily through women's voices that I trace its development. But this association is not absolute, and the contrasts between male and female voices are presented here to highlight a distinction between two modes of thought and to

focus on a problem of interpretation rather than to represent a generalization about either sex. (1982, 2)

> In presenting excerpts from this work, I report research in progress whose aim is to provide, in the field of human develop-ment, a clearer representation of women's development which will enable psychologists and others to follow its course and understand some of the apparent puzzles it presents, especially those that pertain to women's identity formation and their moral development in adolescence and adulthood. (1982, 3)

Notice the apparent inconsistency of aims in these two self-reflections, given that Gilligan's interpretations are illustrated with her research findings.

> These findings were gathered at a particular moment in history, the sample was small, and the women were not selected to represent a larger population. These constraints preclude the possibility of generalization and leave to further research the task of sorting out the different variables of culture, time, occasion, and gender. Additional longitudinal studies of women's moral judgments are needed in order to refine and validate the sequence described. (1982, 126)

Gilligan's research and account of care development, to which the last citations refer, is characterized by gender rather than theme. Chapters three and four of Gilligan's book, which encompass care levels, refer only to Gilligan's abortion study. This study sampled women only, in order to discover how women in particular think about moral issues, construct moral categories, and define moral language. Quite understandably then, Gilligan faults Kohlberg's all-male sampling because he was not researching *male* develop-ment, but, supposedly, human development.

> To derive developmental criteria from the language of women's moral discourse, it is necessary first to see whether women's construction of the moral domain relies on a language different from men and one that deserves equal credence in the defini-tion of development. This in turn requires finding places where women have the power to choose and thus are willing to speak in their own voice. (1982, 70)

Moreover, Gilligan's interpretive analysis of findings from this study focuses on gender difference by organizing the various caring themes of self-survival, feminine virtue and conformity, moral nihilism, and shared (caring) respon-sibility together under gender.

Yet, in addition, Gilligan characterizes her chosen moral issue, as in the abortion study, as focusing on problems of passivity and dependence that have been "most problematic for women," and as requiring a resolution of the conflict between sexist conventions of femininity and women's conception of adulthood (1982, 69, 71). The subject of the study was designed to focus on "how women deal with such choices," "bring(ing) to the core of feminine apprehension . . . that sense of living one's deepest life underwater" (1982, 71).

There is not only a clear emphasis here on gender, then, but a head-on confrontation with sexism. Moreover, this confrontation occurs in an especially sexist context, a sexist crisis. While Gilligan makes the crisis nature of the abortions study clear (1982, 72, 107), she does not make clear how much the crisis is one of sexism itself. However, Gilligan emphasizes from the start the role of sexism in women's spontaneous and distinctive moral judgment more generally. Care orientation is introduced with illustrations from female respondents which show "a sense of vulnerability that impedes these women from taking a (moral) stand, what George Eliot regards as the girl's 'susceptibility' to adverse judgments by others, which stems from her lack of power and consequent inability 'to do something in the world' " (1982, 66). As Gilligan puts this point further: "When women feel excluded from direct participation in society, they see themselves as subject to a consensus or judgment made and enforced by men on whose protection and support they depend and by whose name they are known" (1982, 67). Gilligan illustrates her point vividly, through a respondent.

> As a woman, I feel I never understood that I was a person, that I could make decisions and I had a right to make decisions. I always felt that that belonged to my father or my husband in some way, or my church, which was always represented by a male clergyman. They were the three men in my life: father, husband, and clergyman, and they had much more to say about what I should or shouldn't do. They were really authority figures which I accepted. It only lately has occurred to me that I never even rebelled against it, and my girls are much more conscious of this, not in the militant sense, but just in the recognizing sense. . . . I still let things happen to me rather than make them happen. . . . (1982, 67)

Again, characterizing women's moral judgment *as a whole*, Gilligan notes that,

> The essence of moral decision is the exercise of choice and the willingness to accept responsibility for that choice. To the extent that women perceive themselves as having no choice, they correspondingly excuse themselves from the responsibility that decision entails. Childlike in the vulnerability of their

dependence and consequent fear of abandonment, they claim
to wish only to please, but in return for their goodness they
expect to be loved and cared for. This, then, is an "altruism"
always at risk, for it presupposes an innocence constantly in
danger of being compromised by an awareness of the trade-off
that has been made. (1982, 67)

More significant, then, is a continuing emphasis on the sexism problem
throughout Gilligan's discussion and her excerpts from respondents. This
continuing emphasis is found even when Gilligan's deliberate emphasis is
elsewhere. When Gilligan and her respondents speak of relationships, over
two chapters, there is scarce mention of the relational network of siblings and
friends that supposedly defines care's relational orientation. One would expect
some emphasis on a close female friend or two in an open-ended interview
about one's abortion decision. While there are some abstract generalizations
about caring for "others," or for a "future child," in this text, the only actual
ongoing relationships emphasized are with "the boyfriend" or "lover."
Moreover, the egregiously sexist nature of these relationships and of women's
situations in them (especially regarding abortion) are emphasized in each case.

In discussing level I of care, for example, Gilligan notes that as a general
phenomenon, "Relationships are for the most part disappointing" (1982, 75).
A respondent illustrates this point, "the only thing you are ever going to get
out of going with a guy is to get hurt" (1982, 75). Gilligan then notes that "as
a result, women sometimes choose isolation to protect themselves against hurt"
(1982, 75). Yet whether women choose isolation or not, the overall orientation
of self-care at level I is self-protective, not merely self-concerned (75-77). And
what women are protecting themselves against primarily, in the responses that
Gilligan cites, are the threats posed by characteristically sexist rejection in love
relationships, and in social responses to the abortion crisis.

Gilligan's respondent Betty, for example, had her first abortion after being
raped. Afterwards she felt "helpless and powerless to obtain contraception for
herself because she did not have any money and she believed she needed her
parents' permission; she also felt powerless to deal with her boyfriend's continuing harassment. In the end, she gave in to his assurance that he knew what
he was doing and would not get her pregnant, influenced by her belief that if
she refused, he would break up with her" (1982, 109). She became pregnant
again because "no one was willing to help." "After I went to bed with him he
just wanted me to do everything he wanted to do . . . (disregarding) the fact
that I wanted my freedom." Thus Betty becomes preoccupied with her own needs,
as Gilligan puts it, "to ensure her own survival in a world perceived as exploitative."

At care level I, a woman's thinking "focuses on taking care of herself because
she feels all alone. The issue is survival." Gilligan continues, "In this mode of
understanding, the self . . . is constrained by lack of power that stems from

feeling disconnected" (1982, 75). It is notable that Kohlberg's stages also trace an egoistic "concern for self" at his level I (stages 1 and 2). However, this egoism simply expresses self-interest, not protection against hurt and threat, especially not hurt or threat that puts one's very survival at stake. Presumably this is because Kohlberg and other moral developmentalists are trying to tap general competence in responding to the broad spectrum of moral problems, not to especially oppressive or threatening ones. However, adolescents and adults are observed to retreat to this egoistic level functionally, when faced with oppressive crises and threats (as in a prison environment). In this regard it is important to note in the above citations (and those following) how often the self-protective response of self-concern at level I seems to follow, not precede, the level II concern with "maintaining one's love relationship." It is important to note how often this concern sets care up for its fall. (This ordering of concerns, by levels, is not what we would expect in a developmental sequence.)

We see this regressive "retreat from care," from hurt in love relationships, in the reaction of moral nihilism and confusion which is the corollary to self-protection in Gilligan's account.

> Lisa, a fifteen year old, believing in her boyfriend's love, acceded to his wish "not to murder his child." But after she decided not to abort the child, he left her and "thus ruined my life. . . ."I don't know what to do with my boyfriend gone. I'm still in love with him, no matter what he has done, and that really confuses me, because I don't know why I still do. . . . "I can't get him out of my mind." (1982, 123-124)

We see a similar reaction in a woman already working out of such reactions near the highest level of care.

> Sarah (a third respondent) had discovered the first pregnancy after her lover left her, and she terminated it by an abortion which she experienced as a purging expression of her anger at having been rejected. Remembering the abortion only as a relief she nevertheless describes that time in her life as one in which she "hit rock bottom." Having hoped to "take control of my life" she instead resumed the relationship when the man reappeared. Two years later, having again "left my diaphragm in the drawer," she became pregnant. Although initially ecstatic at the news, her elation dissipated when her lover told her that he would leave her if she chose to have the child. (1982, 90-91)

Level II care is said to show a general concern for serving others' needs sacrificially and thereby winning their approval. It tries to go along with shared norms and values which define the expectations others have of you. In this respect, it seems akin to Kohlberg's conventional stage 3 in which respondents play their "good boy"/"good girl" roles as others expect of them. Gilligan faults Kohlberg's system for classifying women's judgment at such a childlike level of care (1982, 70).

However, in the excerpts Gilligan cites from respondents, the orientation of level II is tailored much more to serving "the boyfriend's" needs and sexist expectations in particular. A secondary focus is on living up to peculiarly sexist conventions of love relations, marriage, and family. There is an emphasis here, as we saw above, on "trying to please" out of the "vulnerability of dependence" and "fear of abandonment," and in the "expectation of being loved or cared for." The prescribed manner of pleasing invokes peculiar "feminine stereotypes" such as "deference to male judgment and strength," and "gentleness and tact" (1982, 69, 79, 80). None of these key features of Gilligan's "altruism at risk" are key to Kohlberg's "good girl" orientation at conventional stage 3.

Consider the type of conventionality care espouses. Gilligan notes that respondents in her abortion study get pregnant in hopes of "making the baby an ally in the search for male support and protection or, that failing, a companion in male rejection" (1982, 72). Pregnancy is also seen as "the perfect chance to get married and leave home" to overcome a sense of "powerlessness and disconnection" (1982, 75) or as a way "to concretize our relationship" (1982, 88) or "put the relationship to the ultimate test of commitment" (1982, 72, 119). Yet abortion also is seen as a way to overcome this sense of powerlessness, to "continue the relationship [with the lover] and not 'drive us apart.' " "Since I met him he has been my life. I do everything for him, my life sort of revolves around him" (1982, 81).

Gilligan observes that her respondent Ellen "considered herself 'fairly strong-willed, fairly in control' . . . until she became involved in an intense love affair . . . entertain[ing] vague ideas that 'some day I would like a child to concretize our relationship.' Abjuring, with her lover, the use of contraceptives . . . she saw herself as relinquishing control, becoming instead 'just simply vague and allowing events to just carry me along' " (1982, 87-88). Even in evolving out of level II, as Gilligan sees it, a woman "struggles to free herself from the powerlessness of her own dependence" when "pregnant by the same man" who made her have the abortion that kept them together (1982, 81).

Aside from relationality, which defines the caring perspective overall, "not hurting" is its dominant orientation. Yet when Gilligan introduces this "common thread" in her initial excerpts from women's judgment, the thread that particularizes these concerns is "not hurting *boyfriends*." As one respondent puts it, "Not hurting others is important in my private morals. Years ago I would have jumped out of a window not to hurt my boyfriend. That was pathological. Even today, though, I want approval and love. . . ." As another respondent put it, "My main principle is not hurting people . . . I'm afraid I'm heading for some big crisis with my boyfriend someday, and someone will get hurt, and he'll get more hurt than I will" (1982, 65).

III

SOCIALIZATION AND REFLECTION

The above citations and the way they are cast, I believe, are representative of Gilligan's first two levels of care. Yet Gilligan's depiction of level II care also includes a more general "caring for others" emphasis alongside the focus on "serving males." In recent writings (Gilligan 1987, Gilligan and Wiggins, 1988) an emphasis has been placed on caring in mother/daughter relations. These emphases in care could challenge the hypothesis that care coping is tailored to sexism. However, I believe that the discussions of care and mothering are highly speculative rather than merely interpretive in a social scientific sense. They concern a global "care orientation" that is very difficult to tie to care *levels* and the actual interview data from which they derive. This is why I have relied so heavily on Gilligan's original, book-length account of care in these discussions. And, of course, the "care as liberation" hypothesis does not claim that care *only* involves coping with sexism.

Moreover, the emphasis on care in general, at level II, is precisely what we should expect if care truly is conventional at this level, as Gilligan claims. The key is that care fits traditional sexist socialization here, socialization in "service orientation" or service ideology, or a coping strategy based on this theme. Obviously the effectiveness of such a socialized conventional ideology depends on its somehow rationalizing the subservient role of women relative to men in society. And there is little dispute, I take it, that this socialized ideology does so in part by generalizing women's service orientation to others as a whole. Gilligan acknowledges this tendency by citing the Broverman stereotypes of gentleness, tact and other care-taking traits as "female stereotypes" (1982, 79). These socially approved and fostered traits are to characterize woman's character, her moral self-concept and orientation to others generally, in sexist society. As Gilligan also notes, this very same rationalization, viewing oneself and one's activities as *generally* altruistic, is used explicitly by women at level II. Here it handles inner conflict with the slavishness of conventional care. These are signs of care's strategic and partially reflective quality at level II, as well as its more dominant socialization influence.

Therefore, if sufficient reason can be offered for preferring a socialization and reflection explanation for care over a cognitive-developmental account, the "Care as Liberation" hypothesis is supported. This will be our final task regarding the first two levels of care and, eventually, the third level. Since level III is more complex, it will have to be addressed at more levels. And, since it is a primarily "self-chosen" orientation, rather than a conventional one, we will emphasize the contrast between its reflective, "consciousness-raising" character, and the nature of cognitive-developmental processes. This approach will be clarified briefly at the outset.

While level III care copes with sexism in particular, it also retains the generalized focus on "caring for others" begun at level II. The "Care as Liberation" hypothesis holds three factors responsible for this trend. First, there is the lingering influence of conventional care at this level. This is shown by the continuation of a basic service theme from level I, now applied to oneself as well as others, combined with the failure to notice key deficiencies of this theme during reflection. Second, there is the "slave morality" phenomenon, providing a more elaborate version of level II rationalizing. It "legitimizes" caring service by generalizing its apparent virtues ideologically.[3] Third, there is the influence of truly liberated "consciousness raising" or insightful reflection. In this process, some women uncover many of the morally valid and virtuous components of benevolence, as Gilligan recounts. These components properly express benevolence toward others in general. However, on the "Care as Liberation" hypothesis, Gilligan's account of level III overrates the fullness and adequacy of these discoveries. It also overrates their cognitive developmental form.

To support the role of these three factors at level III, our analysis should identify six features of care here: (1) the significant role of sexist socialization influences; (2) the superior role of reflection; (3) the peculiarly personal, insightful, or otherwise non-generalizable form of that reflection; (4) its social-ideological character; (5) its moral defects, and the defective way that it is personalized and legitimized; (6) the relative lack of evidence for cognitive-developmental processes there, or their significant influence. Since Gilligan cites very few level III respondents, it is difficult to draw extensive support for these features from the text. However, they all receive some support in the citations that follow, especially when considered in the context of Gilligan's research approach. The moral defects of mature care, suggested earlier, are elaborated in detail elsewhere (Puka 1988). The contrast I will outline between Gilligan's research and the approach of cognitive-developmentalists she criticizes is elaborated elsewhere as well (Puka 1990).

The task of our analysis is made easier by the fact that socialization, reflection, and cognitive-developmental processes exert very different degrees of influence on us. As shown in the research literature, and by common observation, socialization plays the dominant role in shaping our motivations, values and ideologies. On this same basis we can assume that the power of female socialization in sexist "service orientation" is great. Gender studies, as a field, has greatly bolstered that assumption. Reflective learning and insight are a powerful factor in forming moral ideologies among adults, where the effects of earlier socialization are weakened or overcome. (The work of Perry (1964) provides excellent evidence for this, which Gilligan countenances greatly in defining level III. This evidence is supported, despite appearances to the contrary, by Belenky, et. al. in *Women's Ways of Knowing*.) The power of reflection here is greatly increased, we commonly observe, when compounded with the social reinforcements of one's reflective peers. In these contexts, the burden of proof is on the moral developmentalist (*any* moral developmentalist) to show that the processes she posits exist at all, and can compete with these others for influence.

Importantly, cognitive-developmental processes arise in the same form across the broad range of social interactions. They operate and evolve by inherent "principles" of cognitive construction, such as integration and differentiation. They form a holistic system for organizing moral experience and affording basic but general competence in facilitating moral judgment. Such cognitive-moral processes will use experience and learn from it. Perhaps they will encompass some reflective processes at the highest developmental levels. But they will not be determined by the peculiar shape of one's experience and socialization or the particular styles and discoveries of personal insight. Thus, for example, coming to believe in one's subservient roles and traits as a woman is not something we would expect to evolve in this way. This ideology is too particularized, too dependent on particular interpretations of fact and value, and on partisan social interests, to arise without being taught or "discovered" by intellect. It is also regressive, presumably, rather than developmental. In the same way, coming to adopt a distinctively feminist perspective or liberal ideology is not likely to be natural and basic to women's cognitive development.

Thus to support the dominant roles of socialization and reflective coping in care, we will merely note their robust role in Gilligan's account and in her research. At the same time, we will cite the weakness of her grounds for conceiving care as cognitive-moral development. Let us begin with the reflective peculiarities of level III, the ways care rests on certain reflective insights into particular sorts of experience, and into oneself.

Raising Consciousness

Gilligan first characterizes the transition to level III care in the responses of Sarah. Here Gilligan aims to show "how closely her transformed moral understanding is tied to changing self-concept" (92). When asked to "describe yourself to yourself," Sarah answers quite self-consciously,

> I have been thinking about that a lot lately, and it comes up different than what my usual subconscious perception of myself is. Usually paying off some sort of debt, going around serving people who are not really worthy of my attention, because somewhere in life I think I got the impression that my needs are really secondary to other people's, and that if I feel, if I make any demands on other people to fulfill my needs, I'd feel guilty for it and submerge my own in favor of other people's, which later backfires on me, and I feel a great deal of resentment for other people that I am doing things for, which causes friction

and the eventual deterioration of the relationship. And I start
all over again. How would I describe myself to myself? Pretty
frustrated and a lot angrier than I admit, a lot more aggressive
than I admit. (92-93)

Notice that the process of actual self-reflection (and even the awareness of
that process) figures into what Gilligan sees as transformation in Sarah's level
of care. As Sarah also notes, "I am suddenly beginning to think . . . the things
I believe and the kind of person I am are not so bad . . . I am a lot more
worthwhile than my past actions have led other people to believe . . . you
realize that that is a very usual way for people to live—doing what you want
to do because you feel your wants and your needs are important" (93-94). At
earlier levels, women could self-reflect when asked, but they do not report
actually doing so "a lot lately."

Notice also that this process of self-reflection uncovers socialization into an
explicitly sexist "service orientation," into "going around serving people," as
a respondent puts it (92). "Somewhere in life I think I got the impression that
my needs are really secondary to other people's." "I am beginning to think that
all these virtues aren't really getting me anywhere" (93). It also uncovers the
"cycle of repetition" and "psychology of passivity" rationalized previously—
"And I start all over again." Sarah's usual subconscious perception of herself
did not reveal these psychological phenomena.[4]

Sarah's explicit process of consciousness raising regarding her approach to
sexist relationships is especially clear in the following passages from Gilligan:

> For Sarah, facing a second abortion, the first step in taking
> control is to end the relationship in which she has considered
> herself "reduced to a nonentity," but to do so in a responsible
> way. Recognizing hurt as the inevitable concomitant of rejec-
> tion, she strives to minimize that hurt by dealing with her lover's
> needs "as best I can without compromising my own. That's a big
> point for me, because the thing in my life to this point has been
> compromising, and I am not willing to do that anymore." (95)

As Gilligan concludes from this case, in Chapter 3,

> Thus, release from the intimidation of inequality finally allows
> women to express a judgment that had previously been with-
> held. What women then enunciate is not a new morality, but a
> morality disentangled from the constraints that formerly con-
> fused its perception and impeded its articulation. (95)

Yet later, picking up the case again, Gilligan notes that in becoming "tired of
always bowing to other people's standards," Sarah "draws on the Quaker
tradition" in which "your first duty is to your inner voice." ". . . when the inner

voice replaces outer ones as the arbiter of moral truth, it frees her from the *coercion* of others (118). As Gilligan continues,

> Reiterating with more confidence and clarity her discovery of an inner voice, she says that her decisions previously "were based elsewhere, I'm not really sure where . . ." . . . the integration of this insight into Sarah's life, the completion of the transition precipitated by the crisis, entailed a long and painful process that lasted for most of a year. Through this experience, she became more reflective: "I see the way I am and watch the way I make choices, the things I do." And she is now committed to building her life on a "strong foundation" of "surprisingly old wisdoms" with respect to her work and her relationships. (122)

Sarah moves on to level III once she starts "watching herself," and "listening" to the "inner voice" she has "discovered after a long and painful process in which she became more reflective." These sorts of reflective responses are offered by Gilligan's other level III respondents as well, such as Diane:

> It is part of a self-critical view, part of saying, "How am I spending my time and in what sense am I working?"

> When I am dealing with moral issues, I am sort of saying to myself constantly, "Are you taking care of all the things that you think are important, and in what ways are you wasting yourself and wasting those issues?"

> The only way I know is to try to be as awake as possible, to try to know the range of what you feel, to try to consider all that's involved, to be as aware as you can be of what's going on, as conscious as you can of where you're walking. (99)

Gilligan shows how heavily level III care relies on reflection by stressing the contextualism of level III thought. This is gauged by Perry's levels of intellectual judgment. In the transition to level III, Gilligan tells us, women start breaking down their absolute equations between selfish and bad, altruistic and good, and start making judgments relative to situational contexts. They tentatively seek out the shades of moral gray in moral reality, as they perceive it (102-104, 166). At level III, this contextualism reaches fruition.

Perry's levels of intellectual development arose primarily from the reflective struggle of college students to deal with conflicts between the theories and belief systems they were exposed to in class. They chart reflective or meta-cognitive orientations and the way they change. These are orientations to our beliefs, values, and ethical systems themselves, rather than to moral problems and social interactions. When Gilligan asks women for self-descriptions relative to moral choice and gets the sort of responses cited above, she is getting at such meta-cognition. The same is true when she asks respondents to define morality itself and elicits responses such as "trying to uncover a right path to live and always in my mind is that the world is full of real and recognizable trouble and is heading for some kind of doom" (99).

By contrast, classic moral development approaches focus on first-order questions of what to do about this or that problem. They encompass only that reflection which we can assume will evolve inherently in anyone as a normal part of trying to deal with socio-moral problems in a basically competent way. For the most part, reflective processes (and their insights) seem determined by particular types of education, exposure to ideologies and culture-specific styles of thinking, as well as the luck of discovery. At level III, as noted, these processes are intermixed.

Social Learning and Moral Ideology

To distinguish the phenomenon of moral development from socialization and personal experience, researchers have evolved a variety of empirical and interpretive methods. Their research interviews feature a standard variety of moral dilemmas accompanied by challenging probe questions. Together these are designed to assure the existence of stable cognitive systems underlying the gamut of moral beliefs and ideologies, and expressed in them. By testing the limits of moral competence, these research probes uncover the stability of these systems, including their resistance to strong situational pulls from the environment on the one hand, and also their capacity to address varied moral situations consistently on the other. Such cognitive competence would differ from the particular skills or *beliefs* we show in performing particular kinds of tasks. Cognitive systems which show such general competence and stability, which take a holistic organizational form, are unlikely to be determined by the varying schedules of situational reinforcement. These include reflective self-reinforcement. Yet moral ideologies and skills, by contrast, seem to arise primarily in this way.

Cognitive developmental researchers also measure the transformation of cognitive systems at regular intervals to chart the mechanisms of change. In this way, they can better distinguish inherently constructional processes from shaping due to socialization, personal experience, or reflection.

By contrast, Gilligan's research uncovered care using open-ended interviews. Here respondents emitted only those dilemmas they found personally salient. Alternatively, a single, real-life dilemma was used, such as abortion. This approach does not focus on general moral competence.[5] Rather than challenging care responses to see if stable cognitive systems lay beneath, Gilligan's interview "follow(s) the language and logic of the person's thought," only "asking questions in order to clarify the meaning of particular responses"

(2). This may very well clarify moral ideology or socialization rather than cognitive-moral competence.

Gilligan's largest study (s=144) was cross-sectional. It did not chart the evolution of care longitudinally at regular intervals. Her other two studies (s=25, s=21) involved only a single follow-up interview (2-3). On this basis, Gilligan gained little empirical sense of what prompted change in care when change occurred. Gilligan never actually observed women go through the levels of care, as noted. But even more important, her writings do not illustrate the holistic structure or functioning of care levels in any *one* respondent. Rather Gilligan reconstructs the care sequence of development *conceptually* in her book, by glimpsing a small interval of development in 8 respondents (108). Care at each level, and as a general orientation, is presented as a reconstructed composite of responses across respondents.

Furthermore, Gilligan's abortion study, so key to defining care levels, pulled for unusual responses. As noted, it utilized a dilemma which all involved considered a desperate personal crisis for respondents (108). In fact, Gilligan's developmental analysis of these responses was termed "magnification of crisis." This indicates Gilligan's stated belief that care development is a form of "response to crisis" in particular (107). As Gilligan sees it, we will move up care levels only if we have sufficient self-confidence and sense of control over our lives when facing crisis. Where we meet rejection and hurt with vul-nerability and despair, we will likely regress (76-78, 82, 123-126). It is unclear how much these psychological states or processes involve cognitive systems at all, much less morally competent and self-constructional ones. In any event, these sorts of processes are highly vulnerable to socialization influences and peculiarities of personal experience. Gilligan does not try to distinguish aspects of cognition that succumb to this vulnerability from those which do not. This is especially problematic in the abortion context where ideological positions on the issue are so prominent in social experience.

On the contrary, "No claims are made about the origins of the differences described" in Gilligan's account, differences in moral theme or self/other perspective or gender. Rather, the account acknowledges the shaping influence on care of social status and power, traditional gender stereotypes, sexual politics, and bad experiences in love relationships. Feelings of loneliness and depression play a role too (2-3).

Finally, Gilligan reports great changes in care during a mere one-year interval. Out of 21 respondents in the abortion study, 8 developed and 4 "got worse" between pre-test and post-test (108). Such a degree of change is unheard of where the inherent, constructional processes of cognitive develop-ment are at work (e.g., integration, differentiation, equilibration). Yet while change of this sort would be expected in moral ideology or reflective beliefs, especially during personal crises, Gilligan never poses such interpretations of her results. She also does not try to distinguish functionally regressive change

.in care performance from regression in the cognitive-developmental organization of care competence.

Against these observations of socialization and personal reflection in care
stand Gilligan's few remarks on how women "construct" care levels, on how
one level is a more "differentiated and comprehensive" transformation of the
level before (73, 76, 78). These are key cognitive-developmental catchwords.
The "Care as Liberation" hypothesis acknowledges that Gilligan has uncovered some strands of cognitive structure in care. However, there is no
indication in her account that these strands are sizable or that existing theories
of development cannot encompass them under other moral themes. Gilligan's
remarks are so sparse, when seen in relation to any standard cognitive-developmental account, that they are best viewed as suggesting a different sort of
account. Otherwise, they bear serious deficiencies.[6]

CONCLUSION

"Care as Liberation" is meant to be a working hypothesis. Its degree of
support is to be compared with Gilligan's "Different Voice" interpretation of
what her observations indicate. In providing this support, I have attempted to
illustrate care's primary concern with women confronting sexism, and the
primary role of socialization, personal reflection and coping involved. I hope
it is obvious how much this discussion and the "care as liberation" hypothesis
extend the feminist potential of care, and of Gilligan's voice.

NOTES

1. Gilligan's sweeping criticisms of Piaget, Erikson and especially Kohlberg have
reduced the credibility of care unnecessarily. (Gilligan 1982, 12-22, 31, 45, 59, 66, 99,
104), (Kohlberg 1984, 338-370), (Broughton 1984).
2. The hypothesis borrows explicitly from "radical therapy" notions of "abstraction"
and "personalization" in the ideological rationalization process. Some observers may find
them questionable. However, these powerful notions might also have been derived from
Gilligan's own consideration of how "abstraction" and "impersonality" enter patriarchal
morality. Likewise the slave morality or "resentment" phenomenon can be identified in
ideologically neutral terms.
3. Again, while some women learn the lessons of sexist abuse at levels I and II and
face the inadequacies of their coping strategies and rationalizations, they mistakenly
personalize responsibility for failure. As they evolve a more balanced and selective
approach to care coping, they rationalize its lingering limitations through the ideology
of selective generalization and equalization of (slavish) care. Thus, care at level III still
constitutes service orientation, service to others generally, but now not to the extent that
oneself is left out.
4. I believe we would term these realizations especially insightful—psychologically
and interpersonally insightful—and recognize that they are tailored to the issue of sexism

primarily. We should not expect "the average woman" across cultures to come up with such distinctive ways of thinking simply because she takes a relational perspective and is therefore concerned with not hurting others.

5. Gilligan used Kohlberg dilemmas in some studies, but primarily for purposes of comparing justice reasoning with the alternative care orientation her interviews uncovered. Gilligan criticized Kohlberg's dilemmas and probe questions for discriminating against care orientation (Gilligan 1982, 100, Gilligan and Belenky 1979).

6. Since Gilligan did not observe development over a significant length of time in these studies, she could only conceptualize how each level of care *might* have been constructed from another, not how they actually appeared to be. Such a constructional analysis might easily be provided of any two conceptually related ideologies, one of which is more conceptually sophisticated than the other. In addition, Gilligan does not actually explicate the difference between levels and transitions, showing how the latter stabilize into holistic equilibrated systems. She does not actually trace each key component of care from one level to the next, showing how it is transformed and reintegrated with each other (and with new cognitive differentiations) to form a functioning whole. Even the three defining features of care—its moral theme of helping and not hurting, its relational perspective, and its notions of responsibility to others—are not depicted at all three levels. Level I seems to lack all of them. The remaining two-level sequences might just as well be conceived as a bi-modal phenomenon, rather than a developmental sequence. Finally, key features of care that distinguish each level pop in or out of the care "sequence" without clearly being transformed, differentiated, or reintegrated in cognitive organization. Among these are, (1) "survival orientation," which disappears at level III, (2) the "concern for good," of level II, which is later *replaced* by the "concern for truth," and (3) the need to be "honest with oneself" in level II-III transition which does not appear to evolve from, or evolve into, any concern like it. (For a more detailed analysis of these points see Puka, 1990) The greatest deficiencies in Gilligan's account, however, were noted earlier. Gilligan's approach to research and interpretation simply does not provide for crucial distinctions between socialization, consciousness-raising, and cognitive development.

REFERENCES

Belenky, M., McVicker Clenchy, B., Rule Goldberg, N. and Mattuck Tarule, J. 1987. *Women's ways of knowing.* NY: Basic Books.

Bettleheim, B. 1943. Individual and mass behavior in extreme situations. *Journal of Abnormal and Social Psychology* 38: 417-452.

Broughton, J. 1984. Men's virtues, women's rationality. *Social Research* (winter).

Chodorow, N. 1978. *The reproduction of mothering.* Berkeley: University of California Press.

Freud, A. 1946. *The ego mechanisms of defense.* NY: International University Press.

Gilligan, C. 1982. *In a different voice.* Cambridge, MA: Harvard University Press.

Gilligan, C. 1985. Reply to critics. *Signs* 9 (2).

Gilligan, C. 1987. Exit-voice/dilemmas in adolescent development. In *Development, democracy, and the art of trespassing,* A. Goxley, M. McPherson and G. O'Donnell, eds. Indiana: University of Notre Dame Press.

Gilligan, C. and Belenky, M. 1979. A naturalistic study of abortion decisions. In *Clinical-Developmental psychology*, R. Selman and R. Yando, eds. San Francisco: Josey-Bass.

Gilligan, C. and Wiggins, G. 1988. The origins of morality in early childhood relations. In *The emergence of morality in young children*, J. Kagan and S. Lamm, eds. Chicago: Chicago University Press.

Jennings, W. and Kohlberg, L. 1983. Effects of just community programs on the moral level and institutional perception of youthful offenders. *Journal of Moral Education* 12.

Jennings, W., Kilkenny, R. and Kohlberg, L. 1983. Moral development theory and practice for youthful and adult offenders. In *Personality, theory, moral development and criminal behavior*, W. Laufer and J. Day, eds. Lexington, MA: Lexington Books.

Johnston, K. 1985. Two moral orientations—two problem-solving strategies: adolescents' solutions to dilemmas in fables. Doctoral dissertation, Harvard Graduate School of Education.

Kohlberg, L. 1984. *The psychology of moral development*. NY: Harper and Row.

Kohlberg, L., Kauffman, K., and Scharf, P. 1975. *Corrections manual*. Cambridge, MA: Moral Education Research Foundation.

Langdale, C. 1983. Moral observations and moral development. Doctoral dissertation, Harvard University Graduate School of Education.

Lyons, N. 1983. Two perspectives: On self, relationships and morality. *Harvard Educational Review* 53.

Miller, J.B. 1976. *Toward a new psychology of women*. Boston: Beacon Press.

Nicholson, L. 1983. Women, morality and history. *Social Research* 50 (3).

Noddings, N. 1985. *Caring*. Berkeley, CA: University of California Press.

Perry, W. 1968. *Forms of intellectual and ethical development in the college years*. NY: Holt, Rhinehart and Winston.

Puka, B. 1988. Ethical caring: Pros, cons, and possibilities. In *Inquiry Into Values*, S. Lee, ed. NY: Mellen Press.

Puka, B. 1990. Interpretive experiments: Probing the care-justice debate in moral development. *Human Development* (forthcoming).

Sanford, N. 1955. The dynamics of identification. *Psychological Review* 51.

Walker, L. 1984. Sex differences in the development of moral reasoning: A critical review. *Child Development* 55.

BEYOND GENDER DIFFERENCE
TO A THEORY OF CARE

JOAN C. TRONTO

The work of Carol Gilligan and her associates, which describes "an ethic of care" that complements an understanding of morality as concerned with justice, has been cited frequently as proof of the existence of a "women's morality."[1] Gilligan has asserted from the first that she does not regard the

The research for this paper was conducted with support from a Scholar's Incentive Award from the City University of New York and with the aid of the research facilities office of the Library of Congress. I am grateful to these institutions for their support. Earlier drafts of this paper were read at the University of Minnesota in May 1985, at Hunter College in October 1985, and at the seminar on "Feminist Ways of Knowing" held at Douglass College in October 1985. I wish to thank the many listeners who raised questions on these occasions. Special thanks are due Mary Dietz and Annmarie Levins, who commented on earlier drafts of this paper.

[1] See Carol Gilligan, "In a Different Voice: Women's Conceptions of Self and of Morality," *Harvard Educational Review* 47, no. 4 (November 1977): 481–517, "Woman's Place in Man's Life Cycle," *Harvard Educational Review* 49, no. 4 (November 1979): 431–46, "Justice and Responsibility: Thinking about Real Dilemmas of Moral Conflict and Choice," in *Toward Moral and Religious Maturity: The First International Conference on Moral and Religious Development* (Morristown, N.J.: Silver Burdett Co., 1980), *In a Different Voice: Psychological Theory and Women's Development* (Cambridge, Mass.: Harvard University Press, 1982), "Do the Social Sciences Have an Adequate Theory of Moral Development?" in *Social Science as Moral Inquiry*, ed. Norma Haan, Robert N. Bellah, Paul Rabinow, and William M. Sullivan (New York: Columbia University Press, 1983), 33–51, and "Reply" in "On *In a Different Voice*: An Interdisciplinary Forum," *Signs: Journal of Women in Culture and*

[*Signs: Journal of Women in Culture and Society* 1987, vol. 12, no. 4]

ethic of care as a category of gender difference.[2] Nonetheless, her work is widely understood as showing that women are different from men, as evidenced in the *Signs* forum on *In a Different Voice.* For example, Linda K. Kerber wrote, "But by emphasizing the biological basis of distinctive behavior . . . Gilligan permits her readers to conclude that women's alleged affinity for 'relationships of care' is both biologically natural and a good thing." Catherine G. Greeno and Eleanor E. Maccoby wrongly assert, "The fact remains, however, that Gilligan claims that the views expressed by women in her book represent a *different* voice—different, that is, from men." Zella Luria also notes that the book seems to belie Gilligan's later assertions that she is not calling for distinctive psychologies for men and women. Carol Stack seems to accept Gilligan's work as representing "a female model of moral development."[3]

Gilligan's point is a subtle one. On the one hand, she wants to say her argument goes no further than the claim that the moral domain must be extended to include justice and care. On the other hand, she also notes that "the focus on care . . . is characteristically a female phenomenon in the advantaged populations that have been studied."[4]

In considering the issue of gender difference and morality, I shall use Gilligan's theory as the primary way to understand the nature of "women's morality." Although other writers might also be identified with women's morality,[5] none has been so widely read and so widely interpreted as an

---

Society 11, no. 2 (Winter 1986): 324–33. Among collaborative works and works by associates, see Carol Gilligan and Mary Field Belensky, "A naturalistic Study of Abortion Decisions," *New Directions for Child development* 7 (1980): 69–90; Carol Gilligan, Sharry Langdale, and Nona Lyons. "The Contribution of Women's Thought to Development Theory: The Elimination of Sex Bias in Moral Development Research and Education" (Washington, D.C.: National Institute of Education, 1982); Susan Pollak and Carol Gilligan, "Images of Violence in Thematic Apperception Test Stories," *Journal of Personality and Social Psychology* 42, no. 1 (January 1982): 159–67, "Differing about Differences: The Incidence and Interpretation of Violent Fantasies in Women and Men," ibid. 45, no. 5 (November 1983): 1172–75, and "Killing the Messenger," ibid. 48, no. 2 (February 1985): 374–75; Nona Lyons, "Two Perspectives: On Self, Relationships, and Morality," *Harvard Educational Review* 53, no. 2 (May 1983): 125–45; and John M. Murphy and Carol Gilligan, "Moral Development in Late Adolescence and Adulthood: A Critique and Reconstruction of Kohlberg's Theory," *Human Development* 23, no. 2 (1980): 77–104.

[2] Gilligan, *In a Different Voice,* 2, and "Reply," 327.

[3] See "On *In a Different Voice:* An Interdisciplinary Forum," in *Signs* 11, no. 2 (Winter 1986): Linda K. Kerber, "Some Cautionary Words for Historians," 304–10, esp. 309; Catherine G. Greeno and Eleanor E. Maccoby, "How Different Is the 'Different Voice'?" 310–16, esp. 315; Zella Luria, "A Methodological Critique," 316–21, esp. 318; and Carol B. Stack, "The Culture of Gender: Women and Men of Color," 321–24, esp. 324.

[4] Gilligan, "Reply," 330.

[5] Nel Noddings, *Caring: A Feminine Approach to Ethics and Moral Education* (Berkeley and Los Angeles: University of California Press, 1984); Sara Ruddick, "Maternal Thinking," *Feminist Studies* 6, no. 2 (Summer 1980): 342–67, "Preservative Love and Military Destruction: Some Reflections on Mothering and Peace," in *Mothering: Essays in Feminist Theory,*

advocate of this concept as Gilligan.[6] I do not mean to misrepresent Gilligan's work. The equation of Gilligan's work with women's morality is a cultural phenomenon, and not of Gilligan's making. Nonetheless, the contemporary discussion about Gilligan's work sets the context for discussions of women and morality.

This essay argues that although an ethic of care could be an important intellectual concern for feminists, the debate around this concern should be centered not in discussions of gender difference but in discourse about the ethic's adequacy as a moral theory. My argument is threefold. The equation of "care" with "female" is questionable because the evidence to support the link between gender difference and different moral perspectives is inadequate. It is a strategically dangerous position for feminists because the simple assertion of gender difference in a social context that identifies the male as normal contains an implication of the inferiority of the distinctly female. It is philosophically stultifying because, if feminists think of the ethic of care as categorized by gender difference, they are likely to become trapped trying to defend women's morality rather than looking critically at the philosophical promises and problems of an ethic of care.

A critique of the gender-difference perspective

Carol Gilligan originally devised her ethic of care when she sought to address problems she saw in Lawrence Kohlberg's psychology of moral development.[7] Her argument provides a psychological and developmental account of why women's moral statements are often expressed in terms of caring, but her approach leaves many questions unexplored.[8] In suggesting that an ethic of care is gender related, Gilligan precludes the possibility

---

ed. Joyce Trebilcot (Totowa, N.J.: Rowman & Allanheld, 1983), 231–62, and "Pacifying the Forces: Drafting Women in the Interests of Peace," *Signs* 8, no. 3 (Spring 1983): 471–89.

[6] See as evidence the *Ms.* article in which Gilligan is proclaimed the magazine's "Woman of the Year": Lindsy Van Gelder, "Carol Gilligan: Leader for a Different Kind of Future," *Ms.* 12, no. 7 (January 1984): 37–40, 101. A quick perusal of the entries in the *Social Science Citation Index* will reveal how widely, and in what diverse scholarly fields, Gilligan's work is being cited. In her survey of developments in psychology of women for 1983–84, Sarah B. Watstein noted, "The very name *Gilligan* has become a buzzword in both academic and feminist circles" (Watstein, "Psychology," in *The Women's Annual, Number 4: 1983–1984*, ed. Sarah M. Pritchard [Boston: G. K. Hall & Co., 1984], 167–86, esp. 178).

[7] See Lawrence Kohlberg, with Charles Levine and Alexandra Hewer, "The Current Formulation of the Theory," in *Essays in Moral Development*, vol. 2, *The Psychology of Moral Development: The Nature and Validity of Moral Stages* by Lawrence Kohlberg (New York: Harper & Row, 1984), 212–319. One extensive bibliography is James S. Leming, *Foundations of Moral Education: An Annotated Bibliography* (Westport, Conn.: Greenwood Press, 1983).

[8] Gilligan herself noted the way in which theories are confined by the questions they seek to address. See her "Do the Social Sciences Have an Adequate Theory of Moral Development?" (n. 1 above), 36.

that care is an ethic created in modern society by the condition of subordination. If the ethic of care is separated from a concern with gender, a much broader range of options emerges. These are options that question the place of caring in society and moral life, as well as questioning the adequacy of Kohlberg's cognitive-developmental model.[9]

Lawrence Kohlberg's cognitive-developmental theory is today the most widely accepted theory of moral development.[10] According to this theory, individuals develop morally as their cognitive abilities to understand the nature of moral relations deepen. Kohlberg claims that the process of moral development proceeds through set, hierarchically arranged stages that correspond to different levels of moral reasoning.

An associate of Kohlberg's, Gilligan was disturbed by an early finding that girls generally were at lower stages of moral development than boys.[11] This finding led her to examine Kohlberg's work for possible gender bias. She discovered that, in general, men and women follow different paths to moral development, that there exists a morally "different voice" from the one that Kohlberg identified as definitive of mature moral judgment.[12]

---

[9] Linda J. Nicholson made a similar point when she warned against overgeneralizing gender differences in "Women, Morality and History," *Social Research* 50, no. 3 (Autumn 1983): 514–36, esp. 515.

[10] See, e.g., William M. Kurtines and Jacob L. Gewirtz, eds., *Morality, Moral Behavior, and Moral Development* (New York: John Wiley & Sons, 1984).

[11] Gilligan, *In a Different Voice* (n. 1 above), 18.

[12] Some scholars have challenged Gilligan's claim of gender difference. John M. Broughton, reviewing the interviews, found both men and women exhibiting both modes of moral expression. See his "Women's Rationality and Men's Virtues: A Critique of Gender Dualism in Gilligan's Theory of Moral Development," *Social Research* 50, no. 3 (Autumn 1983): 597–642. Debra Nails also believes that Gilligan has exaggerated the extent of gender difference in her findings. See her "Social-Scientific Sexism: Gilligan's Mismeasure of Man," ibid., 643–64. Cynthia J. Benton et al., "Is Hostility Linked with Affiliation among Males and with Achievement among Females? A Critique of Pollak and Gilligan," *Journal of Personality and Social Psychology* 45, no. 5 (November 1983): 1167–71, report a failed attempt to replicate Gilligan's findings about violence. Other methodological criticisms are raised by Greeno and Maccoby, and Luria (both n. 3 above). Judy Auerbach, Linda Blum, Vicki Smith, and Christine Williams observe that since Gilligan leaves out considerations such as class and religion, "Gilligan attributes all the differences she does encounter to gender" ("On Gilligan's *In a Different Voice*," *Feminist Studies* 11, no. 1 [1985]: 149–61, esp. 157). Kohlberg's own position on gender difference has changed since his initial finding: he now finds no significant gender difference. His challenge to Gilligan's finding rests on Lawrence J. Walker's extensive review of the literature (Walker, "Sex Differences in the Development of Moral Reasoning: A Critical Review," *Child Development* 55, no. 3 [June 1984]: 677–91; also cited by Grenno and Maccoby, and Luria). Most studies in Walker's review reported no gender differences; those that did find differences found them among women who have been more isolated from "role-taking" opportunities in society, which is how Kohlberg has always explained gender difference (see Lawrence Kohlberg with Charles Levine and Alexandra Hewer, "Synopses and Detailed Replies to Critics," in Kohlberg [n. 7 above], 345–61, esp. 347). Insofar as Walker reviewed "justice-reasoning" tests, Gilligan is willing to concede that there are no

Fully elaborated, Gilligan described this "different voice" as expressing an ethic of care that is different from the ethic of justice that stands at the pinnacle of Kohlberg's moral hierarchy. As Gilligan explained the ethic of care: "In this conception, the moral problem arises from conflicting responsibilities rather than from competing rights and requires for its resolution a mode of thinking that is contextual and narrative rather than formal and abstract. This conception of morality as concerned with the activity of care centers moral development around the understanding of responsibility and relationships, just as the conception of morality as fairness ties moral development to the understanding of rights and rules."[13]

In this passage, Gilligan identifies three fundamental characteristics that differentiate the ethic of care from the ethic of justice. First, the ethic of care revolves around different moral concepts than Kohlberg's ethic of justice, that is, responsibility and relationships rather than rights and rules. Second, this morality is tied to concrete circumstances rather than being formal and abstract. Third, this morality is best expressed not as a set of principles but as an activity, the "activity of care." In Gilligan's different voice, morality is not grounded in universal, abstract principles but in the daily experiences and moral problems of real people in their everyday lives.

Gilligan and her associates found this ethic of care to be gender related. Research by Nona Lyons tied the two different moral perspectives to two notions of the self: those who viewed the self as "separated" from others and therefore "objective" were more likely to voice a morality of justice, while those who viewed the self as "connected" to others were more likely to express a morality of care. Since men are usually "separate/objective" in their self/other perceptions, and women more often view themselves in terms of a "connected" self, the difference between justice and care is gender related. Further, men usually express themselves only in the moral voice of justice, though women are more likely to use both forms of moral expression.[14]

Lyons and Gilligan do not attempt to explain *why* the males and females they interviewed developed different notions of the self. One possibility is that caring "is the constitutive activity through which women achieve their femininity and against which masculinity takes shape." Such psychological theories of gender difference provide the strongest evidence for thinking of

---

gender differences, but, since justice reasoning is only one part of morality, his finding does not address the issue of gender difference in moral reasoning. See Gilligan's "Reply" (n. 1 above), 328. It is perhaps interesting to note that this dispute follows a pattern that should be familiar to social scientists: different methodologies tend to produce different results. Here two groups of investigators are looking at related but different phenomena. Each group claims, using its method, that the findings of the other group are invalid.

[13] Gilligan, *In a Different Voice*, 19.
[14] See Lyons (n. 1 above).

an ethic of care as an intrinsically female characteristic.[15] Yet Gilligan's own work hints at another possible explanation of the origins of caring. In her description of women in the abortion study she and Mary Belenky conducted, Gilligan wrote:

> What begins to emerge is a sense of vulnerability that impedes these women from taking a stand, what George Eliot regards as the girl's "susceptibility" to adverse judgment of others, which stems from her lack of power and consequent inability to do something in the world. . . . The women's reluctance to judge stems . . . from their uncertainty about their right to make moral statements or, perhaps, the price for them that such judgment seems to entail. . . .
>
> When women feel excluded from direct participation in society, they see themselves as subject to a consensus or judgment made and enforced by the men on whose protection and support they depend and by whose names they are known. . . . The conflict between self and other thus constitutes the central moral problem for women. . . . The conflict between compassion and autonomy, between virtue and power. . . .[16]

This passage suggests that whatever psychological dimensions there might be to explain women's moral differences, there may also be a social cause: women's different moral expression might be a function of their subordinate or tentative social position. Alternatively, the psychological causes may be intermediate causes, resting in turn on the social conditions of secondary status. These possibilities suggest that Gilligan's work may be vulnerable to the same kind of criticism that she raised against Kohlberg. Gilligan's samples may lead her to draw a wrong conclusion about the nature of the moral voice that she has identified. For if moral difference is a function of social position rather than gender, then the morality Gilligan has identified with women might be better identified with subordinate or minority status.

There is little doubt that class status affects the level of justice reasoning.[17] A study that compared moral cognitive-development levels of

[15] Hilary Graham, "Caring: A Labour of Love," in *A Labour of Love: Women, Work and Caring*, ed. Janet Finch and Dulcie Groves (London: Routledge & Kegan Paul, 1983), 13–30, esp. 17. Graham draws this conclusion from her examination of the works of Karen Horney, Jean Baker Miller, and Nancy Chodorow. Greeno and Maccoby also review the basis for psychological gender differences.

[16] Gilligan, "In a Different Voice: Women's Conceptions of Self and of Morality" (n. 1 above), 486, 487, and 490. For further support of this finding, see Gail Golding and Toni Laidlaw, "Women and Moral Development: A Need to Care," *Interchange* 10, no. 2 (1979–80): 95–103, esp. 102.

[17] Anne Colby, Lawrence Kohlberg, J. Gibbs, and M. Lieberman, "A Longitudinal Study of Moral Judgment," *Monographs of the Society for Research in Child Development* 48, nos. 1–2 (1983): 1–96, esp. 70.

649

whites, blacks, and Chicanos discovered that white children were ahead of the minority children.[18] Would a study of these groups indicate that, as Gilligan found to be true for women, their moral views were not underdeveloped but simply not captured by Kohlberg's categories?[19]

To my knowledge, no one has examined minority group members using Gilligan's methodology to see if they fit the morality of care better than they fit Kohlberg's categories. Gilligan's abortion study, like Kohlberg's work, is limited in that it focuses solely on the privileged.[20] Yet circumstantial evidence strongly suggests that the moral views of minority group members in the United States are much more likely to be characterized by an ethic of care than by an ethic of justice. For example, Robert Coles's discussions with Chicano, Eskimo, and Indian children revealed frequent criticisms of Anglos for their inattention to proper moral concerns and for their lack of care for others and for the earth.[21] Similarly, in his depiction of core black culture, John Langston Gwaltney reveals that blacks frequently express similar moral concerns.[22] Core black culture, according to Gwaltney, emphasizes basic respect for others, a commitment to honesty, generosity motivated by the knowledge that you might need help someday, and respect for the choices of others. In the case histories that Gwaltney recorded, one person after another invoked these virtues and contrasted

---

[18] Anthony Cortese, "A Comparative Analysis of Cognition and Moral Judgment in Chicano, Black, and Anglo Children" (paper presented at the annual meeting of the American Sociological Association, San Francisco, September 1982), and "Moral Development in Chicano and Anglo Children," *Hispanic Journal of Behavioral Science* 4, no. 3 (September 1982): 353-66.

[19] In asking this question I certainly do not mean to imply that the type of moral reasoning found among privileged American women should be substituted for the morality found among privileged American men as a universal model for moral development. Kohlberg's work has often been criticized for being an ideological embodiment of liberal values. See, e.g., Edmund V. Sullivan, *Kohlberg's Structuralism: A Critical Appraisal*, Ontario Institute for Studies in Education, Monograph Series 15 (Toronto: Ontario Institute for Studies in Education, 1977). However, if we knew *why* privileged women, lower-class children, and minority group members differ from privileged males in Kohlberg's model, we would know a great deal more about the limits of this model as well as about the psychosocial origins of care itself. See Stack (n. 3 above), 321–24.

[20] The abortion sample consisted of interviews conducted with women from various social and ethnic backgrounds, but no analysis of this material has been done from the standpoint of racial or class differences. See Gilligan and Belenky (n. 1 above). The other sample that has been used to generate most of the findings of Gilligan and her associates was that used for the longitudinal study by Murphy and Gilligan (n. 1 above). Those subjects were initially chosen because they took a course in moral development at college. Thus, the sample is already limited by the opportunity, interest, and ability of individuals who go to college. I know of no analysis that considers the racial, ethnic, and class composition of these samples. For a related criticism of the samples, see Luria (n.3 above).

[21] Robert Coles, *Eskimos, Chicanos, Indians* (Boston: Little, Brown & Co., 1977).

[22] John Langston Gwaltney, *Drylongso: A Self-Portrait of Black America* (New York: Random House, 1980).

650

them to the views of the white majority, who were characterized as greedy, cheap, and self-involved, and as people who lie when it proves advantageous. Is this morality less coherent because it is not expressed abstractly? As Gwaltney succinctly put it, "Black Americans are, of course, capable of the same kind of abstract thinking that is practiced by all human cultures, but sane people in a conquest environment are necessarily preoccupied with the realities of social existence."[23]

Gerald Gregory Jackson also has identified characteristics of West African and Afro-American patterns of thought that are closely reminiscent of Gilligan's different voice, except that they are part of a large, coherent account of the place of humans in the cosmos. In contrast to the "analytical, logical, cognitive, rational, step by step" thinking of Europeans and Euro-Americans, African thought relies on "syncretistic reasoning, intuitive, holistic, affective" patterns of thought in which "comprehension [comes] through sympathy."[24] Indeed, Wade W. Nobles relates this different, connected pattern of thought to the fact that black Americans do not seem to have the same self-concept as whites. Nobles characterizes this view of the self, which stresses "a sense of 'cooperation,' 'interdependence,' and 'collective responsibility,'" as the "extended self." The parallel to Lyons's argument is striking.[25]

The possibility of a social and not just a psychological cause for Gilligan's different voice greatly broadens the implications of and possible interpretations of research on an ethic of care. One possible implication is that Kohlberg's theory of proper moral development is correct, so that the failure of women and minority groups to develop properly is just a reflection of a regrettably unequal social order. According to this explanation, social forces retard the moral development of women and minorities. A

---

[23] Ibid., xxix.

[24] Gerald Gregory Jackson, "Black Psychology as an Emerging Point of View," cited by Anne C. Richards in *Sourcebook on the Teaching of Black Psychology*, comp. and ed. Reginald L. Jones (n.p.: Association of Black Psychologists, 1978), 2:175–77. See also Jackson's "Black Psychology: An Avenue to the Study of Afro-Americans," *Journal of Black Studies* 12, no. 3 (March 1982): 241–60.

[25] Wade W. Nobles, "Extended Self: Rethinking the So-called Negro Self-Concept," *Journal of Black Psychology* 2, no. 2 (February 1976): 15–24, esp. 19. Incidentally, we can raise the same questions about the origins of care among black Americans as we can among women. Jackson and Nobles provide a cultural explanation that describes blacks as morally different from whites because of their African roots; this idea parallels the notion that women care because culturally that is what being a woman is about. Other authors have suggested a more positional cause: Janet D. Ockerman suggests that social subordination produces the psychological response of greater group solidarity in *Self-Esteem and Social Anchorage of Adolescent White, Black and Mexican-American Students* (Palo Alto, Calif.: R and E Research Associates, 1979). V. H. Zimmerman explains the different tasks for psychological development that black women face as a result of racial discrimination in "The Black Woman Growing Up, "in *The Woman Patient*, vol. 2, *Concepts of Feminity and the Life Cycle*, ed. Carol C. Nadelson and Malkah T. Notman (New York: Plenum Publishing Corp., 1982), 77–92.

651

second interpretation rejects the view of women and minorities as passively affected by society. One could claim that women and minorities proudly cling to their moral views, even if they are considered "lesser" moral views by the society, as a way of asserting their distinctiveness.

A third possibility differs from the previous two in its rejection of the assumption that from the start Kohlberg's justice reasoning is somehow superior to an ethic of care. By stressing the positive qualities of an ethic of care, this approach would turn Kohlberg's "naturalistic"[26] moral psychology on its head. While white women and minority men and women occupy vastly different positions in the social order, they disproportionately occupy the caretaking roles in our society. Thus, these groups, in terms of having an ethic of care, are advantaged by their social roles. It may be that, in order for an ethic of care to develop, individuals need to experience caring for others and being cared for by others. From this perspective, the daily experience of caring provides these groups with the opportunity to develop this moral sense. The dearth of caretaking experiences makes privileged males morally deprived. Their experiences mislead them to think that moral beliefs can be expressed in abstract, universalistic terms as if they were purely cognitive questions, like mathematical formulae.[27] This interpretation fits best with Lyons's finding that women, more often than men, are capable of using both types of moral reasoning.

Is women's morality inferior?

Even if an ethic of care could primarily be understood as a gender difference, however, the unsituated fact of moral difference between men and women is dangerous because it ignores the broader intellectual context within which "facts" about gender difference are generally received. Despite decades of questioning, we still live in a society where "man" stands for human and where the norm is equated with the male.[28] Gender difference, therefore, is a concept that concerns deviation from the nor-

---

[26] See Lawrence Kohlberg, "From Is to Ought: How to Commit the Naturalistic Fallacy and Get Away with It in the Study of Moral Development," in *Essays in Moral Development*, vol. 1, *The Philosophy of Moral Development: Moral Stages and the Idea of Justice*, by Lawrence Kohlberg (New York: Harper & Row, 1981), 101–89. The essay was originally published in 1971.

[27] "Justice 'operations' of reciprocity and equality in interaction parallel logical operations of relations of equality and reciprocity in the nonmoral cognitive domain" (see Kohlberg, "The Current Formulation of the Theory" [n. 7 above], 306).

[28] See Gilligan, *In a Different Voice* (n. 1 above), chap. 1. See also Nicholson (n. 9 above); and the Introduction by Sandra Harding and Merrill B. Hintikka, eds., to *Discovering Reality: Feminist Perspectives on Epistemology, Metaphysics, Method and Philosophy of Science* (Dordrecht: D. Reidel Publishing Co., 1983).

mal. Given the conservative nature of our perceptions of knowledge,[29] evidence of a gender difference in and of itself is not likely to lead to the widespread questioning of established categories, such as Kohlberg's.[30] Instead, it is likely to lead to the denigration of the "deviation" associated with the female.

Kohlberg's response to Gilligan is instructive. He has decided that although Gilligan has identified a morally different voice, this voice is of limited application.[31] Kohlberg distinguishes "two senses of the word *moral*":

> The first sense of the word *moral* corresponds to . . . "the moral point of view" [that] stresses attributes of impartiality, universalizability, and the effort and willingness to come to agreement or consensus with other human beings in general about what is right. It is this notion of a "moral point of view" which is most clearly embodied psychologically in the Kohlberg stage model of justice reasoning.
>
> There is a second sense of the word *moral*, which is captured by Gilligan's focus upon the elements of caring and responsibility, most vividly evident in relations of special obligation to family and friends.[32]

Kohlberg's example of the second type of moral concern is a woman's description of her decision to divorce.[33] Although Kohlberg does not deny

---

[29] See the description of "normal science" in Thomas Kuhn, *The Structure of Scientific Revolutions*, 2d ed. (Chicago: University of Chicago Press, 1970). Knowledge is conservative in that we tend to conceive new knowledge in existing frameworks; unless knowledge contains a challenge to the context in which it will likely be placed, it reinforces existing perceptions. Since gender differences are currently perceived in terms of a male norm, we can expect that newly identified gender differences will be perceived in the same way. Of course, Lorraine B. Code is correct when she writes, "To assert a difference . . . is not, inevitably, to evaluate. That is an additional step: one which no epistemically responsible person, male or female, should take without careful consideration. This is a fundamental cognitive imperative" (Code, "Responsibility and the Epistemic Community: Women's Place," *Social Research* 50, no. 3 [Autumn 1983]: 537–54, esp. 546–47). But the worlds of power and knowledge are intertwined; we do not live in a world that adheres to Code's ideal of the epistemically responsible community.

[30] See, e.g., Benjamine R. Barber, "Beyond the Feminist Mystique," *New Republic* (July 11, 1983), 26–32. An argument similar to mine is made by Nails (n. 12 above).

[31] Kohlberg, in "Synopses and Detailed Replies to Critics" (n. 12 above), denies that his stages of moral development do reflect a gender difference. Kohlberg believes that Gilligan's most important contribution is her identification of "responsibility" as a separate moral dimension. See Lawrence Kohlberg, "A Reply to Owen Flanagan and Some Comments on the Puka-Goodpaster Exchange," *Ethics* 92, no. 3 (1982): 513–28, esp. 513.

[32] Kohlberg, "The Current Formulation of the Theory," 229.

[33] Ibid., 230–31.

that such decisions involve moral choice, he believes it is clear that these concerns are parochial and private rather than universal and socially significant. If we accept Kohlberg's explanation that there are two different types of moral concerns, and if the two are connected to gender, the pattern is a familiar one: what is male is important, broad, and public; what is female is narrow, special, and insignificant. Feminist scholars have stressed the need to reject a simplistic evaluation of the "public/private split," with its implicit devaluation of the female.[34] Accordingly, then, the concept of women's morality should be disassociated from the private because the public and the private are not separate-but-equal moral realms.[35]

The contours of public morality in large part determine the shape of private morality. Indeed, it is in the public realm that the boundaries of the private are drawn. To use Kohlberg's example, if the universal, consensual norms of society did not permit divorce, then the woman who expressed her personal moral dilemma about divorce would have faced no moral dilemma at all; the boundaries about what would be right and wrong would already be fixed, and she would know that choosing divorce would be wrong.

This last point raises a troublesome possibility. Perhaps women's morality is just a collection of "moral leftovers," of questions that gain significance only because they are left somewhat open-ended by the commandments and boundaries of public morality. Gilligan has noted that the ethic of care is a relational ethic, that it is tied to who one is, to what position one occupies in society. Such concerns have been considered of a secondary importance in the moral life of any community. In other words, the requirements of justice have traditionally set the boundaries of care.

As long as women's morality is viewed as different and more particular than mainstream moral thought, it inevitably will be treated as a secondary form of moral thinking. This is true because, as the etymology suggests, that which is private is deprived in at least one sense: insofar as the boundaries of the private (in this case, private morality as expressed by care) are set by the categories and definitions of the public (in this case, public morality, i.e., the ethic of justice), that which is relegated to the

[34] See M. Rosaldo, "The Use and Abuse of Anthropology: Reflections on Feminism and Cross-cultural Understanding," *Signs* 5, no. 3 (Spring 1980): 389–417. Linda Imray and Audrey Middleton suggest that the problem is not in the public/private dichotomy itself but in our failure to understand that what is essential in the public/private split is not "activity" or "sphere" but power (Imray and Middleton, "Public and Private: Marking the Boundaries," in *The Public and the Private*, ed. Eva Gamarnikow, David H. J. Morgan, June Purvis, and Daphne Taylorson [London: Heinemann, 1983], 12–27).

[35] A different perspective on the problem of public/private life is presented in Jean Bethke Elshtain's "Antigone's Daughters," *Democracy* 2, no. 2 (April 1982): 46–59. For a response to Elshtain, see Mary G. Dietz, "Citizenship with a Feminist Face: The Problem with Maternal Thinking," *Political Theory* 13, no. 1 (February 1985): 19–37.

private is not judged on its own terms. Private morality is not perceived as independent of the "more important" public realm. It is by nature dependent and secondary.

Thinkers who advocate a women's morality have almost always assumed that it is a necessary corrective, not an alternative, to prevailing moral views.[36] By so doing, they have made it relatively easy for critics to dismiss women's morality as secondary and irrelevant to broader moral and political concerns.[37] To argue that women's morality is a corrective to prevailing modes of morality is to make a functionalist argument. To the extent that women's moral difference is viewed as functional to the improvement of the morality of society as a whole, it remains secondary.[38] If, armed with Gilligan's findings and similar work, the best feminists can do is to claim that letting women assert their morality in more important parts of public life will improve life,[39] or that public life is unimportant and women should cultivate morality in the domestic realm,[40] then they are doomed to failure. Such arguments, all of which take the form "we can be useful to

[36] Carol Gilligan, in "Do the Social Sciences Have an Adequate Theory of Moral Development?" (n. 1 above), seems to suggest that care is such a complementary moral theory.

[37] A good example of this phenomenon is the fate of Jane Addams. Addams was enormously popular for her good works during the first two decades of this century. When the United States entered World War I, though, and she continued to maintain a steadfast belief that moral values, including pacifism, should guide political action, she was vilified as a traitor. Although Addams was honored with the Nobel Prize for Peace in 1931, her reputation and political influence never recovered their prewar levels. See Allen F. Davis, *American Heroine: The Life and Legend of Jane Addams* (New York: Oxford University Press, 1977). An argument similar to the one I make here is found in Emily Stoper and Roberta Ann Johnson, "The Weaker Sex and the Better Half: The Idea of Women's Moral Superiority in the American Feminist Movement," *Polity* 10, no. 2 (Winter 1977): 192–217. I should note that my criticism of the misuse of this argument is not directed against Carol Gilligan herself. Auerbach, Blum, Smith, and Williams (n. 12 above) raise a different objection to the political implications of Gilligan's work. While I have emphasized how the women's morality argument can be turned to conservative purposes (a point they make on 159), they also assert that "the problem with [Gilligan's] book is not that its politics are bad, but that it lacks a politics altogether" (160). Gilligan hinted at a response to this criticism when she alluded to the need for both moralities to play a part in "public as well as private life" ("Reply" [n. 1 above], 326). Yet she has not made clear what that interaction might mean.

[38] Several authors have made arguments similar to this one. See especially James C. Walker, "In a Diffident Voice: Cryptoseparatist Analysis of Female Moral Development," *Social Research* 50, no. 3 (Autumn 1983): 665–95; Judith Stacey, "The New Conservative Feminism," *Feminist Studies* 9, no. 3 (Fall 1983): 559–83. My use of the language of functionalism is inspired here by my reading of Susan Moller Okin, *Women in Western Political Thought* (Princeton, N.J.: Princeton University Press, 1978).

[39] See, e.g., Alice Rossi, "Beyond the Gender Gap: Women's Bid for Political Power," *Social Science Quarterly* 64, no. 4 (December 1983): 718–33, esp. 731; and Katherine E. Kleeman's pamphlet, *Learning to Lead: Public Leadership Education Programs for Women* (n.p.: Public Leadership Education Network, 1984), 3: "Psychologist Carol Gilligan provides us with additional justification for bringing more women into public life."

[40] See, e.g., Susan Tenenbaum, "Women through the Prism of Political Thought," *Polity* 15, no. 1 (Fall 1982): 90–102.

you," ignore the fact that privileged men are the adjudicators of what is useful, of what is important, and, therefore, of what stands most in need of correction. Rather than presenting an alternative moral theory, then, privatized women's morality is a supplemental moral theory. And when and how that different moral voice gets heard is beyond the power of the "different" to decide. In this way, as has happened before, women's moral voice, the ethic of care, is easily dismissed.

In arguing that there is a strategic problem with women's morality, I do not mean to imply that strategy overshadows truth. If women were morally different from men, then strategy would not allow us to dismiss this fact. Yet the facts are not so simple, and it is thus legitimate to see if the direction in which the facts are likely to lead requires that we place them in a different intellectual context. I have tried to show that the consequences of a simplistic embrace of the ethic of care as specifically women's morality are potentially harmful. This is not to say that an ethic of care is morally undesirable but that its premises must be understood within the context of moral theory, rather than as the given facts of a gender-based psychological theory.

A contextual theory of care

If an ethic of care is to be taken seriously as a moral position, then its advocates need to explore the assumptions on which such a moral position is founded. Unless the full social and philosophical context for an ethic of care is specified, the ethic of care can be dismissed as a parochial concern of some misguided women. In making this claim, I differ from some recent feminist theorists who have eschewed full-scale theory construction and have instead focused on the practical implications of an ethic of care. Several writers, for example, have focused on the question of peace as exemplary of the way in which care can inform our treatment of a crucial political issue.[41] Their approach, however, ignores the context in which questions of war and peace appear. Out of the context of any broader political and social theory, the question of peace can easily be dismissed for failing to consider other values (e.g., defense or honor), which others may view as broader or more important.[42] Only when care is assessed in its

[41] See Sara Ruddick, "Preservative Love and Military Destruction," and "Pacifying the Forces" (both n. 5 above). Jean Elshtain often seems to support a similar position, but in her most recent essays, she is critical of a simplistic "beautiful souls" argument on the part of women. Nevertheless, she has not yet provided any full theoretical alternative to naive pacifism except to demur about statism. See Elshtain, "On Beautiful Souls, Just Warriors and Feminist Consciousness," in *Women and Men's Wars*, ed. Judith Stiehm (Oxford: Pergamon Press, 1983), 341–49, and "Reflections on War and Political Discourse: Realism, Just War, and Feminism in a Nuclear Age," *Political Theory* 13, no. 1 (February 1985): 39–57.

[42] Consider, e.g., how ephemeral the tremendous wave of interwar pacifism proved to be. See Peter Brock, *Twentieth Century Pacifism* (New York: Van Nostrand, 1970).

relative importance to other values can it begin to serve as a critical standpoint from which to evaluate public life. Such an assessment will require a full-fledged moral and political theory of care.

In addition to defining the concept of care, I suggest three sets of concerns that begin to address "care" at the theoretical level.[43]

The metaethical question

One reason why, from the standpoint of an ethic of justice, care seems to be such an inadequate moral position is that an ethic of care necessarily rests on a different set of premises about what a good moral theory is. As Alasdair MacIntyre noted, the prevailing contemporary notion of what counts as a moral theory is derived from Kant.[44] According to this view, a moral theory consists of a set of moral principles rationally chosen after consideration of competing principles. William Frankena refers to this as "the moral point of view": it is universalizable, impartial, and concerned with describing what is right, and we would expect chosen moral principles to embody these standard notions of morality.[45]

An alternative model for moral theories is contextual metaethical theory.[46] Such theories consist of presumptions about the nature of morality that are different from Kantian-inspired metaethics. In any contextual moral theory, morality must be situated concretely, that is, for particular

[43] Noddings (n. 5 above) distinguishes between the "one-caring" and the "cared-for." Caring, she claims, is not of itself a virtue but rather the occasion for the exercise of virtues.

[44] Alasdair MacIntyre, *A Short History of Ethics* (New York: Macmillan, 1966), 190. Indeed, Gilligan has been criticized for not presenting a Kantian form of ethical theory. See Gertrud Nunner-Winkler, "Two Moralities? A Critical Discussion of an Ethic of Care and Responsibility versus an Ethic of Rights and Justice," in Kurtines and Gewirtz, eds. (n. 10 above), 348–61. For a critique of Kant that follows some of the directions found in an ethic of care, see Jean Bethke Elshtain, "Kant, Politics, and Persons: The Implications of His Moral Philosophy," *Polity* 14, no. 2 (Winter 1981): 205–21.

[45] See William Frankena, *Ethics*, 2d ed. (Englewood Cliffs, N.J.: Prentice-Hall, Inc., 1973). Kohlberg recites Frankena's argument in the quotation cited by n. 32 above.

[46] Contextual moral theories can be teleological, deontological, axiological, or aretaic. The common theme in contextual moral theories is that they eschew a formal and absolute resolution of moral questions. The reader may suspect that I am coining a new phrase only to weaken the position of my opponents. After all, even Kohlberg believes that his theory is situation specific and not universalistic. Indeed, perhaps only the Kantian perfect duties can be described as an unqualifiedly nonsituated morality. If that is the case, then my argument for introducing contextual morality grows stronger because it requires that moral philosophers drop the convenient fiction that their work stops once they have clarified the moral rules. Contextual moral theories involve a shift of the essential moral questions away from the question, What are the best principles? to the question, How will individuals best be equipped to act morally? Many moral philosophers are beginning to claim the need to return to a contextual ethical theory. A good recent collection of essays that shows both the diversity and core concerns of this emerging perspective can be found in Alasdair MacIntyre and Stanley Hauerwas, eds., *Revisions: Changing Perspectives in Moral Philosophy* (Notre Dame, Ind.: University of Notre Dame Press, 1983).

actors in a particular society. It cannot be understood by the recitation of abstract principles. By this account, morality is embedded in the norms of a given society. Furthermore, contextual moral theory directs attention away from the morality of single acts to the broader moral capacities of actors. To be moral is to possess a moral character, or, as Aristotle put it, virtue is a disposition.[47] Thus, morality cannot be determined by posing hypothetical moral dilemmas or by asserting moral principles. Rather, one's moral imagination, character, and actions must respond to the complexity of a given situation. Among prominent examples of contextual morality, I would include Aristotle's moral theory, the "moral sentiments" views of the Scottish Enlightenment, and some contemporary writers on morality.[48]

As a result of a starting concern with character, any contextual moral theory must embody a complex portrait of the self. Theories that are suspicious of nonrational moral motives often explain moral action as the result of rising above selfish passions. Noncontextual moral philosophers rely on rational tests to check self-interested inclinations. Hence the rational and the moral become identified.[49] In contrast, advocates of contextual moral theories often stress moral sensitivity and moral imagination as keys to understanding mature moral life. Rather than positing some ideal rational human being, contextual morality stands or falls on its ability to describe the ways in which individuals progress morally to exhibit concern for others.

As a fully developed moral theory, the ethic of care will take the form of a contextual moral theory. Perhaps the most important characteristic of an ethic of care is that within it, moral situations are defined not in terms of rights and responsibilities but in terms of relationships of care. The morally mature person understands the balance between caring for the self and caring for others.[50] The perspective of care requires that conflict be worked out without damage to the continuing relationships. Moral problems can be expressed in terms of accommodating the needs of the self and of others, of balancing competition and cooperation, and of maintaining the social web of relations in which one finds oneself.

[47] Aristotle, *The Nichomachean Ethics*, trans. J. A. K. Thomson and H. Tredennick (Harmondsworth: Penguin Books, 1976), 91–92 (1103a14–b25).

[48] Among traditional moral theorists, I have in mind especially David Hume and Adam Smith. Among contemporary moral philosophers, a succinct statement of a contextual moral position can be found in John Kekes, "Moral Sensitivity," *Philosophy* 59, no. 227 (1984): 3–19.

[49] John Rawls's description of the "original position" in *A Theory of Justice* (Cambridge, Mass.: Harvard University Press, 1971) is probably the best-known example of this approach. Lawrence Kohlberg's description of reciprocity ultimately hinges on an application of rationality as well. See his "Justice as Reversibility: The Claim to Moral Adequacy of a Highest Stage of Moral Judgement," in *Essays in Moral Development* (n. 26 above), 1:190–226; esp. 198.

[50] Gilligan describes the stages of care in "Do the Social Sciences Have an Adequate Theory of Moral Development?" (n. 1 above), 41–45.

Quite obviously, if such caretaking is the quintessential moral task, the context within which conflicting demands occur will be an important factor in determining the morally correct act. To resort to abstract, universal principles is to go outside of the web of relationships. Thus, despite Kohlberg's dismissal of care as secondary to and dependent on justice reasoning, from a different metaethical perspective, care may set the boundaries of when justice concerns are appropriate.[51]

If feminists recognize a moral tradition that is non-Kantian, they will be able to ground an ethic of care more securely in philosophical theory. Yet there are some serious problems with all contextual moralities, and specifically with an ethic of care. Consequently, as the following analysis will show, an ethic of care requires more elaboration before feminists can decide whether to embrace it as the appropriate moral theory for feminism.

Conventionalism and the limits of care

Universalistic moral theories presume that they apply to all cases; contextual moral theories must specify when and how they apply.[52] Advocates of an ethic of care face, as Gilligan puts it, "the moral problem of inclusion that hinges on the capacity to assume responsibility for care."[53] It is easy to imagine that there will be some people or concerns about which we do not care. However, we might ask if our lack of care frees us from moral responsibility.[54]

This question arises because we do not care for everyone equally. We care more for those who are emotionally, physically, and even culturally

---

[51] This inversion of Kohlberg's position is recommended to us by the logical requirements of making an ethic of care into a full-fledged moral theory. How the caring person would know when to invoke the more remote criteria of justice is obviously a crucial question.

[52] "We have been told nothing about morality until we are told what features of situations context-sensitive people pick out as morally salient, what weightings they put on these different features, and so on" (Owen Flanagan and Jonathan Adler, "Impartiality and Particularity," *Social Research* 50, no. 3 [Autumn 1983]: 576–96, esp. 591–92). A similar point is made by Jonathan Dancy, "Ethical Particularism and Morally Relevant Properties," *Mind* 92, no. 368 (1983): 530–47.

[53] Gilligan, "Do the Social Sciences Have an Adequate Theory of Moral Development?" 44. Aristotle insisted that to try to extend the bounds of familial love to everyone simply destroys family bonds (*The Politics of Aristotle*, trans. E. Barker [New York: Oxford University Press, 1946], 47; 1262b [2.4.8]).

[54] Thus, David Hume understood justice, an artificial passion, as a necessary complement to the natural passion, benevolence. Hume argued that if benevolence were sufficiently strong, there would be no need of justice. Yet the limited range of benevolence made it an insufficient basis for moral life in human society. See David Hume, *Treatise of Human Nature*, ed. L. A. Selby-Bigge and P. H. Nidditch (Oxford: Oxford University Press, 1978), bk. 3, pt. 2, 494–95.

closer to us.[55] Thus, an ethic of care could become a defense of caring only for one's own family, friends, group, nation. From this perspective, caring could become a justification for any set of conventional relationships. Any advocate of an ethic of care will need to address the questions, What are the appropriate boundaries of our caring? and more important, How far should the boundaries of caring be expanded?

Furthermore, in focusing on the preservation of existing relationships, the perspective of care has a conservative quality. If the preservation of a web of relationships is the starting premise of an ethic of care, then there is little basis for critical reflection on whether those relationships are good, healthy, or worthy of preservation. Surely, as we judge our own relationships, we are likely to favor them and relationships like them. It is from such unreflective tastes, though, that hatreds of difference can grow. One of the reasons why impartiality is such an appealing universal moral characteristic is that in theory it can prevent the kind of special pleading in which we all otherwise engage. Yet it may be possible to avoid the need for special pleading while at the same time stopping short of universal moral principles; if so, an ethic of care might be viable.[56]

The possibility that an ethic of care might lead to the reinforcement of existing social patterns also raises the question of relativism. It is difficult to imagine how an ethic of care could avoid the charge that it would embody different moral positions in different societies and at different times. Philosophers do not agree about the seriousness of this type of relativism, however, and contextual moral theories may entail only a milder form of relativism, one that Dorothy Emmet calls "soft relativism." Viewed from the perspective of "soft relativism," cultural variation in certain moral principles does not preclude the discussion of moral issues across cultures.[57] The only way an ethic of care could entirely bypass the charge of relativism would be to posit some caring relationship, for example, the relationship of parent and child, as universal. This path, however, seems fraught with even greater difficulties for feminist scholars and prejudges in an unacceptably narrow way who "caretakers" should be.

Insofar as the difficulty with justice reasoning is that it ignores the

[55] This point was illustrated graphically by the Scottish Enlightenment thinker Francis Hutcheson, who drew an analogy between the relative strength of our closest and furthest emotional ties and the ties of gravity (*Inquiry into the Original of Our Ideas of Beauty and Virtue* [1726] in *Collected Works of Francis Hutcheson*, ed. Bernhard Fabian [Hildesheim, West Germany: George Olms Verlagsbuchhandlung, 1971], 1:198–99). Perhaps some individuals, the saints among us, can resist the greater pull of those closest to us. A provocative account of moral saints is Susan Wolf, "Moral Saints," *Journal of Philosophy* 89, no. 8 (August 1982): 419–39.

[56] Peter Winch, "The Universalizability of Moral Judgments," in his *Ethics and Action* (London: Routledge & Kegan Paul, 1972), 151–70.

[57] See Dorothy Emmet, *Rules, Roles and Relations* (New York: St. Martin's Press, 1966), chap. 5, esp. 91–92.

importance of context, the expansion of a care ethic suggests a much more adequate moral theory. Yet, how to make sure that the web of relationships is spun widely enough so that some are not beyond its reach remains a central question. Whatever the weaknesses of Kantian universalism, its premise of the equal moral worth and dignity of all humans is attractive because it avoids this problem.

Past contextual moral theories usually have addressed the issue by resorting to some abstract impartial observer. This solution is also inadequate, however, since the impartial observer usually places the same limitations on caring as do conventional moral thinkers.[58] The only other way to resolve this problem is to specify how social institutions might be arranged to expand these conventional understandings of the boundaries of care. Thus, the legitimacy of an ethic of care will depend on the adequacy of the social and political theory of which it is a part.

Politics and care

In the final analysis, successful advocacy of an ethic of care requires the exposition of a social and political theory that is compatible with the broadest levels of care. All moral theories fit better with some rather than other social and political institutions. Proponents of an ethic of care must specify which social and political institutions they understand to be the context for moral actors. It perhaps should give us pause that some of the most compelling visions of politics of care are utopian.[59]

Among the questions a convincing theory of care needs to address are the myriad questions crucial to any social and political theory. Where does caring come from? Is it learned in the family? If so, does an ethic of care mandate something about the need for, or the nature of, families? Who determines who can be a member of the caring society? What should be the role of the market in a caring society? Who should bear the responsibility for education? How much inequality is acceptable before individuals become indifferent to those who are too different in status? How well do current institutions and theories support the ethic of care?

[58] For example, Adam Smith posited the existence of an "impartial spectator" in *The Theory of Moral Sentiments* (Oxford: Oxford University Press, 1976), 3.1.2, 110. Richard Brandt is a recent moral philosopher who advocated an "ideal observer" theory, but he has since repudiated it because it provided no way to prevent the ideal observer from invoking what would seem to him to be harmless preferences that might seriously constrict others' choices. (He uses as one example the preference against homosexuality.) See Brandt, *A Theory of the Good and the Right* (Oxford: Clarendon Press, Oxford University Press, 1979), 225–28.

[59] Consider Charlotte Perkins Gilman, *Herland*, introduction by Ann J. Lane (New York: Pantheon Books, 1979); Marge Piercy, *Woman on the Edge of Time* (New York: Fawcett Crest, 1976). Lee Cullen Khanna draws a parallel between Gilligan's ethic of care and Piercy's novel; see her "Frontiers of Imagination: Feminist Worlds," *Women's Studies International Forum* 7, no. 2 (1984): 97–102.

Finally, we need to think about how an ethic of care might be situated in the context of existing political and social theory. An ethic of care constitutes a view of self, relationships, and social order that may be incompatible with the emphasis on individual rights that is so predominant in Western, liberal, democratic societies. Yet, as it is currently formulated by political theorists, the debate between advocates of rights and advocates of community does not offer a clear alternative to feminists who might advocate an ethic of care. As onerous as rights may seem when viewed from the standpoint of our desires for connected, extended selves, they do serve at least somewhat to protect oppressed individuals. While current yearnings for greater community seem to manifest a view of the self that would allow for more caring, there is nothing inherent in community that keeps it from being oppressive toward women and others.[60] Unless feminists assume responsibility for situating the ethic of care in the context of the rights/community discussions, the end result may be that caring can be used to justify positions that feminists would find unacceptable.[61]

Toward a theory of care

I have suggested that feminists should no longer celebrate an ethic of care as a factor of gender difference that points to women's superiority but that they must now begin the arduous task of constructing a full theory of care. Taken together, the arguments in this article suggest that the direction for future feminist moral thinking must be broader and more theoretical. In order to demonstrate this final claim let me consider a less drastic response to the question, What might the ethic of care mean?

One could assert that an ethic of care is just a set of sensibilities that every morally mature person should develop, alongside the sensibilities of justice morality. Rather than rethinking the nature of moral philosophy, then, we need to change the educational or familial institutions that are responsible for making the differences between justice and care gender

[60] See, e.g., Michael Sandel, *Liberalism and the Limits of Justice* (Cambridge: Cambridge University Press, 1981). It seems doubtful that Sandel's vision holds any more promise for women than Rawls's theory that feminists need to be somewhat suspicious of invocations of community. See Brian Barry, review of Sandel, in *Ethics* 94, no. 3 (April 1984): 523–25; and Amy Gutmann, "Communitarian Critics of Liberalism," *Philosophy and Public Affairs* 14, no. 3 (Summer 1985): 308–21.

[61] Consider the argument made by John Hardwig, "Should Women Think in Terms of Rights?" *Ethics* 94, no. 3 (April 1984): 441–55. Hardwig answers this question negatively; among his reasons is that "rights" imply a particular atomistic view of the self. To use rights arguments, he claims, is to adopt this understanding of the self. Women would have to surrender their sense of their connected, female nature if they used rights arguments. Hence, they should not. Alas, Hardwig does not explain how women can convince men who do think in terms of rights to take them seriously.

specific. We should endorse the development of two equal moralities for everyone and leave it to individuals to decide when to apply either morality.

There are two problems with this alternative. First, such a response ignores the evidence about the origins of the current gender differences. Whether the cause of the gender difference in morality is a psychological artifact of femininity, a cultural product of caretaking activity, or a positional result of social subordination, it is difficult to imagine how any of these causes or some combination of them could affect all individuals equally.

In the second place, expressing such an ideal ignores the tendency, in reality, to accommodate two desirable moralities by falling back into a rigid gender division. If there are two desirable moralities and two genders, what is wrong with viewing one as predominantly male and one as predominantly female? Having separate but, supposedly, equal spheres allows the two different moralities to flourish and delineates their boundaries clearly.

The most promising alternative, I have suggested, is to face squarely the difficult task of discussing the ethic of care in terms of moral and political theory. This task would include looking critically at the notion of a women's morality advanced by interpretations of research on morality and gender differences and by situating such interpretations in the context of research on morality and class, racial, and ethnic differences as well. It would also mean recognizing the limitations of a gender-specific moral theory in our culture. Finally, it would entail exploring the promises, as well as the problems, involved in thinking about the ethic of care as an alternative moral theory, rather than simply as a complement to traditional moral theories based on justice reasoning.

Although this task will be a difficult one, there is much to gain from it. Attentive to the place of caring both in concrete daily experience and in our patterns of moral thought, we might be better prepared to forge a society in which care can flourish.

Department of Political Science
Hunter College of the City University of New York

ACKNOWLEDGMENTS

Gilligan, Carol. "In a Different Voice: Women's Conceptions of Self and of Morality." *Harvard Educational Review* 47 (1977): 481–517. Reprinted with the permission of Harvard University, Graduate School of Education. Courtesy of Yale University Sterling Memorial Library.

Gilligan, Carol and Mary Field Belenky. "A Naturalistic Study of Abortion Decisions." In R.L. Selman and R. Yando, eds., *Clinical-Developmental Psychology* (San Francisco, CA: Jossey-Bass, Inc., 1980): 69–90. Reprinted with the permission of Jossey-Bass Publishers. Courtesy of the author.

Smetana, Judith G. "Reasoning in the Personal and Moral Domains: Adolescent and Young Adult Women's Decision-Making Regarding Abortion." *Journal of Applied Developmental Psychology* 2 (1981): 211–26. Reprinted with the permission of the Ablex Publishing Corp. Courtesy of Yale University Sterling Memorial Library.

Lyons, Nona Plessner. "Two Perspectives: On Self, Relationships, and Morality." *Harvard Educational Review* 53 (1983): 125–45. Reprinted with the permission of Harvard University, Graduate School of Education. Courtesy of Yale University Sterling Memorial Library.

Johnston, D. Kay. "Adolescents' Solutions to Dilemmas in Fables: Two Moral Orientations—Two Problem Solving Strategies." In Carol Gilligan, Janie Victoria Ward, and Jill McLean Taylor, with Betty Bardige, eds., *Mapping the Moral Domain: A Contribution of Women's Thinking to Psychological Theory and Education* (Cambridge, MA: Harvard University Press, 1988): 49–71. Reprinted with the permission of Harvard University Press. Courtesy of Yale University Cross Campus Library.

Gilligan, Carol and Jane Attanucci. "Two Moral Orientations: Gender Differences and Similarities." *Merrill-Palmer Quarterly* 34 (1988): 223–37. Reprinted with the permission of the Merrill-Palmer Institute. Courtesy of Yale University Seeley G. Mudd Library.

Brown, Lyn Mikel. "When Is a Moral Problem Not a Moral Problem? Morality, Identity, and Female Adolescence." In Carol Gilligan, Nona P. Lyons, and Trudy Hanmer, eds., *Making Connections: The Relational Worlds of Adolescent Girls at Emma Willard School* (Cambridge, MA: Harvard University Press, 1990): 88–109. Reprinted with the permission of Harvard University Press, copyright 1990 by the President and Fellows of Harvard College, copyright 1989 by Emma Willard School, Prologue and Preface copyright 1989 by Carol Gilligan. Courtesy of Yale University Sterling Memorial Library.

Brown, Lyn M., Mark B. Tappan, Carol Gilligan, Barbara A. Miller, and Dianne E. Argyris. "Reading for Self and Moral Voice: A Method for Interpreting Narratives of Real-Life Moral Conflict and Choice." In Martin J. Packer and Richard B. Addison, eds., *Entering the Circle: Hermeneutic Investigation in Psychology* (Albany, NY: State University of New York Press, 1989): 141–64. Reprinted by permission of the State University of New York Press. Courtesy of Yale University Sterling Memorial Library.

Broverman, Inge K., Susan Raymond Vogel, Donald M. Broverman, Frank E. Clarkson, and Paul S. Rosenkrantz. "Sex-Role Stereotypes: A Current Appraisal." *Journal of Social Issues* 28 (1972): 59–78. Reprinted with the permission of the Society for the Psychological Study of Social Issues. Courtesy of the Society for the Psychological Study of Social Issues.

Broughton, John M. "Women's Rationality and Men's Virtues: A Critique of Gender Dualism in Gilligan's Theory of Moral Development." *Social Research* 50 (1983): 112–39, 597–624. Reprinted with the permission of *Social Research*. Courtesy of the editor.

Bebeau, Muriel J. and Mary Brabeck. "Ethical Sensitivity and Moral Reasoning among Men and Women in the Professions." In Mary Brabeck, ed., *Who Cares?* (New York: Praeger Press, 1989): 144–63. An imprint of Greenwood Publishing Group, Inc., Westport, CT. Reprinted with permission. Courtesy of the editor.

Nunner-Winkler, Gertrud. "Two Moralities? A Critical Discussion of an Ethic of Care and Responsibility versus an Ethic of Rights and Justice." In William M. Kurtines and Jacob L. Gewirtz, eds., *Morality, Moral Behavior, and Moral Development* (New York: John Wiley & Sons, 1984): 348–61. Reprinted by permission of John Wiley & Sons, Inc. Courtesy of Yale University Cross Campus Library.

Colby, Anne and William Damon. "Listening to a Different Voice: A Review of Gilligan's *In A Different Voice.*" *Merrill-Palmer Quarterly* 29 (1983): 473–81. Reprinted with the permission of the Merrill-Palmer Institute. Courtesy of Yale University Seeley G. Mudd Library.

Friedman, William J., Amy B. Robinson, and Britt L. Friedman. "Sex Differences in Moral Judgments? A Test of Gilligan's Theory." *Psychology of Women Quarterly* 11 (1987): 37–46. Copyright 1987 Division 35, American Psychological Association. Reprinted with the permission of Cambridge University Press. Courtesy of Yale University Sterling Memorial Library.

Maccoby, Eleanor E. "The Role of Gender Identity and Gender Constancy in Sex-Differentiated Development." In D. Shrader, ed., *New Directions for Child Development* (San Francisco, CA: Jossey-Bass Inc., Publishers, 1990): 5–20. Reprinted with the permission of Jossey-Bass Inc., Publishers. Courtesy of the editor.

Greeno, Catherine G. and Eleanor E. Maccoby. "How Different Is the 'Different Voice'?" *Signs* 11 (1986): 310–16. Reprinted with the permission of the University of Chicago Press, publisher. Copyright 1986 by the University of Chicago. All rights reserved. Courtesy of Yale University Sterling Memorial Library.

Luria, Zella. "A Methodological Critique." *Signs* 11 (1986): 316–21. Reprinted with the permission of the University of Chicago Press, publisher. Copyright 1986 by the University of Chicago. All rights reserved. Courtesy of Yale University Sterling Memorial Library.

Walker, Lawrence J. "Sex Differences in the Development of Moral Reasoning: A Critical Review." *Child Development* 55 (1984): 677–91. Reprinted with the permission of the Society for Research in Child Development. Courtesy of Yale University Sterling Memorial Library.

Walker, Lawrence J., Brian de Vries, and Shelley D. Trevethan. "Moral Stages and Moral Orientations in Real-Life and Hypothetical Dilemmas." *Child Development* 58 (1987): 842–58. Reprinted with the permission of the Society for Research in Child Development. Courtesy of Yale University Sterling Memorial Library.

Gilligan, Carol. "Reply by Carol Gilligan." *Signs* 11 (1986): 324–33. Reprinted with the permission of the University of Chicago Press, publisher. Copyright 1986 by the University of Chicago.

All rights reserved. Courtesy of Yale University Sterling Memorial Library.

Baumrind, Diana. "Sex Differences in Moral Reasoning: Response to Walker's (1984) Conclusion that There Are None." *Child Development* 57 (1986): 511–21. Reprinted with the permission of the Society for Research in Child Development. Courtesy of Yale University Sterling Memorial Library.

Puka, Bill. "Caring—In an Interpretive Voice." *New Ideas in Psychology* 7 (1989): 295–314. Reprinted with the permission of Pergammon Press Ltd., Headington Hill Hall, Oxford OX3 0BW, UK. Copyright 1989. Courtesy of the author.

Walker, Lawrence J. "Sex Differences in the Development of Moral Reasoning: A Rejoinder to Baumrind." *Child Development* 57 (1986): 522–26. Reprinted with the permission of the Society for Research in Child Development. Courtesy of Yale University Sterling Memorial Library.

Vasudev, Jyotsna. "Sex Differences in Morality and Moral Orientation: A Discussion of the Gilligan and Attanucci Study." *Merrill-Palmer Quarterly* 34 (1988): 239–44. Reprinted with the permission of the Merrill-Palmer Institute. Courtesy of Yale University Seeley G. Mudd Library.

Gilligan, Carol and Jane Attanucci. "Much Ado About . . . Knowing? Noting? Nothing? A Reply to Vasudev Concerning Sex Differences and Moral Development." *Merrill-Palmer Quarterly* 34 (1988): 451–56. Reprinted with the permission of the Merrill-Palmer Institute. Courtesy of Yale University Seeley G. Mudd Library.

Puka, Bill. "Interpretive Experiments: Probing the Care-Justice Debate in Moral Development." *Human Development* 34 (1991): 61–80. Reprinted with the permission of S. Karger, AG. Courtesy of the editor.

Brown, Lyn M. and Mark B. Tappan. "Commentary." *Human Development* 34 (1991): 81–87. Reprinted with the permission of S. Karger, AG. Courtesy of the editor.

Boyd, Dwight. "The Character of Moral Development." In Larry P. Nucci, ed., *Moral Development and Character Education: A Dialogue* (Berkeley, CA: McCutchan Publishing Corporation, 1989): 95–123. Copyright 1989 by McCutchan Publishing Corporation, Berkeley, CA 94702. Permission granted by the publisher. Courtesy of Yale University Divinity Library.

Puka, Bill. "The Liberation of Caring: A Different Voice for Gilligan's 'Different Voice.'" *Hypatia* 5 (1990): 58–82. Reprinted with the permission of Indiana University Press. Courtesy of the editor.

Tronto, Joan C. "Beyond Gender Difference to a Theory of Care." *Signs* 12 (1987): 644–63. Reprinted with the permission of the University of Chicago Press, publisher. Copyright 1987 by the University of Chicago. All rights reserved. Courtesy of Yale University Sterling Memorial Library.